Holding Aloft the Banner of Ethiopia

Caribbean Radicalism in Early Twentieth-Century America

◆

WINSTON JAMES

VERSO

London · New York

First published by Verso 1998
© Winston A. James 1998
Paperback edition first published by Verso 1999
© Winston A. James 1999
Reprinted 2000
All rights reserved

The right of Winston A. James to be identified as the author
of this work has been asserted by him in
accordance with the Copyright, Designs and Patents Act 1988

Verso
UK: 6 Meard Street, London W1V 3HR
USA: 180 Varick Street, New York NY 10014–4606

Verso is the imprint of New Left Books

ISBN 1–85984–140–6

British Library Cataloguing in Publication Data
A catalogue record for this book is available from the British Library

Library of Congress Cataloging-in-Publication Data
A catalog record for this book is available from the Library of Congress

Typeset by SetSystems Ltd, Saffron Walden, Essex
Printed and bound in the USA by R. R. Donnelley & Sons

To my mother and father,
Ruby Cottrell James and Reginald James,
and
to the memory of
Lauretta Tomlinson Campbell and Uriah Campbell

In every field of our American life we find the West Indian pushing ahead and doing all in his power to uphold the dignity of the Negro race. In every industry, in every profession, in every trade, we find this son of the islands holding aloft the banner of Ethiopia.

When the great day of our liberation comes, we will find the West Indian foremost in the ranks of those fighting with his armor on and his sword raised aloft.

Fenton Johnson, 1919

As to the neglect you refer to, I think it may be traced in part to the old hostility between West Indian and American Negroes. Garvey and myself were no doubt considered upstarts by native-born Negro intellectuals in daring to advance solutions for the problems of American Negroes. The Garvey movement, however, being the greatest mass movement in the history of Negro America, could not be ignored, nor could its founder. . . . Another possible explanation may have been our radicalism—both racial and social. [William Monroe] Trotter, too, has been very much ignored.

Cyril Briggs to Theodore Draper,
March 17, 1958

Contents

ILLUSTRATIONS
Illustrations can be found between text pages 54 and 55, 182 and 183, and 246 and 247

Preface and Acknowledgements

About five years ago, while I was researching the life and times of Claude McKay—the Jamaican-born poet, novelist and radical intellectual—two surprising discoveries claimed my attention and demanded further investigation. The first discovery was the conspicuousness of Caribbean migrants—especially during the early twentieth century—in radical movements in the United States: not only black nationalist organizations like the Universal Negro Improvement Association, led by Jamaica's Marcus Garvey, but also the Socialist Party, the Industrial Workers of the World, and (after it was founded in 1919) the Workers' (Communist) Party as well. The second discovery was that the literature on the period, with few notable and qualified exceptions, has either overlooked the phenomenon, distorted it, or offered inadequate analysis. The more I explored the primary sources, including a substantial amount of archival material on Caribbean migrants and American radicalism, the more dissatisfied I became with the quality of the existing literature.

As I investigated the Caribbean presence within American radical movements, several questions came to the fore. What was the precise extent of the Caribbean involvement? How does one measure it? What does it tell us about those who migrated to the United States? What does it tell us about the Caribbean itself? And, most significantly, how does one explain this variant of Caribbean radicalism abroad? How does it help us to understand traditions of resistance within the African diaspora? How does it help us to appreciate the heterogeneity as well as the unity of the African diaspora in the Americas? *Holding Aloft the Banner of Ethiopia* is the result of my attempt to engage with these questions.

I have incurred many debts during the research and writing of this book, which I am pleased to acknowledge.

I benefited from two summer fellowships awarded by the Councils for Research in the Humanities and Social Sciences at Columbia University, and also from the research and study leave that Columbia awards to its junior faculty.

I am grateful for the courteous assistance which I received from librarians and archivists in the United States and elsewhere. I wish to thank those at the Beinecke Rare Book and Manuscript Library, Yale University; the British Library, especially its newspaper division at Colindale; the British

Library of Political and Economic Science, London School of Economics and Political Science, University of London; Columbia University libraries, especially the Rare Book and Manuscript Library, the Inter-library Loan Office, and the Oral History Office; the Ellis Island Immigration Museum; the Historical Association of Southern Florida; the Harry Ransom Humanities Research Center, University of Texas at Austin; the Library of Congress; the Lilly Library, Manuscripts Department, Indiana University, Bloomington; the Moorland-Springarn Research Center, Howard University; the National Archives; the National Library of Jamaica; the Public Record Office, Kew; the Robert W. Woodruff Library, Emory University; the Tamiment Institute Library and Robert F. Wagner Labor Archives, New York University; the West India Reference Library, University of the West Indies, Mona, Jamaica.

In the course of my research, I called upon the resources of three archives more than the rest. The Special Collections at the University of South Florida Library, Tampa, is one of these. Without the support of Paul Camp and his colleagues my putting together the story of Afro-Cubans in Tampa would have been far more difficult than it turned out to be. Mr Camp's help with the reproduction of photographs from the Collection was indispensable. At the archives of the Centro de Estudios Puertorriqueños, Hunter College, City University of New York, Pedro J. Hernández and his colleagues provided a warm and helpful environment in which I delved into the life and world of Jesús Colón; they were unfailingly helpful and kindly permitted the reproduction of Colón's photographs and the portrait of Pedro Albizu Campos in this book. I cannot imagine how I could have written this book without the human and material resources of the Schomburg Center for Research in Black Culture. I am especially grateful to the Schomburg's Chief, Howard Dodson, Diana Lachatanere and André Elizee in the Manuscripts, Archives and Rare Books Division, and Mary Yearwood, Jim Huffmann and Anthony Toussaint in the Photographs and Prints Division.

Benedict Anderson, Elizabeth Blackmar, Nigel Bolland, Paul Buhle, Eric Foner, Linden Lewis, Daryl Scott, Adam Shatz, Curtis Stokes, Hilbourne Watson and Marcia Wright read an early draft of the manuscript and offered helpful comments and and encouragement. John Higginson, Joyce Moore Turner, Colin Palmer and Michael O. West shared their thoughts on the Postscript. Peter Hobbs, who worked with me as a research assistant in the final phases of the book, provided valuable help. I am especially grateful for his assistance with the detective work on Samuel Haynes and Grace Campbell, two important figures who appear in these pages.

An earlier and abbreviated version of Chapter 7 was published in *Centro: Journal of El Centro de Estudios Puertorriqueños* (vol. viii, nos. 1 and 2, Spring 1996), and I benefited from the comments of *Centro*'s editors: Blanca Vázquez, Juan Flores, Roberto P. Rodríguez-Morazzani and Amílcar Tirado Avilés. Agustín Laó, Solsirée del Moral, Miriam Jiménez Román and Palmira Ríos also deserve my thanks for their comments. I drew great strength from the warmth, enthusiasm and encouragement of my Puerto Rican colleagues.

Susan Greenbaum commented on a draft of Chapter 8, willingly shared her considerable knowledge of Afro-Cuban life in Tampa, and provided encouragement. I am, additionally, indebted to Professor Greenbaum for the use of some of the photographs pertaining to Tampa. My debt to the scholarship of others should be evident from the notes and bibliography. But it should, nevertheless, be made explicit here that my writing of this book would have been far more difficult, and certainly more protracted, had it not been for the pioneering work of Robert Hill and his colleagues who put together the *Marcus Garvey and Universal Negro Improvement Association Papers*. Further, without Hill's recovery and re-publication of Cyril Briggs's *Crusader* magazine, the story of the African Blood Brotherhood could not be told as fully as I have attempted here. Professor Hill has, in addition, generously shared with me valuable archival resources, including some photographs which have been reproduced here. I am also indebted to Hill for reading and commenting upon the Postscript and the discussion of the Brotherhood.

At Verso, Colin Robinson was patient, supportive and encouraging. Robin Blackburn, my editor, read the manuscript closely and made a number of helpful suggestions. Despite his heavy responsibilities as editor of *New Left Review*, Blackburn took a keen and enthusiastic interest in all phases of the book, including the illustrations. Justin Dyer, my copy-editor, was kind and understanding beyond the call of duty as I altered and developed the manuscript.

I doubt if Cecil Gutzmore and Clive Harris realize how much I owe them. But for the past two decades or so, I have been nourished by their friendship with me, by our collaboration and shared political and intellectual interests in the African diaspora. Gutzmore and Harris have played an important part in my education through their generosity, encouragement and example. As with all of my other work, they carefully read and provided me with helpful comments on *Holding Aloft the Banner of Ethiopia*.

Barbara Fields, my wife, has lived with this project from its very inception. We have had innumerable discussions about different aspects of it. In addition, despite the great demands upon her time and energy, she managed to undertake a close reading of substantial parts of the manuscript and made helpful suggestions. I am greatly indebted to Barbara for her support, encouragement, understanding and good humor during the researching and writing of this book.

Of course, despite the help and encouragement of others, I alone am responsible for *Holding Aloft the Banner of Ethiopia*, especially for any weaknesses which may remain.

As always, I have been buttressed by the love and solidarity of my brothers and sisters, David, Michael, Colleen, Christine, Beverley and Mark. Over the years, my parents have provided me with unfailing support in a thousand different ways. I can never adequately thank them for what they have done for me. My late grand-aunt, Lauretta Tomlinson Campbell, and her husband, Uriah Campbell, played a vital role in my early life. To their memory and to my parents I dedicate this book as a small token of appreciation.

Prologue

One of the most intriguing sociological and historical facts about American radicalism in the twentieth century has been the prominence and often pre-eminence of Caribbean migrants among its participants.[1] From Hubert Harrison, the "Father of Harlem Radicalism,"[2] who migrated from the Virgin Islands in 1900, to the Trinidadian Stokeley Carmichael (Kwame Turé), a founder of the Black Power movement of the 1960s, a remarkable line of Caribbeans has stood in the vanguard of both radical political movements and radical currents of intellectual activity among black people in the United States. The group has included Marcus Garvey, the Jamaican founder of the largest mass movement among black people in the United States and the world, Cyril Briggs (Nevis), Jesús Colón (Puerto Rico), Frank Crosswaith (St Croix, Virgin Islands), Wilfred A. Domingo (Jamaica), Amy Ashwood Garvey (Jamaica), Amy Jacques Garvey (Jamaica), Otto Huiswoud (Dutch Guiana, now Suriname), C. L. R. James (Trinidad), Claudia Jones (Trinidad), Claude McKay (Jamaica), Richard B. Moore (Barbados), George Padmore (Trinidad), Thomas Patterson (Jamaica), Joel A. Rogers (Jamaica), Arturo Schomburg (Puerto Rico), Ashley Totten (St Croix, Virgin Islands), and Eric Walrond (British Guiana, now Guyana).[3]

Contemporaries recognized this phenomenon early on, and others have done so since. In 1919, the Afro-American Fenton Johnson, radical poet, political activist, editor, and Chicagoan, wrote:

> We of America owe much to the West Indian. We owe much to the intellectuality and the indomitable will of these Islanders. . . .
>
> In every field of our American life we find the West Indian pushing ahead and doing all in his power to uphold the dignity of the Negro race. In every industry, in every profession, in every trade, we find this son of the islands holding aloft the banner of Ethiopia.
>
> When the great day of our liberation comes, we will find the West Indian foremost in the ranks of those fighting with his armor on and his sword raised aloft.

Johnson insisted that the black political and cultural awakening taking place at the time—"this Negro renaissance," he called it—was "due largely to the aggressive mind of our brother from the islands, and for it we thank him and his Creator."[4]

Nine months after Johnson wrote those words, W. E. B. Du Bois suggested in an editorial in the organ of the National Association for the Advancement of Colored People that it was "not beyond possibilities, that this new Ethiopia of the Isles may yet stretch out hands of helpfulness to the 12 million black men of America."[5] A few years later, in 1923, Du Bois was more categorical and forthcoming. "American Negroes," he told a Jamaican migrant, "to a much larger extent that [sic] they realize, are not only blood relatives to the West Indians but under deep obligations to them for many things. For instance without the Haitian Revolt, there would have been no emancipation in America as early as 1863. I, myself, am of West Indian descent and am proud of the fact."[6]

The black revolutionary socialist magazine the *Messenger*, in a 1922 editorial, adjudged the Caribbeans to be "among the foremost fighters in all cities for racial rights." Edited by two of the most courageous and energetic fighters of the time, A. Philip Randolph and Chandler Owen, both Afro-American, the *Messenger* continued: "They [West Indians] are assiduous workers, vigorous fighters, diligent and able students."[7] W. A. Domingo, himself a leading Caribbean revolutionary socialist and from 1919 to 1923 a contributing editor of the *Messenger*, reported from within the inner circles of Harlem radicalism in 1925 that Caribbeans "largely compose the few political and economic radicals in Harlem." Indeed, so significant was this presence that Domingo went so far as to claim that "without them the genuinely radical movement among New York Negroes would be unworthy of attention."[8] Domingo exaggerated, but not by much.

In 1927 Kelly Miller, the distinguished Howard University professor, reflecting on the state of black American politics after the demise of Garvey, declared: "The West Indians were radical beyond the rest."[9] Indeed, Miller went so far as to "define" a Negro radical as "an *over*-educated West Indian without a job."[10] A decade later, Ira Reid, an Afro-American sociologist, concluded that the Negro immigrant — by which he meant, in essence, Caribbeans — was, in his words, "beyond a doubt more radical than the native [Afro-American]." Based upon a Columbia University doctoral dissertation, Reid's book, *The Negro Immigrant*, was the most substantial study of Caribbean migrants in America in the early twentieth century. To this day it stands unrivalled as an analysis of the Caribbean experience in the United States during the first four decades of the century.[11] A Harlem journalist, Roi Ottley, agreed, observing in 1943 that "The development of left-wing organizations among Negroes is largely attributed to him [the West Indian]."[12]

The agents of the Justice Department, the predecessors of the Federal Bureau of Investigation, agreed. Even by the most cynical standards of twentieth-century government surveillance, they kept an amazingly close watch of political activities within the black communities, and especially of Harlem's radical ferment, as their own documents eloquently testify. "I beg to state," reported the indefatigable special agent, code-named "P-138", from the heart of Harlem in March 1921, that nearly all these Negro radicals carry the *Bolshevic* [*sic*] *red card* and pay their monthly dues. . . . It might be interesting to learn that nearly all of them are West Indian men who have not been naturalized or even in possession of their first papers.

In another report, submitted two months later, he told his superiors:

From information I learned that nearly all the Negro radicals and agitators in New York are not citizens at all. They were fellows who were sailors on ships plying between here and the West Indies who had simply left their ships as soon as they reached New York.[13]

It is no exaggeration to say that the FBI files on "Negro Activities" in the United States during the 1920s are also very much intelligence reports on *Caribbean* radical activity in America, and especially in New York City.

Thus, a diverse group of informed contemporary observers were fully aware of the phenomenon of Caribbean involvement in American radicalism in the early twentieth century.

For their part, Caribbeans, as one commentator said recently, were "not unconscious of their strategic role" in the wider black community.[14] But that is an understatement. It is far more accurate to say that many Caribbeans shared a marked tendency to exaggerate and gloat about what they perceived to be their contribution to the struggle. Their attitude reflected ignorance of the history, of the frightening challenges Afro-America has had to face, of the struggles black people in America mounted against the odds. It also reflected the smug *hubris* of those who have never had loved ones plucked from their midst and lynched with impunity, the deed "passing with as little condemnation as a Sunday school recitation," as William Monroe Trotter put it;[15] never had to answer in the dead of night the call of armed men in superior number wearing white from head to foot, burning Calvary-sized crosses against a black Southern sky. Eric Walrond, the distinguished Guyanese author, illustrates the exaggeration of the Caribbean's role: "When the epic of the negro in America is written," he noted in 1923, "it will show the West Indian as *the* stokesman in the furnace of negro ideals."[16] It is true that Caribbeans were stokesmen in the furnace of Negro ideals. But were *all* the stokesmen Caribbean? Or was there just *one* stokesman, as Walrond suggests, and that one Caribbean?

W. A. Domingo, the radical journalist from Jamaica, illustrates the *hubris*, subtly wrapped up—as befits a writer of Domingo's caliber—but still identifiable for what it is:

The outstanding contribution of West Indians to American Negro life is the insistent assertion of their manhood in an environment that demands too much servility and unprotesting acquiescence from men of African blood. This unwillingness to conform and be standardized, to accept tamely an inferior status and abdicate their humanity, finds an open expression in the activities of the foreign-born Negro in America.

Their dominant characteristic is that of blazing new paths, breaking the bonds that would fetter the feet of a virile people—a spirit eloquently expressed in the defiant lines of the Jamaican poet, Claude McKay:

> "Like men we'll face the murderous, cowardly pack,
> Pressed to the wall, dying, but fighting back."[17]

Apart from the obvious absence of women—Caribbean or otherwise—in his depiction of the struggle for black liberation, the implication is that, prior to the arrival of Caribbeans in the United States there was an absence of "the insistent assertion of their manhood" on the part of African Americans. For according to Domingo, this has been *the outstanding* contribution of West Indians to American Negro life." He also clearly implied that black Americans not only accepted their inferior status, but accepted it *tamely*. Domingo's assertions do not comport with the historical evidence.

The Caribbean migrants learned better the longer they stayed in the United States. But postures such as those of Walrond and Domingo, akin to what St Clair Drake—himself the son of Caribbean migrants—called "West Indian arrogance,"[18] did nothing to heal the strained relationship between Afro-Americans and Afro-Caribbeans in New York and elsewhere in the United States, especially in the early 1920s. The relationship between the two groups in Harlem reached its nadir during the notorious "Garvey Must Go" campaign of 1922–23, when one of his Afro-American critics described Garvey as "A Supreme Negro Jamaican Jackass," and when "Don't be a Garvey!" was an abusive term used against Caribbean migrants, regardless of whether or not they supported Garvey.[19] An editorial in New York's oldest black newspaper, the *New York Age*, described the members of the Universal Negro Improvement Association (UNIA) as "undesirable aliens whose presence in this country is a dangerous intrusion." They should, it continued, "be deported to the islands whence they came, the same as any other group of anarchists." With its repeated reference to Garvey's supporters as an unnaturalized "group of aliens," and as an "alien crew," not to mention "undesirable aliens," the *Age* was, in effect, calling for the deportation of all Caribbean migrants. They should be deported, said the *Age*, "so that they may return under the British flag that they honor so greatly. They will play no such monkey shines under that."[20]

Out of this conjuncture came Langston Hughes's little-known poem "Brothers," a direct and healing—if somewhat sentimental—commentary on the troubled relations between the two fractions of the African diaspora:

> We are related—you and I.
> You from the West Indies,
> I from Kentucky.
> We are related—you and I.
> You from Africa,

I from these States.
We are brothers—you and I.[21]

It is inappropriate that Domingo should have cited McKay as he did, since one of the most powerful motifs in McKay's work is the supersession of petty and negative divisions between people of African descent—including those between African Caribbeans and African Americans. He recognized and openly acknowledged the cultural differences and indeed antagonisms between certain sections of the African diaspora. But he equally insisted that in a world dominated by Europe and its destructive diaspora, when all was said and done, pan-African solidarity and loyalty were more sensible than insular, parochial ones. "It is so stupid and idiotic—the jealousies, rivalries and discords between West Indian and American Negro," wrote McKay to a friend.[22]

But the tendency to exaggerate the political militance of Caribbean migrants was not confined to Caribbeans alone. Some Afro-Americans at times attributed almost messianic powers to those whom Du Bois, in his revealing formulation, described as "this new Ethiopia of the Isles."[23] William Sherrill, Baltimorean and Assistant President of the UNIA, in a speech before the 1924 convention declared:

I am an American Negro, born and raised under the Southern psychology. I know what that psychology is—its peculiar oppressive effect. And I tell you ... that if the Negro was ever to have a real, energetic, courageous Negro leader, able to tell his people to be men and to look the world straight in the face—that if our people were ever to have such a leader ... he would have to come from somewhere else than in the United States of America. The Negro of America raised under such conditions finds it difficult to develop the qualities of leadership. The fine material that is fit to lead the race is killed in the American environment. Here the Negro from childhood is jim-crowed, lynched, kicked about, cursed and made to conduct himself as an inferior until he has not grit enough left to be a leader. The West Indian Negro, on the other hand, from the cradle up develops a certain independence and self-reliance that the American Negro never has the courage to exercise. The British government is bound to allow the development of some initiative among individual Negroes, for her position in Jamaica is such that she has to use certain types of Negroes to exercise authority over the others. Of course, those who are used that way are betraying their own people ... but even at that, in Jamaica there is a different psychology that permits some men of independent spirit and self-reliance to develop.[24]

Though not without merit, Sherrill's depiction of Afro-Americans as well as of Afro-Caribbeans is more caricature than fact. It is true that in a direct and immediate way the American environment, in the post-Reconstruction period especially, was more merciless, more brutal, more suffocatingly inhibiting to black people than the Caribbean environment was to their brothers and sisters. But Sherrill forgets that, despite the soul-destroying environment of America, in his own home state of Maryland alone there arose two of the most magnificent figures of the African diaspora, Harriet Tubman and Frederick Douglass: two black fighters who raised their heads above the American wasteland of slavery and oppression. Sherrill's gloss on Jamaica is not only ahistorical, but doubly illegitimate, in that he sees the Caribbean, and the British Caribbean in particular, as Jamaica writ large, or as so many multiplications of a heroic black Jamaica.

Without question then, an important sociological and historical problem has been identified, and has been articulated in myriad ways, with varying degrees of sophistication, for at least three generations: namely, the relation between Caribbean migrants and varieties of American radicalism. In order to negotiate the minefield of hyperbole and distortions surrounding the subject, one needs to establish the facts of Caribbean involvement in radical movements in the United States, especially during the first three decades of the twentieth century, the crucial period of the islanders' settlement and communal formation in America. Second and more crucially, one needs to offer, or a least attempt to offer, an explanation of the phenomenon. These two tasks form the primary undertaking of *Holding Aloft the Banner of Ethiopia*.

For remarkably, the long-standing and pervasive recognition of the over-representation of Caribbeans in radical politics in America is by no means matched by an adequate explanation and theory. Ira Reid, Dennis Forsythe, and Keith Henry have made important contributions to understanding of the problem. Reid's discussion of the subject is pioneering and insightful, but insufficiently developed. He cannot be blamed for that, because he did not set out to explain Caribbean radicalism as such. His object was a more general sociological analysis of black immigrants in the United States. Forsythe's and Henry's contributions are more substantial, and in parts richly textured and documented. But aside from certain factual errors— partly explained by the limited archival resources that they had at their disposal when they researched and wrote in the late 1960s and the early 1970s —I find unconvincing the theoretical framework of both writers: namely, that there was a general metamorphosis on the part of the migrants from "conservatism" in the Caribbean to "radicalism" in the United States; Henry revealingly subtitles his article on the subject "The Passage from Political Quiescence to Radicalism." The schema, though not wholly without merit, is over-stated, as the historical evidence and analysis that I present in the following pages suggest. In fact the paradigm of conservative-to-radical in itself obscures key conceptual and concrete issues one needs to examine in order to explain the radicalism of Caribbeans in America.[25] The most well-known and widely cited analysis of the problem comes from Harold Cruse's *The Crisis of the Negro Intellectual*. But although, in many respects, Cruse's was a bold and important book when it came out in 1967, his discussion of Caribbeans in the United States is so problematic at a variety of levels, and the influence of his book so pervasive, that I have decided to engage with some of his arguments in a postscript to the main text.

I have also attempted here, in marked distinction from previous efforts, to broaden the discussion from a relatively narrow consideration of the anglophone Caribbean to explore the experience of Afro-Caribbeans from the Hispanic Caribbean. Cubans and Puerto Ricans migrated to the United States in significant numbers during the late nineteenth and early twentieth century and therefore ought not to be ignored in any analysis that purports to treat migrants from the Caribbean, and not just the English-speaking Caribbean.[26] Rafael Serra and Sotero Figueroa (Afro-Caribbean brothers in arms with José Martí in the struggle for Cuban and Puerto Rican independence), Jesús Colón and Arturo Schomburg (two distinguished Afro-Puerto Rican fighters), though less well known than Marcus Garvey, George Padmore, and Richard B. Moore, were nevertheless, members and products of that peculiar civilization that developed in the Caribbean. They were Caribbean Africans and they, too, sojourned and fought in the United States. They deserve attention in their own right, as well as for the contrasting light they provide for understanding the radicals from the non-Hispanic Caribbean.

Holding Aloft the Banner of Ethiopia is also offered as a contribution to the wider and more nuanced understanding of the African diaspora in the Americas. I am continually amazed at scholars who make grandiose claims to write about the experience of the African diaspora as a whole while saying little, if anything, about the Caribbean and Caribbeans.[27] Within the context of the Americas, the Caribbean—geographically and demographically—is small, but its historical, political, and cultural contribution to the experience of the African diaspora and the wider world far exceeds its dimensions. And one of the tasks of the book is to illustrate some of the ways in which this is so.

Holding Aloft the Banner of Ethiopia intends to throw new light on the historical and cultural complexity and heterogeneity of the region, and the variation within its diaspora in the United States. The study is also meant as a contribution to the substantial and growing literature on immigrant radicalism in the United States.[28] It is seldom recognized that black people, Caribbeans and to a lesser extent Africans, migrated to the United States prior to the Second World War. Yet between 1899 and 1937 almost 150,000 black people immigrated to these shores. Although most came through New York City, you would never know that from the iconograpy of Ellis Island immigrant studies or, indeed, from the extant and most influential studies of American immigration. As their immigrant status has been invisible, their role as radicals in the mainstream literature on American radicalism has remained unacknowledged, elided or obscured. With rare exceptions—for example, the work of Theodore Draper—the Caribbean presence is generally acknowledged with reference to Garveyism, but hardly in relation to other variants of twentieth-century American radicalism and dissent. And even in Draper's work the acknowledgement of Caribbean involvement with the American left arises only incidentally to his discussion of the Negro Question as handled by the Communist Party and the Communist International.[29]

Through the next eight chapters, I hope to outline the scale and determinants of Caribbean migration to the United States and the migrants' political behavior from the turn of the century up to the Great Depression. From 1899, the immigration authorities began to keep records that provide fairly detailed information about not only the provenance, but also the "race" and ethnicity—as well as other characteristics, such as literacy, age, sex, and occupation—of those who migrated to the United States. This information has made it possible to trace, with reasonable accuracy, the migration of people from the Caribbean to America.

By 1932, with the onset and deepening of the Great Depression, coupled with the restrictive immigration legislation of 1924, the migration flow from the Caribbean to the United States went into reverse: there were more people returning to the Caribbean from the United States than there were migrants from the Caribbean to the United States.[30] This pattern was only broken in the aftermath of the Second World War. From 1900 to 1932, there was a net migration of almost 88,000 persons from the archipelago to America. The analysis is focussed on this first generation of twentieth-century Caribbean migrants to the United States.

Having established the significant presence of Caribbeans in the United States in the first three decades of the century, the book then moves on to examine in greater detail the characteristics of those who left the Caribbean (Chapter 2), and their initial response to American society (Chapter 3). Chapter 4 then engages with the differences between the articulation of race in the Caribbean and the United States—a task essential to understanding the immigrants' response to the new society.

Chapters 5 to 8 measure the involvement of the islanders in different radical organizations, analyze their political ideology and action, and attempt explanations. Included are two chapters (7 and 8) that examine the dimensions of the Afro-Hispanic radical experience in the United States. Chapter 7 discusses the political evolution of two Afro-Puerto Ricans, Arturo Schomburg and Jesús Colón, and the divergent trajectories that they followed. Chapter 8 outlines and engages with the relatively little known but instructive and fascinating story of Afro-Cubans in Florida (Key West and Tampa, primarily), from the late nineteenth century to about 1940.

It is my hope that *Holding Aloft the Banner of Ethiopia* will throw new light and stimulate further research on the Caribbean diaspora in the United States and elsewhere.

1

Caribbean Migration:
Scale, Determinants, and
Destinations, 1880–1932

I see these islands and I feel to bawl,
"area of darkness" with V. S. Nightfall.

Derek Walcott

Never seen
a man
travel more
seen more
lands
than this poor
path-
less harbour-
less spade.

Edward Kamau Brathwaite

It is little wonder that there was so much talk about Caribbean migrants in early-twentieth-century black America. For not only were they conspicuous in political agitation, they were also made conspicuous through distinctive cultural activities and sartorial taste. But most of all, these migrants were conspicuous, especially in New York City, through sheer weight of numbers. It was not that the Caribbean presence was new to America—far from it. Barbadian slaves had been taken by their British owners colonizing South Carolina during the seventeenth century, and earlier in the same century slaves from Barbados constituted an important portion of the black population of Virginia.[1] South Carolina was in fact developed by and in subservience to Barbadian interests, supplying beef, pork, and lumber products to the island in exchange for sugar. And it has been persuasively argued that South Carolina was, even into the eighteenth century, the dependent of little Barbados—"an island master." South Carolina, said Peter Wood, was the "colony of a colony."[2] Small wonder, then, that the settlement was referred to in London as "Carolina in ye West Indies," for South Carolina was an integral member of the Caribbean

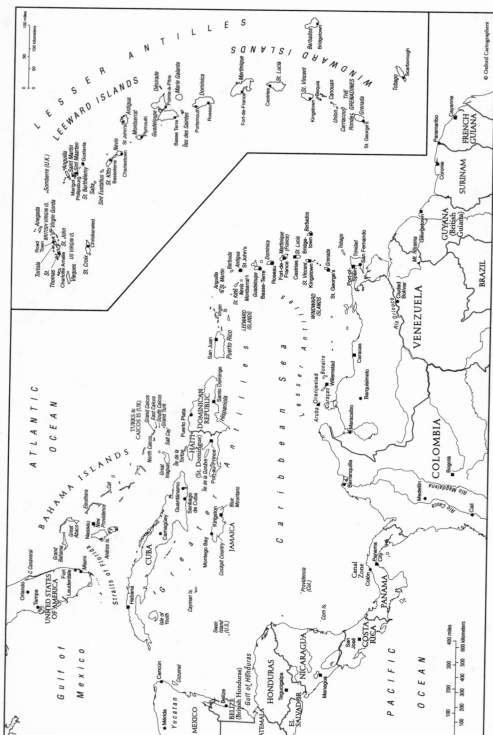

The Caribbean

© Oxford Cartographers

universe of exchange and commerce. In the eighteenth century South Carolina extended and deepened its trading relations with other Caribbean colonies, Jamaica surpassing Barbados as a market for its products. Up to 1700, it is safe to assume that all the slaves in South Carolina came from the Caribbean and Barbados in particular. It has been estimated that between 15 and 20 percent of slaves to South Carolina in the eighteenth century came from the Caribbean.[3] But the degree of intercourse between the two areas, as Jack P. Greene has forcefully argued, was enormous.[4] And the significant influence of the Caribbean on South Carolina endures to this day.

But the pre-twentieth-century Caribbean presence in the United States extends well beyond colonial Virginia and South Carolina. Prince Hall, a Barbadian, established black freemasonry in the United States and was a distinguished leader of black Boston during the eighteenth century. Barbadians and other Caribbeans, apparently, constituted about 20 percent of the black population in Boston at the time.[5] The Caribbean population in the United States was relatively small during the nineteenth century, but it grew significantly, especially after the Civil War. Indeed, the foreign-born black population, which was almost wholly Caribbean in origin, increased fivefold between 1850 and 1900, from 4,067 to 20,236, and distinguished Caribbean migrants populate the annals of nineteenth-century Afro-America.[6]

Denmark Vesey, who in 1822 in Charleston, South Carolina, organized a black uprising, was from the Virgin Islands. The conspiracy was betrayed and Vesey was executed. John B. Russwurm of Jamaica, one of the early New World settlers of Liberia, was one of the first three black people to graduate from an American college—Bowdoin College, Maine, in 1826.[7] In the spring of 1827, Russwurm, with his Afro-American colleague, Samuel E. Cornish, started *Freedom's Journal*, the first black newspaper published in the United States. Russwurm's compatriot, Peter Ogden, organized in New York City the first Odd-Fellows Lodge among the black population. Robert Brown Elliott, the brilliant fighter and orator of the Reconstruction era, claimed Jamaican parentage.[8] David Augustus Straker, a law partner of Elliott's, a fighter for civil rights, educationalist, journalist, chronicler of the dark, post-Reconstruction days, and a distinguished lawyer in his own right, was from Barbados.[9] Jan Earnst Matzeliger, the inventor of a revolutionary shoe-making machine, had migrated from Suriname. Edward Wilmot Blyden, a brilliant man and major contributor to the stream of black nationalist thought in America and abroad, was born in the Virgin Islands.[10] William Henry Crogman, Latin and Greek scholar, a former president of Clark College and one of the founders of the American Negro Academy, came from St Maarten. Bert Williams, the famous comedian, was born in Antigua. And at the beginning of the new century Robert Charles O'Hara Benjamin (1855–1900), journalist, editor, lawyer, and writer, was gunned down—shot in the back six times—in Lexington, Kentucky, because of his work of "uplifting the race," including writing and speaking out against lynching, and defending the constitutional right of black people to vote. On the morning of October 2, 1900, Benjamin had quarrelled with a white man, Michael Moynahan, over the latter's harassment of black people registering to vote. Moynahan struck Benjamin several times with his revolver, for which Benjamin laid assault charges against him. Moynahan was arrested but released on bail within an hour. As Benjamin was returning home in the evening, Moynahan, armed with a rifle, ambushed him. Benjamin attempted to flee, but was cut down by Moynahan's bullets. Despite overwhelming evidence to the contrary, Moynahan was acquitted on grounds of self-defense. Even the white Kentucky newspapers—none of which was a friend of the Negro—thought the verdict an outrage. Benjamin had come from St Kitts and had lived and fought racism in the United States for almost thirty years before moving to Lexington in 1897.[11] Although unfamilar and largely forgotten today, these people were widely known by Afro-Americans in the last century.[12]

A significant number of the nineteenth-century migrants were skilled craftsmen, students, teachers, preachers, lawyers, and doctors. Even more skewed in social origins than those who were to migrate to the United States in the twentieth century, these migrants gained a reputation that distorted Afro-America's perception of the Caribbean reality. For, as Hubert Harrison observed, "It was taken for granted that every West Indian immigrant was a paragon of intelligence and a man of birth and breeding."[13]

What was new in the early twentieth century was, therefore, not the Caribbean presence itself, but the scale of it. The number of black people, and especially Caribbeans, who migrated to the United States increased dramatically, from a trickle of 411 in 1899 to a flood of 12,243 per year by 1924, the high point of the early black migration (see Tables 1.1 and 1.2 and Figure 1.1, pages 355–7, 367 respectively). From a population of twenty thousand in 1900, the foreign-born black population in the United States had grown to almost a hundred thousand by 1930. Over a hundred and forty thousand black immigrants—exclusive of black visitors or tourists—passed through the ports of America between 1899 and 1937. And this occurred despite the viciously restrictive legislation of 1917 and 1924—the figure for those admitted in 1925 was 95 percent below that for the previous year—and the economic and migratory reversals of the Depression thirties. The overwhelming majority of these migrants came from the Caribbean islands, over 80 percent of them—if we include those of Caribbean origin coming from Central America—between 1899 and 1932 (see Table 1.2, pages 356–7). During the peak years of migration, 1913 to 1924, the majority headed not only for the state of New York, but also for New York City (see Table 1.3 and Figure 1.2, pages 358, 368). By 1930, almost a quarter of black Harlem was of Caribbean origin.

A series of interweaving developments, processes, and events triggered and sustained this massive exodus from the islands. And behind the surge of Caribbean migration in the late nineteenth and early twentieth centuries lay the long history of colonialism and the political economy of sugar.

By 1900 the islands had undergone four centuries of European colonial domination. This experience of prolonged colonialism has been the most important force in the Caribbean's historical formation. And colonialism was accompanied for almost its entire duration by chattel slavery.

The European colonialists shaped the economies of the region to the benefit of the metropole and to the severe disadvantage of the overwhelming majority of the Caribbean people. The term "underdeveloped" (meaning relative retardation or economic regression) is often used to describe the economies of the Caribbean. This is overly generous and therefore is a misapplication of the concept, for the historical relationship between the Caribbean and Europe has, in essence, been a more brutal one than the term suggests. The Caribbean islands were annexed, their indigenous peoples (Arawaks and Caribs) subjugated and decimated. Having created a virtual *tabula rasa* of them, as it were, partly through genocide, the islands were then newly populated by the conquerors and by the forced migration of enslaved Africans.

Unlike Africa and Asia, and, indeed, much of continental (especially South) America, where the indigenous population form the base of the colonial edifice, in the Caribbean the native population was not only conquered but also—deliberately and partly inadvertently—destroyed. Upon the bones of the vanquished the Europeans created a new society fashioned essentially according to their colonial desires. The absence, at a remarkably early stage of colonialism, of an indigenous base is one of the most extraordinary, if not unique, features of Caribbean social formations. Caribbean societies, then, were literally *new*, not through the subordination and transformation of old forms but through the destruction of the latter and the creation of new ones.

Rather than having been a victim of "underdevelopment," the Caribbean has quintessentially been a site of plunder and of the unrestrained fabrication of wealth uninhibited by the "inconvenience" of an indigenous presence. It is in more ways than one that the Caribbean has been a construction of Europe—albeit a perennially contested one.

John Stuart Mill's interesting observation in the nineteenth century that Britain and its Caribbean possessions had a relationship of town and country has the merit of drawing attention to the organic nature of the economic relationship between the center and the periphery—what some would later call the relationship of metropolis and satellite, imperial center and colony. "If Manchester," observed Mill, instead of being where it is, were on a rock in the North Sea . . . it would still be a town of England, not a country trading with England: it would be merely, as now, the place where England finds it convenient to carry on her cotton manufactures. The West Indies, in like manner, are the place where England finds it convenient to carry on the production of sugar, coffee, and a few other tropical commodities. All the capital employed is English capital; almost all the industry is carried on for English uses; there is little production of anything except the staple commodities, and these are sent to England, not to be exchanged for things exported to the colony and consumed by its inhabitants, but to be sold in England for the benefit of the proprietors there.[14]

But this formulation—leaving aside the counterfactual and therefore problematic nature of the argument—also over-simplifies the relationship, for the Caribbean colonies were never simply the country to Britain's town. As colonies, they were organic to Britain, but they were also *foreign*, overseas; here as part of Empire, but always there, in "the West Indies." As a part of Empire, they were defined as British and thus central, but by the very same token—as colonies—they were, by definition, marginal, paradigmatically Other. This was the fundamental and inherent tension of the Imperial Idea. Despite the ideological smokescreens, however, it was always very clear that not only politically but also economically the colony was subordinate and subordinated to the imperial heartland—the colony *belonged* to the "Mother Country."[15]

At the beginning of the century, the world was undergoing momentous transformations and the Caribbean was in the throes of extraordinarily rapid and profound changes. By 1890, Africa—from the Mediterranean to the Cape—was writhing in agony as the imperial powers of Europe hacked away at the continent, like butchers with cleavers, to take possession of their self-allocated segments. At the Berlin Congress of 1884–85, they had decided how they would distribute the spoils of their handiwork of co-ordinated and pre-meditated plunder. No longer confined to the coast, imperial Europe was busy penetrating Africa's vast hinterland, joining its conquests from the Atlantic to the Indian Ocean.

Africa, however, was not the only victim of the times. In Asia and Latin America an increasingly vigorous penetration of capital, characteristically accompanied by the displacement of peasants from the land, was underway. An increase in the level of poverty and a widening of economic inequality attended the process. By the beginning of our century, the Philippines, Guam, Cuba, and Puerto Rico had fallen under the overt tutelage of the United States of America. Emerging by this time to be by far the most powerful industrial nation in the world, the United States had transformed the Caribbean sea into a *de facto* American lake.[16]

But the changes in the archipelago were complex and profoundly uneven. There was, on the one hand, the tumult of the sugar revolution in the Hispanic Caribbean, especially in Cuba, and the relatively profitable adjustments of the planter class in Guyana and Trinidad to economic competition on the world sugar market. In marked contrast to these economies, the older British colonies such as Barbados, St Kitts, and Jamaica entered the doldrums as far as the sugar industry was concerned. Indeed, it was a period of catastrophic decline and painful reorganization of the sugar industry in the British Caribbean as a whole. Thus, while the British Caribbean produced in the 1820s just under 56 percent of the total average annual output of 331,000 tons of Caribbean sugar, in the first decade of the twentieth century it contributed only 11 percent of the annual average of 2,217,000 tons produced within the region. Cuba's output corresponded inversely with that of the British Caribbean. From an average of 57,000 tons per annum in the 1820s, amounting to only 17.2 percent of the Caribbean total, Cuba was, by the first decade of the twentieth century, the unrivalled leader in the production of Caribbean sugar, accounting for just under 75 percent of the regions' total output (see Tables 1.4 and 1.5, and Figure 1.3, pages 359–60, 369).[17]

The working people of the Caribbean, especially those in the older British territories, were to experience severe hardship during this period. And it comes as no surprise that Jamaica supplied by far the largest group of migrants from the region during the late nineteenth and early twentieth centuries. The fact that the island was the most populous of the northern European possessions in the archipelago does not fully account for the large number of its citizens who migrated to Panama, Costa Rica, Honduras, Mexico, Guatemala, Nicaragua, Cuba and the United States from 1850 to 1930. In 1881 the island was home to about 40 percent of the British Caribbean population, yet it provided more than half of the net emigration from the area between 1881 and 1914.[18] The proportion would doubtless have been greater had the colonial authorities allowed the Isthmian Canal Commission, the American company that organized the building of the Canal, to recruit on the island with the same freedom that the authorities permitted in Barbados. Of the 23,037 British Caribbeans recruited by the Commission agents on the islands between 1904 and 1913, 19,900 were from Barbados and only 47 came from Jamaica. Unlike the agents' recruits from Barbados and elsewhere, the Jamaicans did not get free passage to the Isthmus. In one way or another they had to pay their own passage, plus a departure tax, as discussed later. Between 1904 and 1914, the years during which the Canal was built, it costed £1. 5s. to travel by deck (with meals) from Jamaica to Panama.[19] This was a considerable sum of money given the prevailing low wages on the island. "Since most of the West Indians who emigrated were unemployed or poorly paid laborers, one may well wonder," Velma Newton wrote, "how they could have afforded to pay these fares." Yet between 1905 and 1915 there were almost 90,000 recorded departures from the island to Panama.[20] Without an understanding of the economic crisis of Jamaica in the late nineteenth and early twentieth centuries it is impossible to appreciate why the island was the site of this astonishing exodus, the primary Caribbean source of labor supply for the rest of the Americas. And as we will see, many of the problems that afflicted Jamaica at the time similarly plagued the older British colonies, especially Barbados, which was second only to Jamaica in its disgorging of people. Let us then look closer at the forces which laid behind the Jamaican migrants' backs as they left the island, saddened by the separation that is migration but filled with hope of a better life elsewhere.

Sugar and the workings of the political economy of sugar hold the key to understanding the fortunes of the island and its people. Indeed, the sugar industry which had been the island's *raison d'être* since the seventeenth century had collapsed well before the end of the nineteenth century. Out-competed by Cuban and Brazilian cane sugar, substituted by subsidized beet sugar in Europe, under-capitalized, encumbered by massive debts to London creditors, and mercilessly exposed to international market forces by Britain's removal of tariffs against its rivals, King Sugar by 1890 had been well and truly dethroned in Jamaica.

In 1836 the price of Jamaican sugar stood at 41 shillings (s.) per hundredweight (cwt). It went up to as high as 48s. in 1840, but for the rest of the century it followed a sharply downward trend: 23s. in 1870, 20.5s., 13.0s. and 11.25s. per cwt in 1880, 1890, and 1900, respectively.[21] It was only with the First World War's unintended devastation of Europe's broad acres of beet sugar that an increase in the price of sugar occurred; and the favorable prices did not last much longer than the war (see Figure 1.4, page 370).

The fall in the number of sugar estates was even more precipitous. From 670 in 1836 this dropped to an estimated 162 in 1890 and dwindled to 74 by 1910.[22] In 1838 Jamaica exported 1,053,000 cwt of sugar, by 1890 sugar exports fell by over 64 percent to 378,000 cwt; in 1910 it was still only 399,000 cwt.[23] Although there were many cases of amalgamation and consolidation of estates during the nineteenth century, the area under sugar cultivation nevertheless shrank considerably. Within the space of only a generation—between 1869 and 1900—the area under sugar cultivation had declined by 45 percent.[24]

But the decline of sugar was by no means evenly distributed geographically across the island. King Sugar had been dethroned but he was by no means dead. He strategically retreated to the western plains of Jamaica while still maintaining a foothold in the flat lands of southern Clarendon. There was ruthless capitalist re-organization and rationalization under the whip of international competition.[25] Consequently, although the number of sugar estates substantially declined, the average size of the surviving ones had increased by almost 60 percent between 1880 and 1910, from 185 to 294 acres.[26] The average yield per acre had also increased from 0.74 to 0.92 tons between 1846 and 1896; not especially impressive, but it constituted improvement. With the amalgamation of the estates the average output per sugar factory doubled between 1880 and 1910.[27] Not surprisingly, the upshot of this dialectic of decline and rationalization was that there were fewer jobs available in the Jamaican sugar industry than previously. Thus between 1891 and 1911 male employment in the sugar industry fell by just under a third from 19,206 to 13,153.[28] And this had repercussions well beyond the immediate impact and well-being of those who lost jobs—families and relatives relied heavily upon the income of the lucky ones who had work, one wage feeding many mouths.

During the last two decades of the nineteenth century, however, a new agricultural sector had emerged into prominence almost overnight, eclipsing sugar with astonishing rapidity. This was the "banana trade." The banana was introduced into Jamaica in the sixteenth century. It was a humble but valued fruit cultivated primarily by slaves on their provision grounds and in the post-emancipation era by the peasantry. The Gros Michel, introduced from Martinique in the nineteenth century, became the most popular variety. To flourish, the banana needs fertile soil with vegetable mould along with good rainfall and drainage. It therefore thrived in the "black soils" of Portland, St Mary, St Thomas, and St Catherine—areas with the heaviest rainfall in the island, the eastern parishes of Jamaica.[29] Up to the late 1870s, bananas remained an essentially peasant crop. According to Lord Olivier, a former Governor of the island, banana cultivation was "despised as a backwoods 'nigger business,' which any old-time sugar planter would have disdained to handle, or, if tempted by undeniable prospects of profit, would have thought an apology was required."[30] Thus in 1879, only one large estate was under banana cultivation.[31] However, large-scale banana cultivation began to occur the following year. Jamaican merchants and professionals "whom their neighbours regarded as cranks," Olivier tells us, moved into the "nigger business" on a grand scale;[32] fourteen of St Thomas' eighteen sugar estates had changed over to banana cultivation by 1899.[33] There was money to be made.

The revolution in banana cultivation and marketing was initiated by an American, Lorenzo Dow Baker, who, unburdened by the historical snobbery of sugar cultivation, had proven in 1871 the feasibility and profitability of large-scale banana shipment to the United States. By the 1880s, acutely aware of the profit to be made, Baker was busy purchasing and leasing thousands of acres in eastern Jamaica for the growing and export of bananas. Others were to follow in Baker's footsteps in the banana trade, but the Bostonian and his corporate creations the Boston Fruit Company, which later developed into the notorious United Fruit Company, were not to be denied. Beneath his beatific New England smile was the mind of a ruthless and shrewd capitalist.[34] But it was not only his capitalist rivals who were punished and vanquished by Baker—the peasants of eastern Jamaica suffered an historic defeat at his hands. Baker had friends in high places: he was aided and abetted by the colonial state and Joseph Chamberlain's policy of encouraging large land-holdings in the British Caribbean.[35]

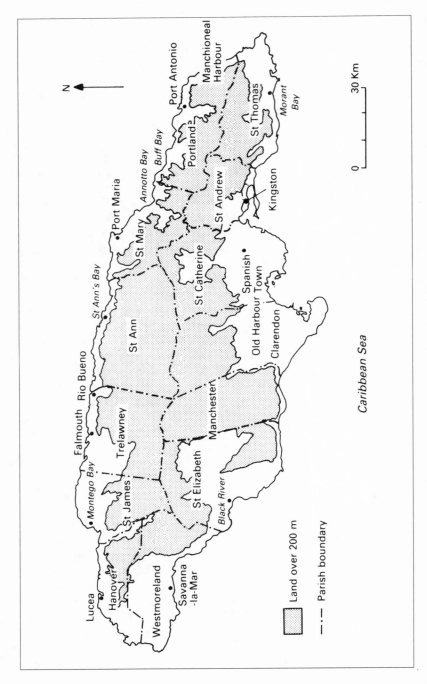

Jamaica and its parishes

The area under banana cultivation in 1894 was 17,297 acres; that under sugar cane was 31,555. By 1900, 28,163 acres were under banana cultivation compared to 26,121 under sugar cane. From 2,000 stems in 1869, Jamaica was producing in 1900 an astonishing 8,248,000 stems of banana.[36] The island was the world's premier producer of bananas for over two generations, from 1876 to 1929, when it fell behind Honduras.[37] The rise was meteoric. In 1870 sugar accounted for 44.5 percent of the island's export earnings, bananas a negligible 0.06 percent. By 1900 bananas were the most important agricultural export earner at 35.6 percent compared to sugar's 10.8 percent of total agricultural export value.[38] Indeed, while sugar and rum together in 1900 earned £325,873, banana alone earned over £600,000. Ten years later bananas furnished 52 percent while sugar and rum combined brought in only 14.1 percent of Jamaica's export earnings.[39] By 1911 bananas employed 77 percent more people than the sugar industry did.[40] The humble Gros Michel had upstaged King Sugar.

However, as intimated, the consequences of the expansion of banana cultivation under the *de facto* hegemony, if not total monopoly, of Baker were not all happy ones. With initially high prices, Baker lured the peasantry of St Mary, Portland, and St Thomas into agreements to exclusively supply his company with bananas. Having captured the market, he then controlled the prices.[41] Baker instructed his agents to bargain hard with the peasant producers. And by insisting that the producers bring their fruit to the ports, he not only avoided the cost of transportation, but also adroitly obviated the risk and cost of damage—such as the all too common bruising—of the bananas en route; the suppliers would bear these burdens. Baker was profoundly aware of the powerful position that he had successfully maneuvered himself into. "You need not make any extra exertion for bananas," he told his son. "Tell the people if they wish to sell their fruit they must bring it down." Baker briefed his agents to accept only top-quality bananas, and to reject all fruit deemed below his prescribed standards; sentiment had no place in such transactions with the peasants: "Never mind what people say," Baker told his son, "throw it back on their barrels, let them suffer for it if they will not mind you."[42]

In addition, Baker's Boston Fruit Company and later United Fruit Company, through their various acquisition of land, significantly contributed to the raising of the price of land beyond the reach of the peasantry. Indeed, some were reduced to becoming tenants on Baker's estates.[43] As one historian recently observed, with the growth in the monopoly power of Baker's United Fruit company, peasant growers

> came to resemble even more the household production workers of England's prefactory textile industry. By the early twentieth century, ... the Jamaican banana trade was controlled from production to marketing by one multinational corporation, rendering the formerly independent peasant cultivators a virtual proletariat.[44]

But Baker's impact on the peasantry and agro-proletarians did not end there: the rapid expansion of banana cultivation and the extensive irrigation it demanded meant that malaria—a disease carried by mosquitoes that breed in stagnant water—became more prevalent in the eastern parishes as a direct result of large-scale banana growing. Indeed, according to one authority: "The extension of banana cultivation to some of these areas . . . made malaria a *typical* disease of banana workers."[45]

In global terms the peasantry fared increasingly badly in late nineteenth-century Jamaica. Veront Satchell, in his pioneering study of land transactions in Jamaica from 1866 to 1900, has shown in laudable detail the mechanisms through which the peasantry was systematically squeezed during this period. The 1860s marked the expansion and consolidation of peasant holdings. This was so despite the fact that through the removal of "squatters" there were numerous losers amongst the peasantry.[46] Smallholders (those in possession of land 5 acres or less in size) were sold public land (i.e., Crown land under the control of the state) at five times the price paid by large landowners (those with acquisitions over 500 acres.) Indeed, Satchell noted that: "While large properties were sold at an average of 8 [shillings] per acre, small lots attracted prices of 45 [shillings] per acre."[47] This was partly due to the fact that from the 1870s to the 1890s the colonial government had a policy of selling land in large tracts which, of course, the peasantry could not afford. And so when small units came on the market there was apparently fierce competition between members of the peasantry to acquire them.[48] Thus, of the 19 lots sold in the 1870s, only 26.3 percent were under 50 acres, and in the 1880s of the 74 sales just 16.2 percent were holdings under 50 acres.[49] The land acquired by the peasantry was far less fertile, more hilly, and less accessible than that acquired by the merchants and planters. Furthermore, the expansion of Crown land inflicted one of the most devastating blows upon the peasants. It artificially reduced the supply of land, thus increasing its price. Between 1867 and 1912 some 240,368 acres had reverted to the colonial government as Crown land. This vigorous consolidation was concentrated at the very end of the century: 128,000 acres of the total-had reverted to the Crown during the eight years between 1894 and 1901.[50]

According to Satchell, by the mid 1890s, 81 individuals had become the owners of no less than 97 percent of the area of rural land offered by the government for sale. A similar dynamic of expansion and consolidation of large plantations at the expense of smallholders occurred in private land transactions over the same period.[51] It was not surprising then, that by the end of the nineteenth century the peasantry were acquiring considerably less land than they had been in the 1860s. They were boxed in by corporate capital and a resurgent plantocracy. With the exception of parts of the Windward Islands, this was characteristic of the anglophone Caribbean at the turn of the century. Woodville Marshall describes the period as that of "saturation," when the peasantry in the British Caribbean as a whole failed to expand its holdings and, indeed, experienced contraction in a number of instances, including in Jamaica.[52]

With the boom in banana cultivation, it became more and more difficult for smallholders to acquire land in the banana parishes. Thus the 1890s were marked by rapid consolidation of landholdings in the eastern parishes. In fact so much so that by 1900 four landholders, including Baker, came to acquire over 65,000 acres of land in the principal banana parishes during the late nineteenth century.[53] In addition to this, the colonial government had offered 76,800 acres of land (79 percent of which was in Portland and St Thomas) to an American syndicate, the West India Improvement Company, for extending the island's railway by 116 miles.[54]

At a time that prices put a plot of land beyond the reach of the peasants, those who were lucky enough to find work soon discovered that they were hardly paid for their labor; unable to live as peasants, they were mercilessly exploited as proletarians. In 1838—the year in which slavery finally came to an end with the close of the apprenticeship system—an agricultural worker could expect to earn between 7 pence, and 1 shilling and 2 pence for a day's labor. In 1890, the figure was between 9 pence, and 1 shilling and 9 pence; and in 1910 the range was 6 pence to 1 shilling and 6 pence.[55] This meant that *nominal*—not to mention real—agricultural wages had remained stagnant over three generations. The African Jamaicans had left the realm of chattel slavery only to enter a world of wage slavery—with hardly any wages at all. In fact, in certain respects conditions were worse in the post-slavery period than they were during the years of bondage. A good example of this is medical provision. Forced by the Slave Acts to provide medical care for their slaves, plantation owners employed doctors at the rate of 6 shillings per annum per slave. As a result, many doctors were said to be "extremely prosperous" during the early part of the nineteenth century. No doubt attracted by the lucrative venture, 200 doctors practiced in Jamaica in 1830—a doctor for every 1,855 people. In 1846 and 1860 there were 139 and 50 doctors, respectively, throughout the whole island. The "market" in medically attending to slaves was no longer there. The former slaves were no longer the charge of their erstwhile masters. Poverty-stricken, they had none of what neo-classical economists would call "effective demand" for the relative luxury of a doctor's care. Thus in 1860, there was 1 doctor to every 8,822 people and as late as 1921 it was still a ratio of only 1:6,129 inhabitants.[56] "In no other country, probably, does there exist such a paucity of qualified medical practitioners," missionary George Blyth remarked.[57] Doctors, as early as the 1840s, were concentrated in Kingston (the island's capital), and commanded a fee between £1 12 shillings and 6 pence (£1 12s. 6d) and £5 6 shillings and 8 pence (£5 6s. 8d) *per visit*. "I am quite unable," said Blyth, "to perceive the justice of three or four medical men confining their attention to a town containing only a small proportion of the inhabitants of the parish to the neglect of the estates." Some doctors returned to Britain; others took up residence in the United States and Canada, and a significant number remained in the island but received the bulk of their income from other lines of work such as operating drug stores; still others left the profession altogether to pursue careers such as becoming planters.[58] It therefore comes as no surprise that given the conditions under which ordinary people existed—including the abysmally low wages paid to workers—their health deteriorated. Infant mortality increased from 158.4 per 1,000 in 1881–85 to 192.0 per 1,000 in 1906–10. It is true that the latter figure was exceptionally high partly because of the Kingston earthquake of 1907, but the average for the five-year period 1911–15 was still 179.2 per 1,000. In 1910, 70 percent of the population suffered from hookworm.[59]

While Jamaica's population increased by 43 percent (from 580,804 to 831,383) between 1881 and 1911, that of Kingston over the same period increased by 55 percent. There was a discernible drift from the Jamaican countryside to the towns. Indeed, while the island's population increased by 10.1 percent between 1881 and 1891, those of the three main banana parishes (St Thomas, Portland, and St Mary) over the same period experienced an increase of only 4.4 percent—a rate of growth less than half that of the national average.[60] In fact, the population of St Thomas actually fell by 5.2 percent between 1881 and 1891.

The proportion employed in agriculture declined from 68.0 percent in 1871 to 58.5 percent of the labor force in 1911. Not insignificantly, those employed in "domestic service" increased over the same period from 10.2 percent to 14.8 percent of the labor force.[61] This was reflective of the disruptive effect of agrarian capitalism in the late nineteenth century. The capitalist transformation in the countryside was powerful enough to disturb, uproot, and displace the peasant but insufficiently dynamic to absorb the latter and transform him or her into a fully fledged agrarian proletarian. And in the absence of a rapidly expanding manufacturing sector to absorb their labor power, these peasants and rural workers were displaced into domestic service, petty trading and, of course, into the long-term unemployed;[62] the latter category of workers forming what Marx aptly described as the "lazarus-layer" of the working class—those mercilessly disgorged and thrown to the winds by capitalist upheaval.[63] From 18 percent in 1891, the proportion of the female workforce in Kingston and St Andrew who were domestic servants increased to 24.9 percent in 1911, and up to 28.6 percent by 1921.[64] Gisela Eisner observed that:

> The large increase in female domestic servants was no evidence of a high standard of living enjoyed by a small section of the community. On the contrary, it was the response of a much wider community to the needs of surplus rural population. By the end of the century the custom had grown up to provide shelter, food and training to "school-girls" in return for service. This cheap labor

supply enabled far lower income groups to enjoy personal services than is usually found in more fully developed societies.[65]

But there was far less reciprocity in such arrangements than Eisner makes out. Abuse and exploitation were more typically the lot of domestic servants. Employers quite often took advantage of the economic vulnerability of domestics. In late and post-Victorian Jamaica, even relatively humble persons indulged in conspicuous consumption and keeping-up-with-the-Joneses' pretensions at the expense of their domestic servants. "It will be apparent," one contemporary observed in 1913, "that if out of a population of less than nine hundred thousand, most of whom serve themselves, the number of domestic is forty thousand, almost everybody who has the slightest pretensions to be considered anybody employs a servant. In fact, you are not respectable if you have not a servant. That at least is one law of Jamaica life."[66]

Despite the revolt of the Jamaican peasants at Morant Bay in 1865, one of whose main contributory causes was the conspicuously unfair and regressive taxation system, such a system was to remain essentially unchanged well into the twentieth century.[67] Between 1870 and 1910 custom and excise duties—regressive *per se* (they are exacted regardless of income) but made doubly so by the higher rate imposed on items consumed by the masses—accounted for between 70 and 80 percent of government revenue. There was no income tax. In the 1890s, the tax on housing was so designed that "the heaviest burden [fell] on the poorest class."[68] As Eisner concludes: "If the criterion of a just system of taxation is ability to pay then the Jamaican system could not be called just."[69]

These were perplexing, difficult, and traumatic times for Jamaican peasants and workers. But for good measure, the planter class conspired to undermine the already low wages of the poor by bringing into the island thousands of Indian and Chinese indentured laborers.[70] To compound the injury—to add injury to injury, so to speak—the very taxes extracted unfairly out of the Jamaican masses would be used to help defray the cost of importing cheap Indian labor.[71]

For the workers and peasants of Jamaica, the late nineteenth century and early twentieth century were extraordinarily bleak. Their suffering and complaints were captured well by by Claude McKay in his aptly titled 1912 poem "Hard Times," in which he tried to articulate their feelings in their own language:

> De mo' me wuk, de mo' time hard,
>   I don't know what fe do;
> I ben' me knee an' pray to Gahd,
>   Yet t'ings same as befo'.
>
> De taxes knockin' at me door,
>   I hear de bailiff's v'ice;

Me wife is sick, can't get no cure,
　But gnawin' me like mice.

De picknies [children] hab to go to school
　Widout a bite fe taste;
And I am working like a mule,
While buccra [the white man], sittin' in the cool,
　hab 'nuff nenyam [food] fe waste.

De clodes is tearin' off dem back
　When money seems noa mek;
A man can't eben ketch a mac [shilling],
　Care how him 'train him neck.

De peas won't pop, de corn can't grow,
　Poor people face look sad. . . .[72]

But four powerful shafts of light relieved the darkness over the land. First was the evident and grim determination on the part of the peasants and workers to survive, despite the severity of the hardship. "I won't gib up, I won't say die,/ For all [although] de time is hard," said the narrator of McKay's poem.[73] And this sturdy resilience manifested itself in myriad ways: through the persistent attempts to make a living out of a recalcitrant soil; through diversification of crops; through sheer hard work; through the migration to the cities; through petty trading and domestic work; and most of all, through the solidarity of poor black people in the countryside and in the towns supporting one another in struggle—cleaving to the black, as Paul Bogle, their martyred leader of Morant Bay, had told them to do.[74]

Second, despite the punishing times in which they lived, the typical worker and peasant were anxious and determined that their children should acquire an education. This was as true, if not more true, for those who had no education themselves as for those who had conquered a rudimentary one. And the education that the Jamaican masses acquired, basic though it was, did not come cheaply. In 1867, the government agreed to help finance the denominational schools which provided elementary education. But the state also insisted that these schools, in order to be eligible for state support, should charge fees for the children that they taught. Fees ranged from 1.5 pence to 6 pence per week—a considerable sum given the low wages prevalent at the time. In 1871–72 the fees collected amounted to £5,873; the government grant was £9,897. Parents suffered the fees for their children and were unrelieved of the charges up to 1892, when they were finally abolished. After 1892 the poor would still pay, but this time indirectly, through additional taxation. In spite of all the obstacles, the literacy rate increased dramatically from 31.3 percent in 1861 to 62.3 percent by 1911, with those being able to write as well as read increasing from 13.3 percent to 47.2 percent over the period.[75] The percentage of children (those between the ages of five and fourteen years) enrolled in schools increased from 36.9 percent in 1861, reaching a peak of 60.7

percent in 1891, falling back with the hard times of the *fin de siècle* to 58.0 percent in 1911. The actual number attending school tripled over the two generations, rising from 40,800 to 125,500 between 1861 and 1911.[76] Given the obstacles, these were mammoth accomplishments. The herculean effort of the little people perplexed their overlords. In October 1899, Sir A. W. Hemming, the governor of the island, wrote privately to Sydney Olivier, then an official in the West India department of the Colonial Office, of the poorer classes "being curiously tenacious & sensitive" on the question of education, and Olivier himself noted in 1899 that it was the issue on which the elected members were most afraid of their constituents.[77]

The Jamaican masses then, over the course of these two generations became substantially more educated and arguably less manipulable. They also, apparently, became more articulate. The voices of the children of the slaves, as well as those of the children of the children of the slaves, became more audible and distinct. Thus in May 1895 when 800 to 1,000 wharf laborers went on strike in Kingston, one of them took time out to publicize their grievances. In a letter to the *Daily Gleaner*, the island's most influential newspaper, he wrote:

> I ask you to occupy a space in your paper concerning the striking of the labourers. We the labouring classes do strike for higher wages, for we are under the advantage of the Agents of ships, we asked for more wages so that we may be able to sustain ourselves and families in a respectable manner. We have to support our families, pay rent, and tax and water rates. Our Island will increase more. It will enable us to spend more, and the merchants will receive more, for we will be able to pay our tax, and in a better way. We won't be having to trouble the Governments often for coffins, and hole for the burial of the dead; we will be able to bury them ourselves if we get suitable wages. The Alms House won't be having so much paupers on the list. All those owing from the want of more wages. Look at our sister island of Trinidad, where the labouring classes are getting 5/- [5 shillings] per day and feeding, then why we Jamaicans can't do the same, we are not behind hand, we been suffering a long time under the tyranny of small wages, so it is time now we look around ourselves ... We mean to be determined for good wages, in our Island—and everybody will inherit the benefit thereof. Three and two shillings are no pay at all for a working man. There are more stealing going on now than if we were getting good wages, if we got good pay, there is no need for us to steal; but on account of the wages is so small, we have to steal, we are going to prison and disgrace ourselves.[78]

Some of the descendants of the enslaved Africans in Jamaica—the "children of the emancipated," as one black organization described them— had acquired higher education and had entered into the professions. These were teachers, lawyers, doctors, dentists, clergymen. There was remarkable growth in the number of those employed in the professions in the late nineteenth and early twentieth centuries; included among these were some of the descendants of enslaved Africans (see Table 1.6, page 360).

A significant segment of this cohort were to form a contingent of organic intellectuals of the black masses, giving voice to their suffering and strivings. The emergence of these intellectuals constituted the third significant positive development of the time.[79] One of these was E. Ethelred Brown, who was to become an ordained Unitarian minister and radical political activist in Harlem in the 1920s. In a pioneering and—especially given the slender resources to hand—impressively documented essay on "Labor Conditions in Jamaica Prior to 1917," he wrote:

> Some progress has been made and there are signs of improvement, but the majority of laborers, the men and women and children who till the banana fields and work on the sugar plantations, are no better off than previously. These are still beasts of burden, still the victims of an economic system under which they labor not as human beings with bodies to be fed or clothed, with minds to be cultivated and aspiring souls to be ministered unto, but as living machines designed only to plant so many banana suckers in an hour, or to carry so many loads of canes in a day. After seventy-eight years in this fair island, side by side, with the progress and improvements above referred to, there are still hundreds and hundreds of men and women who live like savages in unfloored huts, huddled together like beasts of the field, without regard to health or comfort. And they live thus, not because they are worthless or because they are wholly without ambition or desire to live otherwise, but because they must thus continue as economic slaves receiving still the miserable pittance of a wage of eighteen pence or 36 cents a day that was paid to their forefathers at the dawn of emancipation.[80]

Brown was by no means alone in the articulation of such views. There were others, including, Claude McKay's eldest brother and mentor, Uriah McKay, as well as the young Claude McKay himself.

The fourth shaft of light was provided by emigration and especially emigration to Panama and later Cuba. The opportunity to participate in the construction of the Panama Railroad and of the Panama Canal appeared to Caribbean workers and peasants almost like acts of divine intervention. Hemmed in on the islands—under-paid, over-worked, unfairly taxed, exploited, often unemployed—they were suddenly, like a clap of thunder out of a clear blue sky, being pursued by foreigners vying for their labor in the Isthmus. The stream began in the 1850s during the building of the Panama Railroad. An estimated 5,000 Jamaicans worked on the Railroad which was constructed between 1850 and 1855.[81] But the first major wave of migration occurred during the 1880s when the French made their abortive bid to construct the Canal. Although the *Compagnie Universelle* went bankrupt, it provided work for nine years, 1880 to 1889, when people were desperate in Jamaica. Approximately 78,000 Jamaicans migrated to the Isthmus between 1881 and 1890. And between 1891 and 1915, no less than 91,000 left the island for Panama.[82] Between 1904 and 1914, work on the Canal was resumed and completed under the American-controlled Isthmian Canal Commission.

Unskilled workers building the Panama Railroad in the 1850s received approximately 80 cents or 3 shillings and 2 pence per day—more than double the rate that prevailed in Jamaica at the time for agricultural workers. In 1886 unskilled workers on the Canal were earning between $1.50 and $2.00 per day. Men working through contracting firms could choose to work on a piece rate basis and be paid 20 cents for each cartload of soil removed from the channel. "This way," Newton informs us, "many unskilled British West Indians were able to earn as much as $5.00 a day or more if they worked quickly."[83] Skilled workers earned between $2.00 and $5.00 per day depending, like the rate paid to the unskilled workers, on whether the individual worker had signed up directly with the *Compagnie Universelle* or through a contracting firm. During their control of the construction of the Canal, the Isthmian Canal Commission (ICC) instituted a very complex hierarchy of skill and payment over-laid with American Jim-Crow racism.[84] What is nevertheless very clear was that wages were higher than they were in the islands. That tens of thousands still clamored to go to Panama despite the racism of the ICC, the diseased environment, and the high death rate tells us far more about the conditions in the Caribbean proper than about those in the Isthmus. Between 1906 and 1910, the death rate in Jamaica was 24.36 per thousand, that for black workers in Panama was 34.45 per thousand with a peak of 49.01 per thousand in 1905–06.[85] Yellow fever, malaria, tuberculosis, and pneumonia, and ghastly injuries and deaths through accidents devastated the workforce.[86] And yet between January and March 1906, for instance, a span of merely three months, some 5,174 Jamaicans left the island for Panama. Claude McKay, himself a proud son of the African Jamaican peasantry, once again gave voice to the thoughts of the little people of the island. In 1912 he published in the *Daily Gleaner*, one of the longest poems of his literary career. In "Peasants' Ways O' Thinkin'," a 31-stanza monument, he paid special attention to migration from the island to the Isthmus. The narrator of the poem harbors no illusion about life in Panama, but has come to the conclusion that conditions on his native island have become unbearable for the majority of its inhabitants. Athough the emigrant leaves Jamaica with a heavy heart, there is no alternative but to grasp the opportunity that Panama and other areas of the Isthmus represented. And so, contrary to buccra's advice against migration ("He tellin' us we ought to stay"), "dis is wha' we got to say":

> We hea' a callin' from Colon,
> We hea' a callin' from Limon,
> Let's quit de t'ankless toil an' fret
> Fe where a better pay we'll get.

> Though ober deh de law is bad,
> An' dey no know de name o' God,
> Yet dere is nuff work fe we han's,
> Reward in gol' fe beat de ban's [hunger].

De freedom here we'll maybe miss,
Our ol' rum an our Joanie's kiss,
De prattlin' of our little Nell,
De chimin' o' de village bell,

De John-t'-whits in de mammee tree,
An' all de sights we lub fe see;
All dis, I know, we must exchange
For t'ings dat will seem bad an' strange.

We'll have de beastly 'panish beer,
De never-ceasin' wear an' tear,
All Sundays wuk in cocoa-walk,
An' tryin' fe larn de country's talk;

A-meetin' mountain cow an' cat,
An' Goffs wi plunder awful fat,
While choppin' do'n de ru'nate wood,
Malaria suckin' out we blood.

But poo'ness deh could neber come,
An' dere'll be cash fe sen' back home
Fe de old heads, de bastard babe,
An' somet'ing ober still fe sabe.[87]

But the Jamaican planter class was not going to be easily undermined by the lure of Panama and the "disobedience" of the Jamaican peasants and workers who insisted on leaving the island. If it was impracticable to stop altogether the emigration, then the ruling class was determined to make such migration as difficult as it could get away with. From 1893, when the Emigrant Laborers Protection Law was brought into being, the colonial state placed more and more obstacles in the way of would-be emigrants. The law of 1893 gave the Governor the authority to declare any country he thought appropriate "a proclaimed place." A "proclaimed place" was one to which Jamaicans required a permit in order to emigrate. No permit, no emigration—at least no *legal* emigration. Naturally, Panama, other popular destinations in Central America, and Cuba were to become proclaimed places. The crucial clause of the law required the prospective emigrant to produce two persons with property worth £10 who agreed to repay any money which the Government of Jamaica, British Consular officials, or any other authorities in the proclaimed place spent to assist him or her.[88]

The law was made more draconian in 1895, and by the new Emigrants' Protection Law of 1902. But in February 1904, Acting Governor Sydney Olivier, a so-called Fabian Socialist, appointed a committee to suggest changes to the emigration law. The results of their deliberations were contained in a bill which became law on March 29, 1904. The new legislation amended the Emigrants' Protection Law of 1902 in two important respects. The 1902 law had stipulated that a laborer who was not hired by a recruiting agent would be granted a permit to emigrate to a proclaimed place only if he or she could find two persons with property worth no less than £10 to act as guarantors for him or her. With the new amendment, the prospective emigrant was required to deposit £1 5s. in the Treasury to be credited to the Distressed Emigrants' Fund, and used to repatriate him or her if necessary. The previous legislation had required recruiting agents to pay £1 for every laborer hired in the island; the new amendment required them to pay £2.[89]

Even a member of the merchant class of Kingston, A. N. Henriques, conceded that this was a punitive piece of legislation. Henriques thought that a 1 shilling deposit by each emigrant would be ample to cover repatriation costs from Central America if the need arose. Dr J. Robert Love of the *Jamaica Advocate*, a vigorous promoter of black rights, was, as usual, on the job in no time. He recognized class war legislation for what it was. In an editorial written before the bill had become law, he described it as "a damnable cut-throat law." It was in his view "an infernal piece of legislation . . . calculated to crush to earth the class upon which so much of the prosperity of the country depended."[90] One of the most pernicious aspects of this calculation to crush the Jamaican workers was the usage of what was effectively a "departure tax" to strengthen the very chains that held them enthralled. For the money raised, Olivier admitted, would be used to facilitate Indian indentureship on the island by helping to meet the increasing cost of the Immigration Department, and of the medical treatment provided East Indians in hospital.[91] It was not unusual to see in Kingston harbor at this time a boat loaded with hapless Indian indentured laborers dropping anchor next to one taking poor Jamaican laborers to the Isthmus. This is the sort of statecraft that a near-namesake of Olivier— Oliver North of President Ronald Reagan's administration—some four generations later would perhaps have described as a "neat idea."

As Sir Alexander Swettenham, the new Governor of the island, told the United States Secretary of War, Howard Taft, and the Isthmian Canal Company officials at a meeting in 1904, the local employers were "very jealous of emigration of able-bodied laborers."[92] The emigrants would therefore be punished with effectively having to pay for "exit visas" to escape the island and its "tyranny of small wages."

Despite the obstacles placed in the Jamaican workers' path, traffic between the island and the Isthmus was heavy and brisk with at least 168,888 departures and 119,407 people returning between 1882 and 1915. And when Claude McKay left for the United States in 1912, there was, beginning in that very year, a new wave of migration to Cuba to partake in the "dance of the millions," that island's spectacular boom in sugar production and profits in the early twentieth century. The authorities imposed even more punitive taxes upon the departing Jamaicans, but the migration continued unabated. Between 1919 and 1931 an estimated 83,805 Jamaicans had migrated to Cuba.[93] There were many places that Jamaicans desired to be in preference to their native land in the late nineteenth and early twentieth centuries and they were determined to leave.

After Jamaica, Barbados was the major source of Caribbean emigration in the late nineteenth and early twentieth centuries. At 166 square miles small, the island is just over one and half times the size of Martha's Vineyard. Yet Barbados disgorged 150,000 of its sons and daughters between 1861 and 1921, a figure equivalent to the entire population of the island in 1861. An estimated 104,000 settled abroad.[94] While Jamaica lost through emigration an estimated 146,000 people between 1881 and 1921, Barbados, over the same period, lost 82,400. But Jamaica is over twenty-six times the size of Barbados and, at 581,000 people in 1881, its population was over three times that of Barbados. Thus, while Jamaica's loss over the forty-year period amounted to a quarter of its 1881 population, Barbados's loss was almost half the size of its population in 1881.[95]

Why did Barbados lose so many of its people through migration? Simply put, life on Barbados was hard for the mass of its people. Jamaica was tough, but Barbados was tougher still. While wages in Jamaica were low, they were higher than Barbados's.[96] The peasantry expanded considerably in Jamaica in the aftermath of emancipation, while in Barbados the plantocracy gobbled up the land even more fully than their counterparts did in Jamaica. And unlike Jamaica there was no Crown land for the landless to squat on.[97] The price of land in Barbados was generally several times that of Jamaica.[98] While the depression of the 1880s and 1890s effectively destroyed Jamaica's sugar industry, despite the precipitous fall in sugar prices, Barbados continued to produce sugar. But this was done at the enormous expense of the masses of its people, primarily through slashing wages.[99] While banana production provided an alternative—albeit a limited one—to sugar as a source of employment, Barbados remained fundamentally monocultural—the sugar island par excellence. The Jamaican peasants, and indeed some of the planters, shifted production to a number of other crops as the price of sugar collapsed, but Barbados—except for a brief, marginal, and unsuccessful attempt at producing cotton—remained with sugar. And so the Barbadian workers' fortunes were inextricably tied, without the consent of the workers, to the fortunes of the island's sugar industry, which was in catastrophic decline.[100]

The price that ordinary Barbadians were forced to pay for the vagaries of the international sugar market, and for the inertia and folly of their ruling class, was enormous. Like their Jamaican counterparts, they often went hungry. But, by all accounts, the scale and depth of their deprivation were even greater than they were in Jamaica. And contemporaries noticed this. Testifying before the Royal Commission sent out in 1897 to investigate the conditions of the islands, the Reverend C. T. Oehler, a Moravian minister familiar with both islands, could not help but draw comparisons. Unlike Barbados, land was much cheaper in Jamaica, and the ordinary people there could take advantage of unoccupied, mountainous Crown

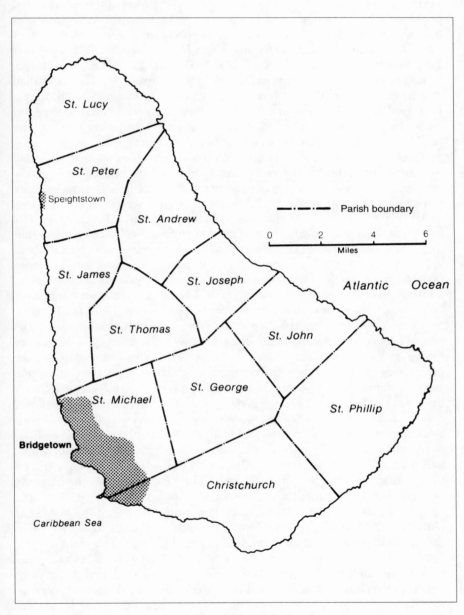

Barbados and its parishes

land for mangoes, citrus, firewood, and other provisions.[101] Oehler may
have overstated the extent to which black Jamaicans enjoyed a state of
wellbeing, but the basic point about the relative condition of the two
populations was fundamentally sound.[102] And this was reflected most
tellingly in the infant mortality rate. The average number of deaths of
infants under one year per 1,000 live births for the years 1900 to 1904 was
282. In Jamaica it was 171; Nevis, 197; Dominica, 185; Trinidad, 162;
British Honduras, 139; British Guiana, 185; St Kitts, 247. The Barbadian
rate worsened over the next few years, rising to 420 in 1906 and dropping
back to 302 in 1907. But in 1906 conditions had deteriorated to the level
where half the infants of St Michael parish died before they were a year
old.[103] St Michael was Barbados's most populous parish.

The hardship of the people in Jamaica and Barbados was compounded
by a series of natural disasters—droughts, floods, and hurricanes—following one another with a speed and intensity exceptional even for the
Caribbean, an area familiar with nature's dreadful wrath. In 1879, 1884,
1885, 1909 and 1912–14 Jamaica was afflicted, to a lesser or greater
extent, by drought. Owing to the fact that they generally receive less rain
than most of the island, the central and southern parishes of St Elizabeth
and Manchester were especially affected during these years. To make
matters worse, spells of drought were often broken by heavy rain, flooding,
and cyclones. Thus, in 1912 one calamity replaced another as drought gave
way to cyclone. Droughts brought suffering to both rural and urban poor.
In the countryside, crops dried up and died and animals often perished; the
people expended precious energy in fetching water, frequently walking over
twelve miles to the nearest source. Hunger became widespread.[104] The
urban poor felt the effects in the rising prices of staples from the countryside
such as yams, potatoes, breadfruit, and vegetables. And the merchants
often took advantage by raising the price of imported items like flour,
cornmeal, and rice. Hurricanes, storms, and floods visited the island with
even more frequency than droughts at the close of the nineteenth and the
opening decades of the twentieth centuries. One hurricane and two storms
struck in the 1880s. In 1899, Portland and St Mary were again hit by
storms that damaged the banana crop. The new century started quietly
enough, but in August 1903 the silence was broken by the roar and
destruction of what the *Handbook of Jamaica* described as a "Great
Hurricane." At least sixty-five people perished and £2,500,000 worth of
damage was done to the island and its trade.[105] In less than a year, in June
1904, there was another storm. This was followed two-and-a-half years
later by the catastrophic Kingston earthquake, which claimed the lives of
about twelve hundred people, injured thousands, and destroyed property
worth over two million pounds sterling.[106] It mangled the city's infrastructure, triggered fires in many parts of Kingston, and shook and frightened
Jamaicans almost a hundred miles away in the west of the island. Those
who felt it never forgot its ferocity and the sudden dread it induced in

children as well as adults. A little eight-year-old schoolgirl felt the vibration, let go of the hand of the six-year-old boy she was walking, dropped to her knees and cried out "Lord—have mercy." Another witness "vividly remember[ed] that there was a coconut tree in the yard and a man had climbed it, reaching almost into the bower and shouting: 'I am going up to heaven, Lord! I am going up to heaven!'"[107] Suffering, disruption, and economic dislocation were major consequences of the earthquake. However, to at least some of Jamaica's artisans it brought temporary respite, as much of the city had to be completely rebuilt. But the number of indirect benefici-aries of the disaster was minuscule compared to the tens of thousands who were made homeless and destitute. After January 14, 1907, Panama and the United States must have looked even more attractive than they had before; green pastures looking even greener set against Kingston's sea of rubble and destruction. But Mother Nature was not finished with the little island. Heavy and destructive rains came in November 1909; and on top of the drought and cyclone of 1912, she brought another hurricane in August 1915 reinforced by a storm the following month. Another big hurricane came in August 1916, and another in September 1917.[108] But things can always get worse, and they did in 1918: the influenza pandemic killed thousands in the island and was mainly responsible for the record number of deaths that year—29,600.[109]

Rarely have so many catastrophes—natural and otherwise—followed one another with such rapidity and destructiveness. Hurricanes struck Jamaica an estimated thirty-seven times between 1685 and 1975.[110] Thus over those 290 years, the island was hit on average once every 7.8 years. Three hurricanes hit Jamaica between 1915 and 1917, a rate of one a year for three years in a row. It normally took 23.4 years—a generation—for that many hurricanes to strike. Although the island experienced seismic disturbances over the centuries, earthquakes of the kind that hit Kingston in 1907 were extremely rare events. The Kingston area has experienced only one major earthquake before or since 1907, and that was the notorious Port Royal earthquake that destroyed the city over two centuries before in 1692. By any measure, then, the conjuncture that spans the generation from 1890 to 1920 was exceptionally bad as far as natural disasters were concerned; one may even say that the generation of the *fin de siècle* was particularly unlucky. And people left the island as their suffering was compounded. A Methodist missionary in Morant Bay, St Thomas, emphasized the exceptional nature of the hardship incurred by the drought of 1914 in his area. The drought, he said, was "the most severe in living memory of anyone. It extended right up the Blue Mountain valley and over the hills to the Yallahs circuit. Our people were *literally* without any food from their fields for about six months."[111] Another reported that the 1917 hurricane had destroyed in the Manchioneal circuit of Portland alone: 901 residences, 1,522 fowls, 3,470 breadfruit trees, 1,130 avocado pear trees, 115 pigs, 116 goats, 5 donkeys, 38,882 coconut trees in Manchioneal, 16,850 coconut trees in Kensington, 15,766 coconut trees in Hector's River, 95 percent of citrus in Hector's River, 90 percent of citrus in Grange Hill, 30 percent of citrus in Darlington, 80 percent of citrus in Reach, 98 percent of citrus in Williamsfield, 90 percent of citrus in Muirton, 50 percent of citrus in Betty's Hope, 75 percent of citrus in Kensington.[112] It should be emphasized that all this destruction and accompanied suffering and sorrow was concentrated in a small part of one parish, and Jamaica has fourteen parishes which were similarly hit by the hurricane. The Reverend A. Cresser ought to be remembered, and thanked, if only posthumously, for his registering and cataloguing this trail of destruction. For the *Handbook of Jamaica*, despite all that Reverend Cresser saw in his little district, simply states for 1917: "Hurricane (Sept. 23) damage to crops."[113] The losses from the hurricane, wrote Cresser in his laudably detailed audit, "are driving our young men and women to Cuba and the USA to work. This circuit has lost many this way."

Like Jamaica, Barbados was similarly afflicted by natural catastrophes during the years of the exodus. The island had always been drought-prone, but during these years, by all accounts, the drought spells were longer, more unrelenting, and more frequent. A year-long drought in 1863 caused such horrible suffering that the iron-fisted plantocracy on the island loosened its emigration restrictions and allowed two-and-a-half thousand Barbadians to emigrate to St Croix and Antigua. But severe droughts recurred in 1891, 1894, and 1895. The 1894 drought was accompanied by typhoid and dysentery. And in 1895 many of the starving were driven by their pangs of hunger to raid neighboring plantations and provision grounds in search of potatoes and edible fruit. In July 1898 a group of 400 men and women similarly raided the potato fields of a plantation in St John parish, and expropriated provisions for several days' sustenance. Nineteen were convicted and sentenced. According to Hilary Beckles, "such events were not uncommon in the 1890s, and reports of starvation in the countryside were numerous."[114] Drought occurred in 1908, and returned with varying severety between 1910 and 1920, but was especially harsh during 1912 and 1919 when there was a six-month dry spell.[115] Unlike Jamaica and the Leeward Islands, Barbados is seldom hit by hurricanes; its southeastern Caribbean location is on the very fringes of the hurricane zone. Indeed, at the time of writing, Barbados has not received a direct hit by a hurricane since 1955, a rare and probably unique blessing for an island in the Caribbean Sea. But in 1898 and again in 1922, Barbados was hit directly and hard by two devastating hurricanes. The September 10, 1898, hurricane killed 112 people, innumerable livestock, and destroyed more than 11,000 dwellings of the Barbadian poor. An appeal was made for assistance and the island received £40,000 for working-class assistance and £50,000 for sugar plantation repairs. The suffering of the people was made worse by outbreaks of typhoid and dysentery in the hurricane's aftermath. An epidemic of smallpox broke out in February 1902, lasted for more than a year, and killed 118. Then in 1908 yellow fever struck on an epidemic scale, the first since 1881. "[C]hronic pauperism ... like a chronic disease is ... undermining the population of this island," reported Barbados's medical officer in 1910.[116] In 1912 the medical officer of St Philip parish reported that the people "passed through a terrible ordeal of drought, pestilence, and famine, the like of which I have never seen before ... even in the months succeeding the hurricane of 1898." Dysentery was epidemic in parts of St Philip.[117]

The effects of natural catastrophes such as hurricanes, earthquakes, and droughts are profoundly mediated by social, economic, and political relations. Put simply, God may send hurricanes, but their consequences are not God-given.[118] The damage that hurricanes, floods, and droughts do is clearly related to the degree of power one has over the effects of these natural phenomena, and the mechanisms at one's disposal to cope with their aftermath. And so the capacity to withstand the destructive forces of nature is conditioned by the power and resources that one possesses. For example, the unspeakable suffering of poor Barbadians after the 1898 hurricane was directly related to their positions in the class structure and the broader network of economic and political relations. The masses of the people lived in "chattel houses." These were physical structures specifically developed by the people to help them cope with the tenantry system. The tenantry system—rather akin to the tied cottage system that came out of feudal relations in Britain—allowed space on the plantation owner's land for a small house in exchange for working on the landlord's estate. When disputes arose between owner and tenant, planters readily evicted the tenant and with impunity.[119] Thus in order to minimise their vulnerabilty, the tenant builds a dwelling that he or she may easily dismantle and carry away to an alternative site. It made no sense, given the social relations, to build more permanent and immobile dwellings. Virtually all of these structures were made of wood and raised from the ground by wooden stakes. With the aid of a donkey cart and the help of a few friends, one of these chattel houses could be taken apart, moved, and reassembled within hours.[120] Small (sometimes no more than 10 feet by 10 feet), portable, the product of the people's genius for adaptation, the chattel house was no match for a hurricane or a flood. Thus these dwellings, profoundly conditioned if not determined by the social relations on the plantation, were challenged by the hurricane of 1898 and found woefully wanting. And so the people died in large numbers and were left homeless in their tens of thousands, not because of the hurricane *per se*, but because of the fragility and flimisiness of their dwellings which can only be understood in the context of the power relations between plantation owner and plantation worker. Similarly, had there been prompt and sympathetic relief of the people's needs in the aftermath of hurricanes and drought, the suffering, the contraction and rapid spread of contagious diseases, and the death rate would have been lowered.[121] Had Reverend Cresser's parishioners in

Manchioneal insurance or meaningful government support to compensate them for the losses, there would not have been the same need to flee destitution through emigration.

In the late seventeenth century Barbados acquired the reputation of being the most densely populated territory in the Americas and one of the most crowded areas of the entire world. The island carried the dubious distinction into the twentieth century. It is for this reason that neo-Malthusian prejudices have crept into discussions of black poverty on the island and black emigration in the late nineteenth and early twentieth centuries. The empiricist lure of over-population in Barbados has caught some of the most sophisticated scholars of the region, including George Roberts and David Lowenthal. Roberts writes of the island's "disastrous overcrowding" and, like Lowenthal, speaks of Barbados's "super-abundant population."[122] Even more disturbing is the self-imposed limitation of theoretical horizons when discussing Barbados. Writing in 1955, Roberts declared:

> But for emigration on a relatively large scale, Barbados, already very densely settled in 1844 ... might by now [have] reached a disastrous state of over-crowding, relief from which would have been possible *only* by widespread starvation, disease and death.

Two years later, in discussing the Barbadian crisis in the 1870s, Lowenthal similarly declared that "pestilence or emigration were the only alternatives."[123] Thankfully, the substance of the analyses of both Roberts and Lowenthal have been better than the authors' formal pronouncements and theoretical framework. For the actual content of their work on Barbados undermines many of their own empiricist presuppositions. But the over-population lore is old, commonplace and enduring. And it comes as no surprise that it finds expression in the novel of Barbadian life and youth published at mid-century. In George Lamming's fine *Bildungsroman, In the Castle of My Skin*, the "Old Man" reported to his wife what he heard the politically ambitious black teacher, Mr Slime, tell a crowd about the Barbadian situation:

> He use a word call em'gration as what an' what he would do here an' now for this present generation. An' he give a full an' proper explanation of it all, what will happen an' what an' what they got to do. Says 'twus more people in this island than the lan' could hold or the law allow. 'Twus a high burnin' shame to put on a piece o' land no more than a hundred an' something square miles, that's as he call it, square mile, 'twus a shame as he say to keep two hundred thousand people on it. Then he give them all the facts an' figures as he understan' them, and they head start to swim with facts an' figures. You an' me an' all o' we he says when you put us together from top to bottom wus that amount of people, something hundred thousand, an he says wus a record population for the size o' the piece of land anywhere in this God's world. An' he go on to say the only manner of way to deal with that sort o' thing wus to get rid o' some; an' since it ain't in your power or mine or his own nor right in the sight o' God to shoot

them down, he says 'twus best to send them where there wus too much square mile for the handful o' people living there. An' 'tis as he say he will do.[124]

Thus, "widespread starvation, disease and death," "pestilence," or "shoot[ing] them down," have been posited as the dismal alternatives to emigration. Yet it takes little reflection to see that such prognoses are ahistorical and superficial. Moreover, historically, other alternatives were known and proposed, if not pursued.

First, there is no causal relationship between population density, poverty and emigration. Think not only of the proverbial Calcutta slums, but think also of Manhattan, Hong Kong, Singapore. Grenada was second only to Barbados in the density of its population in the late nineteenth and early twentieth centuries, yet the proportion of its population that migrated was (for reasons discussed later) minuscule compared to that of Jamaica which had half the population density of Grenada (see Table 1.7, page 361). Similarly, the density of the population of St Kitts–Nevis was generally lower than that of St Vincent, yet a far greater proportion of Kittians and Nevisians migrated than Vincentians. And although Grenada had a population density much higher than that of St Kitts–Nevis, by all accounts and indicators life was much better for black Grenadians than it was for the black inhabitants of St Kitts–Nevis. A number of scholars have also shown that in trying to understand the migration from the islands after the Second World War, so-called demographic attempts at explanation are inadequate, if not completely useless.[125]

To understand the massive levels of black migration from Barbados we need to look at the balance of forces on the land, in the way that I have attempted above—not through counting black heads on the island, but by recognizing white power and black oppression. In the list of alternatives to migration mentioned earlier, there is not a word about land reform, a more equitable distribution of land among the population. As late as 1929, despite the influx of Panama money and money from the United States, only 17,000 acres of the cultivable land was owned by smallholders (who number about 18,000), while some 90,000 acres were under the control of the small white oligarchy. The plantocracy bitterly resisted the growth of a black peasantry in Barbados. The island would be a sugar island under the control of a small group of white men who would monopolize the land. As the Governor of the island, Sir J. S. Hay, told the West India Royal Commission of 1897:

> There is, I think, another argument in favour of the estates being held by the present class of proprietors. Were the island ultimately to fall into the hands of small holders, the land would suffer from want of proper cultivation and the yield, which is at present between 2 and 3 tons an acre, would rapidly fall to 1.[126]

Hay's worship of sugar was so complete that he did not even imagine that a black peasantry would want to plant yams and potatoes, peas and tomatoes, instead of "sweet malefactor," sugar cane. The land, in any case, would remain in the same old hands. Despite its fixation on sugar production, even the 1897 Commission recognized the need for land reform on the basis of the observation that "no reform affords so good a prospect for the permanent welfare in the future of the West Indies as the settlement of the laboring population on the land as small proprietors."[127] Of course, such notions were ignored by the local Barbadian ruling class. There is no doubt that had there been a more equitable distribution of land on the island fewer Barbadians would have had and felt the need to migrate. Considering the number who left, it may seem paradoxical to suggest that Barbadians were reluctant migrants. But from a wide variety of historical accounts, it appears that no group of black Caribbeans had a stronger emotional attachment to their native island than black Barbadians. Travellers to and through the region, including fellow black Caribbeans, from at least the eighteenth century to the present have almost invariably remarked upon the black Barbadian's love for his or her native land. It is a passion so strong that it appears to be irrational, but that is only because no one has adequately explained it.[128] Derek Walcott, in a rather bitter essay on the region, suggested that Caribbeans undertake "migration without remorse."[129] It is not true for Caribbeans in general, least of all for Barbadians. That Barbadians have left in such astonishing numbers is largely a reflection of the absence of domestic options and existence of greater opportunity abroad. Given the island's condition, they were glad to go, but always sorry to leave. There were streams of tears at the quayside in Bridgetown, and heavy hearts on the Panama-bound boats, too, as they weighed anchor.[130]

The Barbadian exodus is less rooted in the density of its population and more in the power of its small ruling class that engrossed the land. The neo-Malthusians, from James Anthony Froude down, have been busy counting black people, castigating their having children, and blaming them for their own suffering.[131] At the same time they are happy to ignore the green ocean of sugar cane that floods the land, washing black Barbadians to its stony shores, blocking access to the soil of their birth, worked without pay by generations of their ancestors.

To economic distress and natural disaster must be added colonial policy that had direct bearing upon migration. In 1911, the colonial government in Jamaica ended competitive examinations for positions in the civil service. This effectively blocked black people, especially the dark-skinned bright children of the peasantry, from entering the service. Competitive examinations had been introduced in 1885, but in response to opposition from the privileged white and light-skinned middle class, including some within the civil service itself, the colonial authorities made changes, allowing specific exemptions from the examinations. In 1905, open competition returned, only to be disbanded again six years later.[132] An important avenue for upward social mobility for educated black people was thus turned, over-night, into a cul-de-sac. The alienation and anger that this policy provoked has hardly been registered, never mind appreciated, despite the fact that they can hardly be over-stated. In fact, this foreclosure of civil service careers to dark-skinned people radicalized many and doubtless contributed to the outward flow of black talent from the island. Indeed, in Claude McKay's novel *Banana Bottom*, set in turn-of-the-century Jamaica, one character, Bab, a bright and ambitious young son of the peasantry, left for the United States specifically and explicitly because of the government's change in policy. And in the novel, published almost a generation after the author had left the island, the flame of McKay's anger over the policy burned white-hot, raging undiminished by time and exile.

Bob had "fixed his hopes" on entering the service. He had studied hard for the examinations, only to be told that they had been abandoned for a system of selection. "The selection was made by the special recommen-dation of people in respectable and responsible positions. And the result of this new order was to limit the minor Civil Service posts to the light-coloured middle classes and bar aspirants from the black peasantry." McKay noted that a group of noncomformist ministers and "especially the descendants of the pioneers had registered a telling opposition to the change." But he also noted that "some of the strongest Government support had come from a group of black men, most of whom had near-white or white wives and light-colored children." McKay aimed his burning spear of rage with deadly accuracy at one of these men who was a member of the island's colonial legislature. He was a noted orator, reported McKay, "although the thought behind the glittering display, when not empty, was always commonplace."

> He had been picked up straight off of a plantation by the missionaries and educated by the ministry. He had a magnificent voice and could stir audiences mightily and he had won the appellation of the silver-tongued parson. He had charge of one of the largest and best-paying churches in the colony. From that it was only a step to become a representative of the people in the island's Legislature. His wife was a lady from Great Britain who had come out to the island as an officer of the Salvation Army. And they had a large family of freckled reddish-colored children.
>
> This reverend black man, who represented a constituency about seven-eighths of which was black peasants, was the most eloquent advocate of the change. With this silver tongue he derided the idea that Civil Service posts should be given to peasant youths fresh from the huts, who possessed no "background" but were clever enough to pass the examinations. Civil Service candidates, he said, should come from respectable and refined homes.
>
> The fact was that perhaps because of their lack of refined things and sharpened by adversity, the black candidates often won the examinations way ahead of their more socially-favoured competitors. At this time it was remem-bered by aged white-headed blacks who knew the early origin of the honourable

and reverend black legislator that he had not even had the benefit of a hut as "background" but that the missionaries found him when the roof over his head was the trash-house of the sugar-cane plantation and his bed the trash-heap.[133]

This is one of McKay's angriest literary outbursts; and he was not a man known for moderation in anything. The remarks underscored the depth of his feeling over the policy and his seering contempt for the white black men who betrayed their humble roots, abused their talents, turning their swords upon the very group, the weak, from which they sprung. The black legislator, is of course, a fictionally drawn character, but there were people of similar formation expressing the views articulated in the novel. And McKay and his older brother and mentor, U. Theo McKay, knew people of such background and ideological bent. *Banana Bottom* is, far more than the critics are aware, a highly autobiographical novel.[134] But in addition to the views explicitly expressed, McKay's contempt inheres in the very way in which he draws the character of "the reverend black man."

Similarly, J. A. Rogers, a light-skinned Jamaican, deeply radicalized by American racism, poured scorn on the new policy in the pages of the *Messenger* in 1922. And Garvey, in his first published article, like his fellow dark-skinned Jamaican, McKay, railed against the policy. Writing in 1913 he angrily remarked:

> [W]hen the Government twenty or thirty years ago, threw open the doors of the Civil Service to competitive examination, the Negro youths swept the board, and captured every available office, leaving their white competitors far behind. This system went on for a few years, but as the white youths were found to be intellectually inferior to the black, the whites persuaded the Government to abolish the competitive system, and fill vacancies by nomination, and by this means kept out the black youths. The service has long since been recruited from an inferior class of sycophantic weaklings whose brains are exhausted by dissipation and vice before they reach the age of thirty-five.[135]

The Rev. E. Ethelred Brown, one of the few dark-skinned Jamaicans to work within the service, continued to denounce the colonial government for its action long after he had left Jamaica for Harlem. And he made this issue the centerpiece of his address at the first mass meeting of the nationalist Jamaica Progressive League held in New York in October 1936. "Why had the examination system been discontinued?" he asked. "I venture this guess; too many poor boys passed the open competition examinations."[136] In the 1920 UNIA "Declaration of Rights of the Negro Peoples of the World," racism within the civil service was a primary complaint:

> In the Civil Service and departmental offices we are everywhere discriminated against and made to feel that to be a black man in Europe, in America and the West Indies is equivalent to being an outcast and a leper among the races of men, no matter what the character attainments of the black men may be.[137]

Even where civil service employment remained open to black Caribbeans, the institution often proved a locus of unrest. Throughout the

Caribbean, but especially in Jamaica, from the late nineteenth century right down to independence in 1962, the service has been a site of nationalist agitation and colonial discontent. This has been so primarily because in both the recruitment to the service, and the treatment of black people who made it into the civil service, racism was transparent and explicit. And this was one of the only institutions of colonial rule on the islands in which racism was plain for all to see. Generally, the racism practiced by the British was far more opaque, cloaked and insidious. It comes as no surprise then, that Jamaica's first explicitly nationalist organization, the National Club, was begun by a disgruntled colored civil servant with bitter grievances over his treatment in the service. Marcus Garvey and W. A. Domingo served their political apprenticeship under Sandy Cox, the founder of the Club.[138]

Some dark-skinned Caribbean men and women in certain parts of the archipelago were given a chance to get lower-level government work. But they resented the restricted opportunity, the paper-pushing drone work, the hum-drum and brain-dead life of the colonial civil service. It was high-status work—for the dark-skinned bright children of the peasantry, that is. And they, the lucky ones who escaped the midday sun of the cane fields, were expected—by the ruling class and its colored lackeys—to count their blessings, to be happy that they used pens, not machetes, that they wore white shirts to work and that they did not get dirty. Those who could, left. And the hidden injuries of race and color festered for years. Almost two generations after leaving his native Trinidad, C. L. R. James—who perhaps more than any other Caribbean migrant intellectual consistently down-played the effect of racism on his life—remarked:

> Albert Gomes told me the other day: "You know the difference between all of you and me? You all went away; I stayed." I didn't tell him what I could have told him: "You stayed not only because your parents had money but because your skin was white; there was a chance for you, but for us there wasn't—except to be a civil servant and hand papers, take them from the men downstairs and hand them to the man upstairs."[139]

"We went one way," said James of his black contemporaries, "these white boys all went the other way. We were black and the only way we could do anything along the lines we were interested in was by going abroad; that's how I grew up."[140]

There was, thus, no shortage of compelling reasons for black people—from the poor to the aspiring professional class—to escape, insofar as they could, these islands.

But the propensity to migrate was greater in some areas of the Caribbean than others. In the smaller old sugar colonies such as St Kitts, Nevis, Antigua and Montserrat, the economic pressures—reinforced by natural disasters—worked in similar ways to those in Jamaica and Barbados to induce migration. And in these areas a high proportion of the population migrated, headed in the same direction as the Jamaicans and Barbadians— Central America, Cuba, the United States and further afield. The sugar plantations of the Dominican Republic attracted thousands of Kittitians, Nevisians, and Anguillans at the turn of the century.[141] Conditions were terrible, but—as a group of petitioners to the King of England pointed out in 1905—they were better than at home:

> The cause why we have left our native land and are in this island [Santo Domingo] is because the British islands failed to furnish us employment and yet were levying upon us taxes of the most exorbitant nature, consequently those who were unable to bear the condition in which they were placed come over to this country, as it is adjacent and passage cheap.

And in 1899 one contemporary noted in pointed language that "Her Majesty's black and colored subjects in the West Indies . . . have to choose between death from starvation in their native islands and suffering and ill-treatment in St Domingo, where many have sought employment under the circumstances that their native islands are merely Islands of Death."[142]

Unlike those of St Kitts and Nevis, the economies of Grenada, St Lucia, and Dominica were more diversified, less dependent upon sugar. Moreover, the black peasantries had a foothold on the land (especially in Grenada) that provided greater political autonomy and economic self-sufficiency.[143] Thus a lower percentage of the population of these islands joined the stream of migrants to Central America, Cuba, and the United States (see Figure 1.5, page 371). In a similar manner, relatively few Trinidadians and Guyanese migrated. Trinidad and Guyana were the powerhouses of British Caribbean sugar production in the late nineteenth and early twentieth centuries (see Table 1.5, page 360). In addition to possessing some of the most fertile soil in the region, they attracted far more capital to their sugar economies than did the older British colonies. Their ruling classes invested in the most modern sugar manufacturing equipment in the British Caribbean. Sparsely populated, they attracted labor from the rest of the Caribbean, and indeed brought into their territories hundreds of thousands of indentured laborers from the Indian subcontinent and elsewhere in the aftermath of slavery.[144] Moreover, their economies, especially that of Trinidad, was far more diversified than most and thus less vulnerable to the vagaries of the sugar market. In both Trinidad and Guyana, wages were higher, land was cheaper, opportunity for advancement greater than in the older British colonies of Jamaica and Barbados. Virtually all of the English-speaking eastern Caribbean was attracted to Trinidad in the late nineteenth and early twentieth centuries. Vincentians, Grenadians, Kittitians, Nevisian, Union Islanders along with large numbers of Barbadians, and even some Jamaicans, all the way from the western end of the Caribbean, made the thousand-mile journey to Trinidad.[145] As the striking Jamaican dock worker in his letter to the *Gleaner* pointed out, in "our sister island of

Trinidad ... the laboring classes are getting [5 shillings] per day and feeding." But like the rest of the Caribbean, Trinidad's and Guyana's sugar suffered in the US market in the early twentieth century. For in addition to the competition from Louisiana sugar, Cuban, Puerto Rican, and Domincian Republic sugar entered the United States on highly preferential terms at the turn of the century. Trinidad, however, increased the production of its highly prized cocoa from 23.5 million pounds in 1896 to 48.1 million pounds in 1913, which helped offset its sugar difficulties. Cocoa in fact surpassed sugar in importance and in 1913 covered three-quarters of the cultivated area of the island. But Ghanaian (Gold Coast) cocoa, though inferior in quality, would in a few years lower prices and squeeze Trinidadian cocoa out of the world market. And after reaching a peak of $23.90 per *fanega* (110 lb) in 1919–20, the price of cocoa collapsed, falling to $9.50 the following year. Prices recovered somewhat in the 1920s, but the "golden age" (1870–1920) of Trinidad cocoa was over.[146] Despite such setbacks, especially for the cocoa producing black peasantry in Trinidad, the island was still far more attractive to other Caribbean workers than Barbados and Jamaica.[147] The large-scale exploitation of its oil in the twentieth century simply reinforced Trinidad's economic pre-eminence in the eyes of the region's workers. It is for these reasons that relatively few Trinidadians and Guyanese were among the growing colonies of British Caribbeans abroad in the late nineteenth and early twentieth centuries. And it appears that the migrants from these two territories were more middle class in origin than the rest of the diaspora.

In the Bahamas, the growing economic difficulties at home and the ample opportunities in Florida in the late nineteenth and early twentieth centuries generated a significant flow to the United States.[148] Similarly, economic dislocations in the Danish Virgin Islands triggered an exodus to the United States that increased after the Islands were acquired by the United States in 1917.

Thus the forces that started and sustained the flow from the British Caribbean islands, especially Jamaica and Barbados, were fundamentally economic and political. But hardship and suffering do not in themselves explain why people move. For migration to take place there has to be the desire to migrate, the opportunity to migrate, and the transportation to effect migration. And all of these were in place during the period of the exodus. Moreover, by the end of the nineteenth century, Caribbeans had been more than familiar with large-scale and long-distance migration. Caribbeans had travelled to and settled in Liberia and Sierra Leone. Some had worked as teachers, doctors, civil servants, and missionaries in various parts of Africa; others had gone there with the British (and the French) as soldiers of imperialism. And some went as ordinary workers as early as the mid nineteenth century. By the end of the nineteenth century Caribbean people had established a complex web of institutions adapted to continuous and large-scale migration from the islands.[149]

And so when the Panama Canal, the banana plantations of Central America, the boom of the "dance of the millions" in Cuba, and industrializing America beckoned, the Jamaicans, the Barbadians, the Kittians, and thousands of other islanders answered their call. Despite reports, few were prepared for the actual hardship they would encounter in Panama. They knew, though, that in Panama they would have a job, they would be paid more than they were getting in Barbados, Jamaica, and St Kitts, and they could escape the torment of their island oppressors.

The Barbadian ruling class, like its Jamaican counterpart, tried to deter workers from going to Panama with scary and exaggerated reports of harsh conditions on the isthmus. But such tactics were as unsuccessful in Barbados as they had been in Jamaica. A Barbadian newspaper in 1905 carried a cartoon of two black men discussing the merits of migration. Thomas took for granted the discouraging words of his manager about migrating. But Jones was determined to go and see Mr Brewster, the recruiting agent for the Canal company:

> *Thomas*: Bwoy, wah yu gwine to Panama fuh? I allus hare muh mangah seh, bettah fuh bare de ill we hab, dan fuh fly to dem we duzzn no nuffin bouk.
> *Jones*: Da is berry good tawk fuh a mangah, but ess he bin hah uh wife, seben childun an a mudder-in-lah, an no wuk fuh do he wudda fly heself sumwa. Ta, ta man Ise gwine fuh se missa Brusta nung, muhself fuh I is orf to Panama.[150]

J. Challenor Lynch, a member of Barbadian ruling class, told the island's Legislative Council in July 1907 of a terrible incident he had heard of. As a Panama-bound crowd of exuberant, young, black men passed a field where a gang of sugar estate workers were being supervised by a plantation manager a member of the crowd shouted out: "Why you don't hit de manager in de head, and come along wid we!" Lynch, of course, was incensed at such brazen incitement.[151] Panama gave hope, and brought new, sweet thoughts and words to the lips of oppressed Barbados.

> We want more wages, we want it now,
> And if we don't get it, we going to Panama
> Yankees say they want we down there,
> We want more wages, we want it now.[152]

Not since the glory days of Bussa's slave revolt in 1816, when some of the white ruling class were literally frightened to death, had such joyous noise been heard on the island. The escape to Panama was the next best thing to revolution in Barbados. And the revolution would not come.

But the treasures of Panama were not unalloyed, nor did they bring lasting or comprehensive relief. For, among other things, the massive flow of money that the exodus brought into the islands' economies, especially that of Barbados, was, at best, a mixed blessing. The rigidity of the Barbadian economy, its minuscule and unresponsive manufacturing base outside of the sugar industry, its powerful and greedy cabal of merchants, its limited supply of land (structurally and geographically) massively outstripped by demand—all these combined to create serious economic dislocation on the island. The primary victims of the crisis were those least capable of withstanding its fury, the very weakest among the black population. Paradoxically, then, one of the consequences of "Panama money" was to exacerbate hardship and set in train further migration. How was this so?

Between 1906 and 1920, according to Bonham Richardson, Barbadians sent home or brought back from Panama well over £1,000,000 to the island. This figure excludes additional items of value such as clothes, jewelry, and gifts similarly sent home or brought by returning migrants.[153] For an economy as small as Barbados's this was a massive inflow of money. In 1912, the total value of the island's exports was £1,085,569. And the government's revenue for the financial year 1912–13 amounted to £234,125 and expenditure came to £230,339.[154] In 1913 alone, £63,816 was sent to Barbados in the form of money orders from the Panama Canal Zone[155]—a figure equivalent to 27.25 percent of government revenue for 1912–13.

A substantial portion of Panama money was used to buy land and build or improve homes. Not surprisingly, the price of land increased dramatically. As late as 1917, land could be bought in the outlying parishes of the island for £20 per acre, but by 1925 prices of £125 per acre were considered normal. In St Michael, the parish in which the island's capital is located, prices skyrocketed to £100 per acre in 1917. And by 1920 land in St John, two parishes removed from high-priced St Michael, fetched as much as £200 per acre. In St Michael itself, according to Francis Mark, land rose to as high as $2,400 (£500) per acre by the late 1920s.[156] White land speculators made massive profits, buying large estates, breaking them up into small lots and selling them on to black buyers at high prices. In 1897 it was estimated that speculators using the same strategy made profits of 50 to 200 percent selling small lots to black Barbadians.[157] There is every reason to believe, given the amount of people with Panama money desirous of land, that profits during the war and the 1920s were even higher for the land speculators. Moved by anger—or jealousy—a member of the Barbadian assembly in 1928 described the speculators as having been engaged over the previous twenty-five years "in the business of sucking the blood out of the people who have to get somewhere to live."[158] But there was a type of landlord who engaged in a species of anti-black class warfare that made the land speculators look like virtuous men. These landlords pointedly refused to sell land to black Barbadians whom they perceived to be a threat to the economic and political status quo. The returnees from Panama fell into this category. Thus in St Andrew parish it was claimed that the plantation owners sold land only to illiterate workers.[159] The plantation owners and their managers were equally discriminating in who they rented land to. As an eighty-year-old Barbadian man in 1990 remembered, they were "very, very keen about, very particular about renting ground out. You couldn't just . . . go at the plantation and get ground so." One had to be considered "dutiful" by the landlord. This meant, as Mary Chamberlain reported, that the renter had to be willing to give labor to the plantation "in much the same way as the laborer who lived on the plantation."[160] In Jamaica, some of the landlords similarly held out against selling to ambitious black people. One old man recalled that he was given the chance to buy a piece of land not only because he could afford it, but because he had worked "cheerfully" as a laborer. He explained to Erna Brodber how he was given the chance to buy:

> The overseer come and say who work cheerful will get a piece of land but who rude can't get any. . . . Well I di de and I really want piece of the land. Well, I work cheerful . . . so mi tell you Maam, mi work cheerful and mi get piece fi buy. Mi name go up. Plenty people name go up and God help me, I succeed.[161]

There were many who were not as lucky. Money was often not the only thing that Jamaicans and Barbadians needed to buy land; a white skin was also required. Market forces—vicious and economically discriminatory though they intrinsically were—were not allowed free reign by the white ruling class. Race and color circumscribed their universe of operation to the disadvantage of black Jamaicans and black Barbadians.[162]

The land speculators in Barbados were, of course, not alone in "sucking the blood out of the people" and making obscene profits. For the merchants, to continue the metaphor, drew blood too from the little people, especially during the war years and the 1920s. In 1913 imported Canadian pitch pine was sold at $44 per 1,000 board feet. By 1920 it trebled in price, fetching between $130 and $145. White pine and spruce were similarly increased in prices.[163] There is no evidence to suggest that the Canadians had similarly increased the cost of the lumber that they supplied to Barbadian merchants. The hike was the result of astronomical mark-ups on the part of the local importers of lumber. And imported lumber was a necessity, used by the people to build and repair their homes.[164]

To be properly appreciated, these skyscraping prices must be seen against the backdrop of low and stagnant nominal wages of ordinary Barbadians. According to official figures, between 1901 and 1910–11 "agricultural laborers" received 8d (16c) per day; in 1911–12, the figure was reportedly raised to 1s (24c). And this prevailed unchanged in the 1920s. Terrible though these figures are, there are good reasons to believe that the reality was even worse than they suggest. And the starvation wages paid were not for light work. In the testimonies presented to the inquiry that the colonial authorities conducted in the aftermath of the 1930s labor revolts, the reality veiled by much official statistics was partially exposed. Theodore

Brancker, the senior member for St Lucy in the House of Assembly, testified that

> There was a class of agricultural laborers . . . whose scale of wages had not been increased in about a century. . . . In some cases they worked for as little as 12 cents per day and the maximum wage was 2/- per day. The cane hole digger was paid 9 cents per 100 holes and as an average day's work was 400 holes he earned 1/6 per day. The forker was paid 8 to 10 cents per 100 holes. A man could do about 400 per day, so he could earn 32 cents per day if he forked 350 holes—an average day's work—10 cents per 100 holes. For planting the canes the laborers received 1/- per 2,000 holes, that was a day's work. For turning up cane stumps he received 5 cents per 100 holes and for an average day's work of 800 holes he received 40 cents. Cane cutters received 16 cents per 100 holes; an average day's work consisted of 300 holes, so that a cane cutter could earn 2/- per day. That was the most lucrative form of agricultural labor.[165]

Had the influx of Panama money not coincided with the steep rise in the price of sugar during and in the aftermath of the First World War, its negative consequences would not have been as dramatic and injurous. But the end of the work on the Canal and the return of the migrants from the isthmus with their money *did* occur at the same time that the price of sugar was at its highest for over a century. And the increase in the price of sugar motivated and rewarded the plantocracy to expand sugar production as much as possible. Marginal land that hitherto had been in the possession of the tenantry laborers and cultivated with yams, potatoes, etc., to supplement their meager diet was now covered with the green gold that sugar had, once again, become. Indeed, many of the smallholders, among whom were returned Panama men, put their small plots of one or two acres under sugar. They, too, wanted to partake in the boom. The inevitable upshot of this was the substantial rise in the price of land, further fuelled by land-hungry Panama returnees. Because of the early domination of the Barbadian landscape by the island's sugar-growing plantocracy, Barbados has always been a poor provider of home-grown food for its inhabitants. Now with the spread of the sugar cane to almost every square inch of the island, the reliance upon imported foodstuff became even greater. Food prices increased under this logic, but were helped on their upward movement by profiteering merchants. The price of potatoes increased by 413 percent between January and October of 1920, from 1.56 cents to 8 cents per pound.[166] Little wonder, then, that during the decade between 1910–12 and 1920–22 the average length of life for Barbadians shortened. For women it fell from 32.5 to 31.9 years. And Barbadian men lived on average 28.5 years, slightly down from the 28.7 years for 1910–12. While Barbadian men were dead before their twenty-ninth birthday, Jamaican men lived to almost 36 and Trinidadians lived to 37.6 years. In 1920–22, Barbadian women died before they were 32, their Jamaican and Trinidadian sisters lived to 38.2 and 40.1 years respectively. Barbados's infant mortality rate rose during most years of the 1920s, reaching an appallingly high 401 in

1921 due to disease and exceptionally bad circumstances that year. In 1925 the rate stood at 312, but in Jamaica it hovered around 176 and in Trinidad, at 134, the rate was less than half what it was in Barbados.[167]

Inflation, therefore, impoverished the Barbadian populace even further. It reduced the spending power of those who had returned with Panama money, devouring their hard-earned cash with astonishing rapidity. Thus, one of the unintended and ironic consequences of the growth in liquidity and the overall increase in the supply of money in Barbados was the devaluation of the very money that triggered and partly fuelled the inflationary spiral. Thus Panama money devoured Panama money, like a beast eating its own tail. Many of the returnees who thought they had earned enough to make a reasonable living in Barbados discovered to their chagrin that they, once again, had to take to the high seas to secure a living. They migrated in their tens of thousands to Cuba, to take advantage of the high wages in Oriente province cutting sugar cane for the Yankees. And Barbadians and other islanders went to Costa Rica, Honduras, and Guatemala to work on the expanding banana plantations. Many of the more educated and skilled tried their luck in the United States. Included among these were Richard B. Moore, W. A. Domingo, Claude McKay, and Cyril Briggs.

A full and comprehensive audit of the consequences of the exodus to Panama and its impact on the masses of the people in the sending societies is yet to be undertaken. But what is already clear, if seldom admitted, is that the results of the exodus were mixed, with clearly negative elements. Those who did not migrate, and those—the overwhelming majority—who did not partake in its benefits, suffered many of the unwanted consequences of Panama and Panama money. The negative impact of Panama money on their lives partly explained the contradictory and somewhat bewildering combination of feelings that the people had toward the returning migrants—admiration, envy, resentment, ambivalence.[168] In the end, the primary beneficiaries of this great migration may very well have been the land speculators, the merchants, and, to a lesser extent, the returning migrants themselves—especially those who took their families to the United States. The chief losers were the poor who did not migrate and existed outside the circuit of Panama money. They were pushed deeper into the vortex of poverty by the powerful hand of inflation, partly nourished by Panama money.

Powered by the same forces, the migration from the Caribbean to the United States was simultaneous with the migration to Panama between 1904 and 1914; the commonly held view that it was sequential is wrong. It is true that the United States as a destination increased in importance after the completion of the Canal in 1914. But there was no sudden or dramamtic increase in the number of Caribbeans entering the United States between

1914 and 1924 (see Table 1.2, pages 356–7). The trend was upward, but not markedly so. Furthermore, the numbers entering the United States fluctuated wildly from year to year, displaying no identifiably meaningful pattern. The sharp increase from 6,580 in 1923 to 10,630 in 1924 reflects effort to enter the country before the immigration act took effect.

Thus during the years of the building of the Canal, the movement to the United States ran temporally parallel to that to Panama. The size of these two migration flows was by no means equal. For while 3,018 Caribbeans entered the United States in 1906, some 10,533 Jamaicans went to Panama, and 6,510 contractor laborers left Barbados the same year.[169] The small stream to the United States was clearly no equivalent to the Mississippi-like flow of Caribbean labor to Panama, but the movements occurred at the same time. There was always some migration from Central America to the United States, but given the tens of thousands who worked on the Canal and banana plantations in the area, it is remarkable how few left—even after the Canal was completed—for the United States. Some of course would have returned to the Caribbean and then migrated to the United States; no one knows precisely how many fell into this category.

By the early twenties, New York was the primary destination of the migrants to the United States (see Table 1.3 and Figure 1.2, pages 358, 368). But it was not the most desperate who escaped by this maritime *marronage*; many of the latter were simply too desperate to effect escape by sea. Who were the people who migrated to the United States? How many men? How many women? What were their educational and occupational backgrounds? What characteristics did they have that help to account for their radicalism? These and others are the questions to which we must now turn.

2

The Peculiarities of the Caribbeans: Characteristics and Forces Conducive to Radicalization

Caribbean migrants to the United States shared a number of character-istics that disposed them toward radical politics. This included their majority consciousness; their prior political and organizational experience; their extensive prior experience of travel and migration; a politically protected status in the United States (at least for those from the British Caribbean) as subjects of the British Crown; a somewhat lesser attachment to the Christian faith and Christian churches; and educational and occupa-tional attainments generally beyond the reach of Afro-Americans. Let us examine these characteristics in more detail.

The black migrants from the Caribbean entered the United States with what we may describe as a majority consciousness; that is, they were accustomed, for the most part, to negotiating a world in which they constituted the overwhelming majority of the population. But even though they migrated primarily to the large urban centers of America, most notably New York City, where the Great Migration brought large numbers of Afro-Americans to settle, the migrants lived in cities in which the vast majority of the population was white and unfriendly, if not overtly hostile. Because of the sardine-tin concentration of black people in Harlem, it is easy to lose sight of the fact that even in New York City—site of the Negro Metropo-lis—black people constituted only 1.9 percent, 2.7 percent, and 4.7 percent of the city's total population in 1910, 1920, and 1930, respectively. The corresponding figures for Manhattan were 2.6 percent, 4.8 percent, and 12.7 percent.[1] Thus the the migrants' unavoidable everyday interaction with white people—often tinged with racism—disposed some of them to radical political activity.

A significant number also came with political and organizational experi-ence. Some had been involved in trade unions, others in nationalist organizations, still others in both. Domingo, for instance, had been an official (second secretary) of a proto-nationalist organization in Jamaica, the National Club, before migrating to the United States in 1910. Marcus Garvey was also an officer (first secretary) of the Club.[2] In addition, Garvey had been a trade unionist when he worked as a printer in Kingston and led a strike at his workplace. More significantly, Garvey began his Universal

Negro Improvement Association in 1914, two years before going to New York.

But Garvey and Domingo were not the only ones to leave the Caribbean as radicals. Claude McKay was one of a handful of freethinkers in Jamaica and a committed socialist, albeit of the Fabian variety, before he left for Tuskegee in 1912. Charles Petioni, Garveyite and Caribbean community leader in New York, arrived in America in 1918 after the colonial government in his native Trinidad "sent word to him," according to one authority, "that his outspoken views about local political and economic conditions had permanently damaged future career opportunities for himself and his family." (It was not only to black Southerners that Harlem served as a "city of refuge.") Petioni had embarked upon a career in business and journalism. Samuel Haynes, a leader of the UNIA in the United States, left British Honduras (now Belize) after helping to lead a large protest movement in his country's capital in 1919.[3] John Sydney de Bourg, former Secretary of Trinidad Workingmen's Association, one of the most important labor organizations in the Caribbean in the early twentieth century, left Grenada in 1920 and joined the leadership of the UNIA in New York. Because of his role in a massive strike in Trinidad in 1919, he was charged with sedition. Born in Grenada, he had lived in Trinidad since 1881. But in the aftermath of the struggle led largely by the Association, the leaders were either imprisoned or deported if they came from elsewhere. (Some, like Bruce McConney from Barbados, were doubly punished: he was imprisoned and then deported after finishing his sentence.) Returning from a labor conference in British Guiana, de Bourg was barred from re-entry and sent to Grenada and was never allowed to set foot in Trinidad for the rest of his life. Although he was 68 at the time, de Bourg still had fight left in him. He was invited by Garvey to represent Trinidad at the historic 1920 convention of the UNIA in New York, where he was elected "Leader of the Negroes of the West Indies, Western Province, South and Central America." In 1921 de Bourg toured Cuba and Jamaica on behalf of the UNIA.[4] The Rev. Edward Seiler Salmon, a Jamaican, was also a leader of the Trinidad Workingmen's Association and in the government crackdown of 1920 was deported to Jamaica. Salmon, like de Bourg, was originally trained as a teacher. But by 1912 he had become a priest in the Anglican Church. He taught for the church in Jamaica, Costa Rica, Trinidad, and elsewhere in the Caribbean. Salmon served as the rector in a church in Port Limón, Costa Rica, for five years but was forced to resign because of his agitation against the British. By 1923, Salmon had migrated to the United States for in that year he joined the African Orthodox Church and was engaged in the supervision of several of the church's missions in New Orleans.[5]

These Caribbean migrants' experience in America further radicalized them, but they had never been the conservatives Kelly Miller and Harold Cruse would let us believe. (Kelly Miller and Harold Cruse's ideas are discussed below.) Nor were they alone: many others, perhaps numbering thousands, were not only disgruntled but radicalized, too, before their arrival in the United States.

Chief among the disgruntled or radicalized were former members of the British West Indies Regiment who served in Europe and the Middle East during the Great War. Any illusions that these soldiers had about their Britishness before going to the "Mother Country" were quickly dispelled by the head-spinning racism meted out to them by white fellow-British soldiers and officers alike.

Even before the men returned, news of their deplorable treatment at the hands of the British had reached relatives and loved ones back in the islands. Some of the more courageous newspapers, such as T. S. Marry-show's *The West Indian* in Grenada, publicized the experience of the men even while the war was in progress. But it was when the men returned after the armistice that the general populace learned of the nightmare that they had experienced. The veterans returned saddened and angry. Almost seventy years later, Leslie Thompson, a black Jamaican musician who knew many of the Jamaican veterans, remembered their dissatisfaction and "deep-seated resentment." Some seemed almost ashamed to relate the racist humiliation they endured abroad at the hands of the British while serving the British in the war. "They wouldn't talk about it," said Thompson, "but one or two fellows would have a drink and a tale would be told."[6] But many talked with less reticence and what they knew, as one of their number said, was "pretty ugly." In 1940, veterans were still complaining about "bonuses, gratuities, awards, pay, etc." owed them but never received. When attempts were made to get what was due, one veteran wrote to the press, "the flimsy excuse of 'lost records' is put forward to close the matter."[7]

The treatment received by members of the British West Indies Regiment profoundly radicalized a significant proportion of these black men. As we will see, they spearheaded many of the struggles in the aftermath of the First World War. But because the general population, in one way or another, learned of the racism the men suffered abroad, the impact of the veterans' experience was, to a certain extent, generalized among thousands of black people in the region. Approximately 16,000 black men served abroad during the war. Over twelve hundred died and almost seven hundred were wounded. They came from every part of the British Carib-bean: from Belize in the west to Guyana in the south east, to the Bahamas in the north.[8] They all had friends and relatives and loved ones; they came from towns and villages. Thus, thousands and thousands of friends, relatives, loved ones, and bereaved were angered and radicalized through this indirect impact of the war. The role of Caribbean veterans in the post-war radical upsurge in the region is insufficiently appreciated. Even less acknowledged and documented is the radical political role of veterans who migrated from the islands to the United States. For these reasons I have given special consideration here to the veterans, with particular reference to the political evolution Corporal Samuel A. Haynes from Belize, who became an ardent Pan-Africanist and leading Garveyite after the war.

The treatment the men received in the army was predetermined by the fact that the British War Office did not want them in the first place. Being good colonials, however, thousands throughout the archipelago volunteered to fight for Britain, which they believed was their country too. In fact, some, soon after the declaration of war, made their way to London, at their own expense (amounting to a far from negligible £25) to enlist in Lord Kitchener's army.[9] After all, were they not an "ancient" part of the British Empire? Had they not been schooled and socialized to believe that they were British? They celebrated the British monarch's jubilee like the British people and like them they, too, celebrated Empire Day and sang "God Save the King" when the monarch was male and "God Save the Queen" when female. They sang "Rule Britannia" with the least excuse and with more gusto than any freeborn Briton—precisely because they were colonials. When war broke out the pro-British ideological offensive increased. C. L. R. James recalled that in Trinidad they had been "deluged" with propaganda;[10] the same was true for the rest of the British Caribbean. In Jamaica, Thomas MacDermot, a white Jamaican, who was later dubbed poet laureate of the island, composed a nine-stanza poem, "Arise O My Country," specifically aimed at winning recruits for the war effort.

> Arise O my Country, the Day of Decision
>   Across thy green border hath come,
> And loud and impetuous trumpets are speaking,
>   And deep is the roll of the drum.
>
> To Arms! for the Day of thy Judgment of Nations
>   Hath come to its fiery birth,
> And the shouts of the Captains, the roar of the battle,
>   They have swept to the ends of the earth . . . .
>
> With war-wasted battalions, see Britain bears forward
>   The banner that freedom hath kissed,
> And Liberty points to the ranks of the Tyrant,
>   And calls to her sons to enlist . . . .
>
> In this day shall the Blackman be proud of his color,
>   And the Whiteman be proud of his strain;
> And each for the other shall strive, and the strength
>   Of the one be the strength of the twain.
>
> To Arms! for the Crusade where God is our Captain,
>   His vengeance we march to perform;
> And bright as his word, doth the Banner of Britain
>   Lead on, through the shadow and the storm.[11]

MacDermot himself disclosed that the poem was written "with the object of having it read aloud or recited at recruiting meetings. The leaflet [i.e. the poem], which was printed at the cost of a gentleman who desired to remain anonymous, was given to the men without charge."[12]

There were people in Jamaica who mocked the soldiers as they marched off to war:

> Lef contingent lef
> Hat ah nuh fi you
> Boot a nuh fi yu
> Lef contingent lef.[13]

But it appears, as Erna Brodber—who recovered this memory through a remarkable series of interviews of elderly Jamaicans—argued, that the objection was not to the war as such and the men going off to it, but to the loss of independence that joining the army entailed.[14] In short, throughout the British Caribbean, people were either highly supportive or indifferent to the war, and the evidence is that far many more were supportive than indifferent. Substantial sums were collected directly from the public in addition to the raiding of the meager treasury of the islands to finance the contingents and the British war effort generally.[15] Yet to be found in the British Caribbean is any sustained intellectual or popular objection to the war and the mobilization in the islands. "Go on England, Barbados is behind you!" are words attributed to a Barbadian public official. It is claimed that they were used in a telegram sent to the British Prime Minister at the beginning of the so-called Boer War in South Africa. Like many good stories, it is probably apocryphal. But the sentiment expressed in those words resonated throughout the British Caribbean during the First World War. Support for the war came from some seemingly unlikely quarters.

The young C. L. R. James, who would become one of the most celebrated radicals of the twentieth century, volunteered to fight. And while Marcus Garvey did not put himself forward, he and his newly formed Universal Negro Improvement Association and African Communities League, as one newspaper reported, held a "farewell meeting . . . and bade good-bye, with hearty good wishes, to members of the Contingent who were present by invitation. The President, Mr Garvey, . . . impressed on the men the good wishes of the meeting, and the duty of every true son of the Empire to rally to the cause of the Motherland."[16] Thus, we find yoked together in their allegiance to Britain and the support of the war, on the one hand, a man who became one of the most distingushed Marxist intellectuals and activists of our century, and, on the other, one who quickly became the pre-eminent and most influential black nationalist that has ever lived.

But to the War Office, none of this history and Caribbean enthusiasm counted. They did not want "black West Indians" to fight white men in Europe. The Colonial Office, the government department superintending the territories conquered overseas by Britain, agreed with the War Office: it

Two Bahamian workers, Thomas and Zebedie, clearing a plot for a pioneer dwelling in Coconut Grove, south of what later became Miami. This photograph was taken around 1886. The black Bahamians who established the first black settlements around Miami were, according to one historian, Arva Moore Parks, the people who taught the white settlers from the north eastern United States in the late nineteenth century how to live in the jungle wilderness. "They provided them with the knowhow they needed to live with the heat and the mosquitoes, showed them the fruits and vegetables they could and could not eat, and provided the labor to bring about the changes." (Photograph from the Ralph Munroe Collection, courtesy of the Historical Association of Southern Florida)

Nat Simpson and Alice Burrows, Bahamian workers at the Peacock Inn, Coconut Grove, dressed in their Sunday best to have their photograph taken, *c.* 1886. (Ralph Munroe Collection, courtesy of the Historical Association of Southern Florida)

Members of the black Bahamian community in Coconut Grove gather to have their photograph tak
outside Ralph Munroe's boathouse, *c.* 1886. Ralph Munroe, a white amateur photographer and
naturalist, was born on Staten Island, New York, and settled in south Florida in the early 1880s.
(Ralph Munroe Collection, courtesy of the Historical Association of Southern Florida)

Ethiopian immigrants as they arrived at Ellis Island, *c.* 1910. They were photographed by Augustu
Sherman (1866–1925), an employee of Ellis Island's Registry Division, between 1892 and 1925. A
amateur photographer, Sherman took over 141 photographs of newly arrived aliens between 1906
and 1925, and was particularly interested in immigrants wearing unusual and "exotic" clothes. Hi
subjects, who were simply taken aside by him to be photographed, often carry expressions of bewil
derment, fear, and annoyance. It is not clear whether the photographing of immigrants was part of
Sherman's official duties; it probably wasn't. (Courtesy of the Ellis Island Immigration Museum)

Three members of the same group. (Courtesy of the Ellis Island Immigration Museum)

Samuel A. Haynes, when President of the Pittsburgh UNIA Division, 1925.
(*The Negro World*, March 21, 1925, courtesy of Robert A. Hill)

Guadeloupean women as they arrived on Ellis Island, April 6, 1911.
(Courtesy of the Ellis Island Immigration Museum)

Three from the same group. (Courtesy of the Ellis Island Immigration Museum)

A portrait of a member of the group.
(Courtesy of the Ellis Island Immigration Museum)

Marcus Garvey, *c.* 1919. (Courtesy of the Schomburg Center for Research in Black Culture,
New York Public Library, Astor, Lenox and Tilden Foundations)

Hubert Harrison, *c.* 1920.
(Courtesy of the Schomburg Center for
Research in Black Culture, New York Public
Library, Astor, Lenox and Tilden
Foundations)

Cyril Briggs, 1930s.
(Courtesy of Robert A. Hill)

Grace Campbell, 1920.
(*The Messenger*, November 1920)

Richard B. Moore, *c.* 1930.
(Courtesy of the Schomburg Center for Research in Black Culture,
New York Public Library, Astor, Lenox and Tilden Foundations)

W. A. Domingo, 1930s.
(Courtesy of Joyce Moore Turner)

would be bad for the imperial connection to have black men killing white men in Europe, even when those white men were Britain's enemies. But the rejection of Caribbean troops was not simply or even primarily made on the basis of the *realpolitik* of colonial rule. It was made, fundamentally, on the grounds of even more narrowly racist reasoning.[17] For public consumption, however, the excuse given for the exclusion was the climate: Europe was too cold for black men to be effective soldiers there. (Privately, the preponderence of opinion was that black men could not be effective soldiers anywhere.) The authorities, from the beginning, welcomed white Caribbeans—as they had accepted offers of contingents from Canada, Australia, and New Zealand—but were firmly set against using Afro-Caribbeans.[18] It is thus not accurate to state, as C. L. R. James did, that at the beginning of the war "The idea that West Indian troops should be sent to fight for the Empire was looked upon as absurd"; no, not West Indian troops, per se, but *black* West Indian troops—that was the perceived absurdity.[19]

For their part, the white and near-white Caribbeans organized a recruitment drive among themselves. Modestly referring to themselves as the "best class" in Barbados and the "better class" in Trinidad, Jamaica, and elsewhere, they successfully pressed the Colonial Office to allow them to join British regiments, and when they enlisted with the British West Indies Regiment they served only as officers over the black men. They went so far as to organize a regional recruitment of members of their class into a Merchants' and Planters' Contingent.[20] Despite knowing that the "rumour was, and the facts seemed to show, that the merchants selected only white or brown people," C. L. R. James went to join the Merchants' and Planters' Contingent in Trinidad. Though "I was dark," he wrote, "I was widely known as a coming cricketer and I kept goal for the college team in the first-class football league." He was also well known as an exceptionally bright young man who attended the island's most prestigious secondary school, Queen's Royal College.

> I was tall and very fit. So on a morning when I should have been at school I went down to the office where one of the big merchants, perhaps the biggest of all, examined the would-be warriors. Young man after young man went in, and I was not obviously inferior to any of them in anything. The merchant talked to each, asked for references and arranged for further examination as the case might be. When my turn came I walked to his desk. He took one look at me, saw my dark skin and, shaking his head vigorously, motioned me violently away.[21]

There was thus a combination of important members of the local ruling class in the Caribbean, the Colonial Office, and the War Office that objected to the participation of black Caribbean men in the war effort in Europe. Nothing less than the intervention of the British monarch, George V, himself, got the War Office to budge from its entrenched position.[22] The West Indies Regiment was created in 1915 and, at its full strength, comprised eleven battalions with over fifteen thousand men, and almost four hundred officers (mainly white and light-skinned). But the War Office, effectively, had its way: the Regiment did not fight in Europe and was stationed for most of the time outside of the European theater.

What happened to the men overseas fell well below their expectations. And the impact of their experience on Caribbean society and history was profound. The political radicalization of the servicemen and, with them, their home societies were some of the main consequences of their partici- pation in the war. Many of those who travelled to the United States were among the radicalized, and indeed, some travelled to the United States precisely because they had already been radicalized.

The experience and political evolution of Samuel Haynes are instructive and illuminating. On the very day that they came off the boat to fight for the Mother Country, Corporal Haynes and his comrades from the British Honduras Contingent were hit between the eyes by British racism. Haynes and the British Hondurans had a horrid 35-day journey across the Atlantic during which the food served was not only inadequate, but ranged from the "far from palatable" to the "unfit for human consumption."[23] They finally disembarked in Alexandria, Egypt, in August 1916. Tired, hungry but relieved, they marched to a Young Men's Christian Association (YMCA) hut reserved for British soldiers singing one of those tunes they had always been taught to believe was theirs, "Rule Britannia." The white soldiers greeted these proud Caribbean men with utter scorn: "Who gave you niggers authority to sing that?" they asked. "Clear out of this building—only British troops admitted here."[24] The welcome given the British Honduras Contingent heralded accurately the treatment it and other members of the British West Indies Regiment would receive over the next three years.

Like Afro-American troops in Europe during the First World War, Caribbean troops were encumbered by their white superiors' racist notions of what black soldiers ought to be allowed to do. The American authorities thought that black soldiers should be used to clean latrines, fetch and bury the dead, load and unload cargo ships. In short, serve as labor batallions— they were most reluctant to let these men engage in combat in Europe.[25] The British held similar views about black soldiers. A contingent of the British West Indies Regiment, after repeated requests to be allowed to fight, learned that it was "against British tradition to employ aboriginal troops against a European enemy."[26] Accordingly, Caribbean soldiers were sent far away from the European theater. Egypt, Mesopotamia, Palestine, the Cameroon, and Tanganyika were their primary locations. Haynes and his compatriots served in Alexandria, Baghdad, Kut, Amara, Kurna, Basra. The British Honduras Contingent spent most of its time on the Inland Water Transport camps along the River Tigris in Mesopotamia (Iraq). In the spring of 1919, they spent a month in India. Other members of the Regiment served in Mombasa, and some, after considerable pressure on the

British military, were eventually allowed to engage in combat in the Jordan valley. They distinguished themselves, winning high honors, fighting valiantly against the Turks in the Middle East, but not allowed to engage the Germans in Europe.[27] Volunteered and recruited as fighting troops, few members of the British West Indies Regiment saw combat. But the discrimination extended well beyond turning men recruited to the infantry into demeaned members of labor battalions. They were exposed to a level of racism that was shocking in its intensity and pervasiveness.

In Kurna, Iraq, while bathing in the British Kraal set aside for British troops, four black men from the British Honduras Contingent were driven away by a Lieutenant Colonel who told them that "no niggers were allowed to bathe in the Kraal."[28] Samuel Haynes and about a hundred other men from the Regiment were transported by cattle trucks "exposed to the sun and with little rations" from Alexandria to Port Suez in Egypt. The journey took ten to twelve hours. Not all of it took place during the day, for Haynes reported that they left in the evening and arrived in the morning. But he and the other men from the Caribbean noticed that the white soldiers were not treated in this way. "I never saw any other troops sent in cattle trucks to Port Suez," he told the Belize commission.[29] The men complained of having to endure filthy conditions on boats transporting them. Below deck where they had to sleep on one of the boats, according to Haynes, "the odour revealed the fact that the vessel was lately used for the conveyance of various animals."[30] White soldiers were not treated this way and the men noticed and resented the discrimination.

The food was generally poor and substandard. And when the men complained they were verbally abused. For three nights Corporal Haynes was provided with nothing to sleep on but the muddy floor of a tent in which he worked as a clerk. He contracted pneumonia. In the hospitals, white soldiers were treated better than black soldiers: the medical attention paid the men from the West Indies Regiment was, in Haynes's words, "exceedingly poor compared with that paid [white] British soldiers." Patients were racially segregated.

> When admitted to hospitals we were generally set apart from Europeans and put in wards with Africans and Asiatics who were ignorant of the English language and Western customs. In wards where Europeans were quartered, tables were set separately for us. In the 33rd British General Hospital in Basra there was an H. Ward. In this ward, there were no sisters to attend to us[,] only [male] orderlies.[31]

Further indignities accompanied their stay in hospital. The orderlies in the hospital where Haynes stayed were in the habit of putting the men on cook house fatigues without the doctor's consent. Drummer McKoy, another British Honduran, also complained about his treatment while in the same hospital. One of the orderlies told him to get up and sweep the hospital. He refused, explaining that "he was too weak to eat his food, much more to sweep the hospital." To this the orderly blurted out, "you black bastards think too much of yourselves."[32] McKoy also testified that, while in the hospital, a white "Tommy" (i.e. a British private), took away a piece of bread from a Corporal Willoughby of the British West Indies Regiment. The corporal took his bread back and the Tommy punched him in the face. Willoughby struck him back. The orderly laid a charge against Willoughby for "striking a white man." The Tommy went unpunished and Corporal Willoughby was reverted to the ranks.[33] While suffering from dysentery, McKoy was placed on a hospital ship together with a Jamaican called Brown. Once again they were segregated from the whites, "placed in the lower hold where some Indians were." McKoy reported that while there, an orderly gave one of the Indians a mug of milk. The Indian drank some but left most of it. Instead of offering the men their own milk, the orderly offered McKoy and Brown what was left in the Indian man's mug. McKoy asked the orderly "what he took them for, if he thought they must drink what an Indian had left." To this the orderly replied: "Damned black bastards, used to nothing better than that in your own home."[34]

A similar contempt must have lurked behind the inferior accommodation provided the black soldiers in Mesopotamia. And once again, the men noticed the difference between what they were offered and what the white soldiers were given. Samuel Haynes told the commission that his group of soldiers arrived in the area in the "height of the winter season and were ushered into mud huts without any flooring."

> We had two blankets, one rubber sheet, and one great coat in our possession. We experienced trying times in the mud and the rain. These huts were always leaking, the roofs not being strong enough to stand the weather. . . . Apart from the British soldiers at the aviation camp, we were the only fighting troops stationed here at that time. The accommodation was rotten. In Tanoma, Khora Creek, the I[nland] W[ater] T[ransport] Dockyard, and the Barge Repair Depot the conditions of the houses were deplorable. It was strongly noticeable that in the huts in which British Soldiers were quartered, electric lights, flooring and winter stoves were introduced, but not in our camp in my time. There was no heat in the camp at all except in the galley. We went to the galley to get warm.[35]

The inferior housing conditions affected the men terribly in summer too. Captain Hulse told of his visit to a camp at Amara. Seventy men from the Regiment were staying there. They were, said Hulse, all alone in a desert patch of very low ground. The authorities provided them with a "small kitchen made of corrugated iron." It was "extremely hot" during the summer months. "Their latrine was out in the desert, and closed with matting, and exposed to the sun. Europeans," Hulse noted, "were provided with proper kitchens and latrines. I pointed out this difference to Captain Butcher, and told him that the men of the B. W. I. Regiment were entitled to the same treatment as the European troops, but could not get him to do anything."[36] The men got sick due to the conditions in the summer as well as in the winter. Heat stroke, dysentery, diarrhoea, malaria, pneumonia, debilitated and killed them. The people charged with looking after the men's health hardly cared. Haynes and others specifically mentioned one Lieut. J. D. Kapur of the Indian Medical Service who was charged with looking after a hundred men at one of the depots. During the summer months, said Haynes, when called to attend to the men, Kapur

> absented himself from the patients until such time as he thought fit. Cases of heat stroke, dysentery, diarrhoea, and malaria were invariably treated as third class matters in spite of the fact that these men were employed on work of a laborious nature. When they reported sick, they received very little attention from Lieut. Kapur ... and he neglected the men in the majority of cases, so much so that he oft-times allowed C[ompany] S[ergeant] M[ajor] Appleby ... to dictate to him who should return to duty or otherwise. Matters of such nature were invariably reported to Major Jeffrey who took no steps to have same redressed.[37]

Although Kapur had responsibility for the men, he, nevertheless, was a victim of the colonial pecking order in the army: he allowed a subordinate, because the latter was white, to dictate to him how his work should be done. The ultimate victims, were, of course, the sick black soldiers. One black sergeant reported that as soon as they arrived at one depot, the men began suffering from dysentery. He had, however, been given orders from the lieutenant in charge, through the orderly sergeant, "not to report more than 6 men per day on the sick report." Some mornings, he said, they had about 15 men sick, "but they were compelled to go to work, although they were suffering."[38] Drummer McKoy explained that although he was suffering from dysentery, Kapur sent him to work. He became so weak that Corporal Haynes and two of his comrades "had to convey me to the latrines, and from the latrines to my hut." It was only then that they consented to his going to hospital.[39]

The distribution of casualties among the men of the British West Indies Regiment underscores the testimonies. Almost six times more men died from illness than killed or died of wounds: while 1,071 died of sickness, mainly pneumonia, only 185 were killed or died of wounds. (Another 697 were wounded.)[40] Even after allowing for the fact that the men had little opportunity for combat, these remained appalling statistics, severely indicting the British army.

The segregation and humiliation extended beyond the hospitals and accommodation. Men were sometimes refused service at the British forces canteen. In Baghdad the British Military Police harassed members of the Regiment—"always at them for some reason or another." Also in Baghdad, British soldiers insulted them when they attended concerts.[41] Drummer McKoy complained that all one winter, along the Tigris, he and three others from the Regiment labored as a ration gang. They had to carry rations to the waterside fully two miles on their heads or shoulders. They could not help noticing, however, that the white soldiers were given bullock carts in which to carry their rations to the waterside. When McKoy asked a senior officer for a bullock cart to carry the heavy load, he was told that the carts were "only for British soldiers." McKoy explained that he was a British soldier and a member of the British West Indies Regiment. But that was not enough to secure him a cart. He and his three black comrades were forced to continue through the wet and muddy winter as before, watching the white soldiers go by, unburdened, sitting in their carts carried by their bullocks.[42]

The inferior status to which Afro-Caribbean men were assigned by the army was graphically illustrated during a month-long stay of some three hundred of them in India. Men from the British Honduras Contingent, including Samuel Haynes, were stationed in Deolalli in March 1919. While there, the men were required to perform fatigues—menial tasks—for white soldiers encamped nearby. As Sergeant McDonald told the Belize commission, "During the time we were there, I can personally say that no Europeans came over to our camp to carry on any sort of work in connection with the [British West Indies Regiment]." Haynes, too, noticed the unreciprocal nature of the relationship. While the black men were required to carry tents, quartermasters' stores, and work of that kind, none of this, he said, was "done in our camp by the Europeans."[43]

Two things are worthy of explicit note here. First is the fact that this inequality was noticed and resented openly by the men, and not just by McDonald and Haynes. Indeed, McDonald was reporting to the commission the fact that his men were "particularly dissatisfied" by this treatment. Second, and perhaps more significantly, is the fact that the men possessed an unbroken dignity, despite three centuries of British colonial rule, which riled up against the relationship established at Deolalli: the men seriously believed that if they had to go to the white soldiers' camp and do their dirty work for them, then the white soldiers, in turn, should come to their camp and render identical services. Failing such an exchange, each camp should do its own dirty work. The radicalization of the men through experience like that at Deolalli cannot be explained outside of their expecations and ideological formation prior to entering the British army.[44]

All recreation, with the exception of cricket, was segregated. And with cricket it was a case of teams made up of black men from the regiment playing against teams made up exclusively of white men. (The Caribbean men invariably beat them at the game.) There was widespread complaint against the YMCAs debarring black men. One army chaplain refused to allow the men in the tent in which he conducted service. Thirty British Honduran soldiers were told that they could sit outside and listen, but not enter. Drummer McKoy had a very bad war. He told the Belize commision about the behavior of another chaplain. At a communion service, McKoy went down to the right of Europeans who were there; the chaplain, noticing this, started on the left with the communion cups. At the following service, McKoy went to the left, the chaplain started from the right. McKoy, who must have had a good sense of humor, informed the members of the commission that "he intended to attend another communion service and kneel down in the centre and see what the chaplain would do." But he never had a chance to carry out his intention as he was sent elsewhere.[45]

Although the men were not allowed to fight within the European theater, they, nevertheless, had an important presence there, especially in France. As was noted above, one of the excuses used by the War Office for not having black Caribbeans as fighting soldiers in Europe was that they would not and could not withstand the rigors of the climate.[46] But after the Bermuda Voluntary Artillery, made up of black Bermudans, had been used in France in the winter of 1915–16, the matter was reviewed. Unlike the Bermuda Volunteer Rifle Corps, made up exclusively of whites, the Bermuda Voluntary Artillery was not allowed to fight in France. They were, instead, used for carrying shells under heavy fire and had distinguished themselves doing so, especially during the winter months. It was in the light of this experience and with an increasing need for more men to do this kind of work that battalions of the British West Indies Regiment were brought into the European theater.[47] From Egypt, the men crossed the Mediterranean and entered France through Marseilles. Thence, they were taken to the front and pointed toward the ammunition dumps. Although the duties were "arduous and dangerous" and "carried at all times under heavy fire," they were more likely to satisfy the expectations of the men for active military service than were the menial tasks of the labor corps that they had been saddled with in Egypt and Mesopotamia.[48] In France, the battalions of the British West Indies Regiment were employed in all the main operations that had taken place, including the battles of the Somme, Arras, Messines, and Ypres. Their work, reported Joseph,

> consisted chiefly of handling ammunition at the railheads and carrying it up to the batteries both day and night, digging cable trenches and emplacements for guns, often under heavy shell fire occasioning heavy casualties. Sometimes detachments were involved in loading and unloading at the docks at Boulogne, and in the construction of light railways. The 3rd battalion was in France from September 1916 up to the armistice, working through both the winters of 1916–17 and 1917–18. Other battalions, like the 4th, spent one winter in France, and the other winter between France and Taranto, Italy, where they worked on the quays in construction work, unloading stores, and loading lighters for ships. The black contingent from Bermuda also served in the same capacity on the ammunition dumps for some time with the Canadian Corps subsequent to the capture of Vimy Ridge, May 1917.[49]

The Commander-in-Chief of the British Armies in France, Field-Marshal Sir Douglas Haig, showered the men with high praise, remarking upon their exceptional physique, excellent discipline, high morale, and the fact that they rendered valuable services at times of great pressure. Despite heavy casualties, the men, he said, showed themselves "willing and cheerful," and the units to which they were attached highly appreciated the assistance rendered. But despite all of this, they were never given a chance to fight in Europe. They were eventually allowed to fight the Turks in Palestine, but not white Germans in Europe.[50] And this they never forgot.

The humiliation of the men—men who had naïvely and full of good intentions volunteered to serve the Mother Country in her moment of need—was unconfined, following them wherever they went, like shadows in the tropics. Complaints were many, but they were inevitably individualized, lodged in isolation, one by one, and easily ignored by the authorities. Beyond building an Everest of complaints, the men resisted, and sometimes violently, the indignity with which they were treated. When the "Rule Britannia"-singing British Hondurans were insulted by the white soldiers at the YMCA in Alexandria, they fought the Tommies for about twenty minutes.[51] Corporal Willouhby lost his stripes, but not before giving the assaulting, racist private a dose of his own medicine. When another member of the Regiment was called a "black son of a bitch" by a white soldier, he never failed to give the latter a sound thrashing.[52] There were numerous cases of this kind, of individual black soldiers defending their dignity against insulting and inhuman treatment. But, inevitably, such resistance was typically carried out on an individual, not a collective, basis. The racist way in which wages were determined and allocated was a complaint of the men from the arrival of the first contingent in Egypt in 1916.[53] However, when, at the close of the war, members of the Regiment discovered that, as a group, they were ineligible for a pay increase granted to other imperial troops, the Rubicon was crossed, and a collective cry of outrage rang out.

Army Order No. 1 of 1918 provided the British soldier with an increase of six pence per day, taking his daily pay to one shilling and six pence, an increase of 50 percent. The West Indians were not entitled to the increase, the War Office ruled, because they were "Natives." Indeed, the basis of the decision was underlined by the War Office when it informed the Colonial Office that the personnel of the Bermuda Volunteer Rifle Corps, an all-white oufit, were entitled to the increase but that the men from the West Indies Regiment were "definitely ineligible."[54] Some men from the Regiment wrote to the governor of Barbados pointing out that the policy was "not only an insult to us who have volunteered to fight for the Empire . . . but also an insult to the whole West Indies." Another, a sergeant, complained, that the men were treated "neither as Christians nor British citizens, but as West Indian 'Niggers'."[55]

At the end of hostilities in November 1918, most of the battalions of the Regiment were stationed at Taranto, in northern Italy. They were once again humiliated, used as labor battalions against the army's own regulations, even put to washing the dirty linen and cleaning the latrines of the Italian Labour Corps.[56] This means that Caribbean men who had enlisted as fighting soldiers were so degraded by the authorities that they were doing the dirty work of men who had been specifically employed as laborers. They became servants of servants; but they were black and the Italian

Labour Corps was white, and so it was acceptable. They were segregated, with their own canteens, and were not allowed to go to the cinemas when British troops were there. When ill, they were sent to a native hospital, instead of the hospital for British troops. According to a white Jamaican officer, several men died from sheer neglect at one of the Native Labour Hospitals.[57] This was only another example of where the treatment of the men ran counter to the commitment given when recruited. Concerned about the inequity, the mounting grievance and discontent among the men, one liberal-minded English officer, Major Thursfield, complained to the camp commandant, Brigadier-General Carey Bernard, a South African. Bernard told Thursfield that, while "perfectly aware" that the men had been promised equal treatment with white British troops, he "intended to take no notice"; that, after all, "the men were only niggers, and that no such treatment should ever have been promised to them; that they were better fed and treated than any nigger had a right to expect." He promised to "force" the men to continue as laborers.[58]

The men of the British West Indies Regiment replied to Bernard's degradation of them. They revolted. It started on December 6, 1918 when members of the 9th Battalion attacked their officers and severely assaulted their unit commander. Men, according to official dispatches, "mutinously refused" to work, a shooting and a bombing occurred, incidents of "insubordination" were widespread and a "generally insubordinate spirit prevailed."[59] On the same day, 180 sergeants sent a petition to the Secretary of State for the Colonies, protesting the the preclusion of black Caribbeans from the benefits of Army Order No. 1, which prevented them from receiving increased separation allowances like other troops, and from being promoted to any rank in the Army.[60] The uprising continued for several days. Finally, the 9th Battalion was disbanded, its members distributed among other units. All battalions of the Regiment in Taranto were disarmed. But even after all this was done, the base commander reported that the situation was "still unsettled," informing the War Office that his need for a battalion of white troops was "absolutely essential." A machine-gun company and a battalion of the Worcestershire Regiment were sent to Taranto. They travelled "in fighting order with ammunition in their pouches."[61]

Most of the men involved in the revolt got three to five years in prison for mutiny. One man was given twenty years, another, who led a subsequent struggle, was executed by a Worcestershire Regiment firing squad.

But the men were not broken. In the aftermath of the revolt, some fifty to sixty sergeants of the Regiment met on December 17, 1918 and formed the "Caribbean League." The League held three to four meetings between December and early January 1919. They discussed a range of issues. The general grievance experienced during the war was an important one. They particularly resented the appointment of white non-commissioned officers in place of black non-commissioned officers. No doubt, some of them felt that had their skin been of a different color, they, too, would have been NCOs. Through the commingling of men from different parts of the archipelago and their bonding through common suffering, a pan-Caribbean identity had emerged out of the crucible of war. The League, made up of sergeants from Britsh Guiana in the south, to the Bahamas at the northern end of the chain, not surprisingly called for closer union among the islands. They sought self-determination for the Caribbean. Indeed, at its second meeting, one man told his comrades that the black man "should have freedom and govern himself in the West Indies" and "force must be used, and if necessary bloodshed to obtain that object." The members of the League agreed to organize a general strike for higher wages when they got back home. They talked of having a Caribbean-wide body with head-quarters in Kingston, Jamaica, but some disagreed with this location. They talked and disagreed over whether the men as a whole in the Regiment should be told about the League. But before the Caribbean League could sprout wings a sergeant of the 8th Battalion betrayed his comrades, revealing the existence and the activities of the League to his commanding officer. The British authorities thought the League had "seditious designs" that they feared would be acted upon when the men returned home. Realizing that they had been betrayed, the radicals discontinued their meetings. But although the League as an association of like-minded men came to an end, the ideas they articulated and the desires they gave voice to were very alive and endured long after the League itself had died.[62]

Despite the suppression of the revolt and the disbanding of the League, the British realized that concessions had to be made to these angry young men returning to the volatile colonies in the Caribbean. Accordingly, the Colonial Office prevailed upon the War Office about the treatment of the West Indies Regiment. And in February 1919 the men from the Regiment got, in full, under the terms of Army Order No. 1, the money previously denied them. The Jamaican legislature, in a similar vein, passed a bizarre law allowing ex-soldiers to vote in the next election—but only in that election. In the same year, changes in the law made it easier for workers to organize in unions; an employers' liability law was also passed. Two-thirds of the members of the West Indies Regiment, about ten thousand men— including most of the Taranto rebels and the leaders of the Caribbean League—came from Jamaica. The colonial authorities thus had compelling reasons to offer concessions there.[63]

But in Trinidad and British Honduras, ex-servicemen led labor revolts and protests in 1919, which shook the colonial structure to its very foundation. And in both cases the race-conscious spirit—what one colonial official called the "mutinous spirit"—of Taranto was in evidence.[64] Merchants in the Caribbean used the war as a cover for the most extraordinary profiteering, pushing prices into the sky. According to the *Port of Spain Gazette,* on the very day that the government announced that war had broken out in Europe prices leapt in Trinidad. Milk went up from 5 pence to 8 pence per tin, rice and flour from 1½ to 3 pence per pound, salted fish from 5 pence to 8 pence per pound, and sugar from 1½ to 3 pence per pound.[65] In Jamaica the wartime rises finally peaked in 1920. Over the previous six years food increased by 45 percent, clothing by 100 percent, and household linen and furnishings increased also by 100 percent.[66] In Trinidad the rise was even more astronomical: 145 percent for the colony generally and 126 percent in Port of Spain.[67] Similar rises occurred in British Honduras, British Guiana, and elsewhere in the Caribbean. While prices rose, wages were brutally held down. And the merchants and planters fattened themselves on the differential between wages and prices. John Smith, owner of a business called the Bonanza in Port of Spain, was on the verge of bankruptcy when war broke out in 1914. When he died in 1919 he left an estate valued at £250,000. Miraculous turnarounds in the fortunes of people like Smith were not uncommon. The Governor reported that even though the Chamber of Commerce in Trinidad had "generally agreed" that wages in the colony were too low, they refrained from doing anything about workers' pay, especially since they did not want to upset the big planters.[68]

The uprisings in the British Caribbean in 1919, especially in Trinidad and British Honduras, were, thus, fueled by material privation on the part of the masses of workers and urban dwellers as well as the accumulated rage borne by the returning ex-servicemen. On top of all this, many of the veterans had difficulty finding work and sustaining themselves and their families, especially given the high prices. But unlike most of the uprisings that occurred in the late nineteenth century, those of 1919 and the 1920s had a nationalist, and racial, ideological charge that were exceptionally strong. The leaders of the strike in Port of Spain, Trinidad, were said by the authorities to be "imbued with the idea that there must be a black world controlled and governed by the black people of their own race."[69] In July 1919, a group of prominent white citizens wrote to the Colonial Secretary seeking, among other things, the arming of the white population, the establishment of a body of white regular troops, and the suppression of the most militant newspaper on the island. They were especially worried and made these proposals because "a substantial minority of the black population openly proclaims that it has no further use for the white man, and means to eliminate him." They went on to say that "the palpable absurdity of such an idea in no way robs it of its danger or diminishes its attractiveness to the negro mind."[70] The fear was excessive, but it signaled a real change in the political climate of the colony, and the remarkable determination and combativity of strikers and protesters in Trinidad. One ex-serviceman in Trinidad, according to the police, was found "to be engaged upon the making of bombs with condensed milk tins and pieces of iron piping."[71]

In Belize, British Honduras's capital, the rebels believed that the colony should be "the black man's country." The rage of the crowd on the night of July 22 was not easily forgotten. "We are going to kill the white sons of bitches tonight. . . . This is the black man's night," a group of ex-servicemen are reported to have said.[72] Women were active in the protest and, like the men, they helped themselves, handily, to some of the necessities of life in the stores. They were seen "with tremendous loads of loot, . . . passing with their dresses full . . . and coming back again for more, and getting it and passing again." "The black men have no pluck," complained one Belize woman during the heat of rioting. "The women have to be behind them all the time, or else they do nothing."[73] Captain H. B. Stoyle, the Acting Director of Public Works, told the Commission of the "terrible language, threatening and foul language," directed to himself and all white men by one of the men from the British Honduras Contingent, who called them "'white up-starts' and everything he could lay his tongue to." The ex-serviceman held a stick over Stoyle's head and threatened to kill him. The following day, while going through the town, Stoyle heard remarks such as, "Here's another son of a bitch," and "Another bloody white man." A lot of the jeering came from boys, which Stoyle reported finding "rather extraordinary."[74] Major Schnarr, a white settler, told the Belize Commission: "The crowds I saw appeared to be furious—terribly furious; and the[i]r fury appeared to be directed against the white element." Although he did not spell it out, Schnarr believed that the people acted irrationally, as Negroes are prone to do. He made it clear that the white people of Belize were all innocent of any wrongdoing against black people in the colony. "To my knowledge," he said, "absolutely nothing has been done by the white element in this town."[75]

Like their counterparts in Trinidad and elsewhere, the whites of British Honduras were able to sleep more soundly as the colonial authorities mobilized and shipped in reinforcements. Jamaica and Grenada were similarly, though not as profoundly, affected by labor disturbances in 1919.[76]

Significantly, in each of the uprisings, from Taranto to Port of Spain, the *Negro World* and its influence was present and profound. Ex-servicemen were among the earliest converts to Garveyism,[77] and they did not all stay in the islands: many moved to the United States to help build the new black world that Garvey and the UNIA promised and yearned for. Ex-Corporal Samuel A. Haynes became General Secretary and the "driving force" behind the British Honduras branch of the UNIA. (The Second Vice-President of the branch, Benjamin Adderley, was also an ex-serviceman, who, like Haynes, had been stationed in Mesopotamia.)[78] Haynes also served as Secretary of the British Honduras Contingent Committee and as such would have penned the forceful letter to the editor of the conservative *Clarion* newspaper in August 1919. At the end of his successful tour of the colony in 1921, Garvey recruited Haynes to the parent organization in the United States. Haynes left British Honduras vowing, according to a police report, to fight for black advancement more enthusiastically than he had "for the Empire in the European War."[79] True to his words, Haynes joined his struggle with that of Afro-America, selflessly serving the UNIA on the mainland in Pittsburgh, Newport News, Baltimore, Philadelphia, South Carolina, North Carolina, and Delaware. When Garvey was sent to jail in 1925, Haynes became one of the four-member Committee of Presidents of the UNIA. In January 1934 he became Garvey's representative—*de facto*, National Leader—in the United States.[80] He had a column in the *Negro World* even before he was announced as a contributing editor in 1927.[81] His column received praise from rank and file and fellow leaders of the UNIA. Arthur S. Gray, for instance, who offically became the High Commissioner for the States of Arizona, Utah, Nevada, and California in 1928, wrote to the *Negro World* in praise of Haynes, describing him as brilliant and "worthy of our sincerest praise." This is the type of Garveyism, Gray wrote, "that fires the enthusiasm and strengthens our hopes."[82] Haynes was extraordinarily loyal to Garvey and it pained him enormously to have to break with the man who brought him from Belize many years earlier. But in 1936, after concerted and repeated attempts to get Garvey to change his negative attitude toward the Emperor Haile Selassie and his opposition to black people supporting the fight against the Italian occupation of Ethiopia, Samuel Haynes publicly broke with Garvey. He remained a Garveyite of old and invoked Garvey's name and would somehow mention him in a positive light, quite often gratuitously, in almost everything he wrote. Haynes had tried his best to keep the UNIA going and he was one of the last people to give up on the organization, but by 1936 he recognized that the glory days of the UNIA were long gone and were unlikely to return. Riven by factions, depleted through defections, its leader in miserable exile in London and increasingly distanced ideologically from the people he had helped to form, the UNIA was effectively dead.[83]

With the demise of the UNIA, Haynes worked on the *Philadelphia Tribune*, the *Norfolk Journal and Guide*, and the Baltimore *Afro-American* during the 1930s and 1940s.[84] He also served as contributing editor and later editor of the *African*, an influential Pan-Africanist journal published in Harlem from the mid-1930s to about 1950. Although George Schuyler, the black satirist and conservative, called him in 1927 a "lampblacked klansman,"[85] Haynes was in fact a gentle and cultivated man seeking nothing more than basic justice for people of African descent around the world. Having accused Schuyler of being an example of a "white mind encased in a black body," Haynes more reasonably wrote:

> If telling the Negroes the truth about certain phases of life as I see and understand it, if inviting Negroes to redeem Africa from the hands of those who exploit and ravish her is preaching hatred against white folks, then I have no apology to

offer. In July, 1919, I saved a number of white men—British, Scot, Irish, German and American—from probably wholesale massacre at the hands of an infuriated contingent of returned soldiers in a British colony, receiving the commendation of the Secretary of State for the Colonies in a special dispatch to the Governor of the Colony for my restraining influence. I volunteered for service in 1915 and served for four years in Egypt and Mesopotamia, earning two medals and an honorable discharge. Hatred finds no haven in my youthful life. I am for peace and good will between men and races. I don't believe in hypocrisy, in deceit between races. Herein lies the incentive to race hatred which the UNIA, to which I am proud to belong is endeavoring to wipe out. No one need waste his time preaching to Negroes to hate white folks. Only white folks can make Negroes hate them.[86]

As his articles in the *African* showed, Haynes had fine humanistic instincts. "The highest patriotism, the highest loyalty, is to humanity," he declared in 1937.[87] Knowledgeable about international affairs, he was particularly astute in his analysis of the machinations of the imperial powers. He wrote poetry and in "Warning," a sixty-line poem of protest, he concluded:

> Listen, white man,
> Listen well:
>
> We who are black and courageous
> Will not retreat one inch
> In the uncompromising struggle
> For unqualified citizenship
> And the protection of our life and property.
> We shall stand where we are —
> Stand, and fight, and die
> Until we are free Americans, equal with all men.[88]

He called for the end of empire, and especially that of the British, in bold, unequivocal terms. "The civilization fostered by British imperialism is damned and doomed," he said in 1946, responding to Winston Churchill's iron-curtain speech in Fulton, Missouri.

> The sooner the British empire is dissolved, and its enslaved and exploited possessions be freed from its tyranny and thraldom to endure as free and independent nations and communities, the sooner we can be assured of peace and security throughout the wor[l]d.[89]

When British Honduras became the independent nation of Belize in 1981, one of Samuel Haynes's poems, "Land of the Gods," was put to music to form the national anthem. "No tyrants here linger, despots must flee/ This tranquil haven of democracy," it declares. "Arise! ye sons of the Baymen's clan," its chorus commands,

> Put on your armour, clear the land!
> Drive back the tyrants, let despots flee —
> Land of the Gods by the Carib Sea![90]

Haynes did not live long enough to hear his poem put to music. But he undoubtedly would have been pleased to see his compatriots leave behind "God Save the Queen" and hear them burst into song with "Land of the Gods." Rarely has the muse of history allowed such a generous turn of events. Here is a black British man who was verbally abused by white British ruffians for singing "Rule Britannia"—which is indeed a white man's song—giving a new song to his new nation at dawn. But, unfortunately, despite giving them their national anthem, Samuel Haynes and his contribution to their struggle for justice and nationhood are hardly remembered by the Belizeans. Similarly, in the United States, despite his considerable and sustained contribution to the black struggle his name is hardly known, unmentioned in the primary chronicles of Afro-America, never mind celebrated.

Among the ex-servicemen from the British West Indies Regiment, Samuel Haynes rose the highest within the UNIA in the United States. But there were other prominent men within the UNIA who had also served in the Regiment. Arnold Ford of Barbados served in the First World War and went on to write the lyrics of the immensely popular Universal Ethiopian Anthem of the UNIA. He was musical director of the UNIA at Liberty Hall. He later became a leader of the black Jews in Harlem, migrated to Ethiopia in the early 1930s and died in Addis Ababa in 1935. St William Grant, one of the most flamboyant, if rather thuggish, figures among Harlem's Garveyites in the 1920s and 1930s, was also an ex-serviceman from the islands.[91] There were Caribbean ex-soldiers, too, who did not return to the islands, but proceeded directly from Europe to Harlem in the aftermath of the war.[92] Indeed, there were enough Caribbean veterans in New York for them to form their own organization, British West Indian World War Veterans' Association, during the 1920s.[93]

In addition to former servicemen, a number of idealistic, radicalized and ambitious young men and women went to Harlem, not only to make a living, but expressly to contribute to Garvey's grand project.[94] Caribbean radicalism in the United States in the 1920s was, therefore, partly attributable to the fact that a significant number of already radicalized people chose to migrate to America. (There was undoubtedly a similar pattern to the movement North of black people in the South: in general, the more discontented and radicalized moved North. Moreover, radicalized black American veterans were one of the main groups lending support to the black awakening of the 1920s.) While it is true, as one scholar observes, that "Whatever the extent and nature of their former political awareness, migration tends to push [black Caribbeans] towards greater militance,"[95] one should not assume, that all those who left were "conservatives," because it simply is not true.

George Schuyler, the Afro-American satirist and journalist, described

Cyril Briggs as an "octoroon", and as someone who "could 'pass' for a white man, a fact that Marcus Garvey would never let him forget." Of the African Blood Brotherhood, headed by Briggs, he said: "There was not an African in its following but all were mixed bloods," further describing the Brotherhood as "chiefly a West Indian anti-Garvey organization [that] plugged the Communist line."[96] Schuyler spoils an acute observation with exaggeration. Yes, Briggs was very light-skinned—his father was a white Trinidadian, his mother a woman of color from the island of Nevis, where he was born—and Garvey did accuse him of being "a white man trying to pass as a Negro" (for which he successfully sued Garvey and won damages). The *New York News* described him as an "angry blond Negro."[97] It is also true that Otto Huiswoud and W. A. Domingo were so-called mulattoes, and that Richard B. Moore was of a light-brown complexion, but to give the impression that not only the leaders, but all the followers of the African Blood Brotherhood were "light-skinned Negroes" is demonstrable nonsense. The presence of dark-skinned black people like Claude McKay, Lovett Fort-Whiteman, Harry Haywood, Benjamin Burrell, and Theophilus Burrell, leading members of the Brotherhood, refutes Schuyler's contention. Nevertheless, the presence of light-skinned Caribbeans among the radicals was significant, and probably disproportionate, and may very well have partially resulted from the downgrading of their social position by American racism: the intermediary position—colored, mulatto, mixed, or the like—which they held in the islands was abolished in America, collapsed into an undifferentiated "Negro" category. And this might have contributed to their radicalization.[98] There is some suggestion that a large proportion of those who migrated from the islands were relatively light-skinned, but the evidence is mainly indirect, being primarily extrapolation from the class characteristics of the migrants.[99] Bearing in mind the nature of the phenomenon, it is probable that this is the best evidence we will ever have on the subject. However, given the fact that a disproportionate amount of those who migrated came from the skilled, educated, and professional classes, and given the fact that there was considerable overlap between color and class in the islands, the idea that a disproportionate number of migrants may have been light-skinned is not implausible. If true, the racial downgrading may have contributed to the radicalization of a larger number of Caribbean people than previously imagined.

Wide travel contributed, as well, to the radicalization of Caribbeans before their arrival in the United States. Both before and after the abolition of slavery, Caribbeans moved extensively—an experience not confined to the intelligentsia but embracing all classes, especially skilled workers. Thus, many Caribbean migrants to the United States had travelled elsewhere before their arrival. A substantial number worked on the Panama Canal, some on banana plantations elsewhere in Central America, and still others on sugar plantations in Cuba, Puerto Rico, and the Dominican Republic, before going to America. Many had even more extensive international experience. Some had ranged as far away as India and China, others lived for a time in West Africa and the Middle East, and even more had lived in Europe or had served in the British army in Europe, Egypt, Iraq, and Palestine during the First World War. Garvey, for instance, had lived and worked for several years in Europe and Central America before journeying to New York. Like Garvey, many of these travelled Caribbeans developed an internationalist, pan-Africanist perspective through interacting with black people from different countries and through observing the common oppressed condition of black humanity around the world. In one of his few autobiographical writings, Garvey describes the processes of his own racial and pan-Africanist awakening, a process that was organically connected to travelling. His political journey overlapped his actual journeying. At eighteen, said Garvey,

> I started to take an interest in the politics of my country, and then I saw the injustice done to my race because it was black, and I became dissatisfied on that account. I went traveling to South and Central America and parts of the West Indies to find out if it was so elsewhere, and I found the same situation. I set sail for Europe to find out if it was different there, and again I found the same stumbling block—"You are black." I read of the conditions in America. I read "Up From Slavery," by Booker T. Washington, and then my doom—if I may so call it—of being a race leader dawned upon me in London after I had traveled through almost half of Europe.
>
> I asked, "Where is the black man's Government?" "Where is his King and his kingdom?" "Where is his President, his country, and his ambassador, his army, his navy, his men of big affairs?" I could not find them, and then I declared, "I will help to make them."[100]

It is easier for those who have travelled than for those who have not, to develop a pan-Africanist consciousness. It is no accident that the Caribbean, being the area that has historically produced the most peripatetic of all African peoples, has also thrown up an extravagantly disproportionate number of pan-Africanist political activists and intellectuals. Edward Wilmot Blyden, H. Sylvester Williams, J. Albert Thorne, J. Robert Love, Theophilus Scholes, Anténor Fermin, René Maran, Hubert Harrison, Marcus Garvey, Claude McKay, Una Marson, J. A. Rogers, Jean Price Mars, Ras Makonnen, C. L. R. James, Aimé Césaire, Leon Gontran Damas, and—perhaps the most under-rated of them all—the great George Padmore of Trinidad: all hailed from this remarkable chain of tiny islands and all participated in and were products of its peripatetic tradition. In more recent times, the region produced Frantz Fanon as well as Walter Rodney.

It is noteworthy that among the black migrants to New York were thousands of mariners who, by the very nature of their work, were international travellers, and often long-distance travellers.[101] Black sailors and seamen around the world served as important couriers of Garvey's *Negro World*—often, at great personal risk, defying colonial law in Africa and the Caribbean to do so. Sailors and the travelled made up a substantial part of the leadership of the UNIA. By the 1930s, they were also a noticeable force on the black left in Harlem, including within the trade union movement. Ferdinand Smith, a Jamaican migrant, and one of Harlem's leading radicals during the 1930s, helped to found the National Maritime Union in 1937 and became its first secretary and its vice-president. His countryman, David E. Grange, was a militant vice-president of the International Seaman's Union.[102]

In contrast to the Caribbeans, Afro-Americans never enjoyed the same opportunity, nor were they driven by comparable economic necessity, to travel abroad as extensively as Caribbeans have. Indeed, up to the First World War, formidable political and economic constraints were imposed upon black people attempting to leave the South for the North, let alone go abroad.[103] Until then, apart from a privileged layer of the Northern black intelligentsia, Afro-Americans hardly travelled overseas. When the opportunity came, however, for Afro-Americans to go abroad—as it did for 200,000 who served in France during the First World War—the experience had a profound impact upon the radicalization of Afro-America. Returning black soldiers, having experienced the freer air of Europe and France in particular, became politically restive upon their arrival in the United States. This occurred in the aftermath of the First as well as Second World War. In both instances, but especially after the First World War, black veterans acted as leaven in the political agitation of Afro-America, playing a leading role in defending black Chicago and black Washington when these communities were attacked by white mobs during the "Red Summer" of 1919. Small wonder, then, that they were especially targeted and attacked by the Klan and the lynchers: at least ten of the seventy-seven black people lynched in 1919 were veterans in uniform.[104]

As British subjects, the migrants were entitled to—and in some instances, especially in New York City, actually enjoyed—the support of the local British consulate. In New York, they readily, and often successfully, called upon the consulate in times of difficulty. From the end of the First World War, when the then Consul General "adopted the policy of being friendly with them" partly to check the influence of Garvey, up to the Italian–Ethiopian crisis, when Britain refused to support an Ethiopia invaded and pillaged by Mussolini's army, Caribbean New Yorkers were generally satisfied with the services received from the British Consulate in the city. "We, the undersigned," declared a memorial sent by a group of Caribbeans in December 1933,

> deeply appreciating the very many efforts His Majesty's Consulate put forth on behalf of His Majesty's West Indian Subjects and others rendering every available assistance possible when and wherever needed, desire to show our gratitude by registering this Memorial.
> We desire to make especial mention of
> Mr Walter F. James,

Pro Consul, who has at all times and under various trying circumstances, and ofttimes at great inconvenience and personal sacrifice to himself, aided us in solving our many difficulties, thereby endearing himself to us as a true and worthy representative of The Crown.

We pray that this memorial be filed.

We have the honor to be

Your Obedient Servants, . . .[105]

The British Consul General in Philadelphia intervened on behalf of Caribbean migrants and claimed to have been, in one case, "successful in obtaining the reprieve of a condemned murderer."[106]

Relations were by no means always this cosy between British diplomatic representatives and British Caribbean migrants. Throughout the Americas, but especially in Panama and Cuba, a profound ambivalence marked the relations between the two parties. The black migrants and their press, especially the *Negro World*, were by no means reticent in leveling criticism at British officials who failed in their duty to British subjects abroad.[107] For their part, the British officials grumbled, patronizingly, about the demands black migrants made upon them. In his covering letter submitting the above-mentioned memorial to London, Sir Robert Lindsay, the British Ambassador to the United States, said that the black Britishers in New York are apt to have "an exalted idea of the nature of the help that a consular officer can render them *vis-à-vis* the local authorities and even the law courts." As a result, "while they are loyal, friendly and possess an attractive sense of humour, the responsibility of looking after them is no light task, especially seeing that most of them live at the other end of New York from the Consulate General, i.e. in one of the better quarters of Harlem." That Mr Campbell and Mr James should have won their "whole-hearted affection and esteem" in such circumstances "seems to me no small achievement."[108]

Nevertheless the tangible support that issued, however inconstantly, from the status of being a British subject is one of the reasons why a large number of British Caribbean migrants were reluctant to relinquish their British citizenship in order to take out American citizenship. Paradoxical though it may seem, the ability to rush to the British Consulate, which Afro-Americans noted with resentment, disdain, and ridicule — "I'm going to see my consul," they teased — might very well have emboldened many of these British Caribbean migrants to engage in political agitation in New York, believing themselves sheltered beneath the protective umbrella of the Union Jack. On top of this, there was also the option — not an ideal one, mind — of returning to the islands if the United States became too hot to hold them.[109]

It is somewhat paradoxical, too, but nevertheless true, that in New York, and other Northern cities such as Boston and Philadelphia, Caribbeans — at least those from the British Caribbean — enjoyed a level of freedom for political organization and protest that they did not enjoy in the islands. Massively outnumbered by the colonized, the British always stood ready to deal repressively with those they regarded as troublemakers, always attempting to intimidate the ringleaders, isolating them and trying to pluck them away from the "volatile" masses. In the British Caribbean, the repression was seldom generalized and rarely needed to be. The policy was to identify, isolate, and persecute individuals or small groups of individuals who were especially troublesome and were in danger of developing a following among the ordinary people. As in the ideal case of precision bombing, there was little collateral damage to alienate and antagonize the general population. Sandy Cox, founder of the National Club in Jamaica, was effectively driven out of the island by the sustained harassment of the colonial authorities.[110] Repressive laws, such as those against sedition, were readily mobilized to silence opposition. The right to "free speech" was always more of a myth in the colonies than in the metropole. The *Negro World* was banned in every British possession in the Caribbean, at one time or another, between 1919 and 1920. Moreover, the British government brought pressure to bear—albeit unsuccessfully—on the American authorities to proscribe or interdict the export of radical black publications emanating from the United States, such as the *Crusader*, the *Messenger*, and the *Negro World*, which all, with impressive success, wended their way across the sea to the islands.[111] If Marcus Garvey expected greater freedom to carry on political agitation in his native Jamaica than he enjoyed in the heyday of the UNIA in New York, he was gravely mistaken. He, too, was effectively hounded out of the island by the British colonialists.[112] W. A. Domingo visited Jamaica, his native land, in 1941 and was immediately clapped in irons—in fact, he was arrested aboard ship—and held in a detention camp under war-time emergency powers by the colonial authorities, despite the fact that he had previously proclaimed his support for the British war effort.[113] "Does the Minister not consider it a remarkable thing for a person to be charged with an offence which he has not committed but which he might commit, and to be interned for a long period?" asked a Labour Member of Parliament in the House of Commons. To this he received the reply, apparently with a straight face: "He [Domingo] was not charged with an offence. . . . He was detained to prevent him from acting in a manner prejudicial to public safety." They locked up Domingo for twenty months without trial.[114] Glad, for their part, to be rid of him, the American authorities blocked Domingo's re-entry into the country. Despite the sustained agitation of the Jamaican lobby in New York, aided by the American Civil Liberties Union, it was not until 1947—six long years after what he had intended to be a short visit to Jamaica—that Domingo was allowed to return to the United States.[115]

Otto Huiswoud was similarly harassed by the British in the Caribbean. In 1930, he was expelled from Jamaica, Trinidad, and British Guiana as a Communist agitator. He visited his native Suriname in 1941 and, like Domingo in Jamaica, he was immediately interned by the Dutch authorities.

Released in 1942, he was refused re-entry into the United States. In 1947 he moved to Holland, where he lived up to his death in 1961.[116]

Interestingly, after having been persecuted into exile by the British in Jamaica, Garvey enjoyed upon his arrival in London perfect freedom to organize and agitate politically. The difference between metropolis and colony in relation to political freedom was not lost on him. Soon after he moved to London in 1935, in a commentary on the labor unrest in St Vincent that year, he wrote of the contrast. Because of the disturbances, he noted the colonial authorities on the island had passed

> some severe sedition laws, to prevent the people from ever repeating what they did. The local press is to remain under permanent censorship. To publish anything critical of the Government invites a fine of one thousand pounds. To hold public meetings, and say anything of the same nature means imprisonment. Yet, we have listened to public speakers in Hyde Park here, who have criticized any and everything political, religious and otherwise, and we have never seen or heard of speakers being arrested and imprisoned for free speech.[117]

From London, Garvey published *The Black Man* and he, like many others, spoke regularly at Speakers' Corner at Hyde Park without the slightest hindrance from the authorities.

Garvey was not the only person to notice the staggering difference between the freedom of the metropolitan center and the unfreedom of the colonial periphery. Ras Makonnen, George Padmore, and other colonial radicals could not help but be struck by the contrast. Indeed, Makonnen and Padmore both considered London and Britain in general to be better places for political agitation than New York and the United States. They enjoyed a cathartic thrill from the opportunity that London provided for, as Makonnen put it, "challenging one of the greatest empires in the world. Imagine," he said

> what it meant to us to go to Hyde Park to speak to a race of people who were considered our masters, and tell them right out what we felt about their empire and about them. Despite the suffering of our people, there was never a gloomy moment, particularly when we realized how much we could do in England: write any tract we wanted to; make terrible speeches; all this when you knew very well that back in the colonies even to say 'God is love' might get the authorities after you!

Makonnen recalls Padmore saying:

> There is something to be said for these people, Mak. Imagine, you were abusing that white man today in Hyde Park, and his own people came afterwards and spoke to you. In America do you think we would have been able to do it to the same extent? There you would have to talk about some nebulous class, without naming names. . . . Then the security people, they know we are here; they come into our offices pretending to be buying books or magazines, and sometimes when we are returning from a trip to Russia, they hold us back after crossing the Channel. But you joke with them and say, "We've just been across to get some

Russian gold, and we're coming back to enrich the old country". Instead of giving you the American cattle-prod treatment, they laugh it off.[118]

The situation was not always as cosy as Padmore made out, but the greater political latitude that London availed was palpable, valuable, and the migrants used it to the full. But it is also clear that the agents of the British ruling class were happy to have Garvey, Makonnen, Padmore, C. L. R. James, Jomo Kenyatta, Kwame Nkrumah and others running loose in London, like children at play, because they reckoned these expatriate radicals could do no harm to the sturdy social structure of metropolitan Britain; a Britain, it should be noted, within which ordinary working people over the centuries had won and safeguarded certain fundamental freedoms. In the colonies, however—as in Gramsci's depiction of pre-revolutionary Russia without the trenches and fortresses of a vibrant civil society such as obtained in Western Europe—the ruling class were more vulnerable and more uncertain of their hold on power; hence the persecution of Garvey and Domingo in Jamaica and of others in St Vincent and elsewhere in the Caribbean.[119] The racist contempt, albeit often muted and restrained, in which the colonial authorities held the "native" population also helps to explain the denial of certain freedoms that they deemed inappropriate in the colonies, but that prevailed unquestioned in the white metropolis.

Compared to the situation they faced at home, Caribbean migrants in the United States encountered more favorable conditions for political activity. Although they had to endure the everyday unfreedom of racism in the United States, they faced, especially in cities such as New York, fewer restrictions on political organization—despite the Red Scare of 1919, and notwithstanding the heavy surveillance of the FBI, which the black radicals in Harlem took in their stride. To this extent, then, the American environment was more conducive to radical activity than that of the Caribbean, thus partially accounting for the agitation on the part of the migrants.

Caribbean migrants came to America with a long and distinguished tradition of resistance with few parallels in the New World.[120] They, consequently, entered the United States with a sense of self-confidence and pride that would have predisposed at least some of them to radical activity, as the harsh racism battered their self-esteem.

An important area in which Caribbean migrants differed from most of their Afro-American counterparts was religious faith. They were neither as deeply attached to Christianity nor, in general, as religiously inclined as their Afro-American counterparts. Hubert Harrison remarked in 1917 that there were a few black agnostics in New York and Boston, but added that they were "generally found to be West Indians from the French, Spanish, and English islands." He noted, however, that "Here and there one finds a Negro-American who is reputed to have Agnostic tendencies; but these are seldom, if ever, openly avowed. I can hardly find it in my heart to blame them, for I know the tremendous weight of the social proscription which it is possible to bring to bear upon those who dare defy the idols of our tribe."[121] The racism that infected Christianity in America repelled many Caribbean migrants from attending church and drove some away from Christianity and religion altogether. Richard B. Moore fell into the last group. As a teenager in Barbados, Moore had become a member of a small evangelical group, the Christian Mission. So committed was he to the gospel and the group that he and some young converts proselytized in the streets of Bridgetown, the island's capital. On coming to New York in 1909, Moore received a double blow to his faith. First, he was denied admission to a typing class at the YMCA on 57th Street because he was black. Second, on finding a religious group of the same persuasion to the one he had left behind in Barbados, he was shocked by their conduct. The Christian Missionary Alliance, located on Eighth Avenue, segregated people of color in the gallery. Moore's discovery of this, said his daughter, "evoked no overt reaction; he simply left quietly and never returned." He seethed with indignation, and quickly made his way from Christianity and religion in general to revolutionary socialism.[122]

Some migrants confessed that they had attended church in the Caribbean because they were forced to and, not having anyone to pressure them to attend church in America, declined to do so.[123] Exile made it easier for many of these young migrants to embrace radical ideas precisely because the social pressures abroad were not as great as they were at home. Just as exile enabled them to dance more and smoke more, it also gave them a greater opportunity than hitherto to engage with new political ideas and behavior, including some that would have been definitely frowned upon back home. George Padmore, according to his friend and comrade Ras Makonnen, often remarked upon and appreciated this new freedom.[124]

The Christian racism of America and the easing of social pressure to attend church, coupled with the extraordinarily high level of reading, participation in political meetings, and formal study, led a number to the secular, more rationalist world of "scientific socialism." Hubert Harrison, like Richard B. Moore, had made the journey from a religious worldview to militant rationalism in exile. (Moore in fact was profoundly influenced by Harrison in the development of a secular worldview.) Claude McKay was perhaps alone among his generation of British Caribbean radicals in America in having completed the journey before leaving home. Jesús Colón was a committed socialist, and probably an agnostic if not an atheist, before he left Puerto Rico in 1918. Among the migrants from the Hispanic Caribbean, including black Puerto Ricans and Cubans, especially among cigar makers (*tabaqueros*), there was a highly developed traditon of not only rationalist political thought and dissent, but also a militant anti-clericalism and anti-Christianity which in its intensity had no parallel in the Caribbean and indeed, the New World.[125]

Just as the migrants were less bound than Afro-Americans to the religious status quo, so they were less bound to the political status quo. Lacking Afro-Americans' historical attachment to the Republican Party and the person of Abraham Lincoln, the migrants were relatively unencumbered in the independence and audacity of their political thought and behavior. It is therefore not surprising that the migrants substantially contributed to the breaking of the Republican monopoly on the black vote in New York City. Hubert Harrison, in particular, never tired of telling his black audience that they owed Lincoln nothing, and that the Republican Party should be made to earn their support, not just given it. Thus, black people's support for the Republican Party had been hemorrhaging in New York, more than in any other city, well before the advent of Franklin D. Roosevelt.[126]

In one final respect, Caribbean migrants differed from most Afro-Americans: their greater access to education and educational attainment. "Those from the British West Indies," observed James Weldon Johnson in 1930, "average high in intelligence and efficiency." He noted that there was "practically no illiteracy among them, and many have a sound English common school education." Indeed, as early as 1923, 98.6 percent of the migrants entering the country were literate and by 1932 this figure had risen to 99.0 percent. Only 1.1 percent of adult black migrants to America were illiterate for the period 1918 to 1932.[127] This compares favorably with the levels for the United States, for in 1920 and 1930 the national levels of illiteracy for adults over 21 were 7.1 percent and 5.3 percent, respectively. The illiteracy rates for black American adults in 1920 and 1930 were 27.4 percent, and 20.0 percent respectively. The corresponding figures for white Americans were 5.0 and 3.4 percent.[128] In other words, Caribbean migrants were not only more literate than Afro-Americans, they were more literate than white Americans, whether foreign-born or native.[129] The fact that, as recently as 1946, the level of illiteracy—admittedly for those over ten, not for those over twenty-one years of age—in the British Caribbean was as high as 22 percent[130] underlines the profoundly selective character of the Caribbean migration to the United States earlier in the century.

Allied to the high rate of literacy were two other characteristics that contemporaries often mentioned. One was an extraordinary love of books, education and the written word. The other was a similar attachment to the spoken word, in conversation as well as in the form of public oratory.

The passion for books and reading seem to have come out of the colonial education that the migrants underwent. It was at first instrumental: book learning and education in general were the necessary resources for upward social mobility—the acquiring of white-collar jobs and entry into the professions. Knowledge then was, in a very concrete sense, power, a vital enabler for those without money. It was also linked to bourgeois Victorian notions of cultivation and refinement that the Caribbean aspiring middle class imbibed and spread through the educational system. And at a more general level, reading was regarded as an integral part of efforts at self-improvement. But over time, the practice of reading seemed to have acquired a momentum and logic of its own; it became a habit. Among the educated but discontented ones, books and other forms of literature that examined, questioned and challenged the colonial status quo were highly valued, discussed, and disseminated.

The migrants carried these traditions with them to the United States and harnessed them to even more radical ends than they did in the islands. On all sides the radicals spread the virtues of reading and study. "Read, Read, Read!" declared Hubert Harrison.

> It is not with our teeth that we will tear the white man out of the ancestral land. It isn't with our jaws that we can ring from his hard hands consideration and respect. It must be done by the upper and not the lower parts of our heads. Therefore, I have insisted ever since my entry into the arena of racial discussion that we Negroes must take to reading, study and the development of intelligence as we have never done before.[131]

Harrison spent a considerable part of his street-corner meetings talking about and recommending books to his listeners.[132] And in his journalism he always provided guidance about what to read; reading was to be directed, not indiscriminate. As he put it, "The masses must be taught to love good books. But to love them they must first know them."[133] Garvey saw himself first and foremost as a teacher and Liberty Hall a center of learning. "You must never stop learning," he told his followers.

> One must never stop reading. Read everything that you can that is of standard knowledge. Don't waste time reading trashy novels . . . .The idea is that personal experience is not enough for a human to get all the useful knowledge of life, because the individual life is too short, so we must feed on the experience of others.[134]

Garvey recommended the reading of the best poetry for inspiration. "Read history incessantly until you master it," he said. In a correspondence course which he prepared in the 1930s for his followers he wrote:

> Use every spare minute you have in reading. If you are going on a journey that would take you an hour carry something with you to read for that hour until you have reached the place. If you are sitting down waiting for somebody, have something in your pocket to read until the person comes. Don't waste time. Any time you think you have to waste put it in reading something . . . .Never forget that intelligence rules the world and ignorance carries the burden. Therefore, remove yourself as far as possible from ignorance and seek as far as possible to be intelligent.[135]

Cyril Briggs, Richard B. Moore, Amy Jacques Garvey, were similarly insistent upon the need to read. The *Crusader* magazine and the *Negro*

World informed its readers on a regular basis of the new books that had arrived at the 135th Street Public Library (now the Schomburg Center for Research in Black Culture) in Harlem. Sometimes they even went so far as to point out individual articles in particular journals that their followers might find interesting and rewarding. This obsession with reading and the acquisition of knowledge was, obviously, not unique to these migrants from the Caribbean. But the passion which they had for books and reading were especially pronounced among the strata of Caribbeans that migrated to the United States, especially among those who went to New York. Shirley Chisholm reported that even during the hard times of the Depression her father, who had only a fifth-grade education and worked as a baker, bought two or three newspapers a day. "He was an omnivorous reader."[136] Contemporaries often remarked upon the Caribbeans' heavy use of the public library system.

Oratory and good talking came out of the African tradition. And of course in the diaspora it was also linked to the acquisition and dissemination of different forms of knowledge. Harrison was respected and loved not only because he was a good orator, but also because he was an extraordinarily knowledgeable one. In the islands, public speaking ability and debating skills were highly prized. These were taught at school. But elocution lessons were often offered and paid for privately. The young Garvey is said to have had elocution lessons from one of Jamaica's leading orators at the time, Dr Robert Love. And it is not surprising that Garvey met his first wife at a debating society in Kingston. Public speaking, good conversation, story-telling, the dextrous and elegant manipulation of words, whether in Creole or standard English, were all highly regarded, and emulated. This love of words is a common feature of the African diaspora.[137] But in the Caribbean, unlike the United States, there was a highly developed secular oratorical tradition, practiced especially by lawyers. Preachers were important, but there were also school teachers, journalists, along with lawyers who drew on sources and inspiration outside of the spiritual realm. According to Guyanese pan-Africanist Ras Makonnen, people in the Caribbean loved to hear a good public speaker, especially one who could make allusions to literature, to the extent that "amongst certain people in the West Indies the best entertainment was not actually cricket, but going along to the Law Courts to observe some young [black] man quoting the law and putting the judge on the spot."[138]

The voracious appetite for knowledge, including subversive knowledge, and the ability to speak publicly were often harnessed to the migrants' discontent in America. Thus it comes as no surprise that Harlem's pre-eminent radical street-corner orators were overwhelmingly Caribbean. Garvey, Harrison, Moore, were some of the most outstanding.

Perhaps most significantly, Caribbean migrants had a socio-economic profile at radical variance with that of black America. From 1925 to the end of the 1930s farmers and agricultural workers, the largest occupational category among Afro-Americans, never formed more than 4 percent of their number. Although some 43.5 percent of black migrants had been laborers and servants during the period 1899–1931, and their numbers reached a peak of 51 percent for the period 1906–12, the proportion declined steadily thereafter. It had fallen to 23 percent by the period 1927–31.[139] But the most remarkable feature of the socio-economic profile of the early migrants is the high proportion of their number that held, in their country of origin, professional, white-collar, and skilled jobs. Caribbean teachers and doctors, clerks and accountants, dressmakers and seamstresses, tailors and carpenters emigrated to the United States in disproportionate numbers compared to their unskilled compatriots. From 32.4 percent in the period 1899–1905, the professional and skilled workers had increased to 43.2 percent of the migrating black adults for the years 1927–31. In 1919, the president of the artisans' trade union in Jamaica claimed that his union had collapsed largely because of the massive migration of its members, especially the most "zealous" ones.[140] The occupational distribution of the passengers on the New York City-bound boats from Port Antonio (Jamaica) and from Bridgetown (Barbados) did not reflect that of the societies they were leaving behind. Indeed, a Barbadian migrant, Clyde Jemmott, lamented, albeit in the gloomy language of eugenics prevalent at the time, what he perceived to be the degenerative effect this prolonged selective migration had on his native land:

> When you take away large numbers of the strong, able-bodied and healthful members of a community, then those who are economically among the middle-class, and finally those who are ambitious, progressive and far-sighted, you are practically skimming the cream from that Society, and the results are a preponderant increase in the mediocre members of the community because of their relative numbers and also because of the fact that those lowest down are the fastest breeders, a gradual weakening of the physical and mental vigor of the people, and a lessening in the number of those ambitious, progressive and far-seeing people without whom no Society can go ahead.

Jemmott drew two conclusions. First, because of "favorable selection" the Caribbean migrant, including the Barbadian, in the United States is conceded to be one of "the most progressive elements in the community." And second, the Barbadian left at home, because of "adverse selection," is "self-satisfied, complacent, lethargic, not desirous of change; in other words, he is not progressive."[141] Poor Barbados. As a superior being, it supposedly made sense, then, for Jemmott to have stayed in New York, where his sperm had a better chance of fertilizing equally superior, progressive, exiled Barbadian ova. Similarly, in a 1921 memorial to the Colonial Office in London, the Jamaica League, a black middle-class pressure group, complained that the economic situation in the island was so bad that "Emigration has been proceeding at a rate which threatens to denude the Colony of its working force: the brains of the Island have been going to the United States and the brawn to Cuba to settle down and earn higher wages than they are able to earn in their homeland."[142] Jamaica must then, have been an island of headless and limbless beings—a weird population of torsos. A St Kitts newspaper in 1903 bemoaned "the continual exodus of our respectable people to the States and Canada." And in 1909 during a drought in Antigua another newspaper reported that the laborers were heading for the Canal Zone in Panama and some for work on Mexican railroads, whereas the "middle-class young men and women" headed for the United States and Canada.[143] Crude though some of these formulations are, they point to a genuine pattern that many found alarming: the profoundly selective nature of the migration to America and, in particular, to the disproportionate number of highly skilled emigrants.

Given the selective character of the flow from the Caribbean, the occupational distribution of the migrants differed from that of black America, including even black New York. Accordingly, a disproportionately high number of the black professional and business class of the United States at the time was of Caribbean origin.[144] This pattern, as we saw in Chapter 1, was established in the nineteenth century. It continued into the new century. In a survey carried out in 1906 in New York City it was found that almost 61 percent of the black men who reported that they knew a trade came from the Caribbean. (At the time, Caribbeans made up less than 10 percent of the city's black population.) While 51 percent of the Caribbean men surveyed were skilled, only 13 percent of their Afro-American counterparts were similarly trained.[145] Another and more comprehensive survey, carried out in 1909 by the Columbia-trained black sociologist, George Edmund Haynes, found that just under 22 percent of the black businesses in New York City were run by Caribbeans. This exceeded by 12.4 percent the proportion of the black population that came from the Caribbean.[146] In other words, the proportion of the black businessmen that were of Caribbean origin was twice the proportion of the black population in the city that were born in the Caribbean.[147] In the 1930s, it was claimed that as much as one third of black professionals in New York City, particularly doctors, dentists, and lawyers, were Caribbean.[148] A study of the entries in *Who's Who in Colored America* covering the period 1915 to 1932 yielded a "disproportionately high" presence of black migrants. In 1930 only 0.8 percent of the black population of America was of foreign birth, yet 6 percent of those listed including over 8 percent of the doctors, 4.5 percent of the lawyers, more than 14 percent of the businessmen, 4.5 percent of the clergymen, over 3 percent of the professors and 4 percent of the writers/authors, were migrants.[149] No doubt the proportion would have been higher if the data included those of immigrant *descent*, instead of being limited to those of foreign birth.

The relatively skewed profile of the black migrant community was partly a result of the fact that, of those migrants who returned to the islands, between two-thirds and three-quarters were classified as laborers, servants, and "miscellaneous" workers. The percentage of skilled and professional migrant workers returning home was considerably lower than that of unskilled workers. Between 1908 and 1924, for instance, only 5.6 percent of the black teachers who emigrated to the United States returned to their country of origin. (Teachers were, by far, the largest category among the incoming black professionals.) In marked contrast, 13.3 percent of servants, 38.5 percent of laborers, and over 40 percent of farm laborers did so. Skilled workers such as seamstresses, carpenters and joiners, as well as dressmakers returned in considerably smaller numbers than unskilled workers: the proportion of farm laborers returning to their country of origin was ten times that of seamstresses[150] (see Table 2.2). In other words, the professional and skilled were both more likely than the unskilled to migrate to the United States in the first place and far more inclined to stay than unskilled islanders were. The socio-economic profile of the Caribbean population in the United States was therefore marked by two selective patterns of movement: it was skewed on the way out and skewed on the way back, each in favor of the professional and the skilled. In net terms, then, black migrants from the higher rungs of the occupational ladder would constitute a greater proportion of the migrant population than the gross migration statistics would lead one to believe. Without careful disaggregation the true story remains unrevealed and untold.

Noteworthy, too, is the fact that many of those who remained built upon their education and the skills with which they came to America.[151] They attended night school. They acquired more qualifications. Caribbean teachers, not infrequently, became American doctors and lawyers. Both Harrison and Colón finished their secondary education in the United States. Huiswoud got trained as a printer. Petioni worked as an elevator operator to finance his medical studies at City College and Howard University. One government survey of immigrants in cities found in 1910 that next only to Russian Jews, of all the foreign-born, black migrants had the highest percentage of men aged sixteen years and older at school.[152] The practice of energetically upgrading their educational qualification, of course, skewed the occupational distribution of Caribbeans even further.

The relevance of the distinct socio-economic profile of these migrants to an explanation of their political behavior is not hard to see. These highly qualified migrants—literate, skilled, confident, ambitious, energetic, in short, Jemmott's Caribbean cream—had great difficulty finding jobs that were commensurate with their skills, experience, and aspirations. They, as Domingo—who came from Jamaica in 1910—testified, found it difficult to "adapt themselves to the tasks that are, by custom, reserved for Negroes in the North. Skilled at various trades and having a contempt for body services and menial work, many of the immigrants apply for positions that the average American Negro has been schooled to regard as restricted to white men only." According to Domingo, because of their "persistence and doggedness in fighting white labor," the migrants have been in many cases "pioneers and shock troops to open a way for Negroes into new fields of employment."

> This freedom from spiritual inertia characterizes the women no less than the men, for it is largely through them that the occupational field has been broadened for colored women in New York. By their determination, sometimes reinforced by the dexterous use of their hatpins, these women have made it possible for members of their race to enter the needle trades freely.[153]

One of these Caribbean pioneers of the needle trades, many years later, recalled that "They had signs saying colored people weren't wanted. We tore them down and marched right in to apply. You bet, we got the jobs."[154] This opening up of the needle trades to black women might have been born of frustration, if not desperation, on the part of Caribbean women. Whatever the case might have been, what is clear is that there were thousands upon thousands of Caribbean women who were eminently qualified to work in the needle trades. For between 1899 and 1931 almost thirteen thousand black seamstresses and dressmakers had made their way to the United States, and to New York in particular. This amounts to no less than 10.2 percent of all the adult black migrants who came to America over the period. It appears that they fared relatively well in the new country as only 4.0 percent of seamstresses and 7.7 percent of dressmakers returned to their country of origin over the three decades. The rate of return of seamstresses was the lowest of any group of workers (see Tables 2.1 and 2.2, pages 362–3). Thus, insofar as these women wanted to work in occupations for which they were trained—invariably through costly and demanding systems of apprenticeships back home—they had to fight and participate in attempts to open the trades to black women. This was undoubtedly a radical act. In 1900, of the 646,610 female breadwinners working in the needle trades only 25,270, or 1.9 percent, were in the combined category of "Negro, Indian, and Mongolian."[155]

There are two especially interesting dimensions to this saga of black women and the needle trades. First, had these Caribbean women not been skilled workers, the struggle would not have been necessary; there would have been little or no resistance to their employment. The fact is, however, that they were seeking work not as domestic servants, for example—over which there was far less struggle, if any—but as skilled workers, seamstresses, dressmakers, and so on, in which there was rigorous gatekeeping on the basis of race.[156] In general, then, the more skilled the migrants were, the more resistance they were likely to encounter in the workplace, and this, in turn, would tend to heighten the political nature of their response in the direction of black nationalism, or, indeed, in the direction of revolutionary socialism, or in the direction of trade unionism. It comes as no surprise, then, that by the 1930s, many of these black women were active members of the International Ladies and Garment Workers Union

(ILGWU). In fact, after surveying the position of black people in the garment and textile industry nationally and their relation to the trade union movement, two authorities concluded in 1931 that "The West Indians in New York are perhaps the most active of all the Negro groups" and reported that the "highest union office held by a Negro, membership on the executive committee of the New York Dressmakers' Union, is held by a girl who comes from Jamaica."[157]

The second instructive aspect of this episode in the needle trades is this: ignorance of the racial mores of the society, naïveté, can sometimes redound to the benefit of the ignorant and the foolhardy. Black people from the South, for instance, who had come to New York during the Great Migration, were, perforce, fully aware of the racial codes and, therefore, would not as readily have taken the risk of violating those codes by knocking down the Jim Crow sign and marching into a factory demanding employment. It took "over-confident," "aggressive," "arrogant" — all adjectives used by Afro-Americans for Caribbeans — foreigners to do that sort of thing.[158] Black people who knew better would have kept away from the place. But, by the same token, people who knew better would not have gained jobs in the trades. Ignorance is, at times, a blessing.

The Caribbean seamstress gloated: "You bet, we got the jobs." But, of course, their getting jobs in the needle trades did not follow automatically from the knocking down of the Jim Crow sign and their marching into the factory demanding to be employed. The white employer could quite easily have told them to get out, and he could have called the police — who would have been happy to oblige him — if the women had not left the premises. For whatever reason or reasons, none of which necessarily having anything to do with Caribbean bravado, the women were given work.

It should be noted, too, that sometimes the racists made bizarre allowances for the ignorance of unitiated black people. Sidney Poitier, the black actor, related one such incident. Soon after his arrival from Nassau in 1943, the fifteen-year-old Poitier had to go to a police station in Miami to pick up a document.

I walked into the police station, and the desk sergeant — a big, burly, rough-looking guy — says, "Take off that cap, nigger." I turned around to see who was behind me and then suddenly realized that he was talking to me. So I said, "Are you talking to me?" He said, "Yes, I'm talking to you." I said, "Are you crazy?" He said, "What?" I said, "Are you crazy?" He said, "What did you say, boy?" I say, "My name is Sidney Poitier, you calling me names? Do you know who you're talking to?" The room is full of lots and lots of cops, and at this point they're falling down on the floor with laughter. Never in their lives have they seen such a nutty little black boy — he's got to be insane, or somebody's paid him fifty cents to come in and play this little charade. The guy behind the desk is looking at me — his mouth is wide open — and he says, "What did you say your name is, boy?" I say, "My name is Sidney Poitier — it's not 'boy.'" He says, "Okay, Mr Poitier, would you mind telling us what it is you want?" I said, "I've come here because I want you to give me a pass to go across the Bureau of Vital Statistics to see about my birth certificate." He said, "All right, sir," having decided he would go along with the joke, whatever it was. And then he said to me, "Where are you from?" I said, "I'm from the Bahamas." And he said, "Oh, I see." At which point they realized that I just didn't know what was going on; that I just wasn't familiar with the established behavior pattern, the reflex conditioning, that would activate automatically if I stayed on in Miami much longer.[159]

It is possible that the policeman had picked up Poitier's accent, suggesting a British nationality, which, in turn, frequently meant more indulgence on the part of the racists, especially in the South. Indeed, any foreign accent, the sound of a little Spanish or French, the sight of a turban or a fez—anything suggesting, "Here is a foreign Negro," generally carried in its wake relative leniency. Understandably, Afro-Americans, especially in the South, resented this special treatment.[160]

In his eloquent and passionate polemic of the Depression years, *Negro Americans, What Now?*, James Weldon Johnson talks of the danger of black people "voluntarily and unnecessarily" Jim-Crowing themselves. When this occurs, claims Johnson, timidity is its root cause. Moreover, this timidity undermines the "spiritual integrity" of those black people who are afflicted by it. "We must throw off timidity and break through the barriers whenever we are able to do it," he implores Afro-America. "We often take discrimination for granted where there actually is none or where it is so indefinite that a little courage and pressure would sweep it away."[161] This is fine as far as it goes. But Afro-Americans seldom enjoyed the relief of pushing at open doors; in the black experience, a closed door is often a locked door. Surely timidity was no more at work in such situations as the bitterly accumulated wisdom of patterned racial discrimination? Why is it more spiritually ennobling to endure rebuffs than to avoid them?

Matters were, however, seldom as easy and as straightforward as they apparently were in the needle trades. Getting jobs commensurate with one's skill was the rare exception rather than the general rule for the migrants. Oblivious to, or incredulous of, the racial boundaries and ceilings of occupations in America, it is true that the newly arrived Caribbean person might, as a migrant of a later period put it, scan the Sunday *New York Times* and choose "the jobs that interest him, the ones he thinks he is capable of handling; then he goes out on Monday morning and swings through every door."[162] But the fact remains that although in the mind of the newly arrived migrant there are "fewer boundaries" compared to the ostensibly jaded perception of his/her Afro-American counterpart, the boundaries and the ceilings *do* exist—and, more often than not, are made evident to the migrant. Like the Barbadian man in *Brown Girl, Brownstones*, one may study hard to become qualified as an accountant without ever getting a chance to practice as one. This lack of fit between skill and opportunity provided fertile soil for the growth of frustration and discontent. (The character in Paule Marshall's novel ended up joining one of Father Divine's Heavens in Harlem.)[163] For as one sociologist noted in the 1930s, the black migrant brings into the American socio-economic order skills and experiences for which "little or no opportunity is provided for Negroes in the United States save in the limited occupational field of racial services."[164] Matters are compounded further by the fact that subjectively and educationally these black migrants felt themselves superior to and far more qualified than many of the white people who were slamming the occupational doors in their face or imprisoning them in jobs below the levels of their skills. Here, then, is the rational kernel to Kelly Miller's enigmatic quip about the Negro radical being "an over-educated West Indian without a job."

Some of the disorientation of downward social mobility is captured well by the testimony of a schoolmaster from the Caribbean who became a day laborer in New York:

> I was inducted into American labor one fine Sabbath morning while on my way to apply for an elevator boy's job I had seen in the newspaper want column. While passing through a side street in the lower section of Manhattan I watched and silently criticized the ungodliness of men working on a building construction on the Lord's Day. While musing, a foreman of the laborers' gang came up to me and in his native Irish accent said, "Want to work?" "Yes," was my reply. "Well, god damn it, take that collar and tie off and pitch in." Without stopping to think, I obeyed. I left my coat, collar and tie in the basement, got hold of a wheelbarrow and soon found myself loading it with bricks which I transported to the bricklayers. There were about two dozen of us in the labor gang. It was apparent that these workers were of all races and nationalities. After three or four hours I was shifted to the concrete gang, i.e., to transport concrete. How I did welcome that whistle at mid-day! I was so tired and my hands were so painful that I stretched myself out on a plank to rest. One fellow said to me, "Don't worry, you will break in." I bought some lunch and went back to work. At five o'clock my day's work was done. . . . I went home, washed up and rested. My roommate, whom I saw once or twice per week—he was working on two jobs—asked me once during that week if I was working. "Yes," was my reply. That's all he wanted to know so I said nothing else. But when I had time to reflect I felt rather badly. I wondered at times if I was the same person who lately had been a very successful schoolmaster with hundreds of children and their parents looking up to me as their idol, with someone to do every form of menial work that I required at my least bidding, and here I was, transformed into a day laborer, trucking bricks and concrete.

The complexity of the situation was deepened by the fact that the payment he received for one week's work ("seven days, time-and-a-half for Sunday") as a laborer would have taken him "almost two months to earn" as a schoolmaster back home in the Caribbean. (He later went to medical school.)[165]

This raises an interesting question: could it be that what generally has been described as "West Indian radicalism" was a function of social class, black petty-bourgeois *angst,* having no connection whatsoever to ethnicity or nationality? Class is of undoubted significance here. But the phenomenon of radicalism among Caribbean migrants cannot be explained by class alone, or even *primarily* by class. For, if that were the case, then one would find an *equivalent* manifestation of such a tendency among the American black petty-bourgeoisie. And there is no evidence to suggest that this occurred to the same remarkable *degree* among the Afro-American middle class. This was precisely why the Caribbean radical activists at the time were so conspicuous, not only to the FBI, but also to ordinary observers of the contemporary scene. It is, however, undeniable that some of those who experienced downward social mobility moved in a more radical direction. It is probable that the African American petty-bourgeoisie, in general, was better positioned than the newly arrived Caribbeans, perhaps enjoying better opportunities through the patronage of the Republican Party, for instance.[166] But it is not clear the extent to which Afro-Americans enjoyed such privileges over Afro-Caribbeans, thus reducing the relative frustration of the former compared to that of the latter. Countervailing this argument of Afro-American privilege is the widespread belief—perhaps true though with little hard evidence to hold it up—that white Americans more willingly gave opportunities to Afro-Caribbeans than they did Afro-Americans.

In any case, although a higher proportion of Caribbeans than Afro-Americans were in the professions, that did not mean that in *absolute* terms they exceeded their black American counterparts. Yet, as we have seen, in relative and in some instances in absolute terms as well, they numerically exceeded Afro-Americans in the leadership of radical movements in the early twentieth century.

There is a second objection to this hypothesis. Working-class Caribbeans were also conspicuously involved in the leadership of these movements. This was especially true of the leadership of the Garvey movement, but it was also true of Caribbeans in the trade unions.[167] And of course, it should be remembered that Otto Huiswoud, the first black member—indeed, a charter member—of the Communist Party in the United States had worked as a scullion on a banana boat when he arrived in the United States in 1913, aged nineteen. He then worked as a salesman of tropical products from Puerto Rico and later became trained as a printer.[168] Richard B. Moore came to New York a bright Barbadian school boy of sixteen but he had to earn a living because of the impoverishment of his family after his father's death. He worked as a bellhop in hotels and elevator operator in apartment buildings. This he did for his first four years or so in America. He later got a job, again as an elevator operator, at a silk manufacturing firm. But in this case, after operating the elevator for some time, he was offered a position as a raw silk clerk, and eventually became the head of the department responsible for the stock. He remained with the firm for some ten years, up to 1923.[169] The most famous printer of them all was, of course, Marcus Garvey, who received his training in Jamaica. W. A.

Domingo was a tailor in Jamaica. When he arrived in Boston in 1910 he attended night school to prepare for medical school. But in 1912, he abandoned the idea of becoming a doctor and left for New York. He worked at the Post Office before he went into business, importing Caribbean foodstuff, from which he apparently made a good living.[170]

But because many of these leaders had working-class jobs did not mean that they lacked a good, albeit secondary, education. Even though they did not attend college, Harrison, Huiswoud, Domingo, Briggs, Moore, and many others attended some of the best secondary schools in the Caribbean, which were, in many cases, on a par with the best in Europe and America. They were on intimate terms with the book, and invested it with almost magical powers. Like good Victorians, they were passionate believers in self-improvement, self-cultivation, and much of this came through self-education. The accomplished autodidact was commonplace in the Caribbean and in the diaspora. The *tabaqueros* in Cuba and Puerto Rico were especially accomplished auto-didacts. Some of the best Cuban historians of the twentieth century were cigar makers.[171] They frequently wrote books of their own, which were often self-published or never published at all. It is a remarkable fact that a considerable number of these migrants, Garveyites especially, wrote their own books in this manner. This is the culture out of which these men came and they did not believe that one had to attend university in order to be educated. Hubert Harrison frequently pointed to Herbert Spencer, whom he admired, as a great thinker who never attended college. C. L. R. James, one of the outstanding intellectuals of our century, never felt particularly deprived for not having gone to university. He chose not to go to university, and never regretted the decision.[172]

Was Caribbean radicalism a function of sex and age distribution, and of the marital status of the migrants? Were the Caribbean migrants, in other words, overwhelmingly young, single black men, and as such apparently more prone to have been involved in radical politics? At the level of the individual biography of the radical Caribbean protagonists, the answer to this question is an unequivocally negative one. Harrison, Garvey, Domingo, Huiswoud, Briggs, and Moore were all married at a relatively early age. The question, however, is worth pursuing at the more general demographic level.

As is evident from Table 2.3 (see page 363), the earliest black migrants were predominantly male—60 percent men to 40 percent women for those who migrated to America in 1900 or earlier. However, by 1930, the female proportion of the migrant population had increased to the extent that the sex differential was evened out. It should also be noted that, for the periods 1900–17 and 1918–21 Portuguese-speaking black migrants from the Azores and Cape Verde islands constituted 14.7 percent and 10.0 percent respectively of the black migrants entering the country. (This was to be reduced to 2.0 percent in 1922–24, dwindling to 0.7 percent for the period 1925–32 [see Table 1.2, pages 356–7].) As these migrants were overwhelmingly men—an estimated 84.6 percent who entered the United States between 1900 and 1919 were male—they disproportionately contributed to the total number of black male migrants entering the country in the early years.[173] In short, although there was an excess of male over female, it was on the whole slight, and there was a reasonably balanced sex distribution among the migrants from the Caribbean as they entered the United States. The available data for New York State and New York City—the most popular state and by far the most popular city, respectively, among the Caribbean migrants—tell a similar story. In 1900, 58 percent of the foreign-born black population were men, but by 1930 the differential had been narrowed to a ratio of 51.4 percent to 48.6 percent in favor of men. And indeed, by 1940, there was a slight excess of black foreign-born females (50.6 percent), over their male counterparts.[174]

In fact, analysis of the yearly movement of migrants from 1908—when the immigration authorities started counting entry and departure on the basis of both race and sex—to 1931 indicate that from 1915 to 1931, with the exception of only four years (1917, 1920, 1927, and 1928), the net migration of black women to the United States was consistently higher than that of men (see Tables 2.4 (A) and 2.4 (B), page 364).

There was a difference between the sex distribution of the foreign-born and the native-born black population in New York State. From 1900 onwards, there has been a consistent excess of women over men in the African American population in both the state and in New York City. There was from 1900 to 1930, for instance, a stable 47.5 percent to 52.5 percent male/female distribution, ranging from 46.6 percent to 47.8 percent for the native-born black males in the state.[175]

At the time of entering the United States, approximately 25 percent of the men as well as 25 percent of the women were married.[176] There is no evidence to suggest that there were significant differences between Caribbeans and Afro-Americans in marital status.[177] It is, in any case, highly questionable whether the incidence of legal marriage is an adequate measure for the distribution of settled relationships between black men and women. It is a well-documented fact that for both African Caribbeans and African Americans the number of legal marriages is merely *one* indicator of the actual relationships that exist between men and women.[178]

Apart from the fact that the migration to the United States was an overwhelmingly adult one, there is very little that we have by way of direct comparative data on the age distribution of Caribbean migrants and the Afro-American population.[179] There is, however, some evidence to indicate that in New York City in 1925, 68 percent of Caribbean males were between the ages of twenty-five and forty-four, compared to 48 percent for native-born black men; 59 percent of Caribbean compared to 48 percent of Afro-American women were in this age range. Only 4 percent of Caribbean males and 5 percent of Caribbean females were under fifteen years of age compared to 21 percent of Afro-American males and 20 percent females. Eighteen percent of males and 26 percent of Caribbean females were between the ages of fifteen and twenty-four, compared to 15 percent and 18 percent of Afro-American males and females, respectively, in this category. This meant that 86 percent and 85 percent of the Caribbean males and females respectively were between the ages of fifteen and forty-four, compared to 64 percent and 66 percent of Afro-American males and females in New York City.[180] This differential of 20 percent between the two nationalities must have been of some significance in the proportion of Caribbeans and Afro-Americans who became involved in radical politics— assuming that there is indeed some correlation (if not causal relationship) between youth and early adulthood, on the one hand, and radical politics, on the other.

We have now seen who the migrants were. But what kind of America did they enter? And how did they respond? Chapter 3 attempts to answer these questions.

3

Coming at Midnight:
Race and Caribbean Reactions to America

In order to understand the radicalism of Caribbeans in the United States, not only do we need to be aware of who these migrants were, we also need to know about the America that they entered in the early part of the twentieth century and, in addition, we need to be able to gauge their reaction to American society. So how did they react to the new environment?

The lynchings in the Southland, the segregation, the calculated as well as the routinized and unthinking humiliation of black people in their everyday life, primarily in the South but also in the North, appalled and shocked Caribbean migrants. Young Hugh Mulzac, just turned twenty-one, bursting with excitement about his first ocean-going trip as a sailor, left Barbados (he was born on tiny Union Island, in the Grenadines) for Wilmington, North Carolina, in 1907. His captain, a Norwegian man named Granderson, was also a licensed roving missionary and promised the devout Mulzac to find out where there was "a good Protestant Church" to take him when they reached Wilmington. Granderson and five of his crew, including Mulzac, duly went off to church. The captain entered the church first. Young Hugh, the only black person in the group, brought up the rear. Sixty years later, Mulzac—who in 1918 became the first black person to win a Master's license in the United States—vividly recalled what happened. Just as he reached the threshold a long, white arm stretched out and blocked his way. "I looked up into my first leering southern face," wrote Mulzac.

> "Where you goin', boy?" a voice asked.
> "Why, I'm going in to church," I replied.
> "Oh no you're not . . . not *this* church!"
> "Why not?" I asked, "what have I done?"
> "Oh no," the man replied, "oh no, no, no, no, *no!*"

Captain Granderson intervened. "The boy's with me," explained the good captain, "I've just brought him from Barbados in the West Indies . . . he's a very religious boy. His grandfather's a minister of the gospel." "That don't mean nothin' *here*," the man at the door replied.

Granderson persisted; he explained that he was captain of a barque in Wilmington harbor, the *Aeolus*; he explained that he was a missionary minister. He took his badge out of his pocket and said, "See. This is a missionary's badge. In every country I go to I'm usually asked to preach in the local churches. Why, in God's name, can't my crew join me at your service?"

"Can't help who you are, captain, the boy can't enter. This is North Carolina!" Then he weakened a little and said, "Wait here a minute."

A short time later he returned with the curate, and Captain Granderson again made a detailed explanation. The curate was sympathetic but said, "The trouble is that this is not the church's doing, it's the law of the state. The North Carolina law forbids the mixing of congregations."

"What about heaven," countered Captain Granderson, "when we die and go to heaven is it the law there too?"

"I don't know about the laws there," said the curate, "but we have our own down here and they have to be obeyed."

While we stood there the service got underway. The congregation rose to sing and the words of the captain and curate merged with the strains of the hymn, "O God Our Help in Ages Past." The music apparently inspired the curate.

"I have it! You can all go in and sit down and the boy can go up in the balcony."

"These people are not Christians, but savages!" Mulzac recalled saying at the time. He was "sick" with anger and humiliation. When he returned to the ship, he went straight to his bunk and wrote to his relatives back on Union Island, explaining "the barbaric customs of our northern neighbors." Though much had happened since he left his little island of twenty-two square miles, there was, said Mulzac, "not a word about the crew, the seas, the dolphins, and very few about the fine captain. There were just hot and tear-stained words about the church in Wilmington, North Carolina, and about a word I had learned for the first time—segregation." The contrast with his Caribbean world was sharp: "Discrimination was a new experience for me. There was none in the West Indies," wrote Mulzac. "Throughout our stay in the United States I did not go ashore again."[1] Mulzac became a Garveyite and worked for the Black Star Line as a ship's captain.

Even those, such as Claude McKay, who, prior to migration, had read and had been told (including by black American visitors to Jamaica) about these aspects of American society were unprepared for the raw and merciless racism that they encountered. Writing in 1918, six years after his arrival in the United States, McKay spoke for many others when he reported that "It was the first time I had ever come face to face with such manifest, implacable hate of my race, and my feelings were indescribable. . . . I had heard of prejudice in America but never dreamed of it being so intensely bitter." He had expected more of what he called "prejudice of the English sort," the more insidious, forked-tongued kind of stuff, "subtle and dignified." The prejudice he saw and experienced in the Caribbean was mainly rooted in class distinction, with less emphasis on

race and color. Upon arrival in America, McKay was shocked and alarmed
to find

> strong white men, splendid types, of better physique than any I had ever seen,
> exhibiting the most primitive animal hatred towards their weaker black brothers.
> In the South daily murders of a nature most hideous and revolting, in the North
> silent acquiescence, deep hate half-hidden under a puritan respectability, oft
> flaming up into an occasional lynching—this ugly raw sore in the body of a great
> nation. At first I was horrified, my spirit revolted against the ignoble cruelty and
> blindness of it all. Then I soon found myself hating in return but this feeling
> couldn't last long for to hate is to be miserable.[2]

Those like McKay, Harrison, Domingo, Moore, and Garvey who had
migrated to the United States in the early part of the twentieth century had
entered an America in which, in Rayford Logan's word, black America had
reached its "nadir"—socially, economically, and politically.[3] Harrison
arrived in 1900; Briggs on July 4, 1905; Moore on July 4, 1909; Domingo,
1910; McKay, 1912; Huiswoud, 1913; Garvey, March 24, 1916. The years
between Harrison's and Garvey's arrival were indeed dark times for black
America. Four years before Harrison disembarked in New York City, the
Supreme Court, in the *Plessy* v. *Ferguson* decision, had enshrined racial
segregation in law under the doctrine of "separate but equal." A voluminous outpouring of racist ideology, moving under the legitimizing camouflage of science, flooded the landscape of the new century from across the
borders of the old.[4] Of all the black radicals—"New Negroes," they called
themselves—Hubert Harrison was especially perplexed and preoccupied by
this movement. In 1915, D. W. Griffiths released his film *Birth of a Nation*,
a racist interpretation of Reconstruction based upon the novel *The Clans-
man*, in which black people were depicted as savages, buffoons, rapists,
incompetents—and the Ku Klux Klan as defenders of civilization and
decency. The newly formed NAACP picketed the film in the North to little
avail; it was even shown in the White House and viewed with approval by
President Woodrow Wilson. "It is like writing history with lightning," the
President is said to have remarked after viewing the film. "And my only
regret is that it is all so terribly true."[5] The Ku Klux Klan found the film a
wonderful device to aid recruitment and used it accordingly in innumerable
screenings. During the first two decades of the century, lynching was
commonplace and generally passed unpunished in the South. This was the
era of Booker T. Washington's hegemony, the era of black accommodation-
ism, timid obsequiousness before the powers that be, albeit conditioned by
formidable circumscription.

But most shocking of all, there was—within just over a year of Garvey's
arrival—the horrifying outbreak of the East St Louis massacre of July 1917.
At the base of this pogrom against the black population of East St Louis
was the customary labor competition between black and white workers, an
institutionalized practice of a racist America. White workers kept black

workers out of the unions; black workers, like many non-union white workers, engaged in strike-breaking; and employers took advantage of the division. Then, on July 2, 1917, consumed by a festering accumulation of racist resentments, white East St Louis exploded into a diabolic orgy of indescribable savagery. Black people in that town were slaughtered and burned alive in the most barbaric and outrageous manner by white mobs: escaping black women and children were pinned down by gun-fire or thrown back alive into raging furnaces that had once been their homes; in other cases, the mob first nailed up boards over the doors and windows before setting homes ablaze. On the night of July 2, the chant "Burn 'em out! Burn 'em out!" was heard from white onlookers as one mob went to work.[6] But the mobs of East St Louis were set on burning 'em *up*, not on burning 'em out. As one Congressman remarked at the time, "It is impossible for any human being to describe the ferocity and brutality of that mob."[7] Oscar Leonard, the superintendent of the St Louis Jewish Educational and Charitable Association, went on a tour of the affected neighbourhoods accompanied by a young Russian-Jewish immigrant. Leonard reported the reaction of his companion:

> I was informed that the makers of Russian pogroms could learn a great deal from the American rioters. . . . He told me when he viewed the blocks of burned houses that the Russian "Black Hundreds" could take lessons in pogrom-making from the whites of East St Louis. The Russians at least, he said, gave the Jews a chance to run while they were trying to murder them. The whites in East St Louis fired the homes of black folk and either did not allow them to leave the burning houses or shot them the moment they dared attempt to escape the flames.[8]

The events were enough to shock even a nation that had largely been impervious to the monumental injustices perpetrated against its black citizens. But President Wilson, who was busy with making the world safe for democracy, did nothing; he did not even have the time to meet a delegation to the White House headed by the NAACP's James Weldon Johnson. East St Louis radicalized and galvanized black militants, who called for armed self-defense. And there was, too, "an insistent, angry demand for revenge," on the part of many black people. Hubert Harrison agitated so effectively for black self-defense that the Justice Department explored the possibility of deporting him to the Virgin Islands, even though the islands were by then a part of US territory (having been sold to the Americans by the Danes). Garvey gave one of his most moving speeches a few days after the massacre, later publishing the speech, with additional material, as a pamphlet. Richard B. Moore's biographer said that Moore was "greatly disturbed" by the race riots, especially that of East St Louis; Moore described them as "wholesale massacres."[9] Black Harlem listened, read, and shed more than a tear over the horrors of East St Louis. (Refugees testified in front of rapt audiences in Harlem about the events.) And on July 28, 1917, black New York also marched.

Down Fifth Avenue to the sound of muffled drums, draped with black handerkerchiefs, marched ten thousand black people. They were silent. Little children, not more than five or six, headed the procession. The children were all dressed in white, and all, according to one account, tried "soberly to keep in step." Behind the children were the women, also dressed in white; and behind them, the men, dressed in black. The marchers carried banners that filled the silence: "Mother, Do Lynchers Go to Heaven?" "Give Me a Chance to Live," "We Are Maligned As Lazy And Murdered When We Work," "We Have Fought For the Liberty of White Americans in 6 Wars, Our Reward is East St Louis," "Mr President, Why Not Make America Safe For Democracy?" "Treat Us so that We May Love Our Country," "Patriotism and Loyalty Presuppose Protection and Liberty," "Pray for the Lady Macbeths of East St Louis." In front of the man bearing the Stars and Stripes went a banner with the inscription: "Your Hands Are Full of Blood."[10] Organized by the NAACP and black groups in Harlem, this was the "Silent Protest Parade," aptly described as "one of the strangest and most impressive sights New York has witnessed." James Weldon Johnson, who helped organize the parade, reported that "They marched in silence and they were watched in silence; but some of those who watched turned away with their eyes filled."[11] Black boy scouts distributed leaflets explaining the purpose of the march. Under the caption, "Why We March," it explained that "We march because we deem it a crime to be silent in the face of such barbaric acts."[12]

Without a doubt, then, the midnight darkness of the moment in which these migrants from the islands entered the country contributed to the speed and depth of their radicalization in America. That turn-of-the-century conjuncture constitutes a point in the nation's history when the contrast between the United States and the Caribbean on the question of race must have been one of the sharpest and most disturbing for an islander in America. The contrast no doubt deepened the Caribbeans' discontent with the new country. It was, therefore, not just the place that contributed to their radicalization: the exceptional times—a veritable state of emergency for black America—played their part. It is not surprising nor is it insignificant that Caribbeans in Harlem helped to organize and took part in the Silent Protest Parade.[13]

In written interviews, migrants from the Caribbean have left behind striking testimonies about how they absorbed the impact of American racism. The sometimes archaic and stilted language does not obscure the interviewees' shock and pain.[14]

> Having passed the immigration and customs examiners, I took a carriage for what the driver called "Nigger Town." It was the first time I had heard that opprobrious epithet employed, and then, by a colored man himself. I was vividly

irked no little. Arriving in Colored Town, [Miami], I alighted from the carriage in front of an unpainted, poorly-ventilated rooming house where I paid $2.00 for a week's lodging. Already, I was rapidly becoming disillusioned. How unlike the land from where I was born, I soliloquized. There colored men were addressed as gentlemen; here as "niggers." (189)[15]

My first set-back was when the pangs of segregation closed in on me. The Pennsylvania train arrived at Cape Charles; I boarded the steamer for Old Point, and not knowing the customs walked into the white section only to be reminded a moment later that my color was to determine where I would stay during the two-hour trip across the Chesapeake Bay. What an impression! Why were people of the two races separated? At home such is unheard of. (192)

In the United States I was to gain new experiences. In New York City there were separate churches for colored and white people. . . . I found that discrimination existed in hotels, in the residential sections of the city, and in office buildings, where in many instances colored people must use the freight elevators. In general, I gathered that Negroes were not wanted except to do menial work. (191)

A student who spent three months travelling throughout the Southern states before settling in New York did not disguise her feelings:

The whole situation down South filled me with bitterness and contempt. The utter ridiculousness of the sign in the cars "Whites to the front, colored to the rear". The girl that pointed it out to me was so amused for I could not stop reading it and laughing. They told me of a white Y.W.C.A. leader who came to their meeting, but always stood by until they had eaten before she ate! I wished I could meet her. It did not seem possible to me that such conditions could exist in one of the centres of civilization. (205)

Such responses can only be explained by the *perceived*, if not actual, differences between the place of race in the social structure of the United States, on the one hand, and the place of race within Caribbean societies, on the other. And the differences were neither fictive nor trivial.

Some of these differences may be fruitfully gauged by examining the response of Afro-American visitors to the islands. Surely, if the differences between the way race was articulated in these societies were as great as the Caribbean migrants in America claimed, then Afro-Americans visiting the islands must have taken notice and had something relevant to say. As it happens, the testimonies of Afro-American visitors invariably corroborated the differences observed by the Caribbean migrants. Although sometimes appalled by the prevailing poverty, Afro-American visitors to the Caribbean were, without exception, pleasantly surprised, indeed thrilled, at the relative absence of racism there. Du Bois, Langston Hughes, Paul Robeson, and others reported their visits to the island in such terms. Their response to the racial situation in the Caribbean is of more help in understanding the America they left behind than in understanding the Caribbean societies that they testify about. And so Du Bois's rhapsody about his visit to Jamaica in

1915 tells one more about race in America and more about Du Bois than it does about Jamaica itself, the ostensible object of his report.

Du Bois wrote of Jamaica in superlatives, opening with the statement: "Jamaica is a most amazing island." He continued in the same vein to the very end of his article. To Du Bois, Jamaica was the "most startling" of the lands he had seen, and not only physically. Writing in the organ of the NAACP, the *Crisis*, he told his readers that he was struck by the manner in which Africa, Asia, and Europe met there. "In Jamaica," the 47-year-old Du Bois observed, "for the first time in my life I lived beyond the color line—not on one side of it but beyond its end." To his great but pleasant surprise, he discovered when he sat down beside the mayor at dinner, that "His Worship was colored." Du Bois was also taken aback by the variety of positions occupied by black people. It was, he said, "a strange sort of luxury to ride on railways where engineers, firemen, conductors and brakemen were black." And he noted that the "smart, dark Constables in their gleaming white hats and coats" gave him a double sense of security.

Although Du Bois registered what he called "the tragedy of a poverty almost incomprehensible," he still spoke of the dignity and beauty of those afflicted by it—the black "peasantry"—in a pastoral, romantic tone:

> The peasants . . . were to me perhaps more alluring. I can see now those black, straight and strong and full-bosomed forms, supple of hip and thigh and lithe of limb, sinewy yet fine and calm, treading their silent miles like fate. Soft of word and slow but sweet of smile and uncomplaining, of the blood and tears of such as these was built Jamaica.

Jamaica was a paradox, said Du Bois. Through the predations of European colonialism the island, he acknowledged, lay "poverty-stricken." Despite this, however, Jamaica, to him, was "facing the world proudly with one great gift, the gift of racial peace, the utter overturning of the barbaric war of color, with a chance for men to lift themselves regardless of the complexion of their grandfathers. It is," he concluded, "the most marvelous paradox of this paradoxical western world."[16]

No Jamaican, or, more accurately put, no untravelled Jamaican, would or could have written about Jamaica in such terms. This is Jamaica seen through the eyes of a black American; Jamaica as seen by one who has lived in the dark and cruel shadow of Jim Crow and the lynching tree. And although Du Bois perhaps did not notice this—if he did, he did not tell— this was also Jamaica as seen through the eyes of a "light skinned," "colored," Harvard-educated gentleman. This is how the Jamaicans would have seen him, and this is how they would have treated him, and this was bound to have a bearing on how he perceived Jamaica. "Don't you believe like colored Dr Du Bois that the 'race problem is at an end here'," Garvey wrote Robert Russa Moton, principal of the Tuskegee Institute. Notice that Garvey described Du Bois as "colored," not "black." (Moton visited

Jamaica a year after Du Bois.) "*Black* men here are never truly honoured," Garvey told him.[17]

Five years after his visit and aware of the labor struggles being waged at the time, Du Bois was less sanguine about Jamaica and more critical of its mulattoes. The islands, he admitted, have "become disgusted with their old leadership." He continued:

> These leaders were largely mulattoes and it is British policy to induce them by carefully distributed honors and preferment to identify their interests completely with the whites. The visitor to Jamaica sees no color line in politics or society but he easily fails to note that the great mass of Negro peasantry has no real economic leadership or sympathy but is left to toil at a wretched wage and under disgraceful conditions.[18]

But Du Bois was still enchanted by Jamaica, which to him epitomized beauty. In a characteristically powerful and bleak essay, "On Being Black," also published in 1920, Du Bois suddenly declared, as if frightened by the darkness of the picture he himself had painted in the earlier part of his essay,

> Pessimism is cowardice. The man who cannot frankly acknowledge the "Jim-Crow" car as a fact and yet live and hope is simply afraid either of himself or of the world. There is not in the world a more disgraceful denial of human brotherhood than the "Jim-Crow" car of the Southern United States; but, too, just as true, there is nothing more beautiful in the universe than sunset and moonlight on Montego Bay in Jamaica. And both things are true and both belong to this, our world, and neither can be denied.[19]

"MY NEW LOVE IS JAMAICA!" Hughes chirpily announced in the *Chicago Defender* on his return from visiting the island in 1947. "She is dressed in green, and her face is as dark and as beautiful as any in the world." Robeson, who toured Jamaica and Trinidad the year after Hughes' visit, said of Jamaica: "I felt that for the first time I could see what it will be like when Negroes are free in their own land. I felt something like what a Jew must feel when first he goes to Israel." It is true though, that, like Du Bois before them, they acknowledged the poverty. "Certainly my people in the islands are poor. They are desperately poor," said Robeson. And Hughes on more sober occasions spoke with insight about "color lines" in the Caribbean.[20]

In 1922 J. A. Rogers complained that many Afro-American visitors to the islands, including Moton as well as Du Bois, "give the impression that there is no color line there." Rogers, himself a Jamaican migrant, observed that such also is "the proud boast" of many Caribbean migrants in the United States. Such a view is "very superficial, and far from being correct," said Rogers.[21]

The differences, then, between the articulation of race within the United States, on the one hand, and that in the societies of the Caribbean, on the other, require further investigation. After all, it is these differences that form the rational basis of the response of the Caribbean migrants to the United States, as well as the response of Afro-American visitors, such as Du Bois, to the Caribbean.

4

The Caribbean and the United States:
Patterns of Race, Color, and Class

A lthough there are fundamental, underlying similarities in the articulation of race in Caribbean societies, there are also significant differences. By the "articulation of race" I mean the historical process through which people were defined as and by "race"—thus becoming racialized—and the relationship between "race" and the wider economic, political, and cultural processes within a society.[1] Despite the fact that the dissimilarities in the articulation of race within the Caribbean have discernible—though mediated—concrete consequences for the political behavior of migrants from the region, these differences are generally ignored or seldom identified by commentators. Without an appreciation of these differences, it becomes impossible to understand and explain the distinct political path trodden in the United States by black Hispanic Caribbeans compared to their non-Hispanic counterparts.[2] One of the most striking patterns that emerges from examining the experience of Caribbeans in the United States in the first half of the century is that, among black radicals from the Hispanic Caribbean, there was relative indifference, if not aversion, to black nationalism and a considerable attraction to an unhyphenated socialism. Arturo Schomburg's black Puerto Rican compatriots in New York City during the 1920s and 1930s shared neither his sympathy for black nationalism nor his profound interest and pioneering work in the history of peoples of African descent. It is impossible to account for Schomburg's rather anomalous situation without understanding what race means to people in the Hispanic and non-Hispanic Caribbean. In broad terms, Puerto Rico could not have produced a Marcus Garvey and Jamaica, by the same token, could not have produced a Jesús Colón (the black Puerto Rican nationalist and socialist).[3]

Differences in the articulation of race hold the key to an explanation. It is necessary to outline and analyze, if only briefly, these important but rarely examined differences within the Caribbean—differences that carry over into the diaspora—before discussing the general differences between the place of race and color in the Caribbean, on the one hand, and, on the other, the place of race and color in American society.

*

The Hispanic Caribbean islands up to about 1800 were colonies in which a comparatively large number of Europeans decided to live, or ended up living, on a permanent basis. In comparison to the northern European colonies, landholdings were small, even though the land–population ratio was large. After the center of gravity of Spanish America shifted to the silver riches of Mexico and Peru in the early sixteenth century, the islands became relatively under-exploited, their links to the expanding capitalist world economy not as strong as they were to be for the Caribbean colonies that Britain, France, and Holland acquired in the seventeenth century. In the wake of the exploits of Hernan Cortés, Francisco Pizarro, and other Spanish *conquistadores* on the mainland, the islands' population declined as their inhabitants rushed to partake in the new-found riches. "*Dios me lleve al Perú*" ("God, take me to Peru"), they cried in Puerto Rico. The stampede was so great that the Spanish authorities feared the departure of the entire European population of the islands, thus jeopardizing their hold on them. To obviate this danger, the Council of the Indies issued decrees in the 1520s and 1530s prohibiting unauthorized emigration from the islands. The penalty for illegal departure was death and the confiscation of property.[4] Subsistence farming and ranching became the mainstay of the islands. Cuba, Puerto Rico, and Santo Domingo, from the earliest days of settlement, had African slaves, but the percentage of the black population that was free was consistently higher than that which obtained in the non-Hispanic colonies of the New World.

With capitalism far more developed than in Spain, over the centuries, Britain, France, and Holland had the economic and political infrastructure to exploit their Caribbean possessions far more systematically and intensively than Spain ever did. Apart from its economically inhibiting feudal system, Spain was spoiled by the great wealth extracted from the mainland in the form of precious metals. The islands, previously the center of Spanish colonial attention in the New World, now lacking the precious metals that attracted Spain to the mainland, were by the mid-sixteenth century of minor, if any, intrinsic value to Spain, functioning as handmaidens to the mainland colonies—refuelling stations and garrisons, aiding the protection of convoys on their way to Spain laden with American gold and silver. As Kenneth Andrews observed:

> The Caribbean colonies were the poor relations of the mainland kingdoms, and they were treated as such by the masters of Spain. This is hardly surprising in view of the contents of the American fleets. That which left Havana on 3 July 1581, for example, was estimated to be carrying, from Catagena, nearly four million *pesos* of bullion together with a large consignment of pearls and some emeralds; from New Spain and Honduras, nearly three million *pesos* of bullion and substantial quantities of cochineal, indigo, silk (from the Philippines), wool and sarsaparilla; from Santo Domingo, 78 *arrobas* (25 lbs each) of sugar and 10,000 lbs of ginger. No doubt the Caribbean colonies contributed many of the pearls and no doubt more sugar, hides and minor commodities found their way

thence to Spain that year, but the fact remained inescapable that the *audiencia* of Santo Domingo represented an economically negligible part of the Indies.[5]

Havana's early colonial history is instructive. Significantly, Havana flourished in the late sixteenth century only after the French burned it down in 1555 and it finally dawned upon the Spanish that Cuba and Havana, in particular, had to be held in order to service and safeguard the traffic with the mineral-rich American mainland. Cuba was strategically located and upon its defense depended the protection of Spain's New World. Havana's sheltered and expansive natural harbor had to be defended, not for the security and well-being of Cuba's inhabitants per se, but for its vital role in Spain's maritime trade. Accordingly, garrisons were established in Havana, providing for a resident armed force, fluctuating in number between four hundred and a thousand men. Fortifications were built, protecting the city from Spain's envious rivals. After the 1560s, to minimize the plunder of pirates, Spain's transatlantic shipping sailed under the escort of an armed convoy. The system known as the *flota* consolidated Spain's maritime traffic into two annual fleets to the Americas. On the return to Europe, both *flotas* put in at Havana, preparatory to the long and dangerous journey across the Atlantic, protected by a fleet of armed galleons. For centuries to come, Cuba depended upon Mexican money to subsidize the military and administrative expenses of the island. The Mexican *situados*, which was received by other islands apart from Cuba, would continue into the nineteenth century, clearly indicating the subordinate and auxillary position of the islands to the mainland.

Havana's population grew, and grew well out of proportion to the rest of the island. The extensive construction of houses and forts stimulated economic growth. The *flotas* brought four to five thousand additional people to Havana for weeks at a time, twice a year. Many had come from the mainland with newly acquired fortunes, eager to have a good time before their forty-five-day voyage home. They required entertainment, lodgings, and food. The silver and gold triggered inflation as it stimulated economic growth. Havana quickly acquired the reputation for being the most expensive place in the Indies. It was also during the sixteenth century that Havana became infamous for its gamblers, merchants, vendors, deserters, con-men, thieves, and prostitutes—a reputation that a revolution finally broke four centuries later.

Havana's prosperity rippled through western Cuba. Farmers, cattle breeders, and artisans benefited. But Havana's success was directly connected to the demise of the eastern end of the island. Santiago de Cuba, the island's colonial capital established in 1515, languished in the south-east as the *flotas* and their riches came and went on the north coast of the island, touching land only in Havana. By 1553, the Council of the Indies ordered the governor of the island to transfer his residence from Santiago de Cuba to Havana. In 1594 Havana was officially designated a city (*ciudad*), no longer a mere town (*villa*). Thirteen years later, in 1607, the colonial authorities officially declared Havana the capital of Cuba, the seat of the governor and captain-general—formally acknowledging what had long been a fact.

By 1608, Havana was home to more than half the island's 20,000 inhabitants. Eastern Cuba lay neglected, envious of Havana's contrived and rapid pre-eminence, resentful of the Spanish colonial yoke. Hardly defended by the colonial authorities, eastern Cuba was easy prey to French, British, and Dutch attackers: Santiago and Bayamo were attacked by the French in 1603, and again in 1628 and 1633; in 1652 the French took over Baracoa and attacked Remedios. The English sacked Santiago in 1662, and in 1665 the French busied themselves with destroying Sancti Spíritus. Henry Morgan sacked Puerto Príncipe in 1668 and John Springer plundered the town of Trinidad in 1675. Four years later Puerto Príncipe was attacked again.

Inadequately supplied by Spain, easterners were, nevertheless, forbidden from trading with foreigners. The citizens of Santiago, Bayamo, Baracoa, and other eastern towns ignored Spanish mercantile law and traded with Dutch, British, and French merchants along the coast, developing a vibrant system of smuggling. The Spanish authorities attempted to clamp down on the flagrant violation of their laws, but through a series of spectacular revolts between 1602 and 1607, they learned to turn a blind eye and to leave the locals to their own devices and thriving contraband trade.

Through such historical experience, Havana, and to a great extent western Cuba as a whole, came to be regarded as Spanish colonial possessions, the stronghold of colonial authority. Eastern Cuba, especially Oriente Province, in contrast, is often perceived as *de facto* Cuban, the repository of *Cubanidad*, even when Spain was the nominal possessor of the island.[6]

Outside of Havana and western Cuba, from the mid-sixteenth to the eighteenth century, Spain's insular possessions commercially turned in upon themselves, and enfeebled, transformed into a colonial backwater. It was in this context of relative neglect that the northern European powers were able, by the early seventeenth century, to pluck away, one by one, a number of islands from the Spanish imperial body politic.[7]

But Spain's neglect of the archipelago—and its effective abandonment of eastern Cuba in the late sixteenth century—provided local opportunity for those who lived on the islands. For one thing, imperial nonchalance provided a level of *de facto* autonomy for the inhabitants that they otherwise would not have enjoyed. The development of a substantial (relative to the slave population) black peasantry in the sixteenth right up to the eighteenth century cannot be explained outside of this wider context. It was also such circumstances that facilitated the growth and reproduction of a large (compared to the slave population) white, smallholding, settler population in the Spanish islands.[8] Along with these developments, there occurred a level of interaction between the black and white population that was prolonged and unparalleled in the New World.

By the late eighteenth century, however, the noisy march of European capitalism had disturbed the rustic somnolence of the Spanish Caribbean. Starting with Cuba, the slave trade dramatically expanded, gigantic plantations were laid out and established, the smallholding peasantry finding it increasingly difficult to maintain its cherished independence. For the enslaved Africans, the acquisition of manumission became more difficult as their labor became more valuable. In short, Spain's Caribbean possessions became progressively more like those of their northern European neighbors' as sugar became the crop of choice.

The metamorphosis of the Spanish Caribbean rapidly accelerated after revolution broke out in the richest sugar colony in the New World, St Domingue, in 1791. The Haitian slaves punched a massive hole in the world sugar market. Almost 80,000 tons of sugar were produced on the eve of revolution in 1791. But with the destruction wrought by a devastating war and its new and fiercely independent peasantry shunning the diabolical plantation system, Haiti produced only 8 tons of sugar in 1836.[9] The *hacendados* in the islands, like their counterparts elsewhere, took advantage of this unprecedented and unique opportunity. And so the sugar revolution, which first broke out in the British possessions in the seventeenth century, belatedly took hold of the Hispanic territories, moving east from Cuba in the middle of the eighteenth century, to Puerto Rico and on to the Dominican Republic in the nineteenth and early twentieth centuries.[10] But even during the nineteenth century, during the din and turmoil of King Sugar ascending his throne, dripping with the blood of Africans, the Hispanic territories displayed distinct characteristics, *vis-à-vis* the non-Hispanic areas, carried over from their classic, and relatively prolonged, settler period. And these characteristics, as will be demonstrated later, included the place of race and color in their social structure.

The dissimilar political economy that shaped the two areas of the Caribbean profoundly affected their demographic and ethnic patterns, which, in turn, significantly influenced the articulation of race and color. In this respect, one key difference is that people of predominantly European descent made up a much larger proportion of the population of the Hispanic Caribbean, relative to the proportion found in the non-Hispanic Caribbean. It is true that racial definitions of "white" tended to be more elastic in the Hispanic compared to the non-Hispanic Caribbean, but, even by the most restrictive criteria, the Hispanic areas of the archipelago have always had a relatively high proportion of white people among their inhabitants. Thus, while the Hispanic Caribbean (with the exception of the Dominican Republic) had, for instance in the nineteenth century, identified approximately half of its population as "white," the non-Hispanic Caribbean, typically so identified, had less than 10 percent.[11]

Prior to the abolition of slavery, the Hispanic Caribbean had a much higher manumission rate and a proportionately larger free non-white population compared to that in the non-Hispanic territories. Thus, on the eve of abolition in 1834, fewer than twelve out of every hundred non-white Jamaicans, and only seven out of a hundred non-white Barbadians, were free; all the others were enslaved. By contrast, almost 60 percent of non-white Cubans were free in 1880, six years before abolition, and 90 percent of their Puerto Rican counterparts were free by the time of abolition in 1873 (see Table 4.1, page 364). This distribution of black freedom in the archipelago was not an aberration of the nineteenth century. It was a secular trend. In 1773 less than 1 percent (0.7 percent) of black and mulatto Barbadians were free, 534 out of 69,082. Their Jamaican counterparts hardly fared better; 2.3 percent legally free—4,500 out of 197,300 in 1775. In the same year, 41 percent of non-white Cubans (30,847 out of 75,180) and a stunning 82.2 percent of their Puerto Rican brothers and sisters were free.[12] Why the massive difference between British and Spanish territories? As a number of scholars have argued, the relative economic backwardness of the Spanish possessions and of Spain itself, rather than—as some had previously suggested—the supposedly benign cultural characteristics of Spanish colonialism in the region, account for the contrast. After all it was in Cuba, under the same Catholic Spanish colonial rule, that as sugar became king in the nineteenth century, the rate and ease with which the slaves acquired their manumission diminished, while the slave trade dramatically expanded. Unable to mobilize the resources to import anywhere near as many African slaves as they would have liked during the nineteenth century, the Puerto Rican *hacendados*, in a desperate bid to solve the labor "scarcity" problem, subordinated peasants and workers, black and white alike, to the rule of capital through extraordinarily coercive legislation.[13]

The black and white peasantry underwent similar travails in the Hispanic Caribbean. Reflecting upon the draconian labor laws passed in Puerto Rico in the mid-nineteenth century, one author rightly noted the "color-blindness of the planter class" when it came to coercing labor to work on the haciendas.[14] Adversity often bonded the oppressed, joining black and white together. Because of these historical patterns, blackness was not as profoundly associated with subordination in the Hispanic as in the non-Hispanic areas of the archipelago.[15] The occupational distance between black and mulatto in the Hispanic Caribbean was less than it was in the non-Hispanic Caribbean. In 1872, the year before abolition, it was estimated that 35 percent of Puerto Rican slaves were mulatto or mestizo; indeed, 1.5 percent was described as "white". In 1832, two years before abolition, 14 percent of Barbadian and 10 percent of Jamaican slaves were colored; none was designated as "white."[16]

The distinct pattern of interaction between black and white contributed to the growth of a relatively large colored population in the Hispanic compared to that in the non-Hispanic Caribbean.[17] The sexual relations between black and white in the Hispanic Caribbean, and Puerto Rico in particular, were less marked by the profound imbalance of power that characterized such relations in the non-Hispanic Caribbean, especially in Jamaica and St Domingue. While in Puerto Rico such cross-racial relations were often established between black and white workers and peasants, in Jamaica and St Domingue they were generally ones between white masters or overseers and female slaves in their charge. In the Hispanic Caribbean, especially in Puerto Rico, miscegenation occurred more democratically and consensually, largely among people in the same class category—horizontally, so to speak. In the non-Hispanic areas it almost invariably occurred across the class divide, vertically, more coercively.

The high level of interaction between black and white peasants and workers, and the many points at which their interests and fortunes converge, help to explain another outstanding feature of Hispanic Caribbean society: the high level of black mobilization and enthusiasm for nationalist projects. It is no accident that Oriente Province, the most eastern province of Cuba, was the place that the support for the Ten Years War and the independence struggle against Spain was greatest. Both the 1868 and 1895 insurrections began there. Oriente had a large black and colored free population who had exceptionally good access to land through ownership, rent or squatting. The small peasantry predominated there, black and white, with remarkably similar land tenure patterns. "Oriente was a place of parity and proportion, of equity and equality," one historian wrote, describing the turn-of-the-century milieu. The language is hyperbolic, but there is much truth to it. It is in this environment that the encroachment of the Spanish government and the local *peninsulares* provoked joint revolt.[18] The free people of color (black and mixed-race) in Puerto Rico enjoyed even greater access to the land than their counterparts in nineteenth-century Cuba. In 1860, six years before the revolt in the north-western town of Lares, they made up over 35 percent of the peasant farmers, 34 percent of proprietors, and over 36 percent of the artisans of the island; the free colored population was estimated to make up 46 percent of Puerto Rico's free population at the time.[19] From *El Grito de Lares*, Puerto Rico's nationalist insurrection in 1868, through the Ten Years War and Cuba's war of independence of the 1890s, right up to the victory of the Fidelistas in 1959, black people have not only been present, but have been prominent and distinguished fighters in the anti-colonial struggle. In Cuba's war against Spain, almost half of the fighters were black. Antonio Maceo, Cuba's "bronze titan," and his brother José, fell on the field of battle, as did countless other black Cubans. The sacrifices of war not only strengthened the bonds of fellowship between black and white patriots, it also reinforced the claims of citizenship and belonging.[20] And even when the white ruling class, such as that in Cuba in the aftermath of independence, tightened the screws on black people, this should not be read as simply reflective of white popular opinion and behavior.[21] In Puerto Rico, Ramón Emeterio Betances (1827–98), a mulatto, is, as José Luis González put it, "recognized by all supporters of Puerto Rican independence as the Father of the Nation."[22] Arturo Schomburg and Jesús Colón were only two of a long and distinguished line of black or colored Puerto Rican nationalists: Francisco Gonzalo "Pachin" Marín, Sotero Figueroa, Pedro Albizu Campos, right down to Felipé Luciano, Chairman of the Young Lords (migrant Puerto Rico's equivalent of the Black Panthers) in the early 1970s.

The British, French, Dutch, and Danish Caribbean had no equivalent of the popular cross-racial nationalism that developed in Puerto Rico and Cuba in the nineteenth and early twentieth century. The white creole minority was too small and fearful of the black masses to break with London, Paris, Amsterdam, or Copenhagen. The mulatto elite often harbored nationalist yearnings, at times hating the metropole, and especially its arrogant European-born agents. But their contempt for and fear of the African masses was more powerful than any desire they might have had to sever links with the mother country. The masses, for their part, despised the mulattoes, the white creoles as well as the European-born whites. Moreover, they always viewed the metropolitan center, and the monarchy in particular, as bulwarks against the tyranny of officialdom and the tender mercies of the local oligarchy who vigorously opposed their emancipation. In short, unlike the black and white *criollos* in the Spanish Caribbean—and for that matter, on the continent—no one felt sufficiently desperate, or hated the colonial center enough, to make a bid for independence, nor did they regard themselves powerful enough to succeed in such a venture. Britain and Spain in the nineteenth century were by no means military, political, or economic equivalents.

At a number of levels, then, the Hispanic Caribbean, because of its historical and cultural experience, displays distinct differences with the non-Hispanic Caribbean in the perception and operation of race and color.

But throughout the Caribbean, Hispanic and non-Hispanic, there existed—nationalist collaboration notwithstanding—a hierarchy of race and color where the "whiter" and "lighter" are generally located at the top of the social pyramid, with the "darker" at the bottom. Caribbean societies were and are characterized, to a greater or lesser degree, by what the late Gordon Lewis has aptly dubbed a "multi-layered pigmentocracy."[23] But in spite of this general pattern, individual black or colored people could be found relatively high up the socio-economic ladder. And although after emancipation insidious practices of discrimination occurred, especially in the professions and in the colonial administration of the northern European possessions, no discriminatory legislation, explicitly based upon race, sat on the statute books of the islands.[24] Social class, which overlapped considerably with race and color, was the primary mechanism of overt social stratification and ordering. Thus a black man could vote in Jamaica in the nineteenth century so long as he fulfilled the economic qualifications for the franchise. Of course, few black people had the financial wherewithal to so qualify. Indeed, the financial qualifications to vote were so prohibitive to ordinary Jamaicans that of a population of 600,000 only 9,176 were registered voters in 1884—a mere 1.5 percent of the population. In 1901 when the population was estimated at 756,000 there were only 16,256 registered voters—hardly an improvement.[25] The franchise was clearly skewed in favor of merchants, landowners, and attorneys, the majority of whom were of European and of Levantine extraction, and against the Africans, who made up over 90 percent of the population. Among the non-Europeans, the coloreds—meaning those of "mixed descent"—being more economically well endowed than the "Negroes," constituted a disproportionately large number of the voters compared to those of darker complexion. This meant that virtually all of the voters were members of the plantocracy and merchant class, who were, of course numerically tiny and overwhelmingly white. The discrimination that obtained, then, was only indirectly (but no less effectively) racial—it was mediated by another complex of discriminatory practices based upon social class.

It must be said, however, that in the Hispanic Caribbean, and in Puerto Rico in particular, the degree of overlap between race and class was not as exact and flush as it was in the British and French territories. Thus in nineteenth- and early-twentieth-century Puerto Rico, considerable collaboration between members of the working class and their organizations took place across racial lines. This was especially so among the *tabaqueros* and artisans, many of whom were black and colored. The United States Resident Commissioner, Henry Carroll, with evident surprise, reported at the turn of the century that of the eleven working-class representatives who testified before him, nine were black, and all except one could read and write, and all were decently clothed.[26]

But despite the variations from place to place within the archipelago, black people in the Caribbean were generally kept down. This was, however, not achieved through the *relatively* crude kick-'em-in-the-teeth discipline of Jim Crow, nor by the terror of the lynch ropes and the pyres of the Ku Klux Klan, but by the no less diabolic—though more enigmatic and opaque—tyranny of Mammon. "The difference between the disfranchisement in the Southern States and that in the West Indies is solely that in the latter place the process is more politic," averred Joel Rogers in 1922. "The government of the British West Indies," he said, "like other British Colonies where colored peoples predominate, may accurately be called a Caucasian oligarchy." He was not as accurate as he thought he was, but he was right in regard to *de facto* British rule in the Caribbean at the time.[27] The subtlety of the process did not escape Claude McKay and he grasped its complexity more fully than Rogers did. Writing in 1940 he noted:

The English do not have laws against intermarriage; they do not have Jim-Crow laws separating Negroes from whites in public places and conveyances; they do not disfranchise Negroes; they do not establish a rule of refusal to serve them in hotels, bars, etc. But in reality all such restrictions more or less obtain in the islands. This is easy. The large masses of Negroes live in such a poverty-stricken condition that they cannot aspire to the better life of the British aristocracy of the military and high government officials. Only the members of the entailed mulatto aristocracy can afford to intrude in the privileged area.[28]

But there are other important respects in which the Caribbean differed from the United States in relation to race.

First, the United States was the only society in the Americas, from the days of slavery onward, within which "race" was articulated in a binary manner, with no intermediary position recognized or privileged to any notable degree by the white ruling class.

Second, legalized segregation on the basis of race was commonplace in the South; and *de facto* racial segregation occurred in much of the supposedly more liberal North. In this respect there was hardly any place to hide in America from such practices. Racial segregation as such, at least *de jure*, did not exist in the Caribbean.

Third, lynching—that peculiarly American institution, approaching something of a devilish pastime for whites in the late nineteenth- and early twentieth-century South—was, of course, unknown in the Caribbean. The first two decades of the twentieth century witnessed one of the most sustained waves of lynching, which took some of the most brutal forms, including burning people alive at the stake.[29]

Finally, a significant contrast between the United States and the Caribbean for many of these migrants was that they had left societies in most of which they had formed a solid majority, and entered an America in which they joined the ranks of not just a minority, but an especially oppressed, stigmatized, ridiculed, maligned, and besieged one. Indeed, so peculiar was the status of Afro-America at the time that it had few, if any, genuine counterparts globally.

So what of the socio-cultural characteristics of the migrants?

First, they were, of course, unaccustomed to being a minority—let alone one in such a resolutely hostile environment. This fact constituted part of the shock which they experienced on arrival in America.

Second, being part of the majority—the overwhelming majority in most cases—in the Caribbean, despite the colonial structure which dominated these societies, Afro-Caribbeans had relatively little direct contact with white people. And so, in terms of the structures of racial oppression, they had far more room to maneuver in their everyday life than they were to have in the United States. This sharp contrast clearly contributed to the migrants' state of restlessness and disorientation in America; the situation was not one with which they were accustomed.

Third, and very significantly, Caribbean migrants had come from societies in which black people, from the period of slavery and its aftermath, had established a rich and virtually unbroken tradition and culture of armed and forthright resistance unparalleled among their Afro-American counterparts, and, arguably, unparalleled by any other group of Africans in the New World. But let there be no confusion here. It was possible for this tradition to develop in the islands primarily because of the more favorable balance of forces in the Caribbean which created more conducive conditions for resistance on the part of the oppressed. African Americans were not blessed by such favorable circumstances. They were, for instance, in marked contrast to their Caribbean brothers and sisters, in a minority from the earliest days of slavery. Thus the student of Jamaican slavery asks, in all seriousness: "[W]hy was it that despite the favourable conditions [which existed] the Jamaican slaves failed to overthrow their masters?" while that of American slavery tells us, after years of research: "The wonder, then is, not that the United States had fewer and smaller slave revolts than some other countries did, but that they had any at all."[30] Furthermore, the post-slavery period in the United States was marked by a level of terror—psychological as well as physical—against black people, even during the relatively glory days of Reconstruction, that was unheard of in the archipelago, and was without parallel in the rest of the Americas.[31]

One of the most pervasive misunderstandings of the background of Caribbeans in the United States is the idea that Caribbeans were passive at home and were only roused into militancy in the aftermath of migration. Thus Kelly Miller declared: "The West Indian Negro in America is a political conundrum. Conservative at home, he becomes radical abroad."[32] At home, the West Indians, according to Miller, are "as meek as Moses and as submissive as a lamb ... but crossing the seas seems to fill them with the spirit of irresponsible revolt."[33] Forty years later, Harold Cruse, in his *The Crisis of the Negro Intellectual*, repeated this legend, begun, apparently, by Miller: "The West Indians," said Cruse, "are essentially conservatives fashioned in the British mold."[34] This rather persistent misunderstanding, clearly, deserves some attention.[35]

Rebuttals were penned within days of Miller's remark in the *New York Amsterdam News*. "Where," asked one Randolph Bynoe in a letter to the editor, "does Mr Miller get his information that West Indians at home are 'as meek as Moses and as submissive as a lamb.' Is this statement founded on first-hand experience or is it a product of his imagination?" Dr Charles Petioni was equally intrigued by Miller's statement: "I am wondering whether this is because of ignorance, malice or wish-fulfilment?"[36] Bynoe's and Petioni's bewilderment at Miller's remark is understandable: the most cursory acquaintance with Caribbean history would give the lie to Miller's and Cruse's pronouncements. Miller's mistaken remark about Caribbeans at home might very well be the product of his rather unorthodox and idiosyncratic way of doing Caribbean history. Oblivious to the *non sequitur* in his argument, he wrote in response to his interlocutors:

> During my forty-four years' teaching experience I suppose that I have had to do with the intellectual handling of as many West Indian students as any educator in America. Literally hundreds of them have come under my tuition. I have found them to be intelligent, energetic and enterprising beyond the average of the American student. Great Britain has a great way in dealing with subordinate races, of making them feel satisfied with her complaisant overlordship. The West Indians all but unanimously laud the British sway as being far more equitable and genial than that of America. Small wonder then that they, in numbers out of proportion to their quota, swell the ranks of the restless and dissatisfied element.[37]

It may very well be true that coming face to face with Jim Crow makes John Bull look good, but that does not mean that people in the Caribbean, especially the untravelled, spend their time singing John Bull's praises. In any case, the history of the Caribbean, which encompasses more than the alleged predilection of students from the region—even hundreds—at Howard University, is very much a history of resistance. "For his information," wrote Petioni, "may I state that there has never been a time even before emancipation when there did not exist an active opposition in most of the islands against their system of government as well as against the white man 'per se'."[38] Petioni's rebuff, though insufficiently nuanced, is essentially correct, for, in reality, contrary to Miller's statement, the Caribbean has had some of the most large-scale and prolonged slave revolts in the Americas. The region is distinguished for having given to the world the first and only case in human history of slaves succeeding in wresting state power from their masters. Apart from bringing about such an event, the slaves in St Domingue also brought Haiti into being in 1804, the second independent state in the Americas since the European lightning sequence of conquests of the fifteenth and sixteenth centuries.[39] The Haitians were preceded to independent nationhood in the Americas only by the thirteen former colonies which formed the core of what became the United States of America.

Out of the womb of slave societies in the Caribbean also emerged Maroon communities—communities founded by runaway and rebel slaves as early as the seventeenth century—which have lasted to the present day in Suriname and Jamaica. No area of the Caribbean was left untouched by servile revolt. And in the post-slavery period the tradition of resistance—mediated by time and circumstances, but with definite threads of continuity with the past—persisted, with its advances, setbacks, and fair share of downright defeats, reaching a crescendo in the 1930s with a hurricane of labor revolts ripping through the archipelago.[40]

Of course there are strains of conservatism in all societies, and here the Caribbean is no exception. Nor does any society exist in a state of permanent revolution. The "brown" (so called, mulatto) middle class in the non-Hispanic Caribbean is renowned for its mimetic pseudo-European culture. But even this class cannot be written off as having been completely conservative. For the slights, rejections, and petty spite of the white colonial ruling class have often led to the radicalization of some of its members. Like their American counterpart, they might not have become revolutionaries, but quite often their experience contributes to their becoming tenacious fighters for reform.[41]

Neither were the workers and peasants who resisted most against the post-slavery order in the Caribbean on the war-path at all times. Nor were those in struggle the same persons over time. There was always a complex dialectic at work between accommodation and resistance. No one loved to fight; and like people the world over, they fought when they could, they fought when they thought it was prudent to do so, and they fought when they felt that they had to. Walter Rodney, described this dialectic well:

> Each day in the life of a member of the working population was a day on which there was both struggle and accommodation. Struggle was implicit in the application of labour power to earn wages or to grow crops, while accommodation was a necessary aspect of survival within a system in which power was so comprehensively monopolized by the planter class. Some persons resisted more tenaciously and consistently than others; but there was no simple distinction between those who resisted and those who accommodated. Moments of struggle and moments of compromise appeared within the same historical conjuncture, but ultimately, resistance rather than accommodation asserted itself as the principal aspect of this contradiction.[42]

As a consequence of this different historical experience, Caribbean migrants were less adept at wearing "the mask"—which disguised their true feelings and thoughts in the presence of white people—than their American counterparts, whose very survival in a hostile land was dependent upon their facility with mask wearing. Paul Laurence Dunbar (1872–1906), the pioneering African American poet, captures powerfully and poignantly this practice in his aptly titled poem "We Wear the Mask":

> We wear the mask that grins and lies,
> It hides our cheeks and shades our eyes, —
> This debt we pay to human guile;
> With torn and bleeding hearts we smile,
> And mouth with myriad subtleties.
>
> Why should the world be over-wise,
> In counting all our tears and sighs?
> Nay, let them only see us, while
>   We wear the mask.
>
> We smile, but, O great Christ, our cries
> To thee from tortured souls arise.
> We sing, but oh the clay is vile

> Beneath our feet, and long the mile;
> But let the world dream otherwise,
>   We wear the mask.[43]

Caribbean migrants had come from societies in which more frontal struggles and open modes of encounter with whites were the general norm. Claude McKay remarked on a number of occasions that he was not used to speaking to white people in one way and black people in another. He tended at all times to be "suicidally frank." America conspired against black people who were not Janus-faced. The Caribbean migrants, especially the Jamaicans, found it difficult to adjust to the new reality. It is not that they never wore masks; they did, as does everyone at one time or another— including McKay, despite what he said.[44] The difference between the migrants and their Afro-American counterparts was that in the Caribbean, at least in the post-emancipation period, they had not the *need* to wear the *racial* mask with the same degree of frequency and facility that black people in America did. For one thing, in the Caribbean, black people hardly interacted with white people, for the simple reason that there were hardly any white people around to interact with, willingly or unwillingly; typically, less than one in ten people in the islands was white. The migrants' deficient grasp of what James Weldon Johnson called the "freemasonry of the race" meant that they were perhaps more aggressive than they otherwise would be had they understood better the somewhat esoteric codes and practices, the "myriad subtleties," in the etiquette of race in America.[45]

It is often forgotten that the Caribbean does not constitute a homogeneous whole. One of the frequent mistakes made by commentators on the region—especially by those from the outside—is to assume and imagine a lack of diversity, or to underestimate the degree of diversity, within the area. Such errors do great harm to understanding the complex reality of the Caribbean. Although one may legitimately speak of general tendencies, one needs also to recognize differences and variations. Thus, when one examines the political behavior of ordinary working people in the Caribbean one finds, not surprisingly, that this is by no means uniform throughout the region. There are for instance, even *within* the anglophone Caribbean, noteworthy differences in the general political culture between one island and another; differences that have important implications for the political behavior of migrants from the various territories of the region in the diaspora—including that in the United States.

Jamaica and Barbados, for example, are often perceived in popular and not so popular discourse as counterpoints in this regard. The Jamaican masses are viewed as having a tradition of struggle that is more aggressive and frontal in its approach than that of their Barbadian counterparts. This is often interpreted as symptomatic of the "radicalism" of Jamaicans, compared to the "conservatism" of the Barbadians, a crude and inaccurate extrapolation. The Barbadian masses have struggled as much as the

Jamaican masses; there is no evidence to suggest that black Jamaicans valued liberty and justice more than black Barbadians did. The fact is that the *mode* of struggle adopted by Barbadians and that by Jamaicans—as is universally the case—has been conditioned and circumscribed by their environment. By any yardstick, Jamaica offered a more favorable environment than Barbados for successful struggle, both during and after slavery. The chief reasons for this may be briefly enumerated. First, Barbados had always had a proportionately larger white population compared to Jamaica. Second, the hilly and mountainous terrain facilitated the relatively successful execution of guerrilla warfare in Jamaica during slavery—Barbados is flat. Third, the Barbados militia was better organized and proportionately larger than that of Jamaica. Fourth, the independent peasantry in Jamaica was, in absolute as well as in relative terms, larger than that of Barbados in the post-slavery period. Fifth, the population density of Barbados, ever since the early seventeenth century, has been substantially greater than that of Jamaica. This, among other things, meant that there were fewer open and uninhabited areas for prospective rebel slaves to seek refuge in Barbados than there was in Jamaica. Sixth, Barbados is also unique among the anglophone territories for having had a stable and unbroken history of British colonial rule stretching from 1625 to 1966, when the island became independent.

British historian James Anthony Froude, who travelled through the Caribbean in 1887, was struck by the "thoroughly English" character of Barbados. "On no one of our foreign possessions," said he, "is the print of England's foot more strongly impressed than on Barbadoes." Three generations later, George Lamming—a son of the soil and one of the region's leading novelists—echoed the sentiment when he described the island as "the oldest and least adulterated of British colonies." British cultural hegemony was more deeply rooted there than anywhere else in the Caribbean, including Jamaica. Finally, Barbados—by having been able to reproduce its slave population at a remarkably early date—was to become one of the first genuinely creole societies (that is, those having a majority of their population born in the New World) in the Caribbean. This meant that the reputedly "troublesome" African-born slaves were relatively few and far between, and, correspondingly, African cultural forms were harder to maintain in Barbados.[46] These somewhat contrasting features—almost to the extent of counterpoints—help to explain the differences in the political culture of the two islands.

Despite the fact that Jamaica experienced white terror in the aftermath of the revolts of 1832 (the Sam Sharpe Rebellion) and 1865 (the Morant Bay Rebellion), it is arguable that the ordinary people were not as overwhelmed by these as their Barbadian brothers and sisters were overwhelmed and traumatized by the unprecedented blood-letting carried out by the white plantocracy after Bussa's Revolt of 1816. In the absence of a more favorable balance of forces and structural conditions, frontal assaults such as Bussa's were futile. This knowledge seeped perceptibly into the political calculus of black would-be insurgents in Barbados. Indeed this process of cautious adaptation on the part of the enslaved began as early as the defeat of the 1692 revolt, in the aftermath of which the ruling class took urgent steps to strengthen the repressive arm of the colonial state.[47] In conspicuous exception to the rest of the Caribbean, there was no revolt to speak of in Barbados in the eighteenth century: the defeat of 1692 was apparently still fresh in the popular memory, and by the end of the eighteenth century neither the balance of forces nor the general circumstances had changed in favor of the slaves. Evidently, Bussa and his followers felt that the situation had improved in their favor and that the conjuncture of Easter 1816 was propitious for a strike against the institution of slavery. For a variety of reasons, they experienced one of the bloodiest defeats in the history of servile revolts in the Americas.[48]

Over a period of more than a century, Africans in Barbados discernibly adopted a more cautious and less frontal mode of struggle than had their counterparts in Jamaica. More than any other place in the entire Caribbean, Barbados developed features in relation to the configuration of color that were somewhat akin to the Southern states of America and there was, perhaps, more white terror and paternalism exercised there than anywhere else in the non-Hispanic Caribbean.

Interestingly, although the subject of what we may call the peculiarities of the Barbadians has been the topic of much popular discourse within the Caribbean and within the diaspora—the calypsonians have not been silent on the issue—it has never seriously been analyzed.[49] John Hearne, the Jamaican journalist and novelist, to his credit, found the enigma worthy of consideration, but his answers are far from satisfactory. According to Hearne, "History englished [*sic*]" the Barbadian "by giving him an exclusive association with that potent and wonderful country," just at the time when England was in one of its most creative phases.[50] Hearne, thus, ignored the coercive origins of English cultural hegemony in Barbados. The Barbadian topography, which so negatively conditioned the struggle of generations of black Barbadians, is viewed ahistorically by Hearne as simply another feature—and tautologically as an explanation—of Barbados's "Englishness."[51]

Despite the book's many problems, Froude's *The English in the West Indies*, cast interesting and valuable light on English hegemony in Barbados. For one of the most striking and enduring impressions of Barbados with which one leaves Froude's travelogue is the omnipresence of soldiers, sailors, and police on the island. Froude tours the island on horseback with the chief of the police, an unnamed colonel. He even manages to meet up with an American commodore. He "inspects" police stations,[52] and he talks about the men of the military and the police in such pastoral terms that one is apt to forget who these people really were—the repressive arm of the colonial state—and what their *raison d'être* was—to put the people down if they attempted to get off their knees. "However it may be in the other islands," Froude wrote,

> England in Barbados is still a solid fact. The headquarters of the West Indian troops are there. There is a commander-in-chief residing in a "Queen's House," so called. There is a savannah where there are English barracks under avenues of almond and mahogany. Red coats are scattered about the grass. Officers canter about playing polo, and naval and military uniforms glitter at the side of carriages, and horsemen and horsewomen take their evening rides, as well mounted and as well dressed as you can see in Rotten Row.

In the harbor, the training squadron had gone, "but in the place of it the West Indian fleet was there, and there were also three American frigates."[53] The commander-in-chief of the British military in the islands was a man who had fought against the Zulus in Natal. Little wonder, then, that Froude felt secure in Barbados and assured of the stability of the island's social order, even if the politicians he observed in the Assembly in Bridgetown, the capital, behaved irresponsibly. As he put it: "One feels that there will be something to retire upon when parliamentary oratory has finished its work of disintegration."[54]

This extraordinary presence of red coats "scattered about the grass," the ruling class always feeling that in moments of crisis there will be "something to retire upon," had no parallel in the rest of the British Caribbean. As Froude noted, Barbados was the headquarters of British might in the archipelago. Black Barbadians were cognizant of the fact, and their struggles were accordingly conditioned and circumscribed both by the *knowledge* of the fact, and by the fact *itself*, of ruling class military superiority.

It may very well be the case that the pattern of struggle, conditioned by particular insular experience, continued in the Caribbean diaspora in New York. Is the apparent pre-eminence of Jamaicans and Virgin Islanders relative—taking into account their weight within the overall Caribbean migrant community—to other Caribbeans in both left-wing and black nationalist activity in Harlem, in the period under review, partially explicable by the radical tradition established in those islands?[55] Does the history of Barbados help to account for its relative dearth of radical black activists in Harlem during those years? Does the Barbadian historical experience explain why Richard B. Moore was one of the few visible Barbadians on the black left in the period of the First World War and the 1920s compared to a whole coterie of Jamaicans (Domingo, McKay, Ethelred Brown, Thomas Patterson, the Burrell brothers—Benjamin and Theophilus— among others) and Virgin Islanders (Harrison, Totten, Frank Crosswaith)?[56]

The Barbadians are confined and politically inhibited at home, but the children of Barbadians living elsewhere in the Caribbean (especially in

Trinidad and Guyana) are over-represented among the archipelago's most distinguished radical intellectuals. Many of those celebrated as Trinidadian radicals are also, more often than not, little more than a generation removed from Barbadian soil: Henry Sylvester Williams, the pioneer Pan-Africanist, George Padmore, and C. L. R. James are all of Barbadian ancestry. Seldom noted, too, is the fact that although he was born in St Croix, Hubert Harrison's mother was of Barbadian origin. Samuel Haynes's father was a Barbadian who served in the old West India Regiment in Africa. On returning to the Caribbean, Samuel Haynes senior moved to Belize, where he settled, enlisting in the constabulary. He got married and fathered thirteen children, including Samuel. Hubert Critchlow, founder of the British Guiana Labour Union and the father of trade unionism in the British Caribbean, was born in Georgetown, the son of a Barbadian dockworker and a Guianese woman. Eric Walrond's parents were Barbadian, even though Walrond was himself born in Guyana. The distinguished Coard family of Grenada, including Dr Bernard Coard, the Deputy Prime Minister of the ill-fated People's Revolutionary Government (1979–83), is of Barbadian origin.

The explanation for this remarkable Barbadian antecedent among substantial sectors of the Caribbean radical intelligentsia cannot detain us here beyond the briefest comments. It most probably lay in the superior cultural capital of their parents. From the eighteenth century, Barbadians have been among the most literate and educated black population in the world. In the nineteenth and early twentieth century the British effectively exported Barbadians to other parts of the Caribbean as teachers, civil servants and policemen—along with a good number of the most destitute elements. From as early as the 1840s, Barbadians dominated the lower ranks of the Trinidad police force. By 1895, 301 of the 537-strong Trinidad force were Barbadians, increasing by 1897 to nearly 400 of the 600 policemen in Trinidad; and in 1895, half the domestic servants in Port of Spain were Barbadians.[57] Trinidad's 1891 census reveals the over-representation of British Caribbean immigrants (disproportionately Barbadians) in the professional and skilled occupations. At a time when they made up only 16.5 percent (33,071 out 200,028) of Trinidad's population, British Caribbean immigrants made up 22 percent of Trinidad's teachers; 15 percent of the clergymen; 19 percent of the civil engineers and surveyors; 26 percent of the public officers and clerks; 34 percent of the druggists, dispensers, and midwives; 67 percent of the postal and prison officers; 59 percent of the hospital nurses and wardsmen; 85 percent of the policemen; 40 percent of the carpenters; 68 percent of the shoemakers; 55 percent of the tailors; 40 percent of the blacksmiths; 46 percent of the coopers; 40 percent of the bakers and cake makers; and 30 percent of the painters.[58] Not much encouragement for this exodus was required, for in the nineteenth and early twentieth centuries tens of thousands of Barbadians of their own volition flocked to the greener pastures of Trinidad and Guyana.[59]

The children of the Barbadian immigrants in Trinidad and elsewhere in the Caribbean were triply endowed by their parents. First the educational advantage of their parents over the locals was to the children's advantage in school—children of the educated tend to perform better than the children of the uneducated. Second, the ambition of the immigrant for his or her children contributed to the impetus to perform relatively well. And third, the latter combined with the legendary drive of the Barbadian abroad must have contributed to the relative success of the descendants of Barbadians in Trinidad and Guyana.[60]

In Trinidad, in particular, there was a fourth advantage to the Barbadians and their children: they were English-speaking in a society within which English had become the language of the colonial ruling class, while the masses of native Trinidadians spoke French creole. (Britain formally took possession of Trinidad from Spain in 1797, but the lingua franca of the island at the time was French creole. The pre-eminence of French Creole came from the substantial French presence and influence on the island up to then.) Indeed, so important was the linguistic distinctiveness of the Barbadian immigrants that the concentration of Barbadians in the urban centers of Trinidad was said, by a colonial official in 1888, to have contributed more to helping the urban Trinidadians learn to speak English than had the educational system itself. This was said to be especially true of those who settled in Port of Spain.[61] The fact that the official language of Trinidad and the language of instruction in Trinidadian schools was English clearly advantaged the Barbadian immigrants and their children. It therefore comes as no surprise that the parents of Henry Sylvester Williams, George Padmore, and C. L. R. James had relatively skilled or white-collar jobs, as teachers and low-level civil servants. And insofar as the descendants of Barbadians were over-represented among the black intelligentsia in the new areas of settlement it stands to reason that a disproportionate number of the radical intellectuals, in Trinidad especially, would probably have Barbadian antecedents.[62]

Significantly, unlike Kelly Miller and Harold Cruse who essentially operated at the level of stereotypes about Caribbeans, at least some people in the Colonial Office in Britain were mindful of the differences between their Caribbean colonial "subjects." As noted in Chapter 2, in 1933, a group of "prominent West Indians" living in New York sent a memorial to the British Foreign Secretary. They wanted to register their gratitude, at the highest level, for the help extended to their community by the Pro-Consul in the British Consulate in New York. "Mostly 'badians [that is, Barbadians], I see [and] strangely few Jamaicans," scribbled one sharp-eyed Whitehall official on the covering note of the document.[63] To him, a mandarin of the imperial state, this was, evidently, not a trivial observation. As far as he was concerned, it was a piece of information that ought to be taken into account in weighing the import of the communication from the British Caribbeans in New York. His was also an implied commentary on "'badians" and Jamaicans. To this official, the signatories were not simply "West Indians" — they were individuals, and organizations representing other individuals, from different parts of the Caribbean with their own specific historical experience and idiosyncrasies. The "West Indians" were disaggregated, into Barbadians and Jamaicans, and so on. Evidently, not only members of the colonial ruling class made these fine distinctions between the islands and their inhabitants. Comrades on the left seem to have also made their evaluations. Robert Minor, who in the 1920s and 1930s was the most senior Communist Party member directly responsible for anti-racist work, made some similar observations. In a remarkable document written on Marcus Garvey in 1925, Minor noted:

> A surprisingly large proportion of Jamaicans is found among the men and women who have become prominent in American Negro organizations which profess more or less to recognize the class line in the social struggle. Find a Negro speaker on a soap-box in a New York street who is talking something else than the white ruling class philosophy of the Republican party, and very frequently you will recognize the English accent of the Jamaican. When the Jamaicans first came in fairly large numbers, there was a wave of prejudice against what some jealous American Negro leaders called the "monkey-chasers" with the British accent; but that prejudice has been diminished by time and contact. Today the Jamaican Negro plays a considerable part in the life of the black masses in the big American towns.
>
> And as it turned out, it was a Jamaican who became the most widely-known Negro in America of the present day, in the role of mass leadership. Better-known Negroes there are in books, and in literary and artistic circles, but the best-known among the toiling, unliterary masses is a man from Jamaica: Marcus Garvey.[64]

Bearing the foregoing in mind, it is not only possible but probable that the commitment to radicalism amongst Caribbeans in New York was not at all evenly spread, *regardless* of provenance, as we are led to believe. Indeed, there is strong evidence indicating correlation between island provenance and different political responses in America. Nor is the pattern confined only to those who migrated to America. It is noticeable in the earlier Caribbean experience in Panama and elsewhere in Central America, and later in Britain as well. This is an issue that has hardly been looked at by scholars, even though there are interesting anecdotes and asides. It cannot be delved into here. Yet its further exploration will not only add depth to the understanding of the migrant experience, it will also throw new and valuable light upon the history and sociology of the individual territories in which the migrants have their roots. It is remarkable what one can learn about the different islands of the Caribbean by observing the behavior and the culture of Jamaicans, Barbadians, Trinidadians, Kittians, Guyanese, Grenadians, and others, when they are forced to live side by side in a new environment, be it in Oriente province in Cuba, the Canal Zone in Panama, London or Leeds in Britain, Brooklyn or Miami in the United

States. Not only is it in the diaspora that fellow Caribbeans learn about their similarities and differences, it is also *only* in the diaspora that some of these similarities and differences are ever knowable at all. How else would one know for sure about the coping strategies of Caribbeans in hostile environments away from home except when they are in such environments? How else would we be able to observe the patterned responses?[65]

5

Dimensions and Main Currents of Caribbean Radicalism in America: Hubert Harrison, the African Blood Brotherhood, and the UNIA

Caribbean migrants were indeed present in socialist and black national-ist organizations in numbers well out of proportion to their weight within the American population. Moreover, many held leadership positions within such movements. Caribbeans were in conspicuous evidence within the Socialist and Communist Parties as well as within black nationalist associations such as the Universal Negro Improvement Association. With an estimated membership running into millions globally, the UNIA was the largest black organization the world had ever known.

No one knows what precise proportion of the membership of the Socialist and Communist Parties or the UNIA was of Caribbean—or any other—origin. There are, not surprisingly, no comprehensive or reliable figures disaggregating the membership of these organizations on the basis of race or national origin.[1] There is, however, evidence pertaining to these matters that is good and strong. Contemporaries were insistent that Caribbean membership in the UNIA in the 1920s, especially in New York City, substantially exceeded the Caribbean population's weight of 21.4, 20.0 and 0.7 percent of the black population in Manhattan, New York City, and the United States, respectively.[2] The first black members of the Communist Party of the United States were Caribbeans. And Caribbean conspicuousness among its black members in the party was to continue up to the witch-hunts of the 1950s when leading Caribbeans such as Ferdinand Smith (Jamaica) and Claudia Jones (Trinidad) were deported.[3] But again, there are no precise figures as to how many of the black members in Harlem—for instance, in the 1930s when black membership of the Com-munist Party peaked[4]—were Afro-American and how many were of Carib-bean origin. However, from the uncontradicted and repeated testimonies of contemporaries and other forms of qualitative evidence, one is more than inclined to believe that the proportion of the black membership comprising Caribbeans exceeded the 16.7 percent and 17.7 percent that the latter constituted of the black population in New York City and Manhattan, respectively, in 1930. There is also strong evidence suggesting that a disproportionately high percentage of the *membership*—its founders and leaders are known to have been Caribbean almost to a person—of the African Blood Brotherhood in the United States was Caribbean.

Any discussion of Caribbean involvement in radical movements in the early part of the twentieth century must properly begin with the remarkable Hubert Henry Harrison. A. Philip Randolph called him the "Father of Harlem Radicalism."[5] And as such, a tradition began with Harrison. Significantly, the radical current that Harrison embodied bifurcated into two powerful, but unequal, streams by the beginning of the 1920s. The first was a black socialist one, and the other, black nationalist. A. Philip Randolph and the *Messenger* magazine that he edited with Chandler Owen exemplified the black socialist tradition, while Marcus Garvey and the Universal Negro Improvement Association exemplified the black nationalist and more powerful stream. Harrison's pioneering role in what became known as the New Negro radicalism of the 1920s can hardly be overstated. He exercised a profound influence upon the intellectual and political development of Harlem's first generation of black radicals. Yet there is no biography of Harrison. His two books have never been reprinted. Although his name is gradually becoming more widely known, history has not been kind to him. Seldom has a person been so influential, esteemed, even revered in one period of history and so thoroughly unremembered in the space of a generation. Harrison, as we will see, deserves better than that. It is for these reasons, along with his profound contribution to the Caribbean radical tradition in the United States, that he commands especial attention here.

Born on the tiny island of St Croix in the Virgin Islands on April 27, 1883, Harrison, whose father had substantial landholding on the island was orphaned and impoverished at fifteen. Having travelled the world as a cabin boy on a ship for a year, young Hubert migrated to New York in 1900, where he joined his older sister. There he worked at a succession of menial jobs: hotel hall boy, messenger, elevator operator. He was, however, possessed of outstanding intellectual gifts, which were evident and remarked upon before he left the Caribbean. Graduating from night school in New York, his brilliant accomplishments—attained under the most difficult of circumstances—gained exceptional public notice: "Speaker's Medal to Negro Student: The Board of Education Finds a Genius in a West Indian Night Pupil," ran one newspaper report. Harrison, whom the newspaper described as of "inky blackness," was said to be "exceptionally thorough" in Latin, English literature, and ancient history. Harrison excelled academically, the reporter noted, through "perseverance and study at night." He was "employed all day, and while at school was compelled to remain away two nights of the school week because of his duties." But despite the handicap, in his final examinations for the diploma—exams that his teacher, Professor Henry Carr, described as "rigid"—Harrison, in Carr's words, "passed perfect at 100 percent, the only student in the class having that rating." Professor Carr, in one of those horrible but well-meaning, backhanded compliments, described Harrison as "the most remarkable Negro I had ever met." Carr predicted that Harrison "will be heard from if learning has anything to do with success."[6]

Unable to afford college, Harrison took and passed with ease the Post Office examination and worked there for four years. (A clerical job at the Post Office was one of the most prestigious and financially rewarding jobs a black person could hope for then.) From the earliest days of his arrival in New York, Harrison had devoted himself to the study of African and African American history, the social sciences, literature, as well as keeping thoroughly abreast of developments in the natural sciences. Harrison was a polymath with unbounded intellectual interests. His friends claimed that he frequently read up to six books a day, and often slept only two or three hours per night.[7] He soon became legendary for his encyclopedic knowledge and outstanding gift of oratory. In his time, he was the most famous and effective of the street-corner orators of New York City—in Harlem as well as downtown, where he lectured at Wall Street. From his studies, Harrison had become seriously interested in socialism and in 1909 he joined the Socialist Party, whose leadership immediately recognized and utilized his talents. He was one of their most effective orators and writers.

With a young and growing family to support at the time, Harrison lost his job at the Post Office through the vindictive politics of Booker T. Washington and his cronies. His crime was to have written a letter to the editor of the *New York Sun* criticizing Washington's politics.[8] Charles Anderson, Washington's protégé and New York's most powerful black politician, would see to it that Harrison was punished. "Do you remember Hubert H. Harrison?" Anderson enquired rhetorically, in a letter to Washington.

> He is the man who wrote two nasty articles against you in the New York "Sun." He is a clerk in the Post Office. The Postmaster is my personal friend, as you probably know. Harrison has had charges proffered against him and I think he is liable to be dismissed from the service. If not dismissed, he will get severe punishment. Can you see the hand? I think you can. Please destroy this, that it may not fall under another eye—unless it is Emmett's. I will attend to Harrison. If he escapes me he is a dandy.[9]

Harrison was no dandy and, not long after, Anderson, thoroughly pleased with himself, was able to report to Washington the results of his handiwork:

> I am sure that you will regret to learn that Mr Hubert H. Harrison has been dismissed from his position as clerk in the New York Post Office. I am certain also that you will regret to hear that he is blaming me for his dismissal. As Postmaster Morgan is a *particular personal friend* of mine of long years standing, and as the charge against Mr Harrison was considered (by Harrison) trivial, that

"brother" believes that some sinister influence was at work against him, and that influence was set in operation by me. Well, I can endure the charge with fortitude and good humor. Harrison had a dispute with the Superintendent of the Branch Post Office in which he was employed, and as he had had several of these disputes with this and other Superintendents before, I presume the Postmaster thought it high time to drop him and get a man who would talk less and work more. He is now stumping for the Socialist party, and will probably have plenty of time in the future to learn that God is not good to those who do not behave themselves.[10]

But Anderson and Washington would not escape as lightly as they thought. Harrison's dismissal from the Post Office facilitated his being employed on a full-time basis by the Socialist Party, thus opening up the possibilities for even more "misbehavior". However, after working full-time for the Socialist Party for several years, Harrison resigned in 1914, disgusted by the party's lack of commitment to black workers and the New York leadership's racist treatment of him. Harrison was not blameless in the deterioration of the relations between himself and the Party. He was in fact suspended from the Party for three months for disobeying orders not to participate in a debate. The question debated: "Is Industrial Action more important than Political Action?" was addressed by Harrison in the affirmative, against Party policy. When the Secretary of the Executive Committee wrote, on behalf of the Committee, telling him not to participate in the debate, Harrison scribbled at the bottom of her letter: "Dear Mrs. Sloan: Please tell the Executive Committee to go chase itself. Hubert H. Harrison. P. S. By the way, if my color has anything to do with it this time, I should thank you to let me know." He posted her letter back to her with his comments. In a letter to New York Local dated June 23, 1912, Harrison complained that he had been offered $1.00 a night as a speaker when the year before he was offered $3.00. "I am a much better speaker now than I was then," he wrote. Harrison further pointed out that he knew that some speakers were getting $3.00 a day, and, he said, "since I can render as efficient a service on the stump I don't think that it would be fair to ask me to take less." At his disciplinary hearing he said, according to the minutes, that he treated the Executive Committee with contempt because the Committee was "'picking' at him all the time." Given such evident difficulties, it is hard to imagine why Harrison stayed in the Party as long as he did. It was only after he was suspended in May 1914 that he resigned.[11] He then joined the ranks of William "Big Bill" Haywood's Industrial Workers of the World (IWW) — better known as the Wobblies — attracted by its principled and anti-racist commitment to the working class.

Harrison was the first person to have given a public platform to Marcus Garvey after the latter's arrival in New York in 1916. Harrison's *Voice* ("A Newspaper for The New Negro") first published on the fourth of July 1917 was also the pioneer of the long line of black radical journals which began appearing in New York during and in the immediate aftermath of the First

World War: Randolph's and Owen's *Messenger*, Briggs's *Crusader*, Garvey's *Negro World*, Bridges' *Challenge*, Domingo's *Emancipator*. According to an informed contemporary, Hodge Kirnon, it was Harrison's paper, that "really crystallized the radicalism of the Negro in New York and its environs."[12] In the aftermath of Harrison's untimely death, Kirnon, in an assessment of the man, recalled that the *Voice* was "the first organ to express the new spirit of the Negro. It is to Mr Harrison," he suggested, "that the credit must go for being the first militant apostle of the New Negro. He assisted in molding and directing this new spirit and its accompanying ideals into their most effective channels."[13]

Apart from his many articles and book reviews scattered in the newspapers and journals of the time, from the *New York Times* to the *Negro World*, Harrison also wrote two books and would later edit Garvey's *Negro World*, between 1920 and 1922.[14] In December 1927, during an operation on his ruptured appendix, Harrison died; he was only forty-four years old. "An impoverishment to the community," said Randolph of his untimely departure.[15] Harlem was shocked.

Harrison occupied a very unusual position intellectually and politically. He was a major inspiration for two powerful and seemingly incompatible currents of black radicalism in Harlem: revolutionary socialism, on the one hand, and radical black nationalism, on the other. As suggested earlier, Harrison was, thus, the intellectual father of A. Philip Randolph and the radical socialism of the *Messenger* magazine, as well as that of Marcus Garvey, and the "Race First" black nationalism of the *Negro World*. His twin, but dissimilar, progeny came out of the different phases of Harrison's political career: the early, Socialist and IWW years, and the later, black nationalist, Liberty League of Negro Americans phase. Somewhat ironically, then, both Randolph and Garvey—deadly antagonists during the 1920s—could legitimately claim to be the rightful heirs of Hubert Henry Harrison.

In a fundamental sense, Harrison remained a socialist from the time he discovered Marx to the end of his life. He never wavered from the materialist analysis of society and always felt that the capitalist system could never serve the interests of black people, the most proletarianized layer of the American population. He was vigorous in his denunciation of capitalism as he was rigorous in his analysis of the impact of capitalism on black people. As the Justice Department intelligence reports indicate, and as his own written pronouncements made clear, Hubert Harrison was as ecstatic about the Bolshevik Revolution and its socialist promise as any radical in America. American socialism did not keep faith with Hubert Harrison, Harrison kept faith with socialism. As many black socialists before and after him discovered—including Du Bois—the Socialist Party in America and other formations of the left did not keep faith with the radical egalitarianism of Marx. The Party succumbed to the racist corruption of its American environment. In an editorial in the *Negro World* in 1920, entitled "Race First Versus Class First," Harrison pointed out that even in "the days when the Socialist Party of America was respectable" it permitted color lines to be drawn in the South by its members. The Party, said Harrison, had "no word of official condemnation" for the white Socialists of Tennessee who prevented a leading party spokeswoman in 1912 from lecturing to black people on socialism, either in the same hall with them, or in meetings of their own. The national office of the Party in that same presidential year refused to route Eugene V. Debs in the South because "that Grand Old Man" let it be known that he would not remain silent on the race question while in the South. "They wanted the votes of the South then, and were willing to betray by silence the principles of inter-racial solidarity which they espoused on paper." But as Harrison himself pointed out, there were problems with what the Socialist Party espoused on paper too. He cited, extensively, the majority report of one of the national committees of the Party that came out of a recent—he did not give the precise date—national convention. The report was signed by some of the leading members of the Party. "Race feeling," said the report, "is not so much a result of social as of biological evolution." It went on:

> It does not change essentially with changes of economic systems. It is deeper than any class feeling and will outlast the capitalist system. It persists even after race prejudice has been outgrown. It exists not because the capitalists nurse it for economic reasons, but the capitalists rather have an opportunity to nurse it for economic reasons because it exists as a product of biology. It is bound to play a role in the economics of the future society. If it should not assert itself in open warfare under a Socialist form of society, it will nevertheless lead to a rivalry of races for expansion over the globe as a result of the play of natural and sexual selection.... Class-consciousness must be learned, but race consciousness is inborn and cannot be wholly unlearned....
>
> Where races struggle for the means of life, racial animosities cannot be avoided. Where working people struggle for jobs, self-preservation enforces its decrees. Economic and political considerations lead to racial fights and legislation restricting the invasion of the white man's domain by other races.[16]

It is well that the New Negro should know this, said Harrison, directly addressing the Socialist Party, since it "justifies him in giving you a taste of your own medicine." Referring to himself, Harrison went on to say that "The writer of these lines is also a Socialist; but he refuses in this crisis of the world's history to put either Socialism or your party above the call of his race. And he does this on the very grounds which you yourselves have given in the document quoted above. Also because he is not a fool."[17] Harrison pointed out that he could respect the Socialists of Scandinavia, France, Germany, or England on their record. "But your record," he said to the American Socialists, "so far does not entitle you to the respect of those of us who can see all around a subject. We say Race First, because you have all along insisted on Race First and class after when you didn't need our help."[18] Harrison repeatedly argued that the strategy of Race First emerges from a position of defense, not one of attack. And he spelt this out most clearly in a 1917 programmatic essay, "The New Politics for the New Negro":

> Any man today who aspires to lead the Negro race must set squarely before his face the idea of "Race First." Just as the white men of these and other lands are white men before they are Christians, Anglo-Saxons or Republicans; so the Negroes of this and other lands are intent upon being Negroes before they are Christians, Englishmen, or Republicans.
>
> Sauce for the goose is sauce for the gander. Charity begins at home, and our first duty is to ourselves. It is not what we wish but what we must, that we are concerned with. The world, as it ought to be, is still for us, as for others, the world that does not exist. The world as it is, is the real world, and it is to that real world that we address ourselves. Striving to be men, and finding no effective aid in government or in politics, the Negro of the Western world must follow the path of the Swadesh[i] movement of India and the Sinn Fein movement of Ireland. The meaning of both these terms is "ourselves first."[19]

Harrison's black nationalism was the last resort of a black socialist in a racist land; a land of white workers and black workers, where race is elevated above social class in politics as well as social life. "Every movement for the extension of democracy here has broken down as soon as it reached the color line," he told his party comrades in 1912. "Political democracy declared that 'all men are created equal,' meant only white men. The Christian church found that the brotherhood of man did not include God's bastard children. The public school system proclaimed that the school house was the backbone of democracy—'for white people only,' and the civil service says that Negroes must keep their place—at the bottom." Harrison was a reluctant black nationalist. He was an intellectual steeped in the work of Marx, willingly acknowledging its analytical power in understanding the perplexing world in which he lived. He shared in the vision of classical socialism. As late as 1920 he told the Socialist Party, in the pages of the *Negro World*, no less, that if they send anyone (black or white) up to Harlem to put "the cause of Karl Marx, freed from the admixture of rancor and hatred of the Negro's own defensive racial propaganda, you may find that it will have as a good a chance of gaining adherents as any other political creed."[20] Harrison was, in essence, a black socialist, waiting for a better day that he feared would never come, working in the meantime as a black nationalist. He was, in short, like the later Claude McKay, a socialist who was also a black nationalist.

Such was Harrison's ideological evolution and position, which helped to explain his black nationalist and black socialist progeny among the black intelligentsia of Harlem. He was less successful with the masses. They loved him, were enchanted and stunned by his learning, they claimed him as their own—their own "Black Socrates"; they were proud of his genius, appreciated his prodigious skills as a teacher and the wonderful news and knowledge he brought them; they loved his sense of humor and the ease with which he handled an audience; they loved the fact that he loved them. But most black Harlemites preferred Garvey's magic, to which they surrendered. Harrison was not a good organizer (certainly not as good as Garvey); he was not a leader of men; he did not suffer fools gladly, largely because he was so extraordinarily wise; he was somewhat arrogant and made powerful enemies, black and white, who harmed him. Within two years of Garvey's arrival in Harlem, that is, by 1918, Harrison was eclipsed as the most popular and influential radical in Harlem and he never regained his political pre-eminence; indeed, he later worked for Garvey's paper, though he never joined his movement; he grumbled behind Garvey's back, and he even grumbled about Garvey in Garvey's own paper. He tried not to look up as Garvey rose above him. Furthermore, Harrison seemed to have developed a certain notoriety as a philanderer and this diminished his standing and popularity. McKay, in his autobiography, described Harrison as "erotically ... very indiscriminate," and in a 1921 government intelligence report it was claimed that "One of the chief reasons why Harrison, who is really a very intelligent and highly educated man and scholar, has failed in nearly all his undertakings is said to be his abnormal sexualism, in spite of the fact that he is the father o[f] several children."[21] Garvey, disciplined and driven, in marked contrast, had little time for anything that was not directly connected with what he regarded as the redemption of Africa—and this included his family.[22]

One of the most distinctive features of Harrison's political thought, compared to that of his black radical (socialist and black nationalist) contemporaries and his black nationalist predecessors of the nineteenth century, was his confidence in and humility before the peoples and cultures of Africa. Much of his time was spent in the study of the continent's history and culture. His knowledge on this, as well as on many other subjects, was described as encyclopedic. And this hard-earned knowledge—grounded in the best scientific data available—coupled with his quietly proud identification with the African continuities in his native St Croix, had developed in Harrison a respect for the African past and the African potential that the overwhelming majority of his contemporaries simply did not have. In Harrison's outlook there is none of the arrogant New World "civilization-ism" that one finds, for instance, in Garvey's pronouncements; none of the "civilizing the backward tribes of Africa," as Garvey and the UNIA had aimed and promised to do.[23] For Harrison, Africa was primarily a teacher; not a primitive unschooled child in need of "civilization" and instruction. His unrelenting and systematic study of the African past had convinced him of the mendacity of the ideologies of European colonialism and racism. "[L]et us American Negroes," said Harrison,

> go to Africa, live among the natives and LEARN WHAT THEY HAVE TO TEACH US (for they have much to teach us). Let us go there—not in the coastlands,—but in

the interior, in Nigeria and Nyasaland; let us study engineering and physics, chemistry and commerce, agriculture and industry; let us learn more of nitrates, of copper, rubber and electricity; so will we know why Belgium, France, England and Germany want to be in Africa. Let us begin by studying the scientific works of the African explorers and stop reading and believing the silly slush which ignorant missionaries put into our heads about the alleged degradation of our people in Africa. Let us learn to know Africa and Africans so well that every educated Negro will be able at a glance to put his hand on the map of Africa and tell where to find Jolofs, Ekoisi, Mandingoes, Yorubas, Bechuanas or Basutos and can tell something of their marriage customs, their property laws, their agriculture and system of worship. For not until we can do this will it be seemly for us to pretend to be anxious about their political welfare.[24]

And here again is Harrison writing in September 1919:

If we are ever to enter into the confraternity of colored peoples it should seem the duty of our Negro colleges to drop their silly smatterings of "little Latin and less Greek" and establish modern courses in Hausa and Arabic, for these are the living languages of millions of our brethren in modern Africa. Courses in Negro history and the culture of West African peoples, at least, should be given in every college that claims to be an institution of learning for Negroes. Surely an institution of learning for Negroes should not fail to be also an institution of Negro learning.[25]

Harrison was light years ahead of his time, which largely explains his pre-eminence as an intellectual, and accounts for a substantial part of his relative failure as a politician.

All of the many black radical intellectuals who met Harrison, loved, admired, and deferred to him. "Hubert Harrison was far more advanced than we were," recalled Randolph. "He was older, and he had a very fine mind [−] a good logician [−] quite analytical, and he had a mind that reached in all areas of human knowledge, but he was poor. He had no clothes of any consequence. This was his life . . . and when Marcus Garvey came here, he planned a meeting for him." Randolph described Harrison's English as impeccable, and the co-founder of the *Messenger* remembered almost six decades after the event that when, as two budding black radicals, he and Chandler Owen first met Harrison, the latter wanted to know "What are you going to do?"

We said, "We want to develop a street forum comparable to yours. We don't plan to have any competition, but we want to extend your work, what you're doing."[26]

As W. A. Domingo, another outstanding black radical, stated: "[B]efore [Garvey] there was Hubert Harrison. He was a brilliant man, a great intellectual, a Socialist and highly respected. Garvey like the rest of us [New Negro radicals] followed Hubert Harrison." Richard B. Moore, who, as an orator in twenties Harlem was equalled in eloquence only by Garvey and Harrison himself, said that "More than any other man of his time,

[Harrison] inspired and educated the masses of Afro-Americans then flocking into Harlem."[27]

Harrison's reach went well beyond black Harlem and its New Negro radicals of the time. The young Henry Miller heard him speak at one of his downtown venues and immediately became an ardent fan. Fifty years later, Miller, who was to become a successful novelist, fondly recollected his "quondam idol, Hubert Harrison," and how much he had learned "standing at the foot of his soapbox in Madison Square." On his way to hear another of his idols, W. E. B. Du Bois, Miller recalled having delivered a "long-drawn-out rhapsody" to his friends about Harrison:

> There was no one in those days, I told them candidly, who could hold a candle to Hubert Harrison. With a few well-directed words he had the ability to demolish any opponent. He did it neatly and smoothly too, "with kid gloves," so to speak. I described the wonderful way he smiled, his easy assurance, the great sculptured head which he carried on his shoulders like a lion. I wondered aloud if he had not come of royal blood, if he had not been the descendant of some great African monarch. Yes, he was a man who electrified one by his mere presence. Beside him the other speakers, the white ones, looked like pygmies, not only physically but culturally, spiritually. Some of them, the ones who were paid to foment trouble, carried on like epileptics, always wrapped in the Stars and Stripes, to be sure. Hubert Harrison, on the other hand, no matter what the provocation, always retained his self-possession, his dignity. He had a way of placing the back of his hand on his hip, his trunk tilted forward, his ears cocked to catch every last word the questioner, or the heckler put to him. Well he knew how to bide his time! When the tumult had subsided there would come that broad smile of his, a broad, good-natured grin, and he would answer his man— always fair and square, always full on, like a broadside. Soon everyone would be laughing, everyone but the poor imbecile who had dared to put the question. . . .[28]

Even a white Southerner, John T. Carroll, though burdened with the usual freight of Dixie prejudice, was moved to write to the press in praise of Harrison. According to Carroll, after hearing Harrison's lectures in 1914, he was compelled to "a change of conviction on . . . the subject of the Negro in America and especially in New York." Carroll explained how white people "so often regard the [Negro] race as inferior to ourselves that it comes as a shock to see any of them on plane of intellectual parity with us." He was at first "angry," but by the end of the first Harrison lecture he heard he had "discovered with amazement" that he had been "interested, charmed, and instructed." Carroll went back three more times to hear Harrison lecture on anthropology, economics, and religion and felt "thankful to New York for widening my mental horizon." He was astonished that such a "large and respectable looking white audience" keenly attended Harrison's lectures, turning out "every Sunday afternoon to listen to a man who is not merely colored but black. And they seem to glory in it, as I have almost come to do myself."[29]

Claude McKay paints a charming portrait of Harrison. "He lectured on free-thought, socialism and racialism, and sold books. He spoke precisely and clearly, with fine intelligence and masses of facts. He was very black, compact of figure, and his head resembled an African replica of Socrates." McKay, as well as other contemporaries, remarked upon Harrison's great, "ebony hard" sense of humor. According to McKay, it was Harrison who was responsible for deciphering the acronym NAACP to mean the "National Association for the Advancement of *Certain* People." McKay, fondly recalls that, on one occasion, having told him a funny story, Harrison "exploded in his large sugary black African way, which sounded like the rustling of dry bamboo leaves agitated by the wind."[30]

Harrison's lampooning of the NAACP did not prevent an official of that organization, William Pickens, from falling under his intellectual spell. Pickens, an Afro-American orator of some standing himself, and, indeed, a winner of the prestigious Ten Eyck Prize for Oratory at Yale University, wrote in 1923:

> It is not possible that Socrates could have outdone Hubert Harrison in making the most commonplace subject interesting. Here is a plain black man who can speak more easily, effectively and interestingly on a greater variety of subjects than any other man we have ever met, even in any of the great universities. We do not like a platitude or a hackneyed phrase, but we know nothing better than to say that he is a "walking cyclopedia" of current human facts, and more especially of history and literature.[31]

Even the agents of the state sent to spy on him ended up admiring Harrison—if only grudgingly at times. The local Harlem spook, "P-138," was struck in particular by Harrison's gift of recall. He reported to his paymasters: "[Harrison] got his education chiefly from reading in the library and has a wonderful memory of the books he reads, being able to give the contents almost word for word after reading a book once. He has a public school education." A couple of days later, special agent "P-138" once again reported on a street corner meeting held by Harrison in which the latter, in the aftermath of the Tulsa, Oklahoma, race riot, eloquently defended the right of black people to arm themselves and resist attacks. Speaking to a large crowd, Harrison, wrote the agent with underlined words, was "loudly applauded, after which he took up a nice collection and sold a few books."[32]

Undoubtedly, the most surprising source of compliments for Hubert Harrison was British intelligence. In an extraordinary document emanating from the British Home Office (Directorate of Intelligence), entitled "Unrest Among the Negroes," special and, in places, astonishingly perceptive consideration was given to Harrison. He is, said the report,

> a scholar of broad learning and a radical propagandist. Most of his time is spent in lecture tours in cities having large negro populations. He is not affiliated with any political party and frequently criticises all of them. He differs from other

negro radicals in that his methods are purely scholastic. He typifies the professor lecturing to his classes rather than a soap box orator appealing to popular clamour. One of his favourite themes is to review the history of the exploitation of Africa, India and other countries by the Caucasian races. His lectures on this subject are always interspersed with sarcastic and ironical references to what he terms "the brazen hypocrisy" of the white races, especially the Anglo-Saxon. He also makes frequent attacks upon the Church, asserting that its influence has been inimical to the progress of humanity by enslaving the minds of the people with foolish dogmas and theories that will not bear the light of reason. He pictures the heads of the Church as being in league with the master capitalists in a pact to plunder the proletariat of all nations.

Thoroughly versed in history and sociology, Mr Harrison is a very convincing speaker and his influence is considered to be more effective than that of any other individual radical, because his subtle propaganda, delivered in scholarly language and backed by the facts of history, carries an appeal to the more thoughtful and conservative class of negroes who could not be reached by the "cyclone" methods of the extreme radicals. As a matter of fact, Mr Harrison's lectures might well be considered as a preparatory school for radical thought in that they prepare the minds of conservative negroes to receive and accept the more extreme doctrines of Socialism. Without any deliberate attempt to serve in such a capacity, he is the drill master training recruits for the Socialist Army led by the extreme radicals, Messrs. Owen and Randolph. Mr Harrison's lectures are always well attended and he ranks as one of the very important factors in the dissemination of radical thought among negroes.

And all this in a report dated October 7, 1919.[33]

But the *New York Amsterdam News*'s kind and astute editorial tribute to Harrison in the aftermath of his untimely death—more than the words of British spies—provides a fitting close to the discussion of the man.

The most widely read man in Harlem, he took his learning to the great mass of the people. One of the most familiar sights of Harlem was Hubert Harrison on a soapbox on Seventh [A]venue. Using none of the tricks of the street fakir, he drew hundreds of hearers by the force of his ideas and passed his erudition on to them. In this way he reached and influenced thousands of people who never read a book. A writer generally has a larger audience than a speaker, but Harrison reversed the rule.

In his street speeches he spoke to the Negro in language that the Negro could understand. He decried the slavish imitation of other races, he told the Negro to think for himself, he glorified in the beauty of the Negro woman, he proclaimed that the Negroes had within them a mighty spring of power and called upon them to release it, he used his scholarship to expose the countless fallacies of the white race about the Negro and itself. No one on the street asked him to speak, but once he was started no one wanted him to stop.

Like most original thinkers, he stood alone. He belonged to none of the uplift organizations because he refused to be fettered by any policy but his own, which was to dig out the truth and proclaim it on the highway without fear. He could have had a smug income if he had been more deferential to the powers that want a Negro leader to go so far and no further. But, like Socrates, he bowed to nobody, and that was his strength.[34]

Thus, Hubert Henry Harrison, the man from the Virgin Islands—the most distinguished, if not the most well-known, Caribbean radical in the United States in the early twentieth century.

Of all the radical projects of the 1920s, the one with the most conspicuous Caribbean involvement was the Garvey movement—the Universal Negro Improvement Association. Some of its detractors have often claimed that the UNIA in New York was a wholly Caribbean affair. It was not. But it is also evident that a significant segment of its leadership, and a substantial proportion—although the precise magnitude has not and cannot be determined—of its rank and file members, were of Caribbean origin.

According to one calculation, of 75 UNIA "leaders"—"International officers, writers on the *Negro World*, officials of the Black Star Line and the Negro Factories Corporation, and heads of leading divisions"—36 were from the Caribbean (including 15 Jamaicans and 5 from the francophone Caribbean), 8 from Africa, 1 "from India via the West Indies," and 19 Afro-Americans (including 15 from the South).[35] It should be noted that the Caribbean leaders were not all located in the Caribbean proper. That they were also in New York City is commonplace knowledge. What is less well known or acknowledged is that these Caribbean Garveyites could be found leading divisions in places like Boston, Philadelphia, Pittsburgh, Gary, Baltimore, Newport News, Miami, Detroit, and as far away from the east coast as Los Angeles.[36] This helps to account for the fact that although over 78 percent (842 out of 1072) of the UNIA branches worldwide between 1921 and 1933 were located in the United States, only 25 percent of the organization's leaders were Afro-Americans compared to 48 percent Afro-Caribbeans.[37]

The leadership of the UNIA, like that of most organizations, is easily identified, counted, categorized, and analyzed. Analyzing the membership is a far more difficult and challenging affair. That type of detailed analysis will not be done here, nor is it necessary or even appropriate to undertake such a task for the present purposes. Suffice it to reiterate that it is more than likely that a disproportionately large element of the UNIA membership in New York City, from 1917 onwards, was of Caribbean origin. All the contemporary commentators—some, admittedly, for highly dubious and self-serving purposes—remarked upon the conspicuous and significant Caribbean presence among the UNIA membership in Harlem.[38] One FBI agent who went to a Garvey meeting at Carnegie Hall on August 25, 1919, reported an attendance of "about 2500 composed with but few exceptions of forei[gn] Negroes, men and women and no children, from the West Indies, Central America and South America, etc."[39] The Afro-American writer Wallace Thurman, a keen observer of the Harlem scene during the twenties, went so far as to describe "the West Indian population of Harlem as a nucleus" of the Garvey movement. This statement is simultaneously an exaggeration and an understatement. Exaggeration because it suggests a far too all-embracing incorporation of Caribbean Harlemites in the Garvey movement; not every Caribbean resident in Harlem was a Garveyite. On the contrary, some of Garvey's most formidable critics were to be found among his Caribbean compatriots. Thurman's remark is an understatement as the noun "nucleus"—by all, including the most authoritative, accounts— diminishes the real weight and extent of the Caribbean contingent within the UNIA in Harlem. If the Caribbeans in Harlem constituted a nucleus it must have been an inordinately large one.[40] Another astute contemporary observer, Ira Reid, while disagreeing with those who described the UNIA as a whole as a "West Indian Movement," nevertheless suggested that this "was actually true in New York City and Boston and to a certain extent in Philadelphia."[41]

Although the leadership of the UNIA was disproportionately Caribbean in origin, the organization as a whole—and certainly the UNIA in the United States—was not a "West Indian Movement" in any meaningful sense. The overwhelming majority of the UNIA's membership in America was Afro-American. Indeed, almost 60 percent of its branches (with Louisiana leading the nation with 75) were located in the South, areas with virtually no Caribbean presence (see Table 5.1, page 365). And it was in the Southern states that the organization, with its loyal Afro-American base, operated most smoothly, if clandestinely, during the turbulent years of UNIA in-fighting after the indictment of Garvey in 1922. Garvey recognized and fully acknowledged the importance of his Afro-American supporters. In 1930, some two years after deportation from the United States back to Jamaica, the *Pittsburgh Courier* gave Garvey the opportunity to tell his own story in a series of some thirteen articles. In his final instalment of May 30, he bade a fond and heartfelt farewell to Afro-America, the rock of the UNIA:

> I cannot close these series without returning my personal thanks to the millions of American friends who have rallied around the Universal Negro Improvement Association. But for the splendid loyalty of the American Negroes the Universal Negro Improvement Association would be still in its swaddling clothes. If the movement comes to anything it is due to the stalwart, loyal and race-loving American Negro who allows nothing to divide him from the truth. It is such a Negro that has helped me to make the Universal Negro Improvement Association and if I live and my name lives in history, this will be due to the help of my American brothers. They must share the credit, the glory, [as] well as I. No one can take it away from them.[42]

They, the Afro-Americans, were "the real dreamers," Claude McKay wrote to a friend in 1932. He felt that they invested more in the UNIA, emotionally as well as financially, than their Caribbean counterparts. In a rather harsh formulation—one unkind, simultaneously, to both Afro-Americans and Afro-Caribbeans—McKay declared that Afro-Americans "pursue[d] the chimera of a political utopia for Negroes and they were the ones who bought the fake stocks while the West Indians did the shouting."[43] There is some truth to it, but McKay's remark is hyperbolic. There were thousands and thousands of Caribbean stock holders in the Black Star Line and they dreamt no less passionately than anyone else about Garvey's new Africa. Moreover, the intelligence reports always suggested that the money for the UNIA came largely from the Northern cities such as New York and Philadelphia where incomes were higher than they were in the South. It is possible, however, that Southern Garveyites, compared to their Northern counterparts, gave a greater proportion of their income to the UNIA. Despite the region's importance to American Garveyism, we know relatively little about the operation of the UNIA in the South.[44] Our view of Garveyism is dominated by the massive August conventions, the parades, regalia and speeches all emanating from New York. And our image of Garveyism at its height—what some would regard as the heroic Garveyism of 1919 to 1923—is extraordinarily determined by a black photographer sympathetic to the movement, James VanDerZee. But what happened outside the media capital of the world? How and why did Louisiana have so many branches? What happened in the little hamlets of the South? How did Garveyism survive in the belly of Dixie? Robert Hill and his colleagues on the *Marcus Garvey and Universal Negro Improvement Association Papers* have gathered together through an astonishing feat of scholarship and recovery much of the essential elements, in the form of documents, for answering these questions. Despite the important regional studies of the UNIA carried out by scholars such as Emory Tolbert, C. Boyd James, and Mary Gambrell Rolinson, the analysis has hardly begun and our understanding of Garveyism remains fundamentally New York-centered.[45]

The UNIA was the largest and most powerful black nationalist organization the world has ever known. It gathered under its large black umbrella the scattered children of Africa with those at home. Kano (Nigeria), Sydney (Australia), Los Angeles (California), as well as Manchester, in the industrial north of England, were some of the places that were homes to UNIA chapters and divisions (see Table 5.2, page 366). At its height it perhaps had as many as four million members and close supporters world-wide, approximately half of whom were in the United States alone. Undeniably, it did more than any other organization to advertise, in the most eye-catching manner, the suffering and yearning of Africa and its diaspora in the Age of Imperialism. The UNIA was, for much of the African diaspora and for masses of people in Africa, a gigantic beacon of hope promising to bring to an end the long night of their oppression. And this counted.

Moreover, the UNIA left an astonishingly rich legacy in America that endures to this day. It schooled and inspired future leaders of Africa and the Caribbean. The decolonization struggles in the aftermath of the Second

World War in Africa and the Caribbean have been organically tied to the efforts of Garvey and the UNIA. Kwame Nkrumah of Ghana has most generously and symbolically acknowledged this debt. He revealed in his autobiography that while a student in the United States in the 1930s he read Hegel, Marx, Engels, Lenin, and Mazzini.

> The writings of these men did much to influence me in my revolutionary ideas and activities, and Karl Marx and Lenin particularly impressed me as I felt sure that their philosophy was capable of solving these problems. But I think that of all the literature that I studied, the book that did more than any other to fire my enthusiasm was *Philosophy and Opinions of Marcus Garvey* published in 1923.

Nkrumah told his audience at the closing session of the All-African Peoples' Conference in Accra in 1958 that "Long before many of us were even conscious of our own degradation, Marcus Garvey fought for African national and racial equality." Nkrumah, who led Ghana to independence in 1957, named the Ghanaian merchant marine after the UNIA's shipping line, the Black Star Line; a black star was placed in the center of the country's flag, where it remains today.[46]

The history of the UNIA, its astonishing rise and dramatic collapse, is well known and documented.[47] But, despite—and in some respects, *because* of— the remarkable advance in Garvey scholarship over the last two decades, significant confusion (old and new) surrounds Garvey and the UNIA still. New, exciting and unanswered questions—born partly out of our growth in knowledge, partly out of our changing preoccupations and thinking— present themselves. These, in turn, help to bring into sharp relief dark and vast areas of profound ignorance in need of scholarly exploration and illumination.

The experience, position, and role of women within the movement are key areas of relative neglect. Despite notable contributions of late, much remains to be done. For example, despite the outstanding contributions of women such as Henrietta Vinton Davis, Maymie Turpeau de Mena, and Amy Jacques Garvey, none of them have been honored with a biography. The fact that some of the scholars who have done work on women in the movement sharply disagree with one another in the presentation and interpretation of evidence—that, put side by side, their arguments are, in large measure, incommensurate and contradictory—is even more reason for further probing and analysis.[48] We still have much to learn about the operation of all-female auxillaries like the Black Cross Nurses, and the Universal African Motor Corps, which had memberships that must have run into tens of thousands in the United States alone. What role, in practice, did the "Lady President," which each division was constitutionally required to have, perform? How did Garveyism affect the lives of women Garveyites?

Notwithstanding lacunae and scholarly differences, however, beyond dispute is the fact that women, individually and in groups, made crucial contributions to the formation, development, and nourishment of the UNIA. So what can we safely say about the position and experience of women in the UNIA?

First, after Marcus Garvey himself, a woman, Amy Ashwood (who Garvey later married), was the first member and indeed co-founder of the UNIA when it was launched in Kingston in 1914.[49] When Garvey shifted his headquarters to New York in 1918, three of the six directors of the UNIA were women: Irene M. Blackstone, Carrie B. Mero, and Harriet Rogers. And a majority, eight of the fifteen, of the initial subscribers to the African Communities League (the sister organization to the UNIA) when it was incorporated three weeks later were women.[50]

But despite the formal and concrete backing that women, from the very start, gave the UNIA, their relative importance diminished within the organization as the latter grew. Indeed, the role of women within the UNIA declined in inverse proportion to the size of the movement. Thus, at its height, the UNIA had only one woman, Henrietta Vinton Davis, among its top leaders. It was in the twilight years of the UNIA that women's position improved. Madame de Mena rose to join Davis at the top levels of the UNIA. Amy Jacques Garvey, who became Garvey's second wife, also acquired considerable informal as well as formal power during Garvey's incarceration in the Atlanta Federal Penitentiary between February 1925 and November 1927. Women resisted the subordinate role, and separate and gendered spheres alotted to them within the movement. This was sharply expressed for the first time publicly at the 1922 convention.

We may never know whether it was due to excessive patience, reluctance, even fear, or a combination of some or all three, but for some reason or reasons the women at the 1922 convention made their move on the last afternoon of a thirty-one-day affair. How much significance we should attribute to the fact that Garvey was not in the room when one of the women rose from the audience to speak on women's dissatisfaction in the UNIA is also unclear. (He entered and assumed the chair while the discussion was in progress.) We may also never know why the "Woman Question" was not an item put on the agenda in the first place. In any case, according to the convention report, "feeling that they had not been given proper recognition during all the former sessions and being determined that they would be heard before the convention was closed," Mrs Victoria Turner of St Louis rose on behalf of the disgruntled women. She "craved the indulgence" of the meeting to submit a set of resolutions drafted and signed by the majority of the women delegates. She was granted the opportunity to present the resolutions:

> We, the women of the U.N.I.A. and A.C.L. know that no race can rise higher than its women. We need women in the important places of the organization to help refine and mold public sentiment, realizing the colossal program of this

great organization, and as we are determined to reclaim our own land, Africa, we have resolved to submit the following recommendations:

1. That a woman be the head of the Black Cross Nurses and Motor Corps and have absolute control over those women, and this shall not conflict with the Legions.

2. That women be given more recognition by being placed on every committee, so that she may learn more of the salient workings of the various committees.

3. That more women be placed in the important offices and field work of the association.

4. That women be given initiative positions, so that they may formulate constructive plans to elevate our women.

5. That Lady Henrietta Vinton Davis be empowered to formulate plans with the sanction of the President-General so that the Negro Women all over the world can function without restriction from the men.[51]

The chair opened the floor to other women delegates. A large number expressed their feelings on the status of women in the UNIA. The general feeling expressed was that women "were curbed to a great extent in the exercise of their initiative powers in formulating plans which would make for the good of the organization." Mrs Morgan from Chicago claimed that the women in the convention "had been completely ignored and were not even given the chance to second a motion." The women, she said, were not willing to "sit silently by and let the men take all the glory while they gave the advice." She was not in favor of women "standing behind and pushing the men; they wanted to be placed in some of the executive positions because they felt they were entitled to them." She further called for women to be put in the field as commissioners to organize the women and put them to work. Mrs Hogue, another delegate from Chicago, perhaps was anxious that Mrs Morgan might have been misunderstood. She said it was not the intention of the women to "get in the way of the men or to take the men's places, but they wanted to be at their side." Mrs Scott from Detroit said she found that "whenever women began to function in the organization the men presumed to dictate to them." Mrs Robinson from New Orleans claimed that she was the only woman commissioner in the field. In this capacity, she travelled throughout the South. From her "considerable experience" she did not think the women should take on this kind of work "if they wanted to hold the proper respect of the men. She believed that if the women sent out in the field were not strong women, they would tend to lower the morale of the organization." Mrs Willis from New York disagreed. She was a field representative and had travelled throughout the country, including as the only woman speaker who went with Garvey on his tour across the United States. She believed that the women were as competent as the men to be field representatives and "they could so conduct themselves in their travels to command the respect of the men." Five other women speakers were mentioned in the official report of the session, but their remarks were not recorded.

Garvey, who had returned to the hall and resumed the chair, responded by saying that the organization recognized women; that it was "the only organization, he believed, where a woman was found in the Executive Council." He claimed that

> If there was any difference made in the local divisions, it was not the fault of the policy of the Universal Negro Improvement Association, but it was the fault of individuals. He did not see any reasons for the resolutions, as the women already had the power they were asking for under the constitution. However, it would do no harm to pass the resolutions in a modified form. He suggested that resolution four be changed to the effect that the women be encouraged to formulate plans, and that resolution five be changed to the effect that the women while functioning without restriction by the men would not be interpreted to mean a severance of the men from the women in the work of the organization.

The convention followed Garvey's suggestions and passed the resolutions as he had amended them.[52] In short, the resolutions were shorn of their small horns, made pathetically inoffensive and hardly resembled those bravely presented by Mrs Turner. The seething discontent among many women within the organization was, nonetheless, brought to the fore. The long-term impact of the women's testimonies at the 1922 convention is hard to judge. But when Amy Jacques Garvey started her women's page less than two years later she must have felt the powerful moral authority and support of these women behind her protesting pen. Indeed, she revealed in her column that it was due to "the repeated requests by our women to express themselves on all matters relating to humanity at large, and our race in particular, the Managing Editor [Garvey] saw fit to allot us [a page in the *Negro World*] for the purpose."[53] No doubt the increasing number of women in leading positions in the late 1920s was partly due to the growth in self-confidence and organization among the women of the UNIA that found expression at the 1922 convention.

Although each division had a Lady President, she was constitutionally— contrary to Garvey's response to the protesting women—subordinate to and had to report to her male counterpart, the Male President, who, in turn, was accountable to the overall President-General (Garvey) of the UNIA.[54] In some divisions, however, the male and female presidents operated on a basis of equality. The Black Cross Nurses and the Universal African Motor Corps were relatively lowly units within the hierarchy of the UNIA, but generated a strong sense of *esprit de corps* among its members, the women developing a powerful sisterhood among themselves. Women also were given and exercised considerable authority over the Juveniles, which extended their influence over the young.[55]

It would be a mistake, then, to assume that because of the relatively subordinate positions allocated them that UNIA women were pathetic and helpless. Mariamne Samad, born of Garveyite parents in Harlem, remembered that these women exercised considerable influence, if not formal power, over the rank and file members, male as well as female, and, indeed, within the black community at large. Many years later, she vividly recalled that the husband of a Motor Corps member, "a no-good," who was not a part of the movement, used to beat his wife. Samad's mother was a leading member of the Motor Corps. At a meeting of some of the women at her home, they put it to their battered sister: "You know, you can't take this kind of thing. You don't tolerate this type of thing. Do you want us to come up and take care of him?" As Samad told an interviewer

> I realised that these women were serious. They would have gone there, I don't know whether they would have beaten him or thrown him through the window. They were amazed at her [the battered woman], but she was very much in love with him. So that she went through this abuse from him, and the Motor Corps women told her that they would take care of him. And I heard that not long after when he found that out he left.
> *He left New York?*
> Yes. Because he realised that these women were coming to get him.[56]

Such group solidarity, courage, and support in adversity was probably not uncommon among women Garveyites. But no one, so far, has bothered to find out for sure. Paule Marshall, the distinguished Barbadian-American novelist, grew up, like Samad, in a Garveyite milieu and she powerfully and movingly recalls the "impressive strength, authority, and style" of the women who regularly gathered after work around her mother's kitchen table in Brooklyn.[57]

Ironic though it may seem, the greatest and most uncompromising revolt against male domination within the UNIA was led by Garvey's former private secretary and second wife, Amy Jacques Garvey. Much of this struggle was carried out in broad daylight, as it were, within the pages of the UNIA's own organ, the *Negro World*. Amy Jacques Garvey's page, "Our Women and What They Think," which ran for three years, between 1924 and 1927, provides us with unique data for exploring the most advanced feminist ideas abroad in the UNIA in the 1920s.

Born in Kingston on December 31, 1896, Amy Jacques was the first of seven children born to George Samuel Jacques and his wife, Charlotte South. The family was comfortably middle class. George Jacques, darkskinned, apparently of Haitian descent, was manager of a Kingston cigar factory for many years. He owned seven acres on Mountain View Avenue, a desirable part of Kingston, on which he built the family home. And over the years he acquired five additional properties in Kingston, the rents from which provided his family with an income after he died. Jacques wanted his first child to be a son, but, it is claimed (not entirely convincingly) that when his first-born turned out to be a girl, he nurtured her with the same love, attention, and devotion that he would have a son. He sent his daughter to some of the best schools on the island, providing her with what Derek Walcott would have called a "sound colonial education." She learned the piano and apparently played it well, but she was not happy with her playing, even if others were. Indeed, she claimed she had "no ear for music, and have always felt that whatever I do, I must excel in it." Amy left Wolmer's Girl School, passing her Cambridge University School Certificate Examination, the passport to higher education or a white-collar job.[58]

But during her childhood, George Jacques extended her world beyond that provided by formal schooling. He had lived in Cuba, spoke Spanish fluently, and as a young man had also spent time in Baltimore. He acquired and developed an international perspective on the world. Amy Jacques recalled that he "bought foreign newspapers and periodicals; on Sundays, I—being the eldest child—had to join him in reading them. He explained that this would improve our knowledge of the world and its happenings outside our small island."[59] George Jacques would hold long discussions with his daughter over current affairs, including dispatches about the First World War in the publications he bought.[60] It is to him that she attributes the first glimmerings of her political awakening. Amy's mother seemed to have exercised relatively little influence upon her daughter. The light-skinned daughter of an English farmer, Frank South, and his black wife, Jane, Charlotte Jacques has been described as "soft-natured and house-wifely." And while Amy Jacques talks of her father and his influence upon her in brief but vivid sketches, she hardly mentions her mother, except to say that she had "people" in America who had passed for white and lived as such.[61]

George Jacques wanted his daughter to study nursing in England.[62] But when he died suddenly from a stroke, Amy Jacques, who had previously studied shorthand and typing, became a clerk in his lawyer's office. She worked there for four years until she "became restless and decided to go to England; but when everything was ready, the ships would not take women passengers because of submarine warfare. I then decided to go to America in 1918."[63] She stayed with relatives in New York, heard conflicting reports about the UNIA and decided one Sunday night to hear Garvey for herself. She was impressed with his "fine oratory," told him so after the meeting, and made an appointment to see him at his offices.[64] She later became his private secretary, then his wife, an ardent supporter of the UNIA, and a radical black nationalist up to her death in Kingston in 1973.

Amy Jacques Garvey is another example of that Caribbean creature strangely metamorphized by American society. Like Cyril Briggs, Richard B. Moore, Otto Huiswoud, J. A. Rogers, and Frank Crosswaithe, here was a light-skinned Caribbean person who was radicalized beyond recognition by the American environment. Just as Rogers's middle-class relatives in Jamaica were astonished at his bizarre transformation in America, so were

Amy Jacques's. If her political evolution could not have been foreseen by her family in Jamaica, her choice of Garvey as a husband was even more unimaginable. Garvey was dark-skinned and had all the features that would make the Jamaican brown middle class, from which his wife came, describe him as ugly; and many did. Years later, Amy Jacques Garvey admitted that as a young girl she had been ashamed of her father coming to her school because of his dark complexion.[65] She recalled that on one occasion while carrying her three-months-old son, Julius, she met a former Wolmer's schoolmate on the street in Kingston. She greeted Amy with: "I haven't seen you in ages. What are you doing with this little *black* baby?" The old concept, Mrs Garvey sardonically wrote in her memoir, "of skin-color distinction, and the idea of 'raising one's color' by marriage dies hard with our people."[66]

Even though he had elevated himself to the black artisanry, Garvey was, nonetheless, a son of the impoverished peasantry of St Ann, a group for which the brown middle class had no respect. He was a member of the wandering tribe of Afro-Caribbean proletariat. Yet they were married in New York in 1922 and nourished each other, even though they spent more time apart than together over the course of their marriage. Garvey's travels on behalf of the UNIA, his imprisonment, and final exile in Britain robbed them of time in each other's company. The relationship appears passionless. Garvey had little time for anything that was not directly connected to the great goal of the redemption of Africa, and that included his wife and family. "There is but one purpose I have," he told a Liberty Hall audience, "and that is the purpose of a free and redeemed Africa; and in striving towards that purpose no one will ever stand in my way—no mother, no father, no wife, no sweetheart, no affiliation—for a free and redeemed Africa."[67] And in her memoir, *Garvey and Garveyism*, Mrs Garvey did not, and perhaps could not, camouflage her bitterness at the hardship and privation Garvey put her and their two sons through, especially in the 1930s. Amy Jacques Garvey reported that in 1925, after she had carried out the arduous task of editing, proofreading, and getting published the second volume of Garvey's *Philosophy and Opinions*, she thought she had done "almost the impossible." But Garvey

callously said, "Now I want you to send free copies to Senators, Congressmen and prominent men who might become interested in my case, as I want to make another application for a pardon." When I completed this task I weighed 98 lbs., had low blood pressure and one eye was badly strained. Two doctors advised complete rest. I stayed with southern friends in Montclair, New Jersey; but it was only part-time rest, as I telephoned the flat daily, and went on weekends to clear up accumulated work. After two weeks he telegraphed me to come and bring all acknowledgements of books sent; then he informed me that as soon as I was stronger, I should make a list of the favorable ones, and go to the capital to lobby on his behalf.[68]

Mrs Garvey quotes a stanza from a poem that her husband wrote while in prison and dedicated to her:

> But you have been a light to me,
> A fond and dear and true Amie;
> So what care I for falsest friend
> When on your love I can depend.

She curtly and surprisingly wrote, immediately after citing the poem:

> What did he ever give in return? The value of a wife to him was like a gold coin—expendable, to get what he wanted, and hard enough to withstand rough usage in the process.[69]

Garvey was fully aware of the sacrifices he enforced on his family, and he acknowledged them time and time again, but he evidently felt that the greater goal made them worthwhile. Although they affectionately and privately referred to each other as "Popsie" (he) and "Mopsie" (she), mutual respect and loyalty and a shared dedication to a great cause, rather than love, held them together for over a turbulent decade. Mrs Garvey, the evidence suggests, stayed with her husband for the time that she did from her own deep devotion to the cause of African redemption. His courage, his love of race, his indefatigability and the very single-minded and blinkered commitment to the liberation of Africans at home and abroad that pushed her and their children aside, strangely and paradoxically drew her closer to him through the chemistry of shared political passion. The second volume of *Philosophy and Opinions* carries a prefatory note written in the form of a letter from Garvey to his wife. In it he publicly entrusted the manuscript to his wife and expressed his "implicit confidence" in her getting it published unaltered. She, in turn, wrote:

> I have, at all times, endeavored to serve him who serves and suffers for his race; the compilation of this volume is but a slight effort in that direction. It is an honor and a pleasure to earn the confidence of one who has been, and is, so signally faithful to his sacred trust.[70]

She admired him greatly, and always felt moved to rise to his defense. And after his death she passionately and ferociously defended his good name. They separated through choice and circumstance in 1938, Mrs Garvey returning to Kingston leaving her husband in London, where he died in 1940 in sad and bitter exile.

Amy Jacques Garvey's rise to prominence in the UNIA occurred after her husband's indictment in 1923. She accompanied Garvey on a national speaking tour soon after his release pending appeal against his five-year prison sentence for mail fraud. While she was on the road, Amy Jacques Garvey sent dispatches to the *Negro World* which proved enormously popular with the UNIA rank and file. And everywhere they went crowds greeted her with warmth and enthusiasm.[71] At the first mass meeting after the couple's return to New York, the success of her series of articles was such that the crowd called out, "We want Mrs Garvey," demanding that she should speak before her husband gave the customary closing address. After she spoke, Garvey rose and smilingly remarked, "Now I have a rival, but I am glad she is my wife." The articles and her speech at Liberty Hall made Garvey realize, apparently for the first time, that in addition to being an extraordinarily efficient administrator, a loyal supporter, and devoted wife, Amy Jacques Garvey was of great propaganda value. He asked her to take over a page of the *Negro World*, later making her an associate editor.[72] Her power within the UNIA increased substantially during his imprisonment as she became his eyes and ears while he languished in the Atlanta Penitentiary.

Cyril Briggs, one of Garvey's most forthright radical black critics, got wind of Mrs Garvey's rise within the movement, but exaggerated when he reported in his Crusader News Service that Garvey had "turned over" the UNIA to his wife after his conviction. The release stated that the old guard was resentful of the change and that "the heads of the UNIA divisions throughout the country are reported taking steps to hold a conference to consider the future of the organization."[73] The report was picked up by a number of black newspapers across the country. The *Negro World* published the release under an editorial entitled, "Look Out for Mud," denouncing it as "vicious falsehood" and "evil propaganda." In an apparent defense of Mrs Garvey, it went on to state that "it is beneath the dignity of common decency to attempt to drag the name of an innocent and helpless woman into an arena where she cannot properly defend herself."[74] Amy Jacques Garvey replied to the editorial giving the leading men of the UNIA a good taste of what was to come in her page, "Our Women and What They Think." Here, she made crystal clear, was a woman who was neither innocent nor helpless, able and willing to fight on her own behalf, and indeed others. She pointed out that Briggs's article was shown to her, but since everyone in the UNIA was aware that a Committee of Management had been appointed to run the UNIA during Garvey's incarceration she ignored it. The report, she said, was such a "clumsy, unvarnished lie that it is worthy of the source from which it came, and did not in the least disturb the divisions, branches and chapters" of the UNIA. She was, therefore, surprised to see the *Negro World* giving such news almost a column of valuable editorial space. She was only twenty-six years old at the time, small and thin, but none of that stopped her from taking her gloves off:

> You have characterized me as "innocent and helpless." I am innocent of the honor of having the Universal Negro Improvement Association "turned over" to me by my husband, but I am not innocent of the depths to which colored men can stoop to further their petty personal schemes, even at the expense of a downtrodden race such as ours.

I am not "innocent" of the tactics employed by men of my race to get easy money from alien individuals, groups and sometimes nations.

I am not "innocent" of the undermining influences used by local individuals and rival organizations to destroy my husband and the Universal Negro Improvement Association; because such individuals and rival organizations fear the power and strength of our organization and have not the ability to create anything like unto it.

I am not "innocent" of all this, and, more, I am not "innocent" of the psychology and know how, when, and where to treat with some men. My four and a half years of active service in the Universal Negro Improvement Association under the personal direction of Marcus Garvey has given me a fair knowledge of men and the methods they employ in the organization and out of it.

With my unusual general knowledge and experiences for a young woman, may I not ask it the word "helpless" is not misapplied?

If the editorial was written in my defense, I have to thank you for same, and hope that if ever I am in need of a protector (not to draw his sword in my defense, but to flash his quill), you, sir, will as on this occasion, unsolicited, spill as much ink as will prove my "innocence" and protect me as a "helpless" woman.[75]

The fact is that there was substance to Briggs's report even though he embellished it. The UNIA was riven with factionalism and intrigue at the time. Rumors and gossip flew thick and fast as the Justice Department's intelligence reports amply show. Amy Jacques Garvey and her husband, who was in jail at the time, were fully aware of the plots and back-stabbing, if only because they participated in them. And the very republication of Briggs's release in its entirety, critical editorial commentary notwithstanding, in the organ of the UNIA was a symptom of the crisis and evidence of maneuvering by Garvey's opponents. Briggs's information, if indirectly, came from the fractured power center of the UNIA itself. Mrs Garvey, therefore, aimed her heaviest punches, not at Cyril Briggs, but at those whom she regarded as the enemies within the organization, sitting by her side and coming in and out of the UNIA's offices in Harlem. She revealed in her memoir that she carried a revolver when she worked as Garvey's private secretary and office manager at the UNIA's headquarters. A clerk threatened to throw her down the stairs because she reported to the directors the fact that he had lost a stock book of signed-up Black Star Line certificates. She was not going to be pushed around or down, so, as she put it "I had to get a gun"; she did not say how long she carried it for. According to her, at Garvey's trial it became evident that the clerk "had been 'planted' there to get information."[76]

Amy Jacques Garvey's page in the *Negro World* began on February 2, 1924. Through no fault of her own, the page, it turned out, was misnamed. For "Our Women and What They Think," was overwhelmingly written and edited by her and her alone. Mrs Garvey repeatedly pleaded for contribution from black women, but the response was disappointing. The first general appeal came in the second week of the page's publication.

Boxed, partly written in bold capital letters, and prominently placed at the top of the page, it read: "WOMEN OF THE NEGRO RACE!/ LET THE WORLD KNOW/ WHAT YOU ARE THINKING AND DOING/ Send in your articles, poems/ and essays to Mrs Amy Jacques Garvey" giving the address of the *Negro World* offices. This advertised request was frequently carried by the page. But by the beginning of June she felt obliged to use up half of her column to solicit contributions from women teachers and students and other similarly educated black women. She had directed her appeal to this group because she had been getting contributions that were, as far as she was concerned, unusable. She put it delicately, but forthrightly: "we are sure that it will be taken in good part if we suggest that persons who have not a common school education and who have not studied the rules of composition, of prose or verse, should not send contributions in prose or verse."[77]

She promised the teachers and students that whether or not they were members of the UNIA their contribution would receive sympathetic consideration. Indeed, she opened her entreaty by making it clear where she stood:

> The Editor of The Woman's Page of the *Negro World* desired that the women of the race should understand that her sympathies are as comprehensive as the Negro race. They extend to other races, as a matter of course, but the women of the Negro race, by the nature of the case, have the first call upon her interest and sympathies. Ain't that entirely human? I think so.

She felt that the women of other races also felt that their own came first. "And why not?" she asked rhetorically. However, "the Negro women have a more urgent necessity to have an interest in and sympathy for their own than have women of other race groups."[78] It had little effect. Her sister, Ida Jacques, who was then living in New York, perhaps felt obliged to do her bit by sending in a letter the following week. In August she devoted an entire column, appropriately entitled "Have a Heart," asking black women from anywhere to contribute. They could make their contribution in English, French or Spanish, whichever the writer felt more comfortable with.

> You women who have had the advantage of higher education, use it, and, for God's sake, don't use it selfishly. Help your less-informed sisters. Mix among them a little more; hear their woes and suffering, and let the world know that our race has noble women, living lives of love and service.
>
> Those of us, who, unfortunately, cannot express ourselves on paper, can get some one who is better equipped to clothe our sentiments in proper language and send same to our office. Don't be discouraged because in your day you did not have the educational facilities your children are having.

Describing the objectives of the UNIA for a liberated race and a redeemed Africa, she ended: "Have a heart sister and join us now! The larger the band of workers, the quicker the goal will be reached. Have a heart! Help put it over!"[79] In September, she was again obliged to tell the women "It's

Up to You!" She revealed that although many highly educated women wrote to her expressing their appreciation of the page, "yet they make no effort to maintain it by weekly contributions."[80] In April the following year she asked in yet another editorial on the subject: "Do Negro Women Want to Express Themselves?"[81] She reluctantly concluded that they did not. "It is an awful calamity," wrote Madame De Mena, "when we realized the many intelligent women in the Universal Negro Improvement Association, who are capable of contributing an article to the 'Woman's Page' in the *Negro World* and will not do so."[82]

The repeated requests are perhaps as remarkable as the paltry response. But why were educated women so reluctant to contribute, even if they read the newspaper and the Page? The fact is that educated people in general, men and women, were defecting from the UNIA in large numbers. The factional fights, the expulsions, the scandal of Garvey's indictment, the brutal muder of Rev. James Eason (the Leader of the American Negroes who had broken with Garvey) by known Garveyites in New Orleans, Garvey's intolerance of independent thinkers within the UNIA, Garvey's meeting with the Ku Klux Klan—all these diminished the intellectual layer within the UNIA; and it was not substantial to begin with. As Mrs Garvey pointed out, women were writing in, but they were not the educated women. It was less the case that the educated black women did not want to express themselves than that they did not wish to express themselves within the pages of the UNIA. Private encouragement was extended to Mrs Garvey in the form of letters, but precious few signed articles, letters, poems for publication. The response perhaps would have been different if the women were offered anonymity. It was undoubtedly the case, though, that Amy Jacques Garvey's ideas were far too radical for many black middle-class women.

She believed that women should be free to enter politics; that married men should wear rings, just as women were required to do, indicating their marital status; that women should wear more "scanty" and comfortable clothes, rather than carry the encumberances of "bustles, hoops, stays and long skirts." She welcomed the changes in marriage laws in Russia which gave women greater freedom. She carried the news of Alexandra Kollontai's appointment as the Soviet Union's ambassador to Mexico, as she did the election of Clara Zetkin and Ruth Fischer to to the German Reichstag. She sought an unencumbered and liberated black womanhood as much as she sought the liberation of Africa and Africans around the world. In fact, as she explained, her first loyalty was to black women. The black press, including the radical black press, had nothing like Mrs Garvey's page. The page's politics extended well beyond the genteel and Victorian black feminism that came out of the nineteenth century. Hers was a different voice, and it was perhaps as disturbing to many black women as it undoubtedly was to many of the men within the movement. The fact that she counteracted many of the negative ideas that the black middle class traditionally held about their blackness and perceptions of Africa, again, must have been discomforting to many.

Amy Jacques Garvey, undaunted by the relative lack of support, boldly pressed on with her page. Despite the fact that she suffered ill-health, she frequently worked eighteen hours per day, and often took only three hours sleep per night. For over three years she valiantly edited her extraordinary Woman's Page. She recognized and articulated the differences between her page and others directed at women:

> Usually a Woman's Page in any journal is devoted solely to dress, home hints and love topics, but our Page is unique, in that it seeks to give out the thoughts of our women on the subjects affecting them in particular and others in general. This pleases the modern Negro woman, who believes that God Almighty has not limited her intellect because of her sex, and that the helpful and instructive thoughts expressed by her in her home, with the aid of this page, could be read in thousands of other homes and influence the lives of untold numbers.[83]

Alongside her column of opinion would be published important items of news culled from and attributed to other publications, black and white, domestic and international. Anything that would instruct and bring cheer and good tidings to her sisters was included on the page. Henrietta Vinton Davis wrote two remarkable articles on Harriet Tubman and Sojourner Truth.[84] News of the achievements of women around the world made up a substantial part of the page. Health advice from the New York Black Cross Nurses—who always reminded their readers that they may be consulted at Liberty Hall every Sunday night—was also a regular feature. She carried substantial news on the non-European world and on women in Asia and Africa; and she editorialized on a range of issues, as varied as the French in Africa, women's position in Turkey, and Langston Hughes' debate with George Schuyler in the *Nation*. As to be expected, there were contradictions. One of the sharpest was somewhat extraneous to her own writing but compromised the integrity of the whole Garvey enterprise. For as early as 1923 the *Negro World* carried advertising for hair straightening (sometimes disguised as hair "growing" preparations). These increased as the UNIA experienced growing financial difficulty. "Too much cannot be said in denouncing the 'want-to-be-white' Negroes one finds everywhere," Jacques Garvey wrote. "This race[-]destroying group are dissatisfied with their mothers and with their creator—mother is too dark 'to pass' and God made a mistake when he made black people."[85] In another editorial entitled, "Are We Proud of Our Black Skins and Curly Hair?" she remarked:

> Negroes use laboratories, not to discover serums to prevent disease and experiment in chemicals to protect themselves in case of war, but to place on the market grease that stiffens curly hair, irons that press the hair to look like a horse's mane, and face cream that bleaches the skin over night.

She was attuned to the fact that so-called hair "growers" were a ploy, aimed at reaching similar goals. She wrote that before white women bobbed their hair, "black women in this Hemisphere thought it a crime to have short hair, and they spent as much money trying to make their hair grow and buying false braids and switches as they do to buy shoes and stockings."

> Look at God's black masterpiece, after several years of this straightening and bleaching process, and you will see a being that God Himself in anger and disappointment would not recognize, and white men ridicule, because in trying to look like some one else, you admit the superiority of that person. Hence the white man rides to power on the black man's self-inflicted inferiority and proclaims his "white superiority."[86]

Apart from the problematic nature of the notion of self-inflicted injury in such a situation, the logic of the argument is fairly tight. The problem is that, on the basis of her own argument, the *Negro World* was contributing to the problem. Madame C. J. Walker products were regularly advertised on her page, and on the very same page on which her article denouncing "want-to-be-whites" was printed also appeared an advertisement for the Royal Chemical Company of Jamaica, New York, promising "$500 Reward If I Fail to Grow Hair," and carrying the etched picture of a woman with ridiculously long hair. Perhaps most disgusting of all was the ad for "Zura Kinkout," that made large and regular appearances, especially in 1923, with a large picture of a satisfied black man who had used the product, and almost half a page of pseudo-scientific text in which the promoters wrote, among other, things:

> Why go through life with ugly, nappy hair? Nature intended you to be beautiful and happy. Perhaps you have beautiful eyes, a fine skin and wonderful figure. Only your hair — ugly, crinkly and nappy! O my! It spoils it all. Why not have nice, lovely hair and have people admire you? Are you in love? Do you want to get a job where your appearance is important? A few minutes' application of ZURA KINKOUT and you will hardly know yourself.[87]

Indeed. This is one of the most pathetic manifestations of the decline of the Garvey movement. An ad like this would not have been carried in earlier years, and how they had the stomach to carry it, even in times of adversity, is difficult to understand. So while Mrs Garvey was saying one thing, something else was being said on the very same page, or somewhere else in the paper.

Jacques Garvey's primary focus was the plight and struggles of black women and what she saw as the major failings of black men. Her attacks on black men were often thinly disguised sorties against those whom she regarded as her husband's enemies, or slackers within the UNIA. This was made most explicit in an editorial entitled "Away with Lip Service":

> Our organization has reached a stage where a big speech cannot advance the cause if there is no real thought and action behind it. A great talker is not the type of man to place at the head of affairs, unless he has the attributes of a deep thinker and knowing the art of diplomacy. Again we warn our membership that

the U. N. I. A. is getting too large for some of us, and this is more so evidenced since our leaders imprisonment.

She spoke of the need for the organization to carry its program in "the same aggressive manner" as when Garvey was free to lead it. But instead "we find some Negroes so spineless and cowardly as to give comfort to the enemy, whose aim is—imprison Garvey—keep him in prison—and you can handle his colleagues, who will shrink with fear and hesitate to move forward." She continued:

> But the Negro women of the U. N. I. A. serve notice on you, who are in charge of locals, diplomatic post or headquarters in Africa or America, that if you don't get a move on, to use the common parlance, you will have to go. The longer you remain making set speeches and repeating eloquent meaningless phrases the longer you keep Marcus Garvey in prison and stultify the progress of the organization. You are but agents of the oppressors and consciously or unconsciously doing his bidding.
> Away with lip servers![88]

As her confidence in the men in the UNIA diminished, she became increasingly fierce in the criticism of black men and invested her hope in black women. While many black middle-class uplifters and Pan-Africanists placed substantial blame for their lowly status on primitive Africans and their barbarous behavior, or the uncouth, immoral, and dirty habits of the black poor in America, Amy Jacques Garvey blamed the men and what she repeatedly referred to as their "laziness." For the black Victorians of the nineteenth century, if only Africa was civilized with Christianity white people would treat all those of African descent with greater respect; but for the alley Negroes, with their illegitimate children and crime, white folks would treat the cultivated Negroes better. Let us civilize Africa and let us help these fallen members of our race, if only to help enhance our own status in the eyes of white society, their argument went.[89] Mrs Garvey felt that black men had failed in their duty to black women, to themselves and, therefore, to the race as a whole. They had not taken on the manly task of independent nationhood because they had insufficient ambition and industry. The race was left weak and, thus, vulnerable to the merciless predations of the white man. She even argued that those who condoned miscegenation did so out of laziness. There is a peculiar logic to her argument but it is superficial, and, in fact, profoundly flawed.

> What is the real reason why Negroes want to escape their race? To be perfectly blunt and brief, we say, LAZINESS IS THE ROOT OF THE WHOLE EVIL. The white man has built up great nations, even when he has done so by using the enslaved blacks, and he does not intend to share and share alike with them in the benefits to be derived by citizens of a great nation, caring not how you pray to him, and petition him. He has built up trade, commerce and large industries all over the world, even in the black man's land, and he does not intend to give Negroes an equal opportunity in his economic and industrial life. If the Negro is satisfied to

be used as a peon or a cheap laborer, he can go out and conquer and build like the white man. The yellow and brown races realize the selfish attitude of the white race and they are emulating him in every particular. Now, Mr. Black Man, how long do you expect to close your eyes to the realities, and solve the degraded condition of your race by "jumping the racial fence"?

The Negro masses are to be pitied, but the false leaders are worse than murderers who tell you that miscegenation will cure your ills. That by gradual wholesale absorption of the blacks by the whites, the former will come into their glory, and enjoy all the benefits of white civilization. Lazy, good-for-nothing, as we are looked upon by the whites, is this the highest ideal to which you can aspire?[90]

She implies here, although she knows better, that "the white man" would allow black people to build unhindered powerful nations in Africa in the Age of Imperialism. Even if we were to accept her argument at face value, she does not explain why black people are "lazy": is it genetic? If it is, it would seem that little *can* be done about it. Unclear too, is how the white man can be said to build up this civilization, in the way in which she described it, when she also conceded that black people's labor has been integral to its construction. She did not and could not mention the names of the "false leaders" who suggested that "miscegenation will cure all ills," because there were no such leaders, not even false ones. In any case, the primary practitioners of "miscegenation" were, of course, white, not black, men.

Jacques Garvey saw black women, by default, taking on the burden of liberating the race; the men would not or could not do it, so the women had to take on the task:

Be not discouraged black women of the world, but push forward, regardless of the lack of appreciation shown you. A race must be saved, a country must be redeemed, and unless you strengthen the leadership of vacillating Negro men, we will remain marking time until the yellow race gains the leadership of the world, and we be forced to subserviency under them, or extermination.

We are tired of hearing Negro men say, "There is a better day coming," while they do nothing to usher in the day. We are becoming so impatient that we are getting in the front ranks and serve notice to the world that we will brush aside halting, cowardly Negro leaders, and with prayer on our lips and arms prepared for any fray, we will press on and on until victory is ours.

Africa must be for Africans, and Negroes everywhere must be independent, God being our helper and guide. Mr. Black Man, watch your step! Ethiopia's queens will reign again, and her Amazons protect her shores and people. Strengthen your shaking knees and move forward, or we will displace you and lead on to victory and to glory.[91]

The leading men within the UNIA, with a few notable exceptions, grew more resentful of Mrs Garvey. But she was secure in her position at the *Negro World*. For in addition to being the Associate Editor, in May 1925

Garvey had publicly appointed her and his executive secretary, Norton Thomas, as "directors of the policy of the *Negro World*."[92] Maybe her powerful position on the paper helped to explain why no letters protesting against her editorials were published; she clearly had the power to veto such letters. But in April 1927, she once again blasted the men. Entitled, "Listen Women!" her opening remarks accurately set the tenor of the entire editorial:

> Negro women are the acknowledged burden bearers of their race. Whether this is due to the innate laziness of Negro men, or to their lack of appreciation for their noble women, we are not sure. Perhaps both these reasons are contributing factors, yet the results are the same—an overburdened womanhood, and a backward race. We hope some of our male readers will in defense of their sex supply us with a plausible excuse; that is if they can summon enough energy to do so.[93]

Placed in this position, black women needed to be careful in keeping pace with daily events and training their minds to cope with situations and problems. She counselled black women against imitating the white race, for, she said, "ours is a young, virile race, while the white race is slowly decaying; therefore it is disastrous for us to imitate the old fellow who indulges in excesses, knowing that he will soon depart." Birth control, she said, "suits them, not us." It is the duty of black women to bear and care for the children, so that the race may have good men and women through whom it can achieve honor and power. Black women should not imitate the night life of the whites. "Your recreation must be wholesome and clean," she said. Jacques Garvey then moved on to the subject of black men, whom she described as "our greatest concern." They lack faith in themselves. "Therefore they must be driven to accomplish anything." She surmised that this state of mind may have been caused by "the oppression of slavery, which has dulled their initiative." The achievement of any black man "can always be traced to the push and perseverance of a good woman." She, once again, compared the white man to the black man. White men "idolize their women and for them they will dare anything in order to merit their look of admiration." (Mrs Garvey perhaps got this fictive view of white men from Klan and other white supremacist literature. But why a person as educated as she, attuned to the developments and struggles of the white feminist movement in the United States and Europe, should swallow so easily this notion of white chivalry is still unclear.) She then launched an astonishing attack on black men, happily mixing fact and fiction in her argument:

> Mr. Negro, who has no love for his woman, loses the incentive to achieve, and the race is that much poorer because of his slothfulness. Tell him to go out and get diamonds and adorn his woman; he will readily tell you that he isn't going to risk his life for her; yet his dependency on white people makes every minute of his life a risk. He is always out of a job because he is too lazy to go out and

make a job for himself; he prefers to hang around the white man's factory doors begging for a job, and oftimes gets what he deserves—a kick.

He makes no effort to provide for his woman, nor does he protect her. He will cheerfully sit down to his wife's table and enjoy the good things on it without contributing a nickel to it. When he does find a job he tells her that they must run the home on a fifty-fifty basis; nor does he care if through necessity her morals are fifty-fifty with his. Small matter as long as he can get a free meal sometimes and not be bothered with the landlord every month. Such are the parasites that most Negro women have for husbands; and we appeal to them at this time to be brave and take hope for the future. Their suffering will not be in vain, although their duties are becoming greater.[94]

The source of this fountain of rage, contempt, even hatred, is difficult to fathom. It does appear, however, that the struggle within the leadership of the UNIA, and the desertion of the organization by large numbers of men, may have been a part of it. It is probable that a larger proportion of male than female members left the UNIA during Garvey's imprisonment. And at the leadership level this was undoubtedly true. Henrietta Vinton Davis, Madame De Mena, and Jacques Garvey took on extraordinary responsibilities and work during this time. Norton Thomas and Samuel Haynes were two of the very few men that Garvey and his wife trusted within the organization when Mrs Garvey wrote the editorial. It is noticeable that as the UNIA declined, the proportion of women delegates at the conventions increased. At the height of the movement in 1921, only 12.8 percent of the delegates were women; in 1922 it rose to 21.5 percent, but fell to 19.4 percent in 1924. However, in 1929, when the movement was but a shadow of its former self, 39.5 percent of the delegates were women, rising to 49.1 percent in 1938.[95] The women of the UNIA were, wisely or unwisely, the most faithful and loyal Garveyites; they endured the troubled times, while the men left in large numbers, from the leadership and from the rank and file too.

In any case, Mrs Garvey received at least two responses to her editorial that the *Negro World* published. Arthur Gray, a long-time Garveyite and regional offical, wrote in from Oakland, California. But it is doubtful that his response and prescription impressed Jacques Garvey:

Most men are decidedly sensitive. Encouragement is a far more effective lever than condemnation or ridicule. Man is a self-conscious creature and keenly resents any domination of his masculine spirit. (Especially so, when exhibited by his womanhood.) Most men can be greatly inspired by the influence of a woman—but should she attempt to "drive," compel, or coerce him—he immediately becomes hostile, arrogant, or defiant. Woman's charm and innate art of attraction are her greatest weapons for subduing man. Some men are attracted by personality, some by intellect, some by beauty, while others are won by sympathy and "understanding." In either case he wants to claim victory.

More persausively, he pointed out that, "There are also women of the white race that have a very sad tale to relate because of the neglect or indifference of their men. The women of our race have no monopoly on matrimonial persecution." He further suggested that when the white man "by his HONEST labor can produce and provide for his family needs—then and only then [—] will we applaud his achievements."[96] Lily Culmer, writing from Miami, Florida, conceded that the race had men that were "good-for-nothing, worthless ones."

> But aside from this let us see the men of the race in a different light. Let us see the conditions they are placed in. And let us pity them. We know the odds that are against them daily. Let us feel that their minds to do for us are like unto the minds of other races. Let us see that our men are handicapped. Let us see the barriers that are placed in their way. . . . I am pleased to see how well the thoughtful, ambitious men of our race take care of their wives considering the disadvantages that confront them. . . . So, let us encourage our men, let us see their condition and see that we cannot expect much of them. Let us, as good women, help shoulder the load our poor men have to bear.[97]

It may not have been coincidence that "Listen Women" marked the end of the Woman's Page. Without announcement or ceremony "Our Women and What They Think" was no more. It is difficult to gauge the impact of the page on the women in the movement and the UNIA in general. But, as mentioned earlier, black women wrote to her privately, praising the page. And when she was ill in the fall of 1924, several well-wishers wrote in expressing appreciation for her page. Lena Obey, for example, wrote in from Columbus, Ohio, saying "we all should thank Mrs Garvey, the first lady of the land, who made it possible for the women of the race to express their opinions publicly. We love her and look to her for example, as other races look to their great women." A poem, "To Mrs. Amy Jacques Garvey" ("From Women of Philadelphia, Chapter No. 47") was written in her honor. From Binghampton, New York, Mr Eason expressed his and his wife's "sympathy from the depths our hearts" for Mrs. Garvey and hoped for her speedy recovery. "My wife never misses reading the woman's page first. May God bless our leader and his dear companion. We are not members of the UNIA yet but expect to be soon. We have no division here." Amy Jacques Garvey later publicly thanked her readers, "many of whom have sent her personal letters."[98]

The African Blood Brotherhood was another radical organization in which there was significant Caribbean involvement. Though small in member-ship—probably never exceeding more than three thousand—its influence extended well beyond its numerical size. It was from the African Blood Brotherhood that the Communist Party recruited its first cohort of black cadres in the early 1920s, who in turn would play a key role in bringing other black people into the Party, especially in the 1930s, but also in subsequent decades.

Founded in Harlem in 1919, the signal feature of the organization was its systematic attempt to organically conjoin radical black nationalism with revolutionary socialism. The African Blood Brotherhood structured itself along military lines, aimed at black self-defense and black upliftment. It was in fact born during the Red Summer of 1919. The Brotherhood had different branches, described as "Posts," under the organization's central leadership, the "Supreme Council," based in New York. Its Harlem headquarters was known as "Post Menelik," doubtless named after the Ethiopian emperor, Menelik II, who had routed the Italian invaders of his country at Adowa in 1896. Menelik died in 1913, just six years before the African Blood Brotherhood was formed. Posts could be found in different parts of the United States—including the South—and there were several in the Caribbean. One old-timer fondly remembered the Brotherhood, describing it in a letter to a scholar as "a 'fighting back' organization that counteracted race riots in the early twenties."[99]

Like the UNIA, the Brotherhood was founded by Caribbeans. The prime mover behind the effort was Cyril Briggs. The clearly identifiable members who helped to form the Brotherhood were W. A. Domingo, Richard B. Moore, and Grace Campbell. With the exception of Campbell, whose father was from the Caribbean and whose mother was from Washington, the others were immigrants from the islands.[100] Early members of the Brotherhood included Harry Haywood and his brother Otto Hall, Otto Huiswoud, Lovett Fort-Whiteman, and Claude McKay, who joined soon after his return from London in 1921. Most of its leading members were to join the Communist (Workers') Party soon after the latter was formed from a split within the Socialist Party, in September 1919. (By the end of 1921 most of the Supreme Council of the Brotherhood had joined the Workers' Party.)

Briggs recalled—and there is no good reason to doubt his word—that there was definite Caribbean over-representation in its membership and leadership:

> The Brotherhood never attained the proportion of a real mass organization. Its initial membership was less than a score, and all in Harlem. At its peak it had less than three thousand members. It had posts, however, in many sections of the country, and in several West Indian islands. It was not comprised solely or mainly of West Indian Negroes living in the U.S. West Indians, however, did constitute the bulk of its New York membership and played [a] role on its Supreme Council out of proportion to their total membership *vis-a-vis* native born members.[101]

Despite the African Blood Brotherhood's extraordinary importance as an expression of black radicalism in the 1920s, and despite its pioneering role in the development of black Bolshevism and Marxism in the early twentieth century, the Brotherhood is hardly known, little studied and poorly understood.[102] Given this state of affairs, a discussion of the brotherhood's formation, ideology and development is necessary. The remainder of the chapter is largely devoted to such an analysis.

New Negro ideology may be said to traverse a continuum exemplified at one end by the black nationalism of the UNIA and, at the other, by the orthodox socialism of the radicals around the *Messenger* magazine, edited by Randolph and Owen. The African Blood Brotherhood, from its founding to its effective demise in 1924, moved along this continuum from the black nationalist to the socialist pole. Although the group's ideology maintained a rather unstable equilibrium, at no point did it touch, let alone merge during its independent existence with, the politics represented at either end of the continuum. The Brotherhood's ideological move, however, was always in one direction, toward revolutionary socialism. In the end, it dissolved itself in the Communist Party of the United States of America, providing that party with its nucleus of black cadres which reproduced itself through recruiting Afro-Americans and Afro-Caribbeans over the years. The African Blood Brotherhood cannot be properly understood without an appreciation of the early life and remarkable political evolution of its founder.

Born in St Kitts on May 28, 1888, Cyril Valentine Briggs was the son and only child of Marian M. Huggins, a colored woman, and a white Trinidadian, Louis E. Briggs, overseer of a sugar plantation. His parents were not married. Briggs spent most of his childhood on the sister island of Nevis and did exceptionally well at school, so well, in fact, that he was even offered a scholarship. He turned the scholarship down because he had decided to migrate to America. Briggs's political awakening had begun at school under the influence of the writings of Robert Ingersoll, the great American radical orator and agnostic, whose works he keenly read and admired.[103] Briggs was very light-skinned and was often mistaken for a white person in America. He, nevertheless, steadfastly and rather self-consciously stuck to what he regarded as the African side of his family. For his entire life, however, Briggs was very aware of the incongruity of his skin color and his professed Negro identity. And it seems as if there was always someone to remind him of this fact and to compound the pain by unwarranted extrapolation. At age seventy-four he was still fighting over his Negro credentials. Writing to his close friend, Harry Haywood, he complained bitterly about the malicious gossip of a mutual friend of theirs, a black woman, who

> recently tried to sell a girl on the notion that my light skin would make it impossible for me to feel like a Negro and to resent the treatment accorded our people. The gal knew better, since going out often with me, she has had ample reason to know how sensitive I am on the question, how angrily I resent any expression or hint of white chauvinism, how I pilloried a white waitress, for

example, who in handing us a menu introduced herself as "Miss Julie." After previously having introduced herself at a white table as Julie.

In another letter to Haywood, he wondered, judging from what this woman does with her hair, "if she were as light as me whether she would not damn well be 'passing,' rather than being like myself a Negro by birth *and by choice!*"[104]

Briggs's enemies—including Garvey, with whom he engaged in vicious ideological and personal battles in the 1920s—from early on knew how sensitive and vulnerable he was on the question of his color. Hitting below the belt, Garvey, in the heat of battle, accused Briggs of being a white man trying to pass as a Negro. Briggs sued him and won, the court awarding him a dollar and a written retraction from Garvey published in the *Negro World*. But this was little consolation for the hurt he felt from the remark. Briggs, who had from early childhood suffered from a terrible stammer, on hearing of the calumny is said to have mounted a stepladder and denounced Garvey for over an hour—some said two, others even three hours—for all Harlem to hear. And he never stuttered. Never before or after had Briggs spoken with such fluency. His close friend and comrade, Harry Haywood, noticed that Briggs stuttered less when he was angry. Haywood remembered that Briggs stammered so badly that "it often took him several seconds to get out the first word of a sentence." He also recalled that when Briggs took the floor at meetings the comrades all listened attentively. "[N]o one would interrupt him because we knew he always had something important and pertinent to say. While he spoke we would cast our eyes down and look away from him to avoid making him feel self-conscious, though he never seemed to be." W. A. Domingo went so far as to claim that Briggs stuttered so badly that "it was impossible to understand him or even to hold a conversation with him,"[105] but Domingo exaggerated. The Justice Department spies also remarked on Briggs's speech impediment.

As if to compensate for his speech defect, Briggs developed an extraordinarily fluent and effective writing style, which was in evidence in the most informal of notes to his closest friends as much as in his published journalism and polemics. His tongue failed him, but he wielded his pen with as much dexterity and, at times, devastation as the samurai his sword. A "keen polemicist, a veritable master of invective," Haywood called him.[106] One can hardly help but wonder if Briggs did not also overcompensate for his lightness of skin with the ultra-black nationalism of his early years. Could it be that the mingling of blood that Briggs required of new recruits to the Brotherhood symbolized his deep desire to be re-infused with, as he saw it, the blood of Africa? Is it coincidence that, of all the New Negro organs—including Garvey's *Negro World*—the *Crusader* magazine, which he founded and edited, took the most principled and explicit editorial stand against skin-lighteners and the like, forgoing valuable advertising revenue in the bargain?

Whatever the case, Briggs was clearly loved and respected by a large number of black people, including black black people, like Hubert Harrison, which must have gratified him. And he was to occupy leadership positions not only in the Brotherhood, but later in the Communist Party and its affiliated organizations. He is recalled by his comrades—Moore, Domingo, McKay, Haywood—with genuine affection and deep respect. And the intelligence reports, filed by Briggs's enemies and preserved for posterity, tell of his extraordinary exertions on behalf of those whom he described as "the sons and daughters of Ethiopia." From time to time Briggs may have been wrong on the Negro Question, but he was always principled and unwavering in his commitment to the liberation of black people. "He was a man possessed of great physical and moral courage, which I was to observe on many occasions," Haywood wrote of him in his memoir.[107] Even when he was hauled up in front of the Un-American Activities Committee in 1958, before inquisitors who made big men cry and poets disown their own poems, their own progeny, Cyril Briggs never showed any fear; and if he was frightened, he never revealed that he was. In true New Negro fashion, he fought back:

> Mr. BRIGGS. I want to say this, that I resent being interrogated by a committee whose members include out-and-out white supremacists and people who have been inciting to insurrection in the South against the Supreme Court's integration mandate, and moreover a committee that during its 20 years has never once investigated the Ku Klux Klan.
>
> The CHAIRMAN. Let me interrupt at this point. That is not true. This committee asked the Ku Klux Klan for its first membership and they complied with the request, as I understand it. That is far more than the Communist Party would ever do.
>
> Mr. BRIGGS. Has this committee ever investigated the Southern White Citizens Committee?
>
> The CHAIRMAN. That is not dominated by Russia, and your organization is. That is the difference. Proceed, Mr. Tavenner.
>
> Mr. TAVENNER. Will you answer the question?
>
> Mr. BRIGGS. I want to say this, then, that I will have to assume then that in this committee's opinion lynching Negroes and spitting on little Negro children is
> —
>
> Mr. TAVENNER. You are evading the question.
>
> The CHAIRMAN. Just a minute, Mr. Tavenner. I want to get the record straight. This sort of thing resorted to by Communists hurts the cause that they say they espouse, because they are not sincere in the efforts to improve the conditions of the colored people in this country.
>
> Mr. BRIGGS. I don't know what Communists or communism have to do with my position, because this has been my position since 1912 before there was, as I understand it, a Communist Party in the United States. It will continue to be my position despite any attempt by this committee to intimidate me.[108]

Briggs arrived in the United States on July 4, 1905 and after repeated sackings from a number of publications—including from the editorship of the *Amsterdam News*, one of Harlem's oldest black newspapers—for his radical and outspoken politics, he founded the *Crusader*. The money for starting the magazine was largely provided by a Caribbean businessman, Anthony Crawford, who supported Briggs's race radicalism. Crawford had read and admired Briggs's articles in the *Amsterdam News* and the New York *Globe* where Briggs had called for "Africa for the Africans." He had taken the initiative to contact Briggs. As Crawford explained, he was keen on doing his "bit" for the the race. "In these days when Jewish People are working for a united Israel and Palestine, I feel it my duty to do something towards supporting the ONE VOICE in all America calling for Africa for the Africans."[109] The magazine made its appearance towards the close of the Great War, in September 1918, less than a month after the *Negro World* was launched.

With the notable exception of its emphasis on the need to fight in America, the *Crusader* was politically almost indistinguishable from Garvey's *Negro World*. But from the middle of 1919 the *Crusader* and its editor began to move in a decidedly socialist direction. The line of march to the left can be clearly discerned in the pages of the *Crusader* and in the copious intelligence reports of the Justice Department from 1919 onward. And it was during this leftward shift that the *Crusader* announced the formation of the African Blood Brotherhood. Despite his increasingly close embrace of socialist ideas, Briggs's relation, interestingly, to Garvey and the UNIA, up to 1921, was by no means antagonistic. As late as April 1921, Briggs could urge his readers, "Join the U. N. I. A. and the African Blood Brotherhood. And join now!"[110] Significant, too, is the fact that Briggs did not so much abandon his black nationalism as graft onto it revolutionary socialism, and, in particular, Bolshevism. And this is why he continued to support Garvey for a relatively long time. When the break with Garvey did come it had less to do with sharp ideological differences and far more to do with Garvey's authoritarian practices and financial mismanagement, plus a growing and fierce personal animosity between the men. As one approached the middle of the 1920s, however, it was clear that the socialist graft had outgrown and superseded the black nationalist host and had indeed thrived at the latter's expense. In fact, by 1925, the majority of the the Supreme Council of the Brotherhood had long joined the Communist Party and had helped to create the American Negro Labor Congress, aligned to the Party. Despite this, however, Briggs held dear to his heart certain black nationalist positions that he took with him to his grave. And when the Party kicked him out in the early 1940s they accused him of being a Negro nationalist, and not without good reason.

Despite the fact that the African Blood Brotherhood was formed around October 1919 during Briggs's leftist move, at inception, the organization was distinct from and independent of the Communist Party. It is claimed that Briggs joined the Party in late 1919, but there is strong evidence to suggest that he joined later. Controversy and considerable confusion surround discussions of the relationship between the Communist Party and the founding of the Brotherhood. I shall, albeit briefly, try to clear up some of the misunderstanding.

In his path-breaking essay on the African Blood Brotherhood, Robert Hill criticized Theodore Draper for claiming that the Brotherhood was organized in 1919 "in complete independence of the Communist Party." He further disagreed with Draper's statement that about two years after the formation of the Brotherhood, "the Communists moved into the Brotherhood by winning over the top leaders." Draper himself was countering an earlier "legend" spread abroad by Communists that the Party had founded the Brotherhood.[111] Hill came to the conclusion that:

> On the basis of the close ties, personal and organizational, between the party's first black recruits, it becomes impossible to divorce the African Blood Brotherhood's inception from Briggs's involvement with the Communist Party in the fall of 1919.[112]

But the weight of the evidence—a substantial part of which was not available when Draper wrote his book in 1960—sustains, rather than overturns, the argument that the Brotherhood was begun independently of the Communist Party.

A key component of Hill's argument is Briggs's claim, years later, that he had joined the Party before the Palmer raids, which took place between November 1919 and January 2, 1920. Briggs, it should be said, was emphatic: "I would say off-hand before the Palmers raids of 19[19]. In fact, I am rather sure that was the case."[113] From this, Hill then suggests that the formation of the African Blood Brotherhood coincided with Briggs's membership of the Communist Party in 1919. But there are serious problems with this argument. There is every reason to believe that Briggs was simply mistaken in claiming that he joined the Party before the Palmer raids. This is largely because his own account of the sequence of events around the formation of the Brotherhood and his entry into the Party—which are laid out in his rich and remarkable correspondence with Draper—repeatedly contradicts and brings into question the timing that Hill gives credence to.

First, Briggs points out in another letter that he joined the Party "after several visits to my office by Rose Pastor Stokes and Bob Minor, each representing what they claimed to be the offical CP I chose Rose's group."[114] The Bureau of Investigation's reports do corroborate the visits uptown of Rose Pastor Stokes and Robert Minor to Briggs and the Supreme Council of the Brotherhood. There were at least two other meetings of the "black Reds," as McKay called them, at the offices of the *Liberator* magazine in 1921. McKay, who at the time was an editor of the *Liberator*, arranged the meetings. Briggs, Domingo, Grace Campbell, Harrison, Moore, along with McKay, had discussions with Robert Minor, a representative of the underground faction of the Workers' Party, and a colleague of McKay's on the editorial board of the magazine. And there was at least one meeting of the leaders of the Brotherhood with Rose Pastor Stokes at her Greeenwich Village home, which again included Hubert Harrison, along with Edgar Grey, his faithful lieutenant in the Liberty League. Pastor Stokes represented the faction of the Party that operated publicly.[115] The visits occurred in 1921, and there may have been some in late 1920, but there is no evidence of official contact as early as 1919, let alone solicitation from the Party.[116] If Briggs was right in saying that he joined the Party in the wake of the visits of Pastor Stokes and Minor, then 1919 could not have been the year he became a card-carrying member; it would have to be 1920 or 1921, the years when both factions of the Party, largely prodded by the Comintern, were energetically wooing the black radicals grouped around the Brotherhood.

Second, Briggs pointed out that "Both Huiswoud and Hendricks [the black charter members of the Party] joined the Brotherhood after I had entered the party—presumably on assignment by the party."[117] If this statement is correct, and there is every reason to believe that it is, then Briggs clearly joined the Party *after* the Brotherhood had been founded. Third, the chronology is further clarified by Briggs's statement that Huiswoud was not among the founders of the Brotherhood.[118]

Briggs repeatedly stated that the Brotherhood was begun independently of the Communist Party. "You are quite correct in assuming that the Communist Party had no part in initiating the organization of the Brotherhood," he told Draper.

> Nor did the Brotherhood owe its inspiration to the Communist movement. It was certainly already in existence when I had my first contact with the Communists, through the visits of Rose [Pastor Stokes] and Bob [Minor] to my office at 2299 Seventh Avenue. Nor did the Communists inspire the A. B. B. program you have seen.[119]

Certainly none of the key members of the organization were members of the Party in 1919. Richard B. Moore was not; Theo Burell and his brother Ben Burell were not; Grace Campbell was not—she ran for the New York State Assembly on the Socialist Party ticket in 1919 and again in November 1920. These were the prime movers behind the formation of the Brotherhood and the members who made up the Supreme Council of the organization at its establishment. Harry Haywood, Briggs said, was wrong in suggesting in a 1948 publication that the Brotherhood was formed by black members of the Party and ex-Garveyites. No, insisted Briggs, "None of us were Communists at the time. And to my knowledge there were only two Negroes in the CP in that period—Otto Huiswoud and one Hendricks. With the exception of Huiswoud, the reverse was the case. That is, it was (some) Brotherhood members who later joined the party."[120]

Hill draws attention to the increasingly pro-Bolshevik editorial policy of the *Crusader* and reads this as an expression of Briggs's membership of the

Communist Party. But there are just as many, if not more, enthusiastically pro-Bolshevik commentaries and analyses in the *Messenger* magazine as there were in the *Crusader*, yet its editors, Randolph and Owen, stayed resolutely within the Socialist Party. W. A. Domingo, who in fact authored some of the key Bolshevik-supporting articles in the *Messenger* and would later become a member of the Supreme Council of the Brotherhood, never joined the Communist Party, and remained, like Randolph and Owen, a member of the Socialist Party.

The evidence suggests, then, that, first, when Briggs began the organization he was not a member of the Communist Party, nor were any of the founders; second, that the Brotherhood came into being independently of the Party, organizationally and programmatically; and, third, that by about 1922, the majority of the leaders of the Supreme Council had joined the Party.[121] Some rank and file members followed the leadership into the Party. But it appears that this was a relatively small minority. Others, especially those in the South, remained outside of the Party. And as Briggs himself later explained, even when the Supreme Council had dissolved the Brotherhood, certain posts—and he vividly remembered the one in West Virginia—continued to operate even after Post Menelik, its headquarters in Harlem, had closed down operations. The intelligence reports give a vivid picture of the shift from an autonomous black organization to one which by the end of 1923 had delivered itself over to the Party, in a process akin to voluntary liquidation.

So why the leftward turn on the part of Briggs? And what essentially did the African Blood Brotherhood stand for?

Developments within the United States and in the wider world account for the leftward turn of Briggs along with many black intellectuals of his generation. The combativity of the working class domestically, as manifested in the large number of strikes, and the growth of the revolutionary left were encouraging signs to Briggs. The rampant and conspicuous profiteering from and during the war by capitalists and landlords caused many to question even further the capitalist system. Briggs, as did the *Messenger* group and many others, came to the conclusion that "The Negro's Place is with Labor," as an editorial declared in June 1919.[122] The government's repression of the left during the Red Scare also increased Briggs's radicalization: the deportation of radical aliens such as Emma Goldman; the raid on the Rand School, an institution of the Socialist Party, by the anti-radical Lusk Committee of the New York State Assembly; the disbarring of the democratically elected members from the New York State Assembly; and the fierce repression of the Industrial Workers of the World (the most progressive working-class organization in the country at the time), especially the imprisonment of its leaders, including the the loved and highly respected Afro-American Ben Fletcher.[123] The attacks on black people by mobs of white thugs in twenty-six American cities in 1919, including Washington DC, and Chicago, contributed to disillusionment with the American system and the radicalization of many black people who were appalled at the way in which the authorities refused to protect or were slow in protecting black citizens from marauding whites.[124]

Outside of the United States, the labor uprisings in the Caribbean, especially in Trinidad, Belize, and Jamaica, and the repression used by the state against strikers and protesters, increased doubts about the capitalist system in general and its colonial outposts in particular.[125] The ferocity of the class struggle in Europe, especially in Germany in 1919, clearly demonstrated that repression operated at the level of class as well as race. Despite the bloody setback in Germany accompanied by the brutal slaughter of Rosa Luxemburg and Karl Liebknecht, and the massacre of hundreds of Indian protesters at Amritsar by the British authorities, 1919 was still marked by tremendous optimism on the part of large sections of the revolutionary forces around the world. (The more astute members of the Bolshevik regime in Russia recognized the massive body blow that the German defeat meant for the world revolution.) The belief was abroad that the world was pregnant with revolution, or at least with progressive transformations for the working class as well as for oppressed nations. "The epoch of final, decisive struggle has come later than the apostles of the socialist revolution [Marx and Engels] had expected and hoped. But it has come," said the Manifesto of the Communist International of 1919. The newly formed affiliate to the Comintern, the Communist Party of America, took up the refrain. "The world is on the verge of a new era," it proclaimed in the first line of its first manifesto.

> Europe is in revolt. The masses of Asia are stirring uneasily. Capitalism is in collapse. The workers of the world are seeing a new life and securing new courage. Out of the night of war is coming a new day.

"The Capitalist class is now making its last stand in history," declared the American Socialist Party in the very first sentence of its manifesto of the same year. This optimism was shared by the black radicals, and found expression, perhaps most sharply, in an editorial in the *Messenger* magazine. Entitled "The March of Soviet Government," it declared:

> Still it continues! The cosmic tread of Soviet government with ceaseless step claims another nation. Russia and Germany have yielded to its human touch and now Hungary joins the people's form of rule. Italy is standing upon a social volcano. France is seething with social unrest. The triple alliance of Great Britain—the railroad, transport and mine workers—threaten to overthrow the economic and political bourbonism of "Merry Old England." The red tide of socialism sweeps on in America. South America is in the throes of revolution.
>
> Soviet government proceeds apace. It bids fair to sweep over the world. The sooner the better. On with the dance![126]

Beyond its direct impact upon the course of the class struggle in Europe, Bolshevism had three added attractions to black radicals in the United States, and indeed elsewhere: first, its domestic policies in relation to nationalities and ethnic minorities, especially Jews; second, its uncompromising rhetoric of anti-colonialism, anti-imperialism, and the right of self-determination for oppressed nations; and, third, the creation of the Third or Communist International (generally abbreviated as the Comintern), launched by Lenin in 1919, and the open anti-colonial, anti-imperialist, and anti-racist resolutions which it loudly proclaimed over the years. Moreover, the Comintern, headquartered in Moscow, explicitly encouraged and appealed to the non-European people to rise up against their colonial oppressors, and it supported the legitimacy of their right to self-determination.

The fact that the Bolsheviks had clamped down on anti-semitism and had effectively brought to an end pogroms against Jews in the territories it controlled was the key piece of evidence with which many black intellectuals decided to support the Bolshevik Revolution. It is true that the Bolsheviks' contiguous policy of support of the rights of oppressed nations to self-determination was also important to winning black support—to Cyril Briggs this was the crucial element within Bolshevik policy which commanded his support for the Revolution as a whole—but what was generally regarded as the exemplary policy of the Bolsheviks toward stamping out anti-semitism and other forms of racism was what caught the eye of oppressed Afro-America. The direct and burning question "Did Bolshevism Stop Race Riots in Russia?" forms the title of Domingo's article in the *Messenger*. Having carefully weighed the evidence Domingo came to the conclusion that it did.

> Will Bolshevism accomplish the full freedom of Africa, colonies in which Negroes are in the majority, and promote human tolerance and happiness in the United States by the eradication of the causes of such disgraceful occurrences as the Washington and Chicago race riots? The answer is deducible from the analogy of Soviet Russia, a country in which dozens of racial and lingual types have settled their many differences and found a common meeting ground, a country from which the lynch rope is banished and in which racial tolerance and peace now exist.[127]

Claude McKay, who in 1921 served on the Supreme Council of the Brotherhood, agreed with Domingo, and indeed invoked the article in a debate over Bolshevism with the editor of the *Negro World*, William Ferris. "Every Negro," McKay proclaims,

> who lays claim to leadership should make a study of Bolshevism and explain its meaning to the colored masses. It is the greatest and most scientific idea afloat in the world today that can be easily put into practice by the proletariat to better its material and spiritual life. Bolshevism (as Mr Domingo ably points out in the current *Messenger*) has made Russia safe for the Jew. It has liberated the Slav

peasant from priest and bureaucrat who can no longer egg him on to murder Jews to bolster up their rotten institutions. It might make these United States safe for the Negro. When the cracker slave frees his mind of the nightmare of race equality, when he finds out that his parasite politicians have been fooling him for years, when he takes back the soil from his Bourbon exploiters and is willing to till it alongside of the Negro and tries to forget that he is a "nigger", while the latter ceases to think of him in terms of poor trash, when the Vardamans and Cole Bleases find themselves jobless, then the artificial hate that breeds lynchings and race riots might suddenly die.

If the Russian idea should take hold of the white masses of the western world, and they should rise in united strength and overthrow their imperial capitalist government, then the black toilers would automatically be free! Will their leaders educate them now to make good use of their advantages eventually?[128]

Within less than two years, McKay would once again be crossing swords with another black editor over the significance of the Bolshevik Revolution. In his letter to the editor of the *Crisis*, W. E. B. Du Bois, McKay made an impassioned defense of the Revolution:

I am surprised and sorry that in your editorial . . . you should leap out of your sphere to sneer at the Russian Revolution, the greatest event in the history of humanity; much greater than the French Revolution, which is held up as a wonderful achievement to Negro children and students in white and black schools. For American Negroes the indisputable and outstanding fact of the Russian revolution is that a mere handful of Jews, much less in ratio to the number of Negroes in the American population, have attained, through the Revolution, all the political and social rights that were denied to them under the regime of the Czar.[129]

Socialism was, in McKay's estimation, the most effective and promising vehicle to achieve the goal of black liberation.

Given his black nationalist bent, it comes as no surprise that Briggs found the anti-colonial thrust the most attractive side of Bolshevism. Indeed, he claimed that his interest in Communism was "inspired by the national policy of the Russian Bolsheviks and the anti-imperialist orientation of the Soviet State birthed by the October Revolution. I was at the time more interested . . . in the national liberation revolution than in the social revolution."[130] When in 1921 the *Crusader* appealed to its readers to send contributions to alleviate the famine in Russia, it articulated its request around Soviet Russia's "friendly and fair-minded attitude towards the darker races and her concrete acts of friendship to them." Russia deserved support because

Of all the great powers Soviet Russia is the only power that deals fairly with weaker nations and peoples. She is the only power that has no skeleton of murderous subjugation and wrongdoing in her national closet—no spectre of a brutally oppressed Ireland or Haiti.[131]

In the spring of 1919, news spread abroad that there was a Negro in Lenin's cabinet. The source of this rumor appears to have been a Dr Simon, who testified before a Congressional committee that a Professor Gordon, a black man, was a member of the Bolshevik cabinet. True or false, this was taken up by the black radical press, and the *Crusader*, along with the *Messenger*, saw this as another wonderful black feather in the cap of red Russia. Indeed, in a *Crusader* editorial, aptly entitled "Make Their Cause Your Own," urging its black readers to support socialism, the following remark opened the discussion: "The Soviet Government of Russia is the only government outside of our own Africa and democratic South America in which a Negro occupies a high and responsible position. And Soviet Russia has neither Negro population nor Negro 'colonies'."[132] The *Messenger* magazine wrote a bitingly ironic editorial, concluding: "No better evidence of the demoralization of Bolshevism could be adduced in this country than the fact of a Negro's being in the Soviet Cabinet!"[133] Was there a black man in Lenin's cabinet in 1919? There is no evidence that there was; no evidence of a Professor Gordon or any other black person, for that matter, in the Bolshevik cabinet. (The rumor was spread by people who opposed Bolshevism, and for whom the presence of a black person in such a cabinet was, as the *Messenger* suggests, the ultimate in moral degeneration, the relapse into barbarism.) There were, however, respected black Bolsheviks, mainly descendants of Africans who had settled several generations before along the Black Sea. They fought, distinguished themselves and rose in Trotsky's Red Army, moistened the Russian soil with their blood during the Civil War, and at least one served in the Soviet of Tblisi, the capital of Georgia in the 1920s.[134] Of course, whether or not Professor Gordon existed does not matter for our purposes. What matters is that the black radicals reinforced their support of Bolshevik Russia on hearing of such a phenomenon. And this indicates clearly the way in which the black radicals' perceptions of Russia's policies on race and nationalities underpinned their support for the revolution.

The Bolsheviks, as far as Briggs and the others were concerned, were the deadly enemies of black people's enemies, which meant that Lenin and Trotsky were their friends. Thus it was possible that on the same editorial page of the *Crusader* Briggs could declare in the most certain terms his support of Bolshevism and the doctrine of Negro First without perceiving any contradiction. His angry but considered remarks—written, it should be said, at the height of the "Red Scare"—entitled "Bolshevist!!!" is worth citing at length:

> Bolshevist is the epithet that present-day reactionaries delight to fling around loosely against those who insist on thinking for themselves and on agitating for their rights. We do not know exactly what the reactionaries desire to convey by the term—we do not think that they know themselves. However, if as appears by its frequent use against those who are agitating in the people's interests and for justice for the oppressed, the term is intended to cover those "bad agitators," who are not content that the people shall forever be enslaved in the clutches of the cut-throat, child-exploiting, capitalist-imperialist crew, then assuredly we are

Bolshevists. This epithet nor any other holds any terrors for us. If to fight for one's rights is to be Bolshevists, then we are Bolshevists and let them make the most of it!

And for the further information of the asses who use the term so loosely we will make the statement that we would not for a moment hesitate to ally ourselves with any group, if by such an alliance we could compass the liberation of our race and the redemption of our Fatherland. A man pressed to earth by another with murderous intent is not under any obligation to choose his weapons. He would be a fool if he did not use any or whatever weapon was within his reach. Self-preservation is the first law of human nature.

Immediately following this, and in the very same column, appears his comments under the heading "Negro First!" His remarks are, again, unrestrained in spite of the times:

For the benefit of the serviles and lick-spittles who are shocked because we refuse to profess perfect contentment under oppression or slavishly to designate a *Living Hell* as a "free, grand and glorious country," the editor of *The Crusader* desires to state that, while he is, theoretically, an "American citizen"—with all the surplus of duties and lack of rights which characterize a Negro "American citizen"—he is still and always has been a NEGRO BEFORE ANYTHING ELSE and will continue so to be until Negro "American citizens" are not only American citizens in theory, but in practice as well.

This choice is not voluntary. It is forced upon us and upon every other Negro of spirit—and, we might add, of intelligence—by the open denial to our people of the most ordinary rights of American citizenship—rights that are so ordinary as to be enjoyed even by the unnaturalized white foreigner in the land, but which, most ordinary as they are, and open to the enjoyment of the white alien, are yet denied to us in every section of the country.

The problem is not confined to the United States, said Briggs. It is an international one: the Negro is denied equal rights and the merest justice under any of the existing white governments. "And therein lies the reason," Briggs declared, "why all Negroes with an ounce of spirit and intelligence are, in their own minds as well as in the minds of the whites, NEGRO FIRST, LAST AND ALL TIME!"[135]

This seemingly impossible, double and simultaneous embrace of revolutionary socialism and black nationalism marked the ideology of the Brotherhood.

The manner in which the formation of the African Blood Brotherhood was brought to public attention must rate as one of the most bizarre for any group with political ambition. There was no announcement in one of the many public forums in Harlem; no banner headline on the cover of the *Crusader*, edited by the Brotherhood's founder and leader; it did not appear on the editorial page of the magazine; it was not even signalled on the contents page. Instead, one finds it quietly tucked away on page twenty-seven of the thirty-one-paged *Crusader* of October 1919. There it was, not even boxed like the tailor's advertisement above it asking "Men Why Wear Torn Shirts?" or like the one below boasting "If You Are Awake You Will Read *The Messenger*." Coyly and inconspicuously it simply disclosed in a rectangular space less than two square inches in size: "Mr. Cyril Briggs, Editor of *The Crusader* announces the organization of **The African Blood Brotherhood** for African Liberation and Redemption. Membership by enlistment. No dues, fees or assessment. Those only need apply who are willing to go the limit. Write or call at 2299 Seventh Avenue, New York, USA."[136] No telephone number was given, even though the *Crusader* had a telephone; no program, no list of aims and objectives beyond the broad one of liberating Africa. Remarkably, people wrote in to join from different parts of the United States, the Caribbean, and Central America. Among the first Afro-Americans writing in to join was a disproportionate number of black veterans from the First World War. Given the sparseness of the information about the Brotherhood in the announcement, it is surprising the level of enthusiasm with which some people wrote in to be enlisted. One man asking to be enrolled wrote: "I do not know what it is all about or what your intentions or dreams are; but I have followed your writings quite closely in the past and have the fullest confidence in your sanity, prudence and brain capacity." Another, the writer of the very first of the volunteers' letters published in the *Crusader*, mailed Briggs all the way from Panama for "particulars about enlistment". But one wonders why he asked for them, for he told Briggs:

> In the meantime, please put my name at the head of the list, or as near to the head as you may deem fit, in bold Roman type, as I am one of those Negroes who is prepared to go the limit—and then some—for the liberation of my Race and the Redemption of the Fatherland—Africa. I am with you heart and soul and body in this work and depend upon me to give a good account of myself in whatever way I am called upon to serve.

S. C. Jordan—one of the few whose name was somehow not deleted by Briggs for security purposes—could hardly wait to engage the enemy:

> Now, Mr. Briggs, I am with you, and, of course, that means that I am going the limit. I always liked to play that limit game. I don't know what your game is, but I believe I can play it with you. So enroll me as one of those extreme limit players . . . .[I]f I can render any service for you in your proposition, I am at your service and await the call.[137]

The response would doubtless have been greater if the publicity was better and the aims and objectives of the Brotherhood more fully revealed. So why was the launch so reticent and low-key? The answer appears to have been fairly straightforward: Briggs and the founders of the African Blood Brotherhood were attempting to recruit new members to a secret organization that they wanted to keep secret from white people. When he published the first letter from a man asking to be enlisted in the Brotherhood, Briggs explained that the writer's name was withheld "as it is not our purpose to give the white man any information concerning the membership and *purpose* of this organization."[138] This, of course, in effect meant that the purpose of the Brotherhood was kept secret even from the readers of the magazine, never mind the wider black population. Prospective black recruits would never know the wider aims and objectives of the organization unless they specifically requested them from the Harlem office of the *Crusader*, or have them disclosed by someone who was already a member. But, inevitably, in the beginning there were few members.

The ideal that Briggs and the others aspired to seemed to have been a secret organization with mass black following. It took a good while for the leaders to realize that this was an unattainable goal. It was not until February 1920 that they published a full-page recruitment advertisement for the Brotherhood. Though much bigger than the October announcement, it imparted little more information than the earlier effort. Claiming that over a thousand "red-blooded Negro patriots," including women, had already enlisted in the organization, it declared: "Ethiopia Expects That Every Negro This Day Will Do His Duty!" If you could not join because of family obligations or other responsibilities, then your money would do, but, said the announcement, "we would much rather have YOU!"[139] It took another four months before something resembling a program was published in the magazine. Simply entitled "The African Blood Brotherhood," the article explained that the Brotherhood was probably the first Negro secret organization created in the Western world having as its sole purpose the liberation of Africa and the redemption of the Negro race. It briefly outlined the structure of the organization, with its posts, the "supreme council or war college" of five, which superintended the Brotherhood. It told of the existence of its own rituals, "degrees, pass-words, signs, etc., and a formal initiation ceremony when a solemn oath is taken." At that time there were no stipulated fees or membership dues. "These are left to the patriotism and financial ability of each member." The document also pointed out that under the rules of the organization, the word of the supreme council, when issued in the form of "instructions," "must be considered as law" by members of the Brotherhood. When issued in the form of "suggestions" it is expected "to command at least respectful and careful consideration."[140] A list of sixteen suggestions was issued by the council, covering the patronization of race enterprise; the encouragement of the UNIA, which it described as "the biggest thing so far effected in surface movement"; learning a trade; adopting the policy of race first; organizing literary clubs for the discussion and study of Negro history and problems; waging war against "alien education being taught our children in the white man's school"—"Inculcate race pride in the little ones by instructing them at home in the facts of Negro achievement." Significantly, the first suggestion on this long list reads:

Affiliate yourself with liberal, radical and labor movements. Don't mind being called "Bolsheviki" by the same people who call you "nigger." Such affiliation in itself won't solve our problems, but it will help immensely.[141]

For the first time, the readers of the *Crusader* were made privy to some of the more programmatic ideas and tactics of the Brotherhood's leadership. A separate program was apparently issued in 1920, but never published in the magazine. It called for: a liberated race; absolute race equality; the fostering of racial self-respect; organized and uncompromising opposition to the Ku Klux Klan; a united Negro front with which to oppose the Klan; industrial development along co-operative lines; higher wages for Negro labor, shorter hours and better living conditions; education of the race at all levels and methods, including forums, newspapers, etc.; co-operation with other darker races and with the class-conscious white workers. The Brotherhood was unapologetic and forthright in supporting its controversial promotion of a cross-racial class alliance:

> The Negro masses must get out of their minds the stupid idea that it is necessary for two groups to love each other before they can enter into an alliance against their common enemy. Not love or hatred, but *Identiy of Interest at the Moment*, dictates the tactics of practical people.[142]

Another program was produced in time for the August 1921 Convention of the UNIA in Harlem. This retained the central points of the earlier program, elaborated upon and carefully argued through, but was more polemical in language and purpose. Its primary aim was to help siphon off as many as possible of Garvey's followers attending the convention. Although the UNIA is nowhere mentioned by name in the document, everyone knew who the target of the Brotherhood was. The program concluded:

> To be kidded along with the idea that because a few hundreds of us assemble once in a while in a convention that therefore we are free to legislate for ourselves; to fall for the bunk that before having made any serious effort to free our country, before having crossed swords on the field of battle with the oppressors, we can have a government of our own, with presidents, potentates, royalties and other queer mixtures; to speak about wasting our energies and money in propositions like Bureaus of Passports and Identifications, diplomatic representatives, etc., is to indulge in pure moonshine and supply free amusement for our enemies. Surely, intelligent, grown-up individuals will not stand for such childish nonsense if at all they are serious about fighting for Negro liberation! We must come down to earth, to actual practical facts and realities and build our strength upon solid foundations—and not upon titled and decorated tomfoolery.[143]

In December of the same year, the Brotherhood issued a "Condensed and Tentative Constitution," which, its title notwithstanding, was a detailed and carefully considered document having some twenty-two articles. Significantly, Article II, which lists the organization's Aims and Objects, while essentially retaining the earlier demands, makes no reference to class

alliance across the color line, a prominent constant of previous formulations. This may have been due to two developments. First, the influence of
Bishop George A. McGuire, former Chaplain-General to the UNIA, who
just weeks before had broken publicly and acrimoniously with Garvey and
joined the Council of the Brotherhood, and helped draft the new Constitution to which he was a signatory; and, second, the attempt of the
Brotherhood to increase its success in recruiting disgruntled Garveyites by
apparently down-playing its socialist beliefs.[144] The document announced
the calling of the First International Convention of the African Blood
Brotherhood, which would be a constitutional convention, to revise, amend,
amplify, and ratify the Condensed and Tentative Constitution. The Convention was scheduled for July 16, 1922, and was planned to take place on
July 16 every year—"the anniversary of the death of our illustrious blood
brother, Toussaint L'Ouverture"—but it never happened.[145] And the
Brotherhood was soon transformed through its relation with the Communist Party of the United States of America. It officially ceased—disbanded
by the Supreme Council—in 1925. But from the end of 1923 it lacked any
semblance of an independent organization.

There are two important dimensions to the program and work of the
Brotherhood that hitherto have been ignored by commentators and are
deserving of mention, even though they cannot be fully analysed here.
Much of this work was only known to members of the organization and is
only known by us today because of the extraordinarily intense surveillance
of the organization by government agents through the Bureau of Investigations, operating out of the Justice Department.

First, in addition to its revolutionary political ambitions, the Brotherhood attempted to double up as a mutual aid society. In the fall of 1923
the Supreme Council decided to expend extra effort to establish an
insurance scheme for its members. Why the effort should be made at that
point in the life of the organization is not entirely clear. From the imperfect
evidence available, it appears that the motive was to make the organization
more attractive to potential members and to help retain the existing
members, while providing a set of valuable services to the race. The most
detailed information about the new services offered by the Brotherhood is
contained in a special bulletin sent to members in November 1923. In the
document, addressed to "Dear Sisters and Brothers," the Supreme Executive
Council proudly announced the opening of its Insurance Department. The
services of the Department would be opened to members only. Sickness and
death benefit would now be provided by the Brotherhood. To be eligible,
an initiation fee of $2.00 for persons under forty-six, $5.00 for those
between forty-six and sixty-five, and $10.00 for those between sixty-five
and seventy, would have to be paid. Dues would be charged at fifty cents
per month for all members. Sickness benefit would be paid at the rate of
$6.00 per week for the first forty weeks, and $3.00 per week for another
forty weeks if necessary. Death benefit of one hundred dollars would be

paid within twenty-four hours of notification to the family of the deceased. No member would be eligible for benefit within the first six months of joining the scheme, and the document made further stipulations about the payment of dues. The Council also informed members that "each Post has the right as a branch of a fraternal organization, to ask for contributions from its membership for the purpose of further helping the family of a deceased brother or sister, and may use all constitutional means whereby to raise such monies as they are needed." Coming in the wake of the Black Star Line fiasco and the indictment of Garvey, to allay fears, the Council outlined the measures taken to secure the funds of the scheme. Among these was the separation of the Insurance Department funds from those of the rest of the Brotherhood. And to drive its point home, the document closed with the ringing declaration: "THE A.B.B.—THE NEGRO'S ROCK OF GIBRALTAR!"[146]

It is not known how many members joined the scheme and how well, if at all, it worked. What we do know is that within a year or so, the Brotherhood had dissolved itself, and no doubt the scheme came to an end. It is possible, however, that individual Posts that continued, despite the dissolution from headquarters, might have made their own mutual aid arrangements, albeit on a less ambitious scale.

Unlike the insurance scheme, the idea of co-operative economic arrangements is one that figured early and prominently in the Brotherhood's program. But it, too, gained sustained attention around the same time that the mutual aid system was being pursued. Unlike the first scheme, however, there is no evidence of the Brotherhood ever succeeding in establishing a co-operative. Briggs had grand schemes of twenty-five co-operative stores in the major cities of black settlement, with stocks costing $25.00 each which would be sold to members of the Brotherhood only.[147] The Supreme Council delegated Huiswoud to approach the comrades in the leadership of the Workers' Party to see if they would support a store in Harlem, but nothing came of it. There was also talk of a wholesale store owned by the Brotherhood. Briggs, reported the government spy, lamented the fact that members "had so much trouble getting what they wanted without paying high prices."[148]

There was much talk of co-operatives in 1923 but nothing came of it. The Brotherhood, nevertheless, seemed to have taken the idea seriously. And seriously enough to have an officer on its Supreme Council responsible for Consumers' Co-operatives. Richard B. Moore had apparently held the position in 1921, but by 1923 he carried the title of Educational Director.[149] The position of Director of Consumers' Co-operatives was held by an outstanding member of the Brotherhood, Grace P. Campbell, one of the most important and least known members of the black left from the First World War to her death in 1943.[150]

*

History has been unkind to Grace Campbell. When referred to at all in discussions of black radicalism in the early twentieth century, hardly any information is given about her background and role; and the little that is given tends to be inaccurate. Campbell deserves much better than that. Claude McKay and Richard B. Moore, two of her comrades in the 1920s, remembered her well and kindly, but gave few details about her. McKay spoke of her as a pioneer in the Socialist and Communist parties and admired her work, especially during the Depression. Moore, writing in 1963 of "Africa-Conscious Harlem," mentions Campbell among the militant socialists of the 1920s who "all steadily emphasized the liberation of the oppressed African and other colonial peoples as a vital aim in their worldview." And in a 1969 television broadcast on "Afro-Americans and Radical Politics," he spoke of Campbell runnning on the Socialist ticket for the New York State Assembly after the First World War. He further mentioned that Campbell was a "humanitarian social worker who maintained, largely from her own earnings, a needed home for deserted young mothers."[151] But Campbell was all these and more. She was one of the first women, black or white, to run for public office in the State of New York. She was probably the first black woman to join the Socialist Party; and almost certainly the first to join the Communist Party. As Moore said, she ran a home for young women and their babies, the Empire Friendly Shelter.[152] And this she did while working for the city as a parole officer. She had previously done "valuable work," the *New York Age* reported, for the Association for the Protection of Colored Women, one of the forerunners of the National Urban League.[153] She apparently worked for the City of New York from 1915 up to her death on June 8, 1943, aged sixty. Campbell started her civil service work as a probation officer, she then worked as a parole officer, and finally through her stellar performance in a competitive examination in 1924, she became a court attendant for the Courts of Sessions. In the examination Campbell ranked first out of a field of 164 candidates, scoring 91.32 percent. There was only one vacancy and she got it, earning a salary of $2,500 per annum.[154]

Campbell was the only woman among the founders of the African Blood Brotherhood and she was the only one to serve on its Supreme Council. As I shall show, she was a key force in the Brotherhood. And even if historians do not recognize Grace Campbell's importance to the New Negro radicalism of the African Blood Brotherhood, the Bureau of Investigations did, accurately describing her in a 1923 report as "one of the prime movers in the organization."[155] It is primarily through their tireless surveillance that we have been able to reconstruct the major role that Campbell played in the Brotherhood and the radicalism of the 1920s.

It is often assumed and suggested—perhaps because she moved within an overwhelming Caribbean milieu—that Grace P. Campbell was from the islands. She was not. She was, however, of Caribbean descent on her father's side; it is more than likely that her father, William Campbell, came from Jamaica. Her mother, Emma Dyson Campbell, was an Afro-American woman from Washington, DC, where Campbell spent part of her childhood and youth. Campbell was born in Georgia in 1882. Ten years later, when her sister Mary was born, the family was living in Texas. The family later moved to Washington from where Campbell moved to New York City in about 1905.[156]

Campbell's political evolution prior to 1905 is unknown. But from 1905 to the late 1930s she increasingly joined her relief and racial uplift politics of the Progressive Era with revolutionary socialism. She was a dedicated political activist all her adult life, and somehow managed to combine a successful career in the civil service with radical dissent. She ran on the Socialist ticket for the State Assembly, in 1919 and again in 1920, receiving just over 7 percent and almost 10.5 percent, respectively, of the vote. In the 1920 campaign, the *Messenger* described her as "the first colored woman to be named for public office on a regular party ticket in the United States of America."[157]

But Campbell was quickly moving leftward and away from the Socialist Party. Like the other founders of the African Blood Brotherhood, the Bolshevik Revolution accelerated her radicalization. Her ideological orientation was similar to that of Briggs, although her animosity toward Garvey had developed earlier as she had helped found in 1920, and was an officer of, the Friends of Negro Freedom, an anti-Garvey front. Her home at 206 West 133rd Street served as the meeting place of the Supreme Council of the Brotherhood. She dealt with much of the correspondence of the Brotherhood. When ill, the meetings of the Brotherhood were cancelled. Significantly, not only did this apply to the Supreme Council, but to Post Menelik as a whole. While the Supreme Council sometimes met in the absence of Cyril Briggs, its official leader, it never did when Grace Campbell could not make it. She seemed to have been a tireless agitator, present at every meeting of the Brotherhood, public and private.

Although she often spoke in public, her forte was organizing. Making sure halls were booked, dues collected, comrades delegated to do particular tasks. Campbell tried to bring more black women over to her brand of radicalism but with little success. According to a 1921 Bureau of Investigations report, "[she] is conducting an active campaign among the colored women, but so far is unsuccessful as these women are not at all interested in Socialism and don't care to learn."[158] There were, however, a small, but significant number of black women on the left in the 1920s. In 1921 Campbell served as the Secretary of the Twenty-First Assembly District Socialist Club (generally referred by its participants at the time as the 21st AD Socialist Club), in Harlem. Largely the product of Hubert Harrison's earlier work on behalf of the Socialist Party in the district, with the exception of one Jewish member, the club was a black one. And in the early years of its formation Grace Campbell was, it is claimed, the only woman member.[159] The role she played in the club was noticed by government spies. When "P-138" spoke of nearly all the Negro radicals carrying "the Bolshevic [*sic*] red card," he also noted their paying "their monthly dues, which is [*sic*] collected by MISS GRACE CAMPBELL (colored), secretary of the uptown branch."[160] She was one of the organizers of the People's Educational Forum, which met every Sunday at 4 p.m. in Room 4 of the Lafayette Theatre. The Forum was well covered by the government spies and the activists knew it, but that did not stop them. Indeed, on occasion they taunted the agents.

The Forum, first organized in 1920, was a joint effort of the radicals. The Socialists around the *Messenger* magazine, such as Randolph and Owen, and those who had joined the Communist Party, such as Otto Huiswoud, would all participate in its organization and proceedings. Domingo, Moore, Campbell, Frank Crosswaithe, were all behind the Forum. It was in essence a black socialist political space, aimed, no doubt, at contesting the black nationalists at Liberty Hall. It was lively and earnest, but it was hardly a rival to Garvey's house. Its pluck was reflected in its motto: "Lay on Macduff; And damn'd be him that first cries, 'Hold, enough!'"[161] More prosaically, it would declare in its publicity, "Knowledge is Power." Hubert Harrison, Elizabeth Gurley Flynn, David Berenberg from the Rand School of Social Science, Fenton Johnson, Franz Boas, Du Bois, and Walter White would speak at the Forum. At other times members of the organizing group, such as Chandler Owen, would speak. Richard B. Moore described the Forum as an "intellectual battleground" "an arena" where "he who came there would have to be ready to battle for his ideas."[162] To the government spy the Forum was "the uptown Negro branch of the Bolshevic [*sic*] free lecture room."[163] As a leading member of the Forum, Campbell's participation would be frequently remarked upon in the intelligence reports.

Campbell, unfortunately, never wrote any articles, let alone published a book; there is no evidence that she ever wrote a letter to the press. She frequently spoke but only the gist and snippets were reported. She clearly was not an orator of the "fire eating" variety that Richard B. Moore evidently was. And unlike Cyril Briggs, who despite his stammer was always voluble, revealing his deepest thoughts and dreams—even going through a fire-arms catalog, discussing cost and quality—to a paid informer in the guise of a Brother, Campbell was generally cautious, revealing little, perhaps suspicious of the interloper in their midst. When approached by the press, she would direct them to another member of the Supreme Council. Although she was willing to speak in public at meetings, even from the platform of the Communist Party in the 1930s, she seemed reticent to have her public utterances recorded. She might have feared "jeopardizing her job," as one of her critics within the faction-ridden Party suggested in 1929, but that hardly explains her behavior.[164] In letters to her friends, however, she revealed her inner world. Unfortunately, the few that survive are concerned with the later period of her life.

Campbell commanded the respect of her comrades and was genuinely liked. No doubt, some of her authority stemmed from the fact that she was older than most of the New Negro radicals, including the other members of the Supreme Council of the Brotherhood. But she was able to lead primarily because her comrades recognized her commitment, selflessness, and even goodness. Campbell, who remained single all her life and had no children, unlike many of the members of the black middle class around her, did not simply sit down on her relatively fat civil service salary. She tried, in the spirit of the National Association of Colored Women's Club, to lift as she climbed, expending her own resources to help those in need. She evidently came to the conclusion that the problems of black people in America required something more radical than relief—important though relief was. Like the rest of the Brotherhood, Bolshevism appeared to her to have been the solution. And in September 1922, a Bureau of Investigations special agent reported, not implausibly, that she had joined the Communist Party.[165] Within a year, the leadership of the local branch of the Workers' Party would be holding meetings in her house at 206 West 133rd Street, rather like the Supreme Council of the Brotherhood.

There was so much overlapping between the Brotherhood and the Workers' Party that they must at times have seemed indistinct at the level of leadership. But there were important differences. In the summer of 1923 several reports appeared—one emanating from as far away as Johannesburg—alleging a merger between the African Blood Brotherhood and the Workers' Party of America. "The African Blood Brotherhood," retorted Briggs in the *Crusader Service*, "is not affiliated with the Workers' Party of America, or with any other political party, for that matter, and is not the official Communist organization among Negroes."[166] Briggs was technically correct because although some of the leading members of the Supreme Council of the Brotherhood were members of the Party, the two organizations were distinct. But on November 22, 1923 at a meeting of the Harlem Branch of the Workers' Party, plans were laid for the effective merger of the two organizations. The Workers' Party agreed to help finance an office and a forum jointly run by the local party branch and the Brotherhood. This was a proposition that Briggs had made months before to the Party leadership downtown. But according to the intelligence report, there was an explicit condition laid down by the Party for its support of the Brotherhood: "all these donations were made with the proviso that in the future the Workers' Party of America would be in charge of the activities of the African Blood Brotherhood." The meeting, held at Grace Campbell's house, was chaired by Otto Huiswoud and attended by twenty-three people, twenty of whom were black. A white member of the local branch, a man by the name of Marshall, had brought the news from the Central Executive Committe of the Workers' Party. According to Marshall, the African Blood Brotherhood would in the future be required to inform the local branch whenever a forum was to be held so that a representative of the Workers' Party might be present. Further, the Party wanted each of its members in a trade to join the appropriate union and report to the secretary of the Party branch when they had done so, the object, said the report, "being to have such members spread the Communist propaganda and bore from within the union."[167]

On November 25, three days after the Workers' Party meeting, the Supreme Council of the Brotherhood called a special meeting of its own. At that meeting the Council agreed to the arrangements suggested by the Party. The details of the discussion are not known (the Justice Department spy was not a member of the Supreme Council). But the day after the meeting Briggs is reported to have said that the Supreme Council thought it was

> the best policy as they had no office and the Workers' Party could help the A. B. B. as well as the A. B. B. could help them; that as all the members of the Supreme Council were members of the Workers['] Party the A. B. B. will benefit by their policies as well as making workers out of some of the A. B. B.; that there are things in the A. B. B. that are of advantage to one in the Workers['] Party as the Workers['] Party can have a forum only where directed by the C.[entral] E.[xecutive] C.[ommittee] while on the other hand members of both could run it under the head of the A. B. B.

Briggs remarked, reported the agent, "that he was going to get out some notices for the members to be present at the meeting of the A. B. B. as it will be business of importance."[168] Like a bad omen, bad weather prevented the meeting from taking place as scheduled on the night of November 30; it was re-scheduled for December 7, 1923. We do not know what happened. We do know, however, that by the end of 1923 the African Blood Brotherhood had effectively ceased functioning as an independent political organization. It persisted for a time in name, but its bold, clear, and defiant black voice that brought such cheer to its suffering admirers in the diaspora would in the future be drowned out by the tuneless chorus of the Workers' Party of America.

Why did the Supreme Council so readily succumb to the blandishments of the Workers' Party? Was the independence of the organization sold for the proverbial mess of pottage, less than a hundred dollars a month from the Workers' Party? The answers to these questions are complex, but are of key importance to the understanding of the black left in the United States of America.

Evidently, the Brotherhood had financial problems. It had not the resources to rent an office on its own, nor did it have the money to rent space for holding public meetings on a regular basis. Such circumstances clearly made the proposition from the Workers' Party attractive to the leadership of the Brotherhood. But why did it have money problems in the first place? Briggs blamed the recession of the early 1920s for much of the financial difficulty of the organization and the demise of the *Crusader* magazine, which ceased publication at the end of 1922. And the recession no doubt contributed to the problems of the Brotherhood. But there is far more to the explanation than that. First, because the Brotherhood had a small membership base—certainly nothing remotely approaching the gigantic membership of the UNIA—when the recession came and members became unemployed, dues could not be paid and the organization's revenues inevitably fell. The UNIA experienced a similar decline in dues, partly because of the recesssion, but because it had a larger membership it was able to withstand the fall in revenue more effectively. Therefore, it was not so much the recession itself that adversely affected the Brotherhood but its relatively narrow membership and therefore financial base. Second, after the magazine ceased publication, the Brotherhood made it a priority of the organization to continue a news service. Through the *Crusader Service*, directed by Cyril Briggs, the organization sent out on a weekly basis analyses and news items to over a hundred black newspapers free of charge. A substantial amount of time and resources were spent on the service and the Brotherhood's ideas were disseminated and its influence grew, but how could such an enterprise sustain itself without an income? Claude Barnett made a similar news service—with the important omission of radicalism— the Associated Negro Press, a paying proposition in the 1920s; Briggs and the Brotherhood did not. Third, the vicious fight against Garvey, especially between 1921 and 1922, extensively carried and waged in the pages of the *Crusader*, alienated and antagonized many members and supporters of the Brotherhood. From its inception, the Brotherhood largely shared its constituency and membership with the UNIA and Marcus Garvey, who had an extraordinarily large personal following. With every salvo fired at Garvey by its leaders, members would leave the Brotherhood and complain. True, the Brotherhood made some inroads into disgruntled and disaffected members of the leadership of the UNIA. Members of the black intelligentsia fed up with Garvey would often turn to the ABB, but these could hardly make up for the large number of ordinary rank-and-file members who left the organization. The *Messenger* magazine also suffered for its attacks on Garvey, but it had a sizeable white readership within the Socialist Party, and it relied heavily upon the subsidy provided by the Party of which its editors, Randolph and Owen, were loyal members. Briggs and the Supreme Council of the Brotherhood did not have a similar relationship with the Workers' Party and suffered accordingly. And the *Crusader* with its eclectic mix of black nationalism and socialism did not have the sizeable white readership that the *Messenger* had.

But it would be a travesty, a gross misunderstanding of the African Blood Brotherhood, to assume that the arrangement with the Workers' Party at the end of 1923 was the result of mere financial expediency, a sordid bartering of independence for a few dollars. Nothing could be further from the truth. The fact is, as Briggs explained, that the overwhelming majority of the Supreme Council and certainly the most active and influential members of the Brotherhood, were already members of the Workers' Party by the beginning of 1923. The African Blood Brotherhood and the Workers' Party were in many instances one and the same as far as some of the members of the Brotherhood were concerned. Thus the new arrangement with the Workers' Party to someone like Huiswoud, the National Organizer of the ABB, made no difference in terms of his political life and Party discipline. The problem that arose with the concordat of 1923 was that it left high and dry rank-and-file members and complete posts of the Brotherhood who would not be seen dead within the Workers' Party.

But why the attraction to the Workers' Party in the first place? The answer is straightforward but often misunderstood. The fact is, as we have seen, that the Bolshevik Revolution and what it was seen to stand for were powerful magnets to black radicals. For Cyril Briggs, for Grace Campbell, for Claude McKay, for Richard B. Moore, for Harry Haywood and his brother Otto Hall, the Workers' Party and later the Communist Party were simply the American division of Lenin's international and multinational army of revolutionaries, the Communist International. These black revolutionaries did not join the American party, they had joined the Comintern. They had joined the organization that declared at its founding congress in 1919: "Colonial slaves of Africa and Asia! The hour of the proletarian dictatorship in Europe will strike for you as the hour of your own emancipation!" They had joined the organization that, they observed, had embarrassed the white American comrades to take more seriously the Negro Question; they noted that Lenin had intervened personally in 1920 to see to it that the issue was addressed, and had, further, drafted with his own hands, the "Theses on the National and Colonial Questions." They had joined the Comintern that had so warmly welcomed two of their own comrades from the African Blood Brotherhood, Claude McKay and Otto Huiswoud, at its Fourth Congress in Moscow in 1922; and they noted the resolution on the "Negro Question" that their own Brothers had played a key role in drafting.[169]

They were especially delighted and pleasantly surprised by the extraordinarily generous reception that McKay received from the Russian people; a glimpse into a non-racist future. "Look at Claude McKay in Soviet Russia today," exclaimed Edward Doty, an Afro-American member of the Chicago Post of the Brotherhood, "he is one of our group, and he is received with open arms, and there is no discrimination."[170] No doubt Doty read the press reports about McKay in Russia, but in addition he would have seen McKay's jubilant report of his Russian experience recently published in the *Crisis* in two parts and lavishly illustrated with photographs. "Those Russian days remain the most memorable of my life," McKay wrote.[171] Otto Huiswoud returned from Russia and told his comrades about his experience. McKay remained in Europe but wrote to Grace Campbell and

Briggs, sending the latter a letter from Trotsky on the Negro Question that Briggs published in the *Crusader Service* release of September 24, 1923.[172] They, no doubt, also saw the long letter to the "Negro Workers of America" from the Chairman of the Comintern, Grigory Zinoviev, on "National and Racial Problems." The letter was addressed to "Comrade McKay, American Negro guest at the IV Congress of the III International," which McKay took with him when he left Russia in 1923. The letter in part read:

> It is the duty of the III International to bring about not only the European but also the World Revolution. The World Revolution can be realised only when the nations of the East, the black workers and the yellow are drawn into the Communist Movement.
>
> The IV Congress of the Comintern fraternally calls to all Negro Workers to organise themselves at once, and to join with the class-conscious white workers to solve the racial problem in the one possible way—the proletarian. We know precisely how difficult it is for the Negro workers to organise their own extensive organisation. The Comintern does not forget for a minute the persecutions to which Negro workers are subjected, even in the most civilised bourgeois Republic! Once more, by you [McKay], we call the Negro-workers to organise their own circles, to enter in the Trade-Unions, in every way to strive immediately to create their own mass-organisation and to link up with other divisions of the fighting proletariat.
>
> The Negro-workers must remember that it was the founder of scientific Socialism and the ideal guider of the First International, Karl Marx, who, during the American Civil War appealed ardently to the black workers to put themselves under the banner of Internationalism. It is over half a century since that time. The Communist International firmly hopes that Karl Marx's call will now stir and move the Negro proletariat at this critical period of the class struggle.
>
> Once more we use this occasion to send by you fraternal greetings and best wishes to the Negro workers of America.[173]

To black comrades, the Comintern represented the purest ideals of socialism, untarnished by racism and colonial ambition. It was the guardian of the flame, and even if the white comrades in America were often hypocrites with feet of clay, the Comintern would put them straight. Harry Haywood reported in his autobiography that in the summer of 1922 he told his older brother, Otto Hall, that he felt ready to join the Party. Hall, who was already a member, told him to wait, because the black comrades were having a hard time with some of the white members in their local Chicago branch. Some of the white comrades, Haywood said, were treating the black members "like children and seemed to think that the whites had all the answers." Haywood related that his brother assured him that it was "only a temporary situation." The problem had been reported to the Party District Committee, and if it was not resolved there it would be taken to the Central Committee. "And if you don't get satisfaction there?" Haywood queried. "Well, then there's the Communist International!" Otto replied emphatically. "It's as much our Party as it is theirs." Haywood wrote:

> I was properly impressed by his sincerity and by the idea that we could appeal our case to the "supreme court" of international communism, which included such luminaries as the great Lenin.[174]

To Lenin and Trotsky, the Comintern was the general staff of the world revolution but to Afro-American comrades its executive in Moscow was a stick with which they could bring local comrades into line, an incorruptible supreme court of international communism.

And one could only become a member of the Comintern through its local, national branch. Joining the local Communist Party—the Workers' Party—was the only means by which one could become a member of the Comintern. Harry Haywood was absolutely right in his ranking when he spoke of members of the Brotherhood "gravitat[ing] toward the Third International and eventually join[ing] its American affiliate, the Communist Party."[175] It is against such a background that Richard B. Moore's famous remark at the Yokinen trial should be viewed. "As for myself," said Moore, "I would rather have my head severed from my body by the capitalist lynchers than to be expelled in disgrace from the Communist International"[176]—he did not say the Communist Party. And these black members, for the duration of their lives in the Party, looked to the Comintern to put the Party right in America, to see to it that the Communist Party of America remain faithful to the spirit and letter of the Comintern.

Some forty years after joining the Workers' Party, Briggs told his comrades at a Party meeting in Los Angeles that black members came into the Party "not because they are socialists but because they believe that the Party is conducting a struggle on the Negro field." And he pointed out that when he joined the Party, "I had no understanding toward socialism." He entered the Party simply because it had a progam, even though it was not written and spelt out, "on the Negro field." Significantly, he went on to say that he joined the Party also because of "the solution of the national question in the Soviet Union and because I was confident that the American Party would in time take its lead on that question from its Soviet party which is what it eventually did."[177]

What happens, however, when the Comintern becomes corrupted, its stated ideals compromised by the exigencies of Soviet *realpolitik* and Stalinism? This is an interesting and complex question that falls outside the scope of the present discussion, but it should be noted that, perhaps out of a sense of historical obligation to the Soviet Union, many black members clung to the Comintern through thick and thin. Some of the staunchest Stalinists and supporters of the Soviet Union have been black ones and not only in the United States.

*

Hubert Harrison, Elizabeth Gurley Flynn and William "Big Bill" Haywood, 1909.
(Courtesy of the Elizabeth Gurley Flynn Collection, Tamiment Library, New York University)

Otto Huiswoud and Claude McKay in Moscow during the Fourth Congress of the
Communist International (Comintern), November 1922. Huiswoud, a leader of the
African Blood Brotherhood and an official delegate of the Workers' Party of America
to the Congress, spoke on the Negro Question. McKay also addressed the Congress
on the same subject. McKay and Huiswoud were members of the committee that
drafted the final resolution on the Negro Question for the Comintern.
(Courtesy of the Yale Collection of American Literature, Beinecke Rare Book and
Manuscript Library, Yale University)

George Padmore, *c.* 1937. (George Padmore, *Afrika: Unter Dem Joch Der Weissen*,
Erlenbach-Zurich / Leipzig: Rotapfel-Verlag, [1937])

Ras Makonnen, *c.* 1940.
(Courtesy of Tania Makonnen and Marika Sherwood)

J. A. Rogers, 1931.
(Courtesy of the Schomburg Center for Research in
Black Culture, New York Public Library, Astor,
Lenox and Tilden Foundations)

Captain Hugh Mulzac in his American Merchant Marine uniform during the Second World War. In 1918 Mulzac became the first black man to earn a Master's license in the United States. But it was only after "thirty-five years of rebuff" and during the exigencies of war that he was given a chance to captain an American ship. He served as Captain of the Liberty ship, the *Booker T. Washington*, between 1942 and 1948, when the ship was decommissioned. Mulzac's seafaring career came to a premature end through racist exclusion in the 1940s along with "blacklisting" in the 1950s, when he was deemed a "security risk" by the American authorities. (Courtesy of the Schomburg Center for Research in Black Culture, New York Public Library, Astor, Lenox and Tilden Foundations)

William Monroe Trotter, 1920. (Courtesy of the Schomburg Center for Research in Black Culture, New York Public Library, Astor, Lenox and Tilden Foundations)

Amy Jacques Garvey, 1923.
(*The Negro World*, March 17, 1923, courtesy of Robert A. Hill)

Maymie Leona Turpeau de Mena, 1925. (Courtesy of Robert A. Hill)

Arturo Schomburg and Marcus Garvey at the funeral of John Edward Bruce, 1924.
(Courtesy of the Schomburg Center for Research in Black Culture, New York Public Library,
Astor, Lenox and Tilden Foundations)

Universal African Legions on parade, *c.* 1921. (Amy Ashwood Garvey Papers)

Opening parade of the UNIA Convention of the Negro Peoples of the World, New York, 1920. (Courtesy of the Schomburg Center for Research in

I wish to make a few brief, final observations on some other expressions of radicalism among Caribbeans.

First, coming as many of the earliest black members did from the African Blood Brotherhood, Caribbeans became conspicuous within the Communist Party from the early 1920s right through the 1930s.[178] In addition, Otto Huiswoud and Arthur Hendricks, a theology student from British Guiana were the only two black founding members of the Party. Huiswoud was to experience a meteoric rise within the party hierarchy. He was to be the first black member of the Central Committee of the Party, and was a delegate to the Fourth Congress of the Communist International in 1922. He was also to become the first district organizer of the Party in Buffalo, New York. Huiswoud gained the distinction of having been a candidate-member of the influential Executive Committee of the Communist International based in Moscow.[179] Thus, when Cyril Briggs joined the CP, these were the only black members of the party in the United States.[180] Other Caribbeans, most notably Richard B. Moore, were to become high-ranking members within the Party by the end of the twenties.[181]

Second, Harrison, as we have seen, was a member of the Industrial Workers of the World. He was, in addition, an important participant in the historic Paterson (New Jersey) silk strike of 1913 led by the IWW. But he was not, of course, the only Caribbean Wobbly in America. Claude McKay had also been a member of the IWW and retained a life-long admiration for Big Bill Haywood.[182] Randolph, Owen, Domingo, Moore, and all the radical black socialists who came to political maturity during the First World War had a similar respect for the IWW and its leaders. But the support was not confined to the black intelligentsia: Afro-Americans and Afro-Caribbean workers in the United States joined and extended their support to the IWW. Like the Afro-American ones, the Caribbean members of the IWW were concentrated in Philadelphia where they worked as longshoremen. It was in Philadelphia that they joined the Marine Transport Workers Industrial Union, Local 8 of the IWW.

From a mere 164 in 1896, the number of black longshoremen in the Philadelphia docks increased by 1910 to 1,428 out of a total of 3,522. By 1920 almost 60 percent of the longshoremen were black, 2,409 out of 4,224.[183] The relatively easy entrance of black workers into the Philadelphia docks was not replicated at other American ports. Working alongside the black workers was a large contingent of Polish, Lithuanian and Belgian immigrants who had been excluded from skilled employment elsewhere in the city. For over five years prior to his imprisonment in 1918, Ben Fletcher (1890–1949), an Afro-American born in Philadelphia, was the local's bold and effective leader. With the blessing of the national leadership of the IWW, Fletcher forged a remarkable and resilient bonding of workers across the color line. It was in this context that the bosses and the government took particular note of the black participation in the union. The Caribbean presence was conspicuous enough for the intelligence services of the United

States government to take special interest. Indeed, in November 1918, the Office of Naval Intelligence reported that the membership of Local 8 was "increasing daily, owing to the influx of a large number of West Indian negroes." Apparently at least one of the officials, the secretary, of the Local was a Caribbean immigrant.[184] During a strike in May of the previous year, the Caribbean longshoremen were in evidence supporting the strike.[185] No one has conducted a detailed analysis of Local 8, its ethnic composition and leadership structure, but what is evident, even in the absence of such a study, is the significant presence of Caribbeans among the longshoremen of Philadelphia and their involvement in the Industrial Workers of the World.[186]

Finally, there was also a conspicuous Caribbean presence within the cultural sphere, more narrowly defined. Claude McKay was regarded by many of his contemporaries—from James Weldon Johnson to the young Langston Hughes—as the leading artist of the Harlem Renaissance. He was also the most radical of the poets. Indeed, to one of the most intelligent and unsparing critics of twenties Harlem, McKay was "the only Negro poet who ever wrote revolutionary or protest poetry."[187] But there was also another important Caribbean writer, Eric Walrond of British Guiana. Walrond was among the most distinguished intellectuals of the Renaissance and undoubtedly one of the most gifted and prolific short story writers of his generation.[188] In the mid-twenties, he worked as the managing editor of *Opportunity*, organ of the Urban League and one of the most important black journals of the period. Walrond also worked as Assistant, Associate and Contributing Editor of the *Negro World*, between 1921 and 1923, when he broke with Garvey, only to link up with him once again in London in the 1930s where he helped to edit Garvey's magazine, *The Black Man*. It is also increasingly recognized that the Garvey movement, and its newspaper, the *Negro World*, played a pioneering and key role in the cultural "renaissance" of the 1920s.[189]

To sum up: the Caribbean presence in radical movements in the United States was remarkable in at least three important respects. First, it was out of proportion to the group's numerical weight within the black population. Second, Caribbeans founded and led not only black nationalist organizations like the UNIA, but also important political currents on the revolutionary socialist left. Third, the migrants also provided some of the most distinguished radical black intellectuals at the time. And this was true for both black nationalist and black socialist currents of protest.

6

Race Consciousness, Class Consciousness, and the Political Strategies of William Monroe Trotter and Marcus Garvey

Professor Kelly Miller was wrong on the details, but there is a rational kernel to his remark on Caribbean radicalization abroad. The fact is that, because of the greater salience of race in America compared to the Caribbean, Afro-Americans have historically been more "race conscious" than Caribbeans. Marcus Garvey reiterated that point time and again, especially during his post-deportation wilderness years. The Negroes in the Caribbean, as he put it, "haven't the racial consciousness possessed by the Negroes of the United States nor those of Africa." They generally have developed "more of the white psychology than of the black outlook." "Though black, he is white" was one of Garvey's descriptions of Caribbean man.[1] But the difference in "race consciousness" between the two groups is hardly surprising given the dissimilarities of the societies in which they were formed.[2] This relatively low level of race consciousness was, in general, transformed by migration to societies such as the United States in the early part of the twentieth century in which racism was a pronounced feature. It is in such an environment that Caribbean people—many for the first time—become self-consciously "black" and thus "race conscious" to a greater degree.[3]

The relatively low level of race consciousness combined with a comparatively high level of educational attainment and class consciousness, made it easier for Caribbeans—Hispanic and non-Hispanic—to work with white people in radical organizations such as the Socialist and Communist Parties in the United States. African Caribbeans in general—but in particular those from the Hispanic territories—because of their experience in the Caribbean, were, clearly, not as prone to view white people with the degree of distrust and suspicion that their African American brothers and sisters were.[4] As a Jamaican sociologist observed, Caribbeans are "less fearful of whites and also have less hatred of them."[5] W. A. Domingo, after nine years of living in the United States, was still dismayed and genuinely shocked by the manner in and the extent to which American racism warps "the ordinary human instincts of both whites and negroes." He wrote:

> They both become indifferent to the sufferings of each other and fail to recognize that most of what they suffer is both preventable and of common origin. So

marked is this attitude that it is next to impossible to rouse a white audience of workingmen to the enormity of the crimes committed against society and the black race when the latter is denied elementary justice and fair play. Equally difficult is it to awaken in the breast of negroes any resentment against a vicious system that thrives on the labor of children, the sweating of adults and the robbery of one class by another. Any attempt in that direction among negroes is usually met by them in the same questioning spirit as they meet the tale of any great disaster. If a railroad wreck occurs, or a ship is sunk, the attitude of the average negro is to scan the death list diligently and if none of his race is among the victims, ejaculate "Thank God, they are all white people. There are no colored folks among them." In short, negroes react to prejudice and discrimination by becoming distinctly race conscious, but so far as their class consciousness is concerned, it is not even as much as scratched.[6]

The understandable distrust of white people by black Americans could hardly be overstated. Harry Haywood, one of the pioneering Afro-American members of the Communist Party, vividly recalled some of the difficulties he had in attempting to recruit African Americans to the Party in the 1920s. One of his progressive black friends, whom he thought would be receptive to the idea, told him bluntly: "I'm sorry, [Haywood], but I find being Black trouble enough, but to be Black and red at the same time, well that's just double trouble, and when you mix in the whites, why that's triple trouble."[7]

The Caribbean migrants' relatively low race consciousness but high class consciousness partially explains their "pioneering" role in "white" radical organizations such as the American Communist Party. It is also not insignificant that the longer the early Caribbean Socialists and Communists remained in the United States, the more they became Americanized, the more they moved towards black nationalist positions, the modal Afro-American radical ideology. Indeed, the longer they lived in America, the more they appreciated black America's distrust of white radicals—and white people in general. The pattern began with Hubert Harrison; Claude McKay and George Padmore followed a similar trajectory. Cyril Briggs and Richard B. Moore were expelled from the CP in 1942 for what was alleged to have been their "Negro nationalist way of thinking."[8] Domingo, one of the most subtle and esteemed black socialist thinkers of the 1920s, abandoned his revolutionary socialism for a narrow Jamaican nationalism that was not expansive enough to even embrace the idea of a federation of the British Caribbean in the 1950s.[9] As he grew older Moore also became more involved in Caribbean nationalism, but, unlike Domingo, held to a Pan-Caribbean position.[10]

It is as if there is a hidden and unwritten law of tendency in the United States which states that because of the racism of the labor movement and its organizations, black socialists are almost inexorably pushed to a black nationalist position. This law of tendency may appropriately be called Garvey's Revenge, because it was as if Garvey, from the grave, managed to wreak revenge upon his erstwhile black socialist opponents by diminishing their belief in and commitment to alliances across racial lines for radical transformation. It is indeed remarkable the way in which, in the 1930s and later, many of Garvey's opponents from the 1920s were to move towards more black nationalist positions, punch drunk and weary from the long years of "beating our brains out against the walls of [white] prejudice," as McKay put it in 1940.[11] The classic example is W. E. B. Du Bois's bombshell of an editorial, "Segregation," in the *Crisis* of January 1934. It triggered a major upheaval within the NAACP itself, the "race relations" establishment, and the black left. Du Bois's editorial was nothing less than vintage black self-reliance that Garvey could not have reasonably objected to, even though he still detested Du Bois.[12] McKay, most dramatically Padmore, Richard B. Moore and, albeit to a lesser extent, C. L. R. James were to execute a similar *volte face* in relation to Garvey and black nationalism. Booker T. Washington has also experienced a posthumous revival but not as dramatic as Marcus Garvey's resurrection, especially during and since the 1960s.[13]

In any event, the historical difference between the strategies adopted by black Americans and black Caribbeans in dealing with the challenges posed by white oppression, in many ways, helps to explain the high profile of Caribbeans in radical movements in the United States in the early part of the twentieth century. Caribbeans also brought to the United States as a component of their cultural inventory tried and tested strategies of struggle—strategies of struggle that had become so routinized they were customary—to a new and different terrain. Thus, to a significant degree, their naïveté about the formidable obstacles erected by the power structure of white America against the fulfilment of black demands and aspirations helps to account for this radical option. "I didn't think that they were as realistic as the American Negro," was George Schuyler's observation of Caribbeans in Harlem in the 1920s. Many of their leaders "seemed given to extremism and flights of fancy and all that." Afro-Americans, in contrast, "had their feet on the ground more. But," added Schuyler "I admired their enterprise in business, their pushfulness."[14]

The Caribbean modal strategy of frontal and often audacious assaults on the forces of oppression, what Antonio Gramsci would call the "war of maneuvre" (or "war of movement"), was transferred, almost unthinkingly, to a terrain on which African Americans had been used to pursuing— through bitter experience—*their* modal strategy of a more prosaic, incremental ('inchin' along') and cumulative process of struggle, operating on different fronts. Gramsci would call this strategy "war of position," a kind of trench warfare of social and political struggle.[15] It is almost unthinkable, for example, that an African American leader at the time would have adopted the high profile, noisy, confrontational posture adopted by the Garvey movement in the early part of the century—the Universal African Legions, a proto-military wing of the UNIA, even had a cavalry unit which paraded on the streets of New York on horseback, in full military regalia; it is almost unthinkable, because the historical experience of Afro-America would certainly have ruled out such an option. It was too much of an obvious high-risk gamble.

William Monroe Trotter (1872–1934) is the exception that proves the rule. The beloved son of James Monroe Trotter, a veteran of the Civil War who served as an officer in the legendary black regiment, the Massachusetts Fifty-Fifth, William grew up in comfortable surroundings in Boston.[16] His parents instilled pride of race in him from an early age, an abhorrence of racial bigotry, and a willingness to fight it. He excelled at secondary school, went on to Harvard, where he also excelled, graduating *magna cum laude*. After some years working as a successful businessman in real estate in Boston, Trotter felt driven into radical race politics, partly out of his profound disgust with the growing influence of Booker T. Washington and the latter's conservative politics. Trotter regarded Washington and the politics he represented as obsequious, and degrading to black people. In November 1901, with George Forbes, Trotter founded the *Guardian*, a weekly newspaper. He made his intentions clear from the very first issue: "We have come to protest forever against being proscribed or shut off in any caste from equal rights with other citizens, and shall remain forever on the firing line at any and all times in defence of such rights."[17] For the rest of his life, Trotter never wavered from this commitment. "For Every Right With All thy Might," was the motto carried by the *Guardian* on its editorial page. Actively involved in founding the Niagara Movement, formed to advance the cause of civil rights, he attended the launch of the National Association for the Advancement of Colored People, but he loathed the white money that ran the organization and the white people who controlled it. He formed several political organizations that culminated in the National Equal Rights League, which, under one name or another, could be traced back to 1908. Unlike the NAACP, the National Equal Rights League was "an organization of the colored people and for the colored people and led by the colored people," maintained Trotter.[18]

With the *Guardian* and the League, Trotter maintained a blunt, unbending struggle for his and his people's rights under the Constitution. Fearless, on a visit to the White House in 1914, Trotter told President Woodrow Wilson to his face—in a heated exchange that allegedly lasted some forty-five minutes—exactly what he thought about his segregation policies in Washington. Wilson was shocked by his outspokenness. Trotter's exchange with the president became front page news around the country.[19] Knowing that Trotter intended to expose the chasm between its rhetoric of making the world safe for democracy and its practice of black disenfranchisement, segregation, and other forms of racial oppression, the United States government denied him a passport in order to prevent his attending the Paris Peace Congress in 1919. Hubert Harrison described as "sublimely silly" the UNIA's attempt to send a delegation to the Congress, but he sharply identified the reasons why Wilson did not want Trotter and the others in Europe. "How would it look," Harrison asked rhetorically, "to have Negroes telling all Europe that the land which is to make the world 'safe for democracy' is rotten with race-prejudice; Jim-Crows Negro officers on ships coming over from France and on trains run under government control; condones lynching by silent acquiescence and refuses to let its Negro heroes vote as citizens in that part of the country in which nine-tenths of them live. This wouldn't do at all."[20] Undeterred by the denial of a passport, Trotter made his way to Paris, hiding his true identity, working as a cook on a steamer across the Atlantic.[21]

Trotter had in his soul, said Du Bois, "all that went to make a fanatic, a knight errant. Ready to sacrifice himself, fearing nobody and nothing, strong in body, sturdy in conviction, full of unbending belief."[22] But Trotter's relentless and uncompromising fight along the color line took its toll, defeated, and killed him. On his sixty-second birthday in 1934, lonely, impoverished, his mouthpiece, the *Guardian*, in deep financial trouble, he made his way up to the roof of the three-story building in which he was only a lodger; it was five-thirty in the morning. One of the occupants in the apartment in which Trotter lived heard a noise. Later, Trotter was found unconscious on the sidewalk below. His skull was crushed; he died on the way to the hospital. No one can be sure that Trotter jumped off the roof; his relatives claimed that he accidentally fell. There were no eyewitnesses; but all the evidence suggests that he took his own life. "I can understand his death," wrote Du Bois, of his former ally-turned-adversary. "I can see a man of sixty, tired and disappointed, facing poverty and defeat. Standing amid indifferent friends and triumphant enemies. So he went to the window of his Dark Tower, and beckoned to Death."[23] The direct, inflexible assault against the walls of American racism had earlier cost a substantial fortune, and, worse, had taken effectively the life of his beloved wife, Geraldine, in 1918. Kelly Miller, with whom Trotter had crossed swords many times over the years, was generous in his assessment of the fallen fighter. "Trotter is the only Negro, of my knowledge, who has made a sacrifice for his race," said Miller. "Others have had nothing to sacrifice but have gained honor, place and fortune out of the cause which they espoused."[24]

Significantly, and not by accident, the Caribbean radicals admired and loved Trotter. Harrison, Garvey, Briggs, Campbell and others worked with him, as did Afro-American radicals such as Randolph and Owen of the *Messenger* magazine. Other Caribbeans joined Trotter's National Equal Rights League and held high office in the organization. Isaac B. Allen, a Barbadian immigrant, served as Secretary of the NERL. Indeed, the president of the League up to his death in 1923 was a Jamaican migrant, the Rev. Dr Matthew A. N. Shaw (1870–1923). Trained as a medical doctor, Dr M. A. N. Shaw, as his contemporaries referred to him, also served for twenty-four years as the pastor for the Twelfth Street Baptist Church in Boston. He was Trotter's closest political ally.[25]

Cyril Briggs referred to Trotter as "this fearless spokesman of the Negro race." And when Woodrow Wilson refused to meet Trotter in Paris in 1919, in Briggs's eyes, this was a positive sign of the type of man Trotter was: "Knowing the kind of Negro that President Wilson and the section of this country he eminently represents are willing to recognize as 'leaders' of the Negro race, we cannot help feeling that Trotter should be mighty proud of the fact that Wilson refused to see him. It is a healthy sign of the character, honor and integrity of a Negro leader when a Bourbon will have nothing to do with him."[26]

In the next, September, issue of the *Crusader*, Briggs honored Trotter by carrying his portrait on the cover of the magazine. And there was at least one very happy customer:

> I thank God for the portrait you print of William Monroe Trotter on the cover of your September issue! . . . The facial expression of Trotter here depicted is a holy inspiration. His soul is aflame with the fires of righteous indignation, knowledge of possessing a vital truth and determination to make it known to friend and foe alike, though martyrdom his por[t]ion be.[27]

In the 1920s, there was in fact an extraordinary degree of collaboration between the Brotherhood and Trotter. Frequent meetings were held at Grace Campbell's house between the leadership of the Brotherhood and William Monroe Trotter. And in 1923, Trotter's National Equal Rights League and the African Blood Brotherhood were the prime movers in calling for a united front of black organizations. The effort eventually materialized in a meeting, dubbed the Sanhedrin, of 1924 in Chicago. However, the differences which emerged at the meeting between the NERL and the ABB, on the one hand, and organizations such as Kelly Miller's National Race Congress, on the other, made sustained co-operation impossible between them. Nevertheless, the relation between Trotter's League and the members of the Brotherhood remained strong.[28]

Briggs loved Trotter and never forgot his contribution. He remembered Trotter to the historian Theodore Draper. Trotter's role in the twenties, he told him, has been greatly neglected.

> He was the Stormy Petrel of the times, one of the most militant, dynamic and popular (with the man in the street) leaders of his day. He was utterly selfless in his dedication to the fight for Negro freedom. Nor was he afraid of associating with "Reds"[29]

Joel Rogers, similarly, called Trotter "the most unselfish of the Negro leaders," describing him as "the most persistent, uncompromising, and unselfish crusader against racial injustice since Frederick Douglass." In one of the most finely etched, considered and generous portraits in his *World's Great Men of Color*, Rogers concluded with these words:

If those leaders who compromise with racial injustice in the hope of present gain either for themselves or their group are following the better path, then the sacrifices of William Monroe Trotter have been in vain, and he deserves the name so often given him of fool and obstinate dreamer. But if an American citizen whose skin is dark is entitled to the same rights as one whose skin is fair—for this was, simply, Trotter's stand—then unborn generations will revere him.

They will revere him not because he alone had the vision of an America in which there would be no color injustice, not because he worked harder than others to achieve it, but for the persistency and purity of his ideals.[30]

Strangely, Garvey too, despite Trotter's integrationism—albeit a decidedly militant integrationism—admired the man and worked with him politically. Hearing of Trotter's untimely death, Garvey, back in Jamaica after his deportation from the United States, wrote a long, melancholy obituary. Noting that it probably will be a long time before Trotter's place can be properly filled, "because he was an uncompromising and sincere advocate of equal rights and Negro freedom," Garvey wrote:

The American Negro could have well afforded to lose a thousand of their present-day pseudo-leaders without regret, rather than losing William Monroe Trotter. We knew Mr Trotter well. We admired him very much and watched his career with deep interest. He was not one who assumed leadership for the purpose of enriching himself, and his very death has proved that.

Trotter's loss to America was very great, Garvey reckoned.[31]

Why did the Caribbean radicals love Trotter so? In the best and worst senses, he behaved like them. He behaved as if he did not know better, seemingly ignorant of the rules of American racism. He behaved with apparently childish naivete, expecting America to live up to its vaunted and unrevised creed. "We hold these truths to be self evident . . . ." Unlike Garvey, though, Trotter's politics was predicated upon an unshakeable faith in America's capacity to change and do the right thing by its black citizens. Like Douglass and Du Bois, Trotter intended to remain in America and fight; Garvey also intended to fight, but essentially while in retreat to Africa, protecting his flank and engaging in rearguard action.

Trotter was defeated for a variety of reasons. He was in the wrong place. Boston—genteel, relatively liberal, with its long-established polite black society—was hardly the place where the black revolution would begin at the turn of the century. He too easily made too many unnecessary enemies while being unable to hold on to his friends. He was not a leader of men; he was a maverick, a "free lance," Du Bois rightly called him. He paid insufficient attention to developing a political base. And by the time the Great Migration released new possibilities and energies for black politics favorable to him, Trotter had been superseded by the National Association for the Advancement of Colored People and eclipsed by the meteoric rise of Marcus Garvey and the UNIA.[32] These are important factors that must go into the accounting of Trotter's defeat. But above all, Trotter was defeated because he was too uncompromising, conspicuously walking tall in a land where black men and women were expected to have bent backs—when not invisible. Trotter was a provocation; he, somewhat like Malcolm X after him, enraged his enemies and at the same time, frightened many potential supporters and friends. "Full of unbending belief," he was inflexible to the point of stiffness, tall and politically erect like a magnificent but fragile palm tree, in a land of racist storms. He was blown over by the wind, broken, reduced to martyrdom. And American soil, ever since Jamestown, has consistently received the corpses of black martyrs with greater ease than it has yielded black heroes; it swallowed the body of William Monroe Trotter, as it had those of countless valiant black men and women before him.

Trotter was, in essence, an Afro-American aberration. Garvey behaved rather like Trotter: noisily, confrontationally, boldly. But, unlike Trotter, Garvey was naïve; Trotter behaved as if he was naïve, but he knew better and *had* to know better. His behavior was fueled—almost involuntarily—by his capacious reservoir of optimism and valor, and his yearning to keep faith with his father, the Massachusetts Fifty-Fifth, his late wife Geraldine, and the dream of black emancipation.

John Bruce (nicknamed "Bruce Grit"), an old head—born a slave in Maryland in 1856—and respected supporter of Garvey, foresaw danger for the Garvey movement, similar to those which overwhelmed Trotter. In 1920, Bruce was disturbed by Garvey's flamboyant noisiness and wanted him "to bridle his language."[33] Bruce was in fact echoing an observation that he made of Garvey before he became an ardent supporter of the UNIA and of Garvey himself. In 1918, Bruce, in a sketch of Garvey he left unpublished, accused the latter of "perfervid rhetoric mixed with frenzy— and oral gymnastics." The idea of the UNIA, Bruce believed, was all right, "but the method all wrong—all gas." Mr Garvey, said Bruce,

> is *sui generis*. And he is a wonder, really. A good military strategist, wise statesmen, and shrewd politicians always conceal more than they reveal when talking of their plans. But Garvey *tells all* and so we have his number. You won't do, Mr Garvey, too *muchee talkee*.[34]

Nevertheless, it was not for nothing that Afro-American commentators at the time, even some of his harshest critics, refer time and time again to the boldness—in the words of Kelly Miller (hardly a friendly observer) of the man, the "amazing audacity"—of Garvey.[35] One referred to him as being as "brave as a Nubian lion." And he was; but he was perhaps also in equal measure as brave as he was foolhardy and naïve. "He made the mistake," observed James Weldon Johnson, with characteristic astuteness,

> of ignoring or looking with disdain upon the technique of the American Negro in dealing with his problems of race, a technique acquired through three hundred years of such experience as the West Indian has not had and never can have. If he had availed himself of the counsel and advice of an able and honest American

Negro, he would have avoided many of the barbed wires against which he ran and many of the pits into which he fell.[36]

But Garvey was not alone; and West Indians were not the only ones to follow him. He had millions of followers around the world and hundreds of thousands of paid-up members (not to mention supporters) in America itself. The conjuncture that prevailed during and in the aftermath of the First World War was such that radical leadership of the type offered by Garvey was made more acceptable to black people in the United States and elsewhere than at any other time since the end of slavery. There was the return of disillusioned and angry black soldiers from Europe whose comrades, in their thousands, had given their lives. President Wilson had told them that the war was about making "the world safe for democracy." And even Du Bois entreatied: "Let us, while this war lasts, forget our special grievances and close ranks with our own white fellow citizens and the allied nations that are fighting for democracy."[37] Uncle Sam, Du Bois had miscalculated, would reward black America with full citizenship for its sacrifice. Trotter, while disagreeing vehemently with Du Bois's "Close Ranks" editorial, supported the war effort and expected, like Du Bois, positive changes with the end of hostilities. But it quickly became clear that America would not be made safe for black people, including those who had traveled over three thousand miles to fight for democracy in Europe. Indeed, before the Armistice, a white man in New Orleans seemed to have summed up the general attitude of white America. Addressing a gathering of black people—ostensibly to thank them for their generous contribution to the war effort—he took the opportunity to clear up a lingering question. "You niggers are wondering how you are going to be treated after the war. Well," he said, "I'll tell you, you are going to be treated exactly like you were before the war."[38]

There was, however, a new spirit of defiance and self-confidence abroad among black people, powerfully demonstrated in the resistance that they mounted in the Red Summer of 1919, when twenty-six American cities—most notably Washington, DC, and Chicago—were consumed by rioting as white mobs attacked black people, and black people, in turn, bravely resisted, with unprecedented resolve. Garvey's frontal posture dovetailed neatly with this new psychology exemplified by the New Negro. So although his tactics departed radically from the American norm, in the post-war conjuncture it nevertheless had mass appeal. For, Garvey had, as one contemporary noted, "leaped into the ocean of black unhappiness at a most timely moment for a savior."[39] The times were ripe for Garveyism; Garveyism was ripe for the times. There was astonishing homology between Garveyism and the conjuncture. Indeed, in a fundamental way, Garveyism was itself a product of the conjuncture.

Garvey, nonetheless, underestimated the antagonistic response his movement aroused among the rulers of America, and the powerful forces that would be unleashed against him and the UNIA. And so, what was remarkable about the Garvey movement, at least in hindsight, was not so much its rapid collapse—the prior historical experience of black America would have predisposed one to suppose that this would have been the most likely final outcome of such a venture—as the fact that it managed to achieve what it did *at all*. For Garvey had transferred from one theater of conflict to another a mode of struggle few thought could succeed to the extent that it did in America.

7

The Peculiarities of Afro-Hispanic Radicalism in the United States: The Political Trajectories of Arturo Schomburg and Jesús Colón

While it is true that race consciousness among Afro-Caribbeans developed in and was nourished by racist environments such as the United States, allowance ought to be made for a noteworthy exception to the general tendency for Afro-Caribbean migrants to undergo this metamorphosis. The exception was migrants of African descent—at least, by American standards—from the Hispanic Caribbean. Black Hispanics, and black Puerto Ricans in particular, gave little indication of the heightened race consciousness so sharply manifested in the United States by migrants from other parts of the Caribbean. The characteristic behavior of Afro-Hispanic migrants has historically been to close ranks with fellow "Spanish" compatriots—"black" and "white" together—distinguishing themselves, deliberately or otherwise, from those classified as "Negroes" in the United States. Writing in 1925 of the black migrants from the Caribbean, W. A. Domingo observed that the "Spanish element has but little contact with the English-speaking majority. For the most part they keep to themselves and follow in the main certain occupational lines." Wallace Thurman, the Afro-American critic and novelist, made the same observation a few years later, using almost identical words: "The Spanish Negro . . . stays to himself and has little traffic with the other racial groups in his environment."[1] From time to time, noted a sociologist in the 1930s, "one may see a very dark Negro who will be speaking Spanish more loudly than the rest. They say he does not wish to be mistaken for an American Negro. All are Latins." In *Harlem: Negro Metropolis*, published in 1940, Claude McKay observed that the Afro-American in Harlem "cannot comprehend the brown Puerto Rican rejecting the appellation 'Negro,' and preferring to remain Puerto Rican. He is resentful of what he considers to be the superior attitude of the Negroid Puerto Rican."[2] As late as 1961, Harlem's poet laureate, Langston Hughes, was pleading with local Puerto Ricans. In his aptly entitled poem "Note to Puerto Ricans (On American Confusions)," he wrote:

> Aw, come on —
> Who cares if you

Are half Negro.
Or $\frac{2}{3}$ or $\frac{1}{10}$ white
Or all black?
Who cares if Africa
Is a distant shadow
Behind your back —
Or if you're pure
Spain?
(The shadow
Fell there, too,
In Moorish days)
So who cares?

Puerto Ricans
In the U.S.A.
Let's be friends
Whatever
Others
Say.[3]

Afro-Hispanic Caribbeans played almost no role in black nationalist politics during the heady days of the First World War and early 1920s. It is significant that the Universal Negro Improvement Association (UNIA) branches in Cuba, Costa Rica, Panama, and elsewhere in Latin America consisted, with few exceptions, of migrant workers from the non-Hispanic Caribbean and especially from Jamaica. In Cuba, where the UNIA had its largest organized contingent outside the United States—no fewer than fifty-two branches at its peak—Afro-Cubans would sometimes attend the meetings of the Garveyites, but seldom joined the organization. A similar pattern prevailed throughout the Isthmus, where anglophone and franco-phone Caribbean migrant workers and their descendants in Panama, Costa Rica, Nicaragua, Honduras, and Guatemala accounted for virtually the entire membership of the UNIA.[4] Although a Nicaraguan, Maymie Leona Turpeau De Mena (known affectionately as Madame De Mena within UNIA circles) was one of the movement's most famous, distinguished, selfless, and admired members in the late twenties and early thirties—she became the International Organizer of the UNIA in 1929—Garveyites of Afro-Latino origin were thin on the ground in the Caribbean, rarer still in Central America, and virtually non-existent in the United States.[5] Small wonder, then, that the delegates to UNIA Conventions from Cuba had surnames like Collins, Cunning, and Taite; from Guatemala, Bourne; from Panama, Reid; from Santo Domingo, Van Putten. Going by his name one would be inclined to think that Elie Garcia was Hispanic, but he was in fact Haitian.[6] Domingo was the name of a Jamaican, the first editor of Garvey's newspaper, the *Negro World*. Carlos Cooks (1913–66), an important figure among Harlem's black nationalists from the 1930s to the 1960s who had been born in the Dominican Republic, was brought up in an English-speaking community of British Caribbean migrant laborers on the island. Both his parents, James Henry Cooks and Alice Cooks, had earlier migrated from neighboring St Martin. They were staunch Garveyites, as were many 1920s migrants. As a child, Carlos was taken to UNIA meetings by his father and uncle. Cooks came to the United States in 1929.[7] Carlos Moore, the most outspoken and controversial black nationalist critic of some of the policies of post-revolutionary Cuba, was born in Oriente of British Caribbean parents (Barbadian father, Jamaican mother), and within a milieu of English-speaking migrants who worked on Cuba's sugar plantations.[8]

From a mere 1,513 in 1910, the Puerto Rican population in the United States increased more than thirty-four fold, to almost 53,000, within two decades. The overwhelming majority settled in New York City, but no one knows what proportion of this population was black.[9] However, as we have seen from contemporary accounts, black and brown Puerto Ricans were a significant and conspicuous presence among the migrants to New York; the photo-journalism of the 1920s and 1930s also gives testimony to this presence.[10] But irrespective of the actual number of black Puerto Ricans, with the possible exception only of Carlos Tapia, Arturo Alfonso Schomburg (1874–1938) was probably the most conspicuous black Puerto Rican in New York City. And he was, without doubt, the most conspicuous Afro-Hispanic in black Harlem from the turn of the century to his death. Schomburg was conspicuous because he was a black Puerto Rican who actively supported and identified with black nationalist aspirations, and with the struggles of African Americans.[11] He radically departed from the pattern of Afro-Hispanic politics which I sketched earlier. How do we explain Schomburg's enigmatic political evolution? What light does his political biography shed upon Afro-Hispanic radicalism in the United States? These questions may best be answered by juxtaposing the political trajectory of Schomburg against that of Jesús Colón (1901–74), another radical and distinguished Afro-Puerto Rican migrant to the United States. The exploration of Schomburg's and Colón's political evolution also serves another and important purpose, that of bringing to the fore two outstanding Caribbean radicals whose ideas and contribution are never discussed within the wider context of black radicalism in the United States. Indeed, Schomburg and Colón are, relatively speaking, among the least known of the Caribbean radicals of the time. As I shall show, the ignorance that shrouds their political evolution does not in any way correspond to the intrinsic merit of their ideas and the significance of their political contribution.

Schomburg had more than color and nationality in common with Colón. Both in their youth burned with the fire of Puerto Rican nationalism, both migrated to the United States as young men, both settled, lived, and died in New York City. Yet the two men are seldom mentioned in the same breath.

Each is known, it is fair to say, by a different set of people, with different political and intellectual interests; they made different friendships and associations, and were driven, eventually, by different passions. It is true that Schomburg and Colón were of different generations, but that hardly accounts for the striking difference in their political evolution, and in the perception and remembrance of them. The fact is that, despite similar points of political origin, they followed radically divergent political paths, were absorbed by different objectives, and had dissimilar destinations. Schomburg died an ardent Pan-Africanist, with definite black nationalist sympathies, wedded to the struggles and aspirations of Afro-America. Colón died a socialist and Puerto Rican nationalist with no time for black nationalism. How do we account for the marked difference in the political trajectory of these two men? And how do their divergent paths illuminate the peculiarities of Afro-Hispanic radicalism in America?

One thing is clear from the outset: Arturo Schomburg, not Jesús Colón, was the Puerto Rican political aberration. For one of the most striking patterns that emerges from the examination of the Caribbean experience in the United States in the first half of the century is that among black radicals from the Hispanic Caribbean there was relative indifference, if not aversion, to black nationalism. Such a position contrasted sharply with a noticeable attraction to an unhyphenated socialism.

Schomburg migrated from his birthplace, San Juan, Puerto Rico, to New York City in 1891. His life's project was, in the vocabulary of the time, "the vindication of the Negro race." It was a counter-struggle against racist ideology, characteristically entailing the assiduous documentation—in practice, at enormous personal cost—of the achievements of people of African descent, past and present, around the world. Schomburg dedicated himself to this life-long struggle when, as a schoolboy in Puerto Rico, one of his teachers had told him that black people had no history, no heroes, no great moments. This cruel racist propaganda, inflicted upon him as a child, appeared to have been the primary source of the fuel that drove his lifelong quest. But the fact that he belonged to a youth club in which the study of history was a key element also contributed to his vindication mission. For in this club, "there was a tendency among the whites and near-whites to point with more pride to the achievements of their white ancestors, than the blacks seemed able to their ancestors." Young Schomburg noted this and decided to study up on the achievements of black Puerto Ricans so that when his white associates began to tell of what history white Puerto Ricans had made, "he could talk equally as freely of the history black Puerto Ricans had made." According to Schomburg, a kind of "historic rivalry" developed between the members of the club and he found his researches extending to the Virgin Islands, Haiti, the Dominican Republic, Cuba and the other islands of the Caribbean. When he came to the United States, he pursued his hobby more systematically and extensively and began to collect books on black people, their experience, and, most notably, their achievements across space and time.[12]

J. A. Rogers, who was a personal friend of his, noted that with a family to support and with his "continual outlay for books," Schomburg was often "financially pinched."[13] But Schomburg's passionate collecting of books, prints, manuscripts and paintings by and related to Africans would continue to the end of his life.[14] And in 1926 the Carnegie Corporation bought his collection of "over 10,000 books, manuscripts, newspapers, prints, and other materials"[15]—allegedly, at a fifth of its intrinsic value— for the New York Public Library. The collection, accumulated by Schomburg over a period of thirty-five years, would form the nucleus of what became the Schomburg Center for Research in Black Culture, based at the branch library at the corner of 135th Street and Lenox Avenue in Harlem. Alain Locke, the distinguished Howard University philosopher and close friend of Schomburg's, rightly noted that the price "patriotically" set by Schomburg for his collection "represented a figure so far below the market value of the collection that the transaction must be seen as a joint benefaction of the collector" and not the gift of the Carnegie Foundation solely.[16] With reference to the $10,000 paid for the collection, Schomburg himself explained his action:

> That sum is hardly what the books cost me. Some of those books are actually priceless, and cost a great deal of money. Others, not so rare, cost less. But the whole amount hardly gives me back the money I spent to get them. My time, labor, etc., go free, and I give them gladly. I am proud to be able to do something that may mean inspiration for the youth of my race. I would have gladly given the books outright had I not felt, in a way it would be unfair to the public, for, as a gift they might not have been deeply appreciated as they are by having cost something. Those who know what they cost, naturally feel there must be some real value attached to them.[17]

In a 1925 essay, Schomburg gave an indication of his project, its rationale, and of some of its results. "The American Negro must," he proclaimed,

> remake his past in order to make his future. Though it is orthodox to think of America as the one country where it is unnecessary to have a past, what is a luxury for the nation as a whole becomes a prime necessity for the Negro. For him, a group tradition must supply compensation for persecution, and pride of race is the antidote for prejudice. History must restore what slavery took away, for it is the social damage of slavery that the present generation must repair and offset. So, among the rising democratic millions, we find the Negro thinking more collectively and more retrospectively than the rest, and apt out of the very pressure of the present, to become the most enthusiastic antiquary of all.
>
> Vindicating evidence of individual achievement have as a matter of fact been gathered and treasured for over a century. . . . But this sort of thing was on the whole pathetically over-corrective, ridiculously over-laudatory; it was apolo-

getics turned into biography. . . . There is the definite desire and determination to have a history well documented, widely-known at least within racial circles, and administered as a stimulation and inspiring tradition for the coming generations. . . . [T]he remote racial origins of the Negro, far from being what the race and the world have been given to understand, offer a record of creditable group achievement when scientifically and impartially viewed, and more important still, that they are of vital general interest because of their bearing upon the beginnings and early development of human culture.[18]

Jesús Colón arrived in New York in 1918. A committed socialist before he left Puerto Rico, he became involved in the struggles of Puerto Rican and Cuban cigar makers—*tabaqueros*—in New York, was a member of the Socialist Party (later a Communist Party member), and fighter for Puerto Rican independence. From all the evidence, a charming, urbane, and sensitive man, Colón was remarkably untouched by black nationalism. Schomburg's interest in black history and politics and his apparent drift away from the Puerto Rican struggle remained a mystery to Colón right up to the end of his life: "[S]omething happened whereby Arturo shifted his interest away from the Puerto Rican liberation movement and put all his energy into the [black] movement."[19] Schomburg's behavior evidently raised eyebrows in the Puerto Rican community in New York. According to Bernardo Vega, another of his compatriots, when Schomburg moved "up to the neighborhood where North American Blacks lived," quite a few Puerto Ricans who knew him thought that he was "trying to deny his distant homeland."[20]

Vega might not have been as mystified as Colón was by Schomburg's behavior, but he, nevertheless, found it somewhat bizarre. In his discussion of Schomburg, he set up (no doubt unconsciously) an insidious and disturbing binary opposition between being "black" and being "Puerto Rican." Despite himself, he imparted the feeling that by having been interested in the African experience in the Americas, Schomburg had somehow diminished, if not deserted completely, his Puerto Ricanness. Significantly, Vega never described Colón—who was several shades darker than Schomburg—as "black," but Schomburg is so described. Colón was Puerto Rican, Schomburg became black; Schomburg, apparently, could not have been black and Puerto Rican at the same time—Vega, at any rate, found it difficult to think of Schomburg as black *and* Puerto Rican. In what is, nonetheless, a generous and moving tribute to Schomburg, Vega concludes: "He came here as an emigrant and bequeathed a wealth of accomplishments to our countrymen [Puerto Ricans] and to North American blacks. What a magnificent example of solidarity among all oppressed peoples!"[21] Schomburg, undoubtedly, would have appreciated this warm tribute, especially from such an esteemed and distinguished compatriot as Bernardo Vega. But I am inclined to believe, that as a fervent Pan-Africanist, Arturo Schomburg would prefer that his work be seen as an act of self-help, rather than one of solidarity. And this is so because he counted himself as a member of Africa's scattered children who also happened to have been born in Puerto Rico. Like his mentor, John Edward Bruce, he regarded oppressed people of African descent as belonging to one family. Schomburg used the first person plural "we" when talking of people of African descent.[22] Clearly, this dimension of Schomburg's thinking and political loyalties fell outside Bernado Vega's purview. That he found Schomburg so difficult to classify and conceptualize is not entirely Vega's fault; Schomburg was one of a rare breed of Puerto Ricans, if not a species of one.

The key to the singularity of Schomburg as a Puerto Rican black nationalist lies in his un-Puerto Rican family background. He was unusual in five important respects. First, Arturo's mother, Mary Joseph, was an *extranjera*, not a Puerto Rican. She was a black migrant worker from St Croix, in the Virgin Islands, with strong family ties not only on St Croix but also on the Danish-controlled sister island of St Thomas. Second, Arturo's father was the son of a German immigrant and a Puerto Rican woman. Some sources claim, inaccurately, that Arturo's father was himself a German immigrant from Hamburg.[23] In any case, his father's side of the family not only had strong foreign connections, it also had strong northern European, non-Iberian roots; such a background was hardly typical of nineteenth-century Puerto Rican society. Schomburg, whose parents were unmarried, had little contact with his father. According to his son, Schomburg senior was a merchant who was born in Mayaguez, on the western end of the island. From the questionnaire that Schomburg answered in the 1930s for a study of the black family, it is evident that he knew very little about his father's side compared to his mother's side of his family.[24] Indeed, according to his biographer, there is no evidence that Schomburg's father "recognized him as his son or supported either child or mother. Nothing suggests that Arturo was raised as an heir of the Schomburg family, a name well known in Puerto Rico."[25]

Third, because of the estrangement of his parents from each other, Arturo was brought up by his mother and was thus substantially influenced by the culture of his mother's native land, the Virgin Islands. Moreover, fourth, during his boyhood Arturo spent time—probably several years—in the Virgin Islands, where he lived with his mother's relatives and claimed to have attended St Thomas College, a secondary school. There is, however, no record to corroborate his claim of having gone to the college. Significantly, Schomburg—who was especially fond of his maternal grandfather, Nicholas Joseph, a butcher—clearly enjoyed life among his relatives and friends on St Croix and St Thomas. And it was during his stay in the Virgin Islands that he received a most valuable bit of education. As he recalled many years later, an old man—probably his own grandfather—told him about the tribulations of slavery and of the slave insurrection led by John Buddhoe on St Croix in 1848. That experience had a profound effect upon little Arturo and was of great significance in his political and intellectual formation. In 1910 he opened his article on the revolt with the recollection:

> When I was a boy I remember hearing from the lips of an old Negro man, friendly and paternal, the story of the horrors practiced by the slave owners. He told with precise details the incidents that led to and surrounded the early life of the emancipator of the Negro, [John] Buddhoe . . . .[26]

Schomburg was, evidently, marked by his Virgin Island connections and experience. Indeed, on the basis of reading Schomburg's work on the Islands, the Secretary of the St Thomas Public Library thought that Arturo was a native Virgin Islander. "Your mention of your boyhood days here carries a ring only possible with a son of the soil," he told Schomburg.[27]

Fifth, unlike many Puerto Ricans—and indeed, Hispanic Caribbeans— at the time, Arturo Schomburg was not a Catholic, nominally or otherwise, but an Episcopalian; he adopted the religion of his mother and his maternal grandparents. Furthermore, all of his own children were brought up in the Protestant Episcopal Church. Schomburg, in marked contrast to the Puerto Rican and Cuban *tabaqueros* who migrated to the United States around the same time that he did, was profoundly religious. As discussed later, the *tabaqueros* were renowned for their atheistic and freethinking ways, linked to their political radicalism. It is possible that Schomburg may have grown more religious as he got older, but what is clear is that he harbored a deep religious faith which came from his mother's side of the family. In his published writings as well as in his letters, he often referred to the Bible and made religious allusions; the Bible was, evidently, one of the many books he knew very well. In a 1932 letter, he told a close friend:

> I have a number of Communist friends who are often trying to make me deny the existence of a God, but instead of keeping silent I just turn loose after their method of reasoning and give them Hell. I say for instance, the feeling that there is a God is living within me[;] it was in my mother before me and I noticed it in my grandmother when[,] in her olden days and could sca[r]cely see[,] call[ed] her daughter to read some passage she wanted to hear once more. It is needless for you to try and change me, no more than change the table of multiplication as it was taught to me.[28]

Two months later, in February 1933, Schomburg gathered his hat and coat and stormed out of a Brooklyn meeting at which he was the guest speaker. He left the platform because T. R. Poston, the chairman, a radical Afro-American journalist, interjected his strong disagreement with Schomburg's assessment of Abraham Lincoln's position on the race question. Lincoln was "a man without prejudice," Schomburg was reported to have said. Poston disagreed, saying that if it had been left up to Lincoln, "it is more than probable we would still be slaves." Praise is due, Poston said, to people like William Lloyd Garrison "in preference to Lincoln who only free us to win the [Civil War]." Schomburg was wrong about Lincoln—who, incidentally, he had always had a soft spot for—and Poston was more right than wrong. Several members of the audience, one newspaper reported, were "incensed" at the "uncalled for remark of the chairman." Apparently, Poston had not been asked to comment on Schomburg's hour-long speech and was, therefore, discourteous in commenting at all, let alone criticizing the speaker—and before an audience of four hundred. Poston had clearly exceeded his brief as chair of the meeting. Schomburg was, understandably, angry with Poston. And it was understandable, too, that he walked out of the meeting. But Schomburg took his leave in an uncharacteristically deplorable and undignified manner. For, he left the meeting declaring, one report says, that "he would have no more to say to his Communist friend."[29]

A year earlier, in a vivid portrait of Harlem street-life, Schomburg dismissed a black Communist street-corner orator as "just a sound artist." The man has never been to Russia, Schomburg said, but "waxes eloquent on Lenin and the Five Years Plan [sic], however, were he to have to eke out an existence[,] we believe [he] would fall from grace, a volunteer to a subject he knows nothing whatever."[30]

It is not clear where Schomburg's anti-Communism of the 1930s came from. But it appears that at least one source of his growing opposition was the ideological clash between his religious worldview and what he perceived as the atheistic one of the Communist Party. The extent to which Schomburg's religious outlook contributed to his alienation from the Puerto Rican and Cuban revolutionary nationalists at the turn of the century is by no means clear, but it might have played a role. Certainly, if, as he claimed, his religiosity was as unchanging as the laws of mathematics, then he would have been uncomfortable all along with his comrades in Las Dos Antillas, militant rationalists and freethinkers that they were. One similar, contemporaneous Afro-Cuban group in Tampa, Florida, made no secret of their views. Formed in 1900, they called themselves *La Sociedad de Libre Pensadores de Martí–Maceo* (The Society of Freethinkers of Martí–Maceo).[31] But Schomburg's negative attitude toward the Communist Party and growing profession of religious faith, as we will see, did not make him a conservative.

Asked, in the questionnaire mentioned earlier, who influenced him the most, Schomburg replied that it was his mother. He evidently loved and idealized her. She represented the "painstaking and faithful ideals of womanhood." To her son, Mary Joseph was "a loving mother of high and pure ideal."[32]

In short, though he was born in Puerto Rico and, apparently, spent most of his childhood there, Arturo Schomburg was substantially shaped by the culture of the non-Hispanic and anglophone Caribbean.[33] Schomburg, astonishingly, discouraged his children from learning Spanish.[34] Although he worked for years with Pura Belpré, a black Puerto Rican librarian, he never, reported one writer, spoke to her about their "shared heritage and mother tongue."[35] But, on reflection, given the evidence of Schomburg's formation, it is not surprising, for he had a dual heritage, Hispanic and non-Hispanic. And it now appears that the non-Hispanic heritage was equally as strong as, if not stronger than, the Hispanic one. For most of his life he used the anglicized version of his first name, although he increasingly returned to Arturo toward the end of his life. Less than a year before he died, in one of his most despairing letters, brought on by his daily exposure to black Harlem's desperate plight during the Depression, Schomburg wrote to his close friend and confidante, the Afro-American journalist Wendell P. Dabney: "You request me to practice moderation. I am sick and tired of the conditions that I see every night in Harlem. I am still dreaming," he confessed, "of going to the Virgin Islands and spending the remainder of my life in the calm and solicitude that can only be had in such a restful place."[36] There is no mention of Puerto Rico in the letter, let alone its consideration by Schomburg as a final resting place. After he broke with the Cuban and Puerto Rican nationalists around 1898, Schomburg maintained no close friendships within the Puerto Rican community. In marked contrast, he established, broadened, and cultivated his closest friendships not only among Afro-Americans, but also among fellow Afro-Caribbean migrants from the English-speaking Caribbean, including Hubert Harrison and Casper Holstein from the Virgin Islands.

Given such a background and orientation it comes as no surprise that Schomburg's political trajectory in the United States bore remarkable similarity to that of Caribbean migrants from the non-Hispanic areas of the archipelago. But his disillusionment with Cuban and Puerto Rican exile nationalist politics in America at the turn of the century,[37] his painful experiences of Jim Crow segregation when he visited his children in the South, his membership and leading role in a black masonic lodge, his working in a job that was isolated from other Puerto Ricans, his befriending and being profoundly influenced by leading black nationalists of the day, especially John E. Bruce and Hubert Harrison, all contributed to the direction in which Schomburg's politics and worldview developed.

We should never forget, however, that Schomburg chose to withdraw from Puerto Rican and Cuban nationalist politics, chose to marry Afro-American women, chose to expend his energies on developing the black Prince Hall Lodge, chose the close association with black nationalists such as Bruce and Harrison, chose to live in the black San Juan Hill district of Manhattan at the turn of the century and later black Harlem, rather than live in one of New York's Puerto Rican neighborhoods. All of these choices become comprehensible only in the context of his formation before migrating to the United States. This is not to say that his early biography *determined* the pattern of his choices, but that it *predisposed* him to make the choices he made. After all, his immediate contemporaries and black Hispanic friends in New York, such as Rafael Serra (Cuba) and Sotero Figueroa (Puerto Rico), made different choices and followed a different, more orthodox, path.[38] Schomburg's close friend Claude McKay noted that in appearance Schomburg was like "an Andalusian gypsy, olive-complexioned and curly-haired, and he might easily have become merged in that considerable class of foreigners who exist on the fringe of the white world." But Schomburg, observed McKay, "*chose* to identify himself with the Aframerican [*sic*] group."³⁹ Thus, to view Schomburg's political evolution in the United States as simply the product of his generational location and circumstances is to ignore the clear and concrete choices that he made in his life.

Schomburg's accomplishments, especially given his limited educational background, verged on the miraculous. He was in fact, despite his pretensions to the contrary, an autodidact. He was, in 1892, co-founder and Secretary of *Las Dos Antillas*, a society of Cuban and Puerto Rican revolutionary nationalists, inspired by José Martí. He served as its Secretary up to 1896. Schomburg was struck by the double blow of Martí's and Antonio Maceo's death in combat in 1895 and 1896, respectively, during Cuba's war against Spain. His fellow *Afroborinqueño*, the revolutionary poet "Pachin" Marín, also fell in Cuba's war of independence. The United States declared war against Spain in February 1898 and by July of the same year Spain had surrendered, ceding the Philippines and Guam, along with Cuba and Puerto Rico, to the Americans. The Puerto Rican and Cuban revolutionaries in New York quarrelled among themselves, disagreeing on how to respond to the new and unforeseen set of circumstances. The Puerto Rican section of the Cuban Revolutionary Party dissolved itself in 1898, despite the strictures of Maceo, Martí, and Betances of the need to struggle for full independence, including independence from the United States of America. *"Ni Española ni Yankee"* ("Neither Spanish nor Yankee"), Betances, Maceo, and Martí had all insisted. Schomburg was also appalled by the moral deterioration of the Cuban nationalist movement in the absence of Martí and Maceo, and the overt racism that had come to the fore under the leadership of Tomás Estrada Palma. Estrada Palma's craven capitulation to the racism of the American occupiers in Cuba must have hurt Schomburg.⁴⁰ With a combination of disgust and disillusion, he ended his direct and deep involvement in Puerto Rican and Cuban nationalist politics, turning his attention, almost exclusively, to Afro-America.

Schomburg's subsequent positions and pronouncements on Puerto Rican independence (which, admittedly, are still in need of a thorough charting) were contradictory—at least apparently so—inconstant, confused, and certainly confusing. But to claim, as one writer does, that toward the end of his life Schomburg "advocated statehood for Puerto Rico" is, on the basis of the evidence offered, to misrepresent him.⁴¹ In fact what Schomburg said, in the very letter used to adduce such a conclusion, was this: "*If* the majority of the [Puerto Rican] people are of the opinion they should seek membership in the American Union, I am for it."⁴² Schomburg, whose letter was in response to American objections to Puerto Rican migration to the mainland, pointed out that had President McKinley acceded in 1898 to the petition of the Puerto Rican Revolutionary Party for a plebiscite on independence, Puerto Ricans would perhaps have less need to migrate to the United States. Schomburg, in the 1930s, might very well have advocated statehood for Puerto Rico—who knows?—but I have seen no evidence, nor has anyone presented any evidence so far to suggest that he did. And in the absence of such evidence, it ought not to be claimed that he did.

In 1892, Schomburg joined El Sol de Cuba, a lodge made up of Cuban and Puerto Rican freemasons in New York. By 1911 he was Master of the lodge. In the same year he changed the name to the Prince Hall Lodge, in honor of the founder of black freemasonry in America. In 1775, Hall, a black abolitionist, believed to have been born in Barbados, established the first black lodge in America, African Lodge No. 1, in Boston, Massachusetts, where he was a leader of the black community. By the time Schomburg became its master, El Sol de Cuba had changed considerably in its composition since its founding in 1881. Afro-Americans and English-speaking Afro-Caribbeans constituted the overwhelming majority of its members. According to Harry Williamson, a former deputy grand master and historian of the lodge, after the Spanish–American war the lodge's membership began to "dwindle." It was in this context of declining Hispanic Caribbean participation that Schomburg played an important role in recruiting new members. In 1918, Schomburg was promoted to Grand Secretary to the Grand Lodge of the State of New York, a position he held until 1926.[43]

Schomburg also played an important role in the formation of the Negro Society for Historical Research. In 1911, he co-founded and served as the secretary-treasurer of the society, with his close friend and mentor, John E. Bruce as president. On the recommendation of Bruce, Schomburg became a member of the prestigious American Negro Academy, founded by Alexander Crummell in 1897, to wage intellectual and ideological war against white supremacy and racist propaganda. In 1920, only six years after he had joined, Schomburg became its president. But despite his making important scholarly contributions to the work of the Academy, the institution withered under Schomburg's superintendence. The Academy began its decline before Schomburg became its president, but his living in New York while the organization had its base in Washington, DC, did not help matters. Schomburg over-stretched himself and was inattentive to the day-to-day business of the Academy. It foundered in 1928.[44]

Schomburg's forte was collecting and research, and it was in those areas that he excelled. As McKay delicately put it, he was not "typically literary." And his private taste in books was "inclined to the esoterically erotic." But, said McKay, Schomburg possessed "a bloodhound's nose in tracing any literary item about Negroes. He could not discourse like a scholar, but he could delve deep and bring up nuggets for a scholar which had baffled discovery."[45] The praise that Schomburg received from *cognoscenti* such as that from his close friend Dr John Wesley Cromwell, former president of the American Negro Academy, was expansive. In the aftermath of Schomburg's successful search for some rare publications of Benjamin Banneker, the brilliant black mathematician and astronomer, Cromwell wrote:

> How can I adequately express to you my indebtedness for your rescue of Banneker from the seclusion in which he has been for one hundred and twenty years. Think of it, biographers, bibliophiles, enthusiastic devotees—Latrobe, Bishop Daniel A. Payne, the Banneker Institute, the noble army of admirers, and what-not—have all absolutely failed to cast down their buckets where they were and secure the refreshing waters you have drawn up! You are entitled to more than a vote of thanks for this one act. There can be no disputing the authenticity of the facsimile of a contemporaneous publication.[46]

Schomburg was not a fluent writer, in either English or Spanish.[47] Though his writing often had passages of real eloquence, it lacked the ease and grace with which his compatriot Jesús Colón wrote both languages.[48] But what Schomburg lacked in expression he more than made up for in knowledge. Schomburg is often celebrated as a bibliophile, but he was much more than a bibliophile, outstanding though he was in that area of activity: Schomburg was also an outstanding scholar; even if he could not discourse with the same facility as most scholars, he operated on the basis of the most taxing criteria of intellectual rigor. He was a restless truth-seeker and he would plunge into the archives and great libraries like any self-respecting historian. He did this during his travels in Europe and the Caribbean, as he did in New York City. He further made deep forays into New England, visiting its fine libraries and collections. Thus, at the beginning of June 1933, Schomburg was off to the Boston Public Library, Harvard University Library, thence to Worcester, Massachusetts, to, as he told a friend, "check my Haytian [*sic*] material with extant work and finish prepare [*sic*] my monograph for your critical eyes. That's the program I am going to stick to this summer."[49] And of course, the expense of all this travelling, lodging, and time spent researching came out of his own pocket. It was not only books, prints, and manuscripts that Schomburg spent his slender resources on, he also spent them on research.

What he hated most about much of European and Euro-American historiography was its lies, its pernicious lies, especially against people of African descent. The truth never frightened him. "[T]ruth should prevail whether we like or dislike it," he told a young scholar. This, said Schomburg, is "the essential spirit of research."[50] And through his legendary patience and stamina in the quest for truth, he developed an arguably unrivalled fount of knowledge about people of African descent and their experience over time and space. Celebrated black intellectuals such as W. E. B. Du Bois, Hubert Harrison, James Weldon Johnson, Alain Locke, J. A. Rogers, and Carter G. Woodson have not only drawn upon Schomburg's unequalled collection of books, prints, paintings, and manuscripts, they have also drawn upon his extraordinary knowledge and sure-footed intellectual guidance, which he freely gave. More often than not, Schomburg's contribution was inadequately acknowledged, or unacknowledged altogether, by his more formally educated and credentialled black contemporaries. Alain Locke admitted that Schomburg was the "silent co-author" of many volumes on black history and culture. But Locke said this after Schomburg was dead and buried—and in a manuscript that to this day remains unpublished.[51] As he grew older, Schomburg increasingly resented the ingratitude, and sometimes downright intellectual dishonesty, of some of those whom he helped. He sometimes complained too much, but there was substance to his complaint. "First chance you have at a Library get hold of J. W. Johnson's *Black Manhattan*," he wrote a friend in 1934,

> examine the following material, inside the cover is a copy of the Brooklyn Handicap, picture of Ira Aldridge, a collection of Ira Aldridge photostat playbills [−] since the original were consumed by fire at Wilberforce [University], the only collection ex[t]ant is in the Schomburg Coll.[−] the picture of Frederick Douglass[;] hours spent with the author to select which one he should use. Help him to find exact knowledge that Ira Aldridge was born in N[ew] Y[ork]. That Milburn did originate the melody of "Listen to the Mocking Bird"[,] etc. Then turn to the Preface and see for yourself the passive way this "great American" thanks his fellow man. It is a scream! I mean he thanks the collection and mentions my name for having collected play-bills, no personal reference of a man's thought. It is hell, how some men do things. But the Good Lord has kept me this long for some purpose or other.[52]

James Weldon Johnson was not the only black intellectual to be privately censured by Schomburg in this manner. Du Bois, Alain Locke, and especially Carter G. Woodson were similarly criticized.[53] Despite the enormous assistance that Schomburg provided in the preparation and illustration of Woodson's 1922 book, *The Negro in Our History*, nowhere does Woodson acknowledge Schomburg's help. In the course of a carefully executed and damning review published in the *Negro World*, Schomburg made indirect reference to the fact that Woodson did not acknowledge the help provided. "A charitable appreciation for those who helped Dr Woodson with rare prints, engravings, etc., would not have in any way harmed him in the preface," said Schomburg. "It is one of the few books lacking this feature of long-established custom."[54] A decade later, Schomburg told his friend Boddy, "Woodson is all for himself, he held a meeting of his society [the Association for the Study of Negro Life and History] here in N[ew] Y[ork] and never mentioned one word of the [Schomburg] collection. I know why. You might as well know of it," suggested Schomburg. "I made a report to the American Negro Academy for the publication of a Journal, a committee was appointed made up [of] [Arthur U.] Craig, Woodson and myself. Six months later Woodson came out with his *Journal of Negro History*. That's why he is afraid of me, and treats me with deference. 'Forgive them Father'."[55] Schomburg grew quite bitter about what he perceived as the opportunism of many black intellectuals. Six weeks before his untimely death, in a letter to a close friend, he wrote:

> I notice that since I am not giving out sources of material to these impecunious writers there is a scarcity of books written by Negroes on the market. Many of them have been annoying me for information and I have closed my mouth tighter than a clam. Not even the loving glances of beautiful damsels will make me fall from the pedestal that [*sic*] I have put my information. I have come to the conclusion that lots of them are like a bunch of vultures on the limb of a tree waiting to pounce down on some information that they can offer a publisher.[56]

If Schomburg did indeed clam up, it was not long enough for any of his contemporaries to have noticed. For one of the most recurring descriptions of Schomburg by his contemporaries, albeit after his death, is the generosity with which he shared his knowledge. This sharing of knowledge came from a profound dual obligation that Schomburg felt he had towards black people: on the one hand, an obligation to those who have gone before, remembering their struggle, dreams and accomplishment; and, on the other, an obligation to the next generation, the young, to reinforce and buttress them in a hostile social environment that professes their "racial" inferiority, and often denies their very humanity, the humanity of people of African descent. Schomburg's project is often misconstrued. He was far less interested in persuading white people of black people's humanity and accomplishment than in convincing black people themselves of their own worth and historical stature as members of the human family. Schomburg tried to blast to pieces the centuries-old, granite accretion of black self-doubt and enforced amnesia, and sought the cultivation of a self-confident and historically informed people with the capacity to fight, precisely because they feel that they deserve better. He believed that, for people of African descent, being self-confident in the world and being historically informed went together. It is impossible for a black person to be at ease with him- or herself in the world while believing the lies of Europe about black inferiority, African historylessness and lack of accomplishment. These beliefs and ideas formed the driving force behind Schomburg's extraordinary and strenuous counter-hegemonic exertions.

Schomburg was absolutely delighted when, on rare occasions, his knowledge could be used in a direct way to aid the political struggles of black people. And such an occasion arose in Cuba in 1932 to 1933. Gustavo Urrutia, a distinguished black Cuban journalist, and friend of Schomburg's, translated his article "Notes on Panama and the Negro: Luna y Victoria, First Native Born Bishop of the Catholic Church of America." The article tells the story of a black man of humble origins who became the Bishop of Panama in 1751, making him the first American-born person to become a bishop in the Catholic Church in the Americas. Urrutia had the article published in Havana in 1933. But it was not meant to disinterestedly impart a quaint and interesting piece of information. The article was a sharp weapon in the struggle to have the ordination of a black man into the Catholic priesthood in Havana. According to Schomburg, the Roman Catholic hierarchy in Cuba, "from the Bishop down are against granting orders to [the] black fellow who was born in their city." Schomburg told a friend:

> I am urging them to fight bitterly to see that this fellow receive honor among his own people and not far away. There are sufficient Negroes in Cuba to put this over. So the article has been used as the signal shot to call the faithfuls to fight and I will be in the background to supply the necessary ammunition. I suppose this will show I also have some kind of red corpuscles in my veins. . . . The article . . . will bring many repercussions, for there is much back of it. The Roman Catholic divines will check my statements. So far Mr. Urrutia said it was well received by the papers and people who did not know the first native American promoted to the Bishopric in the R[oman] C[atholic] church was the son of a Negro woman. Selah.[57]

Schomburg, then, was happy to have his scholarship do work on behalf of black people wherever and however possible. And his use of military metaphors was apposite and clearly reflected his feeling that black people are at war with their oppressors, if only ideologically at times.

But Schomburg's concern with the black past was not entirely pragmatic and instrumental. He had a profound and enduring respect for those who had gone before, their pain and anguish, their dreams and aspirations, their humiliation and accomplishment. Toussaint Louverture, Jean Jacques Dessalines, Henri Christophe, and the Haitian revolutionaries would be hard pressed to find a more reverent remembrancer than Arturo Schomburg. It comes as no surprise that his first published essay was a defense of his beloved Haiti.[58] The year before he died, Schomburg wrote his long-time friend Dantés Bellegarde, former Haitian representative to the United States, introducing an Afro-American artist visiting the island. E. Simms Campbell, the artist, was travelling to Haiti to spend three months painting. Describing Haiti as "your great country," Schomburg wrote:

> I am extremely interested in friend Campbell's work and will be very happy if you were to extend the privilege of seeing those in charge of these courtesies for him to be able to paint for posterity the country of Toussaint Louverture, Dessalines and Christophe, its mountains and valleys made historic by their talents and swords, now with peace reigning supreme, nature will unfold its beauties to a great artist.[59]

And he remembered not just the black high and mighty, his imagination traveled with the humble black slave.

> I have always liked and enjoyed the association with slaves and their descendants, without feeling out of place with love for my fellow man, whether or not he felt the stripes and saw the stars that in a less noble sense can be seen in our national flag. For human affection, quaintness of expression, simple philosophy and naive spirit of comradeship the common herd of humanity to my mind represent the real democracy of life as we often see it portrayed in adversity.[60]

Schomburg similarly possessed a warm and human interest in the young and had a profound impact upon those who encountered him at the 135th Street Library in Harlem. Beyond the more widely acknowledged help and encouragement he provided for the young writers and artists of the Harlem Renaissance, he had a deep interest in the education of children. Kenneth B. Clark, the distinguished black psychologist, is one of many who could testify about Schomburg and his relation with the young. Clark, who grew up in the center of Harlem, recalled meeting Schomburg when he was about twelve years old.

> On one of my trips to the library, I decided that I was going to go upstairs to the third floor, that forbidden and mysterious area reserved for adults. As I climbed the last flight, I felt the excitement of an interloper. I was prepared for the risk of a polite or more direct rejection. When I entered the room, a large man, whom I later came to know as Arthur Schomburg, got up from his desk and came over to me and smiled. He didn't ask me what I wanted. He merely put one arm around my shoulder and assumed that I was interested in books. On that first day of meeting Schomburg, I knew I had met a friend. He didn't ask me whether my mother was poor. He never told me to improve myself. He accepted me as a human being and through this acceptance helped me to share his love of, and his excitement in, the world of books.[61]

Schomburg, forever concerned with group survival, became more worried about the prospects for black people in the United States as he grew older. Even though he at times expressed great faith in Franklin D. Roosevelt and the New Deal—he conveyed to the President his "deep appreciation for the great good you are doing to bring sunshine to the nation"[62]—Schomburg remained pessimistic. Less than a year before he died he made a bleak prophecy: "I am becoming very doubtful of the Negro finding a place for himself in the next quarter of a century. I believe that the forces that are working in this nation against radicalism and syndicalism are going to convert their forces like pincers and crush our group. We will either be relegated to the level of the sidewalk or back to Africa in the spirit of the philosophy of Marcus Garvey."[63]

Schomburg was a strong supporter of Marcus Garvey, but he never believed in the idea of a return to Africa. The fact that in all seriousness, albeit in despair, he contemplated such an idea showed the gloom and desperation that invaded Schomburg's thoughts toward the end of his life. But Schomburg's attitude toward Garvey, and, by extension, toward black nationalism, requires elaboration here. These are in fact some of the most under-explored issues surrounding Schomburg's life and politics, yet some of the most crucial to elucidating his politics.

It is somewhat misleading to claim, as one author does, that Schomburg was a Garvey "disciple."[64] Schomburg had more than ample opportunity to join the UNIA, but never did. Having said that, however, Schomburg's support of Garvey was very strong, even passionate, and remarkably enduring.

It appears that from his very earliest encounter with Garvey, Schomburg's rebel heart began to sing. Never a conservative, Schomburg admired Garvey's audacity, his lion-heartedness. His closest friends reacted in a similar manner to the emergence of Garvey and the UNIA. After initial hesitation, John Edward Bruce, Schomburg's spiritual father, threw in his lot with Garvey, became an official, a columnist of the *Negro World*, and one of the UNIA's leading intellectual and staunchest defenders up to his death in 1924, aged sixty-eight. William Ferris, like Bruce, a leading member of the American Negro Academy, became at an even earlier stage than Bruce a fervent supporter of Garvey and an official of the UNIA, editing the organization's newspaper through its most crucial years. (George Schuyler, who hated Garvey, said that Ferris, a graduate of both Yale and Harvard, provided the best philosphical defense of Garveyism that he had ever heard.)[65] Dr John Wesley Cromwell, a former president of the American Negro Academy, and a very close friend of Schomburg's, was also a strong supporter of the UNIA.[66] Schomburg shared some of his innermost thoughts about Garvey and the UNIA with Cromwell, who lived in Washington, DC.

Schomburg evidently attended the 1919 UNIA convention in New York. He reported to Cromwell that "our friend" Ferris delivered a very inspiring address that "shook the timbers of the ceiling" of Liberty Hall. Garvey, he said, "stood out prominently as a man of principle who will be heard a great deal in the days to come for his peculiar and inspiring character. . . . I believe Garvey will give a good account of his stewardship and his name will go down in history for fidelity and integrity in the Negro's cause for righteousness."[67]

In another letter, Schomburg could hardly contain himself. "The *Negro World* is going over the top this week[,] 10 pages! I am mailing you a copy with an article on Garvey." He expressed his delight with the proposed naming of the first three ships of the Black Star Line, incorporated by the UNIA, after Frederick Douglass, Phillis Wheatley, and Booker T. Washington. He hoped the next ship will be named after another Afro-American hero, Paul Cuffee. "The 'Black Star line'," Schomburg exclaimed, "is going to increase its capital from $500,000 to $10,000,000! Then there will be an unusual howl from the doubters. Garvey is the man!"[68] In yet another letter to Cromwell, clearly written in a state of excitement, immediately after acknowledging receipt of Cromwell's letter, Schomburg declared: "Garvey Veni, Vidi, Vici—I think our leaders have gone to the woods none at hand to answer Garvey."[69]

Schomburg wrote for the *Negro World*, translated letters for Garvey, sided with Garvey in his disputes with Du Bois, spoke to UNIA branches up to as late as the mid-1930s, well after Garvey's and the UNIA's star had fallen. If Schomburg had doubts about aspects of Garvey's program, he did not, apparently, express them publicly until the 1930s, well after Garvey had left the American scene. And even then, Schomburg never condemned Garvey as so many others did. In a 1935 newspaper article in which he discussed Garvey, his strongest criticism of the man was Garvey's claim to "control four hundred million followers." Garvey's positive contribution was what attracted Schomburg:

> We cannot forget Marcus Garvey who for several years gave us much inspiration in trying to awaken the dormant mind of our people and in doing so, aroused the ire of his enemies. However, leaving out of the question the right or wrong of his doctrines, we must admire his indomitable courage when he not only talked but got his [1920] convention that held sway for 30 days to appoint a commission to cross the Atlantic ocean and journey to Geneva, where they presented [to the League of Nations] their message in the most exacting manner with diplomatic requirements and the amenities of the day.[70]

A year later, in an implied rebuke of Garvey, Schomburg wrote that "men who battled in and out of season for the American colored people to remain here in the land of their birth rather than to run across the sea [to Africa] chasing rainbows, served posterity best, and now merit our everlasting thanksgiving."[71] Despite this remark (which was explicitly aimed at John B. Russwurn, who left America in disgust for Liberia in the 1830s), Garvey had a special place in Schomburg's heart. In 1935, reflecting upon the Italian invasion of Ethiopia and the ensuing crisis within the League of Nations, Schomburg's thoughts turned to Garvey. Referring to him as "Chief Garvey," Schomburg wrote:

> We may excoriate Marcus Garvey for his titles of nobility but even today, he is nearer the seat of the League of Nations than any of his opponents who are here still lingering with us, self appease [sic] after crumbs from the masters [sic] table. They lack his element of courage, his dignity in prison and his steadfast will in the adversity of the day knowing that Ethiopia shall yet rule.[72]

Schomburg remembered Garvey better than Garvey remembered him— but Garvey did not forget Schomburg. In exile in London, Garvey got news of Schomburg's untimely death. In an editorial entitled, "Passing of a Great Man," published in his magazine, *The Black Man*, Garvey said that they met "once or twice" and that he could not claim any particular friendship with Schomburg, but the two men "shared the mutual friendship of others." Garvey said it was difficult to find anyone more interesting than Arthur Schomburg.

> In sixty-four years of life he wrapped up in himself the highest ambition of usefulness to his race. He in New York particularly, engaged himself in the intellectual details that would ultimately help the Negro to establish his status among other races of the world. He was not known from many platforms, but every platform scholar and every man of intellectual count in America knew that Arthur Schomburg lived and that his work was a living testimony to a man who was devoted to a worthy cause. . . . It is a pity that the race has lost such a useful man at such a time.[73]

Although the Great Depression and its disproportionately harsh impact upon Afro-America got him down, to the very end, Schomburg never gave up, and remained an activist. During the 1930s he travelled to Washington on a delegation from Harlem in support of the "Scottsboro Boys," the nine black boys and young men wrongfully accused of raping two white women and condemned to death in Alabama; he actively supported Claude McKay and the right for black people to organize on their own in the Negro Writers' Guild; he supported the "Don't Buy Where You Can't Work" campaign in Harlem and went on a delegation to Blumstein's store, the focus of much of the protest, seeking the employment of black people in other than menial jobs; he protested against the Italian invasion of Ethiopia and corresponded with Roosevelt over his government's policy on the issue; he sided with Republican Spain against Franco's fascists.

He had an extraordinarily sturdy constitution—"the body and energy of a powerful Spanish bull," claimed McKay—that undergirded his relentless activity on behalf of "the race."[74] But on June 10, 1938, following complications caused by a tooth infection, Schomburg suddenly died—simultaneously shocking and saddening his friends. "I have done my mite," he modestly wrote in a 1934 letter, to "lift up the Negro to a better appreciation of his worth."[75]

In general, Jesús Colón had different dreams and nightmares and moved in different circles to Schomburg. His world was not that of *los negros Americanos*, nor was his preoccupation the fate of Afro-America. Colón had remained faithful to the world of the *tabaqueros*—in whose midst he was born—faithful to the struggles of the Puerto Rican migrant community (especially in Brooklyn and in El Barrio in East Harlem), faithful to that of Puerto Rican nationalism, and international socialism.

Fabián Jesús Colón was born on January 20, 1901, in the dignified working-class world of Puerto Rico's tobacco growers and cigar makers in Cayey. His father, 36-year-old Mauricio Colón y Coto, worked as a baker (*panadero*) and his mother, Paula López Cedeño, was a housewife.[76] One of his earliest childhood memories is of hearing through his window at about ten every morning a clear, strong voice coming from the big cigar factory at the back of his house. He later discovered that the voice was that of *el lector*, the reader, who read to the one hundred and fifty cigar makers as they bent over their desks, silently rolling tobacco leaves into neat cigars. As he reported:

> The workers paid fifteen to twenty-five cents per week each to the reader. In the morning, the reader used to read the daily paper and some working class weeklies or monthlies that were published or received from abroad. In the afternoon he would read from a novel by Zola, Balzac, Hugo, or from a book by Kropotkin, Malatesta or Karl Marx. Famous speeches like Castelar's or Spanish classical novels like Cervantes' *Don Quixote* were also read aloud by "El Lector".[77]

The cigar makers were among the most literate and highly educated groups of workers in Puerto Rico. Interestingly, because of the tradition of *la lectura*, illiteracy was substantially divorced from ignorance. Even though some of the cigar makers were unable to read and write, they were nonetheless highly informed and educated persons. "So you were amazed," reported Colón, "by the phenomenon of cigarmakers who hardly knew how to read and write, discussing books like Zola's *Germinal*, Balzac's *Pere Goriot*, or Kropotkin's *Fields, Factories and Workshops*, during the mild Puerto Rican evenings in the public square."[78]

By the time Colón was born, the expansion of capitalism into tobacco processing was well under way. Independent cigar makers were being transformed from artisans into proletarians, along the lines of the one hundred and fifty who worked in the "big factory" at the back of Colón's house in Cayey. The erosion of their autonomy and the ineluctable compromising of their craft by the logic of capital, mass production, and its accompanying labor process aroused the opposition of the tobacco workers. Coming out of a political culture that respected the dignity of labor, that had nurtured a tradition of *parejería*—disrespect for hierarchy and pride of self—that placed great value upon education and the cultivation of the mind, a culture that had been informed by the most progressive, scientific, rationalist ideas afloat in the world, it comes as no surprise that the artisans, and especially the *tabaqueros*, were in the vanguard of political and social dissent in Puerto Rico.[79] Spurred on by the pressures of capitalist amalgamation and aggregation, the *tabaqueros* embraced, even more passionately, revolutionary socialist and anarcho-syndicalist ideas. Adversely affected, especially after the American conquest of their land in 1898, by rapid economic and social changes, the cigar makers became one of the most class conscious and combative sections of the Puerto Rican working class. It was they who spearheaded the founding of the Puerto Rican Socialist Party in 1915. And significantly, the party was founded in Bernardo Vega's and Jesús Colón's birthplace, the town of Cayey, in the heart of Puerto Rico's tobacco country. Colón, who was only fourteen, joined the Socialist Party that very year.[80] Colón, then, grew up in an environment of radical and socially conscious workers.

As a schoolboy at the Central Grammar School in San Juan, he was bright, had an early passion for writing, was respected by his fellow students, and evidently possessed qualities of leadership. His three-paragraph letter expressing the condolences of his class, his teacher, and the principal over the death of the mother of one of his classmates was deemed the best by his teacher and the principal of the forty submitted by his class of eighth graders, and his was the one sent to the bereaved family. Another of Colón's classmates told their American History teacher that her textbook was missing from her desk. When no one admitted to having seen or taken the missing book, the teacher, a Mr Whole from Montana, imposed a fine of ten cents per student on the entire class. "Everybody shall bring ten cents tomorrow," he commanded, "otherwise he or she will not be allowed to come into my class."

The students were outraged, and the following morning they resolved not to pay. The students elected Colón chairman of a committee of three to present their demands to the principal. The students, *en bloc*, boycotted Mr Whole's class, and from the square where they gathered watched him through the window to see what his next move would be when they did not turn up. Tired of waiting for the students, the teacher went to the principal's office. Colón presented the students' case and finished by saying "very emphatically that the class refused to come in until Mr Whole rescinded the ten cent order." Mr Whole backed down. Not only was this Colón's first strike, it was a successful one.[81]

Around the age of sixteen, Colón was elected by the whole student body of his school to the editorship of the school magazine, *¡Adelante!* (*Forward!*). It was while reminiscing about *¡Adelante!* that Colón revealed a crucial event in his political formation. While his school was being rebuilt in 1917, classrooms were temporarily located in makeshift wooden barracks—dubbed *Barracones* by the students—in a working-class district called Puerta de Tierra, near the docks in San Juan.

During a dock workers' strike, the workers, their wives, and supporters held a demonstration to publicize their cause. Parades and public demonstrations had been outlawed by the authorities during the strike period. Jesús Colón and some four hundred students were enjoying their after-lunch break when the parade of striking dock workers was passing. Distracted by the noise, the students rushed to look, sticking their heads through the slats in the fence for a better view. As they watched the parade of workers and their wives marching down the street, they noticed about a dozen mounted policemen armed with carbines coming from the opposite direction. Undeterred, the marchers continued, "with slogans and union banners flying." Over forty years after the incident, Colón could still remember clearly what happened:

> As the mounted police saw the parade formation coming towards them, they lined up on their large, strong horses, into an impassable fortress from one side of the street to the other.
>
> There was a moment of suspense and indecision on the part of the workers— it might have been fifteen seconds or more. To us boys and girls, with our heads between the fence slats, these seconds of hesitancy were like an eternity.
>
> At last, taking two steps forward, one of the strikers holding a banner began to march forward and sang at the same time:
>
> *Arriba los pobres del mundo*
> *De pie los esclavos sin pan*[82]
>
> He continued marching with head up toward the mounted police. The rest of the strikers with their wives and their sisters followed after him.
>
> The one in charge of the mounted platoon gave a signal, so imperceptible that nobody seemed to notice. The police moved as if by a spring, moving their

carbines to their shoulders and taking aim. It was done rapidly, but coolly, calmly, dispassionately. It seems to me as if I can see them right now. Another almost imperceptible signal and all of them shot at the same time. The worker with the banner was the first to fall pierced by the police bullets.

Colón noticed a "strange thing" happening. Instead of intimidating the marchers, the shooting stiffened their resolve and "incensed them to a fury." The strikers and their supporters continued marching forward until "strikers, horses, women, children and police were in a whirling mass of fighting humanity." Women stabbed the underbelly of the police horses with long hat pins, causing them to dislodge their riders into the melée. "The strikers kept on pushing, singing and fighting the police," said Colón. One of the policemen managed to mount his horse and sped off to summon reinforcement. As the street cleared—the marchers realizing that the police had gone for help—six strikers, "making a human stretcher of their hands and arms woven together, took the body of their dead companion away."

Despite the principal's frenetic ringing of the school bell, calling the children back to class, Colón and his schoolmates looked heedlessly out on to the street, horrified and spellbound as if their young heads were riveted to the slats in the fence.

A sixteen-year-old, Francisco Colón Gordiany, who witnessed the event reported it for *¡Adelante!* In his article, entitled "Honest Struggle of Our Parents," he lamented: "Our dear fathers struggle for bread but they fall vanquished, covered with blood." He grew up to become the President of the Puerto Rican Confederation of Labor. "Nothing in those schoolrooms of old Barracones," said Colón, "has taught me as much as that encounter between the workers and the police that eventful day."[83]

Within a year of the incident, Jesús Colón, empty handed, walked up the gangway from San Juan dock on to the *SS Carolina* and stowed away to New York City. In his new abode, he continued what he had begun in his native Puerto Rico: he expanded his education, earning against the odds his high school diploma by attending night school in Brooklyn, and attended St John's University for two years; he sustained and deepened his love-affair with books, sparked by the *tabaqueros* in Cayey; he worked at the craft of writing and wrote for the working-class and radical publications in New York and Puerto Rico; he became one of the most important organic intellectuals of exiled Puerto Rico: it is not for nothing that he called one of his newspaper columns '*Lo Que El Pueblo Me Dice*' ('What the People Tell Me').[84] For some sixteen years he wrote columns for the Communist press in America, rolling with the punches as the party and its press declined and dwindled. Starting with *The Daily Worker* in 1955, becoming a contributing editor of the magazine *Mainstream*, to *The Worker* (which was no longer daily) from 1958 to 1968, Colón ended his journalistic career with the *Daily World*, from 1968 to 1971, and died three years later.

Colón founded and led numerous cultural and political organizations among the Hispanic population. Included among these were the *Alianza Obrera Puertorriqueña, Ateneo Obrero Hispano, Sociedad Fraternal Cervantes*, the latter being the Spanish-speaking section of the International Workers Order (IWO). A multinational and multi-racial order, the IWO was founded in 1930 by members of the Communist Party and Jewish radicals. It dedicated itself to providing workers with insurance and other services. It played an active role in the formation of the Congress of Industrial Organizations and campaigned for the unemployed during the Depression years. By 1947, the IWO had almost 190,000 members. Colón, by this time, was in charge of thirty Spanish- and Portuguese-speaking lodges affiliated to the IWO throughout the United States.[85] Colón joined the Communist Party in 1933—having, apparently years earlier, left the Socialist Party—and remained a loyal Party member up to his death forty-one years later. Between 1953 and 1968, he made three unsuccessful bids for public office in the New York State Assembly and New York City Council, the last for City Controller on the Communist Party ticket. Like many other radicals at the time, Colón was hauled up in front of the House Un-American Activities Committee; unlike many others dragged before them, he was remarkably unfrightened by the McCarthyites. He was, instead, outraged by them. As his testimony shows, he was courageous and combative, dubbing the witchunters "the Un-Americans," symbolically turning the tables on his persecutors. A man of almost sixty at the time, he apparently escaped unpunished by the authorities.[86] The Cuban Revolution and the guerrilla movements in Latin America fueled his political ardor and optimism, and brought him cheer in the autumn of his life.

Through the course of his life, Colón maintained an unusually straight political line of march: he was and remained an active socialist and an *independentista* from his early youth to the end of his days. Given his background and experience, it is not surprising that Colón was a class man, not a race man, exercised more by issues of class than of ethnicity and race. Thus, of the two, the enigmatic and anomalous figure is not Jesús Colón, the Puerto Rican black socialist, but Arturo Schomburg, the Puerto Rican with strong black nationalist sympathies. *Schomburg*, not Colón, is the Puerto Rican aberration.

Thus, it is more extraneously than by its actual contents that one discovers that the author of the beautifully written, charming, generous, and wise—I have weighed my adjectives carefully—document, *A Puerto Rican in New York and Other Sketches*, was indeed black. The Puerto Ricans' "American hero," Colón accurately wrote in 1961, "was and still is Vito Marcantonio," the remarkable Italian-American radical Congressman from East Harlem who represented the district, almost without break, from 1934 to 1950.[87] While Schomburg bursting with excitement over the Black Star Line proclaimed: "Garvey is the man!" and that "Garvey, Veni, Vidi, Vici," nowhere in Colón's writing do the words "Marcus Garvey" appear. Never once in his more than four hundred pieces of writing is the acronym UNIA to be seen; neither man nor organization was praised or condemned by Colón. It was as if Garvey had never lived and the Universal Negro Improvement Association had never been born. Arriving in New York in 1918 and living in the city right up to his death in 1974, it would have been impossible, even though he lived most of the time in Brooklyn, for Colón not to have heard of Garvey and the UNIA.[88] He clearly had no interest in either.

Significantly, the civil rights movement of the late 1950s and 1960s roused Colón to reflect—publicly and more explicitly—about race and racism in the United States, in his native Puerto Rico and elsewhere. It was as if the movement, triggered by the arrest of Rosa Parks in December 1955, had given him permission to remember painful experiences, hitherto repressed, and had endowed him with the right to speak out more openly about racial oppression. "Little Things are Big" and "Hiawatha into Spanish," two of his most skillfully executed sketches, are at once under-stated and searing indictments of racism. They were both written during the heat of the civil rights movement in 1956. It was also in 1956 that Colón first mentions Schomburg in writing, describing him as "a great Negro Puerto Rican," and "a great figure in the life of the 19th century Puerto Rican in New York."[89] In the following year, Colón encouraged his Puerto Rican compatriots to march on Washington on the Pilgrimage of Prayer, organized by A. Philip Randolph and the civil rights leadership. Colón attended the march, was deeply moved by it, and told his readers about the event. "Phrase Heard in a Bus," published in 1957, like "Hiawatha into Spanish," recalled incidents of racism that he had experi-enced and bottled up for forty years. The school desegregation struggles in Little Rock, Arkansas also commanded a column in 1957.[90]

Colón's deepening race consciousness may also have been quickened by his interaction with black comrades within the Party. He knew Ben Davis, who was elected on the Communist Party ticket to represent Harlem on New York City Council, and he also knew William L. Patterson, a distinguished civil rights lawyer and senior member of the Party. It is unclear, however, how well he knew these two Afro-American comrades. He probably knew Patterson better than Davis, as Patterson also did Party work in Puerto Rico and, at least according to the House Committee on Un-American Activities, at one stage was given responsibilities that included Puerto Rican affairs. He would have had to liaise with Colón in this endeavor. When Colón published "Little Things Are Big" in the *Daily Worker*—which told of his feeling of shame in not offering to help a white woman and her small children up the stairs at a Brooklyn subway station late one night because he feared a racist reaction from her—Patterson wrote and told him how moved he was by the article. "Its poignancy, its gripping exposure of the terribly dehumanizing blight of the cult of white superiority shook me up on the inside. I have gone through the very same experience and acted precisely as you did," he said.[91] Colón also admired and supported Adam Clayton Powell, Jr, with whom he shared, over the years, many public platforms in New York City. And on several occasions, he used his newspaper column to endorse and promote the candidacy of Powell.[92] These personal relationships with Afro-Americans may very well be partly responsible for the changes in Colón's expressed positions on race, but this is hard to document.

Colón, who according to his 1944 FBI interview was an NAACP member, did, it should be said, discuss racism in his earlier writings, if only infrequently. But the language he mobilized was that of anti-facism rather than that of anti-racism. The analysis was unsatisfactory and crude. In fact, it is fair to say that although his understanding of the phenomenon of racism improved significantly over time, even in the 1950s and 1960s, Colón never adequately came to grips with the complexity and embeddedness of racism in American society. This failure was not entirely Colón's; it was also that of the Communist Party of the United States, to which he belonged. Like the Communist Party, he never saw racism as anything other than the direct result of ruling class manipulation, and an expression of false consciousness on the part of white workers. And so in 1943 he perceived the Ku Klux Klan as "the Trojan horse of nazifascism [*nazifascismo*]" in America.[93] Even in the 1950s and 1960s his conception of racism never went much beyond describing the phenomenon as imperialist and capitalist "poison." In his discussion of the crisis at Central High School in Little Rock in 1957, Colón no less than three times in seven short paragraphs used "poison" as a noun or a verb to capture the phenomenon of racism:

> We should not forget, looking at the gains that the basic admission that Negroes ought to have the same rights and privileges as anybody else is not yet recognized flatly and in life without any ifs or buts, by the majority of the white population that has been poisoned for years by those capitalist interests who thrive and profit by this policy of divide and conquer. We progressives of all races, have been as yet unable to win the wide masses of the white people, especially in the South, from this poison of Chauvinism that keeps the working class and the people in general weak and divided.

Writing in the organ of the Communist Party of the United States, he told his comrades that they cannot "exorcize chauvinism from people by ridiculing, insulting, howling and calling them ignorant. By this method of insult and innuendo all that we can achieve is to alienate those who are just getting rid of the capitalist poison."[94]

Having conceptualized racism in such a manner, Colón, not surprisingly, was overly optimistic as to the extent to which socialists could provide the antidote. Education and exemplary deeds on the part of "progressives" were the remedy. Accordingly, he applauded and encouraged every act of class solidarity and human decency that countered racism. He was right to have done so, but he overestimated the effects of his civilized cheer-leading and encouragement in the pages of *The Daily Worker* and *The Worker*.[95] Colón was never comfortable when it came to talking about race. It is interesting that his column on "The Negro in Puerto Rican History" was requested by his readers, not a subject he himself chose to write on. And although he had promised to write the following week on "The Negro in Puerto Rico Today," Colón's essay on the subject appeared not a week, but four columns and over a month later.[96] In the interim he wrote on "Soviet Exhibition in Havana," and other good things, which he apparently thought were subjects more worthy of his attention.

It should be said, however, that Colón's intellectual growth, and the changes in his discussion and perceptions of race, especially in the last five years of his life, are not adequately reflected in his published works. Around the beginning of 1970, Colón prepared a new edition of *A Puerto Rican in New York* for publication the same year by International Publishers, the Communist Party's book publishing arm. He wrote a new foreword, changed the dedication from his late wife, Concha, to his wife at the time, Clara, indicated sketches he wanted to be withdrawn and suggested new insertions. Colón in fact presented to his publishers a nine-page document with over ninety-five changes to the first edition of the book. This was in addition to the new foreword. The suggestions ranged widely, from the ending of a Spanish noun to the insertion of whole paragraphs to the changing of titles of sketches. The new foreword and the list of changes serve together as a window on Colón's mind as his life came to a close. And one of the things that is clearly visible through the window is the increased prominence and awareness of race on his part. In the first edition of *A Puerto Rican in New York*, Colón has the "Puerto Rican Poet Pachín Marín"; for the second, he suggested the "Puerto Rican black poet Pachín (Francisco) Marín"; "Negro" is systematically changed to "black" and "American Negroes" to "Afro-Americans"; in his powerful sketch "The Mother, the Young Daughter, Myself and All of Us" — in which a nine-year-old girl when told by her mother to sit beside Colón in a café blurted out: "I won't sit beside no nigger" — the reader is told of the mother's color. This time round: "A mother" is changed to "A white mother"; "Youth: The Palisades as a Backdrop," the title of a sketch, is now changed to "Black and Youth are Beautiful," which more accurately captures the spirit and content of the piece. These and many more changes, some smaller, some more substantial, were outlined by Colón.

In his new foreword, Colón gave the sharpest evidence of having moved and developed on these questions. The "oppressed" (on the basis of race and nationality) is given pride of place in the struggle over the "exploited" (on the basis of class), even though Colón called for united action by the two groups against the common oppressor. Colón was clearly aware that he had very little time left, but he was throwing his lot, unequivocally, with the fighters for progress, and, as usual, he was full of fine dreams:

> We will be very happy if in the decade of the 1970's this book will help a bit in the Puerto Rican effort to achieve an independent socialist Puerto Rico and aid

Puerto Ricans now living in the United States to understand the necessity of joining with white, brown and black masses in the struggle against the common enemy: American imperialism.

There are instances in which you have to fight with your fists; others in which you have to fight with bricks and sticks or whatever you find at hand. It is even necessary sometimes to use guns to defend human and constitutional rights which the oppressors—in their final acts of desperation—try to deny the oppressed. Unfortunately for the imperialists, the oppressed in the United States led by the blacks, and the exploited all over the world are awakening fast, and learning, through the word and deed how to eliminate the differences among themselves—differences that the exploiters who own the mass media and various repressive and persecution agencies make sure to exaggerate and exploit.

The word is also a powerful weapon.

All that we can do at our age is to sit somewhere, in a sort of an active quietness, and put down in words, with all the ire, irony and emotion that we can muster, the errors and the successes in the experiences—good and bad —through which we passed in almost seventy years of busy living. In that way, those who struggle in the field, don't have to repeat the mistakes we made.[97]

Although scheduled to be published in 1970, the book never appeared until 1982, eight years after Jesús Colón had died and twelve years later than promised. Worst of all, the changes that Colón so painstakingly set down on paper were completely ignored, his fine new foreword, a dead letter, put aside. How and why this happened are not altogether clear, but the reader should know that Colón said more on the issue of race, and indeed on other subjects, than the 1982 edition of *A Puerto Rican in New York* would lead one to think.[98]

It is nevertheless true that right to the end, Colón was at home talking class politics, the Cuban Revolution, the Puerto Rican struggle, and American imperialism in Latin America. He was out of his depth when it came to the madness of race in America. It was as if his mind was too cultivated and civilized, his instincts too decent, generous, and human for him to have plumbed the stinking depths of American racism. And he squared the circle of his analysis by crudely and repeatedly reducing race to class, and racism to bourgeois conspiracy—hence the notion of racism as capitalist poison.[99]

But the emphasis of class and nationality over race by Colón and other Puerto Ricans in New York has substantially been a reflection of the greater relevance of the former, class, compared to race within Puerto Rican society itself. Moreover, the discrimination that they experience in the United States as a group—partly on linguistic and cultural grounds—reinforces the salience of class and nationality.[100] The Spanish language in itself cemented the bonds of national and ethnic identification over more narrowly racial identification. Indeed, Spanish has become so emblematic of Puerto Rican identity that, as Samuel Betances noted, "one cannot separate a Puerto Rican identity from the Spanish language."[101] It also provided the nexus to a wider Latin American cultural identity and transnationality. For Puerto Ricans in New York City in the early twentieth century, as Virginia Sánchez Korrol observes, "read Spanish language newspapers; saw Mexican and Argentinian films; listened to Spanish radio stations; formed associations which promoted Spanish language and culture; danced and listened to Latin music."[102]

Among the Puerto Ricans, the Catholic religion provided a similar force of cohesion—though a far less powerful one than the Spanish language—which transcended race and color.[103] This is not to say that racism and colorism did not exist within the community. They did and do. Even Jesús Colón, that most sanguine of Puerto Rican voices, acknowledged their existence.[104] Indeed, although Colón never spoke about it publicly, Angel, the brother of his childhood sweetheart, Rufa Concepción Fernández (Concha), objected to his marrying her because he was too dark. "And for your brother Angel, being black is a crime," Colón wrote Concha.[105] What the centripetal and shepherding power of a common language and a common religion does in a hostile environment is to act as a countervailing force against the centrifuge of race, color, and difference within the group. Powerful though they were, the centripetal forces could not hold everyone. Bernardo Vega reported that when he arrived in 1916 there were "quite a few black *paisanos* [compatriots]," especially in East Harlem, between 99th and 106th streets. But some of them, like Schomburg, Augustín Vazquez, and Isidro Manzano, "later moved up to the black North American neighborhood," that is, black Harlem proper. Vega, unfortunately, does not explain why this movement took place, nor does he give us the proportion of the black Puerto Ricans who moved in this way. The most we get from his account is that "some" did.[106] And we learn nothing about Vasquez and Manzano apart from the bare facts of nationality and color as they marched up to Harlem and out of the pages of history, unrecovered to this day.

A Puerto Rican scholar recently wrote that "Puerto Ricans were White and Black; Puerto Ricans were neither White nor Black. From the Puerto Rican perspective, Puerto Ricans were more than White or Black."[107] Memorable though the formulation may be, it elegantly obfuscates more than it reveals about the actual relation between dark-skinned and light-skinned Puerto Ricans at home and abroad.[108] Matters were and are far more complex than such a simplistic rendering would lead one to believe. Not only was there racism and colorism, the commitment to non-racist behavior and anti-racism was not evenly spread among the Puerto Rican migrants either. The *tabaqueros* were, apparently and not implausibly, the most committed, and the light-skinned Puerto Rican middle class the least so.[109] Indeed, one *tabaquero* migrant who came to New York in 1913 went so far as to tell Bernardo Vega that "when it came to the so-called better-off people, some of them were even more prejudiced than the Americans."[110] Vega reported that from the earliest years of migration anti-Puerto Rican bigotry pushed some members of the community, "the better-off ones in particular," to try passing for "Spaniards" so as to minimize the prejudice against themselves. Colón reported that some tried to pass as Mexican, Chilean, Costa Rican, and other nationalities. Vega recalled that there were "even those who went so far as to remain silent in public. They made sure never to read Spanish newspapers in the subway or to teach Spanish to their children." As if pre-empting the incredulity of his readers, Vega drove the point home. "That's right," he said "that's what they did, I know it for a fact."[111] Eric Walrond, who grew up in Panama, concurred. "I know the type," he said. "Coming to New York, he shuns the society of Spanish Americans. On the subway at night he reads the *New York Journal* instead of *La Prensa*."[112] Vega contrasted this behavior with that of the working-class Puerto Rican, in whose community "Spanish was always spoken, and on the train we read our papers for all to see. The workers," he said, "were not afraid of being called 'spiks'. They did not deny their origin. Quite the contrary: they struggled because they knew that they were Puerto Ricans and, in a broader sense, Hispanic."[113]

The class divisions among New York's Puerto Ricans also expressed themselves in spatial terms. By the 1920s, it was evident that Brooklyn's Puerto Rican community was not as well heeled as that in Manhattan. Puerto Rican Brooklyn was more working class and darker in complexion, apparently, than its counterpart in El Barrio and elsewhere in Manhattan. Lawyers, doctors, dentists, and other Puerto Rican professionals, as well as merchants, took up residence far more readily in Manhattan than Brooklyn. And because the cigar shops and factories were located largely in lower Manhattan, most of the *tabaqueros*—the most highly regarded and rewarded of Puerto Rico's skilled workers in the city—also resided on the island.

It is no accident that Puerto Rico's black leaders in New York came not from Manhattan but primarily from Brooklyn. Jesús Colón, his brother Joaquín, and his cousin Ramón Colón were all Brooklyn residents. Most significantly, Carlos Tapia, the "ebony giant" from Ponce who defended New York's Puerto Rican community from racist assaults, bravely avenged wrongs perpetrated against his compatriots, and provided alms and support to needy Puerto Ricans, also settled in Brooklyn. Tapia, "a 250-pound, 6-foot-8-inch man"[114] of humble origins and little education, but with enormous courage, generosity, and integrity, was born in Ponce in 1885 and died in New York in 1945. He lived in Brooklyn from 1920 to 1937, when, as his biographer would put it, the Puerto Rican beach-head in that borough was established, defended, and consolidated—with Tapia playing the leading role in the process.[115] Joaquín and Ramón were president and secretary, respectively, of the Brooklyn Puerto Rican Democratic Club. Tapia was also one of the most influential Puerto Ricans in the Democratic

Party in New York in the 1920s. Along with Jesús Colón, these men were also institution builders and active members in the community's civic and cultural life.

There was, at least in certain quarters of Brooklyn's Puerto Rican community, deep resentment against many of their better-off compatriots residing in Manhattan. The bitterness was generally articulated in class terms, but often went beyond class.

Ramón Colón reported that in the 1920s and 1930s, if a Puerto Rican living in Brooklyn needed the help of "a Puerto Rican lawyer, a Puerto Rican medical doctor, a Puerto Rican dentist, or any other Puerto Rican professional," he or she had to go to El Barrio to be attended by one "who would charge him a very substantial fee for his services." According to him, Puerto Rican doctors would charge $75 minimum to visit a patient in Brooklyn from Manhattan. The patient's Puerto Rican nationality did not temper the "exorbitant fee."[116]

Ramón Colón and Carlos Tapia especially resented the fact that the Manhattan middle-class Puerto Ricans reaped unearned benefits from the struggles and sacrifices of their more humble and embattled Brooklyn *compatriotas*. Almost sixty years after arriving in Brooklyn, Ramón Colón recalled with bitterness the difference in the distribution of the burden and benefits of struggle between Brooklyn and Manhattan. "The Brooklyn Puerto Ricans," he insisted,

> were the ones who fought and struggled to establish the foundation of the Puerto Rican political, social and economic force, which the American citizens of Puerto Rican origin wield for their progress and respect in New York today. The others, who ... settled in Manhattan, did not participate in the battles fought by the Puerto Ricans to establish their beach-head in New York. In their sanctuary in Manhattan, they kept away from the battlefield. From their base of operations in Manhattan, they reaped the political and economic benefits conquered by blood, and fire, death and tears, by their fellow "countrymen" in the streets of Red Hook and other sections of Brooklyn, supported and protected by a one-man army, Carlos Tapia, a one-man supply base, Carlos Tapia.[117]

In 1924, a member of El Barrio's Puerto Rican business and professional group told Tapia of the escalating attacks on and harassment of the community carried out by thuggish business rivals. Tapia is reported to have remarked during the conversation,

> I do not see why, when your kind arrives in Brooklyn from Puerto Rico, as soon as they leave the ship, they run to Manhattan to operate there instead of staying in Brooklyn to help us. You can tell them [the professionals and storekeepers in El Barrio] whenever you have a chance, that had they stayed in Brooklyn and put up their businesses, established their law, medical and dental offices here, things would have been more advantageous to them and to us.

Tapia went on to disparagingly describe El Barrio's Puerto Rican middle class as *blanquitos*, a term which literally translates as "little white men," the diminutive of *blancos*, white men. But as Ramón Colón explains, it is an idiomatic expression widely used in Puerto Rico "meaning a self-class conscious or economically independent (white or Negro) individual. One who feels socially superior to his fellowmen—not because actually he is, but because he thinks he is."[118] Tapia said:

> Sooner or later you are bound to ask us to aid you. It is always the case with *blanquitos*. They never do the fighting unless engulfed by the swollen river of the people in revolt against injustice and oppression, in which case they . . . either fight with the people or perish alone. On the other hand they'd rather live on their knees than fight, because their goal is profit and material happiness at the sacrifice and expense of others.[119]

In the summer of 1926, El Barrio's Puerto Rican storekeepers, as well as ordinary Puerto Ricans going about their everyday business, were viciously attacked by thugs apparently at the behest of more well-established white merchants. These assaults were partly triggered by the overflowing resentment of local shopkeepers and merchants at what they saw as the commercial encroachment of Puerto Rican business competitors.[120] The attacks were shocking and bloody. Bernardo Vega vividly recalled the moment:

> Summer that year was steaming. Our people lived in the streets, and singing and laughter were heard everywhere in El Barrio and across Harlem. The sidewalks were filled with groups playing checkers and dominoes. Others would make their way, laughing and joking, toward the lake in Central Park. On every other corner the men who sold *piraguas*, or snowcones, did a thriving business . . . Raspberry, *guanábana* (soursop), and vanilla ices! It was the Puerto Ricans who brought the *piragua* to New York.
>
> It was July 28. Suddenly the noisy gaiety of the afternoon was silenced. People scattered in all directions. Mothers who had brought their children to the park for some sun took them in their arms and hurried away. All the people swarming the streets vanished in a matter of minutes. The tables where the men played were abandoned on the sidewalk. Doors and windows were slammed shut. And in the darkened apartments the talk was of the killed and wounded.
>
> All of a sudden mobs armed with clubs had begun to attack Puerto Ricans with a fury. Several stores owned by Puerto Ricans had been attacked. The sidewalks in front of the *bodegas* were covered with shattered glass, rice, beans, plantains, and tropical vegetables. A *piragua* cart was broken to bits on the corner, the gutter littered with broken bottles. . . . Terror gripped El Barrio.[121]

After the first attack some fifty people laid injured, some critically. The attacks continued, sporadically, for two weeks. A distressful El Barrio delegation—two men and a woman—arrived in Brooklyn seeking Tapia's help. A good Puerto Rican, Tapia organized a posse that traveled from Brooklyn in a convoy of seven cars. According to Ramón Colón, they took care of business in El Barrio with ease, Tapia "[making] sure the victims knew the reason for our attack."[122] No anti-Puerto Rican mass assault of the type that took place in the summer of 1926 was ever repeated after

Tapia and his men had visited El Barrio. But Tapia was ambivalent about the action he took in defense of the Manhattan Puerto Ricans. The day after the incident he told Ramón Colón, his faithful disciple whom he affectionately called Colóncito, that

> The only thing that bothers me is that we have made it secure for a type of Puerto Rican, the *blanquitos* whose only interest in our community . . . is purely material. This kind of Puerto Rican is the same kind who in our island are to blame for the unsettled political status we are in. I am afraid that these ingrates will never do anything to help either our people's struggle for integration here or our brothers' cause for civic dignity in Puerto Rico because this kind of Puerto Rican[,] as long as their bellies are full and their bank accounts keep growing[,] do not care for our civic dignity or progress.[123]

Of course, it is not true that Puerto Ricans in Manhattan were mere opportunistic bystanders who did none of the fighting; neither is it true that the 1926 attacks in El Barrio were repulsed and avenged under the exclusive guidance of Carlos Tapia, important though Tapia's intervention was. The three sixteen-year-old Puerto Rican youths arrested during disturbances on the night of July 26 were local, El Barrio, residents, not Brooklynites.[124] And there is no evidence that they acted under Tapia's direction. Ramón Colón's book on Tapia falls within the classical tradition of hagiography. Indeed, the material on which it is based was expressly gathered and written to help make the case to the New York Board of Education for naming P. S. 120 in Brooklyn the Carlos Tapia School.[125] There are obvious exaggerations and omissions; you would never know, for instance, from reading *Carlos Tapia: A Puerto Rican Hero in New York* that Tapia was apprehended by the police in 1926 during his intervention in the troubles in El Barrio.[126] What Colón reports is Tapia's own interpretation of events, that the whole operation "worked like a clock."[127] But although it is appropriate to be skeptical about some of the details in Ramón Colón's portrait of Tapia, it would be a grave mistake to dismiss the text *in toto*; that would amount to dismissing valid and valuable information contained in the book—throwing out the baby with the bath water. It would also elide the key question of what was it about Carlos Tapia, what qualities did he possess, that generated such an extraordinarily passionate and loving portrait of him by Colón? Clearly, Tapia had fine qualities: generosity, courage, hatred of injustice, loyalty. There is a mountain of evidence outside of Colón's own recollection to support this contention. "Carlos Tapia helped the Puerto Ricans in every way," an old Puerto Rican told a scholar in the late 1970s. "He even used to help them physically and economically. By physically I mean any abuse the Puerto Ricans got they used to go to Carlos Tapia. And he and his people would correct everything. They didn't go to the police, they went to Carlos Tapia."[128] This type of testimony, depicting Tapia as a saint or an avenging angel, can be multiplied many times over.[129] Tapia's action and moral position evidently had a profound impact upon Colón. But one of the forces that drives Ramón Colón's book and his anti-El Barrio position is the notion that Tapia has not been honored by people who have benefited from his sacrifices; that was the primary source of his bitterness and his protective embrace of Tapia's memory. "It is to be noted," Colón wrote,

> that more than twenty-five years have passed since Carlos Tapia's death and that, if one analyzes the present Puerto Rican *blanquitos* of New York, they are still functioning the way he prophesied they would. The Brooklyn Puerto Ricans have honored him. The Manhattan Puerto Ricans and the island's Puerto Ricans may someday be grateful and also honor him. . . . [130]

In addition to ressurecting a black Puerto Rican hero, Ramón Colón has performed the important service of providing substantial evidence of class tensions within the New York Puerto Rican community in the early years of its formation. He has also written the first history of Puerto Ricans in New York that is not El Barrio-centric; a valuable view of Puerto Rican New York, a view from the east bank of the East River, Manhattan from across the Brooklyn Bridge. And despite his own reluctance to say so, what Colón's account implies is that if Tapia had been white he would perhaps have been accorded greater respect and commemoration by the *blanquitos* of Manhattan.

But notwithstanding the class divisions and resentments among Puerto Ricans, the power of external forces against Puerto Rican group cohesion should not be underestimated. Bernardo Vega in his memoirs, tells of the horrendous persecution of his uncle's family in 1900. Antonio Vega's white neighbors on East 88th Street tolerated his presence but drew the line at his having black visitors (Antonio's swarthy compatriots) to his apartment. One Sunday afternoon, nine white men called, unexpectedly, upon Antonio Vega. Looking serious, they all refused to sit down and did not even bother to take their hats off. "We come on behalf of the tenants of this building," said one of them. "We bear no ill feeling toward anybody, but this is a white neighborhood," he declared, contradicting himself. "We have noticed that you frequently have Negroes coming to your house. People around here don't like that. We do hope that in the future you will be more careful about who you invite to your house." When Antonio tried to object, the spokesman closed him down: "See here, we have not come to discuss the matter. If you wish to keep up such friendships, then you should just move out!" Bernardo Vega reported that his uncle tried to speak again, but the visitors "promptly turned on their heels and were gone. And from that day on, not a word was exchanged with the neighbors." That did not mean that the neighbors were not heard from. Soon after the delegation, they went into action:

Someone picked up a baby-carriage that Antonio's wife had left in the hall and threw it into the street. Next a bunch of kids broke it in pieces, with all the neighbors watching. And the next day the wheels of the broken carriage were at the front door of the apartment. The day after that someone threw a rock through the front window, and a few days later they found the hallway in front of their door covered with feces. As if that was not enough, the family's mail was stolen and their gas was shut off.

Life became "unbearable" in the Vegas's nice apartment. Ignoring the behavior of the neighbors, a strategy initially adopted, became impracticable as the harassment escalated. The family had nowhere to turn:

> Calling the police was useless. When they lodged a formal complaint about the disappearance of their mail, the authorities promised to investigate but never even took the trouble to visit the building. The superintendent was part of the scheme, as was the agent who managed the building. Pressure built up all around them to move out!

But one of Antonio Vega's daughters, Vasylisa, valiantly resisted the pressure, insisting that the family not submit to the racists. She followed her own counsel. "One night she hid, waiting to catch by surprise whoever it was that was throwing filth on their doorsteps. It was a woman; she jumped up, grabbed her by the hair, and smeared the feces in her face. The scuffle woke up all the tenants, who were outraged." The entire family was arrested that night. Morris Hillquit, the Socialist leader, bailed them out and later served as the family's lawyer. But Vasylisa was convicted and, for the same crime, lost her job with the Board of Education because of what they called her "improper conduct." Vanquished, Antonio Vega and his family moved from East 88th Street.[131]

Thus, the pressure on light-skinned Puerto Ricans to reject their dark-skinned compatriots in exchange for a quiet life, to behave badly—to behave like the Yanquis, "ugly Americans," as Jesús Colón would put it— was at times enormous. (Of course, quite a number of these white Puerto Ricans behaved like "ugly Americans" back home in the island—they needed no encouragement.) But since the Vasylisas of this world are a precious few, it was only natural that some Puerto Ricans would yield to the powerful forces of bigotry. In more homogeneous Puerto Rican communities like El Barrio, group cohesion across racial lines was better maintained.[132] Speaking of the consolidation of this area of East Harlem as a Puerto Rican community, Bernardo Vega remarked that "Through this entire area, life was very much like it was back home. Following the example set by the *tabaqueros*, whites and blacks lived together in harmony."[133] Even allowing for Vega's touching partiality for the *tabaqueros*—a sentiment that runs through the entirety of his *Memoirs*—the strength of Puerto Rican cohesion along national and class lines, in contrast to racial division, is well documented, undeniable, and remarkable. McKay, looking in from the outside, was struck by the interaction between the "white and the yellow and the brown Puerto Ricans," who he thought "insouciantly mingle on equal terms."[134] Roi Ottley, one of Harlem's leading black journalists in the 1930s, went so far as to claim that, "Within the Spanish-speaking group color prejudice does not exist as a social handicap."[135]

The cross-racial cohesion, which varied in strength over time, among working-class Puerto Ricans at home and in exile, combined with a relatively low race consciousness, and a comparatively high level of educational attainment and class consciousness made it easier for them to work with white people in radical organizations like the Socialist and Communist Parties in the United States.

Given his background and experience, it is perfectly rational and understandable that Colón adopted the political positions that he did. His was the trajectory of the radical Puerto Rican who happened to be black. Schomburg, through background, circumstances and choice, evolved in a different direction. He embraced Afro-America with as much intensity as Colón lovingly clung to his exiled Puerto Rico. Schomburg became a pan-Africanist and worked vigorously to vindicate his disinherited and maligned race. He is remembered and revered by Afro-America primarily for his most conspicuous, monumental, and vibrant legacy, the Schomburg Center for the Study of Black Culture, at the New York Public Library in Harlem. And no history of the Harlem Renaissance is complete without the recognition of Schomburg's enormous contribution to that cultural and political flowering. In general, those who know about Schomburg know nothing of Jesús Colón. Colón is remembered by Puerto Rican New York, its radical intelligentsia and activists. Arturo Schomburg is hardly known in this, Colón's, world. And when known of, he is hardly seen as a member of the Puerto Rican community, even on the minimal basis of descent. He is given over, as it were, to Afro-America, in which he sought his political and intellectual home. The very images that survive of the two men reinforce this reading of their near-counterpointing political lives. Here is a photograph of Schomburg at a reception for the Liberian President-elect; there is Colón at the Pueblos Hispanos annual dinner. There is Schomburg with his black brothers of the Prince Hall lodge; here is Colón with the comrades of the Sociedad Fraternal Cervantes over which he presides. Schomburg writes for the *Negro World*; Colón for *Pueblos Hispanos*.

But the fact that Colón lived and operated in the more liberal environment of the North, as opposed to the more segregated and constricting South, is of major significance and therefore ought to be borne in mind. The political history of the Cuban *tabaqueros* in Key West and Tampa, Florida, is an instructive one that poignantly illustrates the ways in which the unrelenting societal pressure on a group can contribute to, if not directly cause, its transformation, demise, and collapse. Post-Reconstruction, Jim-

Crow Florida placed so much pressure, and an increasing amount of pressure, on the non-racist and cross-racial ethos of the *tabaqueros* and the Cuban community in general, that in the end the bonds of group cohesion broke, black and white Cubans going their separate ways, forming separate organizations. Jim Crow, contrary to the claims of some, was not exclusively responsible for the sundering, but it created a conducive environment within which the division occurred. In New York City, as we have seen, social forces similarly pushed black and white Puerto Ricans apart. But, as the next chapter makes clear, these centrifugal pressures were far weaker than those in Tampa driving black and white Cubans away from each other.

8

From a Class for Itself to a Race on its Own: The Strange Case of Afro-Cuban Radicalism and Afro-Cubans in Florida, 1870–1940

The Cuban community in Florida, dating from the nineteenth century, has always had a black component. This component has been small— certainly far smaller than the proportion of the population that Afro-Cubans make up on the island itself—but it has always been present and its significance outweighs its number. The contribution of Afro-Cubans living in the United States to Cuban émigré radicalism in America, and especially to the struggle for Cuban independence, is as remarkable and glorious as it is little known. The Afro-Cuban community's contribution far exceeded what one could reasonably expect from a group as small as theirs. The fact that there was a continuous shrinking of the black portion of the Cuban population in Florida made this contribution even more outstanding and noteworthy. Black Cubans made up about 21 percent of the Cuban population in Florida in the 1870s, but by the turn of the century they accounted for only 13 percent of the Cuban émigrés.[1] Yet, as we shall see, not only were they present in the vigorous class struggle of Key West and Ybor City, they were at the forefront of it. Not only were the Afro-Cubans in Key West and Tampa staunch supporters of Cuba's struggle for independence, they were among the vanguard in the fight for *Cuba Libre*. But at the beginning of the twentieth century, the Cuban community in Tampa took a peculiar turn that shattered the fellowship between black and white Cubans for which they had been famous. White Cubans, for the first time in the Cuban community's history in Tampa, banned Afro-Cubans from becoming members of one of the key Cuban institutions in the city, *El Círculo Cubano* (The Cuban Circle). This was done, and it was acknowledged by those who did it, for no other reason than the fact that these were black people. The move shocked and appalled Afro-Cubans. How could such a thing have happened? How did the Afro-Cubans respond? What were relations really like between black and white Cubans before this happened?

In an attempt to answer these and other questions I would like to do three things in this chapter. First, I wish to outline the formation of the Cuban community in Key West and Tampa in the late nineteenth century with special reference to its radical political culture. In this process, the position of Afro-Cubans within the community and their role in the latter's radicalism will be examined. Second, I wish to show the way in which Afro-Cuban radicalism was conditioned, tempered, and transformed by its increasingly inhospitable environment. And third, I wish to outline the evolution of the relation between Afro-Cubans and Afro-Americans in Tampa as the fortunes of both the Afro-Cubans and Afro-Americans decline and coincide as the new century progresses.

But none of this can be done satisfactorily without an understanding of the wider context of the Cuban migration to the United States and the peculiar formation and development of Ybor City and Tampa.

The presence of Cubans in nineteenth-century Florida is easily explained. The escalation of Spanish colonial repression, the economic problems of the tobacco industry (exacerbated by the dislocation caused by the wars of independence), combined with the mighty attraction of Key West and Tampa as sites for the fabrication of tobacco, powered the migration of black as well as white Cubans across the Florida Straits. Florida was not, of course, the only destination for Cubans fleeing Cuba. Paris and New York were two other important centers of Cuban émigré life in the nineteenth century. But, as a rule, those who went to Paris and New York differed in important ways to those who went to Florida. The moneyed *hacendados* lived the good life in Paris.[2] Cuban professionals—doctors, lawyers, journalists, intellectuals of one kind or another—who found themselves in opposition to the Spanish colonial regime in Cuba were attracted to New York City. Although, as we have seen earlier, Cuban cigar workers also lived and worked in New York, Key West and Tampa which were pre-eminently centers of Cuban working-class émigré life. These were the sites of refuge for the *tabaqueros* from Havana and its surrounding areas. And just as the Cuban working class were attracted by tobacco and cigar making to Florida, so were the tobacco bourgeoisie. For capitalists as well as tobacco workers experiencing hard times—a consequence of incredibly inept economic policies on the part of the Spanish colonialists (especially as they related to the tobacco industry), foreign competition, and the dislocations caused by the independence wars of the late nineteenth century—left Cuba, especially Havana, for Key West and Tampa.[3]

Vicente Martínez Ybor was the chief protagonist behind the development of Key West and Tampa as America's premier cigar-producing cities in the nineteenth century. Though Spanish-born, in Cuba, Martínez Ybor sided against colonialism, partly because Spanish colonialism in Cuba was so extraordinarily bad for business. A well-established cigar manufacturer, by the outbreak of the Ten Years War (1868–78) he decided to leave Cuba, narrowly avoiding arrest by the Spanish. He first set up business in New York in 1869, but moved his operation to Key West to avoid militant cigar workers' unions. In Key West, however, he was again in conflict with militant workers. In order to once again outflank his workers and to take advantage of the port facilities of Tampa, he shifted his operations one more time, settling in Tampa. In shifting operations to the United States, not only was Martínez Ybor evading the repression of the colonial authorities, he also obviated the burdensome tariff imposed by the Spanish on tobacco exports from Cuba. He received additional benefits from moving across the Florida Straits when the United States Congress passed the Morrison Act in 1883, lowering the duty on imported tobacco leaf while imposing a relatively high tariff on cigars imported from Cuba from where Martínez Ybor had always imported his leaves. Thus, in one fell swoop, his competitors left behind in Cuba were disadvantaged by the American tariff on cigars while he benefited from the lowering of the duty he paid on tobacco imported from the island. He established his company town on the outskirts (two miles east), of Tampa in 1886. Along with his cigar factory, eighty-nine houses were built to accommodate his workers, and Ybor City, as the complex came to be known, also boasted a hotel by the summer of 1886.[4]

Characterized by a combination of shrewd New World capitalist practices and Iberian paternalism, Martínez Ybor's operation prospered and expanded in Tampa, attracting more Cuban *tabaqueros* over time, and ancillary industries to the area. Tampa prospered and grew in tandem with Ybor City. Indeed, Ybor City's tobacco industry was the locomotive that pulled Tampa from its swampy inertia into prosperity and growth, transforming a sleepy Southern backwater into an astonishingly dynamic, modern city by the turn of the century.[5] As Mormino and Pozzetta in their valuable study of Ybor City point out, "The sheer weight of statistics underscores the integral role of cigars in Tampa's economy." In 1886 custom duties collected at the Port of Tampa amounted to 2,508 dollars; by 1900, a mere fourteen years later, the duties approached a million dollars a year—the duties came almost exclusively from tobacco products. In the same year, Tampa's internal revenues accounted for two-thirds of the total revenues of the state of Florida. Again in 1900, Tampa imported 1,180 tons of Cuban tobacco valued at three million dollars that workers fabricated into ten million dollars' worth of cigar exports. In 1886 Ybor City produced a million cigars; in 1900, twenty million; in 1919, four hundred and ten million. In 1911 almost eight million cigars left Tampa by ship and rail—in a single week.[6] By 1900, Tampa's cigar workers were the most highly paid group of workers and the most concentrated workforce in the state. The cigar workers' spending power fuelled Tampa's commercial growth. Tampans admitted their debt to Martínez Ybor and the cigar industry he brought into their midst. In 1895 a local newspaper acknowledged that Tampa's "financial soul" lay in Ybor City. "The cigar industry is to this city what the iron industry is to Pittsburg," it said two years later. And in 1908, as one observer remarked, Tampa's cigar industry was its "very backbone and muscle."[7] Tampa had become, by the end of the century, the world's "Cigar City," surpassing Havana itself, whose decline reflected Tampa's rise.

From only two in 1886 grew 120 factories in less than a decade, employing 4,783 workers in 1895, plus "innumerable" little shops employing small groups of workers. In 1895 West Tampa was established as another cigar-producing enclave of Tampa and grew with a rapidity similar to that of Ybor City. By 1920 over twelve thousand workers were directly employed in Tampa's cigar industry. Thousands more depended upon its prosperity in ancillary trades. Up to the Depression of the 1930s there was hardly any shortage of work in Tampa. It is not surprising, then, that more and more people—including those from abroad—came to Tampa after 1886, attracted by its spectacular growth and sudden wealth.

In 1860, there were only 885 people living in Tampa. During the course of the next two decades, it fell to 720. But thanks to the arrival of tobacco in 1886, by 1890, Tampa's population had reached 5,532—an increase of 668 percent on that of 1880. In the next ten years, the number of people living in Tampa had increased by another 186 percent, reaching 15,839 in 1900. And by 1920, Tampa boasted a population of 51,608, more than three times the number that lived there at the turn of the century.[8]

The arrival of Cubans and, to a lesser extent, Spanish cigar workers, lay behind the initial increase in Tampa's population growth. Around 1890, Italians also increasingly became a part of Ybor City's cigar industry. By the turn of the century, Ybor City had the largest settlement of Cubans in the United States. The census of 1900 enumerated 3,533 persons born in Cuba living in Hillsborough County, the county in which Tampa is located. But this figure is almost certainly an underestimation of the actual number, given the extraordinary mobility of the population. Even so, Tampa's Cuban émigrés exceeded the number of their compatriots in Key West and New York City. The 1900 census also recorded an additional 963 persons living in Hillsborough County who were born in Spain, most entering the United States after years of settlement in Cuba. Twenty years earlier, in 1880, there were only three people born in either Cuba or Spain living in Hillsborough.[9]

Significant though its growth was in absolute terms, the Cuban population, relative to other ethnic groups in Tampa, declined dramatically. From just under 44 percent of the city's population in 1890, the Cuban-born migrants fell to 22.3 percent in 1900, down to 10.2 percent and 6.7 percent in 1910 and 1920, respectively. Between 1890 and 1910, the Cuban-born population grew from 2,424 to 3,859, an increase of just under 60 percent, but this was well below Tampa's astronomical growth rate. Indeed, Tampa's total population grew ten times faster than its Cuban population— 583 percent between 1890 and 1910. On top of the decline in its relative weight, the Cuban population in Tampa, according to the census, fell by 400 between 1910 and 1920, from 3,859 to 3,459. Over the same period, Tampa's residents increased by 36 percent.[10]

Between 1890 and 1920, the Afro-American population in Tampa grew in number but declined in relative weight. From 1,632 in 1890, the Afro-

Americans by 1920 numbered 11,531, but, despite this growth, they dropped from 29.5 percent of Tampa's population to 22.3 percent over the period. Similarly, the native white Southern component declined from just under 45 percent in 1890 to under 29 percent a decade later, stabilizing at around a third of the city's population between 1910 and 1920.[11] The relative decline of this section of Tampa's population is easily explained: it came about as a result of the migration of Cubans, Spaniards, and Italians into Tampa during this period. Thus, by the turn of the century, Tampa's population was ethnically varied—about a third being white Southerners, over a quarter Afro-American, another quarter Cuban, and the remainder being primarily Spaniards, and Italians. (The Cubans, Spaniards and Italians were often thrown together under the label of "Latin".) The reins of power, despite the change in the composition of Tampa's population, remained in white Southern hands, proud heirs of the Confederacy. By the beginning of the twentieth century, Tampa had become—to paraphrase the words of a student of its history—a cracker town with a Latin accent.[12]

An important peculiarity about Tampa's Cuban population deserves additional comment. As mentioned earlier, the Cubans in Florida were extremely mobile. They moved between Havana and Tampa with ease and astonishing frequency, thus making it difficult to gauge their actual number at any given point in time. Indeed, the Committee on Immigration of the US Senate reported in 1893 that the number of persons estimated to pass annually from Cuba to the United States and back was between 50,000 and 100,000. Most of these travelled between Havana and Key West and Tampa. Ramón Williams, the American consul-general in Havana, told a congressional committee in 1892 that the Cubans "look upon Florida as so much a part of their own country." There is "no emigration from the island of Cuba, in the European sense of the word; that is, no emigrant class," he told the committee. "[B]etween Key West and Havana people go as between Albany and New York, or as between New York and Boston on the Sound." Very often, said Williams, the Cubans say " 'I want to go to the Key,' just as in Baltimore they would say, 'I am going over to Washington.' "[13] It took only six to seven hours by steamboat to travel between Havana and Key West. *Tabaqueros* in Tampa would travel to Havana during slack periods and during holidays, going and coming without even having to go through customs when they arrived at Port Tampa. One employer recalled hiring the same worker three separate times in a single year.[14] As a bargaining tool against their employers, striking Havana tobacco workers would use the ability to slip across the straits and find work without trouble. Workers in Key West and Tampa did the same thing, making the reverse journey, but jobs were not as easily found in Havana as they were in Tampa. Such a peripatetic life had its advantages, but it had its disadvantages too. One advantage of such mobility is that it linked the emigrants with family, friends, and—most significantly for workers in struggle—political and social institutions such as trades unions, political parties, and mutual aid societies that flourished in Havana and Tampa during the late nineteenth and early twentieth centuries. It is true that such bonds "combined to make the world of the cigarworkers on both sides of the Florida Straits a single universe."[15] But this was not enough to obviate the major disadvantage of fragility and instability of political institutions created on the American side of the Straits. And with a small population like that of the Afro-Cuban community in Tampa, such mobility militated against the building of strong and stable institutions.

Afro-Cubans were, as Mormino and Pozzetta noted, "in the vanguard" of Ybor City, and as such, one may add, were in the forefront of the development of Tampa.[16] By 1890 they made up an estimated 367 of the 2,424 Cubans living in the town. Ten years later, it is estimated, some 791 Afro-Cubans and their children had settled in Tampa; 540 were said to have been born in Cuba.[17] They constituted a minority within two decreasing minorities: a minority of the Cuban population, and a minority of the black, primarily Afro-American, population in Tampa; they made up less than a tenth of Tampa's black population. Almost all of the men worked as cigar workers—84 percent in 1900, 86 percent in 1910, dropping to 76 and 64 percent between 1914 and 1924.[18] Although the two-thirds of Cuban male cigar workers were married, it appears that they often travelled to Tampa without their wives. There was, thus, a marked imbalance in the male–female distribution of the population of the Cubans. And although there is no separate and direct statistical information on the Afro-Cuban sex distribution, there is every reason to believe that the population was as skewed, if not more skewed than that of the Cuban population as a whole.[19]

So how did this group of Afro-Hispanic Caribbeans evolve in the Southern milieu of Florida?

Contemporaries are clear and unanimous about two aspects of Tampa's history. First, that there was something special, even wondrous and, certainly, pleasantly incongruous within the Southern milieu, about the ease, the tolerance, the basic human decency with which black and white Cubans and the other Latins of Ybor City interacted with one another. The testimony of black and white old-timers from Ybor City converge, becoming univocal. There was, they say, in the early days an absence of racial bigotry in Ybor City. "In those days we grew up together," recalled Afro-Cuban Hipólito Arenas. "Your color did not matter—your family and their moral character did."

José Rivero Muñiz, a white Cuban, claimed that "there had never existed racial prejudice among the black and white Cubans. There had been always the most cordial relations between them." According to him:

> The racial prejudice that predominated in the southern states never took hold among the Cubans. It was due to southern customs that black Cubans were not

able to move without prejudice in public places, but in the factories of Ybor City, in the clubs or in any other place where the black and white Cubans mixed, there was nothing but respect and mutual help when needed.[20]

This is the general remembrance of, what we may call, Ybor City's golden age of racial harmony and amity.

The second aspect of Tampa's history that there is general agreement on is that the golden age came to an end; that relations between the races in Ybor City and Tampa deteriorated. There is no clear or explicit agreement—among contemporaries or historians—as to when this occurred. Some say the late nineteenth century, others the early twentieth century, several years before the beginning of the Great Depression. The historical record lends broad support to the existence of these two moments in Tampa's development. But the evidence also suggests that the scheme needs to be qualified, refined, and nuanced.

Certainly, the evidence unearthed by Gerald Poyo in his diligent excavations of the nineteenth-century émigré community in the United States suggests the need for greater refinement and less unalloyed celebration. For, as early as the presidential election of 1876, a clear and widening cleavage had emerged between Afro-Cubans and a section of the white Cuban community. A substantial section, perhaps the greater portion, of the Cuban and Spanish capitalist class had switched from supporting the Republican Party, the party of Lincoln, and had turned to the Democratic Party, which in places in the South, like Florida, could be described as the party of the Confederacy. It was under the superintendence of the so-called Democratic Party that the dark deeds of the post-Reconstruction period were carried out against black Americans. True, the Grant adminstration—in its lack of support for the Cuban nationalists during the Ten Years War—provoked this turning away from the Republican Party. But this only explains the behavior of some of the nationalists in Key West, and does not justify it. After all, Afro-Cubans, despite the shared disappointment with Grant, could not vote for the Democratic Party. There were, in addition, expressions of racism from within the émigré community, especially from its leadership in New York, during and in the aftermath of the Ten Years War.[21] Such behavior, naturally, aggravated and antagonized Afro-Cubans in Florida, restraining the full embrace of their white compatriots.

It is true that the move to Tampa and the establishment of Ybor City did not occur until 1886, some ten years after the election of Rutherford Hayes to the presidency of the United States and eight years after the Pact of Zanjón that formally marked the end of the Ten Years War. All that is true, but many members of the Spanish and Cuban capitalist class moved from Key West to Ybor City, as did a substantial part of the Cuban *tabaqueros*, especially after the devastating fire on the Key in 1886. There was, in fact, a geographic shift from Key West to Tampa, but much of the personnel, capitalists and workers, was the same; the stage had changed, but the drama and the *dramatis personae* remained unchanged. And so members of the Cuban and Spanish bourgeoisies in Tampa established alliances, some as intimate and as strong as inter-marriage, with members of the Southern, white—so-called Anglo—elite in Tampa, which was overwhelmingly racist.[22]

The Spanish and Cuban cigar bourgeoisie and petty bourgeoisie in Tampa were, admittedly, a relatively small minority among the Cubans in Florida and were therefore unrepresentative of the group. However, they were, given their class position, extraordinarily influential and, more significantly, because many professed a variant of Cuban nationalism, they complicated, some said corrupted, the nationalist politics of the community. The Cuban community, then, was not homogeneous and certainly not all of its members were tolerant anti-racists. It is also probable that among some of the members of the working class—especially those who had more immediate Spanish ancestry but born in Cuba—racist ideas were harbored and perhaps put into practice in Ybor City as they had been in Havana.[23] Such workers were probably in the minority, but that does not mean that they did not exist.

Nevertheless, by the standards of post-Reconstruction Florida, Ybor City was an oasis of tolerance and decency in a desert of bigotry and hatred. And the ambience of enlightenment extended beyond the Cuban community, generally embracing the Latin cigar workers of Tampa. Afro-Cubans worked beside Spaniards and Italians in addition to their white compatriots, male and female, in Ybor City and West Tampa. And members of the Latin enclaves lived side by side, regardless of color. As 85-year-old Laureano Díaz, a black Cuban said, "In Ybor City, you'd live with an Italian on one side, a Spaniard and a Cuban on the other side." Juan Mallea, another Afro-Cuban Tampeno, recalled that "The Caltagirones, Scagliones, the Martinos—all these people lived across from us. There was no such thing as a white section and a black section. The only time you encountered discrimination was when you left Ybor."[24] Manuel Alfonso, an Afro-Cuban who was born in Ybor City, said of his neighborhood, "We used to get on good." And as recently as 1923 that was the case. For, he recalled that when his "grandmommy" died that year "she was buried on Noche Buena—Christmas Eve—which in Cuban homes always had a big celebration. The only black family on that block was my family. And when she died, nobody celebrated Noche Buena on that block out of respect for her."[25] Ybor City workers frequented the same union halls, and up to the turn of the century, if not later, black and white Cubans frequented the same clubs. Juan Mallea remembered that there were "plenty of white men married to black women and nobody paid any attention to them." Novelist José Yglesias, who was born in Ybor City, recalled that his great uncle, Francisco Milián, a white Cuban, was married to a black Cuban woman and lived in Ybor City without molestation from the authorities. He did not think, however, that Milián could have married her "unless they had sneaked back to Cuba, as a few did, gotten married and then sneaked back."[26] But Mallea also tells of "many" white men who had lived with their black wives in Cuba before migrating as couples to Florida. This was acceptable to the authorities, he noted, "as long as they spoke Spanish and as long as the black partner was the female. It was not permitted for a white woman to marry a black man. If this occurred the authorities could come in and arrest them."[27] Thus, the *Tampa Tribune* approvingly reported the case of an Ybor City Chinese man dragged from the bed he shared with the white woman with whom he lived. The raid was carried out, not by the legal authorities, but by outraged white citizens.[28]

There were strong bonds of fellowship across race, on the basis of class. This was powerfully demonstrated in 1900. On Labor Day that year, cigar makers expressed solidarity with their black comrades and kept faith with the higher ideals of the international working-class movement. They boycotted the Labor Day Parade in Tampa. According to contemporary reports only "a very small and insignificant" contingent came from the cigar workers, the largest branch of the city's working class. They kept away because the committee that organized it wanted to "make the parade a white one."[29] It is noteworthy that the cigar makers stayed away from this Jim Crow Labor Day Parade, but it is equally significant that a committee "representing unions throughout the city" had organized the event with explicit racist intent. It is worth noting, too, that *some*—if only a few—of the cigar makers marched in the parade. A decade earlier, they probably would not have taken part at all in such a reactionary and shameful event.

But how does one explain what was—even taking into account the qualifications submitted—the remarkable group cohesion of Ybor City? The cohesion operated at three discernible levels. It operated at the level of social class; at the wider communal level, that is at the level of a Latin communal identity; and at the level of individual nationality. This was especially the case for the Cubans, who were, in general, held together not just by nationality, but also by a profound desire to give that national sentiment concrete expression in the creation of *Cuba Libre*. Let us examine these forces of cohesion more closely.

Ybor City was a company town and was created as such. Virtually everyone within its boundaries was in one way or another associated with the tobacco industry. Not only that, the overwhelming majority of the workers in Ybor City were involved in the making of cigars. Given the political culture that goes with Cuban and Puerto Rican cigar making, discussed in the previous chapter, it is not at all surprising that a strong sense of group identity based on class and transcending color and nationality should develop in Ybor City. It is true that there were clashes from time to time between groups of Spanish and Cuban workers, but these were, apparently, not as frequent in Tampa as they had been in Key West, especially since many of the Spanish workers were themselves radicals (a significant number being anarchists and socialists) who had great sympathy with the Cuban cause. (There were some, however, who as anarcho-syndicalists did not believe that the nationalist struggle should be supported, especially at the expense of the class struggle. This was in fact the position of some of the Cuban workers too, including some black *tabaqueros*.) But within the bounds of Ybor City there did emerge a profound sense of class identity on the part of the workers and this was, to a significant degree, cemented by the reading of working-class and radical literature in the factories. The fact that a substantial number of the Italian immigrants were also anarchists and politically radical also contributed to Ybor City's remarkable ethos.

Less well known is the fact that a substantial part of the working-class leadership, both in Key West and in Tampa, were black. Francisco Segura and Guillermo Sorondo were among the most prominent Afro-Cubans in labor organization in south Florida. They were both leaders of the *Unión de Tabaqueros* founded in Key West in 1879, and they were also leaders of the *Federación Local de Tabaqueros*, founded in Key West in 1887. Because of their prominence in the successful 1889 general strike of cigar workers on the Key, they were driven from the island to Tampa. This did not stop them. Segura collaborated with the socialist leader Ramón Rivero on the radical newspaper *La Revista de Florida*, which was "in the forefront of efforts to promote the interests of Cuban labor in Florida during the last years of the 1880s."[30] One of the most audacious trade unions in the annals of Ybor City was *La Sociedad de Torcedores de Tampa y Sus Cercanías*. Founded in 1899, *La Sociedad* was generally known as *La Resistencia* because of its stated purpose "*to resist* the exploitation of labor by capital." Proudly syndicalist in outlook, *La Resistencia* spearheaded Tampa's fiercest fight against capital in 1901.[31] Its leader during the strike, Cuban general secretary José González Padilla, was described as a "mulatto."[32] Martín Morúa Delgado, who had fled Cuba with his friend and comrade in struggle, Rafael Serra, edited two of the most important radical labor organs, *El Pueblo* and *La Nueva Era*, steadfast supporters of the Cuban working class in Florida and elsewhere.[33] Such profound involvement in the labor movement on the part of Afro-Cubans must have contributed to the consolidation of class identity and solidarity which transcended racial difference. This does not mean, however, that Afro-Cubans had no sense of their distinct ethnic identity. Significantly, Segura, Sorrondo, and Morúa Delgado were also active members of the Afro-Cuban community and helped to build its autonomous institutions, especially in Key West, such as *Colegio Unificación* and *Sociedad El Progreso*.[34] Nevertheless, these men were fully cognizant of the class struggle. Guillermo Sorrondo was in fact an anarchist, and, sensibly, he recognized that he was also an Afro-Cuban in a racist society.

The level of class cohesion and solidarity often expressed itself through strikes. This, at least on the part of Tampa's capitalists, sometimes reached astonishing heights of class warfare. In 1901, for instance, thirteen leaders of a major strike were abducted by Tampa policemen at the behest of an anti-strike Citizens' Committee, put on a boat, dumped on a deserted beach in Honduras a hundred miles from Truxillo, and were warned never to return to Tampa. The men eventually turned up in Key West and told of what had happened to them. They lodged complaints with local officials and wrote to the President of the United States. The local District Attorney was given the job of dealing with the matter. After two weeks he reported that he "was unable to obtain any evidence of violation of laws of the United States."[35] Such desperate measures on the part of the ruling class were an index of the strength and resolve of the workers and their organization; capitalists never kidnap those whom they can easily overwhelm, only fighters.

A Latin identity, largely imposed from without, contributed to another form of cohesion in Ybor City. Anglo Tampa saw in Ybor City a Latin, foreign, cultural wedge that it tolerated for self-interested reasons, but never really liked. And the relation between Ybor City and those outside its borders was often antagonistic. "No Dogs or Latins Allowed" was not an uncommon sign in Tampa. "No dogs, Niggers, or Latins allowed" loudly proclaimed signs at Anglo bathing spots. "They considered us worse than blacks," recalled an Italian man. "And a lot of places had signs 'No Dagoes'. . . . No, the Latins didn't battle too much against each other, but we did with the Anglo-Saxons." Another Italian pointed out that "When fist fights broke out, you knew who your friends were." "We Latins stuck together," he said. When signs were put up at dances banning the entry of Latins, the latter—Italians, Cubans, and Spaniards—would often combine, enter, and fight the Anglos. Those who lived in Ybor City had a clear sense of the community's physical boundaries and the danger that lurked behind them. "A Latin couldn't cross Twenty-second Street," one man remembered.[36]

The stereotypes of the Latins were reinforced and disseminated by the Tampa newspapers. The press discoursed on the "volcanic tendency" of Latins. It spoke of Cubans and Spaniards being "mercurial in temperament and quick to act," but, said the Tampa *Tribune*, "they are not bad when no evil influences are working among them." However, "When subjected to the devilish influences of even one unprincipled socialist, communist or anarchist, they are transformed into little less than madmen."[37] The Italians were largely dismissed *en masse* as mafiosi. But the Cubans were at the bottom of the ethnic pile. The Anglos preferred the Spanish to the other two groups. They especially disliked the Cuban for having fun on the Sabbath, clearly oblivious to the fact that many of the Cubans were unbelievers and freethinkers—not that that knowledge would have made them behave differently.

In general the Anglos regarded the Latins as not being white at all. The Italians were frequently referred to as non-whites, which "never failed to draw protests from Italian residents." To obviate the complications of different skin color among those in Ybor City, the Anglos simply referred to all of them—Italians, Spanish, and Cubans—as "niggers" or "Cuban niggers." "If the crackers really wanted to make us Latins mad," an Italian recalled, "they'd call us Cuban niggers." Honorato Domínguez, a Cuban Tampeno, recalling the proscription and maligning of Cubans, thought it was particularly unjust since, as he put it, "we built Tampa!"[38]

Clearly then, the common oppression of Latins in Ybor City by the Anglos created a sense of group cohesion and common identity. Moreover, in fighting the Anglos they forged powerful bonds of fellowship and mutual regard. However, it should be noted that part of the explanation for the growing fissure between black and white in Ybor City at the turn of the century might very well have been an attempt on the part of white Latins, including Cubans, to avoid their "niggerization" on the part of the powerful Anglos. And, as we will see, at the beginning of the new century life became increasingly hard if one was designated as black, a nigger, by the powers that be. Thus, when the label of Cuban niggers, in particular, was pinned on all Latins, it perhaps worked more against, than in favor of, group cohesion. It probably alerted, frightened, and encouraged some to break away from the darker members of Ybor City; to keep away from the stigmatized Afro-Cubans.

On top of a militant working-class identity and the Latin nationality that brought the groups together, Cubans in Ybor City had the additional cement of a common culture and a common nationalist aspiration. The nationalist aspiration was a particularly powerful force that unified black and white Cubans. But despite the shared desire of a free Cuba, discernible strains existed in the relation between Cubans of different color. The Key West experience during the Ten Years War brought this out very clearly, as did the tensions during the 1880s. But José Martí's emergence on the American scene in the late 1880s was to have a profound, galvanizing effect upon Cuban nationalism in the United States. In Florida, Key West as well as in Tampa, Martí's consistent denunciation of racism and the articulation of his vision of a liberated Cuba free of bigotry had an enormously important effect on dispelling doubts that some Cubans of color had about the nationalist leadership. Martí's moral courage and principled position in this way held Cubans of different color together in the nationalist community. His speeches in Tampa and Key West in November 1891 were rapturously received by the *tabaqueros*. Martí found in these two Cuban enclaves "civilian camps" of the national revolution. The Florida communities were, according to Martí, Creole strongholds "where from all the sufferings and anxieties of life arose all the sublimities of hope." Martí, as one writer puts it, by his eloquence "infused the tobacco workers with his own fire."[39] And Martí's flame was pure and clear. He had set the moral tone of the revolution and became its leader. He had, in addition, the gift of oratory and the poet's words with which to express his moral vision of *Cuba Libre*. Martí loved Ybor City's nationalist ambience and fervor. Ybor City's tobacco workers inspired him. And, in turn, the *tabaqueros* loved and honored Martí and his project with a passion and commitment unparalleled outside of Cuba itself.[40] Martí had more than ample reasons to pronounce the founding of the *Partido Revolucionario Cubano* in Tampa. No place was more appropriate.

Afro-Cubans in Tampa and elsewhere loved Martí. They had read his words with increasing interest and keenly followed his nationalist crusade. They knew that in the 1880s Martí was, as one historian recently put it, "the only nationalist figure who openly condemned racist attitudes within the movement."[41] And even before his visit to Tampa and Key West in 1891, Afro-Cubans in Florida would have known of Martí's work with Rafael Serra y Montalvo (1858–1909) in New York in *La Liga de Instrución*. Founded in 1890, the League educated Cuban and Puerto Rican people of color in New York City. Black tobacco workers and their families made up most of the League. Rafael Serra, who founded it with the help of Martí, was born in Havana of free Afro-Cuban parents. He served his apprenticeship and became a master cigar maker. He established and collaborated on a number of radical and nationalist periodicals before he was driven into exile because of his political activity. He arrived in Key West in 1880, moved to New York soon after, but in the early 1880s, during the course of his nationalist work, lived in Panama, Colombia, and Kingston, Jamaica, before settling back in New York around 1886. Serra, an autodidact, had always been interested in education and had been involved in educational work among black people in Matanzas before his exile. His starting the League was thus in keeping with his ambition, interests, and work while in Cuba. Martí held the positions of *Presidente Honorario e Inspector Maestro* (Honorary President and Inspecting Teacher). He took his role seriously and participated in the teaching at the League during the evenings.[42] Martí's work with the League in New York had thus brought him into very close working relations with black Cubans and Puerto Ricans before his visit to Tampa in 1891.

"The man of color has a right to be treated according to his qualities as a man, with no reference whatsoever to his color," Martí had written during a Key West strike in 1889.[43] *El Yara*, the nationalist periodical begun in 1878 in Key West, informed its readers of Martí's work. So even before *El Maestro's* morally elevated and justly famous Tampa speech—one of his very best and most important—the Afro-Cuban community in Tampa knew that Martí was a courageous fighter for justice, an extraordinary Cuban, and an extraordinary human being. Small wonder, then, that immediately upon his arrival he received the warmest of welcomes from Afro-Cuban leaders in Tampa.[44] Moreover, during his subsequent visits to Tampa, he stayed in the home of a black couple of modest means, Ruperto and Paulina Pedroso. Indeed, the relation between the Pedrosos and Martí became so close that Señora Pedroso was referred to as Martí's "second mother."[45] And yet Paulina Pedroso was one of the few Afro-Cubans in Tampa who did not take immediately to Martí. It was not a case of her not liking the man—she was skeptical about him. Señora Pedroso preferred the men of action over the intellectuals. According to Jorge Mañach, she was an "old-line patriot, a fanatical follower of Gomez and Maceo."[46] But, like so many others, she was won over by Martí, and won over completely. On a fund-raising visit to a Tampa cigar factory, the words "Here comes the bandit" were said loud enough to be heard by both Martí and Paulina Pedroso as they entered the building. (The words, apparently, came from the lips of a Spanish provacateur working to impede the independence struggle.) Pedroso jumped up on the rostrum: "Gentlemen: If any of you is afraid to give his money or go to the savannahs to fight, let him give me his pants and I'll give him my petticoat." The building roared with laughter and applause. Martí embraced Pedroso, and proceeded with a speech that won the hearts of his listeners. Indeed, so devoted were the Pedrosos to Martí that after their discovery of a Spanish attempt to poison El Maestro, Paulina went to Martí's lodgings in his absence, "swept out with all his possessions," and insisted that Martí stayed at their home. To further ensure Martí's safety, at night, Ruperto slept on the floor across the doorway of Martí's room.[47] Sensing "a certain condescension" in the attitude of the white Cubans towards their black compatriots, Martí acted as well as spoke out. In a small but significant gesture, he walked the streets of Ybor City arm-in-arm with Paulina Pedroso.[48] As José Mañach in his tender portrait of Martí wrote, the Pedroso home,

> the little house opposite Martínez Ibor's factory became a place of jubilee. Ruperto affixed a flagpole to the gable of the house and whenever Martí was at home the flag of the budding Republic fluttered from it. Evenings, the Cubans formed groups in the street to watch El Maestro through the windows. The highest windows, those of Martí's room, remained lighted until late at night; at times, in silence, the scratching of his pen could be heard.[49]

Martí almost single-handedly won over Afro-Cubans who had rightly doubted the sincerity of much of the white Cuban leadership of the nationalist movement. José Martí, Afro-Cuban Tampeños determined, was a man they could rally around with all their heart; and that is what they did. "We don't understand him," a black Cuban Tampeño is reported to have said of Marti, "but we are ready to die for him."[50]

Speaking at the Liceo Cubano in Ybor City on the night of November 26, 1891, Martí frontally addressed the age-old fear of black Cuba that the Spanish colonialists, the slaveholders, and the racists had lodged in the minds of many white Cubans. This fear partly accounted for the postponed liberation of Cuba from the Spanish yoke. "Must we be afraid," Martí asked rhetorically, of the Cuban who has suffered most from being deprived of his freedom in the country where the blood he shed for it has made him love it too much to be a threat to it? Will we fear the Negro—the noble black man, our black brother—who for the sake of the Cubans who died for him has granted eternal pardon to the Cubans who are still mistreating him? Well, I know of black hands that are plunged further into virtue than those of any white man I have ever met. From the Negro's love for a reasonable freedom, I know that only in a greater natural and useful intensity does his differ from the white Cuban's love of freedom. I know that the black man has drawn his noble body to its full height and is becoming a solid column for his native liberties. Others may fear him; I love him. Anyone who speaks ill of him I disown, and I say to him openly: "You lie!"[51]

Within a few months of his visit to Tampa, Martí had established *Patria*, the mouthpiece of the newly founded *Partido Revolucionario Cubano*, in which he continued to spread abroad the same message. Significantly, his paper was edited by Sotero Figueroa, a black man from Ponce, Puerto Rico, who had also worked with Serra in the League.[52] It was in the pages of *Patria* that Martí published "Mí Raza" (My Race), in which he famously declared:

A man is more than white, black, or mulatto. A Cuban is more than mulatto, black, or white. Dying for Cuba on the battlefield, the souls of both Negroes and white men have risen together.[53]

"The Negro simply because he is a Negro, is neither inferior nor superior to any other man," Martí declared. Stokely Carmichael in the late 1960s referred to Fidel Castro as "the blackest man in the Caribbean." The description would have been more appropriately applied to Martí in the 1890s. Fernando Ortiz, the distinguished Cuban historian, remembered that his grandfather—a Spanish Loyalist and retired soldier—hated the *independentistas*. Ortiz's grandfather, a self-confessed racist, was convinced that all those who rebelled against Spain in Cuba had their "drop of colored blood." He conceded, however, that Martí was white, but added an important rider: "Martí was not colored, but . . . he might just as well have been; he was a mulatto inside."[54] High praise, indeed, for the man whom revolutionary Cuba, at home and abroad, called *El Apóstol*. Beside Wendell Phillips (1811–84), it is hard to think of any white person other than Martí, resident in the Americas in the second half of the nineteenth century, so committed materially, intellectually, politically, and publicly to abolitionism *and* anti-racism in theory and practice.[55] How Martí managed to so radically transcend the racism of his times is, to me, one of the great and abiding mysteries in the history of the Americas. His own explanation is one of the least convincing:

I was born of myself, and from myself the tree of the world budded before my eyes, which warmed it like suns. Now, when a man is born, philosophy, religion, political systems stand next to his cradle with large strong bandages ready in

José Martí in Kingston, Jamaica, where a group of nationalist Cuban *tabaqueros* had settled and worked in the late nineteenth century.

Ramón Emeterio Betances, described as the father of the Puerto Rican nation (*Padre de la Patría*) in exile in Paris. (Courtesy of Félix Ojeda Reyes)

General Antonio Maceo, the "Bronze Titan" of Cuba's wars of independence.

Pedro Albizu Campos, leading Puerto Rican nationalist of the twentieth century and the only other Puerto Rican given the title of *Padre de la Patría*. (Courtesy of the Ruth M. Reynolds Papers, Centro de Estudios Puertorriqueños, Hunter College, City University of New York)

Arturo Schomburg, *c.* 1896, when he was Secretary of *Las Dos Antillas*, a nationalist group aligned to the *Partido Revolucionario Cubano*, founded by José Martí. The group agitated for the independence of both Cuba and Puerto Rico. (Courtesy of the Schomburg Center for Research in Black Culture, New York Public Library, Astor, Lenox and Tilden Foundations)

Afro-American artist Aaron Douglas (left) presents "Aspects of Negro Life: Song of the Towers" to Schomburg in 1934. (Courtesy of the Schomburg Center for Research in Black Culture, New York Public Library, Astor, Lenox and Tilden Foundations)

Schomburg among Masons and Odd Fellows at the cornerstone laying of the Ionic Temple, Claremont Avenue, Brooklyn, 1922. (Courtesy of the Schomburg Center for Research in Black Culture, New York Public Library, Astor, Lenox and Tilden Foundations)

Jesús Colón (right) and his brother Joaquin, c. 1918. (Courtesy of the Jesús Colón Papers, Centro de Estudios Puertorriqueños, Hunter College, City University of New York, Benigno Giboyeaux, for the Estate of Jesús Colón)

An elderly Colón with Lenin's *Collected Works* behind him. (Courtesy of the Jesús Colón Papers, Centro de Estudios Puertorriqueños, Hunter College, City University of New York, Benigno Giboyeaux, for the Estate of Jesús Colón)

Colón, Bernardo Vega (center), and unidentified Puerto Rican comrade, c. 1930. (Courtesy of the Jesús Colón Papers, Centro de Estudios Puertorriqueños, Hunter College, City University of New York, Benigno Giboyeaux, for the Estate of Jesús Colón)

Colón with leading members of a Puerto Rican lodge, 1940s. (Courtesy of the Jesús Colón Papers, Centro de Estudios Puertorriqueños, Hunter College, City University of New York, Benigno Giboyeaux, for the Estate of Jesús Colón)

New York Puerto Ricans on a day outing, 1928. Joaquin Colón is standing second from the left. (Courtesy of the Jesús Colón Papers, Centro de Estudios Puertorriqueños, Hunter College, City University of New York, Benigno Giboyeaux, for the Estate of Jesús Colón)

Colón, Afro-American Communist Benjamin J. Davis (right), Elizabeth Gurley Flynn (next to Davis), a leading member of the Communist Party. (Courtesy of the Jesús Colón Papers, Centro de Estudios Puertorriqueños, Hunter College, City University of New York, Benigno Giboyeaux, for the Estate of Jesús Colón)

The workfloor of a Tampa cigar factory, *c.* 1908.
(Special Collections, University of South Florida Library, Tampa)

Part of a photograph showing the founders of *Martí-Maceo* in 1904.
(Special Collections, University of South Florida Library, Tampa)

Paulina Pedroso, Cuban nationalist, community organizer, friend and supporter of Martí in Florida. (Special Collections, University of South Florida Library, Tampa)

Rafael Serra, Cuban *tabaquero*, man of letters, editor, collaborator of Martí in Cuba's struggle for independence; he lived in exile in Jamaica, Central America, Florida and New York in the nineteenth century before returning to Cuba in 1898. ([Pedro N. González Veranes], *Rafael Serra: Patriota y Revolucionario, Fraternal Amigo de Martí*, Havana: [Club Atenas], 1959)

Sotero Figueroa, editor of José Martí's nationalist journal, *La Patría*. (Josefina Toledo, *Sotero Figueroa, Editor de "Patría": Apuntes para una Biografia*, Havana: Editorial Letras Cubanas, 1985)

La Huelga de la Pesa, the Scales or Weight Strike of 1899, lasted sixteen weeks and was won by the cigar workers in Tampa. Soup kitchens were organized to feed the workers and their families. (Special Collections, University of South Florida Library, Tampa)

Members of *Martí-Maceo* on a picnic, *c.* 1900.
(Courtesy of *Sociedad La Unión Martí-Maceo* and Susan Greenbaum)

The Maldonado family posed for this picture in 1937, just before leaving Tampa to settle
in New York City. This was a path taken by many Afro-Cubans in Tampa, as racism,
the Depression, and mechanization of cigar making drove them from Florida.
(Courtesy of Mercedes Torres and Susan Greenbaum)

their hands. And they tie him up, swathe him, and the man is already, for all his life on earth, a bridled horse. I am a horse without a saddle. From no one do I receive law, nor upon anyone do I intend to impose law. I conquer prejudice which comes from the outside, and ambition, which comes from within.[56]

A little over three years after his *Liceo Cubano* speech, José Martí, *El Apóstol*, was dead, fallen on the field of battle, fighting for a free Cuba. News of Martí's sudden death reached Afro-Cubans in Tampa like a body-blow.[57] On hearing the news, Cornelio Brito abandoned his home in Ybor City and went off to fight in Cuba. "[F]or me Martí lives," he told Rafael Serra and Estrada Palma. "To honor him I offered my life and possessions. I first gave my possessions to *la patria*. Martí has fallen and I must keep my promise and honor my pledge. Now, in the name of my brother Martí, I give my life to *la patria*."[58] Martí was a friend, an ally, and, with Antonio Maceo, he was, too, their leader. In the aftermath of Martí's death, the moral degeneration of the white Cuban nationalist leaders—especially in the United States under Tomás Estrada Palma—was as rapid as it was profound.[59] It brought home for all to see how uncommonly noble Martí was and made his absence even more conspicuous and costly. The non-racist and anti-racist cohesion of the Cuban community in Ybor City deteriorated rapidly following Martí's death and in the absence of his vision from the leadership of the PRC.

There is another element to the explanation of Ybor City's tolerant ambience that is never mentioned but, I think, is relevant. It is this. The Italian migration to Tampa came in the wake of the Cubans and the Spaniards. Overwhelmingly Sicilian, the Italians who went to Ybor City knew nothing about cigar making and as such were primarily dependent upon the Cubans to impart to them the secrets of the trade and the rudiments of Spanish, the lingua franca of Ybor City. When the Spanish owners and foremen tried to proscribe the entry of Italians in the cigar factories, the Cubans supported the Italians. As the Cuban cigar maker Domingo Ginésta recalled, "When the Italians first came to Tampa . . . the Spaniards were adversed [*sic*] to allowing them to settle here, and they tried to keep them from working in the cigar factories. At this time we were in revolt against Spain, and we thwarted every move made by the Span-iards."[60] Given the atmosphere of racial tolerance extant among the Cubans prior to the arrival of the Italians, and given the fact that the Italians were dependent upon the Cubans, including black Cubans, there would have been relatively little scope for racist behavior on the part of the Italian immigrants. Thus, it ought not to be thought or implied or claimed that the Italians in Ybor City were enlightened non-racists. There is no reason to believe that those who went to Ybor City were morally superior to those who went to New York, Chicago, Buffalo, and elsewhere in the United

States. Yet in those cities, especially in New York, the Italians quickly (just like other European immigrants), imbibed the racist mores of the dominant society while those in Ybor City behaved differently. Why was this so? Those in Ybor City had a structured relation to black people (meaning here Afro-Cubans) that was radically different to that which obtained elsewhere.[61] And thus at least within the confines of Ybor City, and specifically in relation to Afro-Cubans, Italians behaved in a civil and tolerant manner.[62] This does not mean that they did not harbor stereotypes and even racist ideas—some of them, if not all, did. They simply did not have the power to act upon racist ideas because of their constraining, relatively powerless, circumstances. When these constraints were removed, they behaved differently; that is, relatively badly.

But how and when did the rift develop between black and white Cubans, and between black Cubans, on the one hand, and the rest of the white Latins in Ybor City, on the other?

Cigar maker José Ramón Sanfeliz, a black Cuban, arrived in Ybor City from his native Havana in 1890. The spirit of the enclave took hold of him and he became, in his own words, "somewhat enamored of radical ideas in the proletarian field." Interviewed in 1935, he recalled that "These advanced ideas were, at the time, a sort of 'epidemic' among the cigarmakers here."[63] But he was also a Cuban nationalist and when war broke out in 1895 he helped to found the 24th of February Club, of which he became secretary and collector of funds to aid the fight against Spain. When Antonio Maceo was killed in 1896, he became an organizer and then president of *Los Vengadores de Maceo* (Maceo's Avengers). Soon after, he founded two other nationalist clubs, one of which, the *Oracio S. Rubens* club, was named in honor of Martí's friend and consulting attorney.[64] Señor Ramón Sanfeliz's brother, Serafin, left Tampa and joined the nationalist army in Cuba. He was killed in 1897 while engaged in a fierce battle in Oriente Province. Ramón Sanfeliz seemed to have had a hand in all the nationalist endeavors in Ybor City in the 1890s. When the war ended in 1898, he became the recording secretary of the Association of Cuban Emigrants of the War of Independence. True to form, he was one of the founders of *El Club Nacional Cubano* in 1899. Comprising black and white members, the club was, he recalled, "a sort of rice with black beans. There was no distinction of races [*sic*]." In honor of the new republic promulgated in 1902, the Club changed its name in the same year to *El Círculo Cubano*. But there was more to the change than the name; *El Círculo* was all rice and no beans. "When the *Círculo Cubano* was formed," said Ramón Sanfeliz, "the negroes were left out."[65] Black Cubans were thus locked out of an institution they had helped to fashion; locked out of a club named in honor of the independent nation their loved ones had died to create; in short, locked out of their own house by white Cuban racists.

"Jim Crow made me do it," said the white Cubans. As one of them put it, "in this part of the United States it was necessary to face the reality of the facts." He claimed that "To form the ideal club which all the Cuban immigrants, without distinction of color, could join was impossible."[66] And some Afro-Cubans explained the behavior of their white compatriots in the same way. "The government [state and local]," said Afro-Cuban Juan Mallea, "told them [Cubans] we could not work together, have a society together, and would have to keep the races apart. . . . That was the law of the country."[67] They are correct to draw attention to the proscriptions that existed in Florida and in Tampa in particular. For Jim Crow's seige of Ybor City tightened with every passing day. Outside of the enclave, Afro-Americans were ghettoized, literally marginalized in an area that was, revealingly, called the "Scrub" or "Scrubs." With the collapse of Reconstruction in 1877—the Republican Party withdrawing the federal army and relinquishing enormous powers to the local heirs of the Confederacy in the Southern states—life quickly became harder for Afro-Americans in Florida. They were systematically and blatantly disenfranchised, denied the right to serve on juries, lynched with general impunity.[68] And in 1896, in the *Plessy* v. *Ferguson* case, the Supreme Court ruled segregation legal by its infamous "separate but equal" decision. *De facto* segregation already existed in much of the South, but the Court now gave it the *imprimatur* of law. The highest court in the land, the court of last resort, as it were, had turned its back on black American citizens. The Afro-American freedom train had hit the buffers.

The year before the *Plessy* decision, the Florida state legislature had in fact formally promulgated the segregation of education. The law prohibited anyone from conducting a school in which white and black children attended the same classes, or separate classes in the same building, or classes taught by the same teachers. Violators could be fined or sent to jail. In 1903 racial inter-marriage was outlawed. Two years later, the law said black and white people had to travel in separate sections of streetcars. "Negro nurses travelling with white children or sick persons were exempt." A black prisoner could not be fastened to a white prisoner. Railroad companies had to provide separate waiting rooms and ticket windows for black and white passengers. One way in which the race problem could be solved was through forcibly sending Afro-Americans—American born and bred—to Africa. "Mr Lincoln said that this nation could not exist 'half slave and half free.' I think it is equally true that this nation can not exist *half white* and *half black*," declared Frank Clark, an influential Florida congressman. In his message to the legislature in 1907, the Governor of Florida, Napoleon Bonaparte Broward, proposed the mass removal of black people from the United States.[69] In 1908 a judge in Miami's municipal court publicly praised that city's police department for altering the views of "Nassau [Bahamas] Negroes who upon arrival here consider themselves the social equal of white people."[70] By the 1920s the Ku Klux Klan had established a substantial and visible presence in the state of Florida, including Tampa itself.[71]

The experience of black troops stationed in Tampa in 1898 during the Spanish–American War brought into full relief some of the practices in that city. The soldiers discovered that many shops in Tampa refused to allow black people to make purchases across the same counter as whites. Indeed, some establishments made no secret of the fact that "we don't sell to damned niggers."[72] One of the white officers of the troops tried in vain to find a local restaurant to serve his men before sailing to Cuba to put down "Spanish tyranny." "[T]o have colored men eat in her dining room would ruin her business," one operator informed the officer, typifying the general response.[73] "Regularly taunted by epithets such as 'all niggers look alike to me,'" reported Gatewood, "the black soldiers quickly concluded that nowhere was anti-Negro prejudice more virulent than in Florida." Indeed, the soldiers—alluding to the Confederacy and the Civil War, which were still fresh in the nation's memory—firmly believed that they were stationed in the midst of "a hotbed of rebels." "Prejudice reigns supreme here against the colored troops," one of them wrote.[74] The *Tampa Morning Tribune* was clear about who was to blame for the conflict between the black soldiers and white Tampans. Within a few days of the troops' arrival, the *Tribune* made and promulgated its diagnosis:

> The colored troopers are splendid horsemen and show off to great advantage. The colored infantrymen stationed in Tampa and vicinity have made themselves very offensive to the people of the city. The men insist upon being treated as white men are treated and the citizens will not make any distinction between the colored troops and the colored civilians.[75]

In formal terms, then, the civic culture of Tampa, and Florida generally, grew worse as the nineteenth century progressed and the new century began. Certainly, the Jim Crow laws came thick and fast in the two decades between 1890 and 1910. Shofner argues strongly that these were little more than the formalization of customs into law.[76] The evidence supports him, but only partially, for there was genuine deterioration in the actual status and treatment of black people in Florida and the South in general, from the 1880s to the First World War. There was, in short, deterioration over and above the erosion of rights and legal standing.[77] Those who lived through the period provide strong testimony about how radically times and circumstances had changed.

But these changes, formal as well as concrete, do not explain the decision and the behavior of the white Cubans in *El Círculo Cubano* in 1902; they merely tell us about the circumstances within which the decision was made. The remarks of Rivero Muñiz and Juan Mallea about people having to "face the reality of the facts," and about the force of the law, are not explanations at all. And statements such as "formal segregation had the predictable *effect* of driving a wedge between black and white Cubans,"[78] and "Anglo Tampa pressured Ybor City's white Cubans to dissociate themselves from Afro-Cubans, *resulting* in the organization of separate white and black Cuban societies around the turn of the century," are also unsatisfying as explanations.[79] Problems arise with such statements at two levels, at the methodological level and at the substantive, historical, level. The methodological problem may be summed up by calling attention to the absence of human agency in such schemata: human beings are not machines that react automatically to laws. The fact is that the laws passed are passive, incapable of doing anything; human beings, more or less, *choose* to obey or disobey them. The fact that in most societies most people at any given time choose to obey the law does not mean that they have not exercised a choice, human volition. Because a driver stops at the red light does not mean that he or she could not simply drive through; the consequences for doing so would probably be unpleasant—there could be a fatal accident, there could be severe punishment—but the decision not to drive through red is up to the driver. In short, because Jim Crow laws were passed in Florida, that fact in itself does not tell us *why* white Cubans, apparently, chose to adhere to them.

The substantive problems with such an argument are considerable. Ybor City, as we have seen, had a high degree of autonomy in relation to the wider authorities in Tampa, even though it was formally incorporated into Tampa in 1887. On a number of key occasions Martínez Ybor got the Anglos to back down from threatened interference in the life of Ybor City. For instance, when proposals were made to ban alcohol in Tampa, he threatened to take his business elsewhere, and that was enough the kill the idea. It is true that this autonomy diminished over time, but even in 1902 it was by no means negligible. (Generally, when there was intervention in Ybor City by the larger Tampa authorities, this was done at the behest and with the consent of the cigar ruling class of the enclave.) Black and white worked side by side in Ybor City, men and women together. They generally lived side by side, black and white; they even lived together as racially mixed couples. As we saw earlier, the Jim Crow laws were ignored on the streetcars going in and out of Ybor City, and there is no evidence of the law actively intervening to separate black and white people. The Tampa police did not storm *El Círculo Cubano* and order club members to "Keep the niggers out!" There is not even the evidence of such a threat. Tampa had more than its fair share of vicious thugs, so-called vigilantes. But they focused almost exclusively upon disciplining the workers and labor and trade union radicals in particular. And when they stormed the factories and Labor Temple in Ybor City, they warned and threatened workers about striking, not about black and white mixing. After all, the Latins of Ybor City were, together, an inferior species—"Cuban niggers." Who cares if they mix, when they are already mixed, indeed, "non-white," if not black?

The argument that Cubans were simply obeying the law raises additional questions rather than providing answers. Why did they not abide by the

laws of the United States and refrain from filibustering? Clearly, they chose
to violate the laws of American neutrality by repeatedly sending armed
expeditions to Cuba from American shores—this was as true of the
annexationists of the 1840s as it was of the *independentistas* of the 1880s
and 1890s. Insofar as American laws were not regarded as intrinsically
sacrosanct by white Cubans, the question arises as to why did *El Círculo
Cubano* not choose to break the blatantly iniquitious laws of Jim Crow?

Was there fear of coercion if Jim Crow was denied in Ybor City? Apart
from the fact that there is no evidence of compulsion on the part of the
authorities in relation to what went on between black and white people in
Ybor City, the cigar workers, and especially the Cubans, could hardly be
called cowards. In Key West as well as in Ybor City some of the most
astonishingly courageous pages were written in the annals of the international working-class movement. A more resilient and defiant working
class than that which operated in Ybor City between 1890 and 1930 would
be hard to find—anywhere. For instance, as we saw above, in the strike of
1901, the leaders were kidnapped and taken as far away as Honduras—the
strikers pressed on, despite the fact that the authorities, including the
District Attorney, did nothing; other leaders were driven out of town,
literally and otherwise—the strikers pressed on; strikers and their families
were evicted from their homes—the strikers pressed on; strikers were
charged and prosecuted for vagrancy, many sentenced to hard labor—the
strikers pressed on; the strikers' soup kitchens were invaded by thugs, pots
overturned, food destroyed, equipment smashed—the strikers pressed on;
the vigilantes closed down the strikers' newspaper, destroying the presses,
beating up and intimidating the editor—the strike went on. It was only in
accumulated combination that these measures—and the drying up of funds
from Havana (due to hard times there), Key West and New York, along
with other steps taken by the cigar bourgeoisie of Tampa—defeated the
strike, most of the strikers leaving Ybor City rather than surrendering. The
strike lasted four long months. The union that organized and led the strike,
La Sociedad de Torcedores de Tabaco de Tampa, generally referred to by
its members as *La Resistencia*, collapsed within a year of the strike, in
1902, exhausted and enfeebled by its titanic effort. "[I]t fell," reflected one
of *La Resistencia's* members on his union, "but as a man with his face
toward the sun, honorably and with dignity."[80] Clearly, the white Cubans
had no wish or will to resist Jim Crow in Ybor City, otherwise they would
have done so.

How, then, does one explain the extraordinary turn of events in 1902 at *El
Círculo Cubano* and the racial separation that grew ever wider in subsequent years? Strangely, the knowledge of the precise events which led up
to the split seemed lost with the passage of time.[81] But the testimonies, oral
and otherwise, given by black as well as white Cubans agree on the racial

basis of the dispute and the parting of ways. A number of identifiable forces and processes help to account for the racial separation in Ybor City.

Clearly the departure and death of José Martí in 1895 was a massive blow to community cohesion among Cubans in Tampa and elsewhere. No leader among the nationalists had Martí's moral stature and popular following; none possessed his grand and noble vision of *Cuba Libre* and, simultaneously, his capacity to win masses of his compatriots, black and white, to that lofty and generous vision. Antonio Maceo had enormous following among Cubans of color, to whom he was a hero, but many of the white Cubans—substantially misled by Spanish, and indeed Cuban, racist propaganda—mistrusted him, despite his unimpeachable commitment to a non-racist Cuba. Maceo was, in any case, dead within little over a year of Martí's being killed. Rafael Serra and Sotero Figueroa repeatedly reminded Cubans of Martí's vision as they witnessed with alarm the moral degeneration of the *Partido Revolucionario Cubano*. Indeed Serra, with the assistance of Figueroa and other black comrades who had closely collaborated with Martí in New York, founded a newspaper to spread the Maestro's message. They called their paper *La Doctrina de Martí*. It carried, appropriately, Martí's words in block capitals as its subtitle: "*LA REPÚBLICA CON TODOS Y PARA TODOS*" (The Republic With all and For All). But even though there was evidence of support for this paper in Florida during the war, Serra's and his colleague's views did not prevail under Tomás Estrada Palma's leadership, especially after 1898.[82] Significantly, Martí's sword of justice, the *Partido Revolucionario Cubano*, was dissolved within a year of the American intervention in the war—long before its work was over. Martí had been killed by the Spanish and his moral beacon was put out by the new leadership of the PRC under Estrada Palma. It is nevertheless shocking how quickly after Martí's death the white Cubans of Tampa started to misbehave, apparently forgetful of *El Maestro's* message. It is obviously impossible to tell what would have happened had he lived, but his absence was noticed.

The cohesion of the Cubans in Tampa and Key West shown during the war declined after 1898. And this must have contributed to the racial separation; the basis for unity was, to many, apparently gone. The postwar problems of Cuba convinced many to settle for good in Tampa, transforming themselves from exiles into immigrants. And this decision might have contributed to their coming to terms with the Southern mores of Jim Crow. It is noteworthy, though, that the Southern Americanization of the white Cubans did not extend with the same ease to their accepting American capitalism. In the aftermath of the war, the Cuban resistance to the cigar capitalists of Tampa intensified, taking another three decades, mechanization, and the Great Depression to be tamed.[83]

The decline in the relative weight of the Afro-Cuban population in Ybor City over the period must have contributed to their vulnerability; they became politically weak as their numbers fell. In addition the astonishing mobility of the Afro-Cuban population—a mobility far higher than that of their white compatriots, which in turn was higher than that of the Spanish and the Italians—made it difficult to sink roots, build institutions, and fight racism.[84] In her pioneering research on the community, Susan Greenbaum found:

> Of 19 Afro-Cuban households listed in the 1893 city directory for Tampa, only two reappeared in the 1899 directory, by which time there were 366 Afro-Cuban households listed. Between 1899 and 1900, it appears that virtually all (94 percent) of the Afro-Cubans departed Tampa and were replaced by a comparable, although slightly larger, number of new arrivals. This rather startling level of mobility in a single year may reflect dislocations in Cuba following independence, which could have precipitated large movements in both directions. However, the general pattern seems to have continued into the 1920s: 82 percent of Afro-Cuban households listed in the 1914 directory had not been included in the 1910 census; 91 percent of those listed in the 1914 directory did not reappear ten years later, even though the number of Afro-Cubans listed in 1924 was nearly the same (335 and 376).[85]

This kind of interchange between Tampa and Havana must have brought a certain freshness and depth to the *Afro-Cubanidad* of Ybor City, infusing and re-infusing the community with new blood from the island. Yet such fluidity wreaks havoc with attempts at political organization. The membership of *La Unión Martí–Maceo* reflected the changing and revolving Afro-Cuban population of Tampa. One man joined and rejoined *Martí-Maceo* thirteen times, and many had six or more separate memberships. Moreover, the officers had an even higher level of turnover (average number of joinings/rejoinings), 2.92, than the ordinary members, who had a turnover rate of 2.04. The average length of the officers' memberships period, that is, the mean number of months for each separate membership term, was, however, almost five times longer than that of non-officers.[86] It is true that a number of key personnel within the organization were more rooted locally, but a floating membership, which hardly grew in number and by 1930 was in catastrophic decline, was not an army to fight Jim Crow with. Because of the ever changing Afro-Cuban faces in the factories and in the Latin quarter, many white Cubans might have felt less obligation toward their black compatriots, whom they hardly had a chance to know—had they wanted such a chance.

A substantial part of the Afro-Cuban leadership in both Tampa and New York returned to Cuba to fight in the independence war and to resettle soon after hostilities had come to an end. From Florida, Francisco Segura, Guillermo Sorondo, and Martín Morúa Delgado returned; from New York, the mulatto Puerto Rican poet "Pachin" Marín followed his friend Martí to Cuba, fought at *El Maestro's* side, and, like Martí, was killed on the battlefields of Cuba. Marín's countryman Sotero Figueroa, another close collaborator of Martí's, settled in Havana after the war, as did Rafael Serra. After the bitter strike of 1910 even the Pedrosos, mainstays of the community for two generations, packed up and left for Havana. Three years later, Bruno Roig did the same. The departure of some of Afro-Cuba's most distinguished leaders from the United States in the late nineteenth and early twentieth centuries must have imposed a heavy political and cultural cost on those who remained.

On top of all these negative changes for the community of Afro-Cubans in Tampa was their occupational slippage in the industry that they helped to build in Ybor City. No group of male workers was as dependent upon the cigar industry in Ybor City as were those from the Afro-Cuban community. In 1900, virtually all Afro-Cuban men held jobs in the cigar industry; between 1910 and 1914 their participation slipped from 94 percent to 83 percent. In 1924, 73 percent were so employed and in subsequent years the trend continued ever downward, when by the Depression, there was an almost total shakeout from the industry. Mechanization did not help; neither did the take-over of the industry by American capitalists, in the 1890s and their apparently more racist practices. The fact that men were being replaced in the industry with Italian and white Anglo female labor also adversely affected Afro-Cubans, and the latter, like all black people living in America at the time, were hurt disproportionately by the Great Depression.[87] The crisis manifested itself in the size of the Afro-Cuban population in Tampa. While the Italian population declined by 18 percent, the Spanish by 26 percent and the Cuban population as a whole fell by 35 percent, the Afro-Cuban community lost well over half its members between 1930 and 1940.[88] The membership of *La Unión Martí–Maceo* reflected the crisis. From 100 members in 1908, *La Unión's* reached a peak of 275 in 1911, stabilizing at 150 until the 1930s. In October 1930 the membership fell to 107, a year later it was only 47. Significantly, the main destinations of the migrants, unlike previous departures, were New York and Philadelphia, not Havana.[89]

The fact that Afro-Cubans were locked out of white Cuban society in Ybor City did not mean that they turned to Afro-Americans to join forces. *La Unión's* building, which was officially opened in 1909, had the best dance-hall opened to non-whites in Tampa. The Afro-Cubans were happy to rent out the hall to Afro-Americans, but seldom attended events organized by Afro-Americans. When in 1915 the state required the organization to open membership to persons other than Cubans, the members reluctantly agreed to allow Afro-Americans to join. Of the 62 members present at the meeting in October 1915 deciding whether membership should be opened to Afro-Americans, only 26 voted in favor of Afro-Americans, 4 voted against, and 32 abstained. The meeting decided that candidates for membership had to be recommended by an existing member and had to speak Spanish.[90] In short, in their being apparently forced to open up the membership of *La Unión Martí-Maceo*, the Afro-Cubans decided to effectively block Afro-Americans from joining, while apparently complying with the letter of the law. Juan Mallea reported that after his mother died, his father (who was later president of the club), became involved with an Afro-American woman. When Mallea's father tried to bring his new partner into the club the members "vehemently" objected on the grounds of the woman's nationality. According to Mallea, this was one of the main reasons why his father tried to change the rules of the club. Interviewed decades later, Mallea, nevertheless, remembered clearly that his father had said the Afro-Cubans were "doing the same thing that the others were doing to the Afro-Americans."[91] There were, despite the restrictions, six or seven Afro-American members in the early 1920s.[92]

The basis of the behavior of the Afro-Cubans is clear. Like every other immigrant group entering the United States, including to a certain extent other Afro-Caribbeans, they imbibed some of the contempt that white America had and disseminated about Afro-Americans. Afro-Cubans were highly privileged in relation to Afro-Americans. They were highly paid not only by black, but also by white levels of wages. Indeed, they were among some of the most highly paid workers nationally. They lived, unlike their Afro-American fellow Tampans, in the unsegregated oasis that was Ybor City. They were partly insulated from the coarse quotidian humiliation of Tampa City that Afro-Americans had to endure. They received better treatment by their fellow Latins as well as by white Anglos than did the Afro-Americans. Just as the white Latins resented and dreaded being pulled down to the status of "Cuban niggers" by the presence of Afro-Cubans in their midst, so, it appears, did the Afro-Cubans fear the erosion of privilege by too close an association with America's number one outcast, Americans of African descent. There were, in addition, genuine cultural differences between the two groups of diaspora Africans, one of the most obvious of which was language.

Afro-Americans resented the privileged niche that the Afro-Cubans occupied within Tampa society and the latter's aloofness toward them. They were not blameless for the poor relations that existed between the Afro-Cubans and themselves. They imbibed the nativism of the Anglos, and the teenagers especially, laughed at the accents of the black Cuban kids and the difficulty they had speaking English at school. When the Afro-Cuban teenagers went to the only cinema that was open to them in the city, located in the Afro-American neighborhood called the Scrub, the Afro-American kids regarded them as "alien intruders," calling them "black wops."[93]

But the involuted world of the Afro-Cubans in Tampa was doomed. The combined pressure of Jim Crow, the decline in the Afro-Cuban population and its failure to replenish itself, the crisis of the Cuban economy and diminution of opportunities there (especially for black Cubans), the collapse of employment opportunities in the relatively protected and lucrative world of cigar making, the increasing Americanization that came with each new generation born on American soil, the shock and devastation of the Depression (and the departure of more than half the community) finally broke the relative isolation of the Afro-Cubans from their Afro-American brothers and sisters. By 1940 black Cubans made up only 3 percent of the black population of Tampa and as the cigar industry collapsed and white Latin ex-cigar makers took flight from a declining Ybor City, black Cubans found their fate increasingly joined with that of Afro-Americans. As the whites left Ybor City, the Afro-Americans moved in, in larger and larger numbers. Unlike the white Latins, the Afro-Cubans could not take flight to the white suburbs. They were left behind like beached whales. They were black. And like Afro-Americans they were trapped by race and class in the inner city. By the 1960s, Martin Luther King, Jr would join Martí and Maceo as a hero of Afro-Cuban Tampa.[94] A key step in the racialization, the enforced blackening, of the Afro-Cubans was of course, the rejection they experienced from their white Cuban compatriots. One wonders how the community would have evolved had it not been forced to go it alone.

Significantly, many of those who left Tampa during the Depression lived in El Barrio and joined Hispanic organizations in New York. They all marvelled and relished the freedom of New York City and some vowed never to return to the South.[95] But the greater freedom of the North was not the only major difference between New York and Tampa. A significantly larger Hispanic population, including black Hispanics, in New York was a most important element marking off the two places and their development. Moreover, the Hispanic population in New York replenished itself and grew rapidly; that in Tampa did not. New York never had the massive over-concentration of Hispanics in the cigar industry in the way in which Tampa did. This meant that Puerto Ricans and Cubans in New York, including black Hispanics, were not as vulnerable in the same way that the Afro-Cubans were in Tampa when the cigar industry collapsed under the pressures of mechanization and depression. Indeed, Afro-Cubans who left Tampa for New York were able to find jobs with relative ease. Even though there were undoubted white defections from the Puerto Rican community in New York, it never took on the wholesale and blatantly segregationist character of what the white Cubans did in Tampa. Partly because of the greater freedom of New York City and the greater ease of organization across racial lines politically and culturally, it took less effort for Puerto Ricans such as Jesús Colón to organize on the basis of nationality and class than it did for their counterparts in Tampa. In the end, then, the type of politics possible in New York was not possible in Tampa, given the nature of the changing environment of both locations. The very fact that someone like Jesús Colón could evolve was profoundly conditioned by the environment within which he operated. The Afro-Cubans of Tampa, despite themselves, were shunted from a class and nationalist position to one in which the salience of race had to be acknowledged. Through a series of complex processes, Afro-Cubans in Tampa were forced to bow to the American God of Race.

Epilogue

S trictly speaking, the radicalism of Caribbean migrants in America, paradoxical though it may seem, did not issue from the migrants' Caribbeanness, per se. It issued from a complex combination of inheritance and circumstance. The key elements of this configuration may be enumerated and recapitulated as follows. The migrants moved from majority to a maligned minority status. Those accustomed to the privilege that went with light skin color found themselves reduced to the single category of Negroes. Professionals and artisans, at least initially, lost standing in the pursuit of economic security. Furthermore, many emerged from a cultural and historical tradition of frontal resistance to oppression and failed to master the etiquette of race in America: they either refused to wear the mask or did so clumsily. They had, at least initially, no or relatively little fear of white people. And, in addition, they had the following characteristics: they were highly literate, self-improving, and driven; they had a passion for reading and discussing politics and world affairs; they had a tradition of political organization and petitioning and protest; they were relatively young and removed from some of the social, political, cultural, and psychological constraints of the previous environments; they shared a feeling of educational and cultural superiority to many of their tormentors. Such characteristics were combined with the following circumstances: the entry into a virulently racist society at a particularly gruesome time in its history; a society imposing severe blockages on upward social mobility on the basis of color; a society that perhaps has the most revolutionary creed, as enunciated in the Declaration of Independence, but tramples upon it in keeping black people down; a period in American and world history that was remarkably unstable, characterized by revolutionary agitation in America, revolutionary upheavals in Europe, organized under the banner of socialism (most notably: Russia 1917, Germany 1919, Hungary 1919) and nationalism (most notably Irish nationalism), along with Indian nationalism in Asia. Any person or group of people with such characteristics entering the America of 1900 to 1932 would find that the country was filled, despite its material wealth, with objectionable and intolerable features. Caribbeans were one identifiable group of people who had those characteristics and entered the United States at that point in time.

The migrants from the Caribbean who entered America in the first three decades of the twentieth century were doubly exceptional: they were radically different in their socio-economic and cultural profile from those whom they had left behind in the islands; and they were radically different in their socio-economic and cultural profile from Afro-Americans in the new society. They were new people, an ethnic group *sui generis*, whose uniqueness and complexity the adjective 'Caribbean' does not adequately capture. To be sure, they were from the Caribbean, but they came from a rather narrow band of Caribbean societies. Such was the first generation of Caribbeans in America who laid in place the infrastructure of twentieth-century Caribbean America, including its radical political tradition.

This study stops in 1932. But were we to have gone into the heady politics of the Depression years we would see fundamentally the same pattern: a conspicuous presence of Caribbean folk among the radicals, protesters, and dissenters. Cyril Briggs and Richard B. Moore continued to be at the heart of Harlem radicalism represented by the socialist tradition. Helping to save the Scottsboro Boys became one of Moore's chief duties in the Communist Party at the beginning of the campaign. Grace Campbell, after a period of bitter estrangement from the Party because of her support of the Lovestone faction, returned in about 1932. But the Harlem Tenants' League of which she was Vice-President, got destroyed in the factional fights that involved Richard B. Moore, President of the League, who opposed her.[1] Caribbeans were actively involved in the 'Don't Buy Where You Can't Work' campaign in Harlem. One of the key figures in the campaign was Arthur Reid, an ex-Garveyite from Trinidad.[2] It was also during the Depression that George Padmore came to political maturity and rose as an important black figure within the American Communist Party and later in the Comintern in Moscow.[3] In exile in London, Marcus Garvey, after initially supporting Haile Selassie and denouncing Mussolini and his invasion of Ethiopia, changed his position. Shocked at the unpreparedness and rapid collapse of the Ethiopian army and the flight into exile of the Emperor, Garvey vigorously denounced Haile Selassie. Garvey was further angered by Selassie's snubbing of a black delegation of pan-Africanists (including Garvey) who had gathered to greet him upon his arrival in exile in Britain.[4] But Garvey was out of step with his diminishing band of followers. Against his counsel, Garveyites and, even more, ex-Garveyites—who had been schooled by Garvey himself to love Ethiopia—energetically engaged in the massive effort to aid Ethiopia. Afro-Americans and Afro-Caribbeans (in and outside of America), despite their own needy circumstances during the Depression, rallied to Ethiopia's side in moving and generous ways, thus helping to write the most glorious chapter in the history of pan-Africanism and international black solidarity.[5] In the Spanish Civil War, Afro-Caribbeans fought with their American comrades—black and white—in the Abraham Lincoln Brigade against Franco's fascists. Of the Caribbeans, special mention ought to be made of the effort of Trinidad-born Dr Arnold Donowa, former dean of Howard University's Dental School, for his effort on behalf of Ethiopia and his direct aid to Republican Spain, where he served for eighteen months and was injured.[6] There was substantial Caribbean involvement, especially on the part of ex-Garveyite women, in Father Divine's organization. (Grace Campbell's sister, Mary, joined the organization, as did Madame de Mena, former editor of the *Negro World*.)[7] In short, the Caribbean radical tradition continued in the thirties and later, and in fact, though less pronounced and conspicuous, is alive today among more recent migrants.

Though evident and strong, the legacy of Caribbean radicalism in American society is little recognized. Of all the ideological and political currents of the 1920s, the black nationalist impulse—one that predates the arrival of Marcus Garvey by at least a century but was so powerfully reinvigorated by Garveyism in the aftermath of the First World War—has survived most robustly in the later generations. Elijah Poole, better known as Elijah Muhammad, was substantially influenced if not formed ideologically by Garveyism in his native Georgia and later in Detroit. He developed the Nation of Islam with extensive borrowings, including the regalia of the Nation, from his Garveyite past.[8] And in later years, the movement grew under the extraordinary energy and influence of Malcolm X, son of the Reverend Earl Little and his Grenadian wife, Louise Langdon Norton Little, both staunch Garveyites. Malcolm never forsook his Garveyite roots—on the contrary, he wore them as if they formed a badge of honor—and he grew with them and out of them.[9] Eugene Walcott, better known as Louis Farrakhan, was formed in the milieu of Garveyism in the Caribbean community of Roxbury, in Boston.

A. Philip Randolph, arguably the architect—if there is one—of the modern civil rights movement, traced his political awakening substantially to the Caribbean radical milieu in Harlem, and to the influence of Hubert Harrison. Randolph's trade union activity within the Brotherhood of Sleeping Car Porters was carried on in concert with Caribbean radicals like Ashley Totten, Thomas T. Patterson, and Frank Crosswaith.[10] And in the new day of the Black Power movement in the 1960s and early 1970s, echoes of the radicalism of the 1920s were more than discernible. Not only that, if one knew how to look, one would see many of the children of the earlier generation of Caribbean immigrants fighting shoulder to shoulder with their Afro-American brothers and sisters. Shirley Chisholm, Harry Belafonte, Vincent Harding, and Robert Moses are some of the most notable from that group. Further, a new generation of migrants, represented most visibly by Stokely Carmichael, made substantial contribution to the struggle. In some cases the influence of the older radicals was even more direct. Robert Williams of North Carolina, author of the uncompromising *Negroes With Guns*, admired Cyril Briggs, after whose magazine he named his own bold *Crusader*. And Briggs along with his good friend Harry Haywood, who was by then an old but stalwart black Bolshevik, advised many of the young radicals continuing the old fight.[11] The presence of Caribbean migrants and their descendants within Afro-America's radical and dissenting intelligentsia is also substantial, continuing a rich tradition that goes back to William Crogman in the nineteenth century, extending through Claude McKay, Oliver Cromwell Cox, St Clair Drake, C. L. R. James, and Kenneth B. Clark in the twentieth.

Caribbean radicals of the first three decades of the century have thus made a significant contribution, directly and indirectly, to Afro-American life and have left an impact upon American society that endures to the present. Together with their Afro-American brothers and sisters, they have been strong and firm with their help, as Fenton Johnson noticed in 1919, in holding aloft the banner of Ethiopia.

Postscript

Harold Cruse and the West Indians:
Critical Remarks on
The Crisis of the Negro Intellectual

It is with mixed feelings and some reluctance that I take issue with *The Crisis of the Negro Intellectual*. The book has flaws well beyond the number and seriousness that the reasonable reader ordinarily forgives an author for. Even more disturbing is the fact that as one's knowledge increases about the era, movements, and personalities that form its subject matter, the longer the list of identifiable problems becomes, and the more the authority and trustworthiness of its writer diminish. Some books get better each time we read them; others get worse; a few remain the same; and a small number, like *The Crisis of the Negro Intellectual*, get considerably worse with each additional reading. But despite these serious reservations about the book and its author, Harold Cruse deserves credit for raising big and important questions: What is and what has been the role of the black intellectual? What forces shaped the formation of the black intelligentsia in the early part of the century? What are the relations between politics and black cultural production and expression? Who are the enemies, and who are the friends of black people? What were and have been the relations between Afro-Americans and Jews, especially in the Communist Party? What were and have been the relations between Afro-Americans, Africans, and Afro-Caribbeans? How can black people win for themselves a greater degree of political, social, and cultural autonomy? What is the responsibility of the black intellectual to the wider black community? Cruse may not have satisfactorily answered all or any of these questions, but he poses them clearly and grapples, energetically, with them. He should be praised, too, for attempting to discuss the political questions of the day within the wider historical experience of Afro-Americans. Cruse, in particular, reminds readers of the important political and cultural struggles of the 1920s and 1930s. And his readers, then as well as now, needed and need reminding.

Throughout the book, Cruse names names and writes fearlessly. Even when one disagrees with his judgement and pronouncements, this is made possible, in part, because Cruse is never mealy-mouthed, he never pussy-foots around the important issues of the day, never trembles at the knees; and these qualities, I am reminded by the generally gutless and bloodless intellectual times in which we now live, *are* virtues.

Black intellectuals in the 1960s did much shouting and screaming. This was understandable and justifiable behavior—there was much to shout and scream about. But the heat often obscured the light. In *The Crisis of the Negro Intellectual* there is heat, but there is light too. In a review article published soon after the book appeared, Christopher Lasch declared that:

> When all the manifestoes and polemics of the Sixties are forgotten, this book will survive as a monument of historical analysis—a notable contribution to the understanding of the American past, but more than that, a vindication of historical analysis as the best way, maybe the only way, of gaining a clear understanding of social issues.[1]

As I will explain later, Lasch's prophecy has only partly come true, and could only partly have come true.

Lasch adjudged Cruse a Marxist, "a historical materialist"—a label Cruse himself would be loath to accept, despite the complimentary intent behind it. Lasch was quick to add, however, that Cruse opposes the "obstinate effort to impose on the Negro problem a class analysis which sees Negroes as an oppressed proletariat." Lasch did not explain what he meant when he described Cruse as a historical materialist. But it is evident from *The Crisis of the Negro Intellectual* that Cruse is influenced by Marxism. This is hardly surprising because Cruse, although he never disclosed this in his nearly-six-hundred-page book, was a member of the Communist Party for about seven years, between 1946 and 1953.[2] And his intellectual formation was substantially shaped by the Party. Prior to his break with the Party, all of his published writings appeared in its organs, such as the *Daily Worker*. Indeed, according to his own account, he had a job at the *Daily Worker* as a librarian and part-time reviewer in the cultural department.[3] His preoccupation with causation, process, context, and his acknowledgement of the power of material, especially economic, forces in social change all reveal the mark of historical materialism upon his intellectual formation. But are these sensibilities sufficient to make Cruse a Marxist? I think not: Cruse departs from Marxism substantively as well as methodologically. Despite its genuflection to the idea of black co-operatives, *The Crisis of the Negro Intellectual* is not an anti-capitalist book. And with its heavy emphasis on race in contrast to class, not to mention its rather crude dichotomy of separatism versus integrationism, the book evidently sits squarely within the black nationalist, not the Marxist (black or otherwise), tradition. Cruse's narrow and highly problematic conceptualization of culture, and the inflated role that he assigns to black intellectuals in contrast to ordinary black people in the struggle, also puts him outside the mainstream of historical materialism. His rather mechanistic and undialectical mode of analysis has also caught the attention of his more Marxist critics.[4] Marx's influence is, nevertheless, evident, but it is not strong enough for Cruse to be called a Marxist, even on the dubious basis of method only.[5]

Has *The Crisis of the Negro Intellectual* stood the test of time, a monument to historical analysis, as Lasch predicted? It has endured, but for different reasons. Lasch was overly generous in his praise. For although Cruse undoubtedly has a good sense of history, that is, a desire to relate the present to the past, this is not matched by careful research and judgement. Cruse himself candidly admits that his book has "many flaws," including lack of thoroughness in research.[6] But this admission, unfortunately, was made four long years after its publication, and only in the aftermath of a barrage of withering criticism. Responding to the merciless and devastating critique offered by Ernest Kaiser, archivist at the Schomburg Center at the time, Cruse wrote: "I knew this book had flaws when it was published. There are flaws in organization, lack of thoroughness in research, insufficient data to back up many of my contentions, imperfect conceptualizations, half-developed ideas." He went on to say:

> Kaiser attacked these weaknesses, but the real intent of this book was to inject into the civil rights movement by polemical force a new level of criticism at *any cost*. The intent was *not* to hold back and cater to traditional standards of "scholarship" adhered to by Ernest Kaiser or anyone else in or out of the academic world. If I had postponed my book in order to work up a conformity to the kind of "studies" Ernest Kaiser has been cataloguing in the Schomburg Collection for the last 20 years, *The Crisis of the Negro Intellectual* would never have appeared in time to witness the demise of the Sixties' euphoric expectations.[7]

This shocking admission of polemic at "any cost" must, logically, include polemic at the cost of accuracy. This deduction is further underscored by Cruse's smug disparagement of what he calls traditional standards of scholarship, which he puts in inverted commas. What kind of scholarship was Ernest Kaiser asking for? Was it unreasonable? Kaiser was asking for nothing more than what any reasonable person expects of non-fiction writers: thoroughness in research, clarity of exposition, coherence in argumentation, fidelity to the evidence, honest intentions. Cruse does not tell us what the opposite of "traditional standards of 'scholarship'" is, except to imply that *The Crisis of the Negro Intellectual* operates by such non-traditional (modern?) standards. I can certainly sympathize with the sense of mission and urgency that apparently drove Cruse to put the book out in those pregnant times. But is it not self-defeating to sacrifice so much in polemical engagements? What will critics and adversaries say when they see so many holes in the argument? Or is the author hoping that they will not see the flaws, thus obtaining victory—a Pyrrhic victory in reality— through bluff?

Cruse's book, then, not only through the admission of its own author, but by the evidence of its contents, cannot be seen as a monument of historical analysis. After all, if, as I shall argue, the analysis itself is flawed and the research upon which it is based uneven, inadequate, partial, distorted, too feeble to carry the heavy load of Cruse's many and controversial judgements, how can the book be seen as a historical monument? In parts of the book, the judgements float in the air without any visible, evidentiary support. One cannot but agree with Kaiser when he declared that Lasch's largely uncritical praise for Cruse showed "his ignorance of Negro life, history and culture." Lasch, he said, is "obviously a neophyte in the area of black radical politics and has no qualifications in the field of Negro studies generally."[8]

The Crisis of the Negro Intellectual is valuable and enduring not because it is a monument to historical analysis, bulky though it is, but because it asks monumental questions, however inadequately they are answered by the author.[9] As John Henrik Clarke wrote recently, Cruse in his book

> raises more questions than he has answers for. The greatest value of his book is that it is the work of an alarmist. Alarmists have a role to play in history; however, very often they put a subject on the agenda that they are not equal to handling. Mr Cruse has put many subjects on the agenda for black intellectuals to handle that cannot and should not be ignored if we are to survive as a people.[10]

Cruse's book, in addition, resonates across the generation that produced it to our own because of the persistence and, indeed, deterioration of many of the conditions it describes, and the frustrating absence of effectual political engagement with the current problems of Afro-America as we leave the twentieth century.

Serious internal contradictions vitiate *The Crisis of the Negro Intellectual*. There are clear prejudices expressed within its pages, notably against Jews, Caribbeans, and continental Africans. But an adequate appraisal of the book does not come easily, for *The Crisis of the Negro Intellectual* ranges freely over a wide variety of subjects. It is largely for this reason that, as Arthur Paris pointed out, many of those who reviewed the book when it first came out "little understood what Cruse was talking about, and because he spoke authoritatively, they tended to accept his historical interpretations and quasi-sociological analysis."[11] Thus, to be satisfactorily judged—that is, judged beyond pointing to its internal inconsistencies, and problems of argumentation—the book demands an array of expertise from the would-be critic. What is also clear is that the evidence required to render proper judgement of it, perhaps more than usual, needs to be derived independently of the book's own offering of evidence, given the widely acknowledged unreliability of *The Crisis of the Negro Intellectual*.

Thus, I was not fully aware of some of the weaknesses of the book until I had done my own research on Claude McKay. It was while reviewing the existing literature on McKay and his politics that I was struck by the untrustworthiness of Cruse's account of the man. And in extending my research beyond McKay to other Caribbean radicals in the United States— the research whose results are presented in the present volume—I was taken aback by the difference between the historical record (beyond matters of interpretation) and Cruse's presentation of the subject in his book.

I was surprised, given its inadequacies, that Cruse's book has never been directly challenged on its discussion of Caribbeans.[12] It has been engaged, and sometimes taken apart on a number of other questions, but not on this one.[13] Worst of all, for over a generation, *The Crisis of the Negro Intellectual* has been allowed to stand as the most influential discussion of the subject. Indeed, to this day—and it has continuously remained in print for over a generation—it is seen in most quarters as *the* authoritative text on Caribbeans in America. But, far from being a source of knowledge about the Caribbean experience in the United States, Cruse's book, through its unwarranted and false authority, has been an obstacle to such knowledge. My disagreement is not with the polemical tone of the book: polemical writing has its place, always will, and always should; no, what is disturbing is the author's idiosyncratic and effectively cavalier attitude toward factual accuracy—the historical facts (however defined), as Cruse himself admits, play second fiddle to his polemical zeal.

It is in an attempt to rectify the historical record that the following remarks are offered. My main focus is Cruse's discussion of Caribbean migrants and, in particular, their role in radical politics in the United States from the First World War to the 1950s. There are, in my view, major errors of fact and interpretation that have gone uncorrected and unchallenged since Cruse's book was published thirty years ago. Moreover, these have been picked up and repeated by those who have assumed, through no fault of their own, that Cruse's account is authoritative and reliable. Marx was right when he said: "To leave error unrefuted is to encourage intellectual immorality."[14] But my motives for this critique are far less elevated and more prosaic.[15] I think, as you shall see, that Cruse attacked many of these people unjustly. I happen—I am willing to openly admit—to admire many of those attacked, and the people Cruse attacked are dead and buried and cannot speak for themselves. I cannot speak for them, but I can and wish to bear witness. And I believe that the new information and interpretation should be open to the reading public.

One of the key arguments of Cruse's book is that black people in America have been misled; misled by "integrationists," Marxists, and reformists alike, and indeed misled by simple-minded "black nationalists." The integrationists either operate on the basis of bad faith, or they simply are misguided and do not understand or have chosen not to understand that the United States is a "nation of nations" and that all the ethnic groups in America, except African Americans, act accordingly. The Communist Party and the National Association for the Advancement of Colored People are Cruse's main targets here. To Cruse, America has always been an arena of nationalities and ethnicities competing for power and resources; and black folks have not understood this and are therefore unprepared to recognize what is and what is not in their own best interest as a group. Moreover, African Americans have swallowed the poisonous myth of American individualism and are thus incapacitated when it comes to defending their group interests not only economically, but also politically.

For their part, the black nationalists, especially those whom Cruse calls the "Back-to-Africa" Garveyites, are not only unrealistic in their aspirations but have been devoid of a serious program. This was true, Cruse argues, of Marcus Garvey's Universal Negro Improvement Association in the 1920s as well as of the nationalists operating at the time that he wrote his book in the 1960s.

Insofar as one can discern his own position, Cruse is calling for a black nationalism that is homegrown, profoundly aware of its peculiar American environment, coming out of the American soil. Whether or not one agrees with it, this is a coherent position—as far as it goes. But there are dangers. And one key danger to his thesis is that of being defeated by the difficulty of concretely determining what is American and what is not, what is organic to American conditions and what is not. Regrettably, Cruse dismisses a number of ideas and ideological positions, not on the basis of their intrinsic worth, but on their provenance and, worse, on the grounds of the nationality and ethnicity of their carriers. And so, "Jews" and "West Indians" (by which terms Cruse means those of Jewish descent, including "non-Jewish Jews,"[16] and those of Caribbean descent, including those born in the United States) cannot have anything of value to say to the Afro-American condition as, not only are they not Afro-American, they are also foreign, not American at all. There is a remarkably strong, anti-foreign, nativist streak in *The Crisis of the Negro Intellectual* that does absolutely nothing to advance the more fundamental and important arguments Cruse is trying to put forward. And because he mounts his criticism and arguments on the basis of the ethnicity of those whom he is attacking, he is required to be fully apprised of the ethnicity of everyone in his purview, friend and foe.

This brings us to one of the two sets of problems with *The Crisis of the Negro Intellectual*. These problems may be divided into two broad categories, one *methodological*, the other *substantive*. But both are directly connected with Cruse's discussion of Caribbeans.

Some Methodological Problems of
The Crisis of the Negro Intellectual

In Cruse's worldview, articulated in *The Crisis of the Negro Intellectual*, there is a crude correspondence between ethnicity, on the one hand, and valid ideas, on the other. Claude McKay's ideas, for instance, though viewed somewhat sympathetically by Cruse—a unique accolade for a

Caribbean person in Cruse's book—are nonetheless given short-shrift because McKay is a "typical" West Indian who had a "stand-offish attitude towards the American Negro situation." He was, according to Cruse, "not the type to be embroiled in any action involving the American Negro problem in the United States."[17]

Similarly, in an unwarranted tirade against W. A. Domingo, the alleged weaknesses of the latter's political position is ultimately explained by the fact that he is an "Afro-Britisher." Cyril Briggs and Richard B. Moore, and even the black nationalist Garvey, are likewise dismissed on the basis of their ethnicity. And Paule Marshall, though born in Brooklyn, was dismissed by Cruse partly because she is "a West Indian of traditional 'divided' loyalties."[18] And so one's ideas are condemned or applauded on the basis of one's nationality; the outcome of a crude sociology of knowledge.

But to be consistent in upholding such a position, Cruse would also be obliged to distance himself from a number of people for whom he clearly has admiration, but who, like Paule Marshall, are of Caribbean descent. He would thus have to jettison W. E. B. Du Bois because his father was from the Caribbean. He would also have to jettison James Weldon Johnson, who in his autobiography, *Along this Way*, indicated in great detail the profound influence that his mother and his mother's mother had on the Johnson household and on the children growing up in Jacksonville, Florida. His mother and his mother's mother were both Bahamian.[19] Cruse would also have to jettison Malcolm X, on account of his mother being Grenadian. This is the logical outcome of his methodology.

And because his argument is based on ethnicity, he inevitably gets tangled up into some very uncomfortable knots, and, worse, he often does not even know it. Thus in the course of discussing a 1926 Harlem theatre strike and the positions taken by Moore, Briggs, and Harrison—West Indians, in his vocabulary—he cited with approval a series of articles published in the *Amsterdam News*, written by, as he put it, "one Edgar M. Grey, a leading journalist."[20] What he did not know—or, if he knew, he did not say—is that Edgar M. Grey, a close associate of Hubert Harrison, was also a black migrant of Caribbean origin.[21]

A similar problem arises in relation to Cruse's discussion of Garveyism. Within the space of only five pages Cruse contradicts himself. In the first instance, he maintains that Garveyism was not an Afro-American Nationalist movement, but an "Afro-British" one, coming out of a different social milieu. The membership of the UNIA in the United States was, said Cruse,

> predominantly West Indian and *whatever the number of American Negroes* attracted to Garveyism, it was *not* an Afro-American Nationalist movement engaged in an historical confrontation with the realities of the American situation out of which it sprung. Garveyism was Afro-British nationalism functioning outside its historical British empire context, hence avoiding British confrontation.[22]

So regardless of the number of Afro-Americans it attracted and irrespective of the fact that the UNIA flourished in the United States far more than it ever did in the Caribbean, to Cruse, it nevertheless was not an Afro-American movement. But when, a few pages later, Domingo is quoted as saying in 1919 that the "few Negroes who have become radicals have been in many cases foreigners," Cruse is quick to add: "In 'many cases' this was certainly true, but not all." Wanting to highlight the black radical tradition in the United States, Cruse proclaims that

> [N]ot a single innovation that Briggs, *et al.* formulated in the African Blood Brotherhood was actually new. Every "Back to Africa," "separate state," "emigration" program that Briggs experimented with had been anticipated back in the nineteenth century beginning with Martin R. Delany's work. In 1879 Moses Singleton's migration crusade out of the South towards the West *mobilized as many, if not more, American Negroes* than the Garvey movement. *Every Pan-Africanist trend of the twentieth century, including Garvey's had its roots in the nineteenth century American Negro trends.* The radical elements in these nineteenth-century trends were not Marxian, but native American, in essence.[23]

More carefully formulated, there is little that one could sensibly disagree with in the latter position; it is, in essence, congruent with the historical evidence.[24] But the crucial fact is that such a statement flies in the face of his earlier formulation. Ernest Kaiser noticed that Cruse has a tendency to mount "contradictory arguments on both sides of most issues raised, different answers given at different times to the same questions or just pure nonsense answers to 'win' a point at all costs." It might be an exaggeration to claim that Cruse mounts contradictory arguments on *most* issues raised in the book, but he frequently and conspicuously contradicts himself. It is an attitude of "heads I win, tails you lose," said Kaiser.[25] But I think the contradictions are probably the product of Cruse's inability to superintend, or inattention to superintending, the arguments—not to mention quarrels— in his long, rambling, cantankerous book. The contradiction in his discussion of Garveyism, partly because it occurred within the space of merely five pages, does, however, seem to be a case of wanting to win an argument at any cost.

Some Substantive Problems of *The Crisis of the Negro Intellectual*

There are problems of substance in *The Crisis of the Negro Intellectual* that are even more numerous than those at the methodological level.

First there is the rather simplistic and erroneous idea that Caribbeans are "conservatives fashioned in the British mold."[26] But this has been discussed within the body of the present volume and therefore need not detain us further.

Second, Cruse claims that when the Communist (Workers') Party was formed in 1919, as a breakaway group from the Socialist Party, there was a "split" in allegiance between Afro-Caribbean and Afro-American Socialists. According to him, the split took on "a more or less American Negro vs. West Indian Negro character: The Americans, led by Randolph, refused to join the Communists, while the West Indians—Moore, Briggs and Huiswoud—did. One exception, [Lovett] Fort-Whiteman, an American, did join the Communists."[27] The one problem with this argument is that it is not true. The fact is that in September 1919 when the Communist Party was founded, there were few black people on the revolutionary left in America. Most of them were of Caribbean origin; and it is true to say that the first to join the Communist Party were Caribbeans. Huiswoud, as we have seen, was the only black charter member of the Party and the theology student Hendrickson of Guyana is generally accepted to have been the second black member. Cyril Briggs then joined, followed by Fort-Whiteman, Otto Hall, and his younger brother, Harry Hayward, the last three being Afro-American. But contrary to Cruse's assertion, in 1919, the majority of the Caribbeans stayed within the Socialist Party—Moore, Domingo, Crosswaith, Campbell. By this time, Harrison had given up the Socialist Party in disgust, but never joined the Communist Party, even though he strongly supported the Bolshevik Revolution. Harrison was by then an avowed black nationalist, founder of the Liberty League of Afro-Americans in 1917, advocate of Race First. Moore joined the Party around 1922, but Domingo and Crosswaith, like Randolph and Owen, never did, and remained with the Socialist Party.[28] While it is true that Briggs joined the Communist Party in 1920 or a year or so later, it is not true, as Cruse claims, that he was previously a member of the Socialist Party. And Cruse gives no evidence that Briggs had joined the Socialists; he simply declared that he had. Briggs himself said that he had never joined the Socialist Party. "I did not consider that the S[ocialist] P[arty] had anything to offer the Negro, or any interest in the anti-imperialist struggles of the colonial peoples," Briggs later told a researcher.[29] In short, there was no so-called "American Negro vs. West Indian Negro" split in 1919.

Furthermore, even when there were different party allegiances, in the early 1920s there was considerable co-operation among the black radicals of the left. And up to 1920, black leftists co-operated even with Marcus Garvey. While Domingo edited the *Negro World*, he also wrote for the *Messenger* and published a number of seminal articles in that magazine. In July 1919, for instance, he published in the *Messenger* "Socialism the Negroes' Hope," with the incongruous by-line after his name "Editor of the *Negro World*." Garvey could tolerate his Marxism no longer and fired him the same month. Domingo then became Contributing Editor of the *Messenger* and worked with Randolph and Owen on the magazine until he felt obliged to resign in 1923 over its increasingly anti-Caribbean editorial position during the acrimonious "Garvey Must Go" campaign of

1922–23.[30] But even when he and Moore founded their own magazine, the *Emancipator*, in 1920, Domingo continued as a Contributing Editor of the *Messenger*. Randolph and Owen reciprocated by serving as Contributing Editors of the *Emancipator*. The year before the launch of the *Emancipator*, they described Briggs's *Crusader* in their column, "Suggestions for Good Reading," as "the only other [Negro] magazine besides the *Messenger* worth reading," which, from Randolph and Owen, was high praise indeed. They elaborated upon their judgement of the *Crusader* in an editorial a few months later. Even though they signalled their differences with it, the editors of the *Messenger* warmly welcomed the arrival of the *Crusader*:

> The Crusader, edited by Mr Cyril V. Briggs of New York, is a real addition to the field of Radical Journalism. It represents both intelligence and courage. With a few notable exceptions we agree on the whole with the policy of the Crusader. The magazine is handsomely printed and well gotten up. It is coming in for a part of the attacks of the reactionaries, which is another evidence that it is doing fairly well the work which it has set out to do. Moreover the Crusader has shown the fine spirit of co-operation with The Messenger. We have exchanged lists of agents with mutual profit and fraternity. We welcome the growth of the Crusader and extend Thanksgiving Greetings to it for a long and successful life of usefulness.[31]

Indeed, the *Messenger* dropped its rather lofty sub-title, "The Only Radical Negro Magazine in America" — which itself had superseded its 1917 sub-title, "The Only Magazine of Scientific Radicalsim in the World Published by Negroes" — primarily because another radical Negro magazine, namely the *Crusader*, had appeared.[32] The level of goodwill and fellowship among the black left radicals was so great that in June 1920 the *Messenger*, the *Crusader*, and the *Emancipator* offered their readers what they called a "Combination Offer" of a joint subscription to all three magazines. Readers could have the self-described "Three Leaders in Negro Thought" for $3.00 a year, instead of the $4.00 it would cost if they were to have subscribed to them individually.[33]

Huiswoud, Randolph, Moore, Owen, Domingo, Campbell, Briggs, were all co-founders and members of the People's Educational Forum in 1920 which organized political meetings open to the public. There was no antagonism between them and it was only in the late 1920s that tensions between the Communist and the Socialist parties began to affect relations between their respective black members. The political differences between Moore and Randolph, in particular, became public at this time and worsened in the 1930s.[34] This, however, was the result not of differences in national origin, but political affiliation and practice, along with ideological positions. Moore was a Communist, Randolph a Socialist. (Harry Haywood was just as critical as Moore of Randolph, and, unlike Moore, he did not mellow in his criticism of Randolph with the passage of time.[35]) But once again, Caribbeans as well as Afro-Americans could be found in both political parties, especially in the 1930s. Contrary to Cruse's pronouncements on the subject, one of the most remarkable features of the 1920s was the degree to which black radicals of the left co-operated with one another.

Despite the fact that Cruse talks in an apparently authoritative, indeed, patronising, voice about Claude McKay, closer investigation reveals that he knew little about him and misrepresented McKay, and by so doing once again misled and misinformed the readers of *The Crisis of the Negro Intellectual*. Two particularly glaring inaccuracies are noteworthy. First, drawing upon McKay's autobiography, *A Long Way From Home* (1937), Cruse acknowledges (rather condescendingly) that McKay saw "clearly enough" the problems of Afro-Americans and black people's relationship with the white left in the United States. But according to Cruse, when McKay attended the Fourth Congress of the Communist International in 1922, "he did not tell the Russians his views. . . . McKay should have enlightened the Russians while he was in a position to do so."[36] McKay *had*, in fact, addressed the Congress on "The Negro Question" in America.[37] In addition McKay wrote for and was regularly featured in *Pravda* and *Izvestia* on this issue,[38] and held discussions with Trotsky, Zinoviev, Radek, and Bukharin, among others, on the subject.[39] Moreover, McKay was commissioned to write a book on the subject of *Negroes in America*, which was published in 1923 in Moscow; he even published a small collection of short stories — his first attempt at working in the genre — about black life in America.[40] All of this has apparently gone unrecognized, and certainly unacknowledged, by Cruse.

Second, Cruse maintains that after McKay's collection of short stories, *Gingertown*, was published in 1932, "not much is known here [in the United States] about McKay's literary relationship with the Communist leftwing."[41] In reality McKay returned to the United States in 1934 and immediately threw himself into frenetic journalistic work. His work appeared in the *Nation, American Mercury, Jewish Frontier, New Leader*, and for a time he wrote a weekly column for Harlem's *New York Amsterdam News*. During the Depression McKay had debates with Adam Clayton Powell, Jr, and George Schuyler, among others, in the pages of the *Amsterdam News*, the *Pittsburgh Courier*, and elsewhere. He even had a widely publicized debate on the radio with George Schuyler. Ill and virtually destitute, McKay left Harlem for Chicago in 1944 but he remained politically engaged right up to his death in 1948. The primary object of this work, as McKay saw it, was to help clarify the path Afro-Americans should follow — one which he felt ought to have been pursued independently of the Communist Party of the USA because the latter could not be trusted. Considering that much of *The Crisis of the Negro Intellectual* is concerned with radical politics in Harlem, it is as regrettable as it is astonishing that Cruse is so ignorant of the primary role that McKay played in those stormy debates of the Depression years of the 1930s. What is even more surprising is the fact that McKay's crucial text, *Harlem: Negro Metropolis*, which discusses in detail the relationship between black people and the left, is apparently unknown to Cruse, for, as Wayne Cooper in his biography of McKay noted, McKay's book "contained in essence the core argument later presented by Harold Cruse in his *Crisis of the Negro Intellectual*, minus Cruse's distortions of history, anti-Semitism, personal rancor, petty spite, extreme tediousness, and essential lack of humor."[42]

More than a generation before Cruse, McKay called for black aggregation, black co-operatives, and a more skeptical attitude toward the Communist Party. Like Cruse's, McKay's indictment of the black intellectual was severe. This is McKay in *Harlem: Negro Metropolis*:

> The Communist would . . . readily betray the Negro minority here in America if it suited their purpose. It should be plain why they are seeking to penetrate every Negro organization. The Negro intellectual, apparently becoming neurotic and therefore confused on the issue of Segregation, may not perceive that the Communist maneuver is to make an appendage of his race—a red Uncle Tom of Communism. They are striving for control of the political mind of the Negro so that they may do his thinking for him.
>
> But now, more than ever, Negroes should think for themselves. It is hurting their cause when any organization not truly representative sets itself up as their national and international spokesman. Wild-eyed, panic-stricken neurotic whites who cannot think how to save themselves from the bankruptcy of their own isms, certainly cannot think for the Negro people.

This is Cruse:

> The great dichotomy, the underlying ideological schism that dominates the Negro social outlook in America, is that of integrationism vs. *all* trends that reflect nationalism, separatism or ethnic group identity. Negro integrationists become pro-Marxist Communist, and Negro Marxist-Communists become pro-integrationist because for the Negro Integrationists, Marxism lends a radical flavor to integrationism which in itself is *not* revolutionary in essence. On the other hand, Marxist-Communism becomes pro-integrationist because of its essentially opportunistic pro-Negro policies. Pro-nationalist Negro trends must reject Marxist-Communism, and vice versa, because the latter, being theoretically opposed to independent black power on internationalist premises, must seek to control nationalist trends by directing them into integrationist channels. This has been historically demonstrated.
>
> As a result of these historical findings it has become mandatory today that every pro-nationalist tendency within the Negro movement take stringent steps to ban all Marxist-Communist influences from controlling positions within the movement. These white leftwing influences inevitably divert leadership energies, distort policies, disorient Negroes in terms of specified goals, discourage independent Negro creative thinking.[43]

Apart from the obvious superiority of McKay's prose and coherence of exposition, the substance of these two passages is the same, their political message identical. Had Cruse been more careful in his research he would not have been able to conclude that: "Claude McKay was not the type to be embroiled in any action involving the American Negro problem in the United States."[44]

But, to my mind, the most unsatisfactory aspect of *The Crisis of the Negro Intellectual* is Cruse's discussion of a document written by W. A. Domingo in 1919. Of all the Caribbean radicals discussed in his book, Domingo and Richard B. Moore draw the greatest fire from Cruse. Almost half of the chapter "1920's–1930's—West Indian Influence" is devoted to attacking Domingo. And Moore is given a chapter all to himself, on top of the sniping at him elsewhere in the book.[45] But Cruse's distortion of Domingo's ideas is especially reprehensible.

During the Red Scare of 1919, the Rand School of Social Science, a socialist educational institution, was raided under the aegis of the Joint Legislative Committee Investigating Seditious Activities in the State of New York, generally known as the Lusk Committee, after its chairman, State Senator Clayton R. Lusk.[46] Established in 1906, the Rand School at the time of the raid was located in lower Manhattan, at 7 East 13th Street. Among the items seized on June 21, 1919 was a document, "Socialism Imperilled, or the Negro—A Potential Menace to American Radicalism," written by Domingo. The document, approximately eight thousand words in length, was reproduced in full in the Committee's report.[47] Cruse claims, without a shred of evidence, that the document was "meant to be confidential" and that it came to light "only because of the investigation" by the Lusk Committee. The implication, clearly, is that there is something sinister about Domingo's document. The Report of the Lusk Committee itself nowhere claims that the document was confidential or meant to be so, nor does the document describe itself as "confidential." On the contrary, Domingo, within the body of the text itself, explicitly called it a "booklet," evidently meant for publication by the Socialist Party.[48]

Cruse attacks Domingo, but does not provide his readers with an adequate account of Domingo's views. It is therefore necessary to provide a summary of Domingo's argument before discussing Cruse's response to it. In the essay, Domingo urged the Socialist Party to dedicate more effort and resources to political work among black workers. Perhaps mindful of the great difficulty that Harrison had a few years earlier in trying to get the party to take seriously the "Negro Question," Domingo appealed to the self-interest of the white members.

Given the history of racism in the United States it is not surprising, Domingo argued, that black workers are profoundly "race conscious" but hardly "class conscious." "As a portion of the working class," Domingo observed,

> negroes are industrially unorganized and in most cases bitterly antagonistic to organized labor. This is due to racial discrimination against them, the wages they receive and the kind of work usually reserved for them. They are given low wages and are told to be grateful to those who give them a chance to earn a living, hence, although hating their employers, still they regard them as friends,

in that they are given work to the exclusion of members of their employer's own race.[49]

He argued that it was the duty of the Socialist Party to do all in its power to facilitate the entry of black workers into organized labor and actively to recruit them into the party. The work performed by the Industrial Workers of the World, "those intrepid evangels of industrial unionism," whose appeals were made to all, "and not to particular groups of the working class," should be emulated. If the Socialists follow the methods of the IWW, "they will secure to themselves the adherence of over 12,000,000 people, and active support, without whose help no radical movement in America can hope to succeed."[50]

It would be wise, Domingo argued, for white radicals to engage in this type of work among black people, as in its absence black workers may pose a threat to Socialist revolution in America. Insofar as black workers felt that such a revolution would not serve their interest, they could, said Domingo—drawing upon the analogy of the reactionary war waged against the Bolsheviks in Russia at the time—potentially be "used by the plutocracy as black White Guards, or the Czecho-Slovaks in America."[51] Controversial though the idea may sound, as will be demonstrated, such a position was, at the time—rightly or wrongly—accepted as an article of faith on the black left. Cruse thought this was a "racially unpatriotic position," but it certainly was not one unique to West Indians, as he claims.[52] (And he ought to have known better.) But how did Domingo and others make their way to such an apparently bizarre conclusion?

Domingo developed an elaborate argument. First, as we have seen, he argued, and persuasively so, that the black workers in general hated white workers more than they did their employers. The employers, they reasoned, gave them work while the white workers would rather see black workers starve than allow them into their unions or compete with them on equal terms in the labor market. Incidents such as the East St Louis massacre could hardly improve the image of the white worker in black people's mind.

Second, "subtle control" was exercised by Northern capitalists over black opinion, "through negro schools, colleges, churches and newspapers" that they financed. Due to white Southern opposition to black education, black people have traditionally turned to the North for financial support in founding and running schools and colleges. Such support has come from powerful Northern capitalists: the Rosenwalds, the Carnegies, the Rockefellers. According to Domingo, they controlled the various boards of trustees and shaped the policies of these institutions. Thus, he said—with uncharacteristic crudity—"the curricula are usually framed in such a manner as to train potential industrial scabs, and the students very naturally regard those who endowed the schools as their real friends and benefactors."

The newspapers, for the most part, exist upon "the bounty" of the Republican Party. It is also alleged, said Domingo, that they "receive subsidies from the big corporations for advising their readers to be hostile to organized labor and radicalism in general." The policy of these newspapers is "usually to denounce the white working class, while extolling the virtues of Mr Rosenwald, Mr Carnegie, and their ilk. They usually condemn every form of political and economic radicalism and laud patriotism."[53]

The black churches, "the real source of negro opinion," are usually presided over by graduates of Southern schools endowed by the capitalists, and "true to their training they praise the rich while inveighing against the laboring class." Moreover, these churches have often "had mortgages lifted, organs presented or stained glass windows installed by the philanthropically inclined millionaires."

Following the logic of his argument, Domingo concluded that "every medium of negro thought functions in the interest of capital."

The position of black people within the structure of the American economy is not conducive to the growth of radicalism either. Black people were overwhelmingly located in service jobs, and this had, according to Domingo, important political implications:

> They are mostly cooks, waiters, porters and body servants who because of their inferior social and economic status, place an exaggerated value upon opportunities common to others but denied them. On the trains, in hotels and other places where they work as menials they come in contact with people who can indulge in luxuries, and whose opinions are necessarily of a kind to extol conservatism and condemn radicalism. With the exception of the few who work in the garment industry in New York and come in contact with wholesome radicalism of Russian Jews, the majority of negro men and women are deprived of the stimulating influence of advanced political ideas.[54]

And because of their disproportionate location in these service jobs, they depend upon tips to a large degree, and "the tipper or those in a position to dole out tips take on magnified importance in the eyes of the tip receiver."

All of these influences have had a negative political effect upon black people in America, argued Domingo. They have tended to make the race "docile and full of respect for wealth and authority, while creating an immense gulf between white and black workers." This gulf is widened even further by the racism of the white workers, who refuse to give black people "an opportunity to work under the more favorable conditions achieved by union labor."[55] The downward spiral that such behavior aids is vicious:

> Smarting under the injustice of industrial discrimination and seeing the economic results upon himself and family the average negro worker develops a not unnatural bitterness and hostility towards the white worker who, reacting to the cunning of the capitalist press that is intent on dividing the workers, reciprocates the hostility in terms of race hatred of the vilest and most unreasoning kind.[56]

Flush with the idea that the Revolution was imminent (a view shared widely on the revolutionary left at the time), Domingo pointed out that black soldiers from the United States, France, and Britain—including those from French and British colonies in the Caribbean—had engaged in military action, under their respective national flag, against Bolshevik Russia.[57] It was therefore not inconceivable, were the occasion to arise, that black soldiers might do the same thing on behalf of the capitalist class in the United States itself.[58] And indeed, a number of industrialists and white Southerners have always seen black people as "bulwarks of conservatism against which the waves of American radicalism will dash in vain."[59]

Domingo's argument was not without corroboration. Booker T. Washington boasted about the loyalty of the Negro: "[T]he best free labor in the world," a people "not given to strikes and lockouts."[60] And Kelly Miller, one of his followers, noted with pride, that "[t]he nation looks to the Negro as a great storehouse of conservatism."[61] In an astonishing essay on "The Negro's Place in the Labor Struggle," Miller made clear where he thought black people's interest lay. "The capitalist is prone to a kind and generous attitude toward the black workingman," he wrote. Unlike the white worker, the white capitalist transcends racism; he operates only on the basis of capitalist rationality, and if by some remote chance he "shows race prejudice in his operations, it is merely the reflected attitude of the white workman." When the unions recognize black workers, this is because "they are forced to do so by the attitude of capital." The capitalist stands for an open shop which gives everyone the "unhindered right to work according to his ability and skill." On top of all this: "The employing classes have been wonderfully helpful to the Negro by way of generous philanthropic contributions. They have built his schools and colleges and made the betterment of the race possible," said Miller. Thus, whenever a sharp issue is drawn "between those who have, and those who have not, the Negro's instinct aligns him with wealth and power."[62] Although Booker T. Washington had claimed in 1901 that "the economic, social, and moral progress and advancement of the negro is dependent upon the philanthropic and humane consideration of . . . employers," Miller out-Washingtoned Washington with his anti-labor and pro-capitalist remark.[63] Indeed, in "The Negro and the Labor Unions," an article published in the *Atlantic Monthly* a couple of years before he died, Washington spoke about unions and black membership in them in far more measured and conciliatory terms than Miller did in his writings on the subject.[64] Indeed, Washington was encouraging the unions to allow greater black participation.

Such, then, was the fundamental structure of the argument developed by Domingo. The scenario unfolded by him was entirely hypothetical— "imaginative pictures" was how he described the exercise: what if there was a Socialist Revolution in the United States?[65] A gigantic "if"—even though it looked smaller then than it does from our end of the century. And he spoke about the *potential* menace that a black population, historically locked out of the wider society, might pose to white Socialists.[66] Tactically, what Domingo was trying to do was to twist the arm of the Socialist Party, with the objective of getting it to take the Negro Question in America more seriously. If moral suasion was ineffective, even among avowed Socialists, then enlightened self-interest would be resorted to. Not insignificantly, he attempted to get the Party to release more resources— including more Party support for the *Messenger* magazine—in order that Owen, Randolph, Moore, Crosswaith, Campbell, and he could do their work more effectively among black people.[67] Seven years previously Hubert Harrison tried to persuade the Socialist Party of the importance of "Negro Work"; he did not succeed—despite his formidable powers of persuasion— and he resigned from the Party. Domingo was now having a go for himself.[68]

Hypothetical though the argument was, Domingo made seven concrete recommendations, in the here and now, to the Socialist Party, and American white radicals in general:

1. "They must unequivocally condemn all forms of injustice practiced against negroes," and enshrine this within their declarations of principles, etc.
2. "They must give the negro more prominence in their discussions whether by speech or in their publications relative to injustice in America."
3. "They must seek to attract negroes to their meetings and to induce them to become members of their organizations."
4. "Those who are members of labor unions must work for the repeal of all racially discriminatory practices in their organization and endeavor to gain the admission of negroes into them on terms of equality."
5. "They must have specially prepared propaganda showing negroes how they as a group are likely to benefit and improve their social and economic status by any radical change in the present economic system."
6. "Radical negro publications must be supported financially even if subventions are to be made to them."
7. "Radical white speakers must be instructed to try and reach negro audiences while competent paid negro speakers must be kept touring the country spreading radical propaganda."[69]

Cruse distorts Domingo's argument so profoundly that his rendering bears little resemblance to the original. He claims that Domingo said that the Negro was "unready to embrace socialism," which clearly is inaccurate. Cruse accuses Domingo of being "illogical and racially unpatriotic," but he is unconvincing as to how this is so. He claims that Domingo believed that white workers would be "ready very soon, while having serious misgivings about the Negro"—another false statement, inevitably, unsupported by any direct reference to Domingo's text.[70] He goes so far as to write that Domingo's position was that "[t]he American Negro was not even acceptable Socialist human material."[71] There are many more problems with Cruse's discussion of Domingo's essay but I will focus on just two.

First of all, in *The Crisis of the Negro Intellectual* there is a thoroughly mangled quotation from Domingo's document. Cruse writes: "In clarifying the Socialists on Negro traits, Domingo continued:

> Occupational traits are also developed to a marked degree. Being of slave origins and depending on tips to a large degree. . . *tips take on magnified importance in the eyes of the tip receiver. . . .*
>
> All of [the] foregoing influences exerted upon Negroes have tended to make the race docile and full of respect for wealth and authority, while creating an immense gulf between the white and black workers. . . . [72]

The first paragraph, in fact, says something quite different:

> Servants unconsciously imbibe their masters' psychology and so do negroes. Nobody is more intolerant against foreigners than negroes, despite the fact that their lives are safer in the North where so many foreigners reside than in the South where there are so few. Occupational traits are also developed to a marked degree. Being of slave origin and depending on tips to a large degree, *the tipper or those in a position to dole out tips take on magnified importance in the eyes of the tip receiver.*[73]

I have highlighted the key portion of the passage as quoted by Cruse and as it appeared in the original document. While Domingo is making a subtle sociological point about the relation between structural location within— or in this case, with*out*—the labor process, on the one hand, and class consciousness, on the other, Cruse is bent on distorting the passage. He diminishes it to an intellectually trivial but politically hurtful remark about tips.[74] Having set up a straw man, Cruse then proceeds to destroy it. "Did they [West Indians] not come here to the United States," he asks, rhetorically, "and take jobs with tips, and were not most of them glad to get the tips?"—a completely irrelevant question that falls well below the more elevated point that Domingo was making.[75] Once again, Randolph and the *Messenger* magazine had more in common with Domingo than Cruse would wish to accept. Like Domingo, Randolph acknowledged the skewed distribution of black workers within the labor force but went further than Domingo when he claimed that because of their peculiar structural location they are "sometimes compelled to become sycophant and clownish for a favor, a 'tip'."[76]

The second paragraph quoted by Cruse, as indicated in my discussion above, comes after Domingo had examined and outlined the different forces which militate against the development of class consciousness among black workers. Domingo talks of the "subtle control" exercised by Northern capitalists over the education—schools as well as colleges—the churches and newspapers of black people. He also outlines the peculiar occupational profile of the black labor force—the over-concentration in menial, service jobs, as domestic servants, cooks, elevator operators, and so on—and the way in which this class profile affects the development of class conscious- ness. It is this analysis, along with the argument developed in the paragraph quoted above, that constitutes the "all of the foregoing" of the second paragraph quoted by Cruse.[77]

Finally, as far as Cruse is concerned, Domingo was simply "racially unpatriotic." And this can be explained, like so much else, by his "West Indian Nationalist psychology which was reflected also in Moore, Briggs, and Huiswoud." And for good measure, Cruse includes Garvey too, who, according to him, "had some of the same psychology, but expressed it in another way."[78] Cruse goes into one of his many anti-Caribbean tantrums, extrapolating like mad:

> Here we get deeper into the motivational roots of the American Negro vs. West Indian conflict. Domingo's document serves as a key to the understanding of what motivates the West Indian on every level of Negro–white relations—social, economic, political or cultural. It sheds light on the many mysteries of the early American radical trends of 1919 between Negro and white. It reveals the causes behind the American Negro vs. West Indian split in the Communist movement: the jockeying for power; the duplicity; the subservience to whites camouflaged by super-revolutionary militant phraseology; the ambivalent loyalties; the venal group jealousies; the egotistical lust for status and acceptance by the white revolutionary powers both at home and abroad; even the self-hatred hidden behind nationalism that had to turn to alien philosophies for recognition.[79]

But as has happened so often, there is a serious problem with Cruse's argument. For in the Lusk Report, from which he quotes, is a letter that was also seized by the authorities when they raided the Rand School in 1919. Dated May 16, 1919, and written by David P. Berenberg, of the Correspondence Department of the Rand School, it states plainly:

> There is great need for missionary work among all people and especially among colored people. We have here a very active group of comrades—among them Comrades Chandler Owen and Domingo—who warn us that unless we make headway with the negroes, the capitalists may use them in time of a social revolution much as the Czecho-Slovaks are being used in Russia.[80]

Yes, it said Comrade Chandler Owen, yet Cruse does not utter a peep about this. It is difficult to believe that Cruse could have missed this letter referring to Owen, as in note 17 on page 127 of *The Crisis of the Negro Intellectual* he cites Domingo's document as running from pages 1489 to 1511, in the relevant volume of the Lusk Report. The fact is that the letter containing Owen's "warning" about the potentially counter-revolutionary role of Afro-Americans is quoted in full on page 1511, a page explicitly cited by Cruse. (Domingo's document actually ends on page 1510 of the Report, but the letter from Berenberg is reprinted on page 1511.)

As I indicated at the outset, the position articulated by Domingo in the document was one that was commonly accepted on the black left, including the revolutionary socialist black left.[81] Hubert Harrison and W. E. B. Du Bois, for instance, had made the same argument almost a decade before Domingo did.[82] Furthermore, Du Bois, only a few years after Domingo, would say bluntly: "If American socialism cannot stand for the American Negro, the American Negro will not stand for American socialism."[83] More inconvenient for Cruse's argument is the fact that in the pages of the *Messenger* A. Philip Randolph and Chandler Owen had written an editorial that articulated the very same thesis that Domingo had proffered—and, in fact, in a way that Cruse should find even more objectionable than Domingo's. For instance, while Domingo speaks of the Negro as a "*potential* menace" to radicalism, Randolph and Owen entitled their article "The Negro—A Menace to Radicalism." Published around the same time as the seizure of Domingo's document, the editors of the *Messenger* went so far as to write:

> [T]his much the white radicals must learn that, ten million Negro soldiers and scabs will break the backbone of any radical movement. To maintain that the Negro is not ripe is not only fallacious but suicidal folly. Labor cannot afford to ignore any factor which capital does not ignore. Unhappily, the Negro is the most backward part of the working-class in America and the radical Negroes fear, lest he be used savagely to beat down the more radical wing of the working class. Negro soldiers, if ordered, will shoot down Negro workingmen as quickly as they will white workingmen; just as, for instance, white soldiers shot down white workingmen and women at Ludlow, Colorado, or just as white policemen beat up the heads of white girls striking for a living wage. Add to the Negro's obedience to order the factor of race feeling, and one can conceive of a saturnalia of blood that makes one sick at heart.[84]

Like Domingo, they stressed the disinformation fed to ordinary black people through "the press, pulpit and school, with a view to making them fireproof to all liberal and democratic opinions." When one is uninformed of the nature of a movement that person is "disinclined to entertain it," and misinformation concerning the objects and aims of a movement may lead to its active opposition by the misinformed, said Randolph and Owen. Black opposition to radicalism, in general, and Bolshevism, in particular, was being actively cultivated by "big, hand-picked Negro leaders—and the plutocratic interests" of the country. As an example of this, they cited the remarks made by a black minister—"of reputed light and leading"—before a large convention in Savannah, Georgia:

> Bolshevism was begotten in Germany, or that it is of German parentage, or that it was born in Russia, it took its name from a man named Bolsheviki, an insurrectionist or rioter, who raised an army to overthrow the recognized government of Russia. At that time the Government was tottering under the great blows of the German army. Bolsheviki thought that the time was ripe to establish new ideas and a new government that was somewhat after the idea of the Socialist. The definition or meaning of Bolshevism, as may be determined by

research, is analogous to anarchy, the state of society where there is no law or supreme power, a state of lawlessness and general disorder. A condition where human life and property, human rights and justice, all that is noble and great, [is] trampled under the feet of human beasts.[85]

"This," commented the editors of the *Messenger*, "is a mild sample of the intellectual pabulum served up to Negroes on the problems of world moment."

Hence the need, they argued, for more active work among black people. Like Domingo, Randolph and Owen had their "buts," "ifs," and "unlesses." Thus, "unless the Negro worker is unionized and the Negro public educated as to the nature and aims of radical movements, the Negro constitutes a definite menace to radicalism in America." Without entry into the mainstream of industrial labor, locked out by white working-class racism, and faced, on the one hand, with benefactors who are capitalist and, on the other, with lynchers who are workers, the black worker has very little choice: the Negro "is inclined always to choose the side of capital," wrote the editors of the *Messenger*. "Herein," they declared, "lies the menace of the Negro to the movement toward industrial democracy."[86]

The problem for Cruse here is obvious: Chandler Owen (born and brought up in North Carolina) and Asa Philip Randolph (born and brought up in Jacksonville, Florida) were clearly American, not West Indians, yet, by Cruse's schema, only "racially unpatriotic" West Indians, such as Domingo, could make this type of argument.

Cruse introduces the Domingo document in sensational, if confused, terms. Referring to the bitter and damaging debate between Domingo and Owen in 1923 over the anti-Caribbean posture adopted by the *Messenger* in the "Garvey Must Go" campaign, he writes:

As a radical Socialist Afro-Britisher, Domingo personified more than others a deepseated ambivalence toward the American Negro. As one of Richard B. Moore's closet [*sic*] collaborators, it is difficult to discover what prevented Domingo from following Moore into the Communist Party. At any rate, four years before he had aired his sentiments on the West Indian question in his debate with Chandler Owen in the *Messenger*, Domingo had confidentially revealed his attitudes towards the American Negro. In a long document addressed to the Socialist Party leaders (white) of Rand School, . . . Domingo expressed opinions which, had they been submitted to the *Messenger*, would have increased the bitterness already spewed forth.[87]

There are a number of interesting points here. First, as we have seen, Domingo's "confidential" "attitudes towards the American Negro" were also held in common with Randolph and Owen. Second, the impression is given by Cruse that Domingo was engaged in furtive ("confidential") and treasonous intercourse ("long document addressed to the Socialist Party leaders (*white*) of Rand School") with white Socialists—emblematic of his Afro-Britisher "deepseated ambivalence toward the American Negro." Yet as we have seen from Berenberg's letter, Comrade Owen had spoken to the leadership about the Negro Question in the same terms that Comrade Domingo had done. Moreover, Owen and Randolph as well as Domingo were well-known, highly respected and popular figures at the Rand School and they all taught courses there. Indeed, the May–June 1919 issue of the *Messenger* carried a prominent boxed-advertisement of a course of six weekly lectures on the "Economics and Sociology of the Negro Problem" taught by Randolph and Owen at the School.[88] The notion, then, that Domingo, the "racially unpatriotic" West Indian, was sneaking off Downtown, behind the backs of his Afro-American brothers and comrades, to talk, *sotto voce*, against Afro-Americans to white Socialists is fallacious.

In the final sentence of the passage cited, Cruse claims that had Domingo's opinions contained in the document been submitted to the *Messenger*, they "would have increased the bitterness already spewed forth." We have already seen that the views expressed by Domingo were shared by Randolph and Owen. The "bitterness already spewed forth" to which Cruse refers is the argument between Domingo and Owen, in the pages of the *Messenger* in 1923, over the anti-Caribbean tone of the "Garvey Must Go" campaign. But how could this alleged bitterness be "*already* spewed forth" when it occurred four years *after* Domingo's document? It appears that Cruse is desperately trying to read back into the past—to 1919—the disagreement—which actually took place in 1923—between the editors of the *Messenger* and Domingo. There is not a shred of evidence to support the idea that there was tension, let alone bitter disagreement, between Domingo and the *Messenger* prior to 1923. In fact, up to the break of 1923, Randolph and Owen were both very close friends and not just comrades of Domingo's. Even before Domingo formally broke with Garvey's *Negro World* and became a Contributing Editor of the *Messenger* in 1919, Randolph and Owen had publicly expressed their admiration for him. In the July 1919 *Messenger*, for instance, under an editorial entitled "Suggestions for Good Reading," Domingo's column in the *Negro World* was singled out for special praise. It was described as "the only scholarly and scientific editorial column to be found in any Negro newspaper at present." And Domingo was said to be "a Negro scholar who writes fine English, knows history and economics and has the courage to say just what he thinks." This might have been the last straw for Garvey, for in that very month, as we have seen, he fired Domingo from the *Negro World* for carrying socialist propaganda in his paper. Domingo was immediately snapped up by the *Messenger* magazine, where he formally became a Contributing Editor.[89] He was one of the most influential theoreticians of the New Negro movement, authoring some of its most cogent, strategic, and programmatic articles.[90] Domingo's contribution to New Negro thought is still to be properly weighed.

Randolph had an abiding admiration for Domingo and repeatedly referred to the latter's brilliance. Indeed, this is how he chiefly remembered

Domingo five decades later: "a very brilliant mind", "a brilliant lad", "a brilliant chap", "very fine mind", are the descriptions he applied to his former comrade.[91] Randolph especially admired Domingo's "penetrating and logical mind and [his] thoroughgoing grasp of Marxism."[92] Of the Harlem radicals, only Hubert Harrison ranked higher than Domingo in Randolph's estimation.[93] Contrary to Harold Cruse's depiction of him, Randolph described Domingo as one "free from any personal antagonism against any individual, especially among Negroes." Randolph also pointed out that "Chandler liked him [Domingo] and he liked Chandler." Randolph elaborated in an interview upon the connection between these two powerful polemicists of the twenties: "Chandler liked his writing and he and Chandler were great friends. He too liked Chandler's ruthless exposure of things, you know, with a view to awakening people's interest for or against a question." By then an old man in his eighties, Randolph fondly remembered the heady days of his youth shared with Domingo in Harlem: "[W]e had, oh, some splendid recreational life, where we'd talk about everything. And what was going to happen—insofar as the future of the black people and so forth was concerned, and the Jews, and all of the oppressed people of the world."[94]

Contrary to Cruse's repeated notion of a West Indian versus American Negro split at the *Messenger* (which he dates as early as 1919), the fact is that in 1923 Domingo was the only Caribbean person who severed connections with the magazine.[95] Caribbeans such as Frank Crosswaith continued to write for it; so did Eric Walrond and, most prodigiously, J. A. Rogers, from Jamaica, who continued to make his distinguished contribution.

Cruse's portrait of Domingo as a kind of Caribbean rogue elephant is, thus, belied by the historical evidence. Unsupported also is the rather flippant remark that "Socialist revolutionaries like Domingo did not fight British colonialism in the islands."[96] As it happens, Domingo, as we have seen, was an official (as was Marcus Garvey) of Jamaica's first nationalist organization—the National Club—before he migrated to the United States in 1910, aged twenty-one.

Not only are Cruse's analysis and interpretation highly problematic, it is difficult, as shown, to trust his presentation of "evidence." This is a point Cruse's critics have repeatedly emphasized in relation to one aspect or another of his book. Let me give another example of Cruse bending facts to serve an anti-Caribbean bias. The account presented in *The Crisis of the Negro Intellectual* claims major political differences between two black Communists, Cyril Briggs and Otto Hall, concerning tactics during a 1929 strike in North Carolina. For Cruse, the alleged differences were not between two individuals, but between two antagonistic camps of the African diaspora, with the Caribbean represented by Briggs and Afro-America by Hall. Indeed, Cruse perceives even greater significance. The incident, he says, "brought forth the first theoretical polemic between the American Negro and West Indian factions within the Communist Party over the 'correct' interpretation of the Negro Question."[97] So what actually happened?

In the summer of 1929, the Communist Party-led National Textile Workers Union was in the midst of waging a bitter strike in the textile mills of Gastonia and Bessemer City, North Carolina. At Bessemer City, where black workers had come out on strike with white workers, there occurred what Cyril Briggs called "a most shameful retreat before white chauvinism" on the part of white comrades. The retreat went so far that the organizers of the strike permitted a "Jim-Crow wire to be drawn across the hall, separating the Negro strikers from the whites." Such practices were clearly against Party policy, and in flagrant violation of the resolution recently passed by the Communist International on the Negro question in the United States. Bessemer City, said Briggs, was the worst, but not the only, example of the Party's and Comintern's decisions on the Negro not being taken "seriously to heart" by white comrades who had not energetically set about to combat white chauvinism. Briggs was indignant when he heard that black comrades, including Otto Hall, who had been sent by the Central Committee to North Carolina, made concessions to the racists. But Briggs was apparently misinformed when he reported that Hall had "permitted himself to be stampeded" into proposing that the black textile workers be organized into the American Negro Labor Congress, thus obviating the need for direct, cross-racial contact.[98] For in the July issue of *The Communist*, the one immediately following Briggs's report, Hall explained that

> I did not make the motion to organize the Negro workers into the A. N. L. C. What I did propose was to organize those workers who could not be organized into the N. T. W. U. into the Labor Congress, that is those Negro workers who were not working in the textile industry. This is quite a different thing.[99]

Cruse, in his book, makes no mention of the Jim Crow wire incident that elicited Briggs's cry of indignation. To him, this is just another example of (West Indian) integrationism versus (Afro-American) separatism. And despite the fact that Hall wrote in to *The Communist* clarifying his position and making it clear that Briggs and he were not in disagreement, Cruse is not satisfied. Compare what Hall said (quoted above) to what Cruse reports he said. This is Cruse:

> Hall corrected Briggs in the July issue of *The Communist*, stating that he had proposed that the Negro textile workers be organized into the American Negro Labor Congress (a separate group, organized by the Communists themselves in 1925 for the purpose of bringing Negroes into the labor movement). From any practical point of view, including that of the Communists, Otto Hall's tactic was more intelligent than Briggs's.[100]

Hall, in clear language, made it plain that he had proposed the organization of black workers "who were *not working in the textile industry*" by recruiting them into the American Negro Labor Congress. (This is something that Briggs had no problem with, and was in keeping with Party policy.) Cruse, deliberately or inadvertently, distorts Hall's argument and misleads his readers when he claims that Otto Hall "proposed that the *Negro textile workers* be organized into the American Negro Labor Congress."[101] Needless to say, there were no "American Negro" versus "West Indian" factions in the Party over the Negro Question, or anything else, for that matter. And although Cruse emphasizes the polemic between Harry Haywood and Otto Huiswoud on the Comintern's resolution on self-determination for the Black Belt, differences among the black comrades within the Party did not take the form of a West Indian versus Afro-American split. Cyril Briggs and Richard B. Moore embraced the Comintern's resolution and welcomed the leverage it gave them to tackle "white chauvinism" within the Party. In contrast, Afro-Americans Otto Hall and James Ford opposed the resolution when it was being formulated in Moscow. Haywood reveals in his autobiography the stormy rows he had with Hall, his older brother, and Ford in Moscow's corridors of power in 1928.[102] Haywood never trusted Ford on the Negro question and had his closest ally in the Party in Cyril Briggs who shared his nationalist tendencies. In the 1950s and 1960s, right up to Briggs's death in 1966, the two old Communists had animated discussions about the Negro question and self-determination for the black belt. They stuck to the old line—even though at times they seemed overwhelmed by their own questioning. "With Negro nationalism even then on the increase, as witness the Garvey movement, why did our Negro nation analysis have such little appeal to the Negro people?" Briggs asked Haywood in a 1962 letter. "As you know, many of the thousands who passed through the Party did not fully understand or accept that analysis."[103] In short, the complexity of the actual positions adopted by black protagonists within the Party on the Negro Question are flattened out in Cruse's analysis to one of antagonism between West Indians and Afro-Americans—a far cry from the real situation that existed.

There is another problem with Cruse's depiction of Caribbeans. He speaks of their "subservience to whites camouflaged by super-revolutionary phraseology," yet all the evidence suggests that Caribbeans were among the most outspoken members of the Communist Party, including on racism and on the "Negro Question."[104] Certainly the white leadership of the Party did not regard Briggs, Moore, and Huiswoud as subservient. On the contrary, they felt the three were far too independent-minded and insubordinate, rather like Claude McKay, whom the Party never forgave for speaking out against racism on the American left at the Fourth Comintern Congress in 1922. A decade earlier, another Caribbean, Hubert Harrison, was also regarded to be insubordinate by the leadership of the Socialist Party, many of whom had broken away to form the Communist Party in 1919.

*

A few examples will suffice to show the falsehood of Cruse's charge of subservience. Let us begin with Cyril Briggs. "The Negro Question in the Southern Textile Strikes," and "Further Notes on the Negro Question in the Southern Textile Strikes" both articles written by Briggs and explicitly referred to by Cruse, are clearly not the work of a Red Uncle Tom.[105] Indeed, they constitute two of the most critical articles on the Party's handling of the Negro Question ever published within an organ of the Communist Party of the United States. In his July 1929 article, Briggs even accused *The Communist* of racism in the way in which the editor interfered with his contribution the month before. Although the journal had the title of his article, "The Negro Question in the Southern Textile Strikes," properly captioned at the beginning, Briggs pointed out that the title was made to read in the page heads as "The Negro *Problem*, etc." "And worse yet," he disclosed, "an unauthorized and wholly impermissible change was made in a sentence of the article in which the words 'the Negro Question in the South' were changed to read '*Our* Negro *Problem* in the South'." Embarrased by this, the editor defensively intervened with a footnote stating: "The change to which Comrage Briggs refers as well as the wrong page captions were both due to typographical and technical reasons; but of course Comrade Briggs's remarks are fully justified."[106] But Briggs was not finished with the comrades:

> It should be crystal clear to any Communist who gives this question the serious consideration it deserves that the Communist Party can have no Negro *problem*, South or North. Our problem is rather a problem of white chauvinism among the working class and in the very ranks of the Communist Party itself.
>
> Communists must be careful not to fall into the error of accepting the capitalist estimation of the Negro as a problem. Even viewing the country as a whole the correct Communist viewpoint would be that there is at worst a race problem, not a Negro problem. And certainly *our problem is not what to do with the Negro*, but rather how to overcome the capitalist ideology of race separation and racial hatred in order that we may, as the Party equally of the Negro and white workers, achieve complete working-class unity in the furtherance of our struggle for the overthrow of capitalism.[107]

Thus we have the words of Cyril Briggs, the West Indian subservient. Indeed, his subservience was so notorious that it reached Comintern officials in Moscow that he was: "Severely censured and warned by Party in March 1936 for publishing serious implications against Party leadership in Harlem and for taking a subjective attitude of unprincipled hostility toward a party member (Comrade Ford); instead of the necessary closest cooperation with the Party leadership in Harlem in Negro work worked separately and at crosspurposes."[108]

Cruse conveniently forgot to mention that when the Party wanted to re-establish its rigid orthodoxy in 1933 in Harlem, to rein in what it regarded as black nationalist tendencies, it removed Cyril Briggs and Richard B. Moore from key positions and placed local control in the hands of a more accommodating member of the Party, James Ford, an Afro-American from

Chicago. Briggs and Moore had had more than fifteen years each of revolutionary activity in Harlem. Ford, who had no local experience, along with a number of black and white members, had been parachuted into Harlem to take over from the more independent-minded locals.[109] Partly because of the way in which he was brought into Harlem by the Party, and partly because of his subsequent behavior, Ford, it appears, never had the respect or the support of rank and file members in Harlem, let alone that of the more experienced and senior members whom he was brought in to marginalize, subdue, and control. Harry Haywood, despite a temporary alliance with Ford when he was brought to Harlem, complains bitterly in his autobiography against Ford. Claude McKay was disgusted with Ford's disrespectful denunciation of Grace Campbell from a public platform because she proposed the creation of black co-operatives in Harlem. Manning Johnson, another Afro-American member of the Party in the 1930s, talked of Ford with scorn and anger: "a fellow who couldn't pour water out of a boot with instructions on the heel." Ford, whom he described as having been "set up" by the Party as "the leader of the Negroes," was considered by all the black members as "an incompetent, a 'Charlie McCarthy,'" because he had no ability for leadership.

> He had never participated in any of the so-called mass programs of the Negroes. He didn't rise, as a result of activities of Negroes, from the ranks, and was never considered by them as a leader.
> He was mechanically put into a position of responsibility by the Communist Party, and that is the type of person the Communists want, a person who will follow blindly whatever they tell him.
> James W. Ford never wrote a speech to my knowledge the whole time that he was titular head of the Negro movement in the party. Most of his speeches were written for him and he read them. Where important issues arose involving problems of the Negro, when James W. Ford was asked to take a stand or a position he never did, he would have to consult Browder or Jack Stachel or some of the white leaders, and as a result of that we characterized him as an 'Uncle Tom.' To us his name was synonymous with everything we despise and detest. Some of us were outspoken in our criticism of him, and as a result some of us were called in by the disciplinary commission of the Communist Party.

These are very harsh words, and even though they were uttered as testimony before the notorious Committee on Un-American Activities, they clearly issued from deep and intense, genuine feeling. I doubt that Johnson felt that the Committee would punish Ford because, in his eyes, Ford betrayed the Negroes.[110] Despite his apparently black nationalist stance, and his unrelenting attack upon the Communist Party, there is, strangely, not a word of censure, or even a note of reproach, against Ford in Cruse's book.

Significantly, when both Briggs and Moore were expelled in the early 1940s, they were accused of "Negro nationalist way of thinking." Although the Party has always been reticent to explain Moore's expulsion, one FBI informant correctly reported at the time from within the Party that Moore was "an independent thinker and difficult for leaders to dictate to."[111] In 1977, over thirty years after Moore's expulsion, Abner Berry, who had been a Party organizer in Harlem in the 1940s, explained to an interviewer what happened:

> [Moore] was expelled from the Party, and at that expulsion, I was the prosecutor. I think now wrongly, but at that time I was working [for] the Party. And what he had done was related to a problem that still exists. The problem was whether or not the white labor unions would fight for jobs for Negroes. Now some said, "If you're fighting for jobs for Negroes, you can't stop short of a white worker being fired." Some said, "No, you have to fight for jobs for Negroes and for the white worker's job at the same time." Moore said, "We're just fighting for jobs for Negroes, and we can't be concerned whether a white worker is fired. We're just fighting for this job, right here." Well for that, we chased him out of the Party. The Party had already decided that we would fight for the right of Negroes for jobs, but would guarantee that white workers would not be fired. . . . It [Moore's] was a consistent approach. His approach, by the way was not incorrect. I became the prosecutor and he was expelled for taking a divisive stand. . . . Later, I was very remorseful.[112]

From 1933 right up to his expulsion Moore had had increasing difficulty with Ford and the Party leadership over the jobs campaigns in Harlem; his ouster was the culmination of this running battle.[113]

On one occasion, years later, Moore claimed that the expulsion was the greatest thing the Party ever did for him.[114] But it must have hurt at the time he was thrown out. He had lived the life of a proud member of the Communist Party. For almost twenty years he had selflessly devoted his time, intellect, and energy in the struggle for a better society, only to be thrown out by those whom he viewed as opportunists, negligent in their responsibility to the most oppressed sector of the working class, under the emergency conditions of Depression and war.[115] A decade earlier, in his plea for compassion for August Yokinen, a Harlem-based Finnish member of the Party accused of racism, Moore had said: "We must remember that a verdict of expulsion in disgrace from the Communist Party is considered by a class-conscious worker as worse than death at the hands of the bourgeois oppressors. As for myself, I would rather have my head severed from my body by the capitalist lynchers than to be expelled from the Communist International."[116] Despite his increasing differences with the Party in the 1930s, it is unlikely that Moore's views on expulsion had altered to any significant degree. But although the Party gave every sign of welcoming his return—indeed, Harry Haywood claimed the Party explicitly offered to reinstate his membership—Moore, unlike Briggs, never attempted to rejoin, and never rejoined.[117]

Like Moore and Briggs, Otto Huiswoud showed no sign of the "subservience to whites" talked of by Cruse. For his independent and outspoken dissent from the 1928 and 1930 Communist International line of self-determination for the Black Belt in the United States, Huiswoud was withdrawn from Party work and given "new assignments" in 1931 by the Comintern in Moscow and elsewhere in Europe. He was, in effect, banished from the United States, returning in 1939 only to leave again, and for the last time, in 1941.[118]

Conclusion

One is led inexorably to the conclusion that Harold Cruse's portrait of Caribbean migrants in the United States in the early twentieth century is at best misconceived and unreliable. Whatever its merits in other areas, *The Crisis of the Negro Intellectual*, perhaps more than any other text on the subject, has obfuscated and distorted perceptions of the presence and role of Caribbean migrants in America. *The Crisis of the Negro Intellectual* deserves rebuttal because it still is and has been widely read, and has been extraordinarily influential over the last thirty years, and, as I have endeavored to show, it has serious weaknesses of which most readers would not ordinarily be aware.[119] The effort expended here in criticizing the book, in the end, has little to do with Cruse and far more to do with his readers past, present and future. And it is with that in my mind that I have tried to indicate what I regard as some of the major weaknesses of *The Crisis of the Negro Intellectual*.

It is a fact—and let me make my position absolutely clear here: it is a disgusting, deplorable, shameful, politically retrograde fact—that Caribbean migrants often behaved in an arrogant and disdainful manner toward Afro-Americans.[120] (It is equally true that Caribbeans were quite often treated with the same kind of contempt by Afro-Americans. To the Afro-American's taunt of "monkey-chaser," came the Afro-Caribbean's retort of "coon." Foolishness affected the behavior of both groups, especially in New York City.) Cruse is right when he maintains, as others have pointed out before him, that tension existed between the two groups.[121] But reprehensible behavior on the part of some of the migrants is not legitimate grounds for his anti-Caribbean and politically counter-productive *blitzkrieg*.[122] The genuine and considerable contribution made by Caribbeans is never acknowledged. Cruse sees only discord between the factions of the African diaspora, never noticing the co-operation, friendship, and the genuine warmth and fellowship that also existed. And in his book there is no conceptual space or political room for the type of personal relations Claude McKay had with Afro-Americans. "In America I have always preferred the American Negroes to the West Indians who on all occasions display too much 'class' spirit for my liking," disclosed McKay in 1932, writing from Morocco to a friend, "and when I was there I lived with American in preference to West Indian families. ... [W]hen I did go to work as a menial I found excellent comrades [among Afro-Americans]— strangely nearly all my fights were with West Indians."[123]

As far as Cruse is concerned, Hubert Harrison, Richard B. Moore, W. A. Domingo, Marcus Garvey, Amy Jacques Garvey, J. A. Rogers, Frank Crosswaith, Cyril Briggs, Grace Campbell, Claude McKay, C. L. R. James, Claudia Jones, and all the other Caribbean radicals—socialists and black nationalists alike—were animated and propelled into action by the basest of motives, unrelieved by any unalloyed qualities. Indeed, to Cruse, Caribbean radicalism in America was simply another manifestation of an obsessive quest on the part of the migrants to distance themselves from their Afro-American brothers and sisters. The Caribbean radical's "identi-fication with Africa," says Cruse, "like the West Indian's militant stand on racial discrimination, is motivated more by a psychology of non-identifica-tion with the American Negro status and accommodation to American white bourgeois values, than with other essentials of the American Negro struggle." Similarly, Richard B. Moore's preference in the late 1950s for "Afro-American" over "Negro" is dismissed as "another way of expressing non-identification with the American Negro qua American Negro and his social status in America."[124]

There was only muted reaction to Cruse's book from some of the Caribbean radicals of the 1920s and 1930s who survived beyond 1967, the year *The Crisis of the Negro Intellectual* was published. Cyril Briggs had died in 1966. W. A. Domingo had been incapacitated by a stroke in 1964 from which he never recovered; he died in 1968. Richard B. Moore, seventy-four years old at the time, refrained from publicly responding to the book, but he observed, in a letter to a friend:

> Cruse sought to solve his own crisis by purveying a "Crisis of Negro Intellec-tuals." When he condemns and decries every one but himself, it becomes apparent to thinkers that he seeks deliberately to derogate everyone else in order thereby himself to shine. What he has written about me is mainly false; reflection soon shows that he is guessing and surmising and has no basic knowledge of what he projects, for instance, he states that he really doesn't know whether I *left* or was *expelled* from the Communist party. As a matter of fact, he has no proof that I ever joined or became "bitter" about any experience with this party.

Moore felt that it was beneath his dignity to respond to Cruse. "[I]t is unnecessary to engage in unseemly polemics with such a person," he scornfully wrote.[125] Guyanese pan-Africanist Ras Makonnen, who lived in the United States in the late 1920s and early 1930s, especially criticized the nativism of the book and its rather shallow argument about Caribbean conservatism at home and radicalism abroad.[126] Asked about the book in a 1972 interview, C. L. R. James stated, with characteristic bluntness, "I don't think too much of it. My objection to Cruse's book is that he doesn't like West Indians, he doesn't like Jews, he doesn't like too many people. There is," said James, "too much subjective response to events in the book"—which sums up, in a nutshell, the key weakness of *The Crisis of the Negro Intellectual*.[127]

Notes

Prologue

1. By "radicalism" or "radical politics," in this context, I mean the challenging of the status quo either on the basis of social class, race (or ethnicity), or a combination of the two. By "radicals," therefore, I mean avowed anti-capitalists ("Socialists," "Communists," adherents and practitioners of other variants of Marxism, and non-Marxist anti-capitalists such as anarcho-syndicalists) as well as adherents of varieties of Black Nationalism (emigrationists, pan-Africanists, Garveyites, black statehood supporters, or a combination of these). Included here, too, are those who have attempted to organically conjoin Marxism and Black Nationalism. A classic example of this was the early African Blood Brotherhood, about which more will be said later. Caribbean migrants are those from the archipelago stretching from the Bahamas in the north to Trinidad in the south. The category also includes those from the continental enclaves of Belize (formerly British Honduras) and the three Guianas: Dutch Guiana (now Suriname), British Guiana (now Guyana), and French Guiana, which remains a *de facto* colony of France. I prefer the word "Caribbean" to "West Indies" and "West Indian" for the region and its people, and it is used accordingly.

2. A. Philip Randolph quoted in Jervis Anderson, *A. Philip Randolph: A Biography* (Berkeley: University of California Press 1986), p. 80.

3. A significant number of Afro-Americans with direct Caribbean roots have been involved in radical and civil rights struggles in the United States. W. E. B. Du Bois's grandfather was from the Bahamas, and his father was born in Haiti. James Weldon Johnson's mother was from Nassau, the Bahamas. His father, an Afro-American from Virginia, along with his mother, lived in Nassau for the first eight years of their marriage. Johnson himself was born within less than two years of his parents' having finally returned to the United States. His elder sister, who died in childhood, was born in Nassau. William Patterson's father was a Vincentian who went to San Francisco, where he met Patterson's Virginian mother. Malcolm X's mother was a migrant from Grenada. And Louis Farrakhan's father was born in Jamaica and his mother in St Kitts. Shirley Chisholm, the first black woman elected to the United States Congress, was born in Brooklyn of Barbadian parents. She spent almost six years of her early childhood in Barbados with her grandmother before returning to Brooklyn to join her parents. Throughout her political career she was known as "fighting Shirley" for the best of reasons. Similarly, Harry Belafonte, born in Harlem (Jamaican mother, Martinican father), lived in Jamaica, between the ages of nine and thirteen, before returning to New York with his mother. Du Bois, Johnson, Patterson and Malcolm X all celebrated their Caribbean roots. For Du Bois, see his autobiographical volumes, *Darkwater: Voices from Within the Veil* (1920; New York: Schocken Books 1969), *Dusk of Dawn: An Essay Toward an Autobiography of a Race Concept* (1940; New Brunswick: Transaction publishers 1984), and *The Autobiography of W. E. B. Du Bois: a Soliloquy on Viewing My Life from the Last Decade of Its First Century* (New York: International Publishers 1968); For James Weldon Johnson, see his autobiography, *Along This Way* (1933; Harmondsworth: Penguin Books 1990); for William Patterson, see his autobiography, *The Man Who Cried Genocide* (New York: International Publishers 1971); for Malcolm X, see *The Autobiography of Malcolm X* (1965; Harmondsworth: Penguin Books 1968). Jan Carew's *Ghosts in Our Blood: With Malcolm X in Africa, England, and the Caribbean* (Chicago: Lawrence Hill Books 1994) has provided the most detail about Malcolm's parents and their influence upon his formation. Louis Farrakhan talks about his Caribbean background in Henry Louis Gates, "Farrakhan Speaks: A Conversation with Louis Farrakhan," *Transition*, vol. 6, no. 2, Summer 1996; see also Arthur J. Magida, *Prophet of Rage: A Life of Louis Farrakhan and his Nation* (New York: Basic Books 1996); and Mattias Gardell, *In the Name of Elijah Muhammad: Louis Farrakhan and the Nation of Islam*

(Durham: Duke University Press 1996), esp. pp. 119–22: for Chisholm, see her *Unbought and Unbossed* (Boston: Houghton Mifflin Company 1970); for Belafonte, see Genia Fogelson, *Belafonte* (Los Angeles: Holloway House Publishing Co. 1980). Many others who have been similarly engaged in one degree or another with the black struggle in the United States were born in the Caribbean or have at least one parent from the region. Among these are: Constance Baker Motley, St Clair Drake, Kenneth B. Clark, Maida Springer Kemp, Ewart Guinier (Lani Guinier's father), Margaret Walker, Rosa Guy, Audre Lorde, Paule Marshall, Cicely Tyson, Sidney Poitier, Robert Moses, Vincent Harding, Amiri Baraka, Michelle Wallace, and Kareem Abdul-Jabbar.

4. Editorial, "Credit is Due the West Indian," *Favorite Magazine*, vol. iii (December 1919), pp. 209–10.

5. *Crisis*, Sept. 1920, p. 215.

6. W. E. B. Du Bois to W. A. Domingo, January 18, 1923; in Herbert Aptheker, ed., *The Correspondence of W.E.B. Du Bois*, vol. 1, Selections, 1877–1934 (Amherst: University of Massachusetts Press 1973), p. 263.

7. *Messenger*, April 1922, p. 387.

8. W. A. Domingo, "Gift of the Black Tropics," in Alain Locke, ed., *The New Negro: An Interpretation* (New York: Albert and Charles Boni 1925), p. 346. In 1919 Domingo had noted that "The few negroes who have become radicals [socialists] have been in many cases foreigners." See Senate of the State of New York, Report of the Joint Legislative Committee Investigating Seditious Activities, *Revolutionary Radicalism: Its History, Purpose and Tactics With an Exposition and Discussion of the Steps Being Taken and Required to Curb It*, Apr. 24, 1920, Part I: *Revolutionary and Subversive Movements Abroad and at Home*, vol. 2 (Albany: J. B. Lyon Company Printers 1920), pp. 1507–8.

9. Kelly Miller, "After Marcus Garvey—What of the Negro?" *Contemporary Review*, vol. cxxxi, April 1927, p. 494.

10. Kelly Miller in his column, "Watchtower," *New York Amsterdam News*, Sept. 15, 1934, p. 8, my emphasis; cf. Claude McKay, *Harlem: Negro Metropolis* (New York: E. P. Dutton and Co. 1940), p. 252; and Roi Ottley, *"New World A-Coming": Inside Black America* (1943; New York: Arno Press and the New York Times 1968), p. 47. That a black person should use the term "over-educated" in this way ought not to go unremarked. "Over-education" is a classical colonial and racist adjective applied to "uppity natives" and "uppity niggers". "Over-education" was what the young E. Franklin Frazier, the black sociologist, was accused of by the *Atlanta Independent*, the *Atlanta Constitution*, and the good white citizens of Atlanta as they drove him from Atlanta University in 1927 for writing an article criticizing the racist South. See Anthony M. Platt, *E. Franklin Frazier Reconsidered*, (New Brunswick: Rutgers University Press 1991), pp. 83–4.

11. There are, however, three unpublished but substantial doctoral dissertations that treat various aspects of the subject, albeit with uneven degrees of success: Keith Henry, "The Place of the Culture of Migrant Commonwealth Afro-West Indians in the Political Life of Black New York in the Period Circa 1918 to Circa 1966" (University of Toronto 1973); Dennis Forsythe, "West Indian Radicalism Abroad" (McGill University 1974); and Calvin Holder, "West Indian Immigration in New York City, 1900–1952: A Study in Acculturation," (Harvard University 1976).

12. Ira Reid, *The Negro Immigrant: His Background, Characteristics and Social Adjustment, 1899–1937* (New York: Columbia University Press 1939), p. 221; Ottley, *"New World A-Coming"*, p. 47; Roi Ottley and William J. Weatherby, eds, *The Negro in New York: An Informal Social History* (New York: New York Public Library and Oceana Publications 1967), pp. 191–2; see also Barrington Dunbar, "Factors in the Cultural Backgrounds of the American Southern Negro and the British West Indian Negro that Condition their Adjustments in Harlem" (MA thesis, Columbia University 1935), chap. IV, pp. 26 and 28 (NB: pagination begins anew at the beginning of each chapter of this text); Harry Robinson, "The Negro Immigrant in New York" [June 26, 1939] pp. 14–15, Writers' Program, Federal Writers' Project, "The Negro of New York," Reel 3, New York Public Library, Schomburg Center for Research in Black Culture; Leo Nemiroff, "Radicalism Among the Negroes of New York," [July 31, 1939] p. 10, Writers' Program, ibid., Reel 5; Wallace Thurman, *Negro Life in New York's Harlem* (Girard, Kansas: Haldeman-Julius Publications 1928), pp. 18–20; article on Harlem by William Jourdan Rapp and Wallace Thurman, New York *World*, March 3, 1929, clipping in the L. S. Alexander Gumby Collection of Negroiana, Scrapbook 128, Rare Book and Manuscript Library, Columbia University; "The Reminiscences of George Schuyler,"

New York 1960, Oral History Office, Columbia University 1962, p. 73; idem, *Black and Conservative: The Autobiography of George Schuyler*, (New Rochelle, New York: Arlington House 1966), pp. 120–1, 145; Oscar Handlin, *The Newcomers: Negroes and Puerto Ricans in a Changing Metropolis*, (Cambridge Mass.: Harvard University Press 1959), p. 71.

13. Reports by agent P-138, "Re: Negro Activities," March 2, 1921, and June 14, 1921; Records of the Federal Bureau of Investigation, Record Group 65 (hereafter referred to as RG 65), United States National Archives, Washington DC, (hereafter referred to as NA), file BS 202–600–667; emphasis in original. This description of the radicals is repeated *ad nauseam* in this file, which covers radical political activity on the part of black people during the 1920s in remarkable detail. The pre-eminence of Caribbeans in the African Blood Brotherhood is also noted in the FBI file on the Brotherhood: NA, RG 65, file BS 202–600–2031. See also A. Mitchell Palmer, *Letter From the Attorney General Transmitting in Response to a Senate Resolution October 17, 1919, A Report on the Activities of the Bureau of Investigation of the Department of Justice against Persons Advising anarchy, Sedition, and the forcible Overthrow of the Government* (Washington, DC: Government Printing Office 1919), pp. 161–87; and *Revolutionary Radicalism*, pp. 1476–520. (In 1935 the Bureau of Investigation of the Dept. of Justice became the FBI.) "P-138," who played a major role in intelligence gathering for the Department of Justice in the early 1920s, is believed to be Herbert S. Boulin, a Jamaican immigrant who came to the United States at the turn of the century. Boulin had publicly expressed his anti-Garvey and anti-radical views as early as October 1916 in the *Jamaica Times*. See Robert Hill, ed., *The Marcus Garvey and Universal Negro Improvement Association Papers* (hereafter referred to as *Garvey Papers*), (Berkeley: University of California Press 1983–), vol. i., pp. 196–7, and vol. ii, p. 541, n. 3.

14. Robert Hill, "Introduction—Racial and Radical: Cyril V. Briggs *The Crusader* Magazine, and the African Blood Brotherhood, 1918–1922" (hereafter referred to as "Introduction"), *The Crusader*, edited by Cyril V. Briggs [a facsimile of the periodical edited with a new Introduction], vol. i (New York: Garland Publishing 1987), p. ix.

15. Cited in Stephen Fox, *The Guardian of Boston: William Monroe Trotter* (New York: Atheneum 1970), p. 231.

16. Eric Walrond, "The New Negro Faces America," *Current History*, vol. 17, no. 5, February 1923, p. 787; emphasis added.

17. Domingo, "Gift of the Black Tropics," p. 349.

18. George Shepperson and St. Clair Drake, "The Fifth Pan-African Conference, 1954 and the All People's Congress, 1958," *Contributions in Black Studies: A Journal of African and Afro-American Studies*, no. 8, 1986–87, p. 57.

19. *Messenger*, January 1923, p. 561; Reid, *Negro Immigrant*, p. 179.

20. *New York Age*, August 16, 1924.

21. Langston Hughes, "Brothers," *Crisis*, February 1924, p. 160. The tension between Afro-Americans and Afro-Caribbeans in the United States has been analyzed in a number of places and need not detain us here: Thurman, *Negro Life*, pp. 18–19; Hubert Harrison, *Pittsburgh Courier*, January 29, 1927; Reid, *The Negro Immigrant* esp. pp. 107–24; Harry Robinson, "The Negro Immigrant;" McKay, *Harlem*, pp. 132–5; Ottley, *"New World A-Coming,"* pp. 45–6; Ottley and Weatherby, eds, *The Negro in New York*, pp. 190–4; Lennox Raphael, "West Indians and Afro-Americans," *Freedomways*, vol. 4, no. 3, Summer 1964, pp. 438–45; Orde Coombs, "West Indians in New York: Moving Beyond the Limbo Pole," *New York Magazine*, July 13, 1970, pp. 28–32; idem, "On Being West Indian in New York," in Floyd B. Barbour, ed., *The Black Seventies* (Boston: Porter Sargent Publisher 1970); Gilbert Osofsky, *Harlem: The Making of a Ghetto—Negro New York, 1890–1930* (New York: Harper and Row, 2nd edn., 1971), pp. 131–5; Theodore Vincent, *Black Power and the Garvey Movement* (Berkeley: Ramparts press 1972), pp. 212–14; Theodore Kornweibel, *No Crystal Stair: Black Life and the "Messenger," 1917–1928* (Westport: Greenwood Press 1975), pp. 132–75; David J. Hellwig, "Black Meets Black: Afro-American Reactions to West Indian Immigrants in the 1920s," *South Atlantic Quarterly*, vol. 77, no. 2, Spring 1978, pp. 206–24; John C. Walter, "West Indian Immigrants: Those Arrogant Bastards," *Contributions in Black Studies*, no. 5, 1981–82; *Garvey Papers*, vol. V, pp. 801–2, n. 14, and 803–4; there is also Harold Cruse's polemic, *The Crisis of the Negro Intellectual: From Its Origins to the Present* (New York: William Morrow & Co. 1967), esp. pp. 115–46, 253–66, 420–48 which is at once entertaining, sad, and thoroughly unreliable. For a good index of the deep trough into which this relationship between Afro-Americans and Afro-Caribbeans had

entered—even on the black left—in the early 1920s, see the debate between W. A. Domingo and Chandler Owen in the *Messenger*, March 1923, pp. 639–45; cf. Cruse's distorted rendering of the exchange in Cruse, *The Crisis of the Negro Intellectual*, pp. 120ff.

22. See McKay's sober discussion of the relationship between Afro-Americans and Afro-Caribbeans in *Harlem*, pp. 132–5; Claude McKay to Nancy Cunard, August 20, 1932; Nancy Cunard Collection, Harry Ransom Humanities Research Center, University of Texas at Austin.

23. Cited in Du Bois, "The Rise of the West Indian," p. 215.

24. Cited in Vincent, *Black Power and the Garvey Movement*, pp. 213–14.

25. Reid, *The Negro Immigrant*; Dennis Forsythe, "West Indian Radicalism in America: An Assessment of Ideologies," in Frances Henry, ed., *Ethnicity in the Americas* (The Hague: Mouton Publishers 1976); and Keith S. Henry, "Caribbean Migrants in New York: The Passage from Political Quiescence to Radicalism," *Afro-Americans in New York Life and History*, vol. 2, no. 2, July 1978.

26. There were relatively few migrants, mainly Haitians, from the French-speaking Caribbean. Significantly, their response to American society was similar to that of migrants from the rest of the non-Hispanic Caribbean; many were, for instance, active in the Garvey movement. Migration from the Dominican Republic to the United States is largely a phenomenon of the last four decades or so, not of the early twentieth century.

27. Even more astonishing is that many claim to study the African diaspora without so much as a pretence of knowing anything about black people in Brazil. The fact that Brazil has by far the largest contingent of the diaspora in the New World—some say, not without good reason, it is the largest black nation outside of Nigeria—does not seem to matter; ignorance of the black Brazilian experience is, apparently, not sufficient grounds to attentuate the extravagant claims made.

28. See especially, Nathan Glazer, *The Social Basis of American Communism* (New York: Harcourt, Brace and World, Inc. 1961), chap. 2; Sally Miller, *The Radical Immigrant* (New York: Twayne Publishers, Inc. 1974); Paul Buhle, *Marxism in the United States: Remapping the History of the American Left*, rev. ed. (London: Verso 1991); Paul Buhle and Dan Georgakas, eds, *The Immigrant Left in the United States* (Albany: State University of New York Press 1996); Arthur Liebman, *Jews and the Left* (New York: John Wiley and Sons 1979); Gerald Sorin, *The Prophetic Minority: American Jewish Immigrant Radicals, 1880–1920* (Bloomington: Indiana Univerity Press 1985); idem, *A Time for Building: The Third Migration 1880–1920*, vol. iii of *The Jewish People in America* (Baltimore: Johns Hopkins University Press 1992), esp. chap. 4; David John Ahola, *Finnish-Americans and International Communism: A Study of Finnish-American Communism from Bolshevization to the Demise of the Third International* (Washington, DC: University Press of America 1981); Peter Kivisto, *Immigrant Socialists in the United States: The Case of Finns and the Left* (Rutherford: Fairleigh Dickinson University Press 1984); Charles Leinenweber, "The Class and Ethnic Bases of New York City Socialism, 1904–1915," *Labor History*, vol. 22, no. 1, Winter 1981; idem, "The American Socialist Party and 'New Immigrants'," *Science and Society*, vol. 32, no. 1, Winter 1968; David Waldstreicher, "Radicalism, Religion, Jewishness: The Case of Emma Goldman," *American Jewish History*, vol. lxxx, no. 1, Autumn 1990.

29. See Draper's pioneering study *American Communism and Soviet Russia: The Formative Period* (1960; New York: Vintage Books 1986), esp. chap. 15; see also Carole Charles, "Haitian Life in New York and the Haitian-American Left," in Buhle and Georgakas, eds, *The Immigrant Left in the United States*, but this is about the 1960s to the present.

30. This reverse migration during the Depression was not unique to Caribbeans; many other nationalities left in greater number than they entered the United States.

1. Caribbean Migration: Scale, Determinants, and Destinations, 1880–1932

1. See, in particular, Peter H. Wood, *Black Majority: Negroes in Colonial South Carolina from 1670 through the Stono Rebellion* (New York: Alfred A. Knopf 1974), passim; Jack P. Greene, "Colonial South Carolina and the Caribbean Connection," *South Carolina Historical Magazine*, vol. 88, no. 4, October 1987; Daniel C. Littlefield, "The Colonial Slave Trade to

South Carolina: A Profile," *South Carolina Historical Magazine*, vol. 91, no. 2, April 1990; Edmund Morgan, *American Slavery, American Freedom: The Ordeal of Colonial Virginia* (New York: W. W. Norton & Company 1975), esp. pp. 303–7, 327.

2. Wood, *Black Majority*, pp. 32–4; and Greene, "Colonial South Carolina and the Caribbean Connection," *passim*.

3. Littlefield, "The Slave Trade to Colonial South Carolina," pp. 69–71.

4. Greene, "Colonial South Carolina and the Caribbean Connection."

5. James O. Horton, "Blacks in Antebellum Boston: The Migrant and the Community," in his *Free People of Color: Inside the African American Community* (Washington, DC: Smithsonian Institution Press 1993), p. 27. In 1638, the first group of black slaves/servants were brought to Boston from the Caribbean, thus becoming the first black inhabitants of the city. Ibid., p. 25.

6. Bureau of Census, *Negro Population of the United States, 1790–1915* (Washington, DC: Government Printing Office 1918), p. 61.

7. Recent scholarship runs against the accepted notion that Russwurm was the "first" black person to graduate from an American college. At least one authoritative source now suggests that he may have in fact been the third black person to so graduate, for "Edward Jones received his B.A. degree from Amherst College two weeks before Russwurm's graduation, and Alexander L. Twilight graduated from Middlebury College [Vermont] in 1823." Clarence G. Contee, Sr, "John Brown Russwurm," in Rayford W. Logan and Michael R. Winston, eds, *Dictionary of American Negro Biography* (New York: W. W. Norton & Company 1982), p. 538; cf. Carter G. Woodson and Charles H. Wesley, *The Negro in Our History*, 12th edn (Washington, DC: Associated Publishers Inc. 1972), pp. 269–70. There is no scholarly biography of Russwurm.

8. Elliott had claimed to have been born in Boston of Jamaican parents and attended school in England and Jamaica. His biographer, however, thinks he was probably born in Liverpool. But this in itself does not, of course, preclude Jamaican antecedence. Peggy Lamson, *The Glorious Failure: Black Congressman Robert Brown Elliott and the Reconstruction in South Carolina* (New York: Norton 1973), esp. chap. 1.

9. Glenn O. Phillips, "The Response of a West Indian Activist: D. A. Straker, 1842–1908," *Journal of Negro History*, vol. lxvi, no. 2, Summer 1981.

10. Hollis Lynch, *Edward Wilmot Blyden: Pan-Negro Patriot* (New York: Oxford University Press 1970).

11. Details on Benjamin are drawn from William J. Simmons, *Men of Mark: Eminent, Progressive and Rising* (Cleveland: Geo. M. Rewell & Co. 1887), pp. 991–4; Arnold H. Taylor, "R[obert] C[harles] O['Hara] Benjamin," in Logan and Winston, eds, *Dictionary of American Negro Biography* pp. 39–40; and in particular from George C. Wright, *Racial Violence in Kentucky, 1865–1940: Lynchings, Mob Rule, and "Legal Lynchings"* (Baton Rouge: Louisiana State University Press 1990), pp. 67, 296–7.

12. Further details on the lives of many of those mentioned here may be gleaned from Simmons, *Men of Mark*; Logan and Winston, eds, *Dictionary of American Negro Biography*; J. A. Rogers, *World's Great Men of Color* vol. ii, ([1947] New York: Collier Books 1972); Woodson and Wesley, *The Negro in Our History*. For Crogman's relation to the American Negro Academy, see Alfred A. Moss, Jr, *The American Negro Academy: Voice of the Talented Tenth* (Baton Rouge: Louisiana State University Press 1981).

13. Hubert Harrison in *Pittsburgh Courier*, January 29, 1927; see also William Ferris, in *Pittsburgh Courier*, January 28, and February 4, 1928.

14. John Stuart Mill, *Principles of Political Economy* (London: Routledge and Sons 1900), p. 454.

15. The best overviews of the region's history are: Gordon Lewis, *Main Currents in Caribbean Thought: The Historical Evolution of Caribbean Society in its Ideological Aspects, 1492–1900* (Baltimore: Johns Hopkins University Press 1983); Franklin Knight, *The Caribbean: The Genesis of a Fragmented Nationalism* (New York: Oxford University Press 1990); and Eric Williams, *From Columbus to Castro: The History of the Caribbean, 1492–1969* (London: André Deutsch 1970).

16. These global changes have been admirably summarized by Eric Hobsbawm in *The Age of Empire: 1875–1914* (London: Weidenfeld and Nicolson 1987).

17. For more on the contexts and transformations in the region during the late nineteenth century, see especially Philip Curtin, "The British Sugar Duties and West Indies Prosperity," *Journal of Economic History*, vol. xiv (1954); R. W. Beachey, *The British West Indies Sugar*

Industry in the Late Nineteenth Century (Oxford: Basil Blackwell 1957); S. B. Saul, "The British West Indies in Depression: 1880–1914," *Inter-American Economic Affairs*, vol. xii, no. 3, Winter 1958; H. A. Will, "Colonial Policy and Economic Development in the British West Indies, 1895–1903," *Economic History Review*, 2nd Series, vol. xxiii, no. 1, April 1970; Richard A. Lobdell, "Patterns of Investment and Sources of Credit in the British West Indian Sugar Industry, 1838–97," *Journal of Caribbean History*, vol. 4, May 1972; Manuel Moreno Fraginals, *The Sugarmill* (New York: Monthly Review Press 1974); Bill Albert and Adrian Graves, eds, *Crisis and Change in the International Sugar Economy, 1860–1914* (Norwich: ISC Press 1984); Manuel Moreno Fraginals, Frank Moya Pons, and Stanley Engerman, eds, *Between Slavery and Free Labor: The Spanish-Speaking Caribbean in the Nineteenth Century* (Baltimore: Johns Hopkins University Press 1985); Sidney Mintz, *Sweetness and Power: The Place of Sugar in Modern History* (New York: Viking Penguin 1985); Williams, *From Columbus to Castro*, pp. 328–442; Walter Rodney, *A History of the Guyanese Working People, 1881–1905* (Baltimore: Johns Hopkins University Press 1981).

18. Calculation of the Jamaican proportion of the British Caribbean population made on the basis of census estimates presented in George W. Roberts, *The Population of Jamaica* (Cambridge: Cambridge University Press 1957), pp. 330–31; Velma Newton, *The Silver Men: West Indian Labour Migration to Panama, 1850–1914* (Kingston: Institute of Social and Economic Studies University of the West Indies, 1984), p. 96, estimated that 49 percent of the net migration to Panama up to 1914 came from Jamaica, 63,000, compared to 43,000 or 33 percent from Barbados, and 24,000 or 18 percent from other territories of the British Caribbean. But it is not at all clear on what basis she determined that 70 percent (42,000 out of 60,000) of Barbadians who went to Panama between 1904 and 1914 stayed, and only 49.5 percent (45,000 out of 91,000) of Jamaicans who went there between 1891 and 1915 stayed. Either the proportion of Barbadians who stayed was lower than she estimated or the proportion of the Jamaicans who stayed should be raised. In short, the differential of over 20 percent between the two groups is too high and therefore implausible. Implausible, too, is her estimate of 24,000 British Caribbean migrants other than Jamaicans and Barbadians who migrated to Panama between 1881 and 1914 staying on. Put against her estimate of 62,000 Jamaicans for the same period, it would mean that there were only 2.6 times as many Jamaicans as there were other British Caribbeans, excluding Barbadians, in Panama. The ratio was probably much higher. Newton estimates that over the eleven-year period 1904–14 some 42,000 Barbadians stayed on in Panama, while over a period of twenty-four years, 1891–1915, 45,000 Jamaicans stayed on. This would mean that although the Jamaicans migrated in significantly larger numbers than Barbadians, they stayed on in Panama in roughly the same numbers as Barbadians, and this occurred over a period of migration twice as long as that for Barbadians. More plausibly, George Roberts estimated that between 1881 and 1921 Barbados experienced net emigration to all areas of 82,400, and Jamaica 146,000. Thus, between these two leading sources of Caribbean migration, Jamaica's portion amounted to 63.5 percent. All of this leads me to think that well over half of the British Caribbeans who stayed on in Panama were Jamaicans. See George W. Roberts, "Emigration from the Island of Barbados," *Social and Economic Studies*, vol. iv, no. 3, Sept. 1955 p. 275; and idem, *The Population of Jamaica*, p. 139.

19. For those paying their own way, the same mode of travel from Trinidad, the Windward Islands, and Barbados cost £2 to £2 10s.; Newton, *The Silver Men*, p. 26.

20. Ibid., pp. 26, 40–43, 92; quotation from p. 26. The fare was raised through a variety of means: savings, borrowing from relatives, friends or loved ones, selling chattel or a small plot of land. The fare and the general cost of migration was seen by the would-be migrant and his or her family as an investment.

21. Gisela Eisner, *Jamaica, 1830–1930: A Study in Economic Growth* (Manchester: Manchester University Press 1961), Table XLIII, pp. 244–5.

22. Ibid., Table XXXIV, p. 203.

23. Ibid., Table XLII, pp. 240–3.

24. Veront Satchell, *From Plots to Plantation: Land Transactions in Jamaica, 1866–1900* (Kingston: Institute of Social and Economic Research, University of the West Indies 1990), Table 3.1, p. 38.

25. Ibid., pp. 42–4.

26. Eisner, *Jamaica, 1830–1930*, Table XXXIV, p. 203.

27. Ibid., Tables LVIII and LXI, pp. 294 and 302.

28. Ibid., Table XXVII, p. 171.

29. Satchell, *From Plots to Plantation*, pp. 48–9; Lord Olivier, *Jamaica: The Blessed Island* (London: Faber and Faber 1936), pp. 377–8.

30. Olivier, *Jamaica*, p. 379.

31. Satchell, *From Plots to Plantation*, p. 48.

32. Olivier, *Jamaica*, p. 379.

33. Thomas Holt, *The Problem of Freedom: Race, Labor, and Politics in Jamaica and Britain, 1832–1938* (Baltimore: Johns Hopkins University Press 1992), p. 353.

34. See Olivier, *Jamaica*, pp. 377–98; Ken Post, *Arise Ye Starvelings: The Jamaican Labour Rebellion of 1938 and Its Aftermath* (The Hague: Martinus Nijhoff 1978), pp. 37–8, 63–7; Satchell, *From Plots to Plantation*, *passim*; Holt, *The Problem of Freedom*, pp. 347–56 where a photograph of Baker may be found on p. 351.

35. The Aliens Law Amendment of 1871 gave aliens the right to acquire and dispose of real and personal property in the island. According to Satchell, this law "had the greatest impact on land ownership, as it enabled thousands of acres of prime lands to be transferred to multinational companies and foreign individuals." The Boston Fruit Company and Lorenzo Dow Baker himself were among the main beneficiaries. Satchell, *From Plots to Plantation*, p. 79; H. A. Will, "Colonial Policy and Economic Development in the West Indies, 1895–1903," *The Economic History Review*, Second Series, vol. xxiii, no. 1, April 1970; idem, *Constitutional Change in the British West Indies, 1880–1903* (Oxford: Clarendon Press 1970), chap. 8.

36. Satchell, *From Plots to Plantation*, Tables 3.1, and 3.2, pp. 38 and 41.

37. Post, *Arise Ye Starvelings*, p. 37.

38. Satchell, *From Plots to Plantation*, Table 3.3, p. 41. Satchell's Table 3.3 mistakenly gives 25.6 percent instead of 35.6 percent for the 1900 figure for banana earnings. Cf. Table 3.3 and text on p. 49.

39. Ibid., p. 49; Eisner, *Jamaica, 1830–1930*, Table XLI, p. 238.

40. Calculated from Eisner, *Jamaica, 1830–1930*, Table XXVII, p. 171.

41. Holt, *The Problem of Freedom*, pp. 353–6; Olivier, *Jamaica*, pp. 379–98; Post, *Arise Ye Starvelings*, pp. 37, 64, 117–18.

42. Wilson Randolph Bartlett, "Lorenzo D. Baker and the Development of the Banana Trade between Jamaica and the United States, 1881–1890" (Ph. D. Diss., American University 1977), cited in Holt, *The Problem of Freedom*, p. 356.

43. Holt, *The Problem of Freedom*, p. 353; cf. Satchell, *From Plots to Planmtation*, pp. 103, 106.

44. Holt, *The Problem of Freedom*, p. 356.

45. Eisner, *Jamaica, 1830–1930*, p. 342; emphasis added.

46. As Satchell demonstrated, many so-called "squatters" had legitimate claims to the land from which they were evicted; Satchell, *From Plots to Plantation*, p. 71.

47. Ibid., pp. 106, 110; quotation from p. 106.

48. Ibid., pp. 105–6.

49. Ibid., Table 5.7, p. 100, and pp. 101–2.

50. Eisner, *Jamaica, 1830–1930*, pp. 221–2.

51. Satchell, *From Plots to Plantation*, pp. 109, 111–50.

52. See Woodville Marshall, "Peasant Development in the West Indies since 1838," in P. I. Gomes, ed., *Rural Development in the Caribbean* (London: C. Hurst & Company 1985).

53. Satchell, *From Plots to Plantation*, p. 133.

54. Ibid., pp. 108–9.

55. Eisner, *Jamaica, 1830–1930*, Table I, p. 379.

56. Ibid., pp. 337–9, and 341; see also Nadine Wilkins, "The Medical Profession in Jamaica in the Post-Emancipation Period," *Jamaica Journal* vol. 21, no. 4, November 1988–January 1989, p. 31, where it is claimed that doctors' fees during slavery could be as high as 40 shillings a head per annum.

57. Cited in Ibid., p. 32.

58. Ibid., pp. 31–2.

59. Eisner, *Jamaica, 1830–1930*, pp. 340, 137, and 342.

60. Calculated from Satchell, *From Plots to Plantation*, Table 3.7, p. 56.

61. Eisner, *Jamaica, 1830–1930*, Table XX, p. 163.

62. Between 1891 and 1911, the number of women involved in petty trading more than doubled from 1,500 to 3,200. Ibid., p. 350.

63. Karl Marx, *Capital*, vol. 1 (London: Lawrence and Wishart 1974), p. 603.

64. Richard Lobdell, "Women in the Jamaican Labour Force, 1881–1921," *Social and Economic Studies*, vol. 37, nos. 1 & 2, March–June 1988, pp. 213–14, and Tables 9, 11, and 13, pp. 229–33.

65. Eisner, *Jamaica, 1830–1930*, p. 351.

66. H. G. De Lisser, *Twentieth Century Jamaica* (Kingston: Jamaica Times Limited 1913), p. 97; for an overview of domestic service in the island, see B. Higman, "Domestic Service in Jamaica since 1750," idem, ed., *Trade, Government and Society in Caribbean History, 1700–1920: Essays Presented to Douglas Hall* (Kingston: Heinemann 1983).

67. For more on the Morant Bay Rebellion, see Don Robotham, *"The Notorious Riot": The Socio-Economic and Political Bases of Paul Bogle's Revolt* (Kingston: Institute for Social and Economic Research 1981), and Gad Heuman, *"The Killing Time": The Morant Bay Rebellion in Jamaica* (Knoxville: University of Tennessee Press 1994).

68. Eisner, *Jamaica, 1830–1930*, p. 368, and Table LXXIV, p. 369.

69. Ibid., p. 367.

70. Some 36,412 Indian indentured laborers were brought into Jamaica from the 1840s to 1917, when indentureship ended. There were significantly fewer Chinese indentures: 510 were brought into the island in 1854 and another 696 in 1884 from Hong Kong; and although unindentured Chinese migrated to the island in the late nineteenth and early twentieth centuries, by 1911 there were only 2,111 on the island. Sources: K. O. Laurence, *Immigration into the West Indies in the 19th Century* (Aylesbury: Caribbean Universities Press/Ginn and Co. Ltd 1971), p. 26; Roberts, *The Population of Jamaica*, p. 132; Orlando Patterson, "Context and Choice in Ethnic Allegiance: A Theoretical Framework and Caribbean Case Study," in Nathan Glazer and Daniel P. Moynihan, eds, *Ethnicity: Theory and Experience* (Cambridge, Mass.: Harvard University Press 1975), pp. 323–4.

71. Ethelred Brown, "Labor Conditions in Jamaica Prior to 1917," *Journal of Negro History*, vol. iv, no. 4, October 1919, pp. 353–4; Douglas Hall, *Free Jamaica, 1838–1865: An Economic History*, (New Haven: Yale University Press 1959), pp. 54 and 108; Williams, *From Columbus to Castro*, pp. 357–8.

72. Claude McKay, "Hard Times," in idem, *Songs of Jamaica* (Kingston: Gardner 1912) pp. 53–4.

73. Ibid., p. 54.

74. Post, *Arise Ye Starvelings*, pp. 63–65; Sidney Mintz, *Caribbean Transformations* (Chicago: Aldine Publishing Co. 1974); Don Robotham, "The Development of a Black Ethnicity in Jamaica," in Rupert Lewis and Patrick Bryan, eds, *Garvey: His Work and Impact* (Kingston: Institute of Social and Economic Research, University of the West Indies 1988); Swithin Wilmott, "The Growth of Black Political Activity in Post-Emancipation Jamaica," in ibid.; Lorna Simmonds, "Civil Disturbances in Western Jamaica, 1838–1865," *The Jamaican Historical Review*, vol. xiv, 1984; Patrick Bryan, *The Jamaican People, 1880–1902: Race, Class and Social Control* (London: Macmillan 1991), pp. 266–82.

75. Eisner, *Jamaica, 1830–1930*, p. 332, Table LXVII, p. 333.

76. Ibid., Table LXVIII, p. 335.

77. Will, *Constitutional Change in the British West Indies*, p. 66.

78. Cited in Bryan, *The Jamaican People*, pp. 268–9.

79. For a valuable discussion of this group, see ibid., pp. 239–65.

80. Brown, "Labor Conditions in Jamaica,", pp. 351–2.

81. Newton, *The Silver Men*, p. 22 and Table XI, p. 96.

82. Ibid., Table XI, p. 96.

83. Ibid., p. 118.

84. See ibid., pp. 131–59.

85. Eisner, *Jamaica, 1830–1930*, Table VI, p. 136; Newton, *The Silver Men*, Table XIX, p. 154.

86. For the conditions of these workers in Panama, see Lancelot Lewis, *The West Indian in Panama: Black Labor in Panama, 1850–1914* (Washington, DC: University Press of America 1980); Elizabeth McLean Petras, *Jamaican Labor Migration: White Capital and Black Labor, 1850–1930*, (Boulder: Westview Press 1988) pp. 71–5, 187–203; Newton, *The Silver Men*, pp. 119–30, 139–59.

87. Claude McKay, "Peasants' Ways O' Thinkin'," *Daily Gleaner*, January 27, 1912.

88. Newton, *The Silver Men*, p. 59.

89. Ibid., pp. 62–3.

90. Cited in ibid., p. 63.

91. Ibid.

92. Ibid., p. 64.

93. See Franklin Knight, "Jamaican Migrants and the Cuban Sugar Industry, 1900–1934," in Fraginals et al., eds, *Between Slavery and Free Labor*, pp. 97, 100, and Table 5.2, p. 101.

94. Roberts, "Emigration from the Island of Barbados," pp. 276, 285.

95. Calculations based on Roberts, *The Population of Jamaica*, pp. 139, 330–31; and idem, "Emigration from the Island of Barbados," p. 275.

96. Newton, *The Silver Men*, p. 16.

97. Marshall, "Peasant Development in the West Indies since 1838," p. 4; Bonham Richardson, *Panama Money in Barbados, 1900–1920* (Knockville: University of Tennessee Press 1985) pp. 16–18; Hilary Beckles, *A History of Barbados: From Amerindian Settlement to Nation-State* (Cambridge: Cambridge University Press 1990), pp. 114–16.

98. In the 1840s, the price of land was more than ten times higher than that in Jamaica: £60–£200 in Barbados compared to £4–£20 in Jamaica. See W. Emanuel Riviere, "Labour Shortage in the British West Indies after Emancipation," *Journal of Caribbean History*, vol. 4, May 1972 pp. 18–19; Beckles, *A History of Barbados*, p. 114.

99. David Lowenthal, "The Population of Barbados," *Social and Economic Studies*, vol. 6, no. 4 December 1957, pp. 453–4; Richardson, *Panama Money in Barbados*, pp. 32–3; Beckles, *A History of Barbados*, p. 132.

100. For a good analysis of how different territories of the British Caribbean adapted to the crisis, see S. B. Saul, "The British West Indies in Depression: 1880–1914"; see also Will, "Colonial Policy and Economic Development in the British West Indies, 1895–1903"; Ward, *Poverty and Progress in the Caribbean, 1800–1960*.

101. Richardson, *Panama Money in Barbados*, p. 16.

102. Sydney Olivier, who played a key role on the 1897 Commission, noted similar differences between the islands. Olivier, *Jamaica*, esp. pp. 160–61.

103. Richardson, *Panama Money in Barbados*, pp. 77–8. Barbados's overall death rate from the late nineteenth right up to the middle of the twentieth centuries was always higher than Jamaica's. See Roberts, *Population of Jamaica*, p. 185, Table 48.

104. *Handbook of Jamaica* (various years) (Kingston: Government Printing Office); Newton, *The Silver Men*, p. 17; Olivier, *Jamaica*, pp. 355–60; Erna Brodber, "The Second Generation of Freemen in Jamaica, 1907–1944" (Ph.D. diss., University of the West Indies 1984), pp. 52–3, 136–7.

105. *Handbook of Jamaica 1937–8*, p. 46.

106. Vaughan Cornish, "The Jamaica Earthquake (1907)," *The Geographical Journal*, vol. xxxi, no. 3, March 1908, p. 247. Strangely, after almost a century, Cornish's remains, to my knowledge, the most detailed discussion of the 1907 earthquake. His essay is also far more geological than social. But he was by chance in Kingston when the earthquake occurred and he talks about his experience, the environment, and the aftermath instructively, if only *en passant*.

107. Leslie Thompson, *An Autobiography* (Crawley: Rabbit Press Ltd 1985), p. 2; Claude McKay, *My Green Hills of Jamaica* (Kingston: Heinemann Educational Books, Caribbean Ltd 1979), p. 53.

108. *Handbook of Jamaica* (various years).

109. Roberts, *Population of Jamaica*, pp. 183–4.

110. Colin Clarke, *Kingston, Jamaica: Urban Development and Social Change, 1692–1962* (Berkeley: University of California Press 1975), p. 2.

111. Grant to Andrews, July 15, 1915, Jamaica Methodist Missionary Society Records 742; cited in Brodber, "The Second Generation of Freemen in Jamaica, 1907–1944," pp. 136–7.

112. The Rev. A. Cresser to Andrews, November 23, 1917, Jamaica Methodist Missionary Society Records 743; cited in ibid., pp. 137–8.

113. *Handbook of Jamaica*, 1937–8, p. 48. It is worth noting that unlike the hurricane of 1903, the *Handbook* did not describe that of 1917 as "great."

114. Richardson, *Panama Money in Barbados*, p. 15; Beckles, *A History of Barbados*, pp. 138–40.

115. Newton, *The Silver Men*, p. 17; Richardson, *Panama Money in Barbados*, pp. 73, 181–3.

116. Richardson, *Panama Money in Barbados*, pp. 15, 36–7; Beckles, *A History of Barbados*, pp. 137, 140.

117. Cited in Richardson, *Panama Money in Barbados*, p. 181.

118. I am leaving aside for the moment the moot issue of the extent to which human interaction with the natural world may influence the frequency of hurricanes, droughts, floods, etc.

119. The law stipulated that tenants should be given four weeks' notice of eviction. The constricted life under the tenantry system is vividly and movingly recalled by elderly Barbadians interviewed by Mary Chamberlain and reported in her remarkable essay, "Renters and Farmers: The Barbadian Plantation Tenantry System, 1917–1937," *Journal of Caribbean History*, vol. 24, no. 2, 1990.

120. Richardson has a good description of these structures and the context of their evolution: Richardson, *Panama Money in Barbados*, pp. 58–60.

121. Richardson, *Panama Money in Barbados*, pp. 73–9; Leonard P. Fletcher, "The Evolution of Poor Relief in Barbados, 1838–1900," *Journal of Caribbean History*, vol. 26, no. 2, 1992.

122. Roberts, "Emigration from the Island of Barbados," p. 245; Lowenthal, "The Population of Barbados," p. 448.

123. Roberts, "Emigration from the Island of Barbados,", p. 245, emphasis added; Lowenthal, "The Population of Barbados,", p. 454.

124. George Lamming, *In The Castle of My Skin* (London: Michael Joseph 1953), p. 86.

125. Barbara Welch, "Population Density and Emigration in Dominica," *Geographical Journal*, vol. 134, pt 2, June 1968; Ceri Peach, *West Indian Migration to Britain: A Social Geography* (London: Oxford University Press 1968); Hilbourne Watson, "Theoretical and Methodological Problems in Commonwealth Caribbean Migration Research: Conditions and Causality," *Social and Economic Studies*, vol. 31, no. 1, March 1982; Clive Harris, "British Capitalism, Migration and Relative Surplus-Population," *Migration*, vol. 1, no. 1, 1987; idem, "Post-war Migration and the Industrial Reserve Army," in Winston James and Clive Harris, eds, *Inside Babylon: The Caribbean Diaspora in Britain* (London: Verso 1993); Elizabeth Thomas-Hope, *Explanation in Caribbean Migration* (London: Macmillan 1992).

126. Quoted in Christine Barrow, "Ownership and Control of Resources in Barbados: 1834 to the Present," *Social and Economic Studies*, vol. 32, no. 3, September 1983, pp. 94–5.

127. Ibid., p. 95.

128. I gave some thought to the subject in "'A Simian Exhibition'? Symbol and Meaning in the Celebration of King George VI's Coronation by Caribbean Migrants in Harlem, May 1937," paper presented to the "Conference on Caribbean Culture," University of the West Indies, Mona, Kingston, Jamaica, March 3–6, 1996.

129. Derek Walcott, "What the Twilight Says: An Ouverture," in his *Dream on Monkey Mountain and Other Plays* (New York: The Noonday Press 1970), p. 21.

130. This is powerfully evoked in Carlos Russell's prose-poem monologue, *An Old Woman Remembers: The Recollected History of West Indians in Panama, 1855–1955* (New York: Caribbean Diaspora Press 1995).

131. Froude wrote a notoriously racist travelogue on the Caribbean, *The English in the West Indies or the Bow of Ulysses* (London: Longmans, Green, and Co. 1888). The book provoked a celebrated riposte from the black Trinidadian, John Jacob Thomas, *Froudacity: West Indian Fables by James Anthony Froude* (1889; London: New Beacon Books 1969). Froude is further discussed in Chapter 4.

132. Post, *Arise Ye Starvelings*, pp. 213–14; *Garvey Papers*, vol. i, p. 33 n. 15.

133. Claude McKay, *Banana Bottom* (New York: Harper and Row Publishers 1933), pp. 234–6.

134. See Winston James, *Claude McKay: The Making of a Black Bolshevik, 1889–1923* (forthcoming).

135. Marcus Garvey, "The British West Indies in the Mirror of Civilization. History Making by Colonial Negroes," *African Times and Orient Review*, October 1913; reprinted in *Garvey Papers*, vol. i, p. 30; J. A. Rogers, "The West Indies: Their Political, Social and Economic Condition," *Messenger*, October 1922, p. 506.

136. Quoted in Post, *Arise Ye Starvelings*, p. 214; see also Mark D. Morrison-Reed, *Black Pioneers in a White Denomination*, 3rd edn (Boston: Skinner Howe Books 1994), pp. 31–111.

137. UNIA Convention, "Declaration of Rights of the Negro Peoples of the World," August 13, 1920, *Garvey Papers*, vol. ii, p. 572.

138. Richard Hart, "Jamaica and Self-Determination, 1660–1970," *Race*, vol. xiii, no. 3, January 1972, pp. 282–3.

139. C. L. R. James, "Discovering Literature in the 1930s", *Journal of Commonwealth Literature*, July 1969; reprinted in his *Spheres of Existence: Selected Writings* (London: Allison & Busby 1980), pp. 237–44; citation, p. 239.

140. Ibid., pp. 238–9.

141. Bonham Richardson, *Caribbean Migrants: Environment and Human Survival on St Kitts and Nevis* (Knoxville: University of Tennessee Press 1983), pp. 122–31; and Patrick E. Bryan, "The Question of Labor in the Sugar Industry of the Dominican Republic in the Late Nineteenth and Early Twentieth Centuries," in Fraginals et al., eds, *Between Slavery and Free Labor*.

142. Cited in Bryan, "The Question of Labor in the Sugar Industry of the Dominican Republic in the Late Nineteenth and Early Twentieth Centuries," p. 241.

143. For the formation of the peasantry in these areas in the post-slavery period, see Marshall, "Peasant Development in the West Indies since 1838"; idem, "Metayage in the Sugar Industry of the British Windward Islands, 1838–1865," and "Social and Economic Problems in the Windward Islands, 1838–1865," both in his *Social and Economic Problems of the Windward Islands, 1838–1865* (Kingston: Department of History, University of the West Indies n.d.); Riviere, "Labour Shortage in the British West Indies After Emancipation"; George Brizan, *The Grenadian Peasantry and Social Revolution, 1930–1951*, Working Paper No. 21 (Kingston: ISER 1979); idem, *Grenada: Island of Conflict* (London: Zed Books 1984), esp. chaps 10 and 16; Yvonne Acosta and Jean Casimir, "Social Origins of the Counter-Plantation System in St. Lucia," in Gomes, ed., *Rural Developments in the Caribbean*; Michel-Rolph Trouillot, *Peasants and Capital: Dominica in the World Economy* (Baltimore: Johns Hopkins University Press 1988); Bonham C. Richardson, "Human Mobility in the Windward Caribbean, 1884–1902," *Plantation Society*, vol. ii, no. 3, May 1989.

144. Williams, *From Columbus to Castro*, chap. 20; Rodney, *A History of the Guyanese Working People*; Lobdell, "Patterns of Investment"; Saul, "The British West Indies in Depression"; Will, "Colonial Policy and Economic Development"; Howard Johnson, "Immigration and the Sugar Industry in Trinidad During the Last Quarter of the 19th Century," *Journal of Caribbean History*, vol. 3, November 1971; Kusha Haraksingh, "Labour, Technology and the Sugar Estates in Trinidad, 1879–1914," in Albert and Graves, eds, *Crisis and Change in the International Sugar Economy, 1860–1914*; Walton Look Lai, *Indentured Labor, Caribbean Sugar: Chinese and Indian Migrants to the British West Indies, 1838–1918* (Baltimore: Johns Hopkins University Press 1993); K. O. Laurence, *A Question of Labour: Indentured Immigration into Trinidad and British Guiana, 1875–1917* (Kingston: Ian Randle Publishers 1994).

145. See Marianne Ramesar's helpful and pioneering essay, "Patterns of Regional Settlement and Economic Activity by Immigrant Groups in Trinidad, 1851–1900," *Social and Economic Studies*, vol. 25, no. 3, September 1976. The extent and significance of Barbadian migration to Trinidad and Guyana are discussed further in Chapter 2.

146. Donald Wood, *Trinidad in Transition: The Years After Slavery* (Oxford: Oxford University Press 1968), pp. 97–104; Saul, "The British West Indies in Depression," pp. 20–1; Bridget Brereton, *A History of Modern Trinidad, 1783–1962* (London: Heinemann 1981), pp. 90–95, 207–10.

147. Howard Johnson has shown that some of the difficulties of the cocoa-producing peasantry had roots in the late nineteenth century when merchants dispossessed many through usurous rates of interest on credit extended to black smallholders. The extent of the dispossession is not, however, clear. Johnson gives no figures as to what proportion of the black peasantry was so deprived. See Johnson, "Merchant Credit and the Dispossession of the Cocoa Peasantry in Trinidad in the Late Nineteenth Century," *Peasant Studies*, vol. 15, no. 1, Fall 1987. No doubt some people migrated after the collapse of the price of cocoa. Claudia Jones, a leading member of the American Communist Party in the 1940s and 1950s, reported that her parents left Trinidad in 1922 "when their economic status . . . had been worsened as a result of the drop in the cocoa trade from the West Indies which had impoverished the West Indies and the entire Car[i]bbean." They had been involved in cocoa cultivation themselves. Claudia Jones to William Foster, December 6, 1955; Howard "Stretch" Johnson Papers, Tamiment Collection 166, Tamiment Institute Library and Robert F. Wagner Labor Archives, New York University.

148. Howard Johnson, *The Bahamas in Slavery and Freedom* (Kingston: Ian Randle Publishers 1991), esp. chaps. 4, 5, 6, and 10; Raymond A. Mohl, "Black Immigrants: Bahamians in Early Twentieth-Century Miami," *Florida Historical Quarterly*, vol. lxv, no. 3,

January 1987; Gail Saunders, *Bahamian Society After Emancipation* (Kingston: Ian Randle Publishers 1994).

149. For a detailed discussion of these institutions, see Thomas-Hope, *Explanation in Caribbean Migration.*

150. *Weekly Illustrated Paper*, February 4, 1905, quoted in Richardson, *Panama Money in Barbados*, p. 111.

151. Cited in Richardson, *Panama Money in Barbados*, p. 106.

152. Quoted in Richardson, *Panama Money in Barbados*, p. 132.

153. Richardson, *Panama Money in Barbados*, p. 160.

154. E. Goulbourn Sinckler, *The Barbados Handbook, 1914* (London: Duckworth and Co. 1914), p. 45.

155. Richardson, *Panama Money in Barbados*, p. 157.

156. Francis Mark, *The History of the Barbados Workers' Union* (Bridgetown: Barbados Workers' Union n.d.), pp. 20–21; Richardson, *Panama Money in Barbados*, pp. 191–2; Beckles, *A History of Barbados*, pp. 145, 147.

157. Barrow, "Ownership and Control of Resources in Barbados," p. 94.

158. Cited in Richardson, *Panama Money in Barbados*, p. 191.

159. Chamberlain, "Renters and Farmers," p. 223, n.28.

160. Ibid., pp. 206–7.

161. Brodber, "A Second Generation of Freemen in Jamaica, 1907–1944," p. 156.

162. The Hon. Rev. A. A. Barclay and Mr William Cradwick of the Jamaica League, reported the frustration of a returned Jamaican migrant. The man had been born into severe poverty but after years of hard work in Cuba, he went home with "some hundreds of pounds saved." He tried to buy land but had "the greatest difficulty," in getting some to buy. He could not afford a large property, and managed to buy 10 acres near Gibraltar in St Mary. He wanted more to buy but encountered such reluctance to sell from local planters that, in the end, he resorted to buying 80 acres of badly situated Crown land. Barclay and Cradwick reported that the "lack of roads had so discouraged him that he was tempted to sell it again for whatever he could get and return to Cuba." One of the ways in which the merchants and planters maintained control of land was the opposing and vetoing of road and rail extensions. Thus in Brown's Town, St Ann, the businessmen opposed the creation of new roads as it would divert business away from them. Similarly, in Clarendon the planters objected to the extension of the railway as they feared competition for produce from the peasantry and the latter's reduced dependence on plantation work. When poor black people in Barbados tried to combine their resources through friendly societies, the ruling class stymied their effort. As Hilary Beckles pointed out, these black organizations attracted the attention of the legislature "for the principal reason that the large sum of capital they collected could be used against the interests of the white community if properly mobilised. For example, societies could purchase land on behalf of members and influence the pattern of land distribution." The 1905 Friendly Societies Act saw to it that that did not happen. The Act made it illegal for friendly societies to hold "land exceeding one acre in extent." See C. O. 137/742, despatch 711, Governor Probyn to Viscount Milner, Secretary of State for the Colonies, October 23, 1920; enclosure of report by Barclay and Cradwick, Oct. 9, 1920; also C. O. 137/746, Memorial from T. Gordon Somers and C. A. Wilson, on behalf of the Jamaica League, to Winston Churchill, Secretary of State for the Colonies, May 12, 1921; and Beckles, *A History of Barbados*, p. 151.

163. Richardson, *Panama Money in Barbados*, p. 185.

164. The alleged and documented profiteering of merchants substantially contributed to the revolts in Trinidad, Belize, and Jamaica in 1919. Some among the British authorities were appalled and embarrassed by the profiteering of the merchants in the Caribbean during and in the aftermath of the war. The subject is discussed in Chapter 2.

165. Quoted in Mark, *The History of the Barbados Workers' Union*, pp. 22–3.

166. Calculated on the basis of figures quoted in Richardson, *Panama Money in Barbados*, p. 185.

167. Roberts, *The Population of Jamaica*, pp. 187, 195; Richardson, *Panama Money in Barbados*, p. 202; Beckles, *A History of Barbados*, p. 164. The tenderness with which the colonial authorities looked upon the plight of the people is typified by the remark of Edward Wood, Under Secretary of State for the Colonies, who in a 1922 report declared that the "problem of infantile mortality" in the British Caribbean was "largely the result of ignorance and apathy on the part of parents." Of course, he was in a perfect position to pass such expert judgement: he had spent all of two months in the Caribbean, did rigorous research by drinking

rum and gallivanting with the planters and merchants, and spent a considerable amount of time at luncheons and official dinners. From the evidence of his own diary it appears that he never spoke to a black person in Barbados. Honourable E. F. L. Wood, *Report on Visit to the West Indies and British Guiana (December, 1921-February, 1922)* [Cmd. 1679], (London: H. M. Stationery Office 1922), pp. 58, 94–8.

168. For a good fictionalized exploration of some of these responses see McKay, *Banana Bottom*, esp. pp. 65–70. See also Walter Jekyll, *Jamaican Song and Story: Annancy Stories, Digging Sings, Ring Tunes, and Dancing Tunes* (1907; New York: Dover Publications, Inc. 1966), p. 246. The unsuccessful returnee in Barbados was mocked in song: "Look de Panama man come home from sea/ As skinny as a Church rat/ An' all he had in he grip fo' me/ Was a wide-brim Panama hat." (Quoted in Richardson, *Panama Money in Barbados*, p. 151.) In Jamaica they sang: "One, two three, four/ Colon Man a come/ with him watch chain/ a knock him belly/ Bam Bam Bam/ Ask him what's the time/ And he look upon the sun/ with him watch chain/ a knock him belly/ Bam Bam Bam." (Quoted in Olive Senior, "The Colon People," part 1, *Jamaica Journal*, vol. 11, nos 3 and 4, March 1978, p. 64.)

169. Table 1.2; Newton, *The Silver Men*, p. 92; Richardson, *Panama Money in Barbados*, p. 123. The Barbadian figure does not, of course, include the thousands who made their own way to Panama without first securing a contract in the island.

2. The Peculiarities of the Caribbeans: Characteristics and Forces Conducive to Radicalization

1. US Dept of Commerce, *Fifteenth Census of the United States: 1930*, vol. 2, Table 23, p. 70.

2. Hart, "Jamaica and Self Determination," pp. 282–3; *Garvey Papers*, vol. i, pp. 20–2, 527–30.

3. Robert G. McGuire, "Petioni, Charles, A.," in Logan and Winston, eds, *Dictionary of American Negro Biography*, pp. 490–91; *Garvey Papers*, vol. ii, pp. 578–9 n. 1; Haynes's background is discussed further below.

4. W. F. Elkins, "A Source of Black Nationalism in the Caribbean: The Revolt of the British West Indies Regiment at Taranto, Italy," *Science & Society*, vol. xxxiv, no. 1, Spring 1970; Brinsley Samaroo, "The Trinidad Workingmen's Association and the Origins of Popular Protest in a Crown Colony," *Social and Economic Studies*, vol. 21, no. 2, June 1972, pp. 216–17; idem, "The Trinidad Disturbances of 1917–20: Precursor to 1937," in Roy Thomas, ed., *The Trinidad Labour Riots of 1937: Perspectives 50 Years Later* (St. Augustine, Trinidad: Extra-Mural Studies Unit, University of the West Indies 1987), pp. 41–2; Kelvin Singh, *Race and Class Struggles in a Colonial State: Trinidad 1917–1945*, (Kingston: The Press—University of the West Indies 1994), pp. 14–40; *Garvey Papers*, vol. ii, p. 579 n.6.

5. Samaroo, "Trinidad Workingmen's Association," p. 216; *Garvey Papers*, vol. iii, p. 295 n. 4.

6. Thompson, *An Autobiography*, p. 26.

7. Vere Johns, "A Veteran's Viewpoint," *Public Opinion*, May 11, 1940, pp. 11, 15; see also "Another Veteran's Point of View," *Public Opinion*, May 25, 1940, p. 13.

8. C. L. Joseph, "The British West Indies Regiment, 1914–1918," *Journal of Caribbean History*, vol. 2, May 1971, p. 124.

9. Significantly, those who were white or light enough to pass for white were accepted. The black ones were turned away. Joseph, "The British West Indies Regiment 1914–1918," provides the most cogent and comprehensive analysis of the Caribbean participation in the First World War; see also C. L. R. James, *The Life of Captain Cipriani: An Account of British Government in the West Indies* (Nelson: Coulton & Co. Ltd 1932), esp. pp. 22–39; Elkins, "A Source of Black Nationalism" and Glenford D. Howe, "In the Crucible: Race, Power and Military Socialization of West Indian Recruits During the First World War," *Journal of Caribbean Studies*, vol. 10, no. 3, Summer and Fall 1995.

10. C. L. R. James, *Beyond a Boundary* (London: Hutchinson & Co. 1963), p. 39.

11. Thomas MacDermot wrote under the name Tom Redcam, an inversion of his last name. "Arise O My Country," was first published on October 29, 1915; see "The Poetical Works of Tom Redcam, Poet Laureate of Jamaica, 1910–1933" (ms. presented to the Institute

of Jamaica by the Poetry League 1957), p. 33; unpublished ms National Library of Jamaica, Kingston.

12. Ibid.

13. Cited in Erna Brodber, "A Second Generation of Freemen in Jamaica, 1907–1944," p. 114.

14. Ibid., pp. 113–14.

15. James, *Life of Captain Cipriani*, pp. 22–3; Samaroo, "The Trinidad Workingmen's Association," p. 210; Joseph, "The British West indies Regiment," pp. 100–101, 108–9; *The Grenada Handbook and Directory 1946*, 1st ed. (Bridgetown: The Advocate Company 1946), p. 348.

16. James, *Beyond a Boundary*, pp. 39–40; *Jamaica Times*, 13 November 1915; reprinted in *Garvey Papers*, vol. i, p. 163.

17. See Joseph, "The British West Indies Regiment," esp. pp. 94–101.

18. They were even less inclined to use Indo-Caribbean troops, even those who spoke perfect English, but, strangely, accepted the use of Indian troops from the sub-continent in Europe. Joseph said that the decision to have Indian troops in Europe, "piloted by Curzon, the former Viceroy of India, was not an easy one, and it challenged the policy of the War Office on the use of Indian or other non-white troops on the European front" ("The British West Indies Regiment," pp. 95–96). But, unfortunately, beyond this, he does not explain this apparent anomaly.

19. James, *Life of Captain Cipriani*, p. 23.

20. Samaroo, "The Trinidad Workingmen's Association", pp. 211–12.

21. James, *Beyond a Boundary*, pp. 39–40.

22. Joseph, "The British West Indies Regiment," pp. 98–99.

23. *Report of the Commission appointed by the Governor to enquire into the origin of the riot in the Town of Belize which began on the night of 22nd July 1919*, dated 10 October 1919, CO 123/296, Public Record Office, Kew; hereafter referred to as the *Belize Report*, appended evidence of Corporal Samuel A. Haynes, p. 1.

24. Statement of Haynes, pp. 1–2; see also letter of the British Honduras Contingent Committee to the editor of *The Clarion*, dated August 9, 1919, published in the *Belize Independent*, August 13, 1919, reprinted as Appendix N to *Belize Report*.

25. The most thorough and detailed discussion of the subject is to be found in Arthur E. Barbeau and Florette Henri, *The Unknown Soldier: Black American Troops in World War I* (Philadelphia: Temple University Press 1974), esp. pp. 89–110.

26. See British Honduras Contingent Committee, letter to the editor, *The Clarion*, August 9, 1919.

27. Joseph, "The British West Indies Regiment," pp. 115–118.

28. *Belize Report*, Appendix O, "Alleged Grievances of the B[ritish] H[onduras] C[ontingent] on Foreign Service," p. 1. On July 22, 1919, widespread and serious rioting broke out in Belize, the capital of British Honduras. Ex-servicemen were actively involved and led the protest. The Commission of Inquiry appointed by the Governor of the colony and charged with investigating the causes, heard from the ex-servicemen about their grievances accumulated during the war.

29. Ibid., p. 2, and statement by Haynes, p. 2, in *Belize Report*.

30. Statement by Haynes, pp. 2–3.

31. Ibid., pp. 3–4, 7.

32. "Alleged Grievances," p. 4.

33. Ibid.

34. Ibid., pp. 3–4.

35. "Alleged Grievances," p. 8; see also evidence of Captain Hulse, ibid., pp. 6–7.

36. "Alleged Grievances," p. 6.

37. Haynes statement, pp. 6–7.

38. "Alleged Grievances," pp. 8–9.

39. Ibid., p. 9.

40. Joseph, "The British West Indies Regiment," p. 124.

41. "Alleged Grievances," p. 3.

42. Ibid., p. 4.

43. Ibid., p. 10; Haynes statement, pp. 8–9.

44. See Chapter 4, below.

45. "Alleged Grievances," p. 3.

46. Of course, the notion that black men could not fight under European climatic conditions was completely unscientific and erroneous. No one had bothered to ask the men themselves what their thoughts were on the subject. Throughout the war and in its aftermath, the French successfully used African soldiers in Europe. The Afro-American, 369th Regiment fought oustandingly with the French army and was awarded the *croix de guerre*.

47. Joseph, "The British West Indies Regiment," provides the most detailed analysis of British official policy and practices in relation to these matters.

48. Ibid., pp. 106 and 108.

49. Ibid., pp. 112–13.

50. Ibid., pp. 113, 115–18.

51. Haynes statement, pp. 1–2.

52. "Alleged Grievances," p. 4.

53. See, for examples, ibid., p. 9.

54. Cited in Joseph, "The British West Indies Regiment," p. 101.

55. Cited in Elkins, "A Source of Black Nationalism in the Caribbean," p. 100; see also Howe, "In the Crucible", pp. 170–4.

56. James, *Life of Captain Cipriani*, p. 33.

57. Ibid., pp. 33–34; Joseph, "The British West Indies Regiment," p. 119.

58. Thursfield cited in James, *Life of Captain Cipriani*, pp. 33–34.

59. Joseph, "The British West Indies Regiment," p. 118; Elkins, "A Source of Black Nationalism in the Caribbean," p. 101.

60. Elkins, "A Source of Black Nationalism in the Caribbean," p. 101.

61. Ibid., p. 101; Joseph, "The British West Indies Regiment," p. 118.

62. Joseph, "The British West Indies Regiment," pp. 119–21; Elkins, "A Source of Black Nationalism in the Caribbean," pp. 101–2.

63. Joseph, "The British West Indies Regiment," p. 124; Elkins, "A Source of Black Nationalism in the Caribbean," pp. 101–3.

64. Cited in Elkins, "A Source of Black Nationalism in the Caribbean," p. 103.

65. Figures from *Port of Spain Gazette*, 6 August 1914, as quoted in Samaroo, "The Trinidad Workingmen's Association," pp. 210–11.

66. O. W. Phelps, "Rise of the Labour Movement in Jamaica," *Social and Economic Studies*, vol. 9, no. 4, December 1960, p. 421.

67. Samaroo, "The Trinidad Workingmen's Association," p. 212.

68. Ibid., p. 212.

69. Elkins, "A Source of Black Nationalism in the CAribbean," p. 103; idem, "Black Power in the British West Indies: The Trinidad Longshoreman's Strike of 1919," *Science & Society*, vol. xxxiii, no. 1, Winter 1969, p. 75; Singh, *Race and Class Struggles*, pp. 14–40; see also the fine essay by Tony Martin which effectively links the racial and class dimensions of the struggle in Trinidad: "Revolutionary Upheaval in Trinidad, 1919: Gleanings from British and American Sources," *Journal of Negro History*, vol. lviii, no. 3, July 1973, reprinted in Tony Martin, *The Pan-African Connection: From Slavery to Garvey and Beyond* (Cambridge, Mass.: Schenkman Publishing Company 1983), pp. 47–58.

70. Cited in Martin, "Revolutionary Upheaval in Trinidad," p. 51.

71. Cited in Elkins, "Black Power in the Caribbean," pp. 74–5.

72. *Belize Report*, Appendix B, "Threats Against White Men and Excitement of the Crowd," p. 1.

73. Ibid.

74. Ibid., pp. 1–2.

75. Ibid., p. 1.

76. Richard Hart, "Trade Unionism in the English-Speaking Caribbean: The Formative Years and the Caribbean Labour Congress," in Susan Craig, ed., *Contemporary Caribbean: A Sociological Reader*, vol. 2 (Port of Spain: Susan Craig 1982), pp. 64–5; idem, "Origin and Development of the Working Class in the English-speaking Caribbean area 1897–1937," in Malcolm Cross and Gad Heuman, eds, *Labour in the Caribbean: From Emancipation to Independence* (London: Macmillan 1988), pp. 52–3; Phelps, "Rise of the Labour Movement in Jamaica," pp. 419–21; George Eaton, "Trade Union Development in Jamaica," *Caribbean Quarterly*, vol. 8, no. 1, 1962, pp. 50–3; W. F. Elkins, "Hercules and the Society of Peoples of African Origin," *Caribbean Studies*, vol. 11, no. 4, January 1972, pp. 53–5; George Brizan, *Grenada: Island of Conflict* (London: Zed Books 1984), pp. 278–9.

77. *Garvey Papers*, vol. i, p. cxiv; Elkins, "Black Power in the British West Indies,"

pp. 72–73; idem, "The Suppression of the *Negro World* in the British West Indies," *Science & Society*, vol. xxxv, no. 3, Fall 1971, pp. 344–7; idem, "Marcus Garvey, the *Negro World*, and the British West Indies: 1919–1920," *Science & Society*, vol. xxxvi, no. 1, Spring 1972; and Martin, "Revolutionary Upheaval in Trinidad, 1919".

78. In 1920, at a time when the population of the colony numbered only 16,000, the UNIA had 800 members in British Honduras. (Peter Ashdown, "Marcus Garvey, the UNIA and the Black Cause in British Honduras, 1914–1949," *Journal of Caribbean History*, vol. 15, 1981, p. 46.) In relative terms this must have made the British Honduras branch one of the most successful in the world at the time.

79. Cited in Ashdown, "Marcus Garvey," p. 49.

80. Elkins, "Marcus Garvey, the *Negro World*," pp. 65–6; *Garvey Papers*, vol. iii, p. 789; idem, vol. iv, p. 830 n. 4; idem, vol. vii, pp. xlvi, 669–73; idem, vol. vii, p. 980; Tony Martin, *Race First: The Ideological and Organizational Struggles of Marcus Garvey and the Universal Negro Improvement Association* (Westpoint, Conn.: Greenwood Press 1976), p. 276; *Negro World*, August 13, 1927. Ashdown, "Marcus Garvey," p. 49.

81. Starting out as "Some Things Garveyites Should Know," Haynes' column became "Through Black Spectacles" in 1927 and continued into the 1930s.

82. *Negro World*, April 16, 1927.

83. For evidence of Haynes' desperate effort to save the UNIA, see *Garvey Papers*, vol. vii, esp. pp. 663–664; 669–73.

84. See biographical profile of Haynes in the *African*, July–August 1945, p. 22.

85. *Negro World*, August 13, 1927.

86. Ibid.

87. Haynes, "The Highest Patriotism," *African*, December 1937, p. 66; see also idem, "World Horizon," "The Cross of Intolerance," and "The Philosophy of Force," *African*, October 1937, November 1937, March–April 1938, respectively.

88. Samuel A. Haynes, "Warning," in Beatrice M. Murphy, ed., *Ebony Rhythm: An Anthology of Contemporary Negro Verse* (New York: The Exposition Press 1948), p. 82.

89. Haynes, "Let the Empire Perish," *African*, May 1946, p. 7.

90. My thanks to Nigel Bolland for providing me with the lyrics of "Land of the Gods."

91. *Garvey Papers*, vol. iii, p. 789; idem, vol. iv, p. 830 n. 4; idem, vol. vii, pp. xlvi, 669–73; *Negro World*, August 13, 1927. There is a good profile of Grant in *Garvey Papers*, vol. vii, pp. 309–310, n. 4; but for more on Grant's career see Post, *Arise Ye Starvelings*, and Naison, *Communists in Harlem During the Depression* (Orbana: University of Illinois Press, 1983).

92. Some 260 black people migrated from Britain to the United States during the fiscal years ending June 30, 1919 to 1921. One hundred and twelve came in 1921 alone, after which there was a sharp fall in the number entering the country: thirteen in 1922; twenty-four in 1923; twenty-four in 1924; five in 1925. Given the small number who came from Britain before the First World War, and the drop in number after 1921, it is reasonable to assume that most of those who migrated during this period were Caribbean people associated with the war effort. It is probable that included in the group would also be people leaving Liverpool and Cardiff after the race riots in those cities earlier in 1919. Source: US Department of Labor, Bureau of Immigration, *Annual Report of the Commissioner General of Immigration to the Secretary of Labor*, 1919–1925.

93. *New York Amsterdam News*, February 1, 1928.

94. See, for instance, the extraordinary memoir of the veteran Guyanese black nationalist, Ras Makonnen, *Pan-Africanism from Within*, recorded and edited by Kenneth King (Nairobi: Oxford University Press 1973), pp. 31–4, and p. 36 n. 18.

95. Dennis Forsythe, "West Indian Radicalism in America," in Frances Henry, ed., *Ethnicity in the Americas* (The Hague: Mouton 1976), p. 306.

96. Schuyler, *Black and Conservative*, pp. 123–4, 145.

97. Hill, "Introduction" p. vi, and *Garvey Papers*, vol. i, pp. 521–7.

98. This American downgrading undoubtedly contributed to the light-skinned Jamaican J. A. Rogers' frenetic research for the stated purpose of "vindicating the Negro race." Arriving in 1906, Rogers, like the rest of his Caribbean compatriots, was not prepared for American racism. Rogers deserves but has yet to find a biographer. W. Burghardt Turner has written a fine profile of Rogers in the tradition of Rogers' own *World's Great Men of Color*: "Joel Augustus Rogers: An Afro-American Historian," *Negro History Bulletin*, vol. 35, no. 2, February 1972, pp. 34–8.

99. Richard Frucht, "Emigration, Remittances, and Social Change: Aspects of the Social Field of Nevis, West Indies," *Anthropologia*, vol. x, no. 2, 1968, esp. pp. 198–9; Richardson, *Caribbean Migrants*, pp. 24–5, 133–4.

100. Marcus Garvey, "The Negro's Greatest Enemy," *Current History*, September 1923; reprinted in *Garvey Papers*, vol. i, pp. 3–12; citation p. 5.

101. Between 1899 and 1926, 5,213 black mariners migrated to the United States; this accounted for over 4 percent of the total adult black migration to the United States over the period; calculated from *Immigration Reports*, 1899–1926.

102. Anon., "Ferdinand C. Smith (1894–1861), Jamaican Fighter for Democracy and Socialism," *Socialism!* (Organ of the Workers' Liberation League, Jamaica), vol. 2, no. 1, January 1975; Philip S. Foner and Ronald L. Lewis, eds, *Black Workers: A Documentary History From Colonial Times to the Present*, (Philadelphia: Temple University Press 1989), p. 42; Reid, *The Negro Immigrant*, p. 122; Naison, *Communists in Harlem During the Depression*, pp. 245, 261, 294.

103. See William Cohen, *At Freedom's Edge: Black Mobility and the Southern White Quest for Racial Control 1861–1915* (Baton Rouge: Louisiana State University Press 1991).

104. See Barbeau and Henri, *The Unknown Soldier*; Jack Foner, *Blacks and the Military in American History* (New York: Praeger Publishers 1974), chap. 6; Robert Mullen, *Blacks in America's Wars* (New York: Pathfinder Press 1973); Bernard Nalty, *Strength for the Fight: A History of Black Americans in the Military* (New York: Free Press 1986), pp. 101–24; and the testimony of Harry Haywood of his own experience in the army in France during the war, *Black Bolshevik: Autobiography of an Afro-American Communist* (Chicago: Liberator Press 1978), chap. 2. The radical black press at the time carried a number of important reports, testimonies and analyses of the experience of black soldiers. *The Messenger* magazine was especially copious in its reportage; see January 1918; March 1919; May–June 1919; July 1919; August 1919; and October 1919. Cf. *The Crusader*, December 1919; January 1920; May 1920; and June 1920. The *Crisis* (May 1919) carried a powerful exposé of the treatment of the black troops in France: W. E. B. Du Bois, "Documents of the War"; see also idem, "An Essay Toward a History of the Black Man in the Great War," *The Crisis*, June 1919; William Tuttle, "Views of a Negro During 'The Red Summer' of 1919: A Document," *Journal of Negro History*, July 1966.

105. See, Sir R. Lindsay [British Ambassador to the United States] to Foreign Secretary, "Memorial Presented to Consul General Campbell, New York by West Indians in New York and Brooklyn," January 17, 1934, FO 369/2379, Public Record Office, Kew, London.

106. Sir R. Lindsay, "Reports on West Indian Groups in the United States," March 8, 1934, F.O. 369/2379, Public Record Office, Kew, London.

107. For an appreciation of the condition of British Caribbean migrants in Cuba and their relations with British consulate officials there see FO371/9535 [Public Record Office, Kew, London], and especially the 1924 "Petition of Natives of all the West Indian Islands Residing in Cuba. Prepared and Fowarded [*sic*] Under the Auspices of the West Indian Workers Union." See also Anni Midwood, "Anglo-Cuban Relations 1918–1925," paper presented to the Society for Caribbean Studies Annual Conference, June 1989, Hoddesdon, Hertfordshire, England.

108. Lindsay, "Memorial Presented."

109. I have encountered not a single case of a prominent radical voluntarily returning for good to the islands during the period under review. Radicals were deported especially in the 1930s, 1940s, and 1950s, but apparently—with the exception of a few students who returned after their studies, especially medical students—they seldom returned unforced. Nevertheless, the knowledge that one could always retreat to the islands if things got bad in America must have provided a great sense of security. Indeed, during the Depression many Caribbeans left the United States for good.

110. Hart, "Jamaica and Self-Determination, 1660–1970" pp. 282–283; *Garvey Papers*, vol. i, n. 2, p. 21.

111. Elkins, "Suppression of the *Negro World* in the British West Indies"; and idem, "Marcus Garvey, the *Negro World*, and the British West Indies: 1919–1920."

112. Amy Jacques Garvey, *Garvey and Garveyism* (New York: Macmillan 1970); Rupert Lewis, *Marcus Garvey: Anti-Colonial Champion* (London: Karia Press 1987), pp. 197ff.

113. *Garvey Papers*, vol. i, pp. 527–30.

114. "Jamaica: Detention of W. A. Domingo," CO 968/68/6. After keeping the file on this disgraceful incident secret for over fifty years, the British authorities finally released it on

January 1, 1994—weeded of all its previous content, barring that which was already in the public domain.

115. Robert Hill, "Domingo, W. A.," in Bernard Johnpoll and Harvey Klehr, eds, *Biographical Dictionary of the American Left* (Westpoint, Conn.: Greenwood Press 1986), p. 116.

116. Idem, "Huiswoud, Otto," in ibid., pp. 219–21. Maria Van Enckevort, "The Caribbean Diaspora in France in the 1930s," paper presented to the Association of Caribbean Historians, Kingston, Jamaica 1994.

117. Jacques Garvey, *Garvey and Garveyism*, p. 233.

118. Ras Makonnen, *Pan-Africanism from Within*, pp. 123–4.

119. For Gramsci's discussion of the difference in the relation between state and civil society in Eastern and Western Europe see, his *Selections from the Prison Notebooks* (London: Lawrence and Wishart 1971), esp. pp. 234–8.

120. The argument is developed in Chapter 4 below.

121. Hubert Harrison, *The Negro and the Nation* (New York: Cosmo-Advocate Publishing Company 1917), pp. 45–6. A. Philip Randolph and Chandler Owen were two Afro-Americans who were not only openly agnostic, but atheistic. They certainly fell in the category of those whom Fenton Johnson condemned as "extreme rationalists."

122. W. Burghardt Turner and Joyce Moore Turner, eds, *Richard B. Moore: Caribbean Militant in Harlem: Collected Writings 1920–1972* (Bloomington: Indiana University Press 1988), pp. 22–7.

123. See, for instance, Garrie Ward Moore, "A Study of A Group of West Indian Negroes in New York City" (Master's thesis, Columbia University 1913), pp. 38–9.

124. Ibid., pp. 28–42; Makonnen, *Pan-Africanism from Within*, pp. 99–100.

125. The world of the cigar makers and Afro-Hispanic migrants is discussed in Chapters 7 and 8, below.

126. Hubert Harrison, *The Negro and the Nation*; idem, *When Africa Awakes: The "Inside Story" of the Stirrings and Strivings of the New Negro in the Western World* (New York: The Porro Press 1920); Jeffrey Babcock Perry, "Hubert Henry Harrison, 'The Father of Harlem Radicalism': The Early Years— 1883 Through the founding of the Liberty League and 'The Voice' in 1917" (Ph.D. diss., Columbia University, 1986), chaps i and ii; Calvin Holder, "The Rise of the West Indian Politician in New York City, 1900–1952," *Afro-Americans in New York Life and History*, vol. 4, no. 1, January 1980; Nancy Weiss, *Farewell to the Party of Lincoln: Black Politics in the Age of FDR*, (Princeton: Princeton University Press 1983). I discuss Harrison and his ideas in greater detail in Chapter 5.

127. James Weldon Johnson, *Black Manhattan* (New York: Alfred Knopf 1930), p. 153; Reid, *The Negro Immigrants*, pp. 84–5; *Immigration Reports*, 1899–1932.

128. US Dept of Commerce, *Fifteenth Census*, Table 5, p. 1224. The illiteracy rate amongst foreign-born whites were in 1920 and 1930, 13.7 percent and 10.3 percent, respectively.

129. On top of the inevitable self-selection involved in the migration process, prospective immigrants were required, beginning in 1917, to pass a literacy test in order to be admitted to the country. The literacy test, thus, screened the black population that entered the United States. For the background to the test, see Maldwyn A. Jones, *American Immigration* (Chicago: University of Chicago Press 1960), pp. 259ff., John Higham, *Strangers in the Land: Patterns of American Nativism 1860–1925* (New York: Atheneum 1963), esp. pp. 202–3.

130. It should be noted that although the mean for the region was 22 percent, there was great variation in the level between the territories. Barbados stood, at one extreme, with only 7.3 percent, while Dominica stood at the other with 44.8 percent. David Lowenthal, "The Population of Barbados," Table 6, p. 468.

131. Harrison, *When Africa Awakes*, p. 123.

132. Harrison's life and career are discussed at length in Chapter 5.

133. Harrison, *When Africa Awakes*, p. 125.

134. Marcus Garvey, *Life and Lessons*, edited by Robert Hill and Barbara Bair (Berkeley: University of California Press 1987), p. 184.

135. Ibid., p. 189.

136. Chisholm, *Unbought and Unbossed*, p. 13.

137. The best study of oratory and the performative use of words in the Caribbean is Roger D. Abrahams, *The Man-of-Words in the West Indies: Performance and the Emergence of Creole Culture* (New Haven: Johns Hopkins University Press 1983); see also Peter J.

Wilson, *Crab Antics: A Caribbean Case Study of the Conflict Between Reputation and Respectability* (Prospect Heights, Ill.: Waveland Press 1995).

138. Makonnen, *Pan-Africanism From Within*, p. 98.

139. See Table 2.1. The Portuguese-speaking black migrants from Cape Verde and the Azores—the largest group of black migrants after the Caribbeans—had educational and occupational profiles markedly different to those of the Afro-Caribbeans. Their level of literacy was considerably lower, and a significantly smaller proportion were in skilled and professional occupations. Thus, from 1914 onwards, as the proportion of Portuguese-speaking migrants declined, so, too, did the aggregate levels of illiteracy and unskilled labor among the black migrants.

140. George Eaton, "Trade Union Development in Jamaica," *Caribbean Quarterly*, vol. 8, no. 1, 1962, pp. 49–50; for a fine discussion of the problems of artisans in early twentieth-century Jamaica, see Erna Brodber, "A Second Generation of Freemen, 1907–1944", pp. 125–9.

141. Clyde Jemmott, "Emigration and Barbados: Reflections," *The West Indian-American*, November 1927, p. 4.

142. CO 137/748, Dispatch 391, June 1921, enclosure: The Jamaica League, "The Right Honourable Colonel Winston Churchill, P. C.[,] His Majesty's Principal Secretary of State for the Colonies," May 1921, pp. 3–4. No doubt the memorialists were mindful of the fact that E. Ethelred Brown, one of the two founders of the League, had left Jamaica for good the previous year to settle in Harlem. For more on the League see James Carnegie, *Some Aspects of Jamaica's Politics, 1918–1938* (Kingston: Institute of Jamaica 1973), esp. pp. 97–8, 102–4; for more on Ethelred Brown, see Mark D. Morrison-Reed, *Black Pioneers in a White Denomination*. Brown's papers are deposited at the Schomburg Center for Research in Black Culture, New York Public Library.

143. *Saint Christopher Gazette and Charibbean* [*sic*] *Courier*, Sept. 14, 1903; *St. Kitts Daily Express*, June 21, 1909, both cited in Richardson, *Caribbean Migrants*, p. 133.

144. Domingo, "Gift of the Black Tropics," pp. 344–45; Reid, *The Negro Immigrant*, pp. 83–4.

145. Helen Tucker, "Negro Craftsmen in New York," *Southern Workman*, vol. xxvi, no. 10, October 1907, pp. 549–50; George Edmund Haynes, *The Negro at Work in New York City: A Study in Economic Progress* (New York: Columbia University 1912), p. 58.

146. This figure includes 2.1 percent from South America, most of whom, apparently, turned out to be Guyanese.

147. Haynes, *The Negro at Work in New York City*, pp. 100–101, 108.

148. Reid, *The Negro Immigrant*, p. 121. Cf. Herbert G. Gutman, *The Black Family in Slavery and Freedom, 1750–1925* (New York: Pantheon Books 1976), where a radically different pattern of occupational distribution is given for 1925; see Tables A-41 and A-42, pp. 512–14. Unfortunately, the reliability of Gutman's figures is called into question by his methodological silence: we are not given any information about how he arrived at these magnitudes (was there some kind of sampling involved? if so, what kind?), nor, for that matter, are we even enlightened about the source of the raw data. He apparently used the New York State manuscript census, but he is explicit about this as a source only in relation to his figures for 1905 and the Tenderloin district of Manhattan (pp. 450–5).

149. J. C. Walter and J. L. Ansheles, "The Role of the Caribbean Immigrant in the Harlem Renaissance," *Afro-Americans in New York Life and History*, vol. 1, no. 1, January 1977, pp. 51–2. Carter G. Woodson, *The Negro Professional Man and the Community* (Washington, DC: The Association for the Study of Negro Life and History 1934), p. 165, similarly reported that 9 percent of black dentists were from the Caribbean. Also see A. M. Wendell Malliet, "Some Prominent West Indians," *Opportunity*, November 1926, p. 351; and Alfred E. Smith, "West Indian on the Campus," *Opportunity*, August 1933.

150. The fact that during this period dressmakers and seamstresses in the Caribbean were hit hard by imported ready-to-wear clothing, and the breakthrough of Caribbean migrant women in the New York needle trades, largely account for their low rate of return to the islands. See Rhoda Reddock, "Women and Garment Production in Trinidad and Tobago 1900–1960," *Social and Economic Studies*, vol. 39, no. 1, March 1990, pp. 89–125; idem, *Women, Labour and Politics in Trinidad and Tobago: A History* (London: Zed Books 1994), pp. 85–88; Rosalyn Terborg-Penn, "Survival Strategies Among African-American Women Workers: A Continuing Process," in Ruth Milkman, ed., *Women, Work and Protest: A Century of US Women's Labor History* (Boston: Routledge & Kegan Paul 1985), pp. 147–51.

151. In looking at the training of black physicians in the United States, Woodson reported that because of their better elementary education Caribbean students generally did much better than their Afro-American counterparts, especially those from the South, in medical school. He wrote, emphatically: "In the case of those [students] coming over from the West Indies, . . . the elementary schools attended were at strategic points where thorough training was easily obtained. This had a telling effect in the advantage which these West Indian trained students have had over Negro medical students who have been handicapped by the lack of thorough training in the backward parts of this country. Several deans in medical schools, where Negroes especially have been trained, have thus testified." Woodson, *The Negro Professional Man*, p. 83.

152. Reid, *The Negro Immigrant*, pp. 196–197; Alfred Smith, "West Indian on the Campus"; US Senate, *Abstracts of Reports of the Immigration Commission, with Conclusions and Recommendations and Views of the Minority*, vol. 1, (Senate Doc. no. 747, 61st Cong., 3rd sess.) (Washington DC: Government Printing Office 1910), p. 761, Table 34.

153. Domingo, "Gift of the Black Tropics," pp. 344–5; Reid, *The Negro Immigrant*, p. 122.

154. Quoted in Raphael, "West Indians and Afro-Americans," p. 444.

155. US Immigration Commission, *Abstracts of Reports of the Immigration Commission*, vol. 1, Table 17, pp. 808–9; of the 78,342 female breadwinners in the needle trades in New York City in 1900, 87 percent were foreign-born white women, or women with foreign-born parents (p. 807).

156. Rosalyn Tagenborg-Penn claims that many of these women pass for white, but such light-skinned women could not have been numerous enough to account for the significant Caribbean presence in the needle trades within a relatively short period of time. Tagenborg-Penn, "Survival Strategies Among African-American Women Workers," pp. 147, 150–1.

157. Sterling D. Spero and Abram L. Harris, *The Black Worker: The Negro and the Labor Movement* (New York: Columbia University Press 1931), p. 341; Maida Springer-Kemp, who was born in Panama of an Afro-Panamanian mother and a Barbadian father and grew up in Harlem, became a high-ranking official in the ILGWU in the 1930s and 1940s; see Yevette Richards, "'My Passionate Feeling About Africa': Maida Springer-Kemp and the American Labor Movement," (Ph.D. diss., Yale University 1994); and "Maida Springer Kemp," in Ruth Edmonds Hill, ed., *The Black Woman Oral History Project*, vol. 7 (Westport: Meckler Publishing 1991), pp. 39–145.

158. For a discussion of some of the stereotypes see Reid, *The Negro Immigrant*, pp. 107–12; see also Ottley, "*New World A-Coming*," p. 47.

159. Sidney Poitier, *This Life* (New York: Alfred A. Knopf 1980), p. 46. Poitier had been prematurely born in Miami when his parents, peasant farmers Evelyn and Reginald Poitier, had made a trip to the city. The Poitiers had gone to Miami, as they had on previous occasions, to sell about a hundred boxes of their tomatoes at the Produce Exchange. They had travelled by boat from Cat Island in the Bahamas, where they lived, in the hope of selling their produce to the highest bidder. Evelyn Poitier was seven months pregnant, but on the evening of February 20, 1927, she went into labor and gave birth to Sidney. The unexpected arrival of Sidney, who weighed only three pounds when he was born, detained the Poitiers for three months in Miami. Sidney did not return to the United States until 1943. His childhood was spent on Cat Island and Nassau.

160. See Makonnen, *Pan-Africanism from Within*, pp. 61–5; and Claude McKay, *A Long Way From Home: An Autobiography* (New York: Lee Furman 1937), pp. 8–9.

161. James Weldon Johnson, *Negro Americans, What Now?* (New York: Viking Press 1934), p. 103.

162. Raphael, "West Indians and Afro-Americans," p. 445.

163. Paule Marshall, *Brown Girl, Brownstones* (New York: Random House 1959).

164. Reid, *The Negro Immigrant*, p. 84.

165. Ibid., pp. 196–7.

166. This seem to have been the case in New York in the first half of the century; see Holder, "The Rise of the West Indian Politician."

167. See, for example: Vincent, *Black Power and the Garvey Movement*, pp. 152 and 267–70; Reid, *The Negro Immigrant*, pp. 96 and 121–2; Anderson, *A. Philip Randolph* pp. 153ff; William H. Harris, *Keeping the Faith: A Philip Randolph, Milton P. Webster, and the Brotherhood of Sleeping Car Porters, 1925–1937* (Urbana: University of Illinois Press 1977); John C. Walter, "Frank R. Crosswaith and the Negro Labor Committee in Harlem,

1925–1939," *Afro-Americans in New York Life and History*, vol. 3, no. 2, July 1979; John Seabrook, "Black and White Unite: The Career of Frank B. Crosswaith," (Ph.D. diss., Rutgers University 1980). Important information on Caribbean working-class activity in Harlem can also be gleaned from two important studies of Harlem during the Depression years: Naison, *Communists in Harlem During the Depression*, and Cheryl Greenberg, *"Or Does It Explode?" Black Harlem in the Great Depression* (New York: Oxford University Press 1991).

168. Hill, "Huiswoud, Otto," pp. 219–20.

169. Turner and Turner, eds, *Richard B. Moore*, p. 24.

170. *Garvey Papers*, vol. i, pp. 527–529; "Rèminiscences of A. Philip Randolph," p. 175; Anderson, *A Philip Randolph*, pp. 80–81; Ras Makonnen, who first met Domingo in the late 1920s, gives more detail than anybody else about Domingo's business activity. The fact that Makonnen was from a business family in Guyana, and that he became a highly successful and radical businessman in England in the 1940s, perhaps explains the keenness of his observation of Domingo's business. He claimed that Domingo had a turnover of about $25,000 during the 1920s. "It consisted," reported Makonnen, "of importing from the West Indies the ingredients for pepper sauce, and in his own little factory in Harlem he would chop them and produce the various chutneys and sauces. You can see something of his ability by the fact that Woolworths took his products—and they don't play ball with anybody who doesn't deliver goods on time." Makonnen, *Pan-Africanism from Within*, p. 89.

171. Jean Stubbs, *Tobacco on the Periphery: A Case Study in Cuban Labour History, 1860–1958* (Cambridge: Cambridge university Press 1985), pp. 74–5, 184 n. 5; Fernando Ortiz, *Cuban Counterpoint: Tobacco and Sugar* (New York: Alfred A. Knopf 1947); Gary R. Mormino and George E. Pozzetta, "'The Reader Lights the Candle': Cuban and Florida Cigar Workers' Oral Tradition," *Labor's Heritage*, Spring 1993; Angel Quintero–Rivera, "Socialist and Cigarmaker: Artisans' Proletarianization in the Making of the Puerto Rican Working Class," *Latin American Perspectives*, vol.x, nos 2 and 3, Spring and Summer 1983; the tradition is further discussed in Chaps. 7 and 8 below.

172. See in particular, James, *Beyond A Boundary*, esp. pp. 13–54.

173. Reid, *The Negro Immigrant* p. 81; Marilyn Halter, *Between Race and Ethnicity: Cape Verdean American Immigrants, 1860–1965* (Urbana: University of Illinois Press 1993), p. 46.

174. Calculated from US Dept of Commerce, *Sixteenth Census of the United States: 1940*, Population, vol. II, part 5, Table 4, p. 14.

175. Ibid.; for New York City itself, the distribution in 1930 for the foreign-born black population was 51.3 percent male to 48.7 percent female; for the native-born black population it was 47.2 percent male to 52.8 percent female; ibid., Table C 36, p. 157; cf. Gutman, *The Black Family in Slavery and Freedom, 1750–1925*, Table A-40, pp. 511–12.

176. Reid, *The Negro Immigrant*, Table X, p. 243.

177. Gutman, *The Black Family in Slavery and Freedom, 1750–1925*, pp. 453–5, and Table A-44, p. 515.

178. For African Americans, Gutman, (ibid.) is the classic text, and for the Caribbean see the remarkable synthesis of Raymond T. Smith, *Kinship and Class in the West Indies: A Genealogical Study of Jamaica and Guyana* (Cambridge: Cambridge University Press 1988).

179. Ira Reid made some comparisons between the age distribution of the overall black population and black migrants arriving in 1930. This exercise is, however, of limited value for two reasons: (a) it provides information only on those entering in one particular year, not on those who already resided in the United States; and (b) 1930 was by no means representative of the previous years of migration—indeed, it was atypical.

180. Gutman, *The Black Family in Slavery and Freedom, 1750–1925*, Table A-40, p. 511. I have already sounded a note of caution about Gutman's figures for New York City in 1925. Nevertheless, these particular figures are by no means implausible as an overall reflection of the two populations.

3. Coming at Midnight: Race and Caribbean Reactions to America

1. Hugh Mulzac, *A Star to Steer By* (New York: International Publishers 1963), pp. 26–32.

2. Claude McKay, "A Negro Poet and his Poems," *Pearson's Magazine*, September 1918, p. 275.

3. Rayford Logan, *The Negro in American Life and Thought: The Nadir 1877–1901* (New York: The Dial Press 1954).

4. Stephen Jay Gould, *The Mismeasure of Man* (New York: W. W. Norton 1981); George Frederickson, *The Black Image in the White Mind: The Debate on Afro-American Character and Destiny, 1817–1914* (New York: Harper & Row 1971); idem, *The Arrogance of Race* (Middletown: Wesleyan University Press 1988).

5. John Hope Franklin, "*The Birth of a Nation*: Propaganda as History," in idem, *Race and History: Selected Essays, 1938–1988* (Baton Rouge: Louisiana State University Press 1989), p. 16; see also Jack Temple Kirby, *Media Made Dixie: The South in the American Imagination*, rev. edn (Athens: University of Georgia Press 1986), chap. 1, "Griffith, Dunning, and 'the Great Fact of Race'," pp. 1–22.

6. Elliott Rudwick, *Race Riot at East St. Louis, July 2, 1917* (Carbondale: Southern Illinois University Press 1964), p. 48.

7. Johnson, *Black Manhattan*, p. 239.

8. Oscar Leonard, "The East St. Louis Pogrom," *Survey*, July 14, 1917, p. 331.

9. Johnson, *Black Manhattan*, pp. 231ff; Rudwick, *Race Riot at East St Louis*; the text of Garvey's speech is reprinted in the *Garvey Papers*, vol. i, pp. 212ff; Turner and Turner, eds, *Richard B. Moore*, p. 35.

10. Mary White Ovington, *The Walls Came Tumbling Down* (New York: Harcourt, Brace and Company 1947), pp. 180–1; Johnson, *Black Manhattan*, p. 236; Rudwick, *Race Riot at East St Louis*, pp. 134–135.

11. Johnson, *Black Manhattan*, pp. 236–237; see also Ovington, *The Walls Came Tumbling Down*, p. 181.

12. Johnson, *Black Manhattan*, p. 237.

13. *New York Amsterdam News*, March 23, 1927; Henry, "The Place of the Culture of Migrant Commonwealth Afro-West Indians" pp. 313–314.

14. The testimonies are reprinted in Reid, *The Negro Immigrant*; page references are given parenthetically in the text.

15. Conditions in Colored Town, Miami, at the time when this migrant arrived there is helpfully discussed by Paul S. George in "Colored Town: Miami's Black Community, 1896–1930," *Florida Historical Quarterly*, vol. lvi, no. 4, April 1978, and "Policing Miami's Black Community, 1896–1930," *Florida Historical Quarterly*, vol. lvii, no. 4, April 1979.

16. W. E. B. Du Bois, "An Amazing Island," *Crisis*, June 1915, pp. 80–81.

17. Marcus Garvey to Moton, Feb. 29, 1916, reprinted in the *Garvey Papers*, vol. i, pp. 179–183, citation from p. 182, emphasis added.

18. W. E. B. Du Bois, "The Rise of the West Indian," *Crisis*, September 1920, p. 214.

19. Du Bois, "On Being Black," *The New Republic*, February 18, 1920, p. 340.

20. Langston Hughes, *The Chicago Defender*, November 29, 1947; Arnold Rampersad, *The Life of Langston Hughes: Vol. II: 1941–1967: I Dream A World* (New York: Oxford University Press 1988), pp. 138–9; Langston Hughes, *I Wonder as I Wander: An Autobiographical Journey*, (New York: Rinehart 1956), pp. 6–37; Charles Nichols, ed., *Arna Bontemps–Langston Hughes Letters, 1925–1967* (New York: Dodd, Mead & Co. 1980), p. 235; Paul Robeson, *The National Guardian*, December 20, 1948, reprinted in Philip Foner, ed., *Paul Robeson Speaks: Writings, Speeches, Interviews 1918–1974* (New York: Citadel Press 1978), pp. 190–191; Martin Duberman, *Paul Robeson* (New York: Alfred Knopf 1988), p. 336.

21. J. A. Rogers, "The West Indies: Their Political, Social and Economic Condition," *The Messenger*, September 1922, p. 484.

4. The Caribbean and the United States: Patterns of Race, Color, and Class

1. Such a formulation obviates the pitfalls of the "race relations" paradigm which latter takes for granted far too much of what needs to be explained in the first place, including the very notion of "race" itself. The race relations paradigm is predicated upon a reified idea of "race" located in nature, as it were, instead of seeing the phenomenon as a product of human society, human history, and human invention conditioned by power relations between different groups of people.

2. By "Hispanic Caribbean" I mean the Spanish-speaking Caribbean (Cuba, the Dominican Republic, and Puerto Rico), and people from the Spanish-speaking Caribbean. By "non-Hispanic Caribbean" I mean territories in the Caribbean that were under northern European colonial rule. Thus, the term refers collectively to British, Danish, Dutch, and French colonies in the region, plus the independent republic of Haiti, and to people from these territories.

3. Jesús Colón (1901–74) was a black Puerto Rican who migrated to the United States in 1918 and quickly became active in left-wing and Puerto Rican politics in New York City and elsewhere, but remained surprisingly unmoved and unprovoked by black nationalism. Colón and Schomburg (1874–1938) are discussed at length in Chapter 7.

4. James Dietz, *The Economic History of Puerto Rico: Institutional Change and Capitalist Development* (Princeton: Princeton University Press 1986), pp. 6–7; Eric Williams, ed., *Documents of West Indian History, 1492–1655* (Port of Spain: PNM Publishing Company 1963), pp. 38–40; Louis A. Pérez, *Cuba: Between Reform and Revolution*, 2nd ed. (New York: Oxford University Press 1995), pp. 31–34; Kenneth R. Andrews, *The Spanish Caribbean: Trade and Plunder 1530–1630* (New Haven: Yale University Press 1978); Knight, *The Caribbean*, p. 40; Arturo Morales Carrión, *Puerto Rico: A Political and Cultural History* (New York: W. W. Norton 1983), chap. 2; Fernando Picó, *Historia General de Puerto Rico*, 5th edn (Rio Piedras: Ediciones Huracán 1990), pp. 72–97.

5. Andrews, *The Spanish Caribbean*, p. 64.

6. The foregoing discussion of Havana and Cuba has drawn upon Knight, *The Caribbean*, pp. 44–6, and especially upon the excellent analysis of Pérez, *Cuba*, pp. 34–48; see also John Robert McNeill, *Atlantic Empires of France and Spain: Louisbourg and Havana, 1700–1763* (Chapel Hill: University of North Carolina Press 1985), esp. pp. 85–92, 97–104; Alan J. Kuethe, "Guns, Subsidies, and Commercial Privilege: Some Historical Factors in the Emergence of the Cuban National Character, 1763–1815," *Cuban Studies*, no. 16, 1986; idem, "Havana in the Eighteenth Century," in Franklin W. Knight and Peggy K. Liss, eds, *Atlantic Port Cities: Economy, Culture, and Society in the Atlantic World, 1650–1850* (Knoxville: University of Tennessee Press 1991).

7. Andrews, *The Spanish Caribbean*, has an excellent discussion of this transition.

8. Because of this pattern of rural settlement in Puerto Rico up to the eighteenth century Angel G. Quintero Rivera, in an insightful article, described the island as a "counter-plantation" society. But such a description is hardly apt as there was no plantation system to speak of in Puerto Rico, as there was, for instance, in Barbados, prior to the eighteenth century. Thus, there was no plantation system as such for the rural settlers to counter. Michiel Baud, in a similar discussion of Española, speaks of a "counter economy." This is a far more accurate term than "counter plantation" for what was taking place. See Rivera, "The Rural–Urban Dichotomy in the Formation of Puerto Rico's Cultural Identity," *Nieuwe West Indische Gids/New West Indian Guide*, vol. 61, nos. 3 and 4, 1987; and Baud, "A Colonial Counter Economy: Tobacco Production on Española, 1500–1870," *Nieuwe West Indische Gids/New West Indian Guide*, vol. 65, nos 1 and 2, 1991.

9. Production statistic from Knight, *The Caribbean*, Table 3, p. 365.

10. For a good overview of this process see Fraginals et al., eds, *Between Slavery and Free Labor*; the classic analysis of the transition in Cuba is provided by Manuel Moreno Fraginals, *El ingenio: El complejo económico social cubano del azúcar. Tomo 1, 1760–1860* (Havana: UNESCO 1964); but also see Franklin Knight, *Slave Society in Cuba During the Nineteenth Century* (Madison: University of Wisconsin Press 1970); and Rebecca Scott, *Slave Emancipation in Cuba: The Transition to Free Labor 1860–1899* (Princeton: Princeton University Press 1985). Mintz, *Caribbean Transformations*, Gordon Lewis, *Puerto Rico: Freedom and Power in the Caribbean* (New York: Monthly Review Press 1963), Francisco A. Scarano, *Sugar and Slavery in Puerto Rico: The Plantation Economy of Ponce, 1800–1850* (Madison: University of Wisconsin Press 1984), and James L. Dietz, *Economic History of Puerto Rico*, provide valuable accounts of the transition in Puerto Rico. Harry Hoetink, *The Dominican People, 1850–1900: Notes for a Historical Sociology* (Baltimore: Johns Hopkins University Press 1982) provides a good account of the transition in the Dominican Republic.

11. See Knight, *The Caribbean*, Table 4, pp. 366–7, for a statistical overview of the ethnic composition of the islands during the early nineteenth century. Ethnic composition and identity formation in the Dominican Republic were, of course, over-determined by the latter's troubled relation with Haiti. See Harry Hoetink, "The Dominican Republic in the Nineteenth Century: Some Notes on Stratification, Immigration, and Race," in Magnus Mörner, ed., *Race and Class in Latin America* (New York: Columbia University Press 1970); idem, *The*

Dominican People; Frank Moya Pons, "The Land Question in Haiti and Santo Domingo: The Sociopolitical Context of the Transition from Slavery to Free Labor, 1801–1843," in Fraginals et al., eds, *Between Slavery and Free Labor*.

12. Jerome Handler, *The Unappropriated People: Freedmen in the Slave Society of Barbados* (Baltimore: Johns Hopkins University Press 1974), p. 18; Douglas Hall, "Jamaica," in David Cohen and Jack Greene, eds, *Neither Slave Nor Free: The Freedmen of African Descent in the Slave Societies of the New World* (Baltimore: Johns Hopkins University Press 1974), p. 194; Kenneth Kiple, *Blacks in Colonial Cuba, 1774–1899* (Gainesville: University Presses of Florida 1976), p. 3; Luis M. Diaz Soler, *Historia de La Esclavitud Negra en Puerto Rico* (Rio Piedras: Universidad de Puerto Rico 1981), p. 94. The distribution of slave and free in the French, Danish, and Dutch Caribbean was similar to that of Barbados and Jamaica; see articles by Léo Elisabeth, Gwendolyn Midlo Hall, and Harry Hoetink, in Cohen and Greene, eds, *Neither Slave Nor Free*; and Neville Hall, *Slave Society in the Danish West Indies: St. Thomas, St. John and St. Croix* (Kingston: The Press—University of the West Indies 1992), p. 5.

13. See Knight, *Slave Society in Cuba During the Nineteenth Century*; Rebecca Scott, *Slave Emancipation in Cuba*; Mintz, *Caribbean Transformations*, esp. pp. 82–94; Dietz, *Economic History of Puerto Rico* pp. 34–53; Francisco Scarano has shown that between 1812 and 1828, while the free population in Puerto Rico's sugar growing districts of Mayaguez, Ponce, and Guayama increased by an average of 62 percent, the slave population grew by 296 percent; the rate of surplus extraction intensified, the treatment of slaves deteriorated as sugar boomed: Scarano, *Sugar and Slavery in Puerto Rico*, pp. 25–34.

14. Mintz, *Caribbean Transformations*, p. 94.

15. See the excellent essay on the subject by Harry Hoetink, "'Race' and Color in the Caribbean," in Sidney Mintz and Sally Price, eds, *Caribbean Contours* (Baltimore: Johns Hopkins University Press 1985), and also the very sharp observations of Gordon Lewis in relation to Puerto Rico, in his *Puerto Rico*, esp. pp. 281–8, as well as those of Mintz, *Caribbean Transformations*, pp. 55–8 and 126–30; for a useful analysis of the similarities and differences between Cuba and Puerto Rico on these matters see Jorge Duany, "Ethnicity in the Spanish Caribbean: Notes on the Consolidation of Creole Identity in Cuba and Puerto Rico, 1762–1868," *Ethnic Groups*, vol. 6, 1985.

16. Benjamín Nistal-Moret, "Problems in the Social Structure of Slavery in Puerto Rico During the Process of Abolition, 1872," in Fraginals et al., eds, *Between Slavery*, pp. 146–7; B. W. Higman, *Slave Populations of the British Caribbean, 1807–1834* (Baltimore: Johns Hopkins University Press 1984), p. 116; idem, *Slave Population and Economy in Jamaica, 1807–1834* (Cambridge: Cambridge University Press 1976), p. 142.

17. For an overview of the position of this category of people within the Americas during slavery, see Cohen and Greene, eds, *Neither Slave Nor Free*.

18. Louis Pérez, "Politics, Peasants, and People of Color: The 1912 'Race War' in Cuba Reconsidered," *Hispanic American Historical Review*, vol. 66, no. 3, February 1986, p. 512; Robert B. Hoernel provides a very helpful analysis of late nineteenth- and early twentieth-century Oriente in his "Sugar and Social Change in Oriente, Cuba, 1898–1946," *Journal of Latin American Studies*, vol. 8, pt. 2, November 1976; see also Lisandro Pérez, "Iron Mining and Socio-Demographic Change in Eastern Cuba, 1884–1940," *Journal of Latin American Studies*, vol. 14, pt 2, November 1982; Scott, *Slave Emancipation*, esp. pp. 256–259; Ada Ferrer, "Social Aspects of Cuban Nationalism: Race, Slavery, and the Guerra Chiquita, 1879–1880," *Cuban Studies*, no. 21, 1991; Karen Robert, "Slavery and Freedom in the Ten Years' War, Cuba, 1868–1878," *Slavery and Abolition*, vol. 13, no. 3, December 1992; Aline Helg, *Our Rightful Share: The Afro-Cuban Struggle for Equality, 1886–1912* (Chapel Hill: University of North Carolina Press 1995).

19. Diaz Soler, *Historia de la Esclavitud*, p. 256; Olga Jiménez de Wagenheim, *Puerto Rico's Revolt for Independence: El Grito de Lares* (1985; Princeton and New York: Markus Wiener Publishing 1993), p. 22. Strangely, Jiménez de Wagenheim claims that in 1860, "more than half of the peasant farmers, artisans, and proprietors" were members of the free colored population, but the evidence she points to, quoted above, does not sustain her assertion; see ibid., pp. 21–2. José Luis Gonzalez thinks that black Puerto Ricans, even during the period of slavery, had a greater attachment to the island than the whites, many of whom were in fact foreigners. Francisco Scarano forcefully brings out the role of foreigners in Puerto Rico's sugar industry in the nineteenth century. See José Luis González, *Puerto Rico: The Four-Storeyed Country and Other Essays* (1980; Princeton: Markus Wiener Publishing, Inc. 1993), pp. 9–13;

Scarano, *Sugar and Slavery in Puerto Rico*, esp. chap. 4. In both Cuba and Puerto Rico the discriminatory policies of the Spanish toward creoles and especially toward black creoles, helped to trigger and sustain black participation in the revolts.

20. Patricia Weiss Fagen, "Antonio Maceo: Heroes, History, and Historiography," *Latin American Research Review*, vol. xi, no. 3, 1976; Philip Foner, *Antonio Maceo: The "Bronze Titan" of Cuba's Struggle for Independence* (New York: Monthly Review Press 1977); Donna M. Wolf, "The Cuban *Gente de Color* and the Independence Movement, 1879–1895," *Revista / Review Interamericana*, vol. 5, Fall 1975; Helg, *Our Rightful Share*.

21. This is a point that is very effectively made by Pérez in his revionist analysis of the so-called *guerra de razas* of 1912 in Oriente province; see Pérez, "Politics, Peasants"; Helg, in her valuable book (*Our Rightful Share*), tends to understate the level of cross-racial collaboration in Cuban history.

22. González, *Puerto Rico: The Four-Storeyed Nation*, p. 128.

23. G. Lewis, "Race Relations in Britain: A View From the Caribbean," *Race Today*, vol. 1, no.3, July 1969, p. 80; idem, *Main Currents in Caribbean Thought: The Historical Evolution of the Caribbean in its Ideological Aspects, 1492–1900* (Baltimore: Johns Hopkins University Press 1983), p. 9.

24. It is worth noting, though, that the *Cedula de Gracias* that was granted to Puerto Rico in 1815 gave free black immigrants to the island half the amount of land that it granted to free whites, three instead of six acres. Indeed, the free black immigrant was allocated the same amount of land that a white immigrant would be granted for each slave he brought to the island. Dietz, *Economic History of Puerto Rico*, p. 21. In Cuba, a battery of explicitly anti-discriminatory legislation was passed in the 1880s and 1890s, thanks largely to the vigorous agitation of the people of color. Hugh Thomas, *Cuba, or the Pursuit of Freedom* (London: Eyre & Spottiswoode 1971), p. 293; Wolf, "The Cuban *Gente de Color*," pp. 407–8.

25. Lloyd G. Barnett, *The Constitutional Law of Jamaica* (Oxford: Oxford University Press 1977), p. 12.

26. Lewis, *Puerto Rico*, p. 282.

27. Rogers, "The West Indies," *Messenger*, September 1922, p. 484. Rogers skipped too lightly over the genuine differences between the *de jure* and *de facto* condition of black people in the Caribbean *vis-à-vis* their counterparts in the United States.

28. McKay, *Harlem*, p. 134; see also Du Bois, "The Rise of the West Indian," p. 214.

29. US House of Representatives, 66th Cong., 2nd Sess., *Anti-Lynching Bill*, Report No. 1027 (Washington: Government Printing Office 1920), see esp. Memorandum from the NAACP contained therein; Walter White, *Rope and Faggot: A Biography of Judge Lynch* (New York: Alfred Knopf 1929); Robert L. Zangrando, *The NAACP Crusade Against Lynching, 1909–1950* (Philadelphia: Temple University Press 1980).

30. Orlando Patterson, *The Sociology of Slavery: An Analysis of the Origins, Development and Structure of Negro Slave Society in Jamaica* (London: MacGibbon and Kee 1967), p. 280; Eugene Genovese, *From Rebellion to Revolution: Afro-American Slave Revolts in the Making of the Modern World* (Baton Rouge: Louisiana State University Press 1979), p. 50; see also idem, *Roll, Jordan, Roll: The World the Slaves Made* (New York: Pantheon Books 1974), esp. pp. 587–97.

31. The literature on slavery and its aftermath in the Americas is vast and growing. Special mention ought to be made, however, of the audacious effort at comparative synthesis of slave resistance in the Americas: Genovese's, *From Rebellion to Revolution*; Robin Blackburn's *The Overthrow of Colonial Slavery, 1776–1848* (London: Verso 1988) is by far the most ambitious attempt of its kind to date, and is the only book that analyses the operation of chattel slavery across the Americas as a whole; and Eric Foner, *Nothing But Freedom: Emancipation and its Legacy* (Baton Rouge: Louisiana State University Press 1983) provides the best overview of the discordant aftermath of slavery in the Americas. Michael Craton's *Testing the Chains: Slave Rebellions in the British West Indies* (Ithaca: Cornell University Press 1982) provides a good analysis of the intensity of slave resistance in the British Caribbean, while Neville Hall's posthumously published *Slave Society in the Danish West Indies*, provides an excellent survey of the Danish islands.

33. Kelly Miller, "After Marcus Garvey—What of the Negro?" p. 494.

33. Idem in his column in the *New York Amsterdam News*, Sept.15, 1934.

34. Cruse, *The Crisis of the Negro Intellectual*, p. 119; see Postscript for further discussion of Cruse's work.

35. Both Dennis Forsythe and Keith Henry, though incomparably more sophisticated in

their analysis than Miller and Cruse, concede too much to this mistaken position; see Forsythe, "West Indian Radicalism Abroad," and idem, "West Indian Radicalism in America," and Henry, "The Place of the Culture of Migrant Commonwealth Afro-West Indians," and idem, "Caribbean Migrants in New York: The Passage from Political Quiescence to Radicalism."

36. The letters of Bynoe and Petioni were published in the *Amsterdam News*, of September 22, 1934. See also, in the same issue, the letter by an Afro-American radical, George Streator, who accused Miller of being an "intellectual mossback." Oscar Lewis's letter against Miller amounted to nothing more than Caribbean chauvinism of the most intellectually lazy variety. "Why," he asked, "is Kelly Miller so bitter toward the West Indians? Is the old sycophant jealous because he lacks the nerve and power with which our leaders are *inherently* gifted?" *Amsterdam News*, October 6, 1934, p. 8 (emphasis added).

37. *New York Amsterdam News*, Oct. 6, 1934.

38. *New York Amsterdam News*, Sept. 22, 1934.

39. The classic study of the epic of the Haitian Revolution is C. L. R. James, *The Black Jacobins: Toussaint L'Ouverture and the San Domingo Revolution* (London 1938; 2nd edn New York: Vintage Books 1963); in 1990 Carolyn Fick's outstanding analysis of the Revolution, *The Making of Haiti: The Saint Domingue Revolution from Below* (Knoxville: University of Tennessee Press) was published, and in a number of key respects this is a superior analysis to that of James'.

40. An excellent overview of the post-slavery experience is provided by Malcolm Cross and Gad Heuman, eds, *Labour in the Caribbean: From Emancipation to Independence* (London: Macmillan Publishers 1988); a sophisticated and persuasive analysis of profound popular cultural continuity (between the slavery and the post-slavery period) has been recently provided by Mervyn Alleyne, *Roots of Jamaican Culture* (London: Pluto Press 1988), which builds upon the pioneering work of Melville Herskovits and others; Ken Post has written the best case study of the labor revolts in the 1930s in his majestic trilogy on Jamaica: *Arise Ye Starvelings* and *Strike the Iron: A Colony at War—Jamaica, 1939–1945*, 2 vols, (Atlantic Highlands: Humanities Press 1981). I evaluated Post's work in Winston James, "The Hurricane that Shook the Caribbean," *New Left Review*, no. 138, March–April 1983. See also Roy Thomas, ed., *The Trinidad Labour Riots of 1937: Perspectives 50 Years Later* (St Augustine, Trinidad: Extra-Mural Studies Unit, University of the West Indies 1987); Richard Hart, *Rise and Organise: The Birth of the Workers and National Movements in Jamaica, 1936–1939* (London: Karia Press 1989); O. Nigel Bolland, *On the March: Labour Rebellions in the British Caribbean, 1934–39* (Kingston: Ian Randle Publishers 1995).

41. For examples of this middle-class opposition, see Bryan, *The Jamaican People*, chaps. 11 and 12; Bridget Brereton, *Race Relations in Colonial Trinidad, 1870–1900* (Cambridge: Cambridge University Press 1979), chap. 5; Rodney, *A History of the Guyanese Working People, 1881–1905*, chap. 5.

42. Walter Rodney, *A History of the Guyanese Working People, 1881–1905*, p. 151.

43. Paul Laurence Dunbar, *The Complete Poems of Paul Laurence Dunbar* (New York: Dodd, Mead, & Co. 1922), p. 71.

44. When Scotland Yard, in 1920, raided the offices of the radical *Workers' Dreadnought* in London where he worked, McKay did not hesitate to give a "big black grin" to the detective who asked him: "And what are you?" "Nothing, Sir," said he, as he niftily made his way down the stairs and away. The policeman gave a self-satisfied, racist, chuckle to this reply, but McKay, the stupid darky, had on his person the incriminating documents they were looking for. "I learned afterward," McKay recorded in his autobiography, "that he was the ace of Scotland Yard." McKay, *A Long Way From Home*, pp. 82–3.

45. James Weldon Johnson, *The Autobiography of an Ex-Colored Man* (1912; New York: Penguin Books 1990), pp. 14 and 54. See also Richard Wright's searing testimony, "The Ethics of Living Jim Crow," in his *Uncle Tom's Children* (New York: Harper Collins 1993).

46. The foregoing summary has drawn upon the work of Hilary Beckles, *Black Rebellion in Barbados: The Struggle Against Slavery, 1627–1838* (Bridgetown: Antilles Press 1984); idem, *A History of Barbados*; Karl Watson, *The Civilised Island: Barbados—A Social History, 1750–1816* (Bridgetown, Barbados: Caribbean Graphics 1979); Patterson, *The Sociology of Stavey*; Edward Brathwaite, *The Development of Creole Society in Jamaica, 1770–1820* (Oxford: Clarendon Press 1971); Craton, *Testing the Chains*; Knight, *The Caribbean*, Marshall, "Peasant Development in the West Indies since 1838"; James Anthony Froude, *The English in the West Indies or the Bow of Ulysses*, pp. 38, 101, 113–15; George Lamming, *In the Castle of My Skin*, p. 25.

47. Beckles, *Black Rebellion in Barbados*, pp. 48ff.

48. Ibid., chap. 5; Craton, *Testing the Chains*, pp. 254–66.

49. See, for instance, the classic composition of "Lord Kitchener" (Aldwyn Roberts), the Trinidadian calypsonian, "Take You Meat Out Me Rice"; the lyrics of this popular calypso are reproduced in Stewart Brown, Mervyn Morris, and Gordon Rohlehr, eds, *Voice Print: An Anthology of Oral and Related Poetry from the Caribbean* (London: Longman 1989), pp. 126–7; cf. Gordon Rohlehr, *Calypso and Society in Pre-Independence Trinidad* (Tunapuna, Trinidad: Gordon Rohlehr 1990), pp. 510–14.

50. John Hearne, "What the Barbadian Means to Me," in Andrew Salkey, ed., *Caribbean Essays: An Anthology* (London: Evans Brothers Ltd., 1973), p. 18.

51. Ibid., p. 19.

52. Froude, *The English in the West Indies*, pp. 102, 112–16.

53. Ibid., p. 101.

54. Ibid., pp. 111–12.

55. The remarkable history of frontal struggle and self-reliance in the Danish Caribbean, especially St. Croix, is told in Hall, *Slave Society in the Danish West Indies*.

56. The immigration statistics do not indicate the individual islands and territories from which the migrants from the British Caribbean came. There is, however, evidence—the details of which cannot be entered into here—that points to a substantial Barbadian presence among the early migrants. Indeed, before 1915 or so, the Barbadians might very well have been the largest single Caribbean migrant group in New York City. But, by the 1920s, the indications are that Jamaicans, Barbadians, and Virgin Islanders, were, in that order, the most numerous of the island groupings in the city.

57. The British Honduran and the Bahamian police force were also made up of Barbadians. Donald Wood, *Trinidad in Transition: The Years After Slavery* (Oxford: Oxford University Press 1968), p. 66; David Trotman, *Crime in Trinidad: Conflict and Control in a Plantation Society, 1838–1900* (Knoxville: University of Tennessee Press 1986) pp. 97, 101, 284, Table A.13; Howard Johnson, "Barbadian Immigrants in Trinidad, 1870–1897," *Caribbean Studies*, vol. 13, no. 3, 1973, p. 15; idem, "Social Control and the Colonial State: The Reorganization of the Police Force, 1888–1893," in his, *The Bahamas in Slavery and Freedom* (Kingston: Ian Randle Publishers 1991), pp. 110–24; Brereton, *Race Relations in Colonial Trinidad*, pp. 110–14; Ashton Chase, *A History of Trade Unionism in Guyana, 1900–1961* (Ruimveldt, Demerara: New Guyana Company Ltd n.d. [1964]); *Negro World*, October 28, 1922; Carlyle Harry, *Hubert Nathaniel Critchlow* (Georgetown: Guyana National Service Publishing Centre 1977), p. 7; Frederick McDermott Coard, *Bitter-Sweet and Spice* (Ilfracombe, Devon: Arthur H. Stockwell Ltd 1970), p. 20.

58. Ramesar, "Patterns of Regional Settlement and Economic Activity by Immigrant Groups in Trinidad, 1851–1900,"pp. 119 (Table 4), 205.

59. While the daily wage of male agricultural workers in Barbados stagnated at 10 pence between 1878 and 1903, that of his Trinidadian counterpart ranged between 1 shilling and ½ penny (1½/d) and 1 shilling and 8 pence (1/8d) in 1878, and between 1 shilling and 6 pence (1/6d) and 2 shillings (2/-) in 1895. Wages in Trinidad, were thus, more than twice the going rate in Barbados by the early 1890s. Johnson, "Barbadian Immigrants," pp. 6–7. The daily rate for canecutters in Guyana was from 1 shilling and 8 pence (1/8d) to 3 shillings and 4 pence (3/4d) between 1880–1884, which went up to between 2 shillings (2/-) and 4 shillings (4/-) over the years 1885 to 1895. Calculated from Rodney, *History of the Guyanese Working People*, 1881–1995. Table 10, p. 232. These figures, and, indeed, those often used by historians to indicate the differential in wages in the region are imperfect measures of *real* wages. They are silent about prices and therefore price differentials between one island and another. Nevertheless, all the indications are that in the post-emancipation period, Trinidad and Guyana had the highest real wages in the British Caribbean. The Barbadians provided supporting testimony to this fact by the direction of their movement.

60. Brereton, *Race Relations in Colonial Trinidad*, pp. 76, 113–14.

61. H. Johnson, "Barbadian Immigrants," p. 18.

62. See Owen Charles Mathurin, *Henry Sylvester Williams and the Origins of the Pan-African Movement, 1869–1911* (Westport: Greenwood Press 1976); J. R. Hooker, *Henry Sylvester Williams: Imperial Pan-Africanist* (London: Rex Collings 1975); idem, *Black Revolutionary: George Padmore's Path from Communism to Pan-Africanism* (New York: Praeger Publishers 1967); James, *Beyond A Boundary*; Paul Buhle, *C. L. R. James: The Artist as Revolutionary* (London: Verso 1988); Paul Buhle, ed., *C. L. R. James: His Life and Work*

(London: Allison and Busby 1986); Paget Henry and Paul Buhle, eds, *C. L. R. James's Caribbean* (Durham, N Ca: Duke University Press 1992); Brereton, *Race Relations in Colonial Trinidad*, esp. pp. 76, 89, 92–3, 96, 110–15; Johnson, "Barbadian Immigrants" idem, "Labour on the Move: West Indian Migration, 1922–30," in his *The Bahamas in Slavery and Freedom*, pp. 149–62; Roberts, "Emigration from the Island of Barbados"; Walter Rodney, "Barbadian Immigration into British Guiana, 1863–1924," paper presented to the Ninth Annual Conference of the Association of Caribbean Historians, University of the West Indies, Cave Hill, Barbados, April 3–7, 1977; idem, *A History of the Guyanese Working People, 1881–1905*; Makonnen, *Pan-Africanism from Within*, pp. 26–7; Perry, "Hubert Henry Harrison" p. 13; Hildred Britton, "The Negro and his Descendants in British Guiana," pt 1, in Nancy Cunard, ed., *Negro* (London: Nancy Cunard at Wishart and Co. 1934), pp. 501, 503–4; A. A. Thorne, "The Negro and his Descendants in British Guiana," pt. 2, in ibid., p. 506; Richard B. Moore and Hope R. Stevens, "Some Contributions of Barbadians Abroad," Richard B. Moore Papers, box 10, folder 40, Schomburg Center for Research in Black Culture; Francis Drakes, "The Development of Political Organisation and Political Consciousness in British Guiana, 1870–1964: The *Conscientizacao* of the Middle Class and the Masses" (Ph.D. diss., University of London 1989).

63. Sir R. Lindsay to Foreign Secretary, "Memorial Presented to Consul General Campbell, New York by West Indians in New York and Brooklyn." The official was not, strictly speaking, correct in his remark about the signatories. On the basis of provenance, the Barbadians were by far the single largest group of signatories—not the majority as such. Of the 23 signatories, 9 were from Barbados, 4 from St Kitts, 2 each from Jamaica and Trinidad, and 1 each from Antigua, Bermuda, British Guiana, Grenada, Monserrat, and St Vincent.

64. Robert Minor, unpublished and untitled essay, which begins "Eighty miles southward from Cuba," box 12, "Negro 1924–25," Robert Minor Collection, Rare Book and Manuscript Library, Columbia University.

65. The evidence from Panama, Cuba, the United States, Canada and Britain, suggests that on a political continuum of "radical" to "conservative" or "less radical", at the radical end are the Jamaicans accompanied by (in the United States), Virgin Islanders, and at the opposite end would be found Barbadians. Ras Makonnen and Walter Rodney make interesting observations on Caribbeans abroad: Makonnen, *Pan-Africanism from Within*, pp. 33–4, 57–65, 141; Robert Hill, ed., *Walter Rodney Speaks: The Making of an African Intellectual* (Trenton: Africa World Press 1990), pp. 10–12; see also John Western, *A Passage to England: Barbadian Londoners Speak of Home* (Minneapolis: University of Minnesota Press 1992).

5. Dimensions and Main Currents of Caribbean Radicalism in America: Hubert Harrison, the African Blood Brotherhood, and the UNIA

1. For a valiant, but problematic, effort at disaggregation in relation to the early years of the Socialist Party of America see Charles Leinenweber, "The Class and Ethnic Bases of New York City Socialism, 1904–1915," *Labor History*, vol. 22, no. 1, Winter 1981.

2. Strictly speaking these figures are not just for Caribbeans ("West Indians" is the term used in the Census), but for the "foreign-born Negro population." However, as mentioned earlier, between 1900 and 1932, over 80 percent of this population were of Caribbean provenance (see Table 1.2). Caribbeans resided in New York State and New York City in much greater proportion than the other groups of black migrants. See US Department of Commerce, *Fifteenth Census of the United States: 1930, Population*, vol. II, Tables 17 and 23, pp. 41 and 70; US Department of Labor, Bureau of Immigration, *Annual Report of the Commissioner General of Immigration to the Secretary of Labor* (Washington, DC: Government Printing Office 1899–) for the years 1899–1932; Reid, *The Negro Immigrant*, pp. 85–9; Holder, "The Causes and Composition of West Indian Immigration to New York City, 1900–1952," pp. 16–17.

3. It was also at this time that C. L. R. James (Trinidad)—who migrated to the United States, via Britain, in 1938 and very quickly became one of America's leading exponents of Trotskyism—was deported. On James, see Buhle, *C. L. R. James: The Artist as Revolutionary* (London: Verso 1988) and on the life of Claudia Jones, see Buzz Johnson, *"I Think of My Mother"—Notes on the Life of Claudia Jones* (London: Karia Press 1985). Angela Davis,

Women, Race and Class (New York: Random House 1981), pp. 167–71; on Ferdinand Smith, see anon., "Ferdinand C. Smith (1894–1961), Jamaican Fighter for Democracy and Socialism," *Socialism!* (Organ of the Workers' Liberation League, Jamaica), vol. 2, no. 1, January 1975, pp. 4–12.

4. See Naison, *Communists in Harlem During the Depression*.

5. Anderson, *A. Philip Randolph*, p. 80.

6. *The World*, April 5, 1903; J. A. Rogers, "Hubert Henry Harrison," *World's Great Men of Color*, vol. ii (1947; New York: Macmillan 1972), p. 433; Perry, "Hubert Henry Harrison", chaps i and ii.

7. Rogers, "Hubert Henry Harrison," p. 437; Perry, "Hubert Henry Harrison," p. 51.

8. Hubert H. Harrison, "The Negro Appeal to Europe," *New York Sun*, December 8, 1910; Harrison wrote a second letter in response to criticism of his first: Hubert H. Harrison, "The Appeal to Europe," *New York Sun*, December 19, 1910.

9. Charles W. Anderson, to Booker T. Washington, September 10, 1911, in Louis R. Harlan and Raymond W. Smock, eds, *The Booker T. Washington Papers*, vol. xi, 1911–12 (Urbana: University of Illinois Press 1981), pp. 300–1. Emmett Scott was Washington's secretary at the time.

10. Charles W. Anderson, to Booker T. Washington, October 30 1911, in ibid., p. 351.

11. The record of the deterioration and ending of Harrison's relationship with the Socialist Party is preserved in the Socialist Collections in the Tamiment Library, New York University. See especially Collection 5, Reel 8, Series V: 117, and 119; and Reel 9, Series VI: 4, Minutes 1900–1936; and Reel 9, Series VI: 5, Minutes 1900–1936; citations from: Minutes of the Executive Committee of Local New York, Oct. 6, 1913 (Reel 9, Series VI: 5, Minutes 1900–1936); Anna M. Sloan, Acting Executive Secretary, to Hubert H. Harrison, March 31, 1914 (Collection 5, Reel 8, Series V: 117); Harrison to Comrades [Local New York], June 23, 1912 (Collection 5, Reel 6, Series V: 31, Socialist Party, Local New York, Letter Books, 1907–1914); Report of the Grievance Committee, Central Committee, Local New York, May 6, 1914 (Collection 5, Reel 8, Series V: 117); Julius Gerber, Executive Secretary to Hubert H. Harrison, May 18, 1914 (Collection 5, Reel 8, Series V: 117).

12. "Towards the One Common End," *Promoter*, August 1920, p. 8.

13. Hodge Kirnon, "Hubert Harrison: An Appreciation," *New York Amsterdam News*, January 4, 1928.

14. *The Negro and the Nation*, and *When Africa Awakes*.

15. Cited in Anderson, *A. Philip Randolph*, p. 80.

16. Harrison, *When Africa Awakes*, pp. 80–82.

17. Ibid., p. 82.

18. Ibid., p. 81.

19. Ibid., p. 40; also see pp. 83–6. Sinn Fein actually translates as "ourselves alone" while Swadeshi translates as "of one's own country."

20. Hubert Harrison, "Socialism and the Negro," *International Socialist Review*, vol. 13, no. 1, July 1912, pp. 65–8; reprinted in *The Negro and the Nation*, pp. 21–9, citation p. 24; idem, *When Africa Awakes*, p. 86.

21. McKay, *A Long Way From Home*, pp. 118–19; Parker Hitt (Assistant Chief of Staff for Military Intelligence to Director, Headquarters, 2d Corps Area, Governors Island, New York City) to Director, Military Intelligence Division, Washington, DC, June 23, 1921; NA, RG 160, Records of Army Service Forces, Military Intelligence Division, file 10218–424–1.

22. This comes across very strongly in Garvey's widow's memoirs, Jacques Garvey, *Garvey and Garveyism*.

23. *Garvey Papers*, vol. i, p. 65. For an excellent overview of the civilizationist strand in early black nationalist thought see Wilson Jeremiah Moses, *The Golden Age of Black Nationalism, 1850–1925* (New York: Oxford University Press 1988).

24. Harrison, *When Africa Awakes*, pp. 34–5.

25. Ibid., pp. 130–31.

26. "The Reminiscences of A. Philip Randolph," Oral History Research Office, Columbia University 1973, pp. 153–154. (The interviews with Randolph were conducted in 1972.)

27. Interview with W. A. Domingo, January 18, 1958,; Theodore Draper Papers, Box 21, Folder 3, Robert W. Woodruff Library, Emory University; Richard B. Moore, "Afro-Americans and Radical Politics," in Turner and Turner, eds, *Richard B. Moore* p. 217. "Harrison's role as a discoverer and nurturer of Black talent was as important as it has been unacknowledged. In addition to the writers he exposed through his pioneering book review

columns, he was among the first to actively seek out and promote McKay, J. A. Rogers, the South African Solomon Plaatje and, indeed, Marcus Garvey himself." Tony Martin, *Literary Garveyism: Garvey, Black Arts and the Harlem Renaissance*, (Dover, Mass.: Majority Press 1983), pp. 132–3.

28. Henry Miller, *The Rosy Crucifixion, Book Two: Plexus* (New York: Grove Press 1965), pp. 560–61.

29. John T. Carroll, Letter to the Editor, *New York Globe*, Nov. 4, 1914.

30. McKay, *A Long Way From Home*, pp. 41, 113–14.

31. William Pickens, "Hubert Harrison: Philosopher of Harlem," *New York Amsterdam News*, February 7, 1923, p. 12; William Pickens, *Bursting Bonds: The Autobiography of a "New Negro"* (Bloomington: Indiana University Press, 1991), pp. 38–42; Richard B. Moore, "Harrison, Hubert Henry," in Logan and Winston, eds, *Dictionary of American Negro Biography*, pp. 292–3. For more on Harrison, see Philip Foner, *American Socialism and Black Americans: From the Age of Jackson to World War II* (Westport: Greenwood Press 1977), pp. 207–18; Rogers, pp. 611–19; John G. Jackson, "Hubert Henry Harrison: The Black Socrates," *American Atheist*, February 1987; Wilfred D. Samuels, "Hubert H. Harrison and 'The New Negro Manhood Movement,'" *Afro-Americans in New York Life and History*, vol. 5, January 1981. Perry's "Hubert Henry Harrison", is by far the most substantial piece of work on Harrison. Unfortunately, Perry's narrative ends in 1917 and therefore does not cover what is arguably, the most crucial political period of Harrison's life: the decade between the founding of the black nationalist Liberty League of Negro Americans in 1917, and his death in December 1927. With exclusive access to the Harrison Papers, Perry is now completing a two-volume biography of Harrison.

32. Reports by agent "P-138," "Re: Negro Activities," June 8 and 11, 1921; NA, RG 65, file BS 202–600–667.

33. W. F. Elkins, "'Unrest Among the Negroes': A British Document of 1919," *Science & Society*, vol. xxxii, no. 1, Winter 1968, pp. 77–8. The British were fully aware that the black turbulence in Harlem had serious repercussions in their Caribbean and African colonial possessions and were likely to continue to affect them; hence the interest on the part of Whitehall in Harlem radicalism, and its mobile and influential Caribbean protagonists.

34. *New York Amsterdam News*, December 28, 1927.

35. Vincent, *Black Power and the Garvey Movement*, p. 152.

36. Reid, *The Negro Immigrant*, p. 150; Vincent, *Black Power and the Garvey Movement* p. 152, footnote, and pp. 267–270; Elkins, "Marcus Garvey, the *Negro World*, and the British West Indies: 1919–1920," p. 66; Dennis Dickerson, *Out of the Crucible: Black Steelworkers in Western Pennsylvania, 1875–1980* (Albany: State University of New York Press 1986), p. 80; Judith Stein, *The World of Marcus Garvey: Race and Class in Modern Society* (Baton Rouge: Louisiana State University Press, 1986), pp. 231 and 245; Jeannette Smith-Irvin, *Marcus Garvey's Footsoldiers of the Universal Negro Improvement Association* (Trenton: Africa World Press 1989); George, "Colored Town: Miami's Black Community, 1896–1930," pp. 444–6; *Garvey Papers*, vol. iii, pp. 512–15.

37. The figures for branches are based on Table 5.1, below and the sources cited for that table; those for the distribution of the leadership is calculated on the basis of those provided by Vincent, *Black Power and the Garvey Movement*, pp. 152 and 267–70.

38. See Martin, *Race First*, pp. 183, 287, and 299.

39. Cited in *Garvey Papers*, vol. i, pp. 514–15 n. 1. The black migrants from Central America and South America who migrated to the United States during this period were nearly all of Caribbean provenance (overwhelmingly from the British Caribbean, and especially Jamaica and Barbados) who had worked on the Panama railroad and later the Panama Canal. Many of these workers then had moved on to the United States, directly from the Isthmus, especially after 1914 when work on the Canal ended.

40. Thurman, *Negro Life in New York's Harlem*, p. 20.

41. Reid, *The Negro Immigrant*, p. 150; cf. Birgit Aron, "The Garvey Movement" (Masters thesis, Columbia University 1947), where the author cautiously noted that the majority of the founders and a large portion of later membership of the UNIA in New York consisted of West Indians (p. 80). In 1922 one Afro-American critic of the UNIA claimed that none of the fifteen clerks and stenographers in Garvey's office was Afro-American. See Stein, *The World of Marcus Garvey* p. 148 n. 4.

42. Marcus Garvey, *Life and Lessons*, p. 109.

43. Claude McKay to Nancy Cunard, August 20, 1932; the Nancy Cunard Collection, Harry Ransom Humanities Research Center, University of Texas at Austin.

44. Donations of as little as 5 cents, especially from Southern Garveyites, were not infrequent. In 1923, for instance, Alice and Moses Powell from Maringouin, Louisiana gave 5 cents each. The 39 contributors from their division gave a total of $8.00, none giving more than 50 cents (*Negro World*, Oct. 6, 1923). Mary Gambrell Rolinson has done a fine essay on the UNIA in Georgia, which, to my knowledge, is the first substantial study of the UNIA anywhere in the South. Mary Gambrell Rolinson, "The Universal Negro Improvement Association in Georgia: Southern Strongholds of Garveyism," in John C. Inscoe, ed., *Georgia in Black and White: Explorations in the Race Relations of a Southern State, 1865–1950* (Athens: University of Georgia Press 1994).

45. On Los Angeles, Emory Tolbert, *The UNIA and Black Los Angeles: Ideology and Community in the American Garvey Movement* (Los Angeles: Center for Afro-American Studies, UCLA 1980); on Tobago, C. Boyd James, "Primitives on the Move: Some Historical Articulations of Garvey and Garveyism, 1887–1927" (Ph.D. diss., University of California, Los Angeles, 1982); and on Georgia, Rolinson, "The Universal Negro Improvement Association in Georgia."

46. Kwame Nkrumah, *Ghana: The Autobiography of Kwame Nkrumah* (1957; New York: International Publishers 1971), p. 45; Jacques Garvey, *Garvey and Garveyism*, p. 319; Stein, *The World of Marcus Garvey*, p. 1.

47. The literature on Garveyism is a vast and growing one but of particular note are the following: E. Cronon, *Black Moses: The Story of Marcus Garvey and the Universal Negro Improvement Association* (Madison: University of Wisconsin Press 1955 and 1969; Vincent, *Black Power and the Garvey Movement*; Jacques Garvey, *Garvey and Garveyism*; R. Burkett, *Garveyism as a Religious Movement* (Metuchen: The Scarecrow Press 1978); Martin, *Race First*; Stein, *The World of Marcus Garvey*; Lewis, *Marcus Garvey*; and the invaluable and impressively edited, *Garvey Papers*. To date (1997) eight out of a projected ten volume collection have been published.

48. See Mark D. Matthews, "'Our Women and What They Think': Amy Jacques Garvey and *The Negro World*," *Black Scholar*, May–June 1979; William Seraile, "Henrietta Vinton Davis and the Garvey Movement," *Afro-Americans in New York Life and History*, vol. 7, no. 2, July 1983; Tony Martin, "Amy Ashwood Garvey," *Jamaica Journal*, August-October 1987; idem, "Women in the Garvey Movement," in Rupert Lewis and Patrick Bryan, eds, *Garvey: His Work and Impact* (Kingston: Institute of Social and Economic Research, University of the West Indies 1988); Honor Ford-Smith, "Women and the Garvey Movement in Jamaica," in Lewis and Bryan, eds, *Garvey*; Barbara Bair, "True Women, Real Men: Gender, Ideology, and Social Roles in the Garvey Movement", in Dorothy O. Helly and Susan M. Reverby, eds, *Gendered Domains: Rethinking Public and Private in Women's History* (Ithaca: Cornell University Press 1992); idem, "Pan-Africanism as a Process: Adelaide Casely Hayford, Garveyism, and the Cultural Roots of Nationalism," in Sidney Lemelle and Robin Kelley, eds, *Imagining Home: Class, Culture and Nationalism in the African Diaspora* (London: Verso 1994). Eleanor Krohn Herrmann has a valuable and interesting discussion of the role of the Black Cross Nurses in the development of the health services in Belize: *Origins of Tomorrow: A History of Belizean Nursing Education* (Belize City: Ministry of Health, Belize 1985), chap. 3.

49. Martin, "Amy Ashwood Garvey," p. 33.

50. *Garvey Papers*, vol. i, pp. 246, 253–4.

51. *Garvey Papers*, vol. iv, p. 1037.

52. Ibid., pp. 1037–8.

53. *Negro World*, April 11, 1925; also, *Negro World*, September 13, 1924.

54. See UNIA *Constitution and Book of Laws* (July 1918); reprinted in *Garvey Papers*, vol. i, pp. 256–80; see especially Article v, Secs 3–7, of the General Laws, in ibid., pp. 269–70.

55. See "Rules and Regulations Governing the Universal African Black Cross Nurses," "Rules and Regulations Governing the Universal African Motor Corps," and "Rules and Regulations for Juveniles," all three were adopted at the 1921 convention; reprinted in *Garvey Papers*, vol. iii, pp. 766–72.

56. Maxine McDonnough (interviewer), "Sister Samad: Living the Garvey Life," *Jamaica Journal*, August–October 1987, p. 80.

57. Paule Marshall, "Black Immigrant Women in *Brown Girl, Brownstones*," in Constance

R. Sutton and Elsa M. Chaney, eds, *Caribbean Life in New York City: Sociocultural Dimensions* (New York: The Center for Migration Studies of New York 1987), p. 91.

58. Jacques Garvey, *Garvey and Garveyism*, pp. 112–13.

59. Ibid., p. 39.

60. The biographical information in this passage is drawn largely from the valuable profile of Amy Jacques Garvey provided by Rupert Lewis and Maureen Warner-Lewis, "Amy Jacques Garvey," *Jamaica Journal*, August–October 1987, pp. 39–43.

61. Lewis and Warner-Lewis, "Amy Jacques Garvey," p. 40; Jacques Garvey, *Garvey and Garveyism*, p. 113.

62. Jacques Garvey, *Garvey and Garveyism*, pp. 112–13. It is doubtful that George Jacques would have wanted a career in nursing for a first-born son or indeed any son. The suggestion, then, that he "socialized Amy into the surrogate role and interests of a first son" ought to be qualified. Lewis and Warner-Lewis, "Amy Jacques Garvey," p. 40. Lewis and Warner-Lewis wrote that Amy's father had planned to have his daughter articled to his solicitor, but in *Garvey and Garveyism* (pp. 112–13), Amy Jacques Garvey is explicit about nursing being her father's plan for her.

63. Jacques Garvey, *Garvey and Garveyism*, p. 113.

64. Ibid., pp. 39–41.

65. Lewis and Warner-Lewis, "Amy Jacques Garvey," p. 40.

66. Jacques Garvey, *Garvey and Garveyism*, pp. 222–3; emphasis added.

67. Quoted in Robert A. Hill, "Introduction," to Amy Jacques-Garvey, ed., *Philosophy and Opinions of Marcus Garvey*, 2 vols ([1923 and 1925] New York: Atheneum 1992), p. xxxiv.

68. Jacques Garvey, *Garvey and Garveyism*, p. 168.

69. Ibid., p. 169. See "The Love Amie (Dedicated to Mrs. Amy Jacques Garvey)," in Tony Martin, ed., *The Poetical Works of Marcus Garvey* (Dover, Mass.: The Majority Press 1983), pp. 41–2.

70. Jacques-Garvey, ed., *Philosophy and Opinions of Marcus Garvey*, vol. ii, p. viii.

71. Amy Jacques Garvey wrote six long and remarkable articles about the couple's journey to the West and South: *Negro World*, October 20, 27, November 3, 10, 17, and 24, 1923.

72. Jacques Garvey, *Garvey and Garveyism*, pp. 130–32; *Garvey Papers*, vol. v, pp. xxiv-xxv, lv; Hill, "Introduction," *Philosophy and Opinions*, pp. lxviii-lxx.

73. Quoted in Hill, "Introduction," *Philosophy and Opinions*, p. lxix. Briggs and the African Blood Brotherhood which he founded is discussed later in this chapter.

74. *Garvey Papers*, vol. v, pp. 398–9.

75. *Negro World*, July 21, 1923; reprinted in *Garvey Papers*, vol. v, pp. 398–9.

76. Jacques Garvey, *Garvey and Garveyism*, p. 41.

77. *Negro World*, June 7, 1924; a few months later she was more blunt when she wrote that the "few contributions we receive are not of sufficient literary merit to warrant their publication." *Negro World*, September 13, 1924.

78. *Negro World*, June 7, 1924.

79. *Negro World*, August 2, 1924.

80. *Negro World*, September 13, 1924.

81. *Negro World*, April 11, 1925.

82. *Negro World*, October 31, 1925. Mrs Garvey was still making appeals in 1926; see, for instance, *Negro World*, February 6, 1926.

83. *Negro World*, April 11, 1925.

84. *Negro World*, January 3, and 17, 1925.

85. *Negro World*, July 10, 1926.

86. *Negro World*, August 1, 1925.

87. *Negro World*, September 29, 1923. Advertisements for skin bleach were also carried on Mrs Garvey's page. See for instance, that for "DC Skin Bleach", *Negro World*, October 30, 1926.

88. *Negro World*, February 6, 1926.

89. Wilson Jeremiah Moses has a useful discussion of this issue in his book *The Golden Age of Black Nationalism, 1850–1925*.

90. *Negro World*, August 1, 1925.

91. *Negro World*, October 24, 1925.

92. *Garvey Papers*, vol. vi, pp. 150–51.

93. *Negro World*, April 9, 1927.

94. Ibid.

95. *Garvey Papers*, vol. vii, p. 971.

96. *Negro World*, April 23, 1927.

97. *Negro World*, May 14, 1927.

98. *Negro World*, December 13, and 20, 1924; and March 28, 1925.

99. Theodore Burrell to Theodore Draper, n.d. [early April 1958? Burrell's communication was in reply to a letter from Draper dated March 24, 1958]; Draper Papers, Box 21, Folder 2. Burrell was a member of the Supreme Council of the Brotherhood and a member of the editorial board of the *Crusader*.

100. Grace Campbell's background and role in the organization is discussed in detail below.

101. Cyril Briggs to Theodore Draper, March 17, 1958, p. 2; Theodore Draper Papers, Reel 8.

102. The most detailed discussions of the African Blood Brotherhood may found in Draper, *American Communism and Soviet Russia*, pp. 322–32; Theman Ray Taylor, "Cyril Briggs and the African Blood Brotherhood: Another Radical View of Race and Class During the 1920s," (Ph.D. Diss., University of California, Santa Barbara 1981), chaps. 8–10; and Hill, "Introduction."

103. Biographical details of early years drawn from Cyril Briggs, "Angry Blond Negro," unpublished autobiographical notes; Taylor, "Cyril Briggs and the African Blood Brotherhood," pp. 83–87; and Hill, "Introduction," pp. vi-viii. My thanks to Professor Hill for providing me with a copy of Briggs's autobiographical notes.

104. Cyril Briggs to Harry Haywood, July 29, 1962 (addendum), and August 4, 1962; emphasis in original. Harry Haywood Papers, Schomburg Center for Research in Black Culture.

105. Harry Haywood, *Black Bolshevik: Autobiography of an Afro-American Communist* (Chicago: Liberator Press 1978), p. 126; W. A. Domingo interview, January 18, 1958; Draper Collection, box 21, folder 1.

106. Haywood, *Black Bolshevik*, p. 127.

107. Ibid., p. 126.

108. Testimony of Cyril Valentine Briggs, House of Representatives, *Hearings Before the Committee on Un-American Activities*, 85th Congress, 2nd Session, Part 1, September 3, 1958, p. 78.

109. See Crawford's letters to Briggs, January 24, 1918, and February 25, 1918, both published in the *Crusader*, September 1918, p. 22; quotation from second letter.

110. *Crusader*, April 1921, p. 27.

111. Hill, "Introduction," p. xxiv; Draper, *American Communism and Soviet Russia*, pp. 326, 545 n. 34.

112. Hill, "Introduction," p. xxvii.

113. Cyril Briggs to Theodore Draper, April 14, 1958; Draper Collection. It should be noted here that in Briggs's letter the date for the Palmer raids is typed—and not once, but twice—as 1921, but corrected by hand as 1919. It is not clear if the correction was executed by Briggs or by the recipient of the letter, or by someone else. It is therefore possible that Briggs had simply forgotten when the Palmer raids took place, thinking that they occurred in 1921, rather than 1919. If that is the case, all that Briggs was trying to say was that he joined the Party in or before 1921, which comports far more easily with the existing evidence than 1919. It is also possible that Briggs was thinking of the government's raid—commonly known as the Bridgman raid—on the Party during its conference in Michigan that took place in 1922. One is, nevertheless, obliged to proceed on the assumption that Briggs meant 1919, not 1921, in his reference to the Palmer raids.

114. Briggs to Draper, March 17, 1958.

115. For presentation and analyses of the factions on the revolutionary left in the United States in the aftermath of the Bolshevik Revolution, see Draper, *The Roots of American Communism*; James P. Cannon, *The First Ten Years of American Communism: Report of a Participant* (New York: Lyle Stuart 1962); idem, *James P. Cannon and the Early Years of American Communism: Selected Writings and Speeches, 1920–1928* (New York: Prometheus Research Library Books 1992); Farrell Dobbs, *Revolutionary Continuity: Birth of the Communist Movement, 1918–1922* (New York: Monad Press 1983).

116 See reports by special agent, "P-138," "Re: Negro Activities (African Blood Brotherhood and Attempt of Communist Influence of Same)," July 13, 1921, file 202600–2031–6;

also reports dated August 10, 1921, file 202600–2031–7; August 22, 1921, file 202600–2031–8; August 26, 1921, file 202600–2031–9; August 29, 1921, file 202600–2031–10; August 30, 1921, file 202600–2031–11; August 30, 1921, file 202600–2031–12, all in RG 65, General Intelligence Division, Department of Justice, NA. McKay, *A Long Way From Home*, pp. 108–9; Claude McKay to Max Eastman, May 18, 1923, McKay Mss., Manuscripts Deparment, Lilly Library, Indiana University, Bloomington, Indiana; "Communist Party—USA—Brief, Internal Security—C," Chicago letter to Director, September 11, 1947, file 100–3–74–961, Department of Justice, Federal Bureau of Investigation, Washington, DC. I thank Professor Robert Hill, University of California, Los Angeles, for kindly providing me with a copy of this last-mentioned document.

117. Briggs to Draper, March 17, 1958.

118. Ibid.

119. Cyril Briggs to Theodore Draper, March 17, 1958 (first of two letters sent on the same day); Draper Papers.

120. Briggs to Draper, June 4, 1958. In his autobiography, Haywood gives a more accurate account of the formation of the Brotherhood. He also provided fascinating details about the Chicago Post of the Brother, which he joined in 1922: Haywood, *Black Bolshevik*, chap. 4.

121. One government informant claimed that four out of the seven members of the Brotherhood's "Executive Council," which must mean the Supreme Council, were members of the Party by September 1921; report by "P-141," September 28, 1921, file 202600–2031–14, RG 65, General Intelligence Division, Dept. of Justice.

122. *Crusader*, June 1919, p. 7; see also "High Rents and Bolshevism," *Crusader*, May 1919, p. 4, where Briggs noted that "The landlords and real estate agents of Harlem are doing their merry best to increase the converts of Bolshevism in the district. So far they have been highly successful. And the future promises to be even more fruitful of converts." Cf. "And They Wonder at Bolshevism!" *Crusader*, October 1919, p. 8.

123. See, for example, "Make Their Cause Your Own," *Crusader*, July 1919, p. 6; and "The Lusk Committee Makes a Discovery," *Crusader*, August 1919, p. 6.

124. See *Crusader*, September 1919, which is largely devoted to coverage and analysis of the riots.

125. See for instance, W. A. Domingo, "Capitalism the Basis of Colonialism," *Messenger*, August 1919, pp. 26–7; "Wage Slavery in the West Indies," *Crusader*, October 1919, p. 9; "Foreign Notes," ibid., p. 13.

126. "Manifesto of the Communist International to the Workers of the World" (6 March 1919), in Alan Adler, ed., *Theses, Resolutions and Manifestos of the First Four Congresses of the Third International* (London: Ink Links 1980), pp. 27–36, quotation from p. 27; Communist Party of America manifesto quoted in Draper, *American Communism and Soviet Russia*, p. 9; *Manifesto of the Socialist Party* (New York: Socialist Party, New York County [1919]); *Messenger*, May–June 1919, p. 8.

127. Domingo, "Did Bolshevism Stop Race Riots in Russia?" *Messenger*, September 1919 p. 27.

128. *Negro World*, September 20, 1919; cited in *The Palmer Report* pp. 163–4. It is thanks to the intelligence services that we have this citation at all, as the 1919 and earlier issues of the *Negro World*, I have discovered, are almost as rare as hen's teeth.

129. Quoted in W. E. B. Du Bois, "The Negro and Radical Thought," *Crisis*, vol. 22, no. 3, July 1921, p. 102. For whatever reason, Du Bois chose not to print McKay's letter in its entirety and only cites it in his own reply.

130. Cyril Briggs to Theodore Draper, March 17, 1958, Theodore Draper Papers, Reel 8.

131. "Stand By Soviet Russia!" *Crusader*, December 1921, p. 8.

132. *Crusader*, July 1919, p. 6, see also "Bolshevism and Race Prejudice," *Crusader*, December 1919, pp. 9–10.

133. *Messenger*, March 1919, p. 20.

134. See Allison Blakely's pioneering work, *Russia and the Negro: Blacks in Russian History and Thought* (Washington, DC: Howard University Press 1986), esp. pp. 75–80.

135. *Crusader*, October 1919, p. 9.

136. *Crusader*, October 1919, p. 27.

137. *Crusader*, January 1920, pp. 20 and 22; November 1919, p. 21; December 1919, p. 28.

138. *Crusader*, November 1919, p. 21; emphasis added.

139. *Crusader*, February 1920, p. 29.

140. *Crusader*, June 1920, p. 7.

141. Ibid., p. 22.

142. Arthur Preuss, *A Dictionary of Secret and Other Societies* (St Louis, Mo: B. Herder Book Co. 1924), as quoted in Hill, "Introduction," pp. lxvii–lxx; quotation from p. lxviii, emphasis in the original.

143. "Programm of the A. B. B.," *Crusader*, October 1921, pp. 15–18, quotation on p. 18.

144. See "Condensed and Tentative Constitution," *Crusader*, December 1921, pp. 16–19; Bishop McGuire, "Why I Left the U. N. I. A.," and idem, "Why I Joined the A. B. B.," ibid., p. 5; and "He Became a *persona non grata*," ibid., p. 10.

145. "Condensed and Tentative Constitution," pp. 18–19.

146. See document enclosed in Edward J. Brennan, Special Agent in Charge to J. E. Hoover, Director, Bureau of Investigation, November 19, 1923; Department of Justice, file 61–50–474.

147. Joseph C. Tucker, "Special Report," African Blood Brotherhood, August 18, 1923; *Federal Surveillance of Black Radicals*, reel 1.

148. Earl Titus, reports for September 18, and 24, 1923; Dept Of Justice, files 61–1122–8, and 61–1122–12.

149. Joyce Moore Turner, "Richard B. Moore and His Works," in Turner and Turner, eds, *Richard B. Moore*, p. 36.

150. In September 1923 the officers of the Supreme Council were reported to be: Cyril Briggs, Executive Head; Theo Burrell, Secretary; Otto E. Huiswoud, National Organizer; Richard B. Moore, Educational Director; Ben E. Burrell, Director of Historical Research; Grace P. Campbell, Director of Consumers Co-operatives; W. A. Domingo, Director of Publicity and Propaganda; William H. Jones, Physical Director. Earl E. Titus, "Negro Radical Activities," September 24, 1923; Justice Department, file 61–1122–12.

151. McKay, *A Long Way From Home*, p. 109; idem, *Harlem: Negro Metropolis*, pp. 223–24; Turner and Turner, eds, *Richard B. Moore*, pp. 165–6, 217.

152. According to the 1920 census, Campbell and her sister Mary lived at the same address as the Empire Friendly Shelter, 116 West 135th Street in Harlem. Apart from the two Campbell sisters, there were 26 people living in the house, including seven young children between the ages of two months and four years.

153. *New York Age*, September 6, 1924; also see Guichard Parris and Lester Brooks, *Blacks in the City: A History of the National Urban League* (Boston: Little, Brown and Company 1971), esp. chap. 1.

154. *The Chief*, vol. xxviii, no. 19, August 23, 1924, p. 2; *The chief*, vol. xxviii, no. 20, August 30, 1924, p. 2; *The City Record*, vol. liii, no. 15716, (Supplement) January 31, 1925, p. 419; *The City Record*, vol. lvi, no. 16776, (Supplement), July 31, 1928, p. 282.

155. Joseph G. Tucker, "Special Report," September 29, 1923; Justice Department file 61–23–248.

156. Biographical details drawn from manuscript of the *Fourteenth Census of the United States*, 1920, New York City; *New York Age*, September 6, 1924; telephone conversation with Joyce Moore Turner, February 15, 1997; Certificate of Death of Grace Campbell, certificate no. 13623, Bureau of Records, Dept of Health, City of New York.

157. There is much fiction in the secondary literature about these elections. These are the facts: In the 1919 election Campbell ran in the Twenty-First Assembly District, gaining 858 of the 11,956 votes cast (A. Philip Randolph had received almost twice as many in the Nineteenth Assembly District, 1,629 out of 13,394, over 12 percent); in 1920 she ran in the Nineteenth Assembly District, receiving 1,888 of the 18,222 votes cast. In gaining 10.4 percent of the vote in 1920, she did better than almost all the Socialist Party candidates from New York City and certainly much better than the other black Socialist candidates, including A. Philip Randolph, who received less than 7 percent of the vote for State Comptroller (even though the actual number of votes received was impressive, 202,381 out of a total of 2,921,269), and Chandler Owen, who received 6 percent (1,032 out of 17,190) of the votes cast in the Twenty-First Assembly District. The returns for the November 1919 elections are in the *Manual for the Use of the Legislature of the State of New York*, 1920 (Albany: J. B. Lyon Company 1920), p. 842; and for 1920 see *Manual for the Use of the Legislature of the State of New York*, 1921 (Albany: J. B. Lyon Company), esp. pp. 784–6, and 879; the results for the other black Socialist candidates, Frank Poree (Twentieth Senate District) and William B. Williams (Fifth Assembly District) appear on pp. 851 and 877, respectively.

158. P-138, "Negro Radicals," report March 4, 1921; Justice Department, RG 65, file 202–667–801.

159. Turner, "Richard B. Moore," p. 29.

160. Report by "P-138," March 2, 1921; Justice Department, file BS202600–667.

161. Turner, "Richard B. Moore," p. 30; the quotation from *Macbeth* was incorrectly rendered in Turner; publicity about and reports on the forum were carried frequently in the *Emancipator* in the spring of 1920.

162. Richard B. Moore cited in Turner, "Richard B. Moore," p. 30.

163. Report by "P-138," March 2, 1921.

164. Cyril Briggs, "Party Life: The Lovestoneites in Action," *Daily Worker*, October 30, 1929.

165. Andrew M. Battle, "General Negro Activities," September 15, 1922; Justice Department, file 61–746–14.

166. See *Messenger*, September 1923, which cites reports in the June 1923 issue of *Current History*, the *International*, official organ of the Communist Party of South Africa of July 13, 1923, and Briggs's response in the July 2, 1923 issue of the *Crusader Service*.

167. Joseph G. Tucker, "Special Report of Radical Activities Covering Greater New York District, Period Ending November 24, 1923," Justice Department, file 61–23–263; see also Earl E. Titus, "Workers' Party of America," November 27, 1923, Justice Department, file 61–4613–2.

168. Earl E. Titus, "African Blood Brotherhood," November 30, 1923; Justice Department file 61–50–495.

169. See *Theses and Manifestoes of the First Four Congresses of the Third International*, pp. 32, 76–81, 328–31; and Draper, *American Communism and Soviet Russia*, pp. 315–56.

170. Earl E. Titus, "African Blood Brotherhood," Chicago Bureau Office, January 18, 1924; contained in the Claude McKay file, released under the Freedom of Information Action to the author by the US Department of Justice, February 12, 1993, FOIPA No. 364410/190-HQ-1037464.

171. Claude McKay, "Soviet Russia and the Negro," *Crisis*, December 1923 and January 1924, quotation from p. 117; even though he wrote his memoir during his anti-Communist phase (meaning anti-Stalinist and anti-Communist Party of America, not anti-socialist), McKay did not disown those Russian days of hope, but warmly remembered them; "The Magic Pilgrimage," he called his Russian journey. See McKay, *A Long Way From Home*, pp. 153–234.

172. See Earl E. Titus, "African Blood Brotherhood," October 22, 1923; Justice Department, file 61–50–451; Joseph G. Tucker, "Special Report," September 29, 1923, *Federal Surveillance*, reel 1.

173. "Zinoviev on National and Racial Problems," 8 May, 1923, Petrograd. A copy of this document somehow ended up with the NAACP, and may be found in Walter White (Personal Correspondence), box C. 90, in the Papers of National Association for the Advancement of Colored People, Library of Congress, Washington, DC.

174. Haywood, *Black Bolshevik*, p. 121.

175. Ibid., pp. 125–6.

176. Communist Party, USA, *Race Hatred on Trial* (New York: Workers Library Publishers 1931), p. 32.

177. Briggs cited in Hill, "Introduction," p. xxvi.

178. As they had been earlier in the Socialist Party. Apart from the Harrison experience discussed earlier, see the Postscript below; Leinenweber, "The Class and Ethnic Bases of New York Socialism," p. 47.

179. Hill, "Introduction," pp. xxvi, xxviii, and idem, "Huiswoud, Otto," pp. 219–21; Theodore Draper's classic study, *American Communism and Soviet Russia* (New York: Vintage 1960), pp. 315–56, remains the best account of these formative years of black involvement in the Party.

180. "When I joined the party, there were only two other Negroes in it, Huiswoud and Hendricks." Briggs to Draper, March 17, 1958; Theodore Draper Papers, Reel 8.

181. See Naison, *Communists in Harlem During the Depression*, pp. 3–30. The most detailed information on Moore's political career is to be found in Turner, "Richard B. Moore." See also Harvey Klehr, *Communist Cadre: The Social Background of the American Communist Party Elite* (Stanford: Hoover Institution Press 1978), pp. 58–9.

182 Claude McKay's political evolution is explored at length in my *Claude McKay: The Making of a Black Bolshevik, 1889–1923* (forthcoming).

183 Lisa McGirr, "Black and White Longshoremen in the IWW: A History of the Philadelphia Marine Transport Workers Industrial Union Local 8," *Labor History*, vol. 37, no. 3, Summer 1995, pp. 380–81; William Seraile, "Ben Fletcher, I. W. W. Organizer," *Pennsylvania History*, vol. xlvi, no. 3, July 1979, pp. 214, 216–18.

184 Office of Naval Intelligence, "Investigation of the Marine Transport Workers and the Alleged Threatened Combination Between them and the Bolsheviki and Sinn Feiners," December 23, 1918, pp. 31–32, R. G. 165, file 10110–567, *US Military Intelligence Reports. Surveillance of Radicals in the United States, 1917–1941* (University Publication of America 1984), microfilm, Reel 8. It is likely that the secretary of the local was Caribbean as the report states that "with the exception of the colored secretary," all the leaders of the local are American (p. 32).

185 McGirr, "Black and White Longshoremen," p. 377.

186 Lisa McGirr's analysis, "Black and White Longshoremen," is excellent, but it does not disaggregate Local 8 sufficiently, for our purposes; that was not her objective.

187. Wallace Thurman, "Negro Poets and Their Poetry," *The Bookman*, vol. lxvii, no. 5, July 1928, p. 559.

188. See Eric Walrond, *Tropic Death* (New York: Boni and Liveright 1926). There is no biography of Walrond but see Robert Bone, *Down Home: Origins of the Afro-American Short Story* (New York: Putnam 1975), pp. 171–203; Kenneth Ramchand, "The Writer Who Ran Away: Eric Walrond and Tropic Death". *Savacou*, no. 2, September 1970; Martin, *Literary Garveyism*, pp. 124–32; Walter and Ansheles, "The Role of the Caribbean Immigrant in the Harlem Renaissance.,' Incidentally, two other significant figures of the Renaissance had Caribbean connections: the father of Nella Larsen, the novelist, was Caribbean, so was that of William Stanley Braithwaite, the critic and poet. In Larsen's case, however, this fact is relatively negligible as her father deserted her Danish mother when she was only seven years old and she apparently never re-established any connection with her father's side of the family. Braithwaite's situation was very different: although he was born in Boston, his Guyanese father had a major impact upon his intellectual formation and upon his life as a whole. Braithwaite, it should be said, was one of the most conservative figures of the Renaissance.

189. Martin, *Literary Garveyism*; idem, ed., *African Fundamentalism: A Literary and Cultural Anthology of Garvey's Harlem Renaissance* (Dover, Mass.: The Majority Press 1991); see also John Henrik Clarke, "The Impact of Marcus Garvey on the Harlem Renaissance," in idem, ed., *Marcus Garvey and the Vision of Africa* (New York: Vintage Books 1974); John Runcie, "Marcus Garvey and the Harlem Renaissance," *Afro-Americans in New York Life and History*, vol. 10, no. 2, July 1986; Ted Vincent's illuminating and splendid book, *Keep Cool: The Black Activists Who Built the Jazz Age* (London: Pluto Press 1995).

6. Race Consciousness, Class Consciousness, and the Political Strategies of William Monroe Trotter and Marcus Garvey

1. *The Black Man*, Sept–Oct. 1936, p. 14, and Nov. 1938, p. 20; see also, *The Black Man*, May–June 1936, p. 20. Garvey's remark here in relation to Africans is an exaggeration: the overwhelming majority of them would not even have encountered Europeans to facilitate the cultivation of such "race consciousness." However, in the white settler colonies—especially in the large cities—it was easier for such consciousness to develop, and indeed it did, albeit rather unevenly. The first six issues of Garvey's magazine, published in Jamaica between December 1933 and November 1934, carried the title *The Blackman*. But the subsequent issues, which Garvey put out during his exile in London, carried the title *The Black Man*.

2. In a speech in Raleigh, North Carolina, in June 1922, Garvey thanked the white South for having "lynched race pride into the Negroes." Cited in Stein, *The World of Marcus Garvey*, p. 154. The logical corollary of this position is that it is a pity that the Caribbean did not have the Ku Klux Klan to lynch race pride into "West Indian Negroes." Of course, "uppity niggers" like Garvey would have been the first to feel the noose round their necks.

3. For analysis of an equivalent dynamic among Caribbean migrants to Britain in the post-war years, see Winston James, "Migration, Racism and Identity Formation: The Caribbean

Experience in Britain," in Winston James and Clive Harris, eds, *Inside Babylon: The Caribbean Diaspora in Britain* (London and New York: Verso 1993), pp. 231–87.

4. We are relatively familiar with the names of Caribbeans such as Harrison, Domingo, Briggs and Huiswoud in discussions of black radicalism in early twentieth-century America. Yet Colón, as early as 1918—the very year he arrived in the United States—was not only a member of the Socialist Party, but was a member of the first committee within the Party to be made up of Puerto Ricans. César Andreau Iglesias, ed., *Memoirs of Bernardo Vega: A Contribution to the History of the Puerto Rican Community in New York* (New York: Monthly Review Press 1984), p. 112. Amongst the *tabaqueros* in particular, there was a strong radical tradition stretching back into the nineteenth century in both Cuba and Puerto Rico. Colón had in fact joined the Puerto Rican Socialist Party before migrating to America.

5. Forsythe, "West Indian Radicalism Abroad," p. 126, n.28.

6. Senate of the State of New York, Report of the Joint Legislative Committee Investigating Seditious Activities, *Revolutionary Radicalism: Its History, Purpose and Tactics With an Exposition and Discussion of the Steps Being Taken and Required to Curb It*, filed Apr. 24, 1920, 4 vols (Albany: J. B. Lyon Company Printers 1920), part i, vol. ii, p. 1495.

7. See Haywood, *Black Bolshevik* pp. 135–6. Warrington Hudlin's film *The Killing Floor*, set in Chicago around the time of the Red Summer of 1919, sensitively addresses some of these issues of trust and allegiance. George Schuyler adopted a similar position to Haywood's friend in a debate in 1923 against Otto Huiswoud. "I took the position," he said, "that the Negro had difficulties enough being black without becoming Red." See Schuyler, *Black and Conservative*, pp. 145–6; citation from p. 146.

8. See Turner, "Richard B. moore and His Works," pp. 67–68; and Hill, "Introduction," p. xlviii.

9. See W. A. Domingo, "British West Indian Federation—A Critique," in David Lowenthal and Lambros Comitas, eds, *The Aftermath of Sovereignty: West Indian Perspectives*, (New York: Anchor Books 1973). Beyond his Jamaican nationalism, the political evolution of Domingo from the 1940s to his death in 1968 is not entirely clear. It is, however, interesting to note that as late as February 1940, he wrote to a Jamaican socialist active in the anti-colonial struggle: "I want to make it quite clear to you, so that there should be no mistake as to my attitude, that I am opposed to all imperialisms; that I am for the only anti-imperialistic country in the world and that my support of any country stops the moment the U.S.S.R. is involved. Russia, as I see it, is the hope of all the oppressed colonial peoples, especially those of the colored races. Hence my unconditional support of Russia now and in the future." (Domingo to Frank Hill, February 24, 1940; my thanks to Richard Hart for providing me with a copy of this letter.) Domingo never joined the Communist Party. I discuss his politics further in the Postscript below.

10. In the 1950s and 1960s, Moore and Domingo took their differences into the public arena by debating the West Indies Federation (the ill-fated attempt, between 1958 and 1962, at political federation of the British Caribbean) and Caribbean political unity generally. See Turner and Turner, eds, *Richard B. Moore*.

11. McKay, *Harlem*, p. 216.

12. See Marcus Garvey, "Dr. Du Bois Criticised," *The Blackman*, May/June 1934, pp. 1–2.

13. Cronon, *Black Moses*, pp. 202–24 and Preface to the 1969 edition; Richard Hart, "The Life and Resurrection of Marcus Garvey," *Race*, vol. ix, no. 2, 1967; Jacques Garvey, *Garvey and Garveyism*, pp. 299ff; idem, *Black Power in America* (Kingston: Amy Jacques Garvey 1968); and Cecil Gutzmore's fine essay, "The Image of Marcus Garvey in Reggae Orature," in Kwesi Owusu, ed., *Storms of the Heart: An Anthology of Black Arts and Culture* (London: Camden Press 1988), pp. 275–302.

14. "The Reminiscences of George S. Schuyler," p. 73.

15. Gramsci's examples of war of position and war of movement could hardly be more apt: "Gandhi's passive resistance is a war of position . . . . Boycotts are a form of war of position, strikes of war of movement." Gramsci, *Selections From the Prison Notebooks*, p. 229. It was precisely this war of position that was mobilized by Martin Luther King, Jr and the civil rights movement. And King never ceased to acknowledge his debt to Gandhi. It is as though Gramsci was talking about the United States in the heat of the black struggles at mid century when he noted that "The war of position demands enormous sacrifices by infinite masses of people." It "requires exceptional qualities of patience and inventiveness." Gramsci, like an optimistic King, felt that because of its hegemonic strategy, unlike the war of movement, "in politics the 'war of position', once won, is decisive definitively" (pp. 238–9); a

final *faux pas* by the great thinker: no victory in politics is ever decisive definitively; victories have always had to be safeguarded, they do not look after themselves.

16. After the Civil War, James Trotter was appointed, along with several black war veterans, to what his son called "a good clerkship" in the Boston Post Office. He earned a good income but resigned in protest in 1882 when a white man was promoted over his head to a chief clerkship. James Trotter thought he was overlooked because of his color. He made a living by a variety of means after resigning and for two years, 1887 to 1889, earned a lucrative income from his appointment as Recorder of Deeds, the highest office held by a black person in the federal government at that time. The Recorder of Deeds' salary was based on a percentage of the transactions conducted by the office, and business was heavy in Trotter's time. Rogers claimed that James Trotter made about $10,000 per year, but it's not clear on what basis he came to his conclusion. Du Bois claimed that Trotter left the office with a small fortune. When James Trotter died in 1892 he left his son $20,000; the family had invested in real estate in Boston. Fox, *The Guardian of Boston*, pp. 2–22; Rogers, *World's Great Men of Color*, vol. ii, p. 399; W. E. B. Du Bois, "William Monroe Trotter," *Crisis*, May 1934, p. 134.

17. Fox, *The Guardian of Boston*, p. 30.

18. Ibid., p. 140.

19. Ibid., pp. 179–87.

20. Hubert Harrison, *When Africa Awakes*, pp. 31 and 36.

21. Fox, *The Guardian of Boston*, pp. 223–5; Rogers, *World's Great Men of Color*, vol. ii, pp. 402–3.

22. Du Bois, "William Monroe Trotter," p. 134.

23. Fox, *The Guardian of Boston*, pp. 271–2; Du Bois, "William Monroe Trotter."

24. Statement by Kelly Miller in the *Guardian*, April 2, 1934; cited in Fox, *The Guardian of Boston*, p. 281.

25. Harrison, *When Africa Awakes*, p. 10; *Crisis*, May 1924, p. 27; *Garvey Papers*, vol. i, pp. 226 n. 1; 318 n. 1; 516 n. 8; Fox, *The Guardian of Boston*. Shaw was apparently also a member of the African Blood Brotherhood. According to a spy within the organization, the members of the ABB were shocked to hear of Shaw's death. When Grace Campbell told Cyril Briggs who was visiting her home, that Trotter had written, informing the ABB of the death of Shaw, Briggs "nearly fainted and had to sit down for a while." Shaw had spoken to the Brotherhood only three weeks before he died. Earl E. Titus, "Re: Negro Radical Activities," September 24, 1923, Justice Department, file 61–1122–11.

26. *Crusader*, August 1919, p. 9.

27. *Crusader*, October 1919, p. 31; the writer of the letter was a white man who had been born in New Orleans in 1867 and was an ardent disciple of Tom Paine.

28. For some indication of the closeness of the relation between Trotter and the Brotherhood, see Earl E. Titus, "African Blood Brotherhood," August 16, 1923; Justice Department, file 61–50–410; idem, "Radical Negro Activities," September 18, 1923; idem, "Negro Radical Activities," September 24, 1923; Justice Department, file 61–1122–12.

29. Cyril Briggs to Theodore Draper, March 17, 1958; Draper Collection.

30. Rogers, *World's Great Men of Color*, vol. ii, pp. 399, 404–5.

31. "A Negro Leader Dies," *The Blackman*, vol. 1, no. 5, May–June, 1934, pp. 2–4, citations from p. 3. Fox claims that "Trotter and his NERL were among Garvey's more prominent black opponents." But he marshalls no evidence to support his statement and admits that he found "no direct comment by Trotter on Garvey." In fact the president of NERL, Dr M. A. N. Shaw, was an ardent supporter of the UNIA (British intelligence claimed that he was the Massachusetts representative of the organization). He frequently spoke at UNIA rallies. Further, NERL and the UNIA co-operated on a number of important campaigns, such as the Liberty Congress meetings in 1918 and 1919. To drum up support for the purchase of the *SS Yarmouth* in 1920 for the Black Star Line Company, Garvey in a speech in Boston reminded his audience that the *Yarmouth* was the very ship on which Trotter made his clandestine trip to the Paris Congress the previous year. Trotter was frequently used by the UNIA as a stick with which to beat Du Bois, always drawing comparison between the two men, invariably to Du Bois's disadvantage. Fox, *The Guardian of Boston*, p. 251, 251 n.18; *Garvey Papers*, esp. vols i, ii, v, passim; Martin, *Race First*, pp. 276–7, 286, 291–2.

32. Fox, *The Guardian of Boston*, passim; John Daniels, *In Freedom's Birthplace: A Study of Boston Negroes* (Boston: Houghton Mifflin Co. 1914); Willard Gatewood, *Aristocrats of*

Color: The Black Elite, 1880–1920 (Bloomington: Indiana University Press 1990), esp. pp. 109–13.

33. Cited in Vincent, *Black Power and the Garvey Movement*, p. 154.

34. Peter Gilbert, ed., *The Selected Writings of John Edward Bruce: Militant Black Journalist* (New York: Arno Press 1971), p. 146; emphasis in original.

35. Miller, "After Marcus Garvey—What of the Negro?," p. 492.

36. Johnson, *Black Manhattan*, pp. 257–8.

37. See Woodrow Wilson's speech delivered to Joint Session of Congress, April 2, 1917, in, *Messages and Papers of the Presidents*, vol. xvii, pp. 8226–33; citation from p. 8231; W. E. B. Du Bois, "Close Ranks," *Crisis*, July 1918, p. 111.

38. Quoted in Joshua Blanton, "Men in the Making," *Southern Workman*, January 1919, p. 20.

39. Ottley, "New World A-Coming," p. 69; see also, Miller, "After Marcus Garvey— What of the Negro?," pp. 493–4. As one UNIA supporter put it in 1920, Garvey "is giving voice to the cumulative agonies our people have suffered during their slavery and since their emancipation." Cited in Vincent, *Black Power and the Garvey Movement*, p. 154.

7. The Peculiarities of Afro-Hispanic Radicalism in the United States: The Political Trajectories of Arturo Schomburg and Jesús Colón

1. Domingo, "Gift of the Black Tropics," p. 342; Thurman, *Negro Life in New York's Harlem*, p. 17.

2. Reid, *The Negro Immigrant*, p. 101; McKay, *Harlem*, p. 136.

3. Langston Hughes, "Note to Puerto Ricans (On American Confusions)," in idem., *Good Morning Revolution: Uncollected Writings of Social Protest*, edited by Faith Berry (New York: Citadel Press 1992), p. 164; quoted with permission of the Estate of Langston Hughes.

4. See Martin, *Race First*, esp. pp. 49–51; Martin claims, not implausibly, that the Cuban UNIA was "largely Jamaican in composition" (p. 50). See also Lewis, *Marcus Garvey*, pp. 99–123; Bernardo García Dominguez, "Garvey and Cuba," in Rupert Lewis and Patrick Bryan, eds, *Garvey: His Work and Impact*, (Kingston: Institute of Social and Economic Research, University of the West Indies 1988); Pedro Pable Rodríguez, "Marcus Garvey en Cuba," *Anales del Caribe*, vols 7–8, 1987–88; Ted Vincent, "The Harlem to Bluefields Connection: Sandino's Aid from the Black American Press," *Black Scholar*, May/June 1985; Philippe I. Bourgois, *Ethnicity at Work: Divided Labor on a Central American Banana Plantation* (Baltimore: Johns Hopkins University Press 1989), esp. pp. 98–102; Aviva Chomsky, *West Indian Workers and the United Fruit Company in Costa Rica, 1870–1940* (Baton Rouge: Louisiana State University Press 1996), esp. pp. 198, 202–6; Jacques Garvey, *Garvey and Garveyism*. For more on the pattern of migration within and beyond the Caribbean, see Franklin Knight, "Jamaican Migrants and the Cuban Sugar Industry, 1900–1934," in Fraginals et al., eds, *Between Slavery and Free Labor*; Newton, *The Silver Men*; Richardson, *Panama Money in Barbados, 1900–1920*; and idem, "Caribbean Migrations, 1838–1985," in F. Knight and C. Palmer, eds, *The Modern Caribbean* (Chapel Hill: University of North Carolina Press, 1989). See also the special double issue of *Cimarrón* (vol. II, nos 1–2, Spring/ Summer 1989), on "Ethnicity, Class and the State in Central America."

5. The Afro-Panamanian (non-Caribbean) mother of Maida Springer Kemp, the political activist and trade unionist, was one of the few Afro-Latina Garveyites. For more on Maida Springer Kemp, see "Maida Springer Kemp," in Ruth Edmonds Hill, ed., *The Black Women Oral History Project*, vol. 7 (Westport: Meckler Publishing 1991), pp. 39–145, and Yevette Richards, "'My Passionate Feeling About Africa': Maida Springer Kemp and the American Labor Movement," (Ph.D. diss. Yale University 1994). For De Mena's background see *Garvey Papers*, vol. vi, pp. 117–18 n. 1; cf. Smith-Irvin, *Marcus Garvey's Footsoldiers of the Universal Negro Improvement Association*, pp. 59–63.

6. *Garvey Papers*, vol. iii, p. 789, and vol. ii, p. 120 n.1.

7. See Robert Harris, Nyota Harris, and Grandassa Harris, eds, *Carlos Cooks and Black Nationalism: From Garvey to Malcolm* (Dover, Mass.: The Majority Press 1992).

8. Conversations with Carlos Moore, March 1996, Kingston, Jamaica. Moore's most widely known work on Cuba is *Castro, the Blacks and Africa* (Los Angeles: Center for Afro-American Studies, University of California, Los Angeles 1989).

9. In 1920 the population had grown to 11,811 with 62.3 percent of the total living in New York City. By 1930 the total Puerto Rican population in America had reached 52,774; some claimed it was as high as 200,000, but this is more than likely an overestimation. See Manuel Maldonado-Dennis, *The Emigration Dialectic: Puerto Rico and the USA* (New York: International Publishers 1980), Table 1, p. 131, and History Task Force, Centro de Estudios Puertorriqueños, *Labor Migration Under Capitalism: The Puerto Rican Experience* (New York: Monthly Review Press 1979), pp. 223–5, both of whom use the lower estimates, and Virginia E. Sánchez Korrol, *From Colonia to Community: The History of Puerto Ricans in New York City* (Westport: Greenwood Press 1983), pp. 58–66, who leans toward the higher figures while admitting the "debatable" nature of all the estimates. The enumeration of the Puerto Rican migrant community in the United States was complicated by the political status of the migrants.

10. Much of this may be found in the Jesús Colón Papers, Centro de Estudios Puertorri-queños, Hunter College, City University of New York.

11. Elinor Des Verney Sinnette went so far as to claim that Schomburg was a Garvey "disciple," but this, as I argue later, despite Schomburg's undoubted enthusiasm for the UNIA (which, however, he never joined), is an over-statement. See Sinnette, *Arthur Alfonso Schomburg: Black Bibliophile and Collector—A Biography* (New York: New York Public Library and Wayne State University Press 1989), p. 123.

12. Floyd J. Calvin, "Race Colleges Need Chair in Negro History—A. A. Schomburg," *Pittsburgh Courier*, March 5, 1927. Both Ortiz and Sinnette, Schomburg's biographers, mistakenly deduced that this information was first divulged by Schomburg to the black Cuban writer, Gustavo E. Urrutia, during Schomburg's visit to Cuba in the winter of 1933. In fact, Urrutia's article did not come from a direct interview with Schomburg, it is, almost in its entirety, a direct translation of Calvin's article that had been published six and a half years before Schomburg visited Cuba. See Gustavo E. Urrutia, "Schomburg", *Diario de La Marina*, November 2, 1933; Victoria Ortiz, "Arthur A. Schomburg: A Biographical Essay," in the Schomburg Center for Research in Black Culture, *The Legacy of Arthur Alfonso Schomburg: A Celebration of the Past, A Vision for the Future* (New York: Schomburg Center for Research in Black Culture 1986), pp. 18–117 (published in Spanish and English), see pp. 21–3 for reference to Urrutia's article; Sinnette, *Arthur Alfonso Schomburg*, pp. 13–14.

13. J. A. Rogers, "Arthur A. Schomburg: 'The Sherlock Holmes of Negro History' (1874–1938)," in Rogers, *World's Great Men of Color*, vol. ii, p. 452.

14. For more on this most remarkable man, see Calvin, "Race Colleges Need Chair in Negro History"; Simon Williamson, "History of the Life and Work of Arthur Alonzo [*sic*] Schomburg," July 18, 1938, unpublished ms, reel 10, Arthur A. Schomburg Papers; McKay, *Harlem*, p. 139–42; J. A. Rogers, "Schomburg is the Detective of History," *Norfolk Journal and Guide*, July 5, 1930; idem, *World's Great Men of Color*, vol. ii, pp. 449–53; Jean Blackwell Hutson, "The Schomburg Collection," in John Henrik Clarke, ed. *Harlem: A Community in Transition* (New York: Citadel Press 1969), pp. 205–9; Ernest Kaiser, "Schomburg, Arthur Alfonso," in Logan and Winston, eds, *Dictionary of American Negro Biography*, pp. 546–8; Ortiz, "Arthur A. Schomburg: A Biographical Essay"; Sinnette, *Arthur Alfonso Schomburg*; Flor Piñeiro de Rivera, ed., *Arthur Alfonso Schomburg: A Puerto Rican Quest for His Black Heritage* (San Juan: Centro de Estudios Avanzados de Puerto Rico y el Caribe 1989), pp. 17–50.

15. Howard Dodson, "Introduction," in the Schomburg Center for Research in Black Culture, *The Legacy of Arthur Alfonso Schomburg*, p. 7.

16. Alain Locke, "In Memoriam: Arthur Alfonso Schomburg, 1874–1938," foreword to Arthur Schomburg, "Negro History in Outline" (Bronze Booklet No. 8). Alain Locke Papers, Moorland-Spingarn Research Center, Howard University. The Bronze Booklet series was edited by Locke. Booklet No. 8 was never published.

17. Calvin, "Race Colleges Need Chair in Negro History."

18. Arthur A. Schomburg, "The Negro Digs Up His Past," in Locke, ed., *The New Negro*, pp. 231–2.

19. Colón cited from interview in Sinnette, *Arthur Alfonso Schomburg*, p. 23; the second pair of parentheses is Sinnette's. The interview with Colón took place on June 27, 1973 and he died in May 1974. Colón did write a nice, though passionless, little sketch of Schomburg in the early sixties, "Arthur Schomburg and Negro History." It was written for Negro History Week and published in *The Worker*, Feb. 11, 1962. Claude McKay, a very close friend of Schomburg, observed that intellectually, the latter was proud of his Spanish heritage and fond

of Puerto Rico. Yet, Schomburg, he wrote, "cultivated no social contact with Harlem's Puerto Ricans." McKay, who had a keen eye for such matters, also noted that Schomburg was thrice married, "each time to an American Negro woman, and he reared 7 children." McKay, *Harlem*, p. 142.

20. César Andreu Iglesias, ed., *Memoirs of Bernardo Vega: A Contribution to the History of the Puerto Rican Community in New York* (New York: Monthly Review Press 1984), p. 195.

21. Ibid., pp. 66 and 195–6.

22. For the most accessible source of Bruce's views, see Gilbert, ed., *The Selected Writings of John Edward Bruce*; see, for instance, p. 143, where Bruce talks about black people of African descent belonging to "branch[es] of the Hamatic [sic] family the wide world over." Some of Schomburg's own writings are brought together in Piñeiro de Rivera, ed., *Arthur Alfonso Schomburg*. Schomburg's relation with Bruce is traced in Sinnette's *Schomburg*. Curiously, although it carries a portrait of Bruce signed by himself and addressed to "My dear friend A. A. Schomburg," there is no mention of Bruce's relation with Schomburg in the text of the Schomburg Center's own biographical portrait, Ortiz, "Arthur A. Schomburg."

23. For good evaluation of the evidence concerning Schomburg's parents see Ortiz, "Arthur A. Schomburg." pp. 19–25, and Sinnette, *Arthur Alfonso Schomburg* pp. 7–9.

24. The questionnaire was filled out in the 1930s for E. Franklin Frazier's study, *The Negro Family in the United States* (Chicago: University of Chicago Press 1939); Schomburg's completed questionnaire is among Frazier's papers: "A Study of the Negro Family," questionnaire no. 2597, E. Franklin Frazier Papers, Moorland Spingarn Research Center, Howard University.

25. Sinnette, *Arthur Alfonso Schomburg*, p. 14.

26. Arturo Schomb[u]rg, "Una Historia verdadera de la Insurreccion de los esclavos bajo el Cabecilla de Juan Buddhoe, quien está aún venerado, por sus compatriotas," *Prevision* (Havana), February 10, 1910. The slaves of St Croix had the distinction, shared only by those of St Domingue, of achieving the legal abolition of slavery through the direct action of insurrection. For more on Buddhoe and the insurrection, see N. A. T. Hall, "The Victor Vanquished: Emancipation in St. Croix, its Antecedents and Immediate Aftermath," *Nieuwe West-Indische Gids*, vol. 58, nos 1–2, 1984, also in idem, *Slave Society in the Danish West Indies*, chap. 12.

27. Alton Adams to Arthur Schomburg, February 1, 1927, Reel 1, Schomburg Papers. Sinnette, *Arthur Alfonso Schomburg*, pp. 14–17; see also Ortiz, "Arthur A. Schomburg," pp. 23–25.

28. Schomburg to [Dr. J. M.] Boddy, December 15, 1932; Reel 7, Schomburg Papers.

29. *New York Age*, February 18, 1933.

30. Schomburg, "Harlem Echoes," *The Union*, June 30, 1932.

31. Gary R. Mormino and George E. Pozzetta, *The Immigrant World of Ybor City: Italians and Their Latin Neighbors in Tampa, 1885–1985* (Urbana: University of Illinois Press 1987), pp. 186–7.

32. "A Study of the Negro Family," questionnaire no. 2597.

33. The hegemonic culture in the Danish Virgin Islands from the eighteenth century to 1917, when the islands were sold to the United States, was British. The Danes constituted a small minority of the planters on all three islands, the lingua franca was English-Creole-based (even though there was considerable Dutch influence in St Thomas in the eighteenth century), the newspapers were overwhelmingly published in English, and when the authorities decided to educate the slaves the language of instruction was English. Neville Hall reported that a Danish writer in 1840, noting the presence of European "foreigners" in the Virgin Islands, lamented the fact that St Croix had never been colonized by his countrymen and had never been Danish "except in the narrowly political sense. If all it took to be Danish was the flag and the judicial system, then St Croix was Danish. But colonization implied more than territorial claim and a body of laws." Neville Hall "Empire Without Dominion: The Danish West Indies, 1671–1848," in idem, *Slave Society in the Danish West Indies*, pp. 18–19; see also Hall, "Education for Slaves in the Danish Virgin Islands, 1732–1846," in Ruby Hope King, ed., *Education in the Caribbean: Historical Perspectives* (Kingston: Faculty of Education, University of the West Indies 1987).

34. Sinnette, *Arthur Alfonso Schomburg*, p. 166; Ortiz, "Arthur A. Schomburg," p. 99.

35. Ortiz, "Arthur A. Schomburg," p. 99.

36. Schomburg to Dabney, August 19, 1937; Reel 7, Schomburg Papers.

37. See Ortiz, "Arthur A. Schomburg," pp. 25–35, and Sinnette, *Arthur Alfonso Schomburg*, pp. 20–3.

38. See Pedro N. González Veranes, *Rafael Serra: Patriota y Revolucionario, Fraternal Amigo de Martí* (Havana: Club Atenas 1959); Pedro Deschamps Chapeux, *Rafael Serra y Montalvo: Obrero Incansable de Nuestra Independencia* (Havana: Unión de Escritores y Artistas de Cuba 1975); Josefina Toledo, *Sotero Figueroa, Editor de "Patria": Apuntes para una Biografía* (Havana: Editorial Letras Cubanas 1985). The role of Rafael Serra and Sotero Figueroa in Cuban and Puerto Rican nationalist exile politics are discussed, albeit *en passant*, in Iglesias, ed., *Memoirs of Bernardo Vega*, and in Gerald Poyo, *"With All, and for the Good of All": The Emergence of Popular Nationalism in the Cuban Communities of the United States, 1848–1898* (Durham, NC: Duke University Press 1989); and Isabelo Zenón Cruz, *Narciso Descubre su Trasero: El Negro en la Cultura Puertorriqueña*, 2nd edn (Humacao, Puerto Rico: Editorial Furidi 1983), pp. 149–50; Donna M. Wolf, "The Cuban *Gente de Color* and the Independence Movement, 1879–1895," *Revista/Review Interamericana*, vol. 5, Fall 1975, pp. 418–19; Serra's politics after his return to Cuba in 1902 are discussed in Helg, *Our Rightful Share*, pp. 133–6; see also "Sotereo Figueroa" (Reel 11, Schomburg Papers)—this is an English translation of an obituary apparently published in a Havana magazine, *La Discusion*, Oct. 10, 1923. (Figueroa died on Oct. 5, 1923.) The translation was made by Figueroa's son, Pace Figueroa; it was not accompanied by the Spanish original.

39. McKay, *Harlem*, p. 140, emphasis added; McKay wrongly attributed this choice on the part of Schomburg to his "African blood," but, as we have seen, there was more to it than that.

40. These issues are further discussed in Chapter 8 below.

41. Ortiz, "Arthur A. Schomburg," p. 39.

42. Schomburg to the *New York Herald Tribune*, April 24, 1935, emphasis added. The letter was never published.

43. Williamson, a close friend of Schomburg, evaluated the latter's work as a freemason in, "Arthur A. Schomburg: The Freemason" [March 13, 1941], Reel 5, The Harry A. Williamson Papers, Schomburg Center.

44. See Alfred Moss, Jr, *The American Negro Academy: Voice of the Talented Tenth* (Baton Rouge: Louisiana State University Press 1981), which is harsh in its criticism of Schomburg's presidency and more than a bit nativistic in tone; see esp. pp. 221–2.

45. McKay, *Harlem*, p. 141.

46. Cromwell to Schomburg, July 17, 1928, cited in J. A. Rogers, "Schomburg is the Detective of History," *Norfolk Journal and Guide*, July 5, 1930; this article, with minor changes, formed the profile of Schomburg later published in Rogers's *World's Great Men of Color*.

47. Myriam Jimenez first brought to my attention problems in Schomburg's written Spanish. The quality of Schomburg's Spanish, at least in its written form, deteriorated over time. This may very well have been due to the fact that he had little need to use it after 1898, when he broke with most of his Spanish-speaking comrades in the Cuban and Puerto Rican nationalist movements.

48. Much of Schomburg's published work in English went through substantial editing before entering the public domain. Sinnette registers this fact but barely discusses it. Her claim that Schomburg's written Spanish was "impeccable" is, at best, debatable. Sinnete, *Arthur Alfonso Schomburg* p. 13.

49. Schomburg to [J.M.] Boddy, May 31, 1933.

50. Schomburg to Ira De A. Reid, July 18, 1935; Reel 8, Schomburg Papers.

51. Locke, "In Memoriam: Arthur Alfonso Schomburg," p. 1 of unpaginated script.

52. Schomburg to Boddy, New Year's Day 1934; Reel 7, Schomburg Papers.

53. See, for instance, Schomburg to J. M. Boddy, December 15, 1932, and New Year's Day 1934; Schomburg to "My Dear Nestor" [Wendell P. Dabney], undated.

54. Schomburg in *Negro World*, November 4, 1922; reprinted in Theodore G. Vincent, ed., *Voices of a Black Nation: Political Journalism in the Harlem Renaissance* (San Francisco: Ramparts Press 1973), pp. 340–41. A week after Schomburg's review, Bruce also complained in the pages of the *Negro World* about Woodson's behavior. According to Bruce, Woodson had promised to acknowledge photographs provided by the Negro Society for Historical Research (founded and led by Bruce and Schomburg), but never did; Martin, *The Pan-African Connection*, p. 104, citing *Negro World* of November 11, 1922.

55. Schomburg to Boddy, December 15, 1932; Reel 7, Schomburg Papers. As early as

1916, Schomburg complained to Bruce about Woodson "stealing our thunder." (Martin, *Race First*, p. 83.) It was only after a closer reading of Schomburg's voluminous correspondence that I came to understand more fully what McKay—a man who knew Schomburg well— meant when he said that Schomburg was "full of wonderful love and admiration and hate, positively liking his friends and positively disliking his foes." (McKay, *Harlem*, p. 142.) The love came through Schomburg's published work, but the hate hardly showed. "He strangely combined a simple, disarming exterior and obscure inner complexes," observed McKay, shrewdly (ibid.).

56. Schomburg to W. P. Dabney, April 29, 1938.

57. See Schomburg, "Notes on Panama and the Negro," *Opportunity*, July 1928; Schomburg to [J. M.] Boddy, December 15, 1932; Reel 7, Schomburg Papers.

58. Schomburg, "Is Hayti Decadent?" *Unique Advertiser*, August 1904.

59. Schomburg to Dantés Bellegarde, April 8, 1937, Reel 7, Schomburg Papers. There are two letters to Bellegarde bearing the date of April 8, 1937. The one cited opens with "My dear the Hon. Bellegarde," the other one opens with "My dear Doctor Bellegarde." The letters are both typed and signed by Schomburg, but worded slightly differently, and one contained discussion of additional business. It is probable that Schomburg sent the latter directly to Bellegarde by mail, and gave Campbell the other to take with him to Haiti.

60. Schomburg to Wendell Phillips Dabney, Esq., Editor of the Union, n.d. [1935?]; see also Schomburg to Dabney, May 26, 1938, Reel 7, Schomburg Papers.

61. Cited in Piñeiro de Rivera, *Arthur Schomburg*, pp. 42–4.

62. Schomburg to Hon. Franklin Roosevelt, July 12, 1935; Reel 8, Schomburg Papers.

63. Schomburg to Dabney, August 19, 1937, Reel 7, Schomburg Papers.

64. Sinnette, *Arthur Alfonso Schomburg*, p. 123.

65. Schuyler, *Black and Conservative*, p. 144.

66. See John Wesley Cromwell's letter to William Ferris published in the *Negro World*, October 23, 1920; *Garvey Papers*, vol. iii, pp. 63–4.

67. Schomburg to Cromwell, July 28, 1919; John Wesley Cromwell Family Papers, Moorland Spingarn Research Center, Howard University.

68. Schomburg to Cromwell, undated [summer 1920?]; Cromwell Papers.

69. Schomburg to Cromwell, August 4, 1921; Cromwell Papers.

70. Arturo A. Schomburg, "Neroes [sic] in the League of Nations," *New York Age*, September 14, 1936.

71. Schomburg, "Our Pioneers," *New York Amsterdam News*, September 19, 1936.

72. Schomburg, "Neroes in the League of Nations."

73. *The Black Man*, July 1938, pp. 1–2.

74. McKay, *Harlem*, p. 142.

75. Schomburg to Boddy, New Year's Day, 1934; Reel 7, Schomburg Papers.

76. For biographical details see: Colón's birth certificate (*Acta de Nacimiento*) (another certificate issued in 1966, erroneously gave his first name as "Federico" instead of Fabián); Jesús Colón Papers, Series I, box 1, folder 2, Centro de Estudios Puertorriqueños, Hunter College, City University of New York; Jesús Colón, *A Puerto Rican in New York and Other Sketches* (New York: Masses and Mainstream 1961) and the Foreword by Juan Flores to the 1982 edition (published in New York by International Publishers). More details on Colón's life and work are provided by his close friend, compatriot, and comrade, Bernardo Vega (Iglesias, ed., *Memoirs of Bernardo Vega*); and by Edna Acosta-Belén and Virginia Sánchez Korrol, in their introduction, "The World of Jesús Colón," to Jesús Colón, *The Way it Was and Other Writings* (Houston: Arte Público 1993).

77. Colón, "A Voice Through the Window," in *A Puerto Rican in New York*, p. 11.

78. See Quintero-Rivera, "Socialist and Cigarmaker"; Colón, "A Voice Through the Window," p. 11; Bernardo Vega discusses the transfer of this political culture to New York: Iglesias, ed., *Memoirs of Bernardo Vega*, chap 4. See also Louis Pérez, "Reminiscences of a Lector: Cuban Cigar Makers in Tampa," *Florida Historical Quarterly* vol. liii, no. 4, April 1975; Poyo, *"With All, and for the Good of All"*; Patricia Cooper, *Once a Cigar Maker: Men, Women, and Work Culture in American Cigar Factories, 1900–1919* (Urbana: University of Illinois Press 1987), p. 66. The practice of reading while the cigar makers roll began in Cuba in the 1860s, spread to Puerto Rico soon after and traveled with Cuban *tabaqueros* to New York and Florida, in the nineteenth century; see James H. Collins, "Literature and the Cigar Maker," *Bookman*, July 1905; Ortiz, *Cuban Counterpoint*, pp. 88–92; Stubbs, *Tobacco on*

the Periphery, pp. 97–9; and Mormino and Pozzetta, "'The Reader Lights the Candle,'" a lavishly illustrated and fine analysis.

79. Angel Quintero-Rivera has a fine discussion of this culture and the corrosive processes undermining the artisans at the turn of the century; see his "Socialist and Cigarmaker"; also see Dietz, *Economic History of Puerto Rico*, pp. 85, 116–8; Amílcar Tirado has done an excellent analysis of the economic and political changes taking place in Puerto Rico at the time and how these affected tobacco workers, which includes a pioneering discussion of the new gender division of labor occurring in the tobacco factories; Amílcar Tirado, "Workers Responding to a Changing Society: The Case of Puerto Rican Cigar Makers, 1898–1919." (This is a chapter from Tirado's forthcoming doctoral dissertation on the Puerto Rican working class. I am grateful to Amílcar for sharing his work with me.)

80. Acosta-Belén and Sánchez Korrol, "The World of Jesús Colón," p. 22; Iglesias, ed., *Memoirs of Bernardo Vega*, p. xvii and chap 1.

81. Colón, "My First Literary Venture," and "My First Strike," both in *A Puerto Rican in New York*.

82. Lyrics from a Spanish version of 'The Internationale'.

83. Colón, "The Way to Learn," in *A Puerto Rican in New York*, pp. 17–21. Colón did not disclose the article's author, but one of the issues of *Adelante!* kept among his papers carries the article mentioned: Francisco Colón [Gordiany], "Lucha Honrada de Nuestros Padres," *Adelante! Organo de la Central Grammar School*, no. 6, March 31, 1917, pp. 6–7. We also know from other sources, including Colón's own correspondence with him, that Francisco Colón Gordiany was president of the *Confederación General de Trabajadores*. (See for instance, Miles Galvin, *The Organized Labor Movement in Puerto Rico* (Rutherford: Fairleigh Dickinson University Press 1979), pp. 94–9; and Francisco Colón Gordiany to Jesús Colón, December 19, 1941, Jesús Colón Papers, Series II, box 1.) Over the years, Francisco and Jesús maintained their friendship and enjoyed sustained correspondence up to Colón's death. Although they shared a common last name, there is no evidence that the two were related.

84. In *Pueblos Hispanos*, between 1943 and 1944.

85. Roger Keeran, "The International Workers Order and the Origins of the CIO," *Labor History*, vol. 30, no. 3, Summer 1989; Roberto P. Rodriguez-Morazzani, "Linking a Fractured Past: The World of the Puerto Rican Old Left," *Centro: Journal of the Center for Puerto Rican Studies*, vol. vii, no. 1, Spring 1995, p. 24.

86. See Colón's testimony in US House of Representatives, *Hearings Before the Committee on Un-American Activities: Communist Activities Among Puerto Ricans in New York City and Puerto Rico* (New York City—Part 1), 86th Congress, 1st Session, November 16 and 17, 1959, pp. 1537–48; See Colón, "I Appear Before the Un-Americans," *The Worker*, November 29, 1959; idem, "The Un-Americans and the Americans," *The Worker*, December 6, 1959; and "Statement by Jesús Colón to the Walter Committee on Un-American Activities," reprinted in Colón, *The Way it Was and Other Writings*, pp. 100–102. Colón had in fact been interviewed about his political activity by the FBI a decade earlier; see transcript of FBI interview, July 10, 1944, in Colón Papers, Series II, box 1.

87. Colón, *A Puerto Rican in New York*, p. 200; for more on the relationship between Puerto Ricans and Marcantonio, see Salvatore John LaGumina, *Vito Marcantonio: The People's Politician* (Dubuque, Iowa: Kendall/Hunt Publishing Co. 1969), esp. chap. vii; Iglesias, ed., *Memoirs of Bernardo Vega*, pp. 183–90; Felix Ojeda Reyes, *Vito Marcantonio y Puerto Rico: Por Los Trabajadores y Por la Nacion* (Río Piedras: Ediciones Huracán, Inc. 1978), esp. pp. 9–55; idem, "Vito Marcantonio and Puerto Rican Independence," *Centro de Estudios Puertorriqueños Bulletin*, Spring 1992; Sánchez Korrol, *From Colonia to Community*, pp. 187–94; Jeff Kisseloff, *You Must Remember This: An Oral History of Manhattan from the 1890s to World War II*, (New York: Schocken Books 1989), pp. 337–80; Gerald Meyer, *Vito Marcantonio: Radical Politician, 1902–1954* (Albany, New York: State University Press of New York 1989); idem, "Marcantonio and El Barrio," *Centro de Estudios Puertorriqueños Bulletin*, Spring 1992, which is drawn from Meyer's book.

88. Although Colón in his American sojourn lived mainly in Brooklyn, he also lived in Harlem for some time during the First World War and perhaps after. He in fact revealed in more than one of his autobiographical sketches that he, his brother and later the rest of his family, including his mother and father, lived at 143rd Street between Lenox and Seventh Avenue. This was very much the heart of black Harlem at the time. Indeed, Colón wrote that "In those days the few Puerto Ricans around lived in the heart of the Negro neighborhood

together with the Negro people in the same buildings; many times as roomers in their homes." This is an exaggeration. (On the basis of the manuscript census for 1925 Sánchez Korrol concluded that "the incidence of blacks and Puerto Ricans sharing buildings was limited" and less frequent than Puerto Ricans sharing with Jews, Italians, Russians, and Irish. There is no reason to believe that there would have been more black and Puerto Rican sharing of space a few years earlier.) It is true, however, that some black Puerto Ricans, in the early years, did live in the way described by Colón. The point, however, is this: Colón lived in Harlem at a time that the Garvey movement could not have been missed. See Colón, "How to Rent an Apartment Without Money," and "The Day My Father Got Lost," both in *A Puerto Rican in New York*, pp. 43–5, and 46–8; Sánchez Korrol, *From Colonia to Community*, p. 59.

89. Colón, "Little Things are Big," *Daily Worker*, June 27, 1956; "Hiawatha Into Spanish," *Daily Worker*, November 13, 1956; "The Library Looks at the Puerto Rican," *Daily Worker*, March 5, 1956; these were later included in *A Puerto Rican in New York*.

90. "Pilgrimage of Prayer," "I Went to School on Friday in Washington, DC," "Phrase Heard in a Bus," "Little Rock," published in *The Daily Worker*, May 14, 1957; May 21, 1957; July 2, 1957; October 8, 1957, respectively.

91. See testimony of William Lorenzo Patterson, November 17, 1959, in US House of Representatives, *Hearings Before the Committee on Un-American Activities House of Representatives: Communist Activities Among Puerto Ricans in New York City and Puerto Rico*, pp. 1589–91; William L. Patterson to Jesus Colón, n.d. [June 29(?) 1956]; Jesús Colón Papers, Series IX, box 5, folder 8. It should be noted that the tone of the letter indicates clearly that the two men knew each other well. This judgement is supported by Patterson's note at the bottom of the letter: "P.S. Please tell Mercedes to see me at once if you see her."

92. By 1962, however, Colón had publicly distanced himself from Powell. Powell, who had recently married a Puerto Rican, at a commencement address at the Catholic University of Santa Maria at Ponce, Puerto Rico, declared, according to Colón, that "the final solution for the political status of Puerto Rico should be statehood." He fell further in Colón's estimation when on another occasion he suggested that the official and school language in Puerto Rico should be English. And he made the proposal with menace, for the Congressman suggested the withdrawal of financial "help" approved by Congress for Puerto Rico "unless English is made the main language in teaching all subjects in all grades of the public schools, high schools and the University of Puerto Rico." (Powell was surprised when, in the wake of these remarks, locals picketed his luxury home by the sea at Cerro Gordo in Puerto Rico.) Colón was outraged at Powell's statements: "Spanish is the language we Puerto Ricans have been speaking for over three hundred and fifty years. Who can tell us to change it—just like that!—for the English language?" Jesús Colón, "The Language of Puerto Rico," *The Worker*, August 5, 1962.

93. Colón, "Los Otros Estados Unidos," *Pueblos Hispanos*, April 10, 1943, p. 3. It is significant that Colón wrongly referred to the Ku Klux Klan as the "Klux Klux Klan," not once, but twice.

94. Colón, "Little Rock,"; also see *The Worker*, July 12, 1959, where Colón refers to "ugly Americans contaminated with the imperialist poison of race superiority." A decade earlier, he complained that the popular media, such as the *Daily News* and the *Daily Mirror* were, every day, poisoning the minds of his fellow Puerto Ricans against the Negro (*envenan la mente todos los días contra el negro*) and others: "El Prejuicio y la Independencia," *Liberación*, June 19, 1946, p. 7.

95. See especially, Colón, "Is Language a Barrier?" *Daily Worker*, January 30, 1956; also see, idem, "Pilgrimage of Prayer;" "Little Rock;" "Marching in the Snow," *Daily Worker*, March 2, 1958; "As I See it From Here," *The Worker*, Sept. 7, 1958; "The Powell Campaign," *The Worker*, Sept. 14, 1958; "The Question of Voting for Your Own Kind," *The Worker*, Oct. 5, and 12, 1958.

96. "The Negro in Puerto Rican History," and "The Negro in Puerto Rico Today," *The Worker*, February 7, 1960 and March 13, 1960, respectively.

97. Jesus Colón, "Changes Suggested in the First Edition of: *A Puerto Rican in New York*, by Jesús Colón," Series III, box 1, folder 4; and idem, "Foreword to the Second Edition," Series I, box 1, folder 1, both in the Jesus Colón Papers.

98. Juan Flores, who was commissioned to and wrote a fine introduction to the 1982 edition, told me that he was never informed by the publishers of Colón's suggested changes, nor did he know of the foreword.

99. I am at a loss to adequately explain how Jesús Colón, a man of undoubted decency

and integrity, could tolerate the moral stench of the Communist Party through Stalin's purges of the 1930s; through the Hitler Stalin Pact of 1939; the murder of Trotsky by a self-confessed assassin doing Stalin's work in 1940; through Khrushchev's chilling revelations about Stalin in his "secret speech" in 1956; through the invasion of Hungary in 1956; and through Moscow's military suppression of the Prague Spring in 1968. At each of those turning points along the bumpy road of twentieth-century official Communism, the world Communist movement, including the CPUSA, lost members, but not Comrade Colón, who died in 1974, clinging to the Party. His unpublished essay, "A Puerto Rican in Moscow," goes some way toward an explanation, but only part of the way. (Jesús Colón, "A Puerto Rican in Moscow" [1966], Jesús Colón Papers, Series III, box 1, folder 1.)

100. Handlin, *The Newcomers*, pp. 59–60. Colón in his newspaper columns meticulously documented these acts of anti-Puerto Rican discrimination and the responses to them. See, in particular, "A Judge in New Jersey," and "Because He Spoke in Spanish," *The Daily Worker*, January 16, 1956, and April 9, 1957, respectively; and idem, "Ten to 30 Years—For 2 Cigarettes," and "Racism in Glendale and Ridgewood," *The Worker*, November 16, 1958, and July 5, 1959, respectively.

101. Samuel Betances, "African-Americans and Hispanics/Latinos: Eliminating Barriers to Coalition Building," *Latino Studies Journal*, vol. 6, no. 1, January 1995, p. 15.

102. Sánchez Korrol, *From Colonia to Community*, p. 70.

103. It is almost certain that the *tabaqueros* and their families made up the majority of the Puerto Rican community in New York up to the 1930s. (Iglesias, ed., *Memoirs of Bernardo Vega*, p. 98; Sánchez Karrol, *From Colonia to Community*, p. 137; Angelo Falcon, "A History of Puerto Rican Politics in New York City: 1860s to 1945", in James Jennings and Monte Rivera, eds, *Puerto Rican Politics in Urban America* (Westport: Greenwood Press 1984), p. 23. And as they were renowned as radicals and freethinkers, the church would have had negligible influence over the life of the community in the early years. In 1917 Hubert Harrison reflected despondently upon how few black freethinkers there were in America. His spirits soared, however, when his survey endearingly noted that "The Cuban and Porto Rican cigar-makers are notorious Infidels, due to their acquaintance with the bigotry, ignorance and immorality of the Catholic priesthood in their native islands." (Harrison, *The Negro and the Nation* p. 46.) The evidence from Key West and Tampa, Florida, is that the *tabaqueros* there, too, had no time for religion and, least of all Catholicism. Indeed, they were described as "openly antagonistic" toward the church. Thus, up to 1939, only 100 out of the 12,372 Cubans living in Ybor City (Tampa), were members of the Catholic Church—0.8 percent of the population. (DeWight R. Middleton, "The Organization of Ethnicity in Tampa," *Ethnic Groups*, vol. 3, December 1981, pp. 293–4.) For more on this, see Jay P. Dolan and Jaime R. Vidal, eds, *Puerto Rican and Cuban Catholics in the US, 1900–1965* (Indiana: University of Notre Dame Press 1994). (The book in fact comprises two excellent monograph-length essays: Jaime R. Vidal, "Citizens Yet Strangers: The Puerto Rican Experience," pp. 11–143, and Lisandro Pérez, "Cuban Catholics in the United States," pp. 147–208.) For the Puerto Rican and Cuban background to this popular anti-clericalism see Quintero Rivera, "Socialist and Cigarmaker," pp. 26–8; R. del Romeral [Ramón Romero Rosa], "The Social Question and Puerto Rico: A Friendly Call to Intellectuals", in Angel Quintero–Rivera, ed., *Workers' Struggle in Puerto Rico: A Documentary History* (New York: Monthly Review Press 1976), pp. 22–5; Lewis, *Puerto Rico*, pp. 271–80; Sidney Mintz, *Worker in the Cane: A Puerto Rican Life History* (New York: W. W. Norton 1974), pp. 36 and 96; and Vidal, "Citizens Yet Strangers," esp. pp. 11–25; Pérez, "Cuban Catholics," pp. 147–57; for a wider but brief Latin American overview, see Leslie Bethell, "A Note on the Church and the Independence of Latin America," in Leslie Bethell, ed., *The Independence of Latin America* (Cambridge: Cambridge University Press 1987), pp. 227–32.

104. See, for example, Colón, "El Prejuicio y la Independencia"; idem, "The Negro in Puerto Rico Today," *The Worker*, March 13, 1960; and "Angels in My Hometown Church," in *The Way It Was*, pp. 53–4.

105. Jesús Colón to Concha, September 16, 1925; Jesús Colón Papers, Series II, box 7, folder 11.

106. Iglesias, ed., *Memoirs of Bernardo Vega*, p. 12.

107. Clara Rodriguez, *Puerto Ricans, Born in the U.S.A.* (Boulder: Westview Press 1991), p. 51. This, of course, echoes José Martí's descritpion of Cubans as "más que blanco, más que mulato, más que negro." José Martí, "Mi raza," *Patria*, April 16, 1893.

108. See Samuel Betances's classic essay, "The Prejudice of Having No Prejudice in Puerto

Rico," parts I and II, *The Rican*, Winter 1972 and Spring 1973; also see González, *Puerto Rico*; and Angela Jorge, "The Black Puerto Rican Woman in Contemporary American Society," in Edna Acosta-Belén, ed., *The Puerto Rican Woman: Perspectives on Culture, History, and Society*, 2nd edn. (New York: Praeger 1986); and Roberto Santiago, ed., *Boricuas: Influential Puerto Rican Writings* (New York: Ballantine Books 1995).

109. The *tabaqueros* in Florida had the same non-racist reputation, especially in the nineteenth century. The mixture of shades boggled the racist Southern mind. See Durward Long, "The Making of Modern Tampa: A City of the New South, 1885–1911," *The Florida Historical Quarterly*, vol. xlix, no. 4, April 1971, p. 342; Middleton, "The Organization of Ethnicity," pp. 289–90; Susan D. Greenbaum, "Afro-Cubans in Exile: Tampa, Florida, 1886–1984," *Cuban Studies/Estudios Cubanos*, vol. 15, no. 1, Winter 1985, pp. 60–61; Poyo, *"With All and For the Good of All"*, chap. 5. See discussion below in Chapter 8.

110. Iglesias, ed., *Memoirs of Bernardo Vega*, pp. 105–6. As we have seen, Colón acknowledged the existence of racism within the Puerto Rican community, but his discussion was flawed by his overstating of the Yanqui genesis of the phenomenon.

111. Iglesias, ed., *Memoirs of Bernardo Vega*, p. 97; Colón, "El Prejuicio y la Independencia."

112. Eric Walrond, "On Being Black," *The New Republic*, November 1, 1922, pp. 245–6.

113. Iglesias, ed., *Memoirs of Bernardo Vega*, p. 97.

114. Falcon, "A History of Puerto Rican Politics in New York City: 1860s to 1945," p. 29.

115. Ramón Colón, *Carlos Tapia: A Puerto Rican Hero in New York* (New York: Vintage Press 1976).

116. Ibid., pp. 72–3.

117. Ibid., pp. 71–2.

118. Ibid., pp. 74–5.

119. Ibid., p. 75.

120. There is no sustained discussion nor thorough analysis of this important event: the story of the "Harlem Riot" of 1926 is still to be written. Apart from the Vega discussion, which is the most extensive, referred to below, see Sánchez Korrol, *From Colonia to Community* pp. 68–9; Falcon, "A History of Puerto Rican Politics in New York," pp. 26–7; Ruth Glasser, *My Music is My Flag: Puerto Rican Musicians and Their New York Communities, 1917–1940* (Berkeley: University of California Press 1995), p. 109.

121. Iglesias, ed., *Memoirs of Bernardo Vega*, pp. 141–2.

122. Colón, *Carlos Tapia*, pp. 75–7.

123. Ibid., p. 77.

124. The arrested youths were James Monor of 212 East 98th Street, Tony Santos of 74 East 113th Street, and Peter de Jesus of 100 East 115th Street; *New York Times*, July 27, 1926.

125. See Acknowledgement, and the Introduction (written by the Local Brooklyn School Board Chairman, St Clair T. Bourne) to Colón, *Carlos Tapia*.

126. Sánchez Korrol, *From Colonia to Community*, p. 68.

127. Colón, *Carlos Tapia*, p. 76.

128. Cited in Sánchez Korrol, *From Colonia to Community*, pp. 68–9. see also, James Jennings, *Puerto Rican Politics in New York City* (Washington, DC: University Press of America 1977), pp. 23–4.

129. See, for instance, the letter from Mrs Antonia Denis, reproduced in full in Colón, *Carlos Tapia*, pp. 12–15, and the many cases documented by Colón in the book.

130. Ibid., p. 77. Colón must have been angered by the objection to Carlos Tapia of the type advanced by Félix Ojeda: tendentious, mean-spirited, ungrateful, ahistorical. "In March 1917, Carlos Tapia was charged with felonious homicide in San Juan; but he evaded justice on a technicality," Ojeda writes. What on earth is one to make of a bald statement like this, without details, without context, without source? One also wonders what Ojeda would have said had Tapia been convicted of murder. See Félix Ojeda, "Early Puerto Rican Communities in New York," in Oral History Task Force, Centro de Estudios Puertorriqueños, Hunter College, *Extended Roots: From Hawaii to New York—Migraciones Puertorriqueñas a los Estados Unidos* (New York: Centro de Estudios Puertorriqueños 1986), pp. 49–50.

131. Iglesias, ed., *Memoirs of Bernardo Vega*, pp. 85–6.

132. The fact that El Barrio was located in a relatively liberal, Northern state is not insignificant. For among the Cubans in Florida, as the pressures of Jim Crow increased at the

end of the nineteenth century, so did the tendency for separation along color and racial lines. See Chapter 8 below.

133. Iglesias, ed., *Memoirs of Bernardo Vega*, p. 151.

134. McKay, *Harlem*, p. 136.

135. Ottley, *"New World A-Coming,"* p. 51.

8. From a Class for Itself to a Race on its Own: The Strange Case of Afro-Cuban Radicalism and Afro-Cubans in Florida, 1870–1940

1. Poyo, *"With All, and for the Good of All"*, p. 81; Greenbaum, "Afro-Cubans in Exile" p. 59.

2. In 1894 Ramón Betances, writing from Paris to Martí's close aide, Gonzalo de Quesada, advised him to inform Martí not to bother to make a fund-raising trip to Paris. "[T]he revolutionaries," Betances told de Quesada, "are not favorably viewed in this colony." Quoted in Marshall True, "Revolutionaries in Exile: The Cuban Revolutionary Party, 1891–1898" (Ph.D. diss., University of Virginia 1965), p. 178.

3. For a good overview of the problems of the Cuban tobacco industry in the late nineteenth century see Stubbs, *Tobacco on the Periphery*, esp. chaps 1 and 2.

4. Long, "The Making of Modern Tampa"; idem, "The Historical Beginnings of Ybor City and Modern Tampa," *Florida Historical Quarterly*, vol. xlv, no. 1, July 1966, pp. 31–44; Pérez, "Cuban Catholics in the United States," pp. 158–69; Glenn L. Westfall, "Don Vicente Martinez Ybor, the Man and his Empire" (Ph.D.diss. University of Florida 1977).

5. Mormino and Pozzetta speak of a "symbiotic interlinkage" of cigars and the growth of Tampa (*The Immigrant World of Ybor City*, p. 68). But, as their own analysis indicates, the metaphor is inapposite: the relationship was hardly interdependent, equal or reciprocal. In reality, it looked, more than anything else, like a relation of parasitism, with Ybor City being the host.

6. Ibid., pp. 68–9.

7. Ibid., p. 69.

8. Ibid., pp. 49–50.

9. Mormino and Pozzetta, *The Immigrant World of Ybor City*, pp. 49–50; Pérez, "Cuban Catholics in the United States," p. 169.

10. Calculated from Tables 3 and 4 in Mormino and Pozzetta, *The Immigrant World of Ybor City*, pp. 50 and 55.

11. Defined as native white with native parentage.

12. Anthony Pizzo, *Tampa Town, 1824–86: The Cracker Village with a Latin Accent* (Tampa: Hurricane House Publishers, Inc. 1968).

13. Cited in Pérez, "Cuban Catholics in the United States," p. 170.

14. José Rivero Muñiz, "Tampa at the Close of the Nineteenth Century," *Florida Historical Quarterly*, vol. ixv, no. 4, April 1963, p. 339. Mormino and Pozzetta, *The Immigrant World of Ybor City*, pp. 76–7.

15. Pérez, "Cubans in Tampa," pp. 131–2.

16. Mormino and Pozzetta, *The Immigrant World of Ybor City*, p. 78.

17. Ibid., p. 79.

18. Greenbaum, "Afro-Cubans in Exile," pp. 62 and 65.

19. Mormino and Pozzetta, *The Immigrant World of Ybor City*, pp. 268–9. Joan Marie Steffy, "The Cuban Immigrants of Tampa, Florida, 1886–1898" (Masters thesis, University of South Florida 1975), p. 19; Susan Greenbaum, *Afro-Cubans in Ybor City: A Centennial History* (Tampa: n.p. 1986), p. 13. The Spanish population was even more unbalanced than the Cuban, while the Italians in Tampa established sexual parity fairly early on, and certainly by about 1910. See Mormino and Pozzetta, *The Immigrant World of Ybor City*, and idem., "Immigrant Women in Tampa: The Italian Experience, 1890–1930," *Florida Historical Quarterly*, vol. lxi, no. 3., January 1983.

20. Arenas quoted in Mormino and Pozzetta, *The Immigrant World of Ybor City*, p. 79; José Rivero Muñiz, *The Ybor City Story, 1885–1954* (Tampa: n. p., n. d. [1976], [translation by Eustasio Fernandez and Henry Beltran of *Los Cubanos en Tampa* (Havana 1958)]) pp. 128, 134. See also Long, "The Making of Modern Tampa," p. 342; Middleton, "The

Organization of Ethnicity in Tampa," p. 290; Greenbaum, "Afro-Cubans in Exile," pp. 60–61.

21. Gerald Poyo, "Cuban Revolutionaries and Monroe County Reconstruction Politics, 1868–1876," *Florida Historical Quarterly*, vol. lv, no.4, April 1977; idem, "Key West and the Cuban Ten Years War," *Florida Historical Quarterly*, vol. lvii, no.3, January 1979; idem, *"With All and for the Good of All"*, pp. 82–7.

22. Long, "The Making of Modern Tampa," p. 342; Steffy, "The Cuban Immigrants," pp. 59–61; Robert Ingalls, *Urban Vigilantes in the New South: Tampa, 1882–1936* (Knoxville: University of Tennessee Press), pp. 76, 115; Mormino and Pozzetta, *The Immigrant World of Ybor City*, p. 254; Poyo, *"With All and for the Good of All"*, pp. 84–5.

23. Stubbs, *Tobacco on the Periphery*, pp. 69–72, 110–113; and Mormino and Pozzetta, *The Immigrant World of Ybor City*, p. 101.

24. Mormino and Pozzetta, *The Immigrant World of Ybor City*, p. 186; Mormino and Pozzetta mistakenly identified Laureano Díaz as Alfonso Díaz; letter to W. James from S. Greenbaum, Nov. 18, 1996.

25. Ibid., p. 245.

26. Juan Mallea interviewed by Enrique Cordero, July 28, 1983, pp. 17–18; Special Collections, University of South Florida Library, Tampa; José Yglesias, "Martí in Ybor City," in Louis A. Pérez, Jr, ed., *José Martí in the United States: The Florida Experience* (Tempe: Special Studies No. 28, ASU Center for Latin American Studies, Arizona State University 1995), p. 113.

27. Mallea interview, p. 17.

28. *Tampa Tribune*, May 14, 1895, cited in Steffy, "The Cuban Immigrants," p. 142, n. 110.

29. *Tampa Morning Tribune*, Sept. 4, 1900, cited in Mormino and Pozzetta, *The Immigrant World of Ybor City*, p. 153.

30. Poyo, *"With All and for the Good of All"*, pp. 81–2, 106–7; idem, "The Anarchist Challenge to the Cuban Independence Movement, 1885–1890," *Cuban Studies/Estudios Cubano*, vol. 15, no. 1, Winter 1985, pp. 29–42.

31. Aspects of *La Resistencia* and the 1901 strike are discussed below.

32. Nancy Hewitt, " 'The Voice of Virile Labor': Labor Militancy, Community Solidarity, and Gender Identity among Tampa's Latin Workers, 1880–1921," in Ava Baron, ed., *Work Engendered: Towards a New History of American Labor* (Ithaca: Cornell University Press 1991), p. 150.

33. Morúa Delgado began publishing *El Pueblo* in Matanzas in March 1880; by the end of the year he fled to Key West. Pedro Deschamps Chapeaux, *Rafael Serra y Montalvo: Obrero Incansable de Nuestra Independencia* (Havana: Unión de Escritores y Artistas de Cuba 1975), esp. pp. 30–41; Rafael Serra's career is discussed later in the chapter; Poyo, *"With All and for the Good of All"*, pp. 82, 87–8; idem, "Anarchist Challenge," esp. pp. 31–2, 37–8. After his return to Cuba in 1898, Martín Morúa Delgado rose quickly within the political system, becoming President of the Cuban Senate, and compromised his political principles. In 1910, in an attempt to outflank his black political opponents in the *Partido Independiente de Color*, he successfully proposed an amendment to the constitution outlawing any party organized on the basis of color. He died within months of the passing of the law, but it was used as the pretext for the bloody suppression of the *Independientes* and their supporters, culminating in the slaughter in Oriente in 1912 of thousands of black dissidents. The most detailed account of these events is provided in Rafael Fermoselle-Lopez, "Black Politics in Cuba: The Race War of 1912" (Ph.D.diss., American Univ., 1972).

34. Poyo, *"With All and for the Good of All"*, p. 82.

35. See Durward Long, "*La Resistencia*: Tampa's Immigrant Labor Union," *Labor History*, vol. 6, no. 3, Fall 1965, pp. 193–213; idem, "Labor Relations in the Tampa Cigar Industry, 1885–1911," *Labor History*, vol. 12, no. 4, Fall 1971, pp. 551–9.

36. Mormino and Pozzetta, *The Immigrant World of Ybor City*, p. 239. Gary Mormino and George Pozzetta, "Concord and Discord: Italians and Ethnic Interactions in Tampa, Florida, 1886–1930," in Lydio F. Tomasi, ed., *Italian Americans: New Perspectives in Italian Immigration and Ethnicity* (New York: Center for Migration Studies of New York 1985), p. 353.

37. Quoted in Mormino and Pozzetta, *The Immigrant World of Ybor City*, p. 240.

38. Ibid., pp. 241 and 239.

39. Quoted in Ortiz, *Cuban Counterpoint*, p. 88.

40. For an excellent discussion of Martí's role as unifier of the Cuban nationalist forces in the United States see Poyo, "José Martí: Architect of Social Unity in the Emigré Communities of the United States," in Christopher Abel and Nissa Torrents, eds, *José Martí: Revolutionary Democrat* (Durham, NC: Duke University Press 1986), idem, "*With All and for the Good of All*", chap. 6; see also Louis Pérez, "José Martí: Context and Consciousness," in Ann L. Henderson and Gary R. Mormino, eds, *Spanish Pathways in Florida: 1492–1992 / Los Cominos Españoles en La Florida: 1492–1992* (Sarasota: Pineapple Press, Inc. 1991). (The essays in the book are all printed in English as well as Spanish.)

41. Poyo, "*With All and for the Good of All*", p. 105.

42. For biographical details about Serra and his and Martí's work in the League, see Deschamps Chapeaux, *Rafael Serra y Montalvo*, esp. pp. 49–77. See Martí's own reports—and powerfully evocative ones they are too—of the League, "Mondays at 'The League'" and "A Beautiful Night at 'The League'," published in *Patria*, March 26, 1892 and November 4, 1893, respectively; these have been translated and reprinted in José Martí, *On Education: Articles on Educational Theory and Pedagogy, and Writings for Children from 'The Age of Gold'*, edited by Philip S. Foner (New York: Monthly Review Press 1979), pp. 186–91 and 192–6.

43. José Martí, *Our America: Writings on Latin America and the Struggle for Cuban Independence*, edited by Philip Foner (New York: Monthly Review Press 1977), p. 308; Poyo, "*With All and for the Good of All*", pp. 105–6.

44. Poyo, "*With All and for the Good of All*", p. 106.

45. Greenbaum, "Afro-Cubans in Exile," pp. 70 n.8, Poyo "*With All and for the Good of All*", p. 106; Mormino and Pozzetta, *The Immigrant World of Ybor City*, p. 185.

46. Jorge Mañach, *Martí: Apostle of Freedom* (New York: Devin-Adair Co. 1950), p. 282.

47. Ibid., pp. 309–10.

48. Ibid., p. 318; Greenbaum, *Afro-Cubans in Ybor City*, p. 5; Nancy A. Hewitt, "Paulina Pedroso and *Las Patriotas* of Tampa," in Henderson and Mormino, eds, *Spanish Pathways*, p. 260.

49. Ibid., p. 110. The Pedrosos, contrary to Nancy Hewitt's repeated claim, did not sell their house to raise money for the revolution. In a desperate plea for money, Martí had requested the Pedrosos to sell their house, if necessary, to raise the required amount. "[P]ledge for your country's sake the roof that covers you," he pleaded, "Don't ask questions of me. A man like me does not speak this language without reasons." Mañach, who reported this correspondence, said Martí "knew he would pay them with a free country." But the money was raised without the Pedrosos having to resort to extreme measures, and they continued to live in their house until they emigrated back to Cuba in 1910. Nancy Hewitt, "Varieties of Voluntarism: Class, Ethnicity, and Women's Activism in Tampa," in Louise Tilly and Patricia Gurin, eds., *Women, Politics, and Change* (New York: Russell Sage Foundation 1990), p. 75; idem., "Paulina Pedroso and *Las Patriotas* of Tampa," p. 276; idem., "Engendering Independence: Las Patriotas of Tampa and the Social Vision of José Martí," in Pérez, ed., *José Martí in the United States*, p. 30; cf. Rivero Muñiz, *The Ybor City Story*, p. 93; and Mañach, *Martí: Apostle of Freedom*, pp. 309–10; Professor Susan Greenbaum confirmed that the Pedrosos never sold their house in the 1890s. (Telephone conversation October 29, 1996.)

50. Quoted in Yglesias, "Martí in Ybor City," p. 110.

51. José Martí, "With All, and for the Good of All," in idem, *Our America*, p. 259.

52. Josefina Toledo provides the most detailed analysis of Figeroa's work with Martí in her *Sotero Figueroa, Editor de "Patria": Apuntes para una Biografía* (Havana: Editorial Letras Cubanas 1985); in addition to Toledo, see also Deschamps Chapeaux, *Rafael Serra y Montalvo*, for more on the relation between Figueroa and Serra, esp. pp. 115ff.

53. *Patria*, April 16, 1893; reprinted in Martí, *Our America*, pp. 311–14; quotation from p. 313.

54. Fernando Ortiz y Fernandez, "Cuba, Martí and the Race Problem," *Phylon*, vol. iii, no. 3, 3rd quarter, 1942, p. 255.

55. It is no surprise that Martí greatly admired Phillips; he kept a picture of Phillips on his desk. See his warm and generous obituary on Phillips: José Martí, "Wendell Phillips," in his *Inside the Monster: Writings on the United States and American Imperialism* ed. by Philip S. Foner (New York: Monthly Review Press 1975), pp. 55–66.

56. Ortiz, "Cuba, Martí and the Race Problem," p. 259. For some of the more persuasive explanations as to *how*, as opposed to *why*, Martí evolved in the way in which he did, see Jorge Mañach, *Martí*; John M. Kirk, *José Martí: Mentor of the Cuban Nation* (Tampa:

University Presses of Florida 1982); Peter Turton, *José Martí: Architect of Cuba's Freedom* (London: Zed Books 1986); and Chritopher Abel and Nissa Torrents, eds., *José Martí, Revolutionary Democrat* (Durham: Duke University Press 1986).

57. For a discussion of the response to Martí's death in Tampa, see Pérez, "José Martí," pp. 240–42, 254; see also Rivero Muñiz, *The Ybor City Story*, pp. 96–7.

58. Cited in Deschamps Chapeaux, *Rafael Serra y Montalvo*, p. 110. Brito, who had owned a store in Ybor City, several years earlier gave all his wealth—some 11,000 pesos—to Martí for the struggle. See Susan Greenbaum, "José Martí and Jim Crow" unpublished ms, and Chapeaux, *Rafael Serra y Montalvo*, p. 63.

59. Poyo, *"With All and for the Good of All"*, chap. 7; Louis Pérez, *Cuba Between Empires, 1878–1902* (Pittsburgh: University of Pittsburgh Press 1983), pp. 97–8, 110–12; George W. Auxier, "The Propaganda Activities of the Cuban *Junta* in Precipitating the Spanish-American War, 1895–1898," *Hispanic American Historical Review*, vol. xix, no. 3, August 1939.

60. Domingo Ginésta, "A History of Ybor City" (1936), p. 3, Federal Writers' Project, quoted in Mormino and Pozzetta, *The Immigrant World of Ybor City*, p. 105. For more on the support provided by Cubans to the Italians in the early years and the changing economic profile of the Italians in Ybor City, see ibid., pp. 104–11; also see idem, "Concord and Discord," pp. 348ff.

61. The fact that the Cubans, including Afro-Cubans, were more educated than and had a higher literacy rate than the Italians might also have contributed to the relation that developed. (In 1910 "barely half" of Ybor City's Italians over ten years old could read and write in their native language, compared to 97 percent of Cubans and Spaniards. As early as 1899 over 90 percent of Havana cigar makers could read and write.) In addition, the Cubans, who were virtually all from Havana, looked down upon the Italians whom they regarded as country bumpkins, especially when they kept farm animals in their backyard. (Mormino and Pozzetta, *The Immigrant World of Ybor City*, pp. 165, 242–3, 286; Stubbs, *Tobacco and the Periphery*, p. 88.)

62. There is no evidence to suggest that the white Cubans, Spaniards, and Italians accorded black Americans outside (or indeed, the few inside during the early years) of Ybor City the same amount of respect and civility that they gave black Cubans.

63. "Life History of José Ramón Sanfeliz," in Federal Writers' Project, "Social-Ethnic Study of Ybor City, Tampa, Florida," vol. 1, pp. 17–18, Special Collections, University of South Florida Library, Tampa, Florida.

64. Ibid., p. 18.

65. Ibid., pp. 19, 22.

66. Rivero Muñiz, *The Ybor City Story*, pp. 128, 134.

67. Interview with Juan Mallea, cited in Mormino and Pozzetta, *The Immigrant World of Ybor City*, p. 186.

68. C. Vann Woodward, *The Strange Career of Jim Crow* (New York: Oxford University Press 1955), deservedly regarded as a classic text, still stands as the best overview of the rise of Jim Crow. For the Florida experience in particular, see Jerrell H. Shofner, "Custom, Law, and History: The Enduring Influence of Florida's 'Black Code'," *Florida Historical Quarterly*, vol. lv, no. 3, January 1977; idem, *Nor Is It Over Yet: Florida in the Era of Reconstruction, 1863–1877* (Gainesville: University Presses of Florida 1974); Wali R. Kharif, "Black Reaction to Segregation and Discrimination in Post-Reconstruction Florida," *Florida Historical Quarterly*, vol. lxiv, no. 2, October 1985; August Meier and Elliott Rudwick, "The Boycott Movement Against Jim Crow Streetcars in the South, 1900–1906," in their, *Along the Color Line: Explorations in the Black Experience* (Urbana: University of Illinois Press 1976); George, "Colored Town: Miami's Black Community, 1896–1930"; idem, "Policing Miami's Black Community, 1896–1930."

69. Shofner, "Custom, Law, and History," pp. 289–91, original emphasis.

70. Cited in George, "Colored Town," p. 444.

71. David Chalmers, "The Ku Klux Klan in the Sunshine State: The 1920s," *Florida Historical Quarterly*, vol. xlii, no. 3, January 1964.

72. Willard B. Gatewood, Jr, "Negro Troops in Florida, 1898," *Florida Historical Quarterly*, vol. xlix, no. 1, July 1970, p. 6.

73. Ibid., p. 11.

74. Ibid., pp. 5 and 4.

75. *Tampa Morning Tribune*, May 5, 1898; cited in Gatewood, "Negro Troops in Florida,"p. 3.

76. See especially Shofner's "Custom, Law, and History."

77. This is a point made very forcefully by Vann Woodward in *The Strange Career of Jim Crow*, chaps ii and iii.

78. Susan Greenbaum, "Afro-Cubans in Exile," p. 59; emphasis added. Greenbaum, quite sensibly, dropped and rejected this position in her subsequent writings on the subject.

79. Mormino and Pozzetta, *The Immigrant World of ybor City*, p. 186; emphasis added. See also Mormino and Pozzetta, "Concord and Discord," pp. 347, 354.

80. Cited in Long, "*La Resistencia*," p. 213. In addition to Long's pioneering essay, see Ingalls' excellent study, *Urban Vigilantes in the New South*, esp. chap. 3 for the 1901 strike. For more on the labor radicalism of Ybor City, see Long, "Labor Relations in the Tampa Cigar Industry, 1885–1911," idem, "The Open–Closed Shop Battle in Tampa's Cigar Industry, 1919–21," *Florida Historical Quarterly*, vol. xlvii, no. 3, October 1968; Gary Mormino, "Tampa and the New Urban South: The Weight Strike of 1899," *Florida Historical Quarterly*, vol. lx, no. 3, January 1982; Mormino and Pozzetta, "Immigrant Women in Tampa"; Mormino and Pozzetta, *The Immigrant World of Ybor City*, esp. chap. 4; Nancy A. Hewitt, "'The Voice of Virile Labor'"; Pérez, "Cubans in Tampa"; idem, "Reminiscences of a *Lector*."

81. See Greenbaum, *Afro-Cubans in Ybor City*, p. 7; Nancy Raquel Mirabal, "'Más que negro': José Martí and the Politics of Unity," in Louis Pérez, ed., *José Martí in the United States*, p. 62. The split seems to go back to 1899 when a group of Cubans formed the October 10 Club. The club's membership was black and white, but soon after its formation black members were either expelled or felt that they had to withdraw. The remaining members of the October 10 Club renamed the latter *El Club Nacional Cubano* (most accounts state that black Cubans were still allowed to become members for the next two years), which in 1902 became *El Círculo Cubano*, which definitively barred black membership. In the meantime, the former black members of the October 10 Club founded their own organization, *Los Libres Pensadores de Marti Y Maceo*. Bruno Roig, one of its founders, had belonged to a similar organization in Santa Clara, Cuba, named in honor of Antonio Maceo. In 1904, the Society merged with another black organization that was based in West Tampa, *La Unión*, and they jointly became a bona fide mutual aid society (providing, among other things, medical care for its members) and cultural organization. Greenbaum, *Afro-Cubans*, pp. 7–8; Mormino and Pozzetta, *The Immigrant World of Ybor City*, pp. 186–7; Durward Long, "An Immigrant Co-operative Medicine Program in the South, 1887–1963," *Journal of Southern History*, vol. 31, no. 4, November 1965, p. 430; idem, "The Making of Modern Tampa," p. 342.

82. See Deschamps Chapeaux, *Rafael Serra y Montalvo*, pp. 115–47 where a facsimile of the front page of *La Doctrina de Martí* is printed, p. 117; Poyo, "*With All and for the Good of All*", pp. 128ff.

83. For discussions of the intensification of the struggle and changes in the cigar industry in the period after 1898, see Long, "*La Resistencia*"; idem "The Open–Closed Shop Battle"; idem, "Labor Relations in the Tampa Cigar Industry"; Mormino, "Tampa and the New Urban South"; Pérez, "Cubans in Tampa"; Ingalls, *Urban Vigilantes in the New South*, esp. chaps 2–5; Cooper, *Once A Cigar Maker*, is especially good on the social and political impact of technological changes in the early twentieth century.

84. Mormino and Pozzetta, *The Immigrant World of Ybor City*, p. 272.

85. Greenbaum, "Afro-Cubans in Exile," p. 64.

86. Idem, "Economic Cooperation Among Urban Industrial Workers: Rationality and Community in an Afro-Cuban Mutual Aid Society, 1904–1927," *Social Science History*, vol. 17, no. 2, Summer 1993, p. 184.

87. Pérez, "Cubans in Tampa"; idem, "Reminiscences of a *Lector*"; Stubbs, *Tobacco on the Periphery*, chap. 2; Ingalls, *Urban Vigilantes in the New South*, chap. 5; Mormino and Pozzetta, "Immigrant Women"; idem, *The Immigrant World of Ybor City*, chap. 9; Greenbaum, *Afro-Cubans in Ybor City*, p. 10; Hewitt, "'The Voice of Virile Labor'."

88. Mormino and Pozzetta, *The Immigrant World of Ybor City*, p. 289; Greenbaum, "Afro-Cubans in Exile," p. 65.

89. Greenbaum, *Afro-Cubans in Ybor City*, pp. 10, 18; idem, "Afro-Cubans in Exile," p. 65.

90. Greenbaum, "Afro-Cubans in Exile," p. 63; Mirabal, "'Más que negro'," p. 63.

91. Mallea interview, pp. 15–18; quotation from p. 15.

92. Ibid., p. 13.

93. Greenbaum, *Afro-Cubans in Ybor City*, p. 14.

94. Idem, "Afro-Cubans in Exile," p. 67.

95. Idem, *Afro-Cubans in Ybor City*, pp. 18–20.

Epilogue

1. In 1929, at the behest of Joseph Stalin and the Comintern, Jay Lovestone, the leader of the Communist Party of the United States, was expelled by his own party. Lovestone had had the support of the majority of the Party, but with the edict from Stalin, those who remained in the CP followed the Comintern line. Cyril Briggs, Richard B. Moore, and Otto Huiswoud were among the black members who opposed the 'Lovestoneites,' among whom was Grace Campbell. Draper, *American Communism and Soviet Russia*, esp. chap. 18; Naison, *Communists in Harlem During the Depression*, pp. 24–5.

2. For good discussions of the period and the activists, see Naison, *Communists in Harlem During the Depression*; McKay, *Harlem: Negro Metropolis*; Greenberg, *'Or Does it Explode.'*

3. George Padmore, *Pan-Africanism or Communism: The Coming Struggle for Africa* (London: Dennis Dobson 1956); Hooker, *Black Revolutionary*.

4. *Garvey Papers*, vol. vii, pp. xlvii–xlviii, and passim; Lewis, *Marcus Garvey*, pp. 168–75; William Scott, *Sons of Sheba's Race: African Americans and the Italo-Ethiopian War, 1935–1941* (Bloomington: Indiana University Press 1993), pp. 204–7.

5. S. K. B. Asante, 'The Afro-American and the Italo-Ethiopian Crisis, 1934–36,' *Race*, vol. xv, no. 2, 1973; idem, 'The Impact of the Italo-Ethiopian Crisis of 1935–36 on the Pan-African Movement in Britain,' *Transactions of the Historical Society of Ghana*, vol. 13, no. 2, pp. 217–27; idem, *Pan-African Protest: West Africa and the Italo-Ethiopian Crisis, 1934–1941* (London: Longman 1977); J. Ayo Langley, 'Pan-Africanism in Paris, 1924–36,' *Journal of Modern African Studies*, vol. 7, no. 1, April 1969; Makonnen, *Pan-Africanism From Within*, chap. 8; Robert G. Weisbord, *Ebony Kinship: Africa, Africans and the Afro-American* (Westport, Conn.: Greenwood Press 1973), chap. 3; Scott, *Sons of Sheba's Race*; Joseph E. Harris, *African-American Reactions to War in Ethiopia, 1936–1941* (Baton Rouge: Louisiana State University Press 1994).

6. Scott, *Sons of Sheba's Race*, p. 112; Naison, *Communist in Harlem During the Depression*, pp. 196–7; Danny Duncan Collum, ed., *African Americans in the Spanish Civil War: "This Ain't Ethiopia, But It'll Do"* (New York: G. K. Hall and Co. 1992), pp. 70–71.

7. Sworn Deposition of Ralph E. Campbell, October 7, 1943, in Surrogate's Court New York County, Re: Grace P. Campbell, file no. A 2630, 1943, liber 433; *Garvey Papers*, vol. vii, pp. xlvi, 567 n.l; Jill Watts, *God, Harlem U.S.A.: The Father Divine Story* (Berkeley: University of California Press 1992), pp. 113–15.

8. E. U. Essien-Udom, *Black Nationalism: The Rise of the Black Muslims in the U.S.A.* (Harmondsworth: Penguin Books 1966), p. 68; Vincent, *Black Power and the Garvey Movement*, pp. 222–4; Rolinson, 'The Universal Negro Improvement Association in Georgia,' p. 220; Smith-Irvin, *Marcus Garvey's Footsoldiers*, pp. 49 and 72.

9. Jan Carew provides the best account of the politics of the Littles: Carew, *Ghosts in Our Blood*; see also Ted Vincent, "The Garveyite Parents of Malcolm X," *Black Scholar*, March/April 1989.

10. Anderson, *A. Philip Randolph*; William H. Harris, *Keeping Faith: A. Philip Randolph, Milton P. Webster, and the Brotherhood of Sleeping Car Porters, 1925–37* (Urbana: University of Illinois Press 1977); John H. Seabrook, 'Black and White Unite: The Career of Frank R. Crosswaith' (Ph.D. diss., Rutgers University 1980).

11. Hill, 'Introduction,' p. xlviii; Theodore G. Vincent, *Voices of a Black Nation: Political Journalism in the Harlem Renaissance* (San Francisco: Ramparts Press 1973), p. 21; see also Amiri Baraka's enthusiastic review of Haywood's book: Amiri Baraka, *Daggers and Javelins: Essays, 1974–1979* (New York: William Morrow and Company 1984), pp. 234–36.

Postscript

1. Christopher Lasch, "The Trouble with Black Power," *New York Review of Books*, February 29, 1968, p. 10.

2. Julian Mayfield detects "a peculiar and not very pleasant smell" in Cruse's reluctance to

be open about his Communist past and his role in the Party in Harlem: Julian Mayfield, "A Challenge to a Bestseller: Crisis or Crusade?" *Negro Digest*, June 1968, p. 13. Cruse's own explanation of his reticence to mention his political past in the book is unconvincing. "Certain unfriendly critics of my book," he writes, "have complained that I was overly 'modest' in not talking very much about myself and my own political exploits during the forties and fifties. But that would have necessitated another kind of book—a political autobiography, a genre I was not interested in." Harold Cruse, *Rebellion or Revolution?* (New York: William Morrow & Company, Inc. 1968), p. 8; Cruse puts forward the same argument in his response to Mayfield: Harold Cruse, "Replay on a Black Crisis," *Negro Digest*, November 1968, pp. 66–7. Of course, neither Mayfield, nor any other critic, called upon Cruse to write his political autobiography. The call was for greater openness about his past and role, especially in relation to events and incidents discussed in *The Crisis of the Negro Intellectual*. It is not precisely clear when Cruse left the Party. Cruse himself speaks of having left in the "early fifties" as well as the "middle fifties." See Cruse, *Rebellion or Revolution?*, pp. 8 and 193. A helpful sketch of Cruse's background and political evolution is provided in Henry Vance Davis, "From Petersburg to *Crisis*: A Review of the Early Years," *Voices of the African Diaspora: The CAAS Research Review* [published by the Center for Afroamerican and African Studies, University of Michigan, where Cruse has taught since the late 1960s], vol. ix, no. 1, Winter 1994, pp. 12–16. Davis claims that Cruse left "by 1953," p. 15. In a paper prepared for a 1967 conference, Cruse unpersuasively suggests that "[t]he main reason I stayed in the movement as long as I did was to learn more thoroughly *why* the Marxists could be so dogmatically wrong about Negroes." Cruse, *Rebellion or Revolution?*, p. 193; emphasis in original.

3. Cruse, *Rebellion or Revolution?*, p. 15. It is fairly certain that some of the most unpleasant polemical tricks displayed in *The Crisis of the Negro Intellectual* were learned while Cruse was a member of the Party.

4. For some perceptive discussions of the conceptualization of culture in Cruse's work, see Robert Chrisman, "The Crisis of Harold Cruse," *The Black Scholar*, November 1969; idem, "The Contradictions of Harold Cruse: Or Cruse's Blues, Take 2," *Black World*, May 1971; William Eric Perkins, "Harold Cruse: On the Problem of Culture and Revolution," and Ernest Allen, "The Cultural Methodology of Harold Cruse," both in *The Journal of Ethnic Studies*, vol. 5, no. 2, Summer 1977.

5. Georg Lukács, the distinguished Hungarian Marxist philosopher, had suggested in a controversial essay that even if all of Marx's theses were misproven, the genuine Marxist (what he called the "orthodox Marxist") would not renounce his othodoxy for a single moment. For, he said, orthodox Marxism is "not the 'belief' in this or that thesis, nor the exegesis of a 'sacred' book. On the contrary, orthodoxy refers exclusively to *method*." Of course, the question that arises with such a proposition is: Who, apart from brave souls like Lukács, would take a theory or method seriously if all its findings have been shown to be false? See Georg Lukács, "What is Orthodox Marxism?" in his *History and Class Consciousness: Studies in Marxist Dialectics*, trans. Rodney Livingstone (London: Merlin Press 1971), p. 1, emphasis in original.

6. Harold Cruse, "Black and White: Outlines of the Next Stage," *Black World*, January 1971, p. 22.

7. Ibid., p. 22: first emphasis mine; Ernest Kaiser, "The Crisis of the Negro Intellectual," *Freedomways*, First Quarter 1969.

8. Kaiser, "The Crisis of the Negro Intellectual," p. 25.

9. In a similar vein, Ernest Allen, in one of the finest critiques of Cruse, sees the "catalytic role" of the book as its chief merit: Allen, "The Cultural Methodology of Harold Cruse," p. 47.

10. John Henrik Clarke, "*The Crisis of the Negro Intellectual* by Harold Cruse: A Reappraisal of Some of the Neglected Aspects of the Crisis," in his *Africans at the Crossroads: Notes for an African World Revolution* (Trenton: Africa World Press, Inc. 1991), p. 368.

11. Arthur Paris, "Cruse and the Crisis in Black Culture: The Case of Theater, 1900–1930," *Journal of Ethnic Studies*, vol. 5, no. 2, Summer 1977, p. 51.

12. Dissatisfaction is expressed with Cruse's discussion of Caribbeans, but only in passing and briefly, in the following: Dennis Forsythe, "'Roll Call' of the Negro Intellectual: A Critique of Harold Cruse's *Crisis of the Negro Intellectual*," *New World Quarterly*, vol. 5, no. 3, n.d. [1968?]; Mayfield, "A Challenge to a Bestseller"; review by Locksley Edmondson in *Journal of Modern African Studies*, vol. 7, no. 1, April 1969; Allen, "The Cultural

Methodology of Harold Cruse"; and Clarke, "*The Crisis of the Negro Intellectual* by Harold Cruse."

13. In addition to Kaiser, "The Crisis of the Negro Intellectual," and Allen, "The Cultural Methodology of Harold Cruse," see, in particular, Chrisman, "The Crisis of Harold Cruse," idem, "The Contradictions of Harold Cruse: Or Cruse's Blues, Take 2"; Mayfield, "A Challenge to a Bestseller?"; Michael Thelwell, "What is to be Done?" *Partisan Review*, vol. xxxv, no. 4, Fall 1968; Perkins, "Harold Cruse: On the Problem of Culture and Revolution; Paris, "Cruse and the Crisis in Black Culture"; Sterling Stuckey and Joshua Leslie, "Reflections on Reflections about the Black Intellectual, 1930–1945," *First World*, vol. 2, no. 2, 1979; Clarke, "*The Crisis of the Negro Intellectual* by Harold Cruse." See, in addition, the special issue of *Voices of the African Diaspora: The CAAS Research Review* (vol. ix, no. 1, Winter 1994) commemorating the twenty-fifth anniversary of the publication of *The Crisis of the Negro Intellectual*, where Beverly Guy-Shetfall, in "Reconstructing a Black Female Intellectual Tradition: Commentary on Harold Cruse's *The Crisis of the Negro Intellectual*," questions the absence of black women intellectual in Cruse's discussion.

14. This is quoted as the epigraph to E. P. Thompson, *The Poverty of Theory and Other Essays* (London: Merlin Press 1978).

15. In any case, when would we have time to do our own work if we were to correct the many errors we come across every single day? Marx lived very much by this stricture, which substantially explained why, of the many volumes of *Capital* he had planned writing, only the first was finished and published in his lifetime. We shall never be in a position to correct all the errors we know of. Some of us do not bother to correct any at all. Most of us pick and choose which to correct, and whether to correct them implicitly or openly. On what basis do we choose to correct some and not others?

16. The term is Isaac Deutscher's: see his *The Non-Jewish Jew and Other Essays* (Oxford: Oxford University Press 1968), esp., pp. 25–41.

17. Harold Cruse, *The Crisis of the Negro Intellectual: From Its Origins to the Present* (New York: William Morrow & Co. 1967) (hereafter referred to in footnotes as Cruse), pp. 115–17.

18. Ibid., esp. pp. 127–34, 207, 254–5.

19. Johnson, *Along This Way*; see also Lynn Adelman, "A Study of James Weldon Johnson," *Journal of Negro History*, vol. lii, no. 2, April 1967, and Eugene Levy, *James Weldon Johnson: Black Leader, Black Voice* (Chicago: University of Chicago Press 1973).

20. Cruse, pp. 78, 80, 81.

21. For more on Grey's background, see *Garvey Papers*, vol. i, pp. 211–12 n. 3.

22. Cruse, p. 124; first emphasis added. Of course, the UNIA in the United States was not predominantly Caribbean. The fact that Garveyism functioned within the British empire, in the Caribbean, Africa, and even in Australia, has escaped Cruse.

23. Ibid., p. 129; second emphasis added.

24. The remark needs to be qualified in two important respects. First, the nineteenth-century black nationalist and emigrationist trends in the United States had important Caribbean elements. John Brown Russwurm (1799–1851), Edward Wilmot Blyden (1832–1912), and Robert Campbell (1829–84) were the most important Caribbean representatives of these trends. Second, Cruse over-states the number of Afro-Americans "mobilized" by Singleton. The most careful estimate of the 1879 black migration to Kansas under the influence of Singleton and others is twenty-two thousand. An estimated twenty-six thousand are thought to have migrated to Kansas between 1870 and 1880. The membership of the Garvey movement in the United States ranged from hundreds of thousands to more than a million. On the "Kansas Fever" of 1879 see Nell Irvin Painter, *Exodusters: Black Migration to Kansas after Reconstruction* (New York: Alfred Knopf 1977), and the more detailed quantitative analysis of Cohen, *At Freedom's Edge*, pp. 168–97, 299–311. Robert Campbell was in fact a close associate of Delany's. For a fine discussion of Campbell's political evolution see R. J. M. Blackett, *Beating Against the Barriers: The Lives of Six Nineteenth-Century Afro-Americans* (Baton Rouge: Louisiana State University Press 1986), Chap. 3.

25. Kaiser, "The Crisis of the Negro Intellectual," pp. 30–31.

26. Cruse, p. 119.

27. Ibid., p. 118.

28. See Turner and Turner, eds, *Richard B. Moore*, p. 51.

29. Cyril Briggs to Theodore Draper, March 17, 1958 (first of two letters sent on the same day); Theodore Draper Papers, Reel 8, Robert W. Woodruff Library, Emory University.

30. See the the the exchange of letters between Domingo and Chandler Owen in the *Messenger*, March 1923, pp. 639–45; Theodore Kornweibel, *No Crystal Stair*, chap. 5, provides a good account of the "Garvey Must Go" campaign and its repercussions.

31. *Messenger*, July 1919, p. 13; and Thanksgiving Number, December 1919, p. 6.

32. *Messenger* March 1920, p. 11; and November 1917, p. 21.

33. See boxed advertisement in the *Crusader*, June 1920, p. 31.

34. See, for instance, Richard B. Moore, "An Open Letter to Mr. A. Philip Randolph," *Negro Champion*, vol. i, no. 14 (August 8, 1928); reprinted in Turner and Turner, eds, *Richard B. Moore*, pp. 147–150.

35. Haywood, *Black Bolshevik*, pp. 602, 634–5.

36. Cruse, p. 57.

37. McKay's speech to the Fourth Congress of the Communist International was extensively reported on in both *Pravda* and *Izvestia* on November 26, 1922 and the full text was reprinted in *International Press Correspondence*, vol. 3, January 5, 1923, pp. 16–17. Indeed, the *Crisis* carried photographs of McKay in the Soviet Union, including one in which he is speaking to the Congress from the podium in the Throne Room of the Kremlin. These photographs accompanied a long and important article by McKay on his Russian experience; see McKay, "Soviet Russia and the Negro," *Crisis*, December 1923–January 1924, pp. 61–5, 114–18; the *Messenger* of April 1923 (p. 653) had as its first editorial item, "Negroes in Soviet Russia," which mentioned McKay's speech and the fact that he "plead for his race."

38. There are no less than eight articles on McKay, including interviews and poems published in *Pravda* and *Izvestia*, between November 18, 1922 and April 1, 1923. The first was an interview conducted by *Izvestia*, "Rasovy vopros v Amerika—Beseda s tovarish Klod Makkei," ("The Racial question in America—An Interview with Comrade Claude McKay") *Izvestia* November 18, 1922, p. 2, and the last was a long letter addressed to Leon Trotsky, "Pismo Mek-Kaia Tovarishu Trotskomu," ("Letter of McKay to Comrade Trotsky"), *Pravda*, April 1, 1923, p. 3. McKay also published a letter in *Bolshevik*, organ of the Fourth Congress of the Communist International, on December 3, 1922.

39. McKay relates at length in his autobiography, his experience in the Soviet Union—including his conversations with leading Bolsheviks. See McKay, *A Long Way From Home* pp. 153–234; cf. "Soviet Russia and the Negro."

40. Claude McKay, *Negry v Amerike* (Moscow: State Publishing House 1923); idem, *Negroes in America*, trans. Robert J. Winter (Port Washington, New York: Kennikat Press 1979); idem, *Sudom Lyncha* (Moscow: State Publishing House 1925); idem, *Trial By Lynching: Stories About Negro Life in North America*, trans. Robert J. Winter (Mysore, India: Centre for Commonwealth Literature and Research, University of Mysore 1977).

41. Cruse, p. 115.

42. Wayne Cooper, *Claude McKay: Rebel Sojourner in the Harlem Renaissance* (Baton Rouge: Louisiana State University Press 1987), p. 344.

43. McKay, *Harlem: Negro Metropolis*, p. 254; Cruse, p. 263.

44. Cruse, p. 115.

45. Part of the explanation for the extraordinarily negative attention paid to Moore seems to lie in an unpleasant incident that took place at a party a few years before *The Crisis of the Negro Intellectual* was published. Moore and Cruse, at least according to Cruse's letter of complaint, had a heated political exchange at the home of a mutual friend, an African. During the exchange, Moore apparently drove his points home with "the prefatory admonition" to Cruse: *"I don't want you to forget them."* Cruse found Moore's behavior at the party condescending, a "pure and simple display of *arrogance.*" "When you discuss racial matters with me," Cruse told Moore in his letter, *"I don't want you to forget* that you are not talking to an unknowledgeable child." Cruse was hurt and enraged by Moore's behavior and wrote to him in an "attempt to settle and resolve certain ideological differences that exist between us once and for all time." He would no longer engage Moore in discussions over the name "Negro." (Moore had published in 1960 *The Name "Negro": Its Origin and Evil Use* [New York: Afroamerican Publishers, Inc. 1960], a pamphlet linked to a campaign that he was waging.) It is not clear whether Moore responded to Cruse. But from the evidence of *The Crisis of the Negro Intellectual* Cruse had not settled accounts with him. Moreover, Cruse reneged on his promise to "avoid any involvement" in arguments about the word "Negro". Harold Cruse to Richard B. Moore, February 28, 1963; box 2, folder 1, Richard B. Moore Papers, Schomburg Center for Research in Black Culture, New York Public Library.

46. The report of the Committee was published in 1920 in some four volumes which took

over 4,500 pages, see: Senate of the State of New York, Report of the Joint Legislative Committee Investigating Seditious Activities, *Revolutionary Radicalism* (see above, Prologue n. 8) see also Palmer, *Letter from the Attorney General* (see above, Prologue n. 13); for illuminating discussion of the Red Scare see Robert K. Murray, *Red Scare: A Study in National Hysteria, 1919–1920* (Minneapolis: University of Minnesota Press 1955), and Julian E. Jaffe, *Crusade Against Radicalism: New York During the Red Scare, 1914–1924* (New York: Praeger 1972).

47. *Revolutionary Radicalism*, Part I, vol. II (hereafter referred to as Domingo), pp. 1489–510.

48. Cruse, p. 127; Domingo, p. 1504.

49. Domingo, pp. 1493, 1495, 1506.

50. Ibid., pp. 1492–3.

51. Ibid., pp. 1496–7.

52. Cruse, p. 127.

53. Domingo, pp. 1493–4.

54. Ibid., pp. 1494.

55. Ibid., pp. 1494–5.

56. Ibid., p. 1495.

57. "The capitalist class is now making its last stand in history," declared the very first sentence of the Socialist Party manifesto in 1919. *Manifesto of the Socialist Party* (New York: Socialist Party of New York County [1919]).

58. Domingo, pp. 1509–10.

59. Ibid., pp. 1499.

60. Quoted in August Meier and Elliott Rudwick, "Attitudes of Negro Leaders Toward the American Labor Movement from the Civil War to World War I," in Julius Jacobson, ed., *The Negro and the American Labor Movement* (New York: Anchor Books 1968), p. 40.

61. Kelly Miller, "Radicalism and the Negro," in his *The Everlasting Stain* (Washington: Associated Publishers 1924), pp. 33–4; see also idem, *An Appeal to Conscience*, (New York: Macmillan Co. 1918).

62. Kelly Miller, "The Negro's Place in the Labor Struggle," in his *The Everlasting Stain*, pp. 279–89; citations pp. 286–9.

63. Quoted in Philip S. Foner, *Organized Labor and the Black Worker, 1619–1918* (New York: International Publishers 1982), p. 80.

64. Booker T. Washington, "The Negro and the Labor Unions," *Atlantic Monthly*, June 1913; reprinted in Foner and Lewis, eds, *Black Workers*, pp. 285–301.

65. Domingo, p. 1504.

66. Ibid., p. 1504.

67. Ibid., pp. 1505–7.

68. As it happens, he, like Harrison before him, failed in this effort. Turner, "Richard B. Moore and his Works," p. 42. For helpful discussion of the Socialist Party and the "Negro Question," see James Weinstein, *The Decline of American Socialism, 1912–1925* (1967; New Brunswick: Rutgers University Press 1984), pp. 63–74; R. Laurence Moore, "Flawed Fraternity—American Socialist Response to the Negro, 1901–1912," *The Historian*, vol. xxxii, no. 1, November 1969; Sally M. Miller, "The Socialist Party and the Negro, 1901–1920," *Journal of Negro History*, vol. lvi, no. 3, July 1971; Foner, *American Socialism and Black Americans*.

69. Domingo, pp. 1504–5.

70. Cruse, pp. 127–8.

71. Ibid., p. 133.

72. Ibid., p. 130.

73. Domingo, p. 1494.

74. I doubt if Albert Murray fully realized how right he was when, in a favorable review of the book, described *The Crisis of the Negro Intellectual* as "imaginatively documented."

75. Cruse, p. 130.

76. A. Philip Randolph, "The Negro in Politics," *Messenger*, July 1919, p. 21; see also William Tuttle, "Views of a Negro During 'The Red Summer' of 1919," *Journal of Negro History*, July 1966, pp. 211–13, where an Afro-American contemporary, Stanley B. Norvell, speaks in similar terms about tips; Norvell also talks of the existence of what he uncharitably calls "the menial, servitor and flunkey class" among black people.

77. There is, incidentally, nothing between the "receiver" of the first paragraph and the

beginning of the second with "All". The ellipsis, placed by Cruse, after "receiver", therefore ought not to have been there.

78. Cruse, p. 128.

79. Ibid., p. 132.

80. Quoted in *Revolutionary Radicalism*, p. 1511; see also pp. 2007–8.

81. What was fundamentally wrong with such a position is the implicit assumption that black people would be acting irrationally were they to oppose or rise up against such a so-called Socialist Revolution. All the evidence indicates that they would be acting perfectly rationally if they were to take up arms against this Revolution that would effectively devolve more power to Samuel Gompers (the racist head of the American Federation of Labor) and the very same white workers who had murdered black people wantonly in East St Louis and elsewhere. Unless such a Revolution was under the actual and moral leadership of someone like William "Big Bill" Haywood, head of the Industrial Workers of the World—the only working-class organization at the time that attempted to take a principled stance against racism and sexism—then it would have deserved black opposition, and at best black skepticism and vigilance.

82. Harrison, "Socialism and the Negro,"; idem, "The Negro a Conservative: Christianity Still Enslaves the Minds of Those Whose Bodies it Long Held Bound," *Truth Seeker*, vol. 41, no. 37 (12 September 1914); developed as "On a Certain Conservatism in Negroes," in Harrison, *The Negro and the Nation*, pp. 41–7; W. E. B. Du Bois, "A Field for Socialists," *New Review*, January 11, 1913; idem, "Socialism and the Negro Problem," *New Review*, February 1, 1913.

83. Cited in Foner, *American Socialism and Black Americans*, p. 357.

84. *Messenger*, May–June 1919, p. 20.

85. Ibid.; the remarks are quoted from a black weekly, the *Savannah Journal*, Saturday, March 22, 1919.

86. *Messenger*, May–June 1919, p. 20.

87. Cruse, p. 127.

88. *Messenger*, May–June, 1919, p. 31.

89. *Messenger*, July 1919, p. 13; Hill, "Domingo, W. A.," p. 116.

90. See, for example, these by Domingo which appeared in the *Messenger*: "What Are We, Negroes or Colored People?" May–June 1919; "Socialism the Negroes' Hope," July 1919; "Capitalism the Basis of Colonialism," August 1919; "'If We Must Die'," September 1919; "Did Bolshevism Stop Race Riots in Russia?" September 1919; "Private Property as a Pillar of Prejudice," April–May 1920 and August 1920; "Will Bolshevism Free America?" September 1920; "A New Negro and a New Day," November 1920.

91. "The Reminiscences of A. Philip Randolph," p. 133, 140, 175.

92. Randolph's remark in interview with Anderson, cited in Jervis Anderson, *A. Philip Randolph*, p. 80.

93. Ibid., pp. 79–80.

94. "Reminiscences of A. Philip Randolph," pp. 133, 186, 175–6.

95. Cruse, pp. 117–18, 128.

96. Cruse, p. 131.

97. Cruse, p. 140.

98. Cyril Briggs, "The Negro Question in the Southern Textile Strikes," *The Communist*, vol. viii, no. 6, June 1929, pp. 324–8.

99. *The Communist*, vol. viii, no. 7, July 1929, p. 394. Hall's note comes at the end of another article by Briggs on the struggle in North Carolina: Cyril Briggs, "Further Notes on the Negro Question in the Southern Textile Strikes," *The Communist*, vol. viii, no. 7, July 1929, pp. 391–4.

100. Cruse, p. 141.

101. Cruse complains that in June 1977 at a conference on "Black Culture" at the University of Iowa "Stirling Stuckey would not debate my accounts of my *personal* contacts with Robeson unless it was backed up with 'documentary evidence'." (Professor Stuckey is clearly a most unreasonable man.) Harold Cruse, "A Review of the Paul Robeson Controversy" (in 2 parts), *First World*, vol. 2, nos. 3 and 4, 1979 and 1980, p. 32 n. 4; footnotes for both parts of the article were carried in the second part in vol. 2, no. 4, 1980. Cruse's article was in response to Stuckey and Leslie, "Reflections on Reflections About the Black Intellectual, 1930–1945."

102. Haywood, *Black Bolshevik*, esp. chaps. 8 and 9; Draper, *American Communism and*

Soviet Russia, pp. 348–56; Harvey Klehr and William Tompson, "Self-Determination in the Black Belt: Origins of a Communist Policy," *Labor History*, vol. 30, no. 3, Summer 1989, p. 359.

103. Cyril Briggs to Harry Haywood, June 10, 1962, Harry Haywood Papers, Schomburg Center for Research in Black Culture, New York Public Library.

104. Cruse, p. 132.

105. *The Communist*, June 1929, pp. 324–8; and July 1929, pp. 391–4, respectively.

106. "Further Notes on the Negro Question in the Southern Textile Strikes," p. 394. Significantly, there were no typographical and technical problems with the page captions for Briggs's second article.

107. Ibid., p. 394.

108. Comintern Archive documentary quoted to author by Maria van Enckevort; van Enckevort to Winston James, August 21, 1995.

109. For a good discussion of the arrival of James Ford in Harlem, the policies he represented and implemented, see Naison, *Communists in Harlem During the Depression*, pp. 95–114.

110. Haywood, *Black Bolshevik*; McKay, *Harlem: Negro Metropolis*, pp. 223–4; Testimony of Manning Johnson, in US Congress, House of Representatives, *Hearing Before the Committee on Un-American Activities*, Hearings Regarding Communist Infiltration of Minority Groups—Part 2, 81st Congress, 1st Session, July 14, 1949 (Washington: Government Printing Office 1949), pp. 507–8.

111. *Pittsburgh Courier*, November 7, 1942; Turner, "Richard B. Moore and his Works," p. 67; Robert Hill, "Racial and Radical: Cyril V. Briggs, *The Crusader* Magazine, and the African Blood Brotherhood, 1918–1922," introduction to the facsimile edition of *The Crusader* (New York: Garland Publishing, Inc. 1987), p. xlviii.

112. Interview of Abner Berry by Mark Naison, New York City, July 5, 1977, quoted in Turner, "Richard B. Moore and his Works," pp. 67–8.

113. See Naison, *Communists in Harlem During the Depression*, pp. 100–103.

114. Turner, "Richard B. Moore and his Works," p. 68.

115. Greenberg, *"Or Does it Explode?"* documents well the extent of black Harlem's greater suffering compared to that of white New York.

116. Communist Party, USA, *Race Hatred on Trial* (New York: Workers Library Publishers 1931), p. 32.

117. Turner, "Richard B. Moore and his Works," p. 68; Haywood, *Black Bolshevik*, p. 669 n. 2, where Haywood also said that "Briggs was readmitted in the early forties, following mass protests from the rank and file." Haywood may have been right about rank and file support for Briggs's return, but he is mistaken about when Briggs rejoined, which was in 1948.

118. Klehr and Tompson, "Self-Determination in the Black Belt," p. 357; Robert Hill, "Huiswoud, Otto," p. 220. For more on Huiswoud after he left the United States see Gert J. Oostindie, "Prelude to the Exodus: Surinamers in the Netherlands, 1667–1960s," in Gary Brana-Shute, ed., *Resistance and Rebellion in Suriname: Old and New*, Studies in Third World Societies 43 (Williamsburg: College of William and Mary 1990), pp. 241f; and Maria van Enckevort, "The Caribbean Diaspora in France in the 1930s," paper presented to the annual conference of the Association of Caribbean Historians, Kingston, Jamaica, 1993.

119. The reader should not leave with the idea that all of the weaknesses on the subject in Cruse's book have been dealt with here, because they have not. I have simply attempted to highlight and discuss the ones I regard to be most significant; there are many other problems that I have simply not bothered to discuss here, including Cruse's rather unreliable report of the exchange between Domingo and Chandler Owen in the pages of the *Messenger* in 1923.

120. Such behavior is repeated, at least initially, with every wave of black immigrants to the United States. For shocking evidence of the negative attitude of recent Caribbean immigrants and their offspring toward Afro-Americans, see Mary Waters, "The Role of Lineage in Identity Formation Among Black Americans," *Qualitative Sociology*, vol. 14, no. 1, Spring 1991; and idem, "Ethnic and Racial Identities of Second-Generation Black Immigrants in New York City," *International Migration Review*, vol. xxviii, no. 4, Winter 1994.

121. This is an important subject that, in my view, has not been properly analyzed and explained and which I shall attempt to explore elsewhere.

122. The complex and often troubled relations between Afro-Americans and Afro-

Caribbeans, especially in Harlem, cannot be dealt with here. Such relations and Cruse's experience of growing up in Harlem clearly helped to shape, but cannot completely account for, his anti-Caribbean stance. After all Thomas Sowell, the Afro-American economist, like Cruse, was born in Virginia and grew up in Harlem. Yet, while Cruse all but demonizes Afro-Caribbeans, Sowell romanticizes them. In Sowell's superficial and tendentious reading of the Caribbean experience, Caribbeans are viewed as exemplars, one of the "model minorities," that Afro-Americans should emulate. Racism and the role of racism, past and present, in the blighting of Afro-Americans' life chances are downplayed, if not totally denied. And for this argument Sowell is loudly applauded, and rewarded by white conservatives. Sowell develops this thesis in several places, but see in particular his *Ethnic America: A History* (New York: Basic Books 1981), especially pp. 216–20; idem, *Civil Rights: Rhetoric or Reality?* (New York: William Morrow 1984), especially chap. 4. I plan to discuss Sowell's work in greater detail elsewhere.

123. Claude McKay to Nancy Cunard, August 20, 1932; Nancy Cunard Collection, Harry Ransom Humanities Research Center, University of Texas at Austin.

124. Cruse, p. 255.

125. Moore to Reginald Barrow, Sept. 4, 1969; Box 3, Folder 1, Richard B. Moore Papers, Schomburg Center for Research in Black Culture.

126. Makonnen, *Pan-Africanism from Within*, pp. 96–8.

127. Ian Munro and Reinhard Sander, eds, *Kas-Kas: Interviews with Three Caribbean Writers in Texas* (Austin: African and Afro-American Research Institute, The University of Texas at Austin 1972), p. 39. On October 25, 1995, Harold Cruse gave a lecture at Columbia University on the history of the relation between Afro-Americans and Afro-Caribbeans in Harlem. During the discussion that followed, he was asked to what extent he departed from the arguments presented in 1967 in *The Crisis of the Negro Intellectual*. He emphatically declared: "I don't depart from any of them." Cruse then went on to say that the remarks he made in 1967 were "mostly experiential." "Frankly, I had not done much academic research on the question," he said. He had, he continued, "just responded on a social, intellectual, and cultural level" to living day by day with West Indians or West Indian descendants in Harlem. It would have helped readers in deciding how seriously to take his book if Cruse had made this clear when he published *The Crisis of the Negro Intellectual* thirty years ago.

Statistical Appendix

Contents

Tables

Figures

Table 1.1 Black immigrant aliens admitted and black emigrant aliens departed: United States, 1899–1937

Year	Admitted	Departed	Net admission
1899	412	NA	NA
1900	714	NA	NA
1901	594	NA	NA
1902	832	NA	NA
1903	2,174	NA	NA
1904	2,386	NA	NA
1905	3,598	NA	NA
1906	3,786	NA	NA
1907	5,235	NA	NA
1908	4,626	889	3,737
1909	4,307	1,104	3,203
1910	4,966	926	4,040
1911	6,721	913	5,808
1912	6,759	1,288	5,471
1913	6,634	1,671	4,963
1914	8,447	1,805	6,642
1915	5,660	1,644	4,016
1916	4,576	1,684	2,892
1917	7,971	1,497	6,474
1918	5,706	1,291	4,415
1919	5,823	976	4,847
1920	8,174	1,275	6,899
1921	9,873	1,807	8,066
1922	5,248	2,183	3,065
1923	7,554	1,525	6,029
1924	12,243	1,449	10,794
1925	791	1,094	−303
1926	894	865	29
1927	955	870	85
1928	956	789	167
1929	1,254	425	829
1930	1,806	776	1,030
1931	884	737	147
1932	183	811	−628
1933	84	1,058	−974
1934	178	604	−426
1935	246	597	−351
1936	272	502	−230
1937	275	433	−158
1899–1937	**143,397**	**33,518***	**85,731***

Note: "African, black" is the term used by the Bureau of Immigration to describe these migrants. See United States Senate, Document no. 662, 61st Congress, 3rd sess., *Reports of the Immigration Commission: Dictionary of Races and Peoples*, (Washington D. C.: Government Printing Office 1911), pp. 100–1.

* These figures apply for the period 1908–37.

Source: Adapted from US Department of Labor, Bureau of Immigration, *Annual Report of the Commissioner General of Immigration to the Secretary of Labor*, (hereafter referred to as *Immigration Report*), 1899–1937.

Table 1.2 Black immigrants by region of last residence, 1899–1932

Year	Total*	Caribbean		Central America		South America		British North America		Portuguese Atl. (Cape Verde & Azores)		Others	
		No.	%	No.	%	No.	%	No.	%	No.	%	No.	%
1899	411	388	94.4	NA	NA	NA	NA	NA	NA	NA	NA	23	5.6
1900	714	703	98.5	NA	NA	NA	NA	NA	NA	NA	NA	11	1.5
1901	594	520	87.5	NA	NA	NA	NA	NA	NA	NA	NA	74	12.5
1902	832	805	96.8	NA	NA	NA	NA	NA	NA	NA	NA	27	3.2
1903	2,174	1,134	52.2	1	–	2	–	NA	NA	934	43.0	103	4.7
1904	2,386	1,762	73.8	3	–	25	1.0	5	–	439	18.4	152	6.4
1905	3,598	3,034	84.3	37	1.0	66	1.8	9	–	347	9.6	105	2.9
1906	3,786	3,018	79.7	91	2.4	43	1.1	57	1.5	301	8.0	276	7.3
1907	5,233	4,561	87.2	99	1.9	48	–	105	2.0	349	6.7	71	1.4
1908	4,626	3,563	77.0	116	2.5	77	1.7	102	2.2	705	15.2	63	1.4
1909	4,307	3,340	77.5	107	2.5	30	–	172	4.0	615	14.3	43	1.0
1910	4,966	3,769	75.9	120	2.4	38	–	212	4.3	778	15.7	49	–
1911	6,719	4,973	74.0	154	2.3	111	1.7	304	4.5	1,101	16.4	76	1.1
1912	6,759	4,885	72.3	245	3.6	94	1.4	329	4.9	1,103	16.3	103	1.5
1913	6,634	4,891	73.7	277	4.2	91	1.4	338	5.1	972	14.6	65	–
1914	8,447	5,724	67.8	348	4.1	111	1.3	342	4.0	1,711	20.2	211	2.5
1915	5,662	4,104	72.5	252	4.5	38	–	286	5.1	838	14.8	144	2.7
1916	4,616	3,257	70.6	160	3.5	100	2.2	364	7.9	653	14.1	82	1.8
1917	8,011	5,769	72.0	662	8.3	135	1.7	409	5.1	940	11.7	96	1.2
1918	5,706	3,993	70.0	906	15.9	158	2.8	142	2.5	407	7.1	100	1.8
1919	5,823	4,027	69.2	799	13.7	268	4.6	274	4.7	329	5.6	126	2.2

Table 1.2 (cont.)

Year	Total*	Caribbean No.	%	Central America No.	%	South America No.	%	British North America No.	%	Portuguese Atl. (Cape Verde & Azores) No.	%	Others No.	%
1920	8,174	6,059	74.1	417	5.1	193	2.4	415	5.1	845	10.3	245	3.0
1921	9,873	7,046	71.4	543	5.5	197	2.0	414	4.2	1,364	13.8	309	3.1
1922	5,248	4,424	84.3	188	3.6	154	2.9	172	3.3	201	3.8	109	2.1
1923	7,599	6,580	86.6	254	3.3	171	2.3	292	3.8	164	2.2	138	1.8
1924	12,247	10,630	86.8	511	4.2	375	3.1	498	4.1	128	1.0	105	–
1925	791	308	38.9	174	22.0	47	5.9	224	28.3	13	1.6	25	3.2
1926	894	480	53.7	197	22.0	50	5.6	114	12.7	7	0.8	46	5.1
1927	955	581	60.1	125	13.1	53	5.5	153	16.0	2	0.2	41	4.3
1928	956	586	61.3	136	14.2	57	6.0	134	14.0	9	0.9	34	3.6
1929	1,254	803	64.0	169	13.5	89	7.1	123	9.8	8	0.7	62	4.9
1930	1,806	1,388	76.8	112	6.2	158	8.7	106	5.9	0	0	42	2.3
1931	884	674	76.2	77	8.7	61	6.9	30	3.4	9	1.0	33	3.7
1932	183	113	61.7	13	7.1	10	5.5	28	15.3	3	1.6	16	8.7
1899–1932	142,868	107,892	75.6	7,293	5.1	3,050	2.1	6,153	4.3	15,275	10.7	3,205	2.2

Source: Immigration Reports, 1899–1932.

* There are some minor but irreconcilable differences between Tables 1.1 and 1.2 for the total number of black immigrants for the years 1899, 1911, 1915, 1916, 1923 and 1924.

Table 1.3   Principal states of intended residence of black immigrant aliens: United States 1899–1931

Years	Number admitted	New York		Florida		Massachusetts		Other states	
		No.	% of immigrants	No.	% of immigrants	No.	% of immigrants	No.	% of immigrants
1899–1905	10,710	1,847	17.2	5,783	54.0	1,655	15.5	1,425	13.3
1906–12	36,398	12,802	35.2	11,183	30.7	6,337	17.4	6,076	16.7
1913–19	44,817	21,097	47.1	8,006	18.0	7,001	15.6	8,713	19.4
1920–26	44,777	26,084	58.3	7,665	17.1	4,292	9.6	6,736	15.0
1927–31	6,455	3,998	61.9	329	5.1	375	5.8	1,753	27.2
1899–1931	143,157	65,828	46.0	32,966	23.0	19,660	13.7	24,103	17.3

Source: Immigration Reports, 1899–1931.

Table 1.4 Average annual sugar production, 1820–1929 ('000 tons)

Years	British Caribbean	French Caribbean	Cuba	Puerto Rico	Dominican Republic	Total Caribbean	Rest of world, cane	Rest of world, beet	Total world
1820–29	185	53	57	10	–	331	NA	NA	NA
1830–39	190	54	131	25	–	427	NA	NA	NA
1840–49	136	55	192	40	–	449	500	67	1,016
1850–59	162	46	345	45	–	620	624	259	1,503
1860–69	207	58	580	55	–	920	571	579	2,070
1870–79	247	81	645	83	2	1,074	731	1,242	3,047
1880–89	284	87	595	73	10	1,069	1,283	2,505	4,857
1890–99	260	72	638	57	35	1,076	1,990	4,292	7,358
1900–09	244	70	1,655	173	58	2,217	4,290	7,020	13,527
1910–19	246	65	2,647	375	119	3,469	6,738	6,693	16,900
1920–29	312	59	4,335	514	277	5,523	9,134	7,429	22,086

Source: Ward, *Poverty and Progress in the Caribbean, 1800–1969*, p. 27.

Table 1.5 Annual production of sugar in selected British Caribbean territories, 1845–1899 (expressed in five-year averages, tons)

Years	Jamaica	Barbados	Trinidad	Guyana*
1845–49	33,279	20,157	19,270	26,780
1850–54	26,609	30,980	23,101	35,547
1855–59	22,283	31,542	24,321	40,178
1860–64	25,936	33,319	28,191	53,056
1865–69	25,595	43,112	39,716	61,083
1870–74	26,349	37,981	48,820	74,042
1875–79	22,810	44,234	46,920	95,546
1880–84	23,143	48,257	53,178	110,888
1885–89	16,804	54,789	58,270	115,184
1890–94	21,969	57,482	47,560	111,149
1895–99	19,123	43,419	50,080	96,817

* The data for Guyana start a year ahead of the rest in the calculation of the five-year averages. They therefore begin 1846–50 (instead of 1845–49) and end at 1896–1900/1901 (instead of 1895–999).

Sources: Watts, *The West Indies*, p. 496; Mandle, *The Plantation Economy*, p. 20, for Guyana data.

Table 1.6 Growth in professional employment: Jamaica, 1861–1911

Professions	1861	1871	1881	1891	1911
Doctors and dentists	87	84	89	107	182
Lawyers	60	44	37	80	113
Clergy	278	255	261	329	344
Public servants	624	1,203	1,481	1,501	2,241
Teachers	448	871	1,270	1,733	2,207
Others	992	1,911	1,520	3,229	4,124
Total	*2,489*	*4,368*	*4,658*	*6,979*	*9,211*

Source: Adapted from Eisner, *Jamaica, 1830–1930*, Table XXIII, p. 166.

Table 1.7 Population density in the British Caribbean Islands,
1841–1921

(persons per square mile)

Island	1841–44	1881	1911	1921
Jamaica	86	132	188	195
Trinidad	37	86	168	185
Barbados	735	1,033	1,036	943
Grenada	217	319	502	499
St Lucia	90	165	209	221
St Vincent	182	270	279	296
Dominica	74	92	111	121
Antigua	215	205	189	175
St Kitts-Nevis	214	289	283	250
Montserrat	230	315	381	379

Source: Roberts, *The Population of Jamaica*, p. 56.

Table 2.1   Occupational status of black immigrants, 1899–1931

Years	1899–1905		1906–12		1913–19		1920–26		1927–31		1899–1931	
	No.	% of adults	No.	% of adults	No.	% of adults	No.	% of adults	No.	% of adults	No.	% of adults
No. admitted	10,710		36,398		44,817		44,777		5,855		142,557	
Children	1,496		3,264		4,394		6,717		1,051		16,922	
Adults	*9,214*		*33,134*		*40,423*		*38,060*		*4,804*		*125,635*	
Adults without occup.	1,383	15.0	4,010	12.1	4,646	11.5	5,334	14.0	1,393	29.0	16,766	13.3
Adults with occup.	7,831	85.0	29,124	87.9	35,777	88.5	32,726	86.0	3,411	71.0	108,869	86.7
Professional	204	2.2	811	2.4	1,152	2.8	1,286	3.4	,289	6.0	3,742	3.0
Teachers	69	–	248	–	405	1.0	448	1.2	94	2.0	1,264	1.0
Physicians	11	–	31	–	36	–	36	–	16	–	130	–
Skilled	2,787	30.2	9,552	28.9	13,291	32.9	13,802	36.3	1,789	37.2	41,221	32.8
Carpenters and joiners	234	2.5	940	2.8	1,643	4.1	1,574	4.1	120	2.5	4,511	3.6
Dressmakers and seamstresses	298	3.2	2,773	8.4	4,493	11.1	4,645	12.2	632	13.2	12,841	10.2
Clerks and accountants	182	2.0	777	2.3	1,236	3.0	1,563	4.1	320	6.7	4,078	3.2
Servants, farm laborers and laborers	2,645	28.7	16,901	51.0	18,801	46.5	15,150	39.8	1,106	23.0	54,661	43.5

Source: Immigration Reports, 1899–1931.

Table 2.2 Black aliens admitted into and departed from the United States by selected occupation, 1908–1924

Occupation	Admitted	Departed	Departures as % of admissions
Professionals	2,951	424	14.4
Teachers	1,005	56	5.6
Skilled workers	33,233	2,767	8.3
Seamstresses	6,650	269	4.0
Dressmakers	4,041	312	7.7
Carpenters and joiners	3,826	271	7.1
Clerks and accountants	3,348	471	14.1
Servants	22,204	2,961	13.3
Farm laborers	12,338	5,022	40.7
Laborers	12,449	4,789	38.5

Source: *Immigration Reports*, 1908–24.

Table 2.3 Year of arrival of the foreign-born black population by sex, for the United States, 1930

Year of migration	No.			% of total	
	Total	Men	Women	Men	Women
1925–30	7,582	3,806	3,776	50.2	49.8
1930*	302	142	160	47.0	53.0
1929	1,357	632	725	46.6	53.4
1928	1,173	558	615	47.6	52.4
1927	1,261	652	609	51.7	48.3
1925–26	3,489	1,822	1,667	52.2	47.8
1920–24	27,372	13,391	13,981	49.0	51.0
1915–19	18,181	9,699	8,482	53.3	46.7
1911–14	10,951	6,008	4,943	54.9	45.1
1901–10	15,356	9,178	6,178	59.8	40.2
1900 or earlier	7,601	4,551	3,050	60.0	40.0
Unknown	11,577	7,448	4,129	64.3	35.7
Total	106,202	57,887	48,315	54.5	45.5

* *To April.*

Source: Adapted from U. S. Dept of Commerce, *Fifteenth Census of the United States: 1930*, vol. II, Table 4, p. 498.

Table 2.4(A) Black entry and departure by sex, 1908–1931

	Men			Women		
Years	Arrivals	Departures	*Net arrivals*	*Net arrivals*	Arrivals	Departures
1908–12	16,315	3,505	*12,810*	*9,526*	11,064	1,538
1913–17	18,077	5,303	*12,774*	*12,213*	15,211	2,998
1918–22	17,320	4,416	*12,904*	*14,388*	17,504	3,116
1923–27	10,154	2,766	*7,388*	*9,246*	12,283	3,037
1928–31	2,163	1,135	*1,028*	*1,145*	2,737	1,592

Table 2.4(B) Net entry of black migrants by sex, 1908–1931

	Arrivals	% of total
Men	46,904	50.2
Women	46,518	49.8
Total	93,422	100.0

Source: *Immigration Reports*, 1908–31.

Table 4.1 Slave and free non-white population in the nineteenth-century Americas

Colony/nation (year)	Slave	Free non-white	% free non-white
Cuba (1880)	199,885	267,547	57.4
Puerto Rico (1872)	31,635	251,709	88.8
Barbados (1833/34)	82,807	6,584	7.4
Jamaica (1834)	310,000	42,000	11.9
United States (1860)	3,953,760	488,070	11.0
United States (Southern states) 1860	3,953,696	261,918	6.2
Brazil (1872)	1,510,806	4,245,428	73.7

Sources: Cuba: Kenneth F. Kiple, *Blacks in Colonial Cuba, 1774–1899* (Gainesville: University Presses of Florida 1976), p. 70; Puerto Rico: Luis M. Diaz Soler, *Historia de la Esclavitud Negra en Puerto Rico*, 3rd edn (Río Piedras: Editorial Universitaria, Universidad de Puerto Rico 1981), p. 256; Barbados: Jerome S. Handler, *The Unappropriated People: Freedmen in the Slave Society of Barbados* (Baltimore: Johns Hopkins University Press 1974), pp. 18–19; Jamaica: Gad Heuman, *Between Black and White: Race, Politics, and the Free Coloreds in Jamaica, 1792–1865* (Oxford: Clio Press 1981), p. 7; United States: Ira Berlin, *Slaves Without Masters: The Free Negro in the Antebellum South* (New York: Pantheon 1974), pp. 136–7, 396–7; Brazil: Herbert Klein, "Nineteenth-Century Brazil," in David W. Cohen and Jack P. Greene, eds., *Neither Slave Nor Free: The Freedmen of African Descent in the Slave Societies of the New World* (Baltimore: Johns Hopkins University Press 1972), p. 314.

Table 5.1 Distribution of UNIA branches in the United States, 1921–1933

State	No. of branches
Louisiana	75
Pennsylvania	61
North Carolina	58
Mississippi	56
West Virginia	50
Virginia	48
Arkansas	43
New Jersey	41
Ohio	40
Georgia	32
Oklahoma	32
Florida	30 (32)
Missouri	30
Illinois	25
South Carolina	25
California	22
New York	19
Michigan	15
Alabama	14
Indiana	12 (13)
Connecticut	12
Massachusetts	12
Texas	12
Kentucky	11
Maryland	10
Tennessee	9
Kansas	8
Delaware	5
Iowa	5
Arizona	4
Rhode Island	3
Utah	3
Washington	3
Colorado	2 (3)
Minnesota	2
Wisconsin	2
District of Columbia	1 (2)
Hawaii	1
Nebraska	1
Oregon	1

Note: The figures represent the aggregation of a list of cities and towns that hosted UNIA divisions or chapters that reported their activities to the *Negro World*, over the period 1921–33, and/or were listed in the records of the UNIA Central Division, New York, as active in 1925–26.

Sources: Adapted from "Appendix X: Locations of UNIA Divisions and Chapters"; "Appendix XI: Concentration of UNIA Divisions by Regions," in Robert A. Hill, ed., *The Marcus Garvey and Universal Negro Improvement Association Papers*, vol. vii (Berkeley: University of California Press 1990), pp. 986–96, 1001–2; (there is an obvious error in the number of divisions given for Indiana on p. 1001; clearly it should have been 12 and not 112); and Tony Martin, *Race First: The Ideological and Organizational Struggles of Marcus Garvey and the Universal Negro Improvement Association* (Westport: Greenwood Press 1976), Table 1, p. 15. Figures in parentheses are the higher estimates given by Martin.

Table 5.2   Distribution of UNIA branches outside the United States,
c. 1926

Country	No. of branches
Cuba	52
Panama	47
Trinidad	30
Costa Rica	23
Canada	15
Jamaica	11
South Africa	8
Spanish Honduras	8
British Guiana	7
Colombia	6
Dominican Republic	5
Guatemala	5
Nicaragua	5
Barbardos	4
British Honduras	4
Mexico	4
Sierra Leone	3
Canal Zone	2
England	2
Gold Coast	2
Liberia	2
Bahamas	2
South West Africa	2
Wales	2
Antigua	1
Australia	1
Bermuda	1
Brazil	1
Dominica	1
Dutch Guiana	1
Equador	1
Grenada	1
Haiti	1
Nevis	1
Nigeria	1
Puerto Rico	1
St Kitts	1
St Lucia	1
St Thomas	1
St Vincent	1
Venezuela	1

Source: Martin, *Race First*, p. 16.

Figure 1.1 Black immigrant aliens admitted and black emigrant aliens departed: United States, 1899–1937

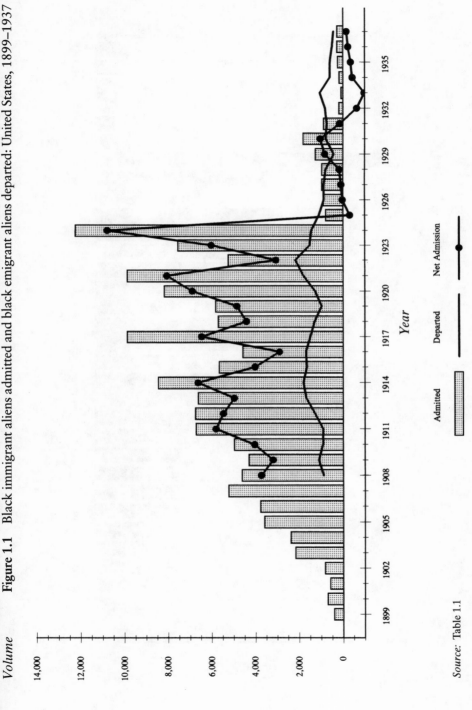

Source: Table 1.1

Volume

Figure 1.2 Principal states of intended residence of black immigrant aliens: United States, 1899–1931

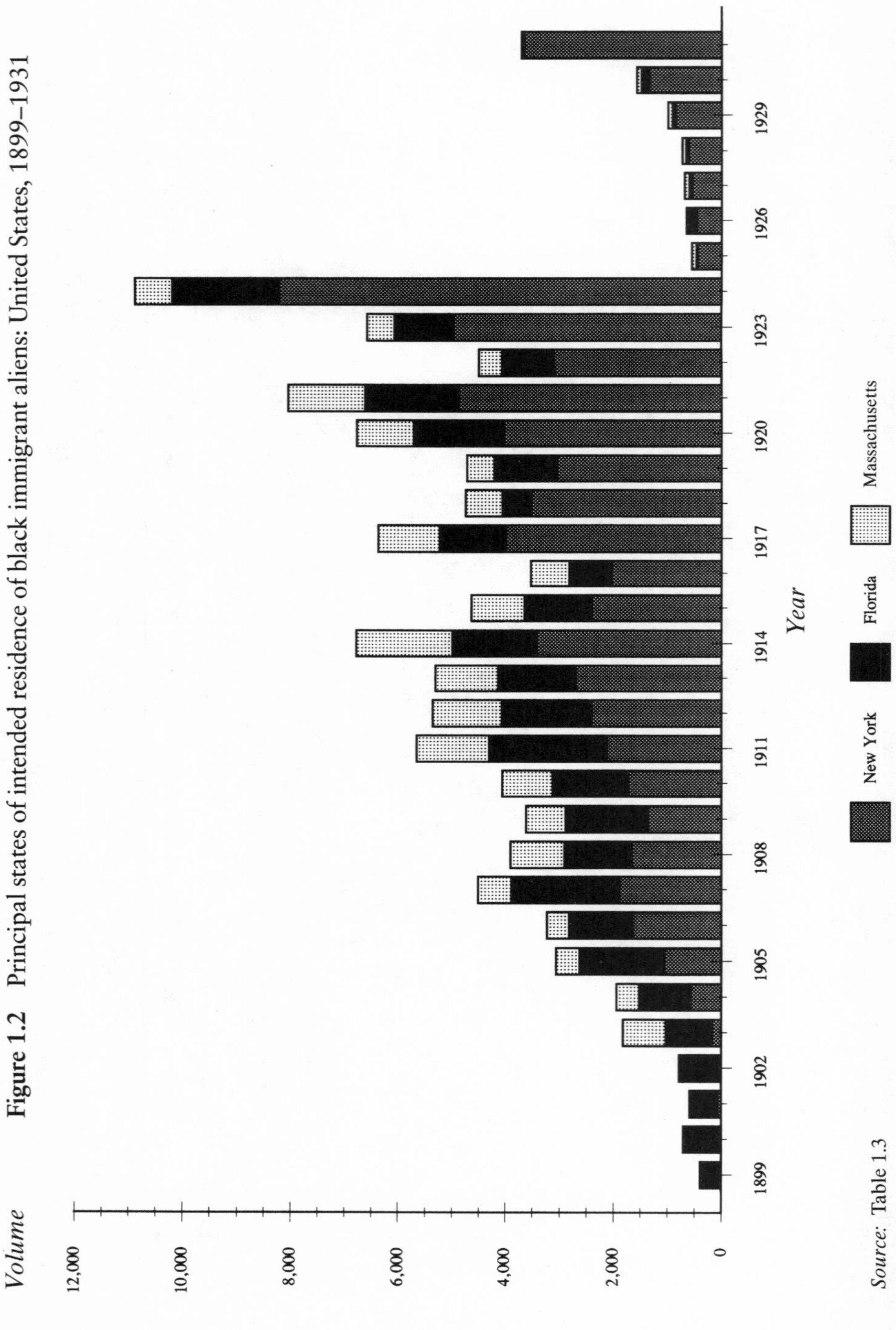

Year

☐ New York   ■ Florida   ☐ Massachusetts

Source: Table 1.3

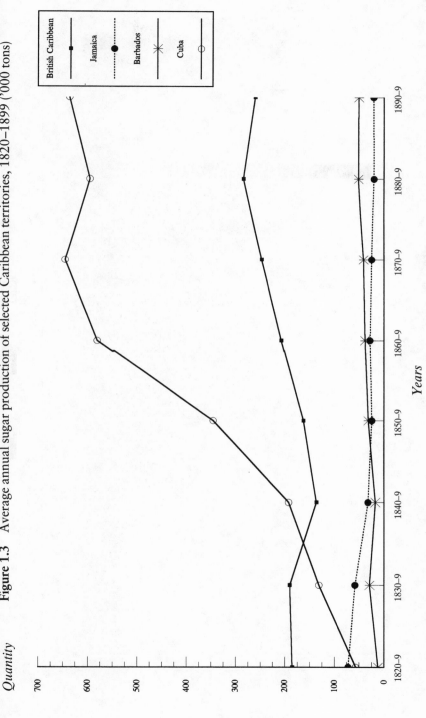

Figure 1.3 Average annual sugar production of selected Caribbean territories, 1820–1899 ('000 tons)

Sources: Tables 1.4 and 1.5; Watts, *The West Indies*, pp. 286, 288; Eisner, *Jamaica, 1830–1930*, p. 240; Levy, *Emancipation, Sugar and Federalism*, p. 182.

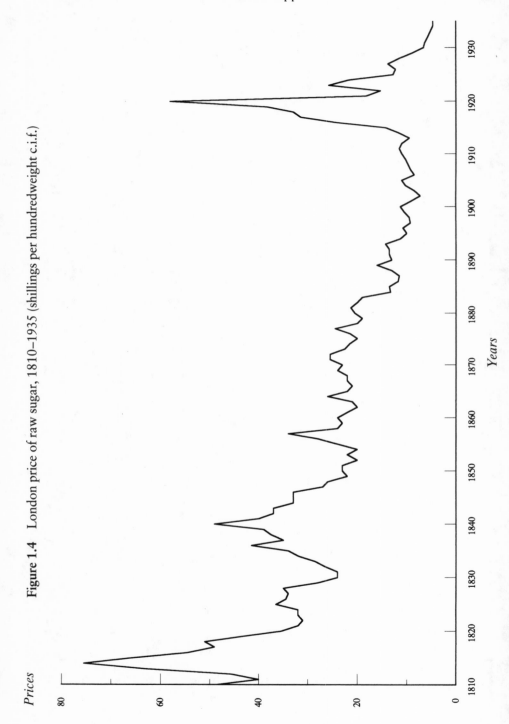

Figure 1.4   London price of raw sugar, 1810–1935 (shillings per hundredweight c.i.f.)

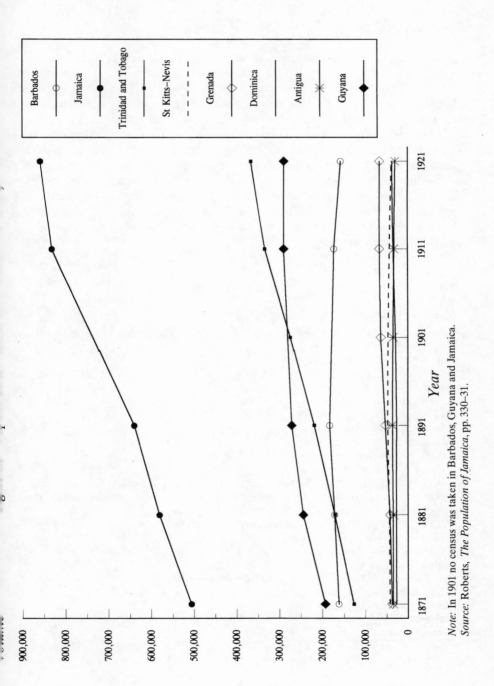

Note: In 1901 no census was taken in Barbados, Guyana and Jamaica.
Source: Roberts, *The Population of Jamaica*, pp. 330–31.

Bibliography

Articles published in contemporary newspapers and magazines such as the *Crusader* and the *Negro World* are not individually listed in the the bibliography; specific citations will be found in the notes. Similarly, in an effort to save space, where several essays published in an edited volume have been cited or found useful, the volume as a whole, rather than the individual items, is listed in the bibliography. As is the case for the articles in newspapers and magazines, the detailed citations for particular items in anthologies of essays will be found in the notes. I have listed in the bibliography the newspapers and magazines that I have found especially useful in doing this study.

Primary Material

Manuscript Collections

Schomburg Center for Research in Black Culture, New York Public Library:
  E. Ethelred Brown Papers
  John Edward Bruce Papers
  J.R. Ralph Casimir Papers
  Ewart Guinier Papers
  Harry Haywood Papers
  Claude McKay Papers
  Julian Mayfield Papers
  Richard B. Moore Papers
  Arthur A. Schomburg Papers
  Harry A. Williamson Papers
  Writers' Program, Federal Writers' Project, "The Negro of New York"
Walter White, Personal Correspondence, Papers of the National Association for the Advancement of Colored People, Library of Congress
Moorland–Spingarn Research Center, Howard University:
  John Wesley Cromwell Family Papers
  E. Franklin Frazier Papers
  Alain Locke Papers
Rare Book and Manuscript Library, Columbia University:
  L. S. Alexander Gumby Collection of Negroiana
  Robert Minor Collection
McKay Mss., Manuscripts Department, Lilly Library, Indiana University, Bloomington, Indiana
Claude McKay Papers, James Weldon Johnson Collection, Beinecke Rare Book and Manuscript Library, Yale University.

Special Collections, University of South Florida Library, Tampa:
  Juan Mallea, President of La Union Marti-Maceo, Transcript of interview conducted by Enrique A. Cordero, July 28, 1983
  Federal Writers' Project, Works Progress Administration, "Life History of José Ramón Sanfeliz," in "Social-Ethnic Study of Ybor City, Tampa, Florida," vol. 1 [1935]
Tamiment Institute Library and Robert F. Wagner Labor Archives, New York University:
  Elizabeth Gurley Flynn Papers
  Howard "Stretch" Johnson Papers
  Socialist Party Papers
  Rose Pastor Stokes Papers
Jesús Colón Papers, Centro de Estudios Puertorriqueños, Hunter College, City University of New York
Nancy Cunard Collection, Harry Ransom Humanities Research Center, University of Texas at Austin
Theodore Draper Papers, Robert W. Woodruff Library, Emory University

Published Papers and Documents

Boehm, Randolph, ed., *US Military Intelligence Reports: Surveillance of Radicals in the United States, 1917–1941* (University Publication of America 1984) [microfilm]
Elkins, W.F., "'Unrest Among the Negroes': A British Document of 1919," *Science & Society*, vol. xxxii, no. 1, Winter 1968
Harlan, Louis R. and Raymond W. Smock, eds, *The Booker T. Washington Papers*, vol. xi, 1911–12 (Urbana: University of Illinois Press 1981)
Hill, Robert, ed., *The Marcus Garvey and Universal Negro Improvement Association Papers* (Berkeley: University of California Press 1983)
Kornweibel, Theodore, ed., *Federal Surveillance of Afro-Americans (1917–1925): The First World War, The Red Scare, and the Garvey Movement* (University Publications of America 1986) [microfilm]

Official Archives

United States
National Archives, Washington, DC:
  Record Group 160, Records of Army Service Forces, Military intelligence Division
  Record Group 65, Records of the Federal Bureau of Investigation
  Record Group 60, General records of the Justice Department
Municipal Archives of the City of New York:
  New York State Manuscript Census, 1920 (*Fourteenth Census of the United States*)
  Records, Surrogate's Court New York County

Britain: Public Record Office, Kew
Colonial Office Records:
  CO 123/296: "Report of the Commission appointed by the Governor to enquire into the origin of the riot in the Town of Belize which began on the night of 22nd July 1919," October 10, 1919
  CO 137/742: Despatch 711, Governor Probyn to Viscount Milner, Secretary of State for the Colonies, October 23, 1920; enclosure of report by Barclay and Cradwick, October 9, 1920

CO 137/746: Memorial from T. Gordon Somers and C.A. Wilson, on behalf of the Jamaica League, to Winston Churchill, Secretary of State for the Colonies, May 12, 1921

CO 137/748: Dispatch 391, June 1921. Encl.: The Jamaica League, "The Right Honourable Colonel Winston Churchill, P.C.[,] His Majesty's Principal Secretary of State for the Colonies," May 1921

CO 968/68: Jamaica: Detention of W.A. Domingo

Foreign Office Records:

FO 369/2379: Sir R. Lindsay [British Ambassador to the United States] to Foreign Secretary, "Memorial Presented to Consul General Campbell, New York by West Indians in New York and Brooklyn," January 17, 1934

FO 369/2379: Sir R. Lindsay, "Reports on West Indian Groups in the United States," March 8, 1934

FO 371/9535: See especially the 1924 "Petition of Natives of all the West Indian Islands Residing in Cuba. Prepared and Fowarded [sic] Under the Auspices of the West Indian Workers Union."

Government and Official Publications

US House of Representatives, 66th Cong., 2nd. Sess., *Anti-Lynching Bill*, Report No. 1027 (Washington, DC: Government Printing Office 1920)

US Senate, *Abstract of Reports of the Immigration Commission, with Conclusions and Recommendations and Views of the Minority*, vol. i, (Senate Doc. no. 747, 61st Cong., 3d sess.) (Washington, DC: Government Printing Office 1910)

US Department of Labor, Bureau of Immigration, *Annual Report of the Commissioner General of Immigration to the Secretary of Labor*, [1899–1932] (Washington, DC: Government Printing Office [1900–1933])

US Dept. of Commerce, *Fifteenth Census of the United States: 1930* (Washington, DC: Government Printing Office 1932)

US Dept. of Commerce, *Sixteenth Census of the United States: 1940* (Washington, DC: Government Printing Office 1942)

Bureau of Census, *Negro Population of the United States, 1790–1915* (Washington, DC: Government Printing Office 1918)

Handbook of Jamaica (various years) (Kingston: Government Printing Office)

Senate of the State of New York, Report of the Joint Legislative Committee Investigating Seditious Activities, *Revolutionary Radicalism: Its History, Purpose and Tactics With an Exposition and Discussion of the Steps Being Taken and Required to Curb It*, filed April 24, 1920, 4 vols. (Albany: J. B. Lyon Company Printers 1920)

Honourable E. F. L. Wood, *Report on Visit to the West Indies and British Guiana (December, 1921–February, 1922)* [Cmd. 1679] (London: H. M. Stationery Office 1922)

US House of Representatives, *Hearing Before the Committee on Un-American Activities: Hearings Regarding Communist Infiltration of Minority Groups—Part 2*, 81st Congress, 1st Session, July 14, 1949 (Washington, DC: Government Printing Office 1949)

US House of Representatives, *Hearings Before the Committee on Un-American Activities: The Southern California District of the Communist Party*, 85th Congress, 2nd. Session, Part 1, September 2 and 3, 1958 (Washington, DC: Government Printing Office 1959)

US House of Representatives, *Hearings Before the Committee on Un-American Activities House of Representatives: Communist Activities Among Puerto Ricans in New York City and Puerto Rico*, 86th Congress, 1st Session, Part 1, November 16 and 17, 1959 (Washington, DC: Government Printing Office 1960)

Hugo, Francis M., ed., *Manual for the Use of the Legislature of the State of New York 1920* (Albany: J. B. Lyon Company 1920)

Lyons, John J., ed., *Manual for the Use of the Legislature of the State of New York 1921* (Albany: J. B. Lyon Company 1921)

US Attorney General, A. Mitchell Palmer, *Letter From the Attorney General Transmitting in Response to a Senate Resolution October 17, 1919, A Report on the Activities of the Bureau of Investigation of the Department of Justice Against Persons Advising Anarchy, Sedition, and the Forcible Overthrow of the Government*, Senate Documents, vol. 12, 66th Congress, 1st Session, May 19–November 19, 1919 (Washington, DC: Government Printing Office 1919)

Memoirs, Autobiographies, Reminiscences, Published Letters

Chisholm, Shirley, *Unbought and Unbossed* (Boston: Houghton Mifflin Company 1970)

Coard, Frederick McDermott, *Bitter-Sweet and Spice* (Ilfracombe, Devon: Arthur H. Stockwell Ltd 1970)

Colón, Jesús, *A Puerto Rican in New York and Other Sketches* (New York: Masses and Mainstream 1961; and International Publishers 1982)

Colón, Jesús, *The Way it Was and Other Writings*, ed. by Edna Acosta-Belén and Virginia Sánchez Korrol (Houston: Arte Público 1993)

Colón, Ramón, *Carlos Tapia: A Puerto Rican Hero in New York* (New York: Vintage Press 1976)

Du Bois, W. E. B., *Darkwater: Voices from Within the Veil* (1920; New York: Schoken Books 1969)

Du Bois, W. E. B., *Dusk of Dawn: An Essay Toward an Autobiography of a Race Concept* (1940; New Brunswick: Transaction Publishers 1984)

Du Bois, W. E. B., *The Autobiography of W. E. B. Du Bois: A Soliloquy on Viewing My Life from the Last Decade of Its First Century* (New York: International Publishers 1968)

Fogelson, Genia, *Belafonte* (Los Angeles: Holloway House Publishing Co. 1980)

Foner, Philip, ed., *Paul Robeson Speaks: Writings, Speeches, Interviews 1918–1974* (New York: Citadel Press 1978)

Garvey, Amy Jacques, *Garvey and Garveyism* (New York: Macmillan 1970)

Haywood, Harry, *Black Bolshevik: Autobiography of an Afro-American Communist* (Chicago: Liberator Press 1978)

Hill, Robert, ed., *Walter Rodney Speaks: The Making of an African Intellectual* (Trenton: Africa World Press 1990)

Hill, Ruth Edmonds, ed., *The Black Woman Oral History Project*, vol. 7 (Westport: Meckler Publishing 1991)

Hughes, Langston, *I Wonder as I Wander: An Autobiographical Journey* (New York: Rinehart 1956)

Iglesias, César Andreu, ed., *Memoirs of Bernardo Vega: A Contribution to the History of the Puerto Rican Community in New York* (New York: Monthly Review Press 1984)

James, C. L. R., *Beyond A Boundary* (London: Hutchinson & Co. 1963)

Johnson, James Weldon, *Along This Way: The Autobiography of James Weldon Johnson* (1933; Harmondsworth: Penguin Books 1990)

Kisseloff, Jeff, *You Must Remember This: An Oral History of Manhattan from the 1890s to World War II* (New York: Schocken Books 1989)

Makonnen, Ras, *Pan-Africanism from Within*, recorded and edited by Kenneth King (Nairobi: Oxford University Press 1973)

Malcolm X, *The Autobiography of Malcolm X* (1965; Harmondsworth: Penguin Books 1968)

Marshall, Paule, "Black Immigrant Women in *Brown Girl, Brownstones*," in Constance R. Sutton and Elsa M. Chaney, eds, *Caribbean Life in New York City: Sociocultural Dimensions* (New York: The Center for Migration Studies of New York 1987)

McDonnough, Maxine, "Sister Samad: Living the Garvey Life," *Jamaica Journal*, August–October 1987

McKay, Claude, *A Long Way From Home* (New York: Lee Furman 1937)

McKay, Claude, *My Green Hills of Jamaica* (Kingston: Heinemann Educational Books, Caribbean Ltd. 1979)

McKay, Claude, "A Negro Poet and his Poems," *Pearson's Magazine*, September 1918

Mulzac, Hugh, *A Star to Steer By* (New York: International Publishers 1963)

Nichols, Charles, ed., *Arna Bontemps–Langston Hughes Letters, 1925–1967* (New York: Dodd, Mead & Co. 1980)

Nkrumah, Kwame, *Ghana: The Autobiography of Kwame Nkrumah* (1957; New York: International Publishers 1971)

Oral History Task Force, Centro de Estudios Puertorriqueños, Hunter College, *Extended Roots: From Hawaii to New York—Migraciones Puertorriqueñas a los Estados Unidos* (New York: Centro de Estudios Puertorriqueños 1986)

Ovington, Mary White, *The Walls Came Tumbling Down* (New York: Harcourt, Brace and Company 1947)

Patterson, William, *The Man Who Cried Genocide* (New York: International Publishers 1971)

Poitier, Sidney, *This Life* (New York: Alfred A. Knopf 1980)

Randolph, A. Philip, "The Reminiscences of A. Philip Randolph," Oral History Research Office, Columbia University 1973

Schuyler, George, *Black and Conservative: The Autobiography of George S. Schuyler* (New Rochelle: Arlington House 1966)

Schuyler, George, "The Reminiscences of George Schuyler," New York 1960, Oral History Office, Columbia University 1962

Thompson, Leslie, *An Autobiography* (Crawley: Rabbit Press Ltd. 1985)

Turner, W. Burghardt and Joyce Moore Turner, eds, *Richard B. Moore, Caribbean Militant in Harlem: Collected Writings 1920–1972* (Bloomington: Indiana University Press 1988)

Walrond, Eric, "On Being Black," *New Republic*, November 1, 1922

Books, Pamphlets and Selected Articles

Adler, Alan, ed., *Theses, Resolutions and Manifestos of the First Four Congresses of the Third International* (London: Ink Links 1980)

Allen, Ernest, "The Cultural Methodology of Harold Cruse," *Journal of Ethnic Studies*, vol. 5, no. 2, Summer 1977

Blanton, Joshua, "Men in the Making," *Southern Workman*, January 1919

Britton, Hildred, "The Negro and his Descendants in British Guiana, pt. 1," and A. A. Thorne, "The Negro and his Descendants in British Guiana, pt. 2," in Nancy Cunard, ed., *Negro* (London: Nancy Cunard at Wishart and Co. 1934)

Brown, Ethelred, "Labor Conditions in Jamaica Prior to 1917," *Journal of Negro History*, vol. iv, no. 4, October 1919

Brown, Stewart, Mervyn Morris, and Gordon Rohlehr, eds, *Voice Print: An Anthology of Oral and Related Poetry from the Caribbean* (London: Longman 1989)

Chrisman, Robert, "The Contradictions of Harold Cruse: Or Cruse's Blues, Take 2," *Black World*, May 1971

Chrisman, Robert, "The Crisis of Harold Cruse," *Black Scholar*, November 1969

Clarke, John Henrik, "*The Crisis of the Negro Intellectual* by Harold Cruse: A Reappraisal of Some of the Neglected Aspects of the Crisis," in his *Africans at the Crossroads: Notes for an African World Revolution* (Trenton: Africa World Press, Inc. 1991)

Communist Party, USA., *Race Hatred on Trial* (New York: Workers Library Publishers 1931)

Coombs, Orde, *Do You See My Love For You is Growing?* (New York: Dodd, Mead and Co. 1972)

Coombs, Orde, "On Being West Indian in New York," in Floyd B. Barbour, ed., *The Black Seventies* (Boston: Porter Sargent Publisher 1970)

Coombs, Orde, "West Indians in New York: Moving Beyond the Limbo Pole," *New York Magazine*, July 13 1970

Cornish, Vaughan, "The Jamaica Earthquake (1907)," *Geographical Journal*, vol. xxxi, no. 3, March 1908

Cruse, Harold, *Rebellion or Revolution?* (New York: William Morrow & Company, Inc. 1968)

Cruse, Harold, *The Crisis of the Negro Intellectual: From Its Origins to the Present* (New York: William Morrow & Co. 1967)

Cruse, Harold, "A Review of the Paul Robeson Controversy," (in 2 parts) *First World*, vol. 2, nos. 3 and 4, 1979 and 1980

Cruse, Harold, "Black and White: Outlines of the Next Stage," *Black World*, January 1971

Cruse, Harold, "Replay on a Black Crisis," *Negro Digest*, November 1968

DeLisser, H. G., *Twentieth Century Jamaica* (Kingston: Jamaica Times Limited 1913)

Domingo, W. A., "British West Indian Federation–A Critique," in David Lowenthal and Lambros Comitas, eds, *The Aftermath of Sovereignty: West Indian Perspectives* (New York: Anchor Books 1973)

Domingo, W. A., "Gift of the Black Tropics," in Alain Locke, ed., *The New Negro: An Interpretation* (New York: Albert and Charles Boni Inc 1925)

Du Bois, W. E. B., "On Being Black," *The New Republic*, February 18, 1920

Foner, Philip S. and Ronald L. Lewis, eds, *Black Workers: A Documentary History from Colonial Times to the Present* (Philadelphia: Temple University Press 1989)

Froude, James Anthony, *The English in the West Indies or the Bow of Ulysses* (London: Longmans, Green, and Co. 1888)

Garvey, Amy Jacques, *Black Power in America* (Kingston: Amy Jacques Garvey 1968)

Harris, Robert, Nyota Harris, Grandassa Harris, eds, *Carlos Cooks and Black Nationalism: From Garvey to Malcolm X* (Dover, Mass: The Majority Press 1992)

Harrison, Hubert, *The Negro and the Nation* (New York: Cosmo-Advocate Publishing Company 1917)

Harrison, Hubert, *When Africa Awakes: The "Inside Story" of the Stirrings and Strivings of the New Negro in the Western World* (New York: The Porro Press 1920)

Haynes, George Edmund, *The Negro at Work in New York City: A Study in Economic Progress* (New York: Studies in History, Economics and Public Law, Columbia University 1912)

Haynes, Samuel A., "Warning," in Beatrice M. Murphy, ed., *Ebony Rhythm: An Anthology of Contemporary Negro Verse* (New York: The Exposition Press 1948)

Hearne, John, "What the Barbadian Means to Me," in Andrew Salkey, ed., *Caribbean Essays: An Anthology* (London: Evans Brothers Ltd., 1973)

Hill, Robert and Barbara Bair, eds, *Marcus Garvey: Life and Lessons, a Centennial Companion to the Marcus Garvey and the Universal Negro Improvement Association Papers* (Berkeley: University of California Press 1987)

Hughes, Langston, *Good Morning Revolution: Uncollected Writings of Social Protest*, edited by Faith Berry (New York: Citadel Press 1992)

Jacques-Garvey, Amy, ed., *Philosophy and Opinions of Marcus Garvey*, 2 vols., Introduction, by Robert A. Hill ([1923 and 1925] New York: Atheneum 1992)

James, C. L. R., *Spheres of Existence: Selected Writings* (London: Allison & Busby 1980)

James, C. L. R., *The Black Jacobins: Toussaint L'Ouverture and the San Domingo Revolution* (London 1938; 2nd. edition New York: Vintage Books 1963)

James, C. L. R., *The Life Captain Cipriani: An Account of British Government in the West Indies* (Nelson: Coulton & Co. Ltd 1932)

Jekyll, Walter, *Jamaican Song and Story: Annancy Stories, Digging Sings, Ring Tunes, and Dancing Tunes* (1907; New York: Dover Publications, Inc. 1966)

Johnson, James Weldon, *Black Manhattan* (New York: Alfred Knopf 1930)

Johnson, James Weldon, *Negro Americans, What Now?* (New York: Viking Press 1934)

Kaiser, Ernest, "The Crisis of the Negro Intellectual," *Freedomways*, First Quarter 1969

Lamming, George, *In the Castle of My Skin* (London: Michael Joseph 1953)

Leonard, Oscar, "The East St. Louis Pogrom," *Survey*, July 14, 1917

Mañach, Jorge, *Martí: Apostle of Freedom* (New York: Devin-Adair Co. 1950)

Mark, Francis, *The History of the Barbados Workers' Union* (Bridgetown: Barbados Workers' Union [1966])

Marshall, Paule, *Brown Girl, Brownstones* (New York: Random House 1959)

Martí, José, *Inside the Monster: Writings on the United States and American Imperialism* ed. by Philip S. Foner (New York: Monthly Review Press 1975)

Martí, José, *On Education: Articles on Educational Theory and Pedagogy, and Writings for Children from 'The Age of Gold'*, ed. by Philip S. Foner (New York: Monthly Review Press 1979)

Martí, José, *Our America: Writings on Latin America and the Struggle for Cuban Independence*, ed. by Philip Foner (New York: Monthly Review Press 1977)

Martin, Tony, ed., *African Fundamentalism: A Literary and Cultural Anthology of Garvey's Harlem Renaissance* (Dover, Mass: The Majority Press 1991)

Martin, Tony, ed., *The Poetical Works of Marcus Garvey* (Dover, Mass.: The Majority Press 1983)

Mayfield, Julian, "A Challenge to a Bestseller: Crisis or Crusade?" *Negro Digest*, June 1968

McKay, Claude, *Banana Bottom* (New York: Harper and Row Publishers 1933)

McKay, Claude, *Harlem: Negro Metropolis* (New York: E. P. Dutton and Co. 1940)

McKay, Claude, *Negroes in America*, trans. Robert J. Winter (Port Washington, NY: Kennikat Press 1979)

McKay, Claude, *Songs of Jamaica* (Kingston: Gardner 1912)

Miller, Kelly, *An Appeal to Conscience* (New York: The Macmillan Co. 1918)

Miller, Kelly, *The Everlasting Stain* (Washington: The Associated Publishers 1924)

Miller, Kelly, "After Marcus Garvey—What of the Negro?" *Contemporary Review*, vol. cxxxi, April 1927

Munro, Ian and Reinhard Sander, eds, *Kas-Kas: Interviews with Three Caribbean Writers in Texas* (Austin: African and Afro–American Research Institute, The University of Texas at Austin 1972)

Olivier, Lord, *Jamaica: The Blessed Island* (London: Faber and Faber 1936)

Ortiz, Fernando, *Cuban Counterpoint: Tobacco and Sugar* (New York: Alfred A. Knopf 1947)

Ortiz y Fernandez, Fernando, "Cuba, Martí and the Race Problem," *Phylon*, vol. iii, no. 3, 3rd. quarter, 1942

Ottley, Roi, *"New World A-Coming": Inside Black America* (1943; New York: Arno Press and the New York Times 1968)

Ottley, Roi and William J. Weatherby, eds, *The Negro in New York: An Informal Social History* (New York: New York Public Library and Oceana Publications 1967)

Padmore, George, *Pan-Africanism or Communism: The Coming Struggle for Africa* (London: Dennis Dobson 1956)

Perkins, William Eric, "Harold Cruse: On the Problem of Culture and Revolution," *Journal of Ethnic Studies*, vol. 5, no. 2, Summer 1977

Pickens, William, *Bursting Bonds: The Autobiography of a "New Negro"* (Bloomington: Indiana University Press, 1991)

Piñeiro de Rivera, Flor, ed., *Arthur Alfonso Schomburg: A Puerto Rican Quest for His Black Heritage* (San Juan: Centro de Estudios Avanzados de Puerto Rico y el Caribe 1989)

Quintero Rivera, Angel, ed., *Workers' Struggle in Puerto Rico: A Documentary History* (New York: Monthly Review Press 1976)

Raphael, Lennox, "West Indians and Afro–Americans," *Freedomways*, vol. 4, no. 3, Summer 1964

Reid, Ira, *The Negro Immigrant: His Background, Characteristics and Social Adjustment, 1899–1937* (New York: Columbia University Press 1939)

Rivero Muñiz, José, *The Ybor City Story, 1885–1954*, trans. Eustasio Fernández and Henry Beltram (Tampa: n. p. 1976)

Rogers, J.A., *World's Great Men of Color*, vol. ii (1947; New York: Collier Books 1972)

Schomb[u]rg, Arturo, "Una Historia verdadera de la Insurreccion de los esclavos bajo el Cabecilla de Juan Buddhoe, quien está aún venerado, por sus compatriotas," *Prevision*, (Havana), February 10, 1910

Simmons, William J., *Men of Mark: Eminent, Progressive and Rising* (Cleveland: Geo. M. Rewell & Co. 1887)

Sinckler, E. Goulbourn, *The Barbados Handbook, 1914* (London: Duckworth and Co. 1914)

Socialist Party, *Manifesto of the Socialist Party* (New York: Socialist Party, New York County 1919)

Spero, Sterling D. and Abram L. Harris, *The Black Worker: The Negro and the Labor Movement* (New York: Columbia University Press 1931)

Stuckey, Sterling and Joshua Leslie, "Reflections on Reflections about the Black Intellectual, 1930–1945," *First World*, vol. 2, no. 2, 1979

The Grenada Handbook and Directory 1946 1st ed. (Bridgetown: The Advocate Company 1946)

Thomas, John Jacob, *Froudacity: West Indian Fables by James Anthony Froude* (1889; London: New Beacon Books 1969)

Thurman, Wallace, *Negro Life in New York's Harlem* (Girard, Kansas: Halde-man–Julius Publications, 1928)

Thurman, Wallace, "Negro Poets and Their Poetry," *The Bookman*, vol. lxvii, no. 5, July 1928

Tucker, Helen, "Negro Craftsmen in New York," *Southern Workman*, vol. xxvi, no. 10, October 1907

Tuttle, William, "Views of a Negro During 'The Red Summer' of 1919: A Document," *Journal of Negro History*, July 1966

Urrutia, Gustavo E., "Schomburg", *Diario de La Marina*, November 2, 1933

Vincent, Theodore G., ed., *Voices of a Black Nation: Political Journalism in the Harlem Renaissance* (San Francisco: Ramparts Press 1973)

Voices of the African Diaspora: The CAAS Research Review, [published by the Center for Afroamerican and African Studies, University of Michigan] vol. ix, no. 1, Winter 1994, Special Issue on Harold Cruse

Walrond, Eric, "The New Negro Faces America," *Current History*, vol. 17, no. 5, February 1923

Walrond, Eric, *Tropic Death* (New York: Boni and Liveright 1926)

Williams, Eric, ed., *Documents of West Indian History, 1492–1655* (Port of Spain: PNM Publishing Company 1963)

Woodson, Carter G., *The Negro Professional Man and the Community* (Washing-ton: The Association for the Study of Negro Life and History 1934)

Newspapers and Magazines

African
Blackman / Black Man
Champion Magazine
Chicago Defender
Chief
City Record
Communist
Crisis
Crusader
Daily Worker
Emancipator
Favorite Magazine
Liberación
Liberator (Harlem)

Messenger
Negro Champion
Negro World
New York Amsterdam News
New York Sun
New York Times
Pittsburgh Courier
Promoter
Public Opinion
Pueblos Hispanos
Revolutionary Age
West Indian–American
Worker

Biographical Dictionaries

Buhle, Mari Jo, Paul Buhle and Dan Georgakas, eds, *Encyclopedia of the American Left* (New York: Garland Publishing 1990)

Johnpoll, Bernard K. and Harvey Klehr, eds, *Biographical Dictionary of the American Left* (Westport, Conn.: Greenwood Press 1986)

Logan, Rayford and Michael Winston, eds, *Dictionary of American Negro Biog-raphy* (New York: W. W. Norton and Co. 1982)

Who's Who in Colored America (various years)

Contemporary Black Biography (various years)

Secondary Literature

Books and Articles

Abel, Christopher and Nissa Torrents, eds, *José Martí: Revolutionary Democrat* (Durham, NC: Duke University Press 1986)

Abrahams, Roger D., *The Man-of-Words in the West Indies: Performance and the Emergence of Creole Culture* (Baltimore: Johns Hopkins University Press 1983)

Adelman, Lynn, "A Study of James Weldon Johnson," *Journal of Negro History*, vol. lii, no. 2, April 1967

Ahola, David John, *Finnish-Americans and International Communism: A Study of Finnish-American Communism from Bolshevization to the Demise of the Third International* (Washington, DC: University Press of America 1981)

Albert, Bill and Adrian Graves, eds, *Crisis and Change in the International Sugar Economy, 1860–1914* (Norwich: ISC Press 1984)

Alleyne, Mervyn, *Roots of Jamaican Culture* (London: Pluto Press 1988)

Anderson, Jervis, *A. Philip Randolph: A Biographical Portrait* (Berkeley: University of California Press 1986)

Andrews, Kenneth R., *The Spanish Caribbean: Trade and Plunder 1530–1630* (New Haven: Yale University Press 1978)

Anon., "Ferdinand C. Smith (1894–1961), Jamaican Fighter for Democracy and Socialism," *Socialism!* [Organ of the Workers' Liberation League, Jamaica], vol. 2, no. 1, January 1975

Asante, S. K. B., *Pan-African Protest: West Africa and the Italo-Ethiopian Crisis, 1934–1941* (London: Longman 1977)

Asante, S. K. B., "The Afro-American and the Italo-Ethiopian Crisis, 1934–36," *Race*, vol. xv, no. 2, 1973

Asante, S. K. B., "The Impact of the Italo-Ethiopian Crisis of 1935–36 on the Pan-African Movement in Britain," *Transactions of the Historical Society of Ghana*, vol. 13, no. 2

Ashdown, Peter, "Marcus Garvey, the UNIA and the Black Cause in British Honduras, 1914–1949," *Journal of Caribbean History*, vol. 15, 1981

Auxier, George W., "The Propaganda Activities of the Cuban *Junta* in Precipitating the Spanish-American War, 1895–1898," *Hispanic American Historical Review*, vol. xix, no. 3, August 1939

Bacchus, M. Kazim, *Education as and for Legitimacy: Developments in West Indian Education Between 1846 and 1895* (Waterloo: Wilfrid Laurier University Press 1994)

Bair, Barbara, "Pan-Africanism as a Process: Adelaide Casely Hayford, Garveyism, and the Cultural Roots of Nationalism," in Sidney Lemelle and Robin Kelley, eds, *Imagining Home: Class, Culture and Nationalism in the African Diaspora* (London: Verso 1994)

Bair, Barbara, "True Women, Real Men: Gender, Ideology, and Social Roles in the Garvey Movement" in Dorothy O. Helly and Susan M. Reverby, eds, *Gendered Domains: Rethinking Public and Private in Women's History* (Ithaca: Cornell University Press 1992)

Baraka, Amiri, *Daggers and Javelins: Essays, 1974–1979* (New York: William Morrow and Company 1984)

Barbeau, Arthur E. and Florette Henri, *The Unknown Soldiers: Black American Troops in World War I* (Philadelphia: Temple University Press 1974)

Barnett, Lloyd G., *The Constitutional Law of Jamaica* (Oxford: Oxford University Press 1977)

Barrow, Christine, "Ownership and Control of Resources in Barbados: 1834 to the Present," *Social and Economic Studies*, vol. 32, no. 3, September 1983

Baud, Michiel, "A Colonial Counter Economy: Tobacco Production on Española, 1500–1870," *Nieuwe West Indische Gids/New West Indian Guide*, vol. 65, nos. 1 & 2, 1991

Beachey, R. W., *The British West Indies Sugar Industry in the Late Nineteenth Century* (Oxford: Basil Blackwell 1957)

Beckles, Hilary, *A History of Barbados: From Amerindian Settlement to Nation-State* (Cambridge: Cambridge University Press 1990)

Beckles, Hilary, *Black Rebellion in Barbados: The Struggle Against Slavery, 1627–1838* (Bridgetown: Antilles Press 1984)

Betances, Samuel, "African-Americans and Hispanics/Latinos: Eliminating Barriers to Coalition Building," *Latino Studies Journal*, vol. 6, no. 1, January 1995

Betances, Samuel, "The Prejudice of Having No Prejudice in Puerto Rico," Parts I and II, *The Rican*, Winter 1972 and Spring 1973

Bethell, Leslie, ed., *The Independence of Latin America* (Cambridge: Cambridge University Press 1987)

Blackburn, Robin, *The Overthrow of Colonial Slavery, 1776–1848* (London: Verso 1988)

Blackett, R. J. M., *Beating Against The Barriers: The Lives of Six Nineteenth-Century Afro-Americans* (Baton Rouge: Louisiana State University Press 1986)

Blakely, Allison, *Russia and the Negro: Blacks in Russian History and Thought* (Washington, DC: Howard University Press 1986)

Bolland, O. Nigel, *On the March: Labour Rebellions in the British Caribbean, 1934–39* (Kingston: Ian Randle Publishers 1995)

Bone, Robert, *Down Home: Origins of the Afro-American Short Story* (New York: Putnam 1975)

Bourgois, Philippe I., *Ethnicity at Work: Divided Labor on a Central American Banana Plantation* (Baltimore: Johns Hopkins University Press 1989)

Brathwaite, Edward, *The Development of Creole Society in Jamaica, 1770–1820* (Oxford: Clarendon Press 1971)

Brereton, Bridget, *A History of Modern Trinidad, 1783–1962* (London: Heinemann 1981)

Brereton, Bridget, *Race Relations in Colonial Trinidad, 1870–1900* (Cambridge: Cambridge University Press 1979)

Brizan, George, *Grenada: Island of Conflict* (London: Zed Books 1984)

Brizan, George, *The Grenadian Peasantry and Social Revolution, 1930–1951*, Working Paper No. 21 (Kingston: ISER 1979)

Bryan, Patrick, *The Jamaican People, 1880–1902: Race, Class and Social Control* (London: Macmillan 1991)

Buhle, Paul, *C.L.R. James: The Artist as Revolutionary* (London: Verso 1988)

Buhle, Paul, ed., *C.L.R. James: His Life and Work* (London: Allison and Busby 1986)

Buhle, Paul, *Marxism in the United States: Remapping the History of the American Left*, rev. ed. (London: Verso 1991)

Buhle, Paul and Dan Georgakas, eds, *The Immigrant Left in the United States* (Albany: State University of New York Press 1996)

Cannon, James P., *James P. Cannon and the Early Years of American Communism: Selected Writings and Speeches, 1920–1928* (New York: Prometheus Research Library Books 1992)

Cannon, James P., *The First Ten Years of American Communism: Report of a Participant* (New York: Lyle Stuart 1962)

Carew, Jan, *Ghosts in Our Blood: With Malcolm X in Africa, England, and the Caribbean* (Chicago: Lawrence Hill Books 1994)

Carnegie, James, *Some Aspects of Jamaica's Politics, 1918–1938* (Kingston: Institute of Jamaica 1973)

Chalmers, David, "The Ku Klux Klan in the Sunshine State: The 1920s," *Florida Historical Quarterly*, vol. xlii, no. 3, January 1964.

Chamberlain, Mary, "Renters and Farmers: The Barbadian Plantation Tenantry System, 1917–1937," *Journal of Caribbean History*, vol. 24, no. 2, 1990

Chomsky, Aviva, *West Indian Workers and the United Fruit Company in Costa Rica, 1870–1940* (Baton Rouge: Louisiana State University Press 1996)

Clarke, Colin, *Kingston, Jamaica: Urban Development and Social Change, 1692–1962* (Berkeley: University of California Press 1975)

Clarke, J. H., ed., *Marcus Garvey and the Vision of Africa* (New York: Vintage Books 1974)

Cohen, David and Jack Greene, eds, *Neither Slave Nor Free: The Freedmen of African Descent in the Slave Societies of the New World* (Baltimore: Johns Hopkins University Press 1974)

Cohen, William, *At Freedom's Edge: Black Mobility and the Southern White Quest for Racial Control 1861–1915* (Baton Rouge: Louisiana State University Press 1991)

Collum, Danny Duncan, ed., *African Americans in the Spanish Civil War: "This Ain't Ethiopia, But It'll Do"* (New York: G.K. Hall and Co. 1992)

Cooper, Patricia, *Once a Cigar Maker: Men, Women, and Work Culture in American Cigar Factories, 1900–1919* (Urbana: University of Illinois Press 1987)

Craton, Michael, *Testing the Chains: Slave Rebellions in the British West Indies* (Ithaca: Cornell University Press 1982)

Cronon, E., *Black Moses: The Story of Marcus Garvey and the Universal Negro Improvement Association* (Madison: University of Wisconsin Press 1955)

Cross, Malcolm and Gad Heuman, eds, *Labour in the Caribbean: From Emancipation to Independence* (London: Macmillan Publishers 1988)

Cudjoe, Selwyn R. and William E. Cain, eds, *C.L.R. James: His Intellectual Legacies* (Amherst: University of Massachusetts Press 1995)

Curtin, Philip, "The British Sugar Duties and West Indies Prosperity," *Journal of Economic History*, vol. xiv (1954)

Daniels, John, *In Freedom's Birthplace: A Study of Boston Negroes* (Boston: Houghton Mifflin Co. 1914)

Davis, Angela, *Women, Race and Class* (New York: Random House 1981)

Deerr, Noel, *The History of Sugar*, vol. 2 (London: Chapman and Hall 1950)

Del Rio, Emilio, *Yo Fuí Uno de Los Fundadores de Ybor City* (Tampa: n. p. 1972)

Deschamps Chapeaux, Pedro, *Rafael Serra y Montalvo: Obrero Incansable de Nuestra Independencia* (Havana: Unión de Escritores y Artistas de Cuba 1975)

Diaz Soler, Luis M., *Historia de La Esclavitud Negra en Puerto Rico* (Rio Piedras: Universidad de Puerto Rico 1981)

Dickerson, Dennis, *Out of the Crucible: Black Steelworkers in Western Pennsylvania, 1875–1980* (Albany: State University of New York Press 1986)

Dietz, James, *The Economic History of Puerto Rico: Institutional Change and Capitalist Development* (Princeton: Princeton University Press 1986)

Dobbs, Farrell, *Revolutionary Continuity: Birth of the Communist Movement, 1918–1922* (New York: Monad Press 1983)

Dolan, Jay P. and Jaime R. Vidal, eds, *Puerto Rican and Cuban Catholics in the US, 1900–1965* (Indiana: University of Notre Dame Press 1994)

Drake, St. Clair and George Shepperson, "The Fifth Pan-African Conference, 1954 and the All People's Congress, 1958," *Contributions in Black Studies: A Journal of African and Afro-American Studies,* no. 8, 1986–1987

Draper, Theodore, *American Communism and Soviet Russia* (New York: Vintage 1960)

Draper, Theodore, *The Roots of American Communism* (New York: Viking Press 1957)

Duberman, Martin, *Paul Robeson* (New York: Alfred Knopf 1988)

Dunbar, Paul Laurence, *The Complete Poems of Paul Laurence Dunbar* (New York: Dodd, Mead, & Co. 1922)

Eaton, George, "Trade Union Development in Jamaica," *Caribbean Quarterly,* vol. 8, no. 1, 1962

Eisner, Gisela, *Jamaica, 1830–1930: A Study in Economic Growth* (Manchester: Manchester University Press 1961)

West Indies Regiment at Taranto, Italy," *Science & Society,* vol. xxxiv, no. 1, Spring 1970

Elkins, W. F., "A Source of Black Nationalism in the Caribbean: The Revolt of the British West Indies Regiment at Taranto, Italy," *Science & Society,* vol. xxxiv, no. 1, Spring 1970

Elkins, W. F., "Black Power in the British West Indies: The Trinidad Longshoreman's Strike of 1919," *Science & Society,* vol. xxxiii, no. 1, Winter 1969

Elkins, W. F., "Hercules and the Society of Peoples of African Origin," *Caribbean Studies,* vol. 11, no. 4, January 1972

Elkins, W. F., "Marcus Garvey, the *Negro World,* and the British West Indies: 1919–1920," *Science & Society,* vol. xxxvi, no. 1, Spring 1972

Elkins, W. F., "The Suppression of the *Negro World* in the British West Indies," *Science & Society,* vol. xxxv, no. 3, Fall 1971

Essien–Udom, E. U., *Black Nationalism: The Rise of the Black Muslims in the USA* (Harmondsworth: Penguin Books 1966)

Fagen, Patricia Weiss, "Antonio Maceo: Heroes, History, and Historiography," *Latin American Research Review,* vol. xi, no. 3, 1976

Ferrer, Ada, "Social Aspects of Cuban Nationalism: Race, Slavery, and the Guerra Chiquita, 1879–1880," *Cuban Studies,* no. 21, 1991

Fick, Carolyn, *The Making of Haiti: The Saint Domingue Revolution from Below* (Knoxville: University of Tennessee Press 1990)

Fletcher, Leonard P., "The Evolution of Poor Relief in Barbados, 1838–1900," *Journal of Caribbean History,* vol. 26, no. 2, 1992

Flores, Juan, *Divided Borders: Essays on Puerto Rican Identity* (Houston: Arte Público Press 1993)

Foner, Eric, *Nothing But Freedom: Emancipation and its Legacy* (Baton Rouge: Louisiana State University Press 1983)

Foner, Jack, *Blacks and the Military in American History* (New York: Praeger Publishers 1974)

Foner, Philip, *American Socialism and Black Americans: From the Age of Jackson to World War II* (Westport: Greenwood Press 1977)

Foner, Philip, *Antonio Maceo: The "Bronze Titan" of Cuba's Struggle for Independence* (New York: Monthly Review Press 1977)

Foner, Philip S., *Organized Labor and the Black Worker, 1619–1918* (New York: International Publishers 1982)

Foner, Philip, "The IWW and the Black Worker," *Journal of Negro History,* vol. lv, no. 1, January 1970

Forsythe, Dennis, "West Indian Radicalism in America: An Assessment of Ideologies," in Frances Henry, ed., *Ethnicity in the Americas* (The Hague: Mouton Publishers, 1976)

Fox, Stephen, *The Guardian of Boston: William Monroe Trotter* (New York: Atheneum 1970)

Franklin, John Hope, *Race and History: Selected Essays, 1938–1988* (Baton Rouge: Louisiana State University Press 1989)

Frederickson, George, *The Arrogance of Race* (Middletown: Wesleyan University Press 1988).

Frederickson, George, *The Black Image in the White Mind: The Debate on Afro-American Character and Destiny, 1817–1914* (New York: Harper & Row 1971)

Frucht, Richard, "Emigration, Remittances, and Social Change: Aspects of the Social Field of Nevis, West Indies," *Anthropologia*, 10 (1968)

Gardell, Mattias, *In the Name of Elijah Muhammad: Louis Farrakhan and the Nation of Islam* (Durham: Duke University Press 1996)

Gates, Henry Louis, "Farrakhan Speaks: A Conversation with Louis Farrakhan," *Transition*, vol. 6, no. 2, Summer 1996

Gatewood, Willard, *Aristocrats of Color: The Black Elite, 1880–1920* (Bloomington: Indiana University Press 1990)

Gatewood, Willard B., Jr., "Negro Troops in Florida, 1898," *Florida Historical Quarterly*, vol. xlix, no. 1, July 1970

Genovese, Eugene, *From Rebellion to Revolution: Afro-American Slave Revolts in the Making of the Modern World* (Baton Rouge: Louisiana State University Press 1979)

Genovese, Eugene, *Roll, Jordan, Roll: The World the Slaves Made* (New York: Pantheon Books 1974)

George, Paul S., "Colored Town: Miami's Black Community, 1896–1930," *Florida Historical Quarterly*, vol. lvi, no. 4, April 1978

George, Paul S., "Policing Miami's Black Community, 1896–1930," *Florida Historical Quarterly*, vol. lvii, no. 4, April 1979

Gilbert, Peter, ed., *The Selected Writings of John Edward Bruce: Militant Black Journalist* (New York: Arno Press 1971)

Glasser, Ruth, *My Music is My Flag: Puerto Rican Musicians and Their New York Communities, 1917–1940* (Berkeley: University of California Press 1995)

Glazer, Nathan and Daniel P. Moynihan, eds, *Ethnicity: Theory and Experience* (Cambridge, Mass.: Harvard University Press 1975)

González, José Luis, *Puerto Rico: The Four-Storeyed Country and Other Essays* (1980; Princeton: Markus Wiener Publishing, Inc. 1993)

Gould, Stephen Jay, *The Mismeasure of Man* (New York: W.W. Norton 1981)

Gramsci, Antonio, *Selections From the Prison Notebooks* (London: Lawrence and Wishart 1971)

Greenbaum, Susan, *Afro-Cubans in Ybor City: A Centennial History* (Tampa: n.p. 1986)

Greenbaum, Susan, "Afro-Cubans in Exile: Tampa, Florida, 1886–1984," *Cuban Studies/Estudios Cubanos*, vol. 15, no. 1, Winter 1985

Greenbaum, Susan, "Economic Cooperation Among Urban Industrial Workers: Rationality and Community in an Afro-Cuban Mutual Aid Society, 1904–1927," *Social Science History*, vol. 17, no. 2, Summer 1993

Greenberg, Cheryl, *"Or Does It Explode?" Black Harlem in the Great Depression* (New York: Oxford University Press 1991)

Greene, Jack P., *Imperatives Behaviors, and Identities: Essays in Early American Cultural History* (Charlottesville: University Press of Virginia 1992)

Greene, Jack P., "Colonial South Carolina and the Caribbean Connection," *South Carolina Historical Magazine*, vol. 88, no. 4, October 1987

Gutman, Herbert G., *The Black Family in Slavery and Freedom, 1750–1925* (New York: Pantheon Books 1976)

Gutzmore, Cecil, "The Image of Marcus Garvey in Reggae Orature," in Kwesi Owusu, ed., *Storms of the Heart: An Anthology of Black Arts and Culture* (London: Camden Press 1988)

Hall, Douglas, *Free Jamaica, 1838–1865: An Economic History* (New Haven: Yale University Press 1959)

Hall, Neville, *Slave Society in the Danish West Indies: St. Thomas, St. John and St. Croix* (Kingston: The Press–University of the West Indies 1992)

Hall, Neville, "Education for Slaves in the Danish Virgin Islands, 1732–1846," in Ruby Hope King, ed., *Education in the Caribbean: Historical Perspectives* (Kingston: Faculty of Education, University of the West Indies 1987)

Halter, Marilyn, *Between Race and Ethnicity: Cape Verdean American Immigrants, 1860–1965* (Urbana: University of Illinois Press 1993)

Handler, Jerome, *The Unappropriated People: Freedmen in the Slave Society of Barbados* (Baltimore: Johns Hopkins University Press 1974)

Handlin, Oscar, *The Newcomers: Negroes and Puerto Ricans in a Changing Metropolis* (Cambridge, Mass.: Harvard University Press 1959)

Harris, Joseph E., *African-American Reactions to War in Ethiopia, 1936–1941* (Baton Rouge: Louisiana State University Press 1994).

Harris, William H., *Keeping the Faith: A Philip Randolph, Milton P. Webster, and the Brotherhood of Sleeping Car Porters, 1925–1937* (Urbana: The University of Illinois Press 1977)

Harry, Carlyle, *Hubert Nathaniel Critchlow* (Georgetown: Guyana National Service Publishing Centre 1977)

Hart, Richard, *Rise and Organise: The Birth of the Workers and National Movements in Jamaica, 1936–1939* (London: Karia Press 1989)

Hart, Richard, "Jamaica and Self-Determination, 1660–1970," *Race*, vol. xiii, no. 3, January 1972

Hart, Richard, "The Life and Resurrection of Marcus Garvey," *Race*, vol. ix, no. 2, 1967

Hart, Richard, "Trade Unionism in the English-Speaking Caribbean: The Formative Years and the Caribbean Labour Congress," in Susan Craig, ed., *Contemporary Caribbean: A Sociological Reader*, vol. 2 (Port of Spain: Susan Craig 1982)

Helg, Aline, *Our Rightful Share: The Afro-Cuban Struggle for Equality, 1886–1912* (Chapel Hill: University of North Carolina Press 1995)

Hellwig, David J., "Black Meets Black: Afro-American Reactions to West Indian Immigrants in the 1920s," *South Atlantic Quarterly*, Vol. 77, No. 2, Spring 1978

Henderson, Ann L. and Gary R. Mormino, eds, *Spanish Pathways in Florida: 1492–1992 / Los Cominos Españoles en La Florida: 1492–1992* (Sarasota: Pineapple Press, Inc. 1991)

Henry, Frances, ed., *Ethnicity in the Americas* (The Hague: Mouton 1976)

Henry, Keith S., "Caribbean Migrants in New York: The Passage from Political Quiescence to Radicalism," *Afro-Americans in New York Life and History*, vol. 2, no. 2, July 1978

Henry, Paget and Paul Buhle, eds, *C.L.R. James's Caribbean* (Durham, North Carolina: Duke University Press 1992)

Herrmann, Eleanor Krohn, *Origins of Tomorrow: A History of Belizean Nursing Education* (Belize City: Ministry of Health, Belize 1985)

Heuman, Gad, *"The Killing Time": The Morant Bay Rebellion in Jamaica* (Knoxville: University of Tennessee Press 1994)

Hewitt, Nancy A., "'The Voice of Virile Labor': Labor Militancy, Community Solidarity, and Gender Identity among Tampa's Latin Workers, 1880–1921," in Ava Baron, ed., *Work Engendered: Toward a New History of American Labor* (Ithaca: Cornell University Press 1991)

Hewitt, Nancy A., "Paulina Pedroso and *Las Patriotas* of Tampa," in Henderson and Mormino, eds, *Spanish Pathways.*

Hewitt, Nancy A., "Varieties of Voluntarism: Class, Ethnicity, and Women's Activism in Tampa," in Louise Tilly and Patricia Gurin, eds, *Women, Politics, and Change* (New York: Russell Sage Foundation 1990)

Higham, John, *Strangers in the Land: Patterns of American Nativism 1860–1925* (New York: Atheneum 1963)

Higman, B. W., *Slave Population and Economy in Jamaica, 1807–1834* (Cambridge: Cambridge University Press 1976)

Higman, B. W., *Slave Populations of the British Caribbean, 1807–1834* (Baltimore: The Johns Hopkins University Press 1984)

Higman, B. W., "Domestic Service in Jamaica since 1750, " in B. Higman, ed., *Trade, Government and Society in Caribbean History, 1700–1920: Essays Presented to Douglas Hall* (Kingston: Heinemann 1983)

Hill, Robert A., "Racial and Radical: Cyril V. Briggs, *The Crusader* Magazine, and the African Blood Brotherhood, 1918–1922," introduction to the facsimile edition of *The Crusader* (New York: Garland Publishing, Inc. 1987)

History Task Force, Centro de Estudios Puertorriqueños, *Labor Migration Under Capitalism: The Puerto Rican Experience* (New York: Monthly Review Press 1979)

Hobsbawm, Eric, *The Age of Empire: 1875–1914* (London: Weidenfeld and Nicolson 1987)

Hoernel, Robert B., "Sugar and Social Change in Oriente, Cuba, 1898–1946," *Journal of Latin American Studies*, vol. 8, pt. 2, November 1976

Hoetink, Harry, *The Dominican People, 1850–1900 : Notes for a Historical Sociology* (Baltimore: Johns Hopkins University Press 1982)

Holder, Calvin, "The Causes and Composition of West Indian Immigration to New York City, 1900–1952," *Afro-Americans in New York Life and History*, vol. 11, no. 1, January 1987

Holder, Calvin, "The Rise of the West Indian Politician in New York City, 1900–1952," *Afro-Americans in New York Life and History*, vol. 4, no. 1, January 1980

Holt, Thomas, *The Problem of Freedom: Race, Labor, and Politics in Jamaica and Britain, 1832–1938* (Baltimore: Johns Hopkins University Press 1992)

Hooker, J. R., *Black Revolutionary: George Padmore's Path from Communism to Pan-Africanism* (New York: Praeger Publishers 1967)

Hooker, J. R., *Henry Sylvester Williams: Imperial Pan-Africanist* (London: Rex Collings 1975)

Horton, James O., *Free People of Color: Inside the African American Community* (Washington, DC: Smithsonian Institution Press 1993)

Howe, Glenford D., "In the Crucible: Race, Power and Military Socialization of West Indian Recruits During the First World War," *Journal of Caribbean Studies*, vol. 10, no. 3, Summer and Fall 1995

Ingalls, Robert, *Urban Vigilantes in the New South: Tampa, 1882–1936* (Knoxville: University of Tennessee Press 1988)

Jackson, John G., "Hubert Henry Harrison: The Black Socrates," *American Atheist*, February 1987

Jaffe, Julian E., *Crusade Against Radicalism: New York During the Red Scare, 1914–1924* (New York: Praeger 1972)

James, Winston and Clive Harris, eds, *Inside Babylon: The Caribbean Diaspora in Britain* (London and New York: Verso 1993)

James, Winston, "The Hurricane that Shook the Caribbean," *New Left Review*, No. 138, March–April, 1983

Jennings, James and Monte Rivera, eds, *Puerto Rican Politics in Urban America* (Westport: Greenwood Press 1984)

Jiménez de Wagenheim, Olga, *Puerto Rico's Revolt for Independence: El Grito de Lares* (1985; Princeton and New York: Markus Wiener Publishing 1993)

Johnson, Buzz, *"I Think of My Mother"—Notes on the Life of Claudia Jones* (London: Karia Press 1985)

Johnson, Howard, *The Bahamas in Slavery and Freedom* (Kingston: Ian Randle Publishers 1991)

Johnson, Howard, "Barbadian Immigrants in Trinidad, 1870–1897," *Caribbean Studies*, vol. 13, no. 3, 1973

Johnson, Howard, "Immigration and the Sugar Industry in Trinidad During the Last Quarter of the 19th Century," *Journal of Caribbean History*, vol. 3, November 1971

Johnson, Howard, "Merchant Credit and the Dispossession of the Cocoa Peasantry in Trinidad in the Late Nineteenth Century," *Peasant Studies*, vol. 15, no. 1, Fall 1987

Jones, Maldwyn A., *American Immigration* (Chicago: University of Chicago Press 1960)

Jorge, Angela, "The Black Puerto Rican Woman in Contemporary American Society," in Edna Acosta-Belén, ed., *The Puerto Rican Woman: Perspectives on Culture, History, and Society*, 2nd. edn. (New York: Praeger 1986)

Joseph, C. L., "The British West Indies Regiment 1914–1918," *Journal of Caribbean History*, vol. 2, May 1971

Keeran, Roger, "The International Workers Order and the Origins of the CIO," *Labor History*, vol. 30, no. 3, Summer 1989

Kharif, Wali R., "Black Reaction to Segregation and Discrimination in Post-Reconstruction Florida," *Florida Historical Quarterly*, vol. lxiv, no. 2, October 1985

Kiple, Kenneth, *Blacks in Colonial Cuba, 1774–1899* (Gainesville: University Presses of Florida 1976)

Kirby, Jack Temple, *Media Made Dixie: The South in the American Imagination*, rev. ed. (Athens: University of Georgia Press 1986)

Kirk, John M., *José Martí: Mentor of the Cuban Nation* (Tampa: University Press of Florida 1982)

Kivisto, Peter, *Immigrant Socialists in the United States: The Case of Finns and the Left* (Rutherford: Fairleigh Dickinson University Press 1984)

Klehr, Harvey, *Communist Cadre: The Social Background of the American Communist Party Elite* (Stanford: Hoover Institution Press 1978)

Klehr, Harvey and William Tompson, "Self-Determination in the Black Belt: Origins of a Communist Policy," *Labor History*, vol. 30, no. 3, Summer 1989

Knight, F. and C. Palmer, eds, *The Modern Caribbean* (Chapel Hill: University of North Carolina, 1989)

Knight, Franklin, *Slave Society in Cuba During the Nineteenth Century* (Madison: University of Wisconsin Press 1970)

Knight, Franklin, *The Caribbean: The Genesis of A Fragmented Nationalism*, 2nd. ed. (New York: Oxford University Press 1990)

Knight, Franklin W. and Peggy K. Liss, eds, *Atlantic Port Cities: Economy, Culture, and Society in the Atlantic World, 1650–1850* (Knoxville: University of Tennessee Press 1991)

Kornweibel, Theodore, *No Crystal Stair: Black Life and the "Messenger," 1917–1928* (Westport: Greenwood Press 1975)

Kuethe, Alan J., "Guns, Subsidies, and Commercial Privilege: Some Historical Factors in the Emergence of the Cuban National Character, 1763–1815," *Cuban Studies*, no. 16, 1986

LaGumina, Salvatore John, *Vito Marcantonio: The People's Politician* (Dubuque, Iowa: Kendall/Hunt Publishing Co. 1969)

Lai, Walton Look, *Indentured Labor, Caribbean Sugar: Chinese and Indian Migrants to the British West Indies, 1838–1918* (Baltimore: Johns Hopkins University Press 1993)

Lamson, Peggy, *The Glorious Failure: Black Congressman Robert Brown Elliott and the Reconstruction in South Carolina* (New York: Norton 1973)

Langley, J. Ayo, "Pan-Africanism in Paris, 1924–36," *Journal of Modern African Studies*, vol. 7, no. 1, April 1969

Lasch, Christopher, "The Trouble with Black Power," *New York Review of Books*, February 29, 1968

Laurence, K. O., *A Question of Labour: Indentured Immigration into Trinidad and British Guiana, 1875–1917* (Kingston: Ian Randle Publishers 1994)

Laurence, K. O., *Immigration into the West Indies in the 19th Century* (Aylesbury: Caribbean Universities Press/Ginn and Co. Ltd. 1971)

Leinenweber, Charles, "The American Socialist Party and 'New Immigrants'," *Science and Society*, vol. 32, no. 1, Winter 1968

Leinenweber, Charles, "The Class and Ethnic Bases of New York City Socialism, 1904–1915," *Labor History*, vol. 22, no. 1, Winter 1981

Levy, Claude, *Emancipation, Sugar, and Federalism: Barbados and the West Indies, 1833–1876* (Gainesville: University Presses of Florida 1900)

Levy, Eugene, *James Weldon Johnson: Black Leader, Black Voice* (Chicago: University of Chicago Press 1973)

Lewis, Gordon, *Main Currents in Caribbean Thought: The Historical Evolution of Caribbean Society in Its Ideological Aspects, 1492–1900* (Baltimore: Johns Hopkins University Press 1983)

Lewis, Gordon, *Puerto Rico: Freedom and Power in the Caribbean* (New York: Monthly Review Press 1963)

Lewis, Lancelot, *The West Indian in Panama: Black Labor in Panama, 1850–1914* (Washington, DC: University Press of America 1980)

Lewis, Rupert, *Marcus Garvey: Anti-Colonial Champion* (London: Karia Press 1987)

Lewis, Rupert and Maureen Warner-Lewis,, "Amy Jacques Garvey," *Jamaica Journal*, August–October 1987

Liebman, Arthur, *Jews and the Left* (New York: John Wiley and Sons 1979)

Littlefield, Daniel C., "The Colonial Slave Trade to South Carolina: A Profile," *South Carolina Historical Magazine*, vol. 91, no. 2, April 1990

Lobdell, Richard A., "Patterns of Investment and Sources of Credit in the British West Indian Sugar Industry, 1838–97," *Journal of Caribbean History*, vol. 4, May 1972

Lobdell, Richard, "Women in the Jamaican Labour Force, 1881–1921," *Social and Economic Studies*, vol. 37, nos. 1 & 2, March–June 1988

Logan, Rayford, *The Negro in American Life and Thought: The Nadir 1877–1901* (New York: The Dial Press 1954).

Logan, Rayford W. and Michael R. Winston, eds, *Dictionary of American Negro Biography* (New York: W.W. Norton & Company 1982)

Long, Durward, "An Immigrant Co-operativbe Medicine Program in the South, 1887–1963," *Journal of Southern History*, vol. 31, no. 4, November 1965

Long, Durward, "*La Resistencia*: Tampa's Immigrant Labor Union," *Labor History*, vol. 6, no. 3, Fall, 1965

Long, Durward, "Labor Relations in the Tampa Cigar Industry, 1885–1911," *Labor History*, vol. 12, no. 4, Fall 1971

Long, Durward, "The Historical Beginnings of Ybor City and Modern Tampa," *Florida Historical Quarterly*, vol. xlv, no. 1, July 1966

Long, Durward, "The Making of Modern Tampa: A City of the New South, 1885–1911," *Florida Historical Quarterly*, vol. xlix, no. 4, April 1971

Long, Durward, "The Open-Closed Shop Battle in Tampa's Cigar Industry, 1919–21," *Florida Historical Quarterly*, vol. xlvii, no. 3, October 1968

Lowenthal, David, "The Population of Barbados," *Social and Economic Studies*, vol. 6, no. 4, December 1957

Lynch, Hollis, *Edward Wilmot Blyden: Pan-Negro Patriot* (New York: Oxford University Press 1970)

Magida, Arthur J., *Prophet of Rage: A Life of Louis Farrkhan and his Nation* (New York: Basic Books 1996)

Maldonado-Dennis, Manuel, *The Emigration Dialectic: Puerto Rico and the USA* (New York: International Publishers 1980)

Mandle, Jay R., *The Plantation Economy: Population and Economic Change in Guyana, 1838–1960* (Philadelphia: Temple University Press 1973)

Marshall, Woodville, *Social and Economic Problems of the Windward Islands, 1838–1865* (Kingston: Department of History, University of the West Indies n.d.)

Marshall, Woodville, "Peasant Development in the West Indies since 1838," in P. I. Gomes, ed., *Rural Development in the Caribbean* (London: C. Hurst & Company 1985)

Martin, Tony, *Literary Garveyism: Garvey, Black Arts and the Harlem Renaissance* (Dover, Mass.: The Majority Press 1983)

Martin, Tony, *Race First: The Ideological and Organizational Struggles of Marcus Garvey and the Universal Negro Improvement Association* (Westport, Conn.: Greenwood Press 1976)

Martin, Tony, "Amy Ashwood Garvey," *Jamaica Journal*, August–October 1987

Martin, Tony, *The Pan-African Connection: From Slavery to Garvey and Beyond* (Cambridge, Mass.: Schenkman Publishing Co. 1983)

Marx, Karl, *Capital*, vol. 1 (London: Lawrence and Wishart 1974)

Mathurin, Owen Charles, *Henry Sylvester Williams and the Origins of the Pan-African Movement, 1869–1911* (Westport: Greenwood Press 1976)

Matthews, Mark D., "'Our Women and What They Think': Amy Jacques Garvey and *The Negro World*," *Black Scholar*, May–June 1979

McGirr, Lisa, "Black and White Longshoremen in the IWW: A History of the Philadelphia Marine Transport Workers Industrial Union Local 8," *Labor History*, vol. 37, no. 3, Summer 1995

McNeill, John Robert, *Atlantic Empires of France and Spain: Louisbourg and Havana, 1700–1763* (Chapel Hill: University of North Carolina Press 1985)

Meier, August and Elliott Rudwick, *Along the Color Line: Explorations in the Black Experience* (Urbana: University of Illinois Press 1976)

Meier, August and Elliott Rudwick, "Attitudes of Negro Leaders Toward the

American Labor Movement from the Civil War to World War I," in Julius Jacobson, *The Negro and the American Labor Movement* (New York: Anchor Books 1968)

Meyer, Gerald, *Vito Marcantonio: Radical Politician, 1902–1954* (Albany: State University Press of New York 1989)

Middleton, De Wight R., "The Organization of Ethnicity in Tampa," *Ethnic Groups*, vol. 3, December 1981

Milkman, Ruth, ed., *Women, Work and Protest: A Century of US Women's Labor History* (Boston: Routledge & Kegan Paul 1985)

Mill, John Stuart, *Principles of Political Economy* (London: Routledge and Sons, 1900)

Miller, Henry, *The Rosy Crucifixion, Book Two: Plexus* (New York: Grove Press 1965)

Miller, Sally M., "The Socialist Party and the Negro, 1901–1920," *Journal of Negro History*, vol. lvi, no. 3, July 1971

Miller, Sally, *The Radical Immigrant* (New York: Twayne Publishers, Inc. 1974)

Mintz, Sidney and Sally Price, eds, *Caribbean Contours* (Baltimore: Johns Hopkins University Press 1985)

Mintz, Sidney, *Caribbean Transformations* (Chicago: Aldine Publishing Co. 1974)

Mintz, Sidney, *Sweetness and Power: The Place of Sugar in Modern History* (New York: Viking Penguin 1985)

Mintz, Sidney, *Worker in the Cane: A Puerto Rican Life History* (New York: W.W. Norton 1974)

Mohl, Raymond A., "Black Immigrants: Bahamians in Early Twentieth-Century Miami," *Florida Historical Quarterly*, vol. lxv, no. 3, Janaury 1987

Moore, R. Laurence, "Flawed Fraternity—American Socialist Response to the Negro, 1901–1912," *Historian*, vol. xxxii, no. 1, November 1969

Morales Carrión, Arturo, *Puerto Rico: A Political and Cultural History* (New York: W. W. Norton 1983)

Moreno Fraginals, Manuel, *The Sugarmill* (New York: Monthly Review Press 1974)

Moreno Fraginals, Manuel, Frank Moya Pons, and Stanley Engerman, eds, *Between Slavery and Free Labor: The Spanish-Speaking Caribbean in the Nineteenth Century* (Baltimore: Johns Hopkins University Press 1985)

Morgan, Edmund, *American Slavery, American Freedom: The Ordeal of Colonial Virginia* (New York: W.W. Norton & Company 1975)

Mormino, Gary R. and George E. Pozzetta, "Concord and Discord: Italians and Ethnic Interactions in Tampa, Florida," in Lydio Tomasi, ed., *Italian Americans: New Perspective in Italian Immigration and Ethnicity* (New York: Center for Migration Studies 1985)

Mormino, Gary R. and George E. Pozzetta, "Immigrant Women in Tampa: The Italian Experience, 1890–1930," *Florida Historical Quarterly*, vol. lxi, no. 3, January 1983

Mormino, Gary R. and George E. Pozzetta, "'The Reader Lights the Candle': Cuban and Florida Cigar Workers' Oral Tradition," *Labor's Heritage*, Spring 1993

Mormino, Gary R. and George E. Pozzetta, *The Immigrant World of Ybor City: Italians and Their Latin Neighbors in Tampa, 1885–1985* (Urbana: University of Illinois Press 1987)

Mormino, Gary R., "Tampa and the New Urban South: The Weight Strike of 1899," *Florida Historical Quarterly*, vol. lx, no. 3, January 1982

Mörner, Magnus, ed., *Race and Class in Latin America* (New York: Columbia University Press 1970)

Morrison-Reed, Mark D., *Black Pioneers in a White Denomination*, 3rd. edn. (Boston: Skinner House Books 1994)

Moses, Wilson Jeremiah, *The Golden Age of Black Nationalism, 1850–1925* (New York: Oxford University Press 1988)

Moss, Alfred A., Jr., *The American Negro Academy: Voice of the Talented Tenth* (Baton Rouge: Louisiana State University Press 1981)

Mullen, Robert, *Blacks in America's Wars* (New York: Pathfinder Press 1973)

Murray, Robert K., *Red Scare: A Study in National Hysteria, 1919–1920* (Minneapolis: University of Minnesota Press 1955)

Naison, Mark, *Communists in Harlem During the Depression* (Urbana: University of Illinois Press, 1983)

Nalty, Bernard, *Strength for the Fight: A History of Black Americans in the Military* (New York: The Free Press 1986)

Newton, Velma, *The Silver Men: West Indian Labour Migration to Panama, 1850–1914* (Kingston: Institute of Social and Economic Studies, University of the West Indies 1984)

Ojeda Reyes, Felix, *Vito Marcantonio y Puerto Rico: Por Los Trabajadores y Por la Nacion* (Río Piedras: Ediciones Huracán, Inc. 1978)

Ojeda Reyes, Felix, "Vito Marcantonio and Puerto Rican Independence," *Centro de Estudios Puertorriqueños Bulletin*, Spring 1992

Oostindie, Gert J., "Prelude to the Exodus: Surinamers in the Netherlands, 1667–1960s," in Gary Brana-Shute, ed., *Resistance and Rebellion in Suriname: Old and New*, Studies in Third World Societies 43 (Williamsburg: College of William and Mary 1990)

Ortiz, Victoria, "Arthur A. Schomburg: A Biographical Essay," in The Schomburg Center for Research in Black Culture, *The Legacy of Arthur Alfonso Schomburg: A Celebration of the Past, A Vision for the Future* (New York: Schomburg Center for Research in Black Culture 1986)

Osofsky, Gilbert, *Harlem: The Making of a Ghetto—Negro New York, 1890–1930* (New York: Harper and Row, 2nd ed., 1971)

Painter, Nell Irvin, *Exodusters: Black Migration to Kansas after Reconstruction* (New York: Alfred Knopf 1977)

Parris, Guichard and Lester Brooks, *Blacks in the City: A History of the National Urban League* (Boston: Little, Brown and Company 1971)

Patterson, Orlando, *The Sociology of Slavery: An Analysis of the Origins, Development and Structure of Negro Slave Society in Jamaica* (London: MacGibbon and Kee 1967)

Patterson, Orlando, "Context and Choice in Ethnic Allegiance: A Theoretical Framework and Caribbean Case Study," in Nathan Glazer and Daniel P. Moynihan, eds, *Ethnicity: Theory and Experience*, (Cambridge, Mass.: Harvard University Press 1975)

Peach, Ceri, *West Indian Migration to Britain: A Social Geography* (London: Oxford University Press 1968)

Pérez, Lisandro, "Iron Mining and Socio-Demographic Change in Eastern Cuba, 1884–1940," *Journal of Latin American Studies*, vol. 14, pt. 2, November 1982

Pérez, Louis, *Cuba: Between Reform and Revolution*, 2nd ed. (New York: Oxford University Press 1995)

Pérez, Louis, ed., *José Martí in the United States: The Florida Experience*, Special Studies No. 28 (Tempe: ASU Center for Latin American Studies, Arizona State University 1995)

Pérez, Louis, *Cuba Between Empires, 1878–1902* (Pittsburgh: University of Pittsburgh Press 1983)

Pérez, Louis, "Cubans in Tampa: From Exiles to Immigrants, 1892–1901," *Florida Historical Quarterly*, vol. lvii, no. 2, October 1978

Pérez, Louis, "José Martí: Context and Consciousness," in Henderson and Mormino, eds., *Spanish Pathways*

Pérez, Louis, "Politics, Peasants, and People of Color: The 1912 'Race War' in Cuba Reconsidered," *Hispanic American Historical Review*, vol. 66, no. 3, February 1986

Pérez, Louis, "Reminiscences of a *Lector*: Cuban Cigar Makers in Tampa," *Florida Historical Quarterly*, vol. liii, no. 4, April 1975

Petras, Elizabeth McLean, *Jamaican Labor Migration: White Capital and Black Labor, 1850–1930* (Boulder: Westview Press 1988)

Phelps, O.W., "Rise of the Labour Movement in Jamaica," *Social and Economic Studies*, vol. 9, no. 4, December 1960

Phillips, Glenn O., "The Response of a West Indian Activist: D.A. Straker, 1842–1908," *Journal of Negro History*, vol. lxvi, no. 2, Summer 1981

Picó, Fernando, *Historia General de Puerto Rico*, 5th ed. (Rio Piedras: Ediciones Huracán 1990)

Pizzo, Anthony, *Tampa Town, 1824–1886: The Cracker Village with a Latin Accent* (Tampa: Hurricane House Publishers 1968)

Platt, Anthony M., *E. Franklin Frazier Reconsidered* (New Brunswick: Rutgers University Press 1991)

Post, Ken, *Arise Ye Starvelings: The Jamaican Labour Rebellion of 1938 and Its Aftermath* (The Hague: Martinus Nijhoff 1978)

Post, Ken, *Strike the Iron: A Colony at War—Jamaica, 1939–1945*, 2 vols. (Atlantic Highlands: Humanities Press 1981)

Poyo, Gerald E., "Cuban Revolutionaries and Monroe County Reconstruction Politics, 1868–1876," *Florida Historical Quarterly*, vol. lv, no. 4, April 1977

Poyo, Gerald E., "Key West and the Cuban Ten Years War," *Florida Historical Quarterly*, vol. lvii, no. 3, January 1979

Poyo, Gerald E., "Evolution of Cuban Separatist Thought in the Emigré Communities of the United States, 1848–1895," *Hispanic American Historical Review*, vol. 66, no. 3, 1986

Poyo, Gerald E., "The Anarchist Challenge to the Cuban Independence Movement, 1885–1890," *Cuban Studies/Estudios Cubano*, vol. 15, no. 1, Winter 1985

Poyo, Gerald E., *"With All, and for the Good of All": The Emergence of Popular Nationalism in the Cuban Communities of the United States, 1848–1898* (Durham, NC: Duke University Press 1989)

Pozzetta, Gary R. Mormino and George E., "Immigrant Women in Tampa: The Italian Experience, 1890–1930," *Florida Historical Quarterly*, vol. lxi, no. 3., January 1983

Quintero Rivera, Angel G., "The Rural–Urban Dichotomy in the Formation of Puerto Rico's Cultural Identity," *Nieuwe West Indische Gids/New West Indian Guide*, vol. 61, nos. 3 & 4, 1987

Quintero Rivera, Angel G., "Socialist and Cigarmaker: Artisans' Proletarianization in the Making of the Puerto Rican Working Class," *Latin American Perspectives*, vol. x, nos. 2 and 3, Spring and Summer 1983

Ramesar, Marianne D., "Patterns of Regional Settlement and Economic Activity by Immigrant Groups in Trinidad, 1851–1900," *Social and Economic Studies*, vol. 25, no. 3, September 1976

Rampersad, Arnold, *The Life of Langston Hughes: Vol. II: 1941–1967: I Dream A World* (New York: Oxford University Press 1988)

Reddock, Rhoda, *Women, Labour and Politics in Trinidad and Tobago: A History* (London: Zed Books 1994)

Reddock, Rhoda, "Women and Garment Production in Trinidad and Tobago 1900–1960," *Social and Economic Studies,* vol. 39, no. 1, March 1990

Richardson, Bonham C., "Freedom and Migration in the Leeward Caribbean, 1838–48," *Journal of Historical Geography,* vol. 6, no. 4, October 1980

Richardson, Bonham C., "Human Mobility in the Windward Caribbean, 1884–1902," *Plantation Society,* vol. ii, no. 3, May 1989.

Richardson, Bonham, *Caribbean Migrants: Environment and Human Survival on St. Kitts and Nevis* (Knoxville: University of Tennessee Press 1983)

Richardson, Bonham, *Panama Money in Barbados, 1900–1920* (Knoxville: University of Tennessee Press 1985)

Robert, Karen, "Slavery and Freedom in the Ten Years' War, Cuba, 1868–1878," *Slavery and Abolition,* vol. 13, no. 3, December 1992

Roberts, George W., "Emigration From the Island of Barbados," *Social and Economic Studies,* vol. 4, no. 3, September 1955

Roberts, George W., *The Population of Jamaica* (Cambridge: Cambridge University Press 1957)

Robotham, Don, *"The Notorious Riot": The Socio-Economic and Political Bases of Paul Bogle's Revolt* (Kingston: Institute for Social and Economic Research 1981)

Rodney, Walter, *A History of the Guyanese Working People, 1881–1905* (Baltimore: Johns Hopkins University Press 1981)

Rodriguez, Clara, *Puerto Ricans, Born in the USA,* (Boulder: Westview Press 1991)

Rodríguez, Pedro Pablo, "Marcus Garvey en Cuba," *Anales del Caribe,* vols. 7–8, 1987–88

Rodriguez-Morazzani, Roberto P., "Linking a Fractured Past: The World of the Puerto Rican Old Left," *Centro: Journal of the Center for Puerto Rican Studies,* vol. vii, no. 1, Spring 1995

Rohlehr, Gordon, *Calypso and Society in Pre-Independence Trinidad* (Tunapuna, Trinidad: Gordon Rohlehr 1990)

Rolinson, Mary Gambrell, "The Universal Negro Improvement Association in Georgia: Southern Strongholds of Garveyism," in John C. Inscoe, ed., *Georgia in Black and White: Explorations in the Race Relations of a Southern State, 1865–1950* (Athens: University of Georgia Press 1994)

Rudwick, Elliott, *Race Riot at East St. Louis, July 2, 1917* (Carbondale: Southern Illinois University Press 1964)

Runcie, John, "Marcus Garvey and the Harlem Renaissance," *Afro-Americans in New York Life and History,* vol. 10, no. 2, July 1986

Russell, Carlos, *An Old Woman Remembers: The Recollected History of West Indians in Panama, 1855–1955* (New York: Caribbean Diaspora Press 1995)

Samaroo, Brinsley, "The Trinidad Disturbances of 1917–20: Precursor to 1937," in Roy Thomas, ed., *The Trinidad Labour Riots of 1937: Perspectives 50 Years Later* (St. Augustine, Trinidad: Extra-Mural Studies Unit, University of the West Indies 1987)

Samaroo, Brinsley, "The Trinidad Workingmen's Association and the Origins of Popular Protest in a Crown Colony," *Social and Economic Studies,* vol. 21, no. 2, June 1972

Samuels, Wilfred D., "Hubert H. Harrison and 'The New Negro Manhood Movement,'" *Afro-Americans in New York Life and History,* vol. 5, January 1981

Sánchez Korrol, Virginia E., *From Colonia to Community: The History of Puerto Ricans in New York City* (Westport: Greenwood Press 1983)

Santiago, Roberto, ed., *Boricuas: Influential Puerto Rican Writings* (New York: Ballantine Books 1995)

Satchell, Veront, *From Plots to Plantation: Land Transactions in Jamaica, 1866–1900* (Kingston: Institute of Social and Economic Research, University of the West Indies 1990)

Saul, S. B., "The British West Indies in Depression: 1880–1914," *Inter-American Economic Affairs*, vol. xii, no. 3, Winter 1958

Saunders, Gail, *Bahamian Society After Emancipation* (Kingston: Ian Randle Publishers 1994)

Scarano, Francisco A., *Sugar and Slavery in Puerto Rico: The Plantation Economy of Ponce, 1800–1850* (Madison: University of Wisconsin Press 1984)

Scott, Rebecca, *Slave Emancipation in Cuba: The Transition to Free Labor, 1860–1899* (Princeton: Princeton University Press 1985)

Scott, William, *Sons of Sheba's Race: African Americans and the Italo-Ethiopian War, 1935–1941* (Bloomington: Indiana University Press 1993)

Senior, Olive, "The Colon People," pt. 1, *Jamaica Journal*, vol. 11, nos. 3 and 4, March 1978

Seraile, William, "Ben Fletcher, I.W.W. Organizer," *Pennsylvania History*, vol. xlvi, no. 3, July 1979

Seraile, William, "Henrietta Vinton Davis and the Garvey Movement," *Afro-Americans in New York Life and History*, vol. 7, no. 2, July 1983

Shofner, Jerrell H., *Nor Is It Over Yet: Florida in the Era of Reconstruction, 1863–1877* (Gainesville: University Presses of Florida 1974)

Shofner, Jerrell H., "Custom, Law, and History: The Enduring Influence of Florida's 'Black Code'," *Florida Historical Quarterly*, vol. lv, no. 3, January 1977

Simmonds, Lorna, "Civil Disturbances in Western Jamaica, 1838–1865," *The Jamaican Historical Review*, vol. xiv, 1984

Singh, Kelvin, *Race and Class Struggles in a Colonial State: Trinidad 1917–1945* (Kingston: The Press—University of the West Indies 1994)

Sinnette, Elinor Des Verney, *Arthur Alfonso Schomburg: Black Bibliophile and Collector—A Biography* (New York: New York Public Library and Wayne State University Press 1989)

Smith, Raymond T., *Kinship and Class in the West Indies: A Genealogical Study of Jamaica and Guyana* (Cambridge: Cambridge University Press 1988)

Smith-Irvin, Jeannette, *Marcus Garvey's Footsoldiers of the Universal Negro Improvement Association* (Trenton: Africa World Press 1989)

Sorin, Gerald, *A Time for Building: The Third Migration 1880–1920*, vol. iii of The Jewish People in America (Baltimore: Johns Hopkins University Press 1992)

Sorin, Gerald, *The Prophetic Minority: American Jewish Immigrant Radicals, 1880–1920* (Bloomington: Indiana University Press 1985)

Starkey, Otis P., *The Economic Geography of Barbados* (New York: Columbia University Press 1939)

Stein, Judith, *The World of Marcus Garvey: Race and Class in Modern Society* (Baton Rouge: Louisiana State University Press, 1986)

Stubbs, Jean, *Tobacco on the Periphery: A Case Study in Cuban Labour History, 1860–1958* (Cambridge: Cambridge University Press 1985)

Thomas, Hugh, *Cuba, or the Pursuit of Freedom* (London: Eyre & Spottiswoode 1971)

Thomas-Hope, Elizabeth, *Explanation in Caribbean Migration: Perception and Image—Jamaica, Barbados, St. Vincent* (London: Macmillan Press Ltd. 1992)

Tolbert, Emory, *The UNIA and Black Los Angeles: Ideology and Community in the American Garvey Movement* (Los Angeles: Center for Afro-American Studies, UCLA 1980)

Toledo, Josefina, *Sotero Figueroa, Editor de "Patria": Apuntes para una Biografía* (Havana: Editorial Letras Cubanas 1985)

Trotman, David, *Crime in Trinidad: Conflict and Control in a Plantation Society, 1838–1900* (Knoxville: University of Tennessee Press 1986)

Trouillot, Michel-Rolph, *Peasants and Capital: Dominica in the World Economy* (Baltimore: Johns Hopkins University Press 1988)

Turner, W. Burghardt, "Joel Augustus Rogers: An Afro-American Historian," *Negro History Bulletin*, vol. 35, no. 2, February 1972

Turton, Peter, *José Martí: Architect of Cuba's Freedom* (London: Zed Books 1986)

Vincent, Theodore, *Black Power and the Garvey Movement* (Berkeley: Ramparts Press 1972)

Vincent, Ted, "The Garveyite Parents of Malcolm X," *Black Scholar*, March/April 1989

Vincent, Ted, *Keep Cool: The Black Activists Who Built the Jazz Age* (London: Pluto Press 1995)

Vincent, Ted, "The Harlem Bluefields Connection: Sandino's Aid from the Black American Press," *Black Scholar*, May/June 1985

Walcott, Derek, "What the Twilight Says: An Ouverture," in his *Dream on Monkey Mountain and Other Plays* (New York: The Noonday Press 1970)

Waldstreicher, David, "Radicalism, Religion, Jewishness: The Case of Emma Goldman," *American Jewish History*, vol. lxxx, no. 1, Autumn 1990

Walter, J.C. and J.L. Ansheles, "The Role of the Caribbean Immigrant in the Harlem Renaissance," *Afro-Americans in New York Life and History*, vol. 1, no. 1, January 1977

Walter, John C., "Frank R. Crosswaith and the Negro Labor Committee in Harlem, 1925–1939," *Afro-Americans in New York Life and History*, vol. 3, no. 2, July 1979

Walter, John C., "West Indian Immigrants: Those Arrogant Bastards," *Contributions in Black Studies*, no. 5, 1981–1982

Ward, J.R., *Poverty and Progress in the Caribbean, 1800–1960* (London: Macmillan 1985)

Waters, Mary, "Ethnic and Racial Identities of Second-Generation Black Immigrants in New York City," *International Migration Review*, vol. xxviii, no. 4, Winter 1994

Waters, Mary, "The Role of Lineage in Identity Formation Among Black Americans," *Qualitative Sociology*, vol. 14, no. 1, Spring 1991

Watkins-Owens, Irma, *Blood Relations: Caribbean Immigrants and the Harlem Community, 1900–1930* (Bloomington: Indiana University Press 1996)

Watson, Hilbourne, "Theoretical and Methodological Problems in Commonwealth Caribbean Migration Research: Conditions and Causality," *Social and Economic Studies*, vol. 31, no. 1, March 1982

Watson, Karl, *The Civilised Island: Barbados–A Social History, 1750–1816* (Bridgetown, Barbados: Caribbean Graphics 1979)

Watts, David, *The West Indies: Patterns of Development, Culture and Environmental Change since 1492* (Cambridge: Cambridge University Press 1987)

Watts, Jill, *God, Harlem USA: The Father Divine Story* (Berkeley: University of California Press 1992)

Weinstein, James, *The Decline of American Socialism, 1912–1925* ([1967] New Brunswick: Rutgers University Press 1984)

Weisbord, Robert G., *Ebony Kinship: Africa, Africans, and the Afro-American* (Westport: Greenwood Press 1973)

Weiss, Nancy, *Farewell to the Party of Lincoln: Black Politics in the Age of FDR* (Princeton: Princeton University Press 1983)

Welch, Barbara, "Population Density and Emigration in Dominica," *Geographical Journal*, vol. 134, pt. 2, June 1968

Western, John, *A Passage to England: Barbadian Londoners Speak of Home* (Minneapolis: University of Minnesota Press 1992)

White, Walter, *Rope and Faggot: A Biography of Judge Lynch* (New York: Alfred Knopf 1929)

Wilkins, Nadine, "The Medical Profession in Jamaica in the Post-Emancipation Period," *Jamaica Journal* vol. 21, no. 4, November 1988–January 1989

Will, H. A., *Constitutional Change in the British West Indies, 1880–1903* (Oxford: Clarendon Press 1970)

Will, H. A., "Colonial Policy and Economic Development in the British West Indies, 1895–1903," *Economic History Review*, 2nd. Series, vol. xxiii, no. 1, April 1970

Williams, Eric, *From Columbus To Castro: The History of the Caribbean, 1492–1969* (London: André Deutsch 1970)

Wilson, Peter J., *Crab Antics: A Caribbean Case Study of the Conflict Between Reputation and Respectability* (Prospect Heights, Ill.: Waveland Press 1995)

Wolf, Donna M., "The Cuban *Gente de Color* and the Independence Movement, 1879–1895," *Revista / Review Interamericana*, vol. 5, Fall 1975

Wood, Donald, *Trinidad in Transition: The Years After Slavery* (Oxford: Oxford University Press 1968)

Wood, Peter, *Black Majority: Negroes in Colonial South Carolina from 1670 through the Stono Rebellion* (New York: Alfred A. Knopf 1974)

Woodson, Carter G. and Charles H. Wesley, *The Negro in Our History* 12th ed. (Washington, DC: Associated Publishers, Inc. 1972)

Woodward, C. Vann, *The Strange Career of Jim Crow* (New York: Oxford University Press 1955)

Worcester, Kent, *C. L. R. James: A Political Biography* (Albany: State University of New York 1996)

Wright, George C., *Racial Violence in Kentucky, 1865–1940: Lynchings, Mob Rule, and "Legal Lynchings"* (Baton Rouge: Louisiana State University Press 1990)

Zangrando, Robert L., *The NAACP Crusade Against Lynching, 1909–1950* (Philadelphia: Temple University Press 1980)

Zenon Cruz, Isabelo, *Narciso Descubre su Trasero: El Negro en la Cultura Puertorriqueña*, 2nd ed. (Humacao, Puerto Rico: Editorial Furidi 1983)

Theses, Dissertations, Papers, and Unpublished Manuscripts

Aron, Birgit, "The Garvey Movement" (Masters thesis, Columbia University, 1947)

Bartlett, Wilson R., "Lorenzo Dow Baker and the Development of the Banana Trade Between Jamaica and the United States, 1881–1890" (Ph.D. diss., American University 1977)

Brodber, Erna, "The Second Generation of Freemen in Jamaica, 1907–1944" (Ph.D. diss., University of the West Indies, 1984)

Chinea Serrano, Jorge Luis, "Racial Politics and Commercial Agriculture: West Indian Immigration in Nineteenth-Century Puerto Rico, 1800–1850" (Ph.D. diss., University of Minnesota, 1994)

Drakes, Francis, "The Development of Political Organisation and Political Consciousness in British Guiana, 1870–1964: The *Conscientizacao* of the Middle Class and the Masses" (Ph.D. diss., University of London, 1989)

Dunbar, Barrington, "Factors in the Cultural Backgrounds of the American Southern Negro and the British West Indian Negro that Condition their Adjustments in Harlem" (M. A. thesis, Columbia University, 1935)

Fermoselle-Lopez, Rafael, "Black Politics in Cuba: The Race War of 1912" (Ph.D. diss., American University, 1972)

Forsythe, Dennis, "West Indian Radicalism Abroad" (Ph.D. diss., McGill University, 1973)

Giusti-Cordero, Juan A., "Labor, Ecology and History in a Caribbean Sugar Plantation Region: Piñones (Loíza), Puerto Rico 1770–1950" (Ph.D. diss., State University of New York, Binghampton, 1994)

Greenbaum, Susan, "José Martí and Jim Crow" (unpublished ms. [1996])

Hellwig, David J., "The Afro-American and the Immigrant, 1880–1930: A Study of Black Social Thought" (Ph.D. diss., Syracuse University, 1973)

Henry, Keith, "The Place of the Culture of Migrant Commonwealth Afro-West Indians in the Political Life of Black New York in the Period circa 1918 to circa 1966" (Ph.D. diss. University of Toronto, 1973)

Holder, Calvin, "West Indian Immigration in New York City, 1900–1952: A Study in Acculturation" (Ph.D. diss., Harvard University, 1976)

James, C. Boyd, "Primitives on the Move: Some Historical Articulations of Garvey and Garveyism, 1887–1927" (Ph.D. diss., University of California, Los Angeles, 1982)

James, Winston, "'A Simian Exhibition'? Symbol and Meaning in the Celebration of King George VI's Coronation by Caribbean Migrants in Harlem, May 1937," paper presented to the "Conference on Caribbean Culture," University of the West Indies, Mona, Kingston, Jamaica, March 3–6, 1996

Moore, Garrie Ward, "A Study of A Group of West Indian Negroes in New York City" (Master's thesis, Columbia University, 1913)

Perry, Jeffrey Babcock, "Hubert Henry Harrison, 'The Father of Harlem Radicalism': The Early Years–1883 Through the Founding of the Liberty League and 'The Voice' in 1917" (Ph.D. diss., Columbia University, 1986)

Richards, Yevette, "'My Passionate Feeling About Africa': Maida Springer-Kemp and the American Labor Movement" (Ph.D. diss., Yale University 1994)

Rodney, Walter, "Barbadian Immigration into British Guiana, 1863–1924," paper presented to the Ninth Annual Conference of the Association of Caribbean Historians, University of the West Indies, Cave Hill, Barbados, April 3–7, 1977

Samuels, Wilfred D., "Five Afro-Caribbean Voices in American Culture, 1917–1929: Hubert Harrison, Wilfred A. Domingo, Richard B. Moore, Cyril V. Briggs, and Claude McKay" (Ph.D. diss., University of Iowa, 1977)

Seabrook, John, "Black and White Unite: The Career of Frank B. Crosswaith" (Ph.D. diss., Rutgers University, 1980)

Sharp, Kathleen A., "Rose Pastor Stokes: Radical Champion of the American Working Class, 1879–1933" (Ph.D. diss., Duke University, 1979)

Steffy, Joan Marie, "The Cuban Immigrants of Tampa, Florida, 1886–1898" (Masters thesis, University of South Florida, 1975)

Taylor, Theman Ray, "Cyril Briggs and the African Blood Brotherhood: Another Radical View of Race and Class During the 1920s" (Ph.D. diss., University of California, Santa Barbara, 1981)

True, Marshall, "Revolutionaries in Exile: The Cuban Revolutionary Party, 1891–1898" (Ph.D. diss., University of Virginia, 1965)

van Enckevort, Maria, "The Caribbean Diaspora in France in the 1930s," paper presented to the annual conference of the Association of Caribbean Historians, Kingston, Jamaica, 1993

Westfall, L. Glenn, "Don Vicente Martinez Ybor, the Man and his Empire: Development of the Clear Havana Industry in Cuba and Florida in the Nineteenth Century" (Ph.D. diss., University of Florida, 1977)

Index

emigration prevention 28–9, 102
Estrada Palma, Tomás 205, 247, 253

Farrakhan, Louis (Walcott, Eugene) 260
Federación Local de Tabaqueros 241
Ferris, William 165, 212
Figueroa, Sotero 7, 246, 253, 254
Fletcher, Ben 163, 183
Florida *see* Afro-Cubans in Florida
Forbes, George 188
Ford, Arnold 69
Ford, James 286, 287–9
Forsythe, Dennis 6
Fort-Whiteman, Lovett 70, 156, 270–71
Froude, James Anthony 38, 115, 116–17

Garvey, Amy Jacques 137, 141–55
  admiration for Garvey, Marcus 144–5
  "Away with Lip Service" 150–51
  background and education 141–2
  criticism of black men 150–55
  "Have a Heart" 147
  on importance of reading and learning 79–80
  "Our Women and What They Think" 140, 145, 145–9, 146–50
  relationship with Garvey, Marcus 143–4
  "want-to-be-whites" and advertisements 150
Garvey, Marcus 191–4
  absence of racism in Caribbean 98–9
  admiration for Trotter, William Monroe 189
  and African Blood Brotherhood 179
  arrival in United States 94
  Black Man, The 75, 184
  on Briggs, Cyril 70
  Bruce, John on 192
  co-operation with by black leftists 270
  colonial policy 40
  Cruse, Harold on 268
  demise 2
  dismissal of Domingo, Wilfred A. from *Negro World* 283
  and Harrison, Hubert 125, 129, 130
  on importance of learning 79
  imprisonment (1925) 67
  indictment (1922) 135, 148, 173
  Johnson, James Weldon on 192–3
  in London 75, 76, 259
  Minor, Robert on 120
  National Club 41, 50, 284
  occupational training 88
  oratory and debate 80
  revival since his death 186–7
  travel in Europe and Central America 71
  see also Negro World; Universal Negro Improvement Association
"Garvey Must Go" campaign (1922–3) 4, 270–71, 282–3
Garveyism 7, 66, 88, 136, 137, 193–4, 260
Ginésta, Domingo 247
Goldman, Emma 163
Gomes, Albert 41
Gramsci, Antonio 76, 187
Grange, David E. 72
Grant, St William 69
Gray, Arthur S. 67, 154
Greenbaum, Susan 254
Greene, Jack P. 11

Grey, Edgar M. 162, 268
Griffiths, D.W. 94
Gurley Flynn, Elizabeth 176

Hall, Otto 156, 180, 181–2, 270, 284, 285–6
Hall, Prince 11
Harrison, Hubert 12, 76–7, 122–34, 268, 281, 284
  agitation for black self-defense 95
  arrival in United States 94
  background and education 118, 123–4
  black nationalism 126, 128
  Bolshevism 126
  and Briggs, Cyril 159
  British intelligence 132–3
  Carroll, John T. on 131
  Communist Party 161–2
  dismissal from Post Office 124–5
  distrust of white radicals 186
  Domingo, Wilfred A. on 130
  editorial tribute 133–4
  education 83, 89
  from religious worldview to militant rationalism 77
  Harlem 128–9
  on importance of reading and learning 79
  Industrial Workers of the World 126, 183
  influence on Randolph, A. Philip 260
  Liberty League of Negro Americans 126
  McKay, Claude on 132
  and Marx, Karl 126, 127, 128
  Moore, Richard B. on 130–31
  National Association for the Advancement of Colored People 132
  "New Politics for the New Negro" 128
  oratory and good talking 80
  on Paris Peace Congress 188–9
  People's Educational Forum 176
  as philanderer 129
  Pickens, William on 132
  "Race First Versus Class First" 127
  Randolph, A. Philip on 130
  and Republican Party 78
  revolutionary socialism 126
  Socialist Party 124–5, 126–8, 175, 278, 286
  study of Africa 129–30
  Voice 125–6
Hay, Sir J.S. 37–8
Hayes, Rutherford 238
Haynes, Corporal Samuel A. 51, 53, 56–60, 66–9, 154
Haynes, George Edmund 82
Haywood, Harry 162, 260, 270, 271
  African Blood Brotherhood 156
  on Briggs, Cyril 157, 158, 159
  Communist (Workers') Party 180, 181–2, 186, 270, 286, 289
  on Ford, James 288
  skin color 70
Haywood, William 125, 183
Hearne, John 116
Hemming, Sir A.W. 25
Hendricks, Arthur 162, 183
Henriques, A.N. 29
Henry, Keith 6
Hill, Robert 136, 161
Hillquit, Morris 229